SKILLS For SUCCESS

with Microsoft®
Access 2016
Comprehensive

CHANEY ADKINS | HAWKINS

PEARSON

Boston Columbus Indianapolis New York San Francisco
Amsterdam Cape Town Dubai London Madrid Milan Munich Paris Montréal Toronto
Delhi Mexico City São Paulo Sydney Hong Kong Seoul Singapore Taipei Tokyo

Library of Congress Cataloging-in-Publication Data

CIP data on file with the Library of Congress.

Editorial Director: *Andrew Gilfillan*
Executive Editor: *Jenifer Niles*
Team Lead, Project Management: *Laura Burgess*
Project Manager: *Anne Garcia*
Program Manager: *Emily Biberger*
Development Editor: *Lori Damanti*
Editorial Assistant: *Michael Campbell*
Director of Product Marketing: *Maggie Waples*
Director of Field Marketing: *Leigh Ann Sims*
Product Marketing Manager: *Kaylee Carlson*
Field Marketing Managers: *Joanna Sabella & Molly Schmidt*
Marketing Assistant: *Kelli Fisher*
Efficacy Implementation: *Candice Madden*

Senior Operations Specialist: *Maura Zaldivar Garcia*
Senior Art Director: *Diane Ernsberger*
Manager, Permissions: *Karen Sanatar*
Interior and Cover Design: *Studio Montage*
Cover Photo: *Courtesy of Shutterstock® Images*
Associate Director of Design: *Blair Brown*
Product Strategy Manager: *Eric Hakanson*
Vice President, Product Strategy: *Jason Fournier*
Digital Product Manager: *Zachary Alexander*
Media Project Manager, Production: *John Cassar*
Full-Service Project Management: *Cenveo Publisher Services*
Composition: *Cenveo Publisher Services*

3 17
ISBN-10: 0-13-4479513
ISBN-13: 978-0-13-4479514

Contents in Brief

Table of Contents

Series Reviewers

We'd like to thank the following people for their reviewing of Skills for Success series:

Focus Group Participants

Rose Volynskiy	Howard Community College	Lex Mulder	College of Western Idaho
Fernando Paniagua	The Community College of Baltimore County	Kristy McAuliffe	San Jacinto College South
Jeff Roth	Heald College	Jan Hime	University of Nebraska, Lincoln
William Bodine	Mesa Community College	Deb Fells	Mesa Community College

Reviewers

Barbara Anderson	Lake Washington Institute of Technology	Deb Fells	Mesa Community College
Janet Anderson	Lake Washington Institute of Technology	Tushnelda C Fernandez	Miami Dade College
Ralph Argiento	Guilford Technical Community College	Jean Finley	Asheville-Buncombe Technical Community College
Tanisha Arnett	Pima County Community College		
Greg Ballinger	Miami Dade College	Jim Flannery	Central Carolina Community College
Autumn Becker	Allegany College of Maryland	Alyssa Foskey	Wiregrass Georgia Technical College
Bob Benavides	Collin College	David Freer	Miami Dade College
Howard Blauser	North GA Technical College	Marvin Ganote	University of Dayton
William Bodine	Mesa Community College	David Grant	Paradise Valley Community College
Nancy Bogage	The Community College of Baltimore County	Clara Groeper	Illinois Central College
Maria Bright	San Jacinto College	Carol Heeter	Ivy Tech Community College
Adell Brooks	Hinds Community College	Jan Hime	University of Nebraska
Judy Brown	Western Illinois University	Marilyn Holden	Gateway Technical College
Maria Brownlow	Chaminade	Ralph Hunsberger	Bucks County Community College
Jennifer Buchholz	UW Washington County	Juan Iglesias	University of Texas at Brownsville
Kathea Buck	Gateway Technical College	Carl Eric Johnson	Great Bay Community College
LeAnn Cady	Minnesota State College—Southeast Technical	Joan Johnson	Lake Sumter Community College
John Cameron	Rio Hondo College	Mech Johnson	UW Washington County
Tammy Campbell	Eastern Arizona College	Deborah Jones	Southwest Georgia Technical College
Patricia Christian	Southwest Georgia Technical College	Hazel Kates	Miami-Dade College, Kendall Campus
Tina Cipriano	Gateway Technical College	Jane Klotzle	Lake Sumter Community College
Paulette Comet	The Community College of Baltimore County	Kurt Kominek	Northeast State Community College
Jean Condon	Mid-Plains Community College	Vivian Krenzke	Gateway Technical College
Joy DePover	Minneapolis. Com. & Tech College	Renuka Kumar	Community College of Baltimore County
Gina Donovan	County College of Morris	Lisa LaCaria	Central Piedmont Community College
Alina Dragne	Flagler College	Sue Lannen	Brazosport College
Russ Dulaney	Rasmussen College	Freda Leonard	Delgado Community College
Mimi Duncan	University of Missouri St. Louis	Susan Mahon	Collin College
Paula Jo Elson	Sierra College	Nicki Maines	Mesa Community College
Bernice Eng	Brookdale Community College	Pam Manning	Gateway Technical College
Jill Fall	Gateway Technical College	Juan Marquez	Mesa Community College

Contributors continued

Alysia Martinez	*Gateway Technical College*	Jeff Roth	*Heald College*
Kristy McAuliffe	*San Jacinto College*	Diane Ruscito	*Brazosport College*
Robert McCloud	*Sacred Heart University*	June Scott	*County College of Morris*
Susan Miner	*Lehigh Carbon Community College*	Vicky Seehusen	*MSU Denver*
Namdar Mogharreban	*Southern Illinois University*	Emily Shepard	*Central Carolina Community College*
Daniel Moix	*College of the Ouachitas*	Pamela Silvers	*A-B Tech*
Lindsey Moore	*Wiregrass Georgia Technical College*	Martha Soderholm	*York College*
Lex Mulder	*College of Western Idaho*	Yaacov Sragovich	*Queensborough Community College*
Patricia Newman	*Cuyamaca College*	Jody Sterr	*Blackhawk Technical College*
Melinda Norris	*Coker College*	Julia Sweitzer	*Lake-Sumter Community College*
Karen Nunan	*Northeast State Community College*	Laree Thomas	*Okefenokee Technical College*
Fernando Paniagua	*The Community College of Baltimore County*	Joyce Thompson	*Lehigh Carbon Community College*
Christine Parrish	*Southwest Georgia Technical College*	Barbara Tietsort	*University of Cincinnati, Blue Ash College*
Linda Pennachio	*Mount Saint Mary College*	Rose Volynskiy	*Howard Community College*
Amy Pezzimenti	*Ocean County College*	Sandra Weber	*Gateway Technical College*
Leah Ramalingam	*Riversity City College*	Steven Weitz	*Lehigh Carbon Community College*
Mary Rasley	*Lehigh Carbon Community College*	Berthenia Williams	*Savannah Technical College*
Cheryl Reuss	*Estrella Mountain Community College*	David Wilson	*Parkland College*
Wendy Revolinski	*Gateway Technical College*	Allan Wood	*Great Bay Community College*
Kenneth Rogers	*Cecil College*	Roger Yaeger	*Estrella Mountain Community College*

Skills for Success Office 2016

With Microsoft Office 2016, productivity is truly possible anywhere, anytime! Understanding this and being able to think and adapt to new environments is critical for today's learners. The *Skills for Success* series focuses on teaching essential productivity skills by providing a highly visual, step-by-step approach for learning Microsoft Office. This concise approach is very effective and provides the depth of skill coverage needed to succeed at work, school, and for MOS certification preparation. Using this approach, students learn the skills they need, and then put their knowledge to work through a progression of review, problem-solving, critical thinking projects, and proficiency demonstration with the NEW *Collaborating with Google* projects. For Office 2016, MOS exam objectives are also woven into the lessons, so students can review and prepare as they learn. Combine the visual approach and real-world projects of the text with the matching, live-in-the-application grader projects and high fidelity Office simulation training and assessments in MyITLab, and you have a truly effective learning approach!

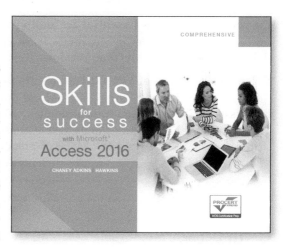

Series Hallmarks

- **Highly Visual Two-Page Landscape Layout** — Gives students the visual illustrations right with the steps—no flipping pages

- **Clearly Outlined Skills** — Each skill is presented in a single two-page spread so that students can easily follow along

- **Numbered Steps and Bulleted Text** — Students don't read long paragraphs or text, but they will read information presented concisely

- **Wide Coverage of Skills** — Gives students the knowledge needed to learn the core skills for work success

Skills for Success with Microsoft Office 2016

Personalized, engaging, effective learning with MyITLab 2016

Using the *Grader* projects and MyITLab *simulations*, students receive immediate feedback on their work to ensure understanding and help students progress.

MyITLab Grader **Live-in-the-application Grader Projects**—provide hands-on, autograded options for practice and assessment with immediate feedback and detailed performance comments. Grader projects cover all the skills taught in the chapter, including a new grader covering all four *More Skills*.

MyITLab Simulation **MyITLab Simulation Trainings and Assessment** provide an interactive, highly-realistic simulated environment to practice the Microsoft skills and projects taught in the book. Students receive immediate assistance with the learning aids, *Read, Watch, Practice,* and *detailed click stream data* reports provide effective review of their work. In the simulation assessments, students demonstrate their understanding through a new scenario exam without learning aids. Please note that for chapters 5–10, the simulations are topic-based; they cover the skills in chapter, but are not based on the same scenario.

Current Content and Essential Technology Coverage

Three Fundamental Chapters cover the latest technology concepts, key Windows 10 skills, and Internet Browsing with Edge and Chrome. Windows 10 skills are covered in the MyITLab Windows 10 simulations.

Extensive coverage of key skills students need for professional and personal success.

Chapters cover 10 Skills through real-world projects to meet the Learning Objectives and Outcomes. All 10 Skills are covered in the MyITLab grader projects and training and assessment simulations.

More Skills are now included in the text instead of online. These projects go beyond the main skills covered to provide additional training and to meet chapter learning objectives. NEW MyITLab grader project covers the skills from all four.

MOS Objective integration ensures students explore the MOS objectives as they are covered in the text for exam awareness and preparation.

Collaborating with Google projects—require students to apply their knowledge with another tool, replicating real-world work environments.

MOS appendix and icons in the text allow instructors to tailor preparation for Microsoft Office Specialist candidates by mapping MOS requirements to the text.

Clearly Defined, Measurable Learning Outcomes and Objectives

Learning *Outcomes* and *Objectives* have been clarified and expanded at the beginning of each chapter to define what students will learn, and are tied to the chapter assessments for clear measurement and efficacy.

Wide range of projects to ensure learning objectives and outcomes are achieved

Objective-based: Matching & Multiple choice, Discussion;

Review projects: Skills Review, Skills Assessments 1 & 2;

Problem-Solving: My Skills and Visual Skills Check;

Critical Thinking: Skills Challenges 1 & 2 and More Skills Assessment

Application Capstone Projects provided for each application help instructors ensure that students are ready to move on to the next application. Also delivered as grader projects in MyITLab.

Integrated Projects follow each application so that as students learn a new application, they also learn how to use it with other applications.

Office Online Projects provide hands-on experience with the web version of the Office applications to ensure students are familiar with the differences and become proficient with working between different versions of the tools.

Effective Learning Tools and Resources

Project Summary Chart—details the end of chapter projects from review, and problem-solving, to critical thinking, and demonstration of proficiency.

Skills Summary Chart lists all the Skills and Procedures and shortcut keys covered in the chapter making remembering what was covered easier!

Watch Skill Videos (formerly Student Training videos) are author-created training videos for each Skill in the chapter! Makes learning and remediation easier. Linked in ebook.

Wide screen images with clear callouts provide better viewing and usability.

Application Introductions provide a brief overview of the application and put the chapters in context for students.

Stay Current

IT Innovation Station keeps you up to date with Office and Windows updates, news, and trends with help from your Pearson authors! Look for the IT "Innovation Station," articles on the MyITLab Community site. These monthly articles from Pearson authors on all things Microsoft Office, include tips for understanding automatic updates, adjusting to and utilizing new capabilities, and optimizing your Office course.

Skills for Success

with Microsoft® Access 2016 Comprehensive

Application Introductions provide students with a concise overview of each application to put the chapters in context

Two Page Chapter Introduction — Briefs students on what is important and sets the stage for the project they will create

Learning Outcomes and Chapter Objectives clearly define what students will learn and achieve

Clock — Tells how much time students need to complete the chapter

File Summary — A quick summary of the files the students need to open and the names of the files they will turn in

Watch Skills Videos (formerly Student Training) for each Skill in the chapter provide a personal, instructor-led walk through

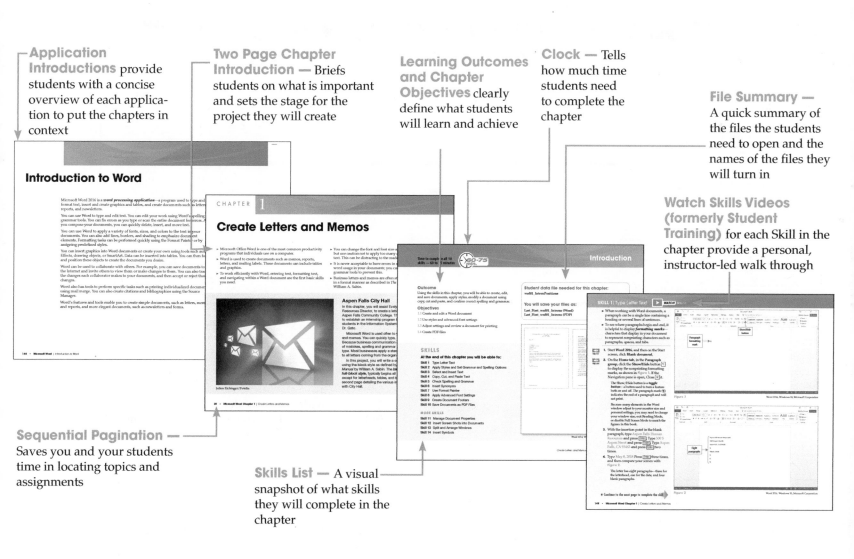

Sequential Pagination — Saves you and your students time in locating topics and assignments

Skills List — A visual snapshot of what skills they will complete in the chapter

Skills for Success

Written for Today's Students — Skills are taught with numbered steps and bulleted text so students are less likely to skip valuable information

Two-Page Spreads — Each skill is presented in a concise, two-page spread to give students the visual illustration right with the steps—no flipping pages

Colored Text — Clearly shows what a student types

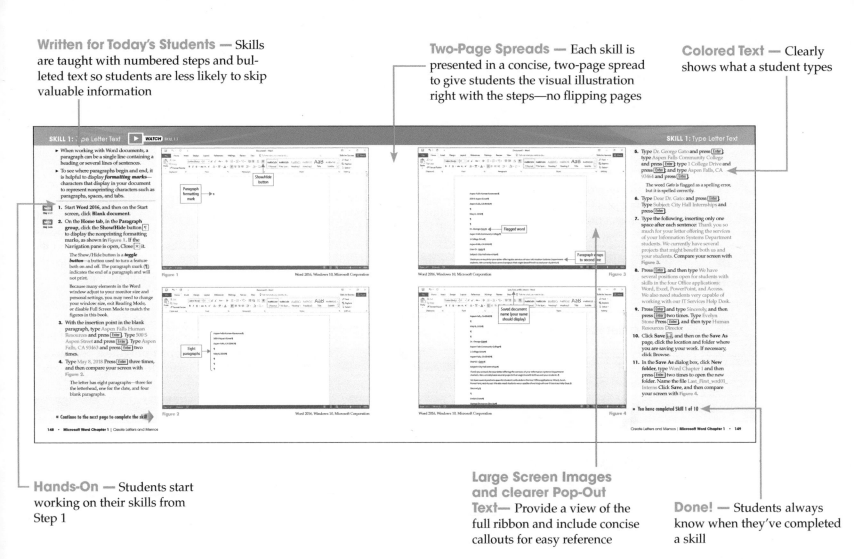

Hands-On — Students start working on their skills from Step 1

Large Screen Images and clearer Pop-Out Text — Provide a view of the full ribbon and include concise callouts for easy reference

Done! — Students always know when they've completed a skill

More Skills — Additional skills previously provided online are now included in the chapter to ensure students learn these important skills.

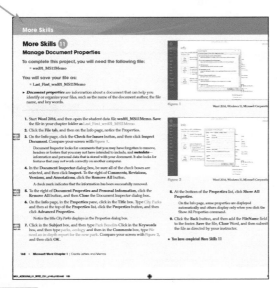

BizSkills Videos and Discussion Questions — Covering the important business skills students need to succeed: *Communication, Dress for Success, Interview Prep,* and more

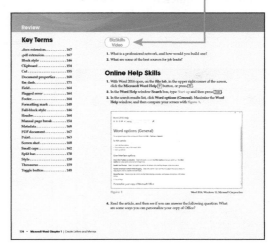

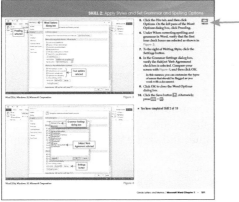

MOS Objectives — Integrated into the text for quick review and exam prep.

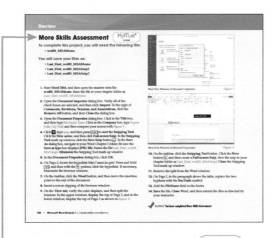

More Skills Assessment — MyITLab® Grader

Covers the core skills from the the four More Skills projects in a linear project that tells students what to do, but not necessarily how to do it.

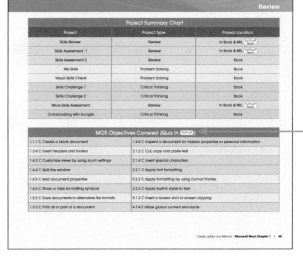

NEW MOS Summary table — Provides quick overview of objectives covered.

Skills for Success

NEW Collaborating with Google — Hands-on projects that allow students to apply the skills they have learned in a Google project to demonstrate proficiency.

Skills and Procedures Summary Chart — Provides a quick review of the skills and tasks covered in each chapter

NEW Project Summary Chart — Provides an overview of project types and locations.

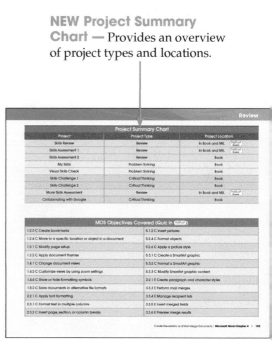

Application Capstones — For each application we provide two comprehensive projects covering all of the Skills. The capstones are available as a Homework and Assessment version, with the Assessment version earning a MIL Badge. Also available as a Grader project in MyITLab.

Office Online (formerly Web App) Projects — Students use Cloud computing to save files; create, edit, and share Office documents using Office Online; and create Windows Live groups.

Create Flyers Using Word Online

Skills for Success

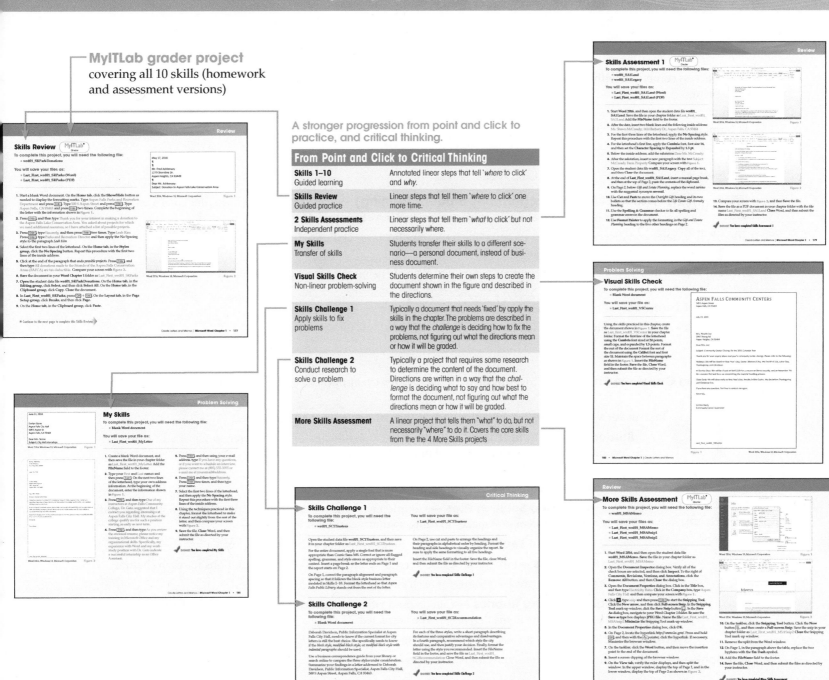

MyITLab grader project
covering all 10 skills (homework and assessment versions)

A stronger progression from point and click to practice, and critical thinking.

From Point and Click to Critical Thinking

Skills 1–10 Guided learning	Annotated linear steps that tell 'where to click' and why.
Skills Review Guided practice	Linear steps that tell them 'where to click' one more time.
2 Skills Assessments Independent practice	Linear steps that tell them 'what to click' but not necessarily where.
My Skills Transfer of skills	Students transfer their skills to a different scenario—a personal document, instead of business document.
Visual Skills Check Non-linear problem-solving	Students determine their own steps to create the document shown in the figure and described in the directions.
Skills Challenge 1 Apply skills to fix problems	Typically a document that needs 'fixed' by apply the skills in the chapter. The problems are described in a way that the challenge is deciding how to fix the problems, not figuring out what the directions mean or how it will be graded.
Skills Challenge 2 Conduct research to solve a problem	Typically a project that requires some research to determine the content of the document. Directions are written in a way that the challenge is deciding what to say and how best to format the document, not figuring out what the directions mean or how it will be graded.
More Skills Assessment	A linear project that tells them "what" to do, but not necessarily "where" to do it. Covers the core skills from the the 4 More Skills projects

Skills for Success

MyITLab (MyITLab®)

Skills for Success combined with MyITLab gives you a completely integrated learning solution: Instruction, Training, & Assessment

- eText
- Training & Assessment Simulations
- Grader Projects

Student Resources and Videos!

 WATCH Watch Skills videos (formerly Student Training) — Each skill within a chapter comes with an instructor-led video that walks students through how to complete the skill.

BizSkills Video — BizSKill Videos and discussion questions cover the important business skills students need to be successful— *Interviewing, Communication, Dressing for Success,* and more.

Student Data Files — are all available on the Companion Website using the access code included with your book.
pearsonhighered.com/skills

PowerPoint Lectures — PowerPoint presentations for each chapter

Audio PPTs —Provide an audio version of the PowerPoint presentations for each chapter

Instructor Materials

Application Capstone Projects — Covering all of the Skills for each application. Also available as MyITLab grader projects

Instructor's Manual — Teaching tips and additional resources for each chapter

Student Assignment Tracker — Lists all the assignments for the chapter; you just add in the course information, due dates and points. Providing these to students ensures they will know what is due and when

Scripted Lectures — Classroom lectures prepared for you

All Student and Instructor Materials available in MyITLab.

Annotated Solution Files — Coupled with the scoring rubrics, these create a grading and scoring system that makes grading so much easier for you

PowerPoint Lectures — PowerPoint presentations for each chapter

Audio PPTs —Provide an audio version of the PowerPoint presentations for each chapter

Prepared Exams — Exams for each chapter and for each application

Detailed Scoring Rubrics — Can be used either by students to check their work or by you as a quick check-off for the items that need to be corrected

Syllabus Templates — For 8-week, 12-week, and 16-week courses

Test Bank — Includes a variety of test questions for each chapter

Margo Chaney Adkins is an Assistant Professor of Information Technology at Carroll Community College in Westminster, Maryland. She holds a bachelor's degree in Information Systems and master's degree in Post-Secondary Education from Salisbury University. She teaches computer application and office technology courses, both online and in the classroom. She enjoys athletic activities, gardening, and traveling with her husband.

Lisa Hawkins is a Professor of Computer and Information Sciences at Frederick Community College in Maryland. She earned a PhD in Information Technology from Capella University. Lisa has also worked as a database administrator, E-commerce manager, and systems administrator. She enjoys adventure sports, gardening, and making glass beads.

A Special Thank You Pearson Prentice Hall gratefully acknowledges the contribution made by Shelley Gaskin to the first edition publication of this series—*Skills for Success with Office 2016*. The series has truly benefited from her dedication toward developing a textbook that aims to help students and instructors. We thank her for her continued support of this series.

Common Features of Office 2016

- ▶ Microsoft Office is a suite of several programs—Word, PowerPoint, Excel, Access, and others.
- ▶ Each Office program is used to create different types of personal and business documents.
- ▶ The programs in Office 2016 share common tools that you use in a consistent, easy-to-learn manner.

- ▶ Some common tasks include opening and saving files, entering and formatting text, inserting pictures, and printing your work.
- ▶ Because of the consistent design and layout of the Office applications, when you learn to use one Microsoft Office application, you can apply many of the same techniques when working in the other Microsoft Office applications.

lculig/Fotolia

Aspen Falls City Hall

In this project, you will create documents for the Aspen Falls City Hall, which provides essential services for the citizens and visitors of Aspen Falls, California. You will assist Janet Neal, Finance Director, to prepare a presentation for the City Council. The presentation will explain retail sales trends in the city. The information will help the council to predict revenue from local sales taxes.

Microsoft Office is a suite of tools designed for specific tasks. In this project, the data was originally stored in an Access database. You will use Word to write a memo to update your supervisor about the project's status. Next, you will use Excel to create a chart from that data, and then use PowerPoint to display the chart to an audience. In this way, each application performs a different function and creates a different type of document.

In this project, you will create a Word document, and open existing files in Excel and PowerPoint. You will write a memo, format an Excel worksheet, and update chart data, and then place a copy of the chart into a PowerPoint presentation. You will also format a database report in Access. In all four applications, you will apply the same formatting to provide a consistent look and feel.

Outcome

Using the skills in this chapter, you will be able to open Office applications, save files, edit and format text and pictures, apply themes, use the Mini toolbar and Backstage view, format worksheets and reports, and paste objects into presentations.

Objectives

1 Explain the common features of Office 2016 applications

2 Modify documents

3 Prepare a presentation

4 Differentiate the uses of each Office 2016 application

5 Create Word, Excel, PowerPoint, and Access files for a presentation

Student data files needed for this chapter:

cf01_Memo (Word)
cf01_Parks (Word)
cf01_RetailChart (Excel)
cf01_RetailSlides (PowerPoint)
cf01_RetailData (Access)

You will save your files as:

Last_First_cf01_Parks (Word)
Last_First_cf01_Memo (Word)
Last_First_cf01_RetailMemo (Word)
Last_First_cf01_RetailChart (Excel)
Last_First_cf01_RetailSlides (PowerPoint)
Last_First_cf01_RetailData (Access)

SKILLS

At the end of this chapter, you will be able to:

Skill 1   Start Office Applications
Skill 2   Open and Save Student Data Files
Skill 3   Type and Edit Text
Skill 4   Format Text and Save Files
Skill 5   Apply Themes and Use the Mini Toolbar
Skill 6   Use Backstage View
Skill 7   Insert and Format Images
Skill 8   Format Worksheets
Skill 9   Copy and Paste Objects and Format Slides
Skill 10 Format Access Reports

MORE SKILLS

Skill 11 Store Files Online
Skill 12 Share Office Files
Skill 13 Install Office Add-ins
Skill 14 Customize the Ribbon and Options

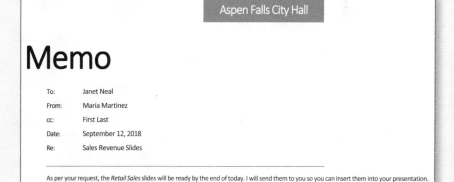

Office 2016, Windows 10, Microsoft Corporation

► The way that you start an Office application depends on what operating system you are using and how your computer is configured.

► Each application's start screen displays links to recently viewed documents and thumbnails of sample documents that you can open.

1. If necessary, turn on the computer, sign in, and navigate to the desktop. Take a few moments to familiarize yourself with the various methods for starting Office applications as summarized in Figure 1.

   One method that works in both Windows 8.1 and Windows 10 is to press ▦ (the Windows key located between Ctrl and Alt) to display the Start menu or screen. With Start displayed, type the application name, verify that Word is selected, and then press Enter .

2. Use one of the methods described in the previous step to start **Word 2016**, and then take a few moments to familiarize yourself with the Word start screen as shown in Figure 2.

   Your list of recent documents will vary depending on what Word documents you have worked with previously. Below the list of recent documents, the *Open Other Documents* link is used to open Word files that are not listed.

■ Continue to the next page to complete the skill ▶

Common Methods to Start Office 2016 Applications	
Location	**Description**
Start screen tile	Click the application's tile
Desktop	Double-click the application's desktop icon
Taskbar	Click the application's taskbar button
Windows 10 Start menu	Click Start and look in pinned or most used apps. Or click All apps and locate the Office application or the Microsoft Office 2016 folder.
All locations	Press ▦, type the application's name, select the correct application, and then press Enter .
Search the web and Windows	Type the application's name, and then press Enter

Figure 1

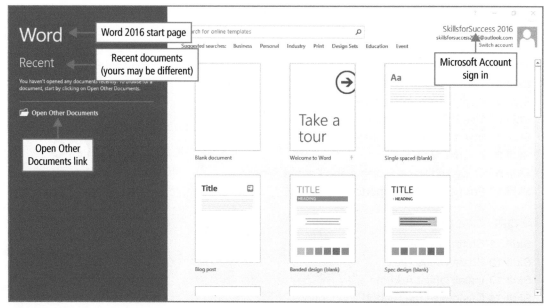

Figure 2

Word 2016, Windows 10, Microsoft Corporation

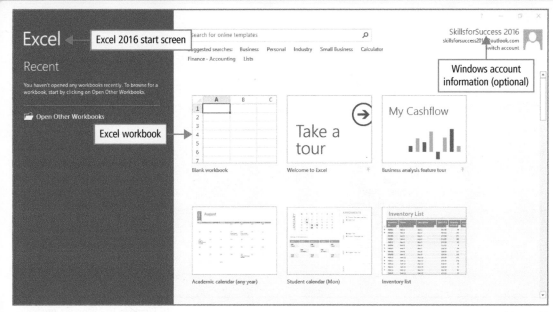

Excel 2016, Windows 10, Microsoft Corporation

Figure 3

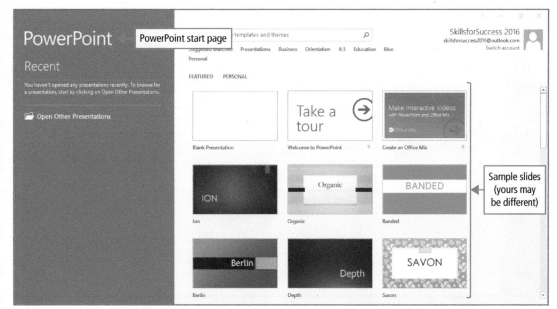

PowerPoint 2016, Windows 10, Microsoft Corporation

Figure 4

3. If desired, click **Sign in to get the most out of Office**, and then follow the onscreen directions to sign in using your Microsoft account.

Logging in enables you to access Microsoft Cloud services such as opening and saving files stored on your OneDrive. Unless otherwise directed, signing in to your Microsoft account is optional in this book. To protect your privacy, you should sign in only if you are already signed in to Windows using a unique username, not a shared account. For example, many public computers share an account for guests. When you are logged in to your Microsoft account, your name and picture will display in the upper right corner of the window.

4. Using the technique just practiced, start **Excel 2016**, and then compare your screen with Figure 3.

Worksheets are divided into *cells*—boxes formed by the intersection of a row and column into which text, objects, and data can be inserted. In Excel, cells can contain text, formulas, and functions. Worksheets can also display charts based on the values in the cells.

5. Start **PowerPoint 2016**, and then compare your screen with Figure 4.

PowerPoint presentations consist of *slides*—individual pages in a presentation that can contain text, pictures, or other objects. PowerPoint slides are designed to be projected as you talk in front of a group of people. The PowerPoint start screen has thumbnails of several slides formatted in different ways.

■ **You have completed Skill 1 of 10**

▶ In this book, you will frequently open student data files.

1. Before beginning this skill, download the student data files for this chapter and unzip or copy them; use **Figure 1** as an example. Follow the instructions in the Getting Started with Windows 10 chapter or provided by your instructor.

2. On the taskbar, click the **Word** button . If necessary, start Word.

3. On the **Word** start page, click **Open Other Documents** to display the Open page. If you already had a blank document open, click the File tab instead.

4. On the **Open** page, click **This PC**, and then click the **Browse** button.

5. In the **Open** dialog box navigation pane, navigate to the student files for this chapter, and then compare your screen with **Figure 2**.

6. In the **Open** dialog box, select **cf01_Memo**, and then click the **Open** button.

7. If the **Protected View** message displays, click the **Enable Editing** button.

   Files downloaded from a website typically open in **Protected View**—a view applied to files downloaded from the Internet that allows you to decide if the content is safe before working with the file.

8. On the **File tab**, click **Save As**. Click **Browse**. Navigate to the location where you will be saving your files. In the **Save As** dialog box, click the **New folder** button, and then type Common Features Chapter

   Save As is used to select the location where you want to save your work. You can choose to save to your OneDrive or other locations on your computer.

▪ **Continue to the next page to complete the skill**

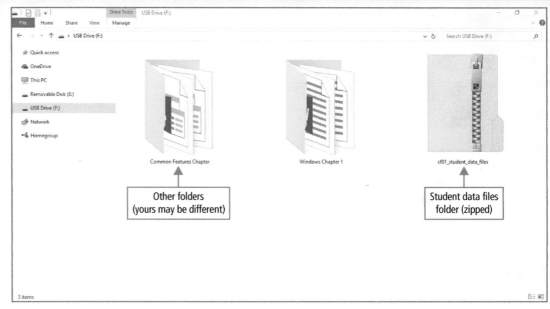

Figure 1   Word 2016, Windows 10, Microsoft Corporation

Figure 2   Word 2016, Windows 10, Microsoft Corporation

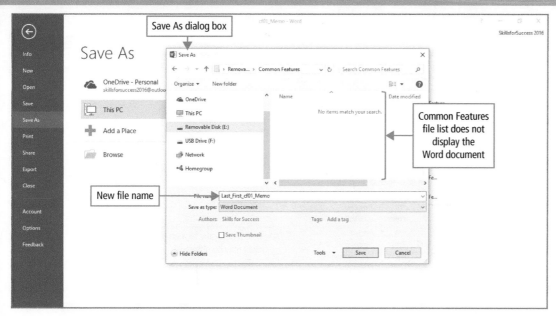

Save As dialog box

New file name

Common Features file list does not display the Word document

Word 2016, Windows 10, Microsoft Corporation

Figure 3

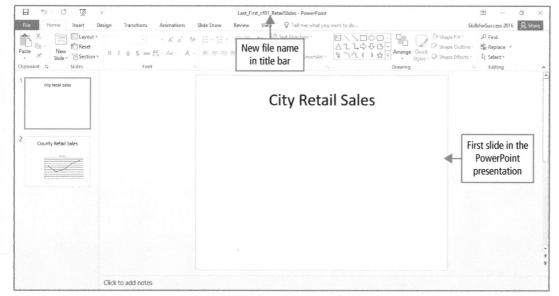

City Retail Sales

New file name in title bar

First slide in the PowerPoint presentation

PowerPoint 2016, Windows 10, Microsoft Corporation

Figure 4

9. Press [Enter] twice. In the **File name** box, change the text to Last_First_cf01_Memo using your own name.

In this book, you should substitute your first and last name whenever you see the text *Last_First* or *Your Name*.

10. Compare your screen with Figure 3, and then click the **Save** button.

You can use Save As to create a copy of a file with a new name. The original student data file will remain unchanged.

By default, the Save As dialog box displays only those files saved in the current application file format.

11. On the taskbar, click the **PowerPoint** button to return to the PowerPoint start screen. If necessary, start PowerPoint.

12. On the **PowerPoint 2016** start screen, click **Open Other Presentations** to display the Open page. If you already had a blank presentation open, click the File tab instead.

13. On the **Open** page, click **This PC**, and then click the **Browse** button. In the **Open** dialog box, navigate to the student files for this chapter, and then open **cf01_RetailSlides**. If necessary, enable the content.

14. On the **File tab**, click **Save As**, and then use the **Save As** page to navigate as needed to open your **Common Features Chapter** folder in the Save As dialog box.

On most computers, your Word and Excel files will not display because the PowerPoint Save As dialog box is set to display only presentation files.

15. Type Last_First_cf01_RetailSlides and then click **Save**. Compare your screen with Figure 4.

■ **You have completed Skill 2 of 10**

▶ New documents are stored in **RAM**—the computer's temporary memory—until you save them to more permanent storage such as your hard drive, USB flash drive, or online storage.

▶ To **edit** is to insert, delete, or replace text in an Office document, workbook, or presentation.

▶ To edit text, position the **insertion point**—a flashing vertical line that indicates where text will be inserted when you start typing—at the desired location or select the text you want to replace.

1. On the taskbar, click the **Word** button ⬜ to return to the *Last_First_cf01_Memo* document.

2. Click the **Date** placeholder—*[Click to select date]*—and then click the **date arrow** to open the calendar. In the calendar, click the current date.

> **Placeholders**—are reserved, formatted spaces into which you enter your own text or objects. If no text is entered, the placeholder text will not print.

3. In the **Subject** placeholder, type Sales Tax Revenues Compare your screen with **Figure 1**.

4. Press Ctrl + End to place the insertion point in the **Type memo here** placeholder—*[Type memo here]*—and then type the following: As per your request, the Retail Sales slides will be ready by the end of today. I will send them to you so you can insert them into your presentation. Let me know if you have any questions. Compare your screen with **Figure 2**.

> Word determines whether the word will fit within the established margin. If it does not fit, Word moves the entire word to the beginning of the next line. This feature is called **word wrap**.

■ **Continue to the next page to complete the skill** ➤

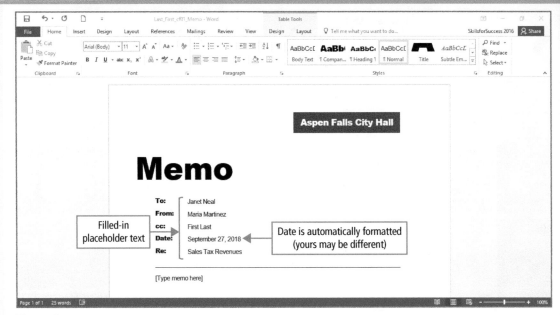

Figure 1

Word 2016, Windows 10, Microsoft Corporation

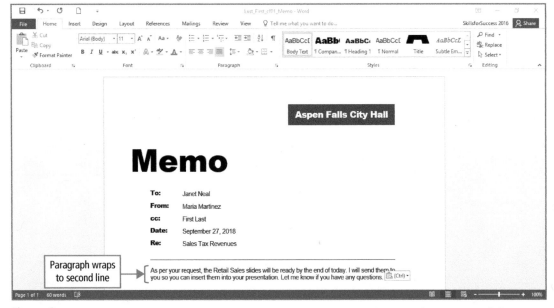

Figure 2

Word 2016, Windows 10, Microsoft Corporation

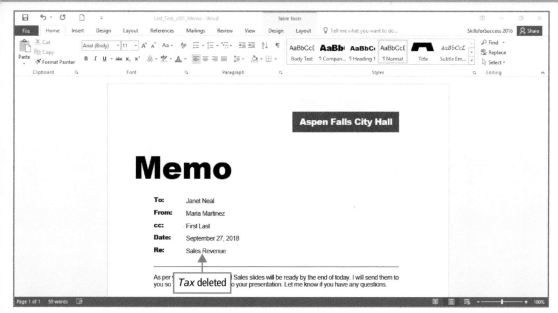

Word 2016, Windows 10, Microsoft Corporation   Figure 3

Word 2016, Windows 10, Microsoft Corporation   Figure 4

5. In the **Re:** line, click to the left of *Tax* to place the insertion point at the beginning of the word. Press Delete four times to delete the word *Tax* and the space following it.

   The Delete key deletes one letter at a time moving from left to right. The name on your keyboard may vary—for example, DEL, Del or Delete. Another option would be to ***double-click***— is to click the left mouse button two times quickly without moving the mouse—or to ***double-tap***—tap the screen in the same place two times quickly—the text to delete the word.

   After selecting text, the ***Mini toolbar***—a toolbar with common formatting commands—displays near the selection.

6. Click to the right of *Revenues*. Press Backspace one time to delete the letter *s*, and then compare your screen with **Figure 3**.

   The Backspace key deletes one letter at a time moving from right to left. The name on your keyboard may vary—for example, BACK, Backspace, or simply a left-facing arrow.

7. Press Ctrl + End. Type Thank you On the Quick Access Toolbar, and then click **Undo Typing** ↺.

8. Click the **Customize Quick Access Toolbar** button, and then from the menu, click **Print Preview and Print** Compare your screen with **Figure 4**.

9. Click the **Print Preview and Print** button 🔍 to view how the memo will look in printed form. Click the **Back** button ← to return to the document. Keep the file open for the next skill.

■ **You have completed Skill 3 of 10**

▶ **WATCH** SKILL 1.4

▶ To **_format_** is to change the appearance of the text—for example, changing the text color to red.

▶ The **_Format Painter_** copies formatting from selected text and applies that formatting to other text.

1. Select the text _Janet Neal_. On the **Home tab**, in the **Font group**, click the **Font Dialog Box Launcher** ⌐ to open the Font dialog box. Compare your screen with **Figure 1**.

2. In the **Font dialog** box, under **Font**, scroll down until you can see the _Calibri_ font. Click **Calibri**, and then under **Size**, click **12**. Click **OK**.

3. Verify that the text _Janet Neal_ is selected. On the **Home tab**, in the **Clipboard group**, double-click the **Format Painter** button.

4. With the **Format Painter** selected, double-click the word **Maria** to apply the formatting from the text _Janet Neal_.

5. **_Drag_**—press and hold the left mouse button while moving the mouse—to select the text **Martinez** to apply the formatting from the text _Janet Neal_. Use the techniques just practiced to apply the formatting to **First** and **Last** name, the **date**, and **Sales Revenue**. Compare your screen with **Figure 2**.

   The Calibri font and font size of 12 are copied from the text _Janet Neal_ and applied to the other text.

■ **Continue to the next page to complete the skill** ⟩

Figure 1   Word 2016, Windows 10, Microsoft Corporation

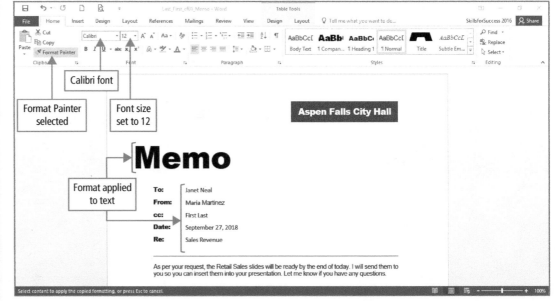

Figure 2   Word 2016, Windows 10, Microsoft Corporation

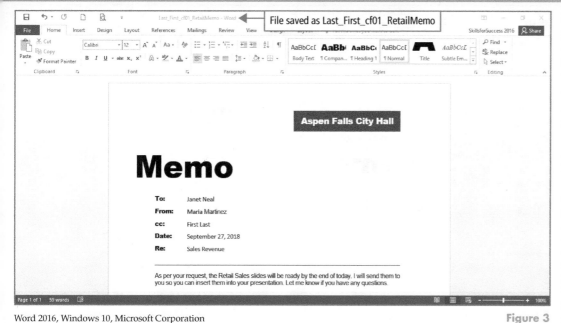

Word 2016, Windows 10, Microsoft Corporation   **Figure 3**

Word 2016, Windows 10, Microsoft Corporation   **Figure 4**

6. Click the **Format Painter** button to deselect it.

   When you single-click the format painter, you can apply the formatting to one other text selection. When you double-click the format painter, it will remain active until you click it again to deselect it.

7. In the **cc:** line, replace the text **First Last** with your first and last names. Click the **File tab**, and then click **Save As**.

8. Click **Browse** to navigate to your **Common Features Chapter** folder, and then in the **Save As** dialog box, change the **File name** to Last_First_cf01_RetailMemo

9. Click **Save**, and then compare your screen to **Figure 3**.

10. In the **Re:** line, click to the right of *Revenue* to place the insertion point at the end of the word. Type Sildes

11. Click the **Review tab**. In the **Proofing group**, click the **Spelling & Grammar** button. Compare your screen with **Figure 4**.

    The Spelling pane provides suggested spelling corrections.

12. In the **Spelling pane**, if necessary, click the first option **Slides**, and then click **Change** to correct the spelling of the word **Slides**. Read the dialog box message, and then click **OK**.

    After the document is saved, the name of the file displays on the title bar at the top of the window.

13. Leave the memo open for the next skill.

■ **You have completed Skill 4 of 10**

▶ When formatting an Office document, it is a good idea to pick a ***theme***—a prebuilt set of unified formatting choices including colors and fonts.

1. Click the **Design tab**. In the **Document Formatting group**, click the **Themes** button, and then compare your screen with Figure 1.

Each theme displays as a thumbnail in a ***gallery***—a visual display of selections from which you can choose.

2. In the **Themes** gallery, point to—but do not click—each thumbnail to preview its formatting with ***Live Preview***—a feature that displays what the results of a formatting change will be if you select it.

3. In the **Themes** gallery, click the third theme in the second row—**Retrospect**.

A ***font*** is a set of characters with the same design and shape. Each theme has two font categories—one for headings and one for body text.

4. Click anywhere in the text *Aspen Falls City Hall* to make it the active paragraph. With the insertion point in the paragraph, click the **Home tab**.

5. In the **Paragraph group**, click the **Shading arrow** ⬛▾. In the first row of the gallery under **Theme Colors**, click the sixth choice—**Orange, Accent 2**. Compare your screen with Figure 2.

In all themes, the Accent 2 color is the sixth choice in the color gallery, but the color varies depending on the theme. Here, the Retrospect theme Accent 2 color is a shade of orange.

■ **Continue to the next page to complete the skill** ➤

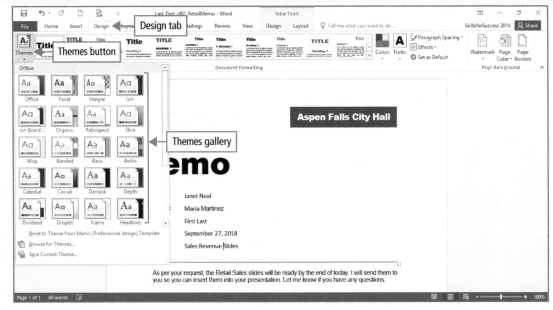

Figure 1   Word 2016, Windows 10, Microsoft Corporation

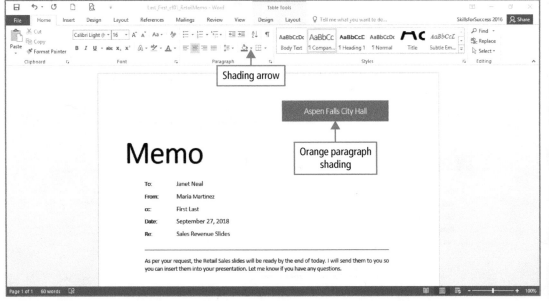

Figure 2   Word 2016, Windows 10, Microsoft Corporation

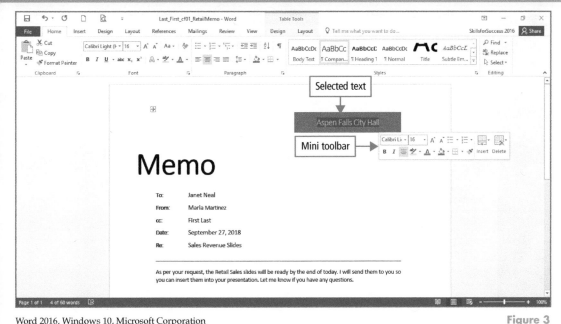

Word 2016, Windows 10, Microsoft Corporation

Figure 3

Word 2016, Windows 10, Microsoft Corporation

Figure 4

6. In the upper right corner, select the text *Aspen Falls City Hall*, and then compare your screen with Figure 3. To select by dragging with a touch display, tap in the text and then drag the selection handle.

If the Mini toolbar does not display, you can right-click or tap the selected text.

7. On the Mini toolbar, click the **Font Size arrow** ⬚, and then from the list, click **20** to increase the size of the selected text. On the Mini toolbar, click the **Bold** button ⬚.

8. On the Mini toolbar, click the **Font Color arrow** ⬚, and then under **Theme colors**, click the first color in the first row—**White, Background 1** Alternatively, on the Home tab, in the Font group, click the Font Color arrow.

9. In the paragraph that begins *As per your*, drag to select the text *Retail Sales*. From the Mini toolbar, click the **Italic** button ⬚.

Alternatively, you can use a **keyboard shortcut**—a combination of keys that performs a command. To apply italic, you could press ⬚ Ctrl ⬚ + ⬚ I ⬚.

10. Click a blank area of the document, and then compare your screen with Figure 4. Carefully check the memo for spelling errors. If spelling errors are found, use the techniques previously practiced to correct them.

11. **Save** ⬚ the file.

■ **You have completed Skill 5 of 10**

▶ **Backstage view** is a collection of options on the File tab used to open, save, print, and perform other file management tasks. In Backstage view, you can return to the open document by clicking the Back button.

1. Click the **File tab**, and then compare your screen with Figure 1.

2. On the **File tab**, click **Print** to display the Print page. In the lower right corner of the **Print** page, click the **Zoom In** button until the zoom level displays **100%**, and then compare your screen with Figure 2.

The Printer list displays available printers for your computer along with their status. For example, a printer may be offline because it is not turned on. The **default printer** is automatically selected when you do not choose a different printer—indicated by a check mark.

In a school lab or office, it is a good idea to check the list of available printers and verify that the correct printer is selected. It is also important that you know where the printer is located so that you can retrieve your printout.

The size of the print preview depends on the size of your monitor. When previewed on smaller monitors, some documents may not display accurately. If this happens, you can zoom in to see a more accurate view.

3. If you are printing your work for this project, note the location of the selected printer, click the **Print** button, and then retrieve your printouts from the printer.

■ **Continue to the next page to complete the skill**

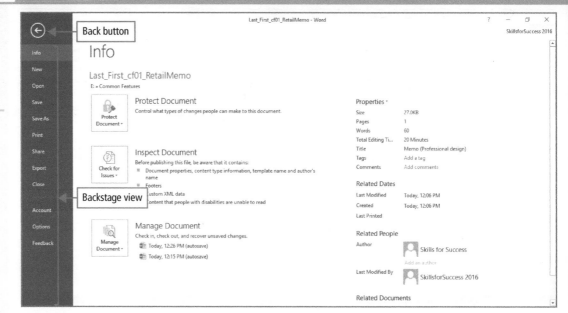

Figure 1   Word 2016, Windows 10, Microsoft Corporation

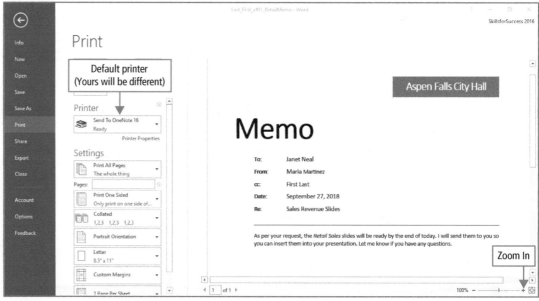

Figure 2   Word 2016, Windows 10, Microsoft Corporation

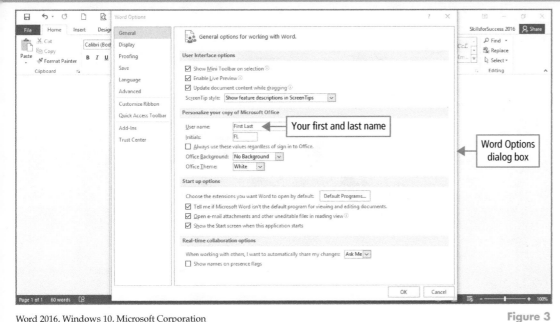

Word 2016, Windows 10, Microsoft Corporation

Figure 3

Word 2016, Windows 10, Microsoft Corporation

Figure 4

4. If necessary, click the **File tab**, and then click **Options**.

5. Under **Personalize your copy of Microsoft Office**, in the **User name** text box, replace the existing text with your First and Last name. Compare your screen with Figure 3.

6. Press Tab to select the text in the **Initials** text box, and then type your initials. Compare your screen to Figure 4, and then click **OK**.

7. Click the **Layout tab**. In the **Page Setup group**, click the **Margins** button.

8. Click the second option in the list— **Moderate**—to adjust the margins of the document.

> When changing the margins of the document, you should verify that the document will still print properly.

9. Click the **File tab**, and then click **Print**.

10. Under the **Settings** options, click the **Portrait Orientation** button, and then click **Landscape Orientation**.

> In Portrait Orientation, the page is taller than it is wide. In Landscape Orientation, the page is wider than it is tall.

11. Click the **Back** button ⊙, and then click **Save** 🖫. **Close** ✕ the file.

- **You have completed Skill 6 of 10**

▶ You can insert images into documents from files or online resources.

▶ Images can be resized or rotated or the color of the picture can be changed. You can also add frames and artistic effects to images.

1. Start **Word 2016**, and then open the student data file **cf01_Parks**. On the **File tab**, click **Save As**. Click **Browse**, navigate to the folder for this chapter, and then save the file as Last_First_cf01_Parks

2. If the Security Warning message displays, enable the content.

3. If necessary, click the upper left portion of the document, to place the insertion point in the blank area above the *Park Events* title.

4. Click the **Insert tab**. In the **Illustrations group**, click the **Online Pictures** button.

5. In the **Insert Pictures** dialog box, in the **Bing Image Search** text box, type Forest and then press Enter. Compare your screen with **Figure 1**.

6. Scroll down to view the available images. Select an image of a forest. Compare your screen with **Figure 2**, and then click **Insert**. If you are unable to locate the image shown in the figure, choose a similar picture.

7. If necessary, scroll down so you can view the entire image. With the **Resize** pointer, drag the lower right corner of the image upward and to the left until the right edge of the image aligns with the space between the words *Park* and *Events* in the document title.

■ **Continue to the next page to complete the skill**

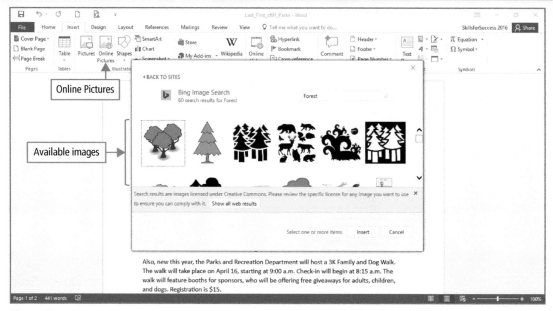

Figure 1   Word 2016, Windows 10, Microsoft Corporation

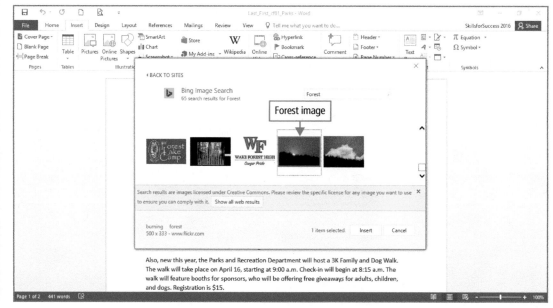

Figure 2   Word 2016, Windows 10, Microsoft Corporation

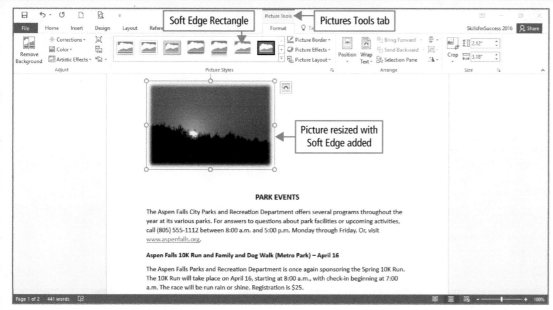

Lassedesignen/Fotolia; Word 2016, Windows 10, Microsoft Corporation

Figure 3

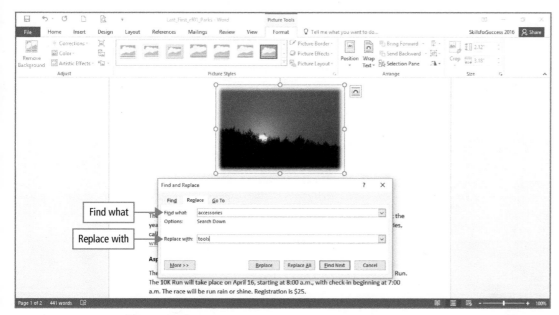

Lassedesignen/Fotolia; Word 2016, Windows 10, Microsoft Corporation

Figure 4

8. On the **Picture Tools Format tab**, in the **Picture Styles group**, click the sixth option—**Soft Edge Rectangle**. Compare your screen with Figure 3.

9. With the image still selected, press Ctrl + E to center the image on the page.

Keyboard shortcuts can be used to edit text, change the position of images on a page, or navigate throughout the document.

10. Next to the **Format tab**, click **Tell me what you want to do…**, and then type Find and Replace Press Enter.

11. In the **Find and Replace dialog box**, in the **Find what** text box, type accessories In the **Replace with** text box, type tools and then compare your screen with Figure 4.

12. In the **Find and Replace dialog box**, click **Replace All**.

13. Read the message, and then click **Yes**. Read the next message, and then click **OK**.

14. In the **Find and Replace dialog box**, click **Close**.

15. Click **Save** 🖫, and then **Close** ✕ the file.

■ **You have completed Skill 7 of 10**

▶ To keep formatting consistent across all Office files, the same themes are available in Word, Excel, PowerPoint, and Access.

▶ To format text in Excel, you select the cell that holds the text, and then click the desired formatting command.

1. On the taskbar, click the **Excel** button. On the **Start** screen, click **Open Other Workbooks**. Click **Browse** to navigate to the student data files, and then double-click **cf01_RetailChart**.

2. Click the **File tab**, and then click **Save As**. Navigate to the folder for this chapter, and then save the file as Last_First_cf01_RetailChart

3. Click cell **B9**—the intersection of column B and row 9—to select the cell. Compare your screen with **Figure 1**.

   A selected cell is indicated by a thick, dark-green border.

4. With cell **B9** selected, type 4.37 and then press Enter to update the chart.

   The chart is based on the data in columns A and B. When the data is changed, the chart changes to reflect the new values.

5. On the **Page Layout tab**, in the **Themes group**, click the **Themes** button, and then click the **Retrospect** thumbnail. Compare your screen with **Figure 2**.

   The Retrospect theme applies the same colors, fonts, and effects as the Retrospect theme of other Office applications. Here, the font was changed to Calibri.

➡ **Continue to the next page to complete the skill**

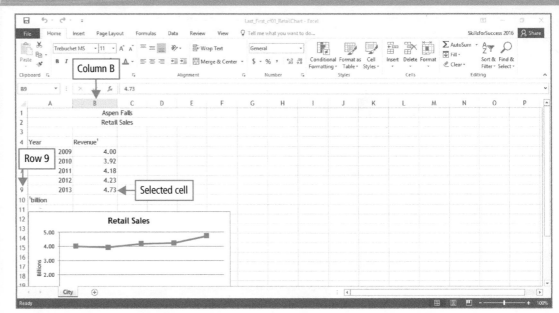

Figure 1   Excel 2016, Windows 10, Microsoft Corporation

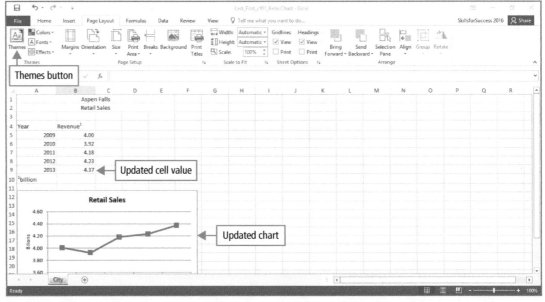

Figure 2   Excel 2016, Windows 10, Microsoft Corporation

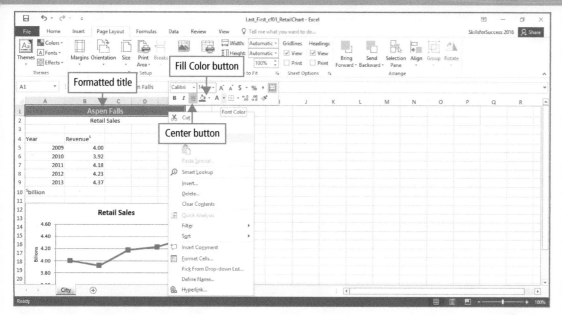

Excel 2016, Windows 10, Microsoft Corporation

Figure 3

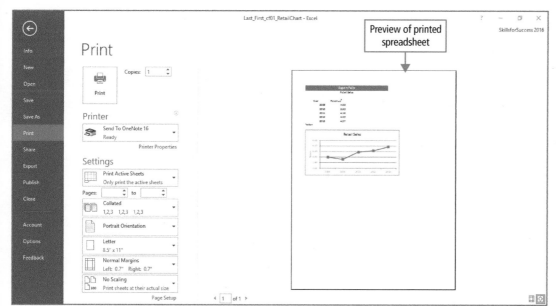

Excel 2016, Windows 10, Microsoft Corporation

Figure 4

6. Right-click cell **A1** containing the text *Aspen Falls* to display the Mini toolbar. Click the **Font Size arrow**, and then click **14** to increase the font size. Click the **Center** button to center the title.

7. With cell **A1** still selected, on the Mini toolbar, click the **Fill Color arrow**, and then under **Theme Colors**, click the sixth choice—**Orange, Accent 2**.

8. On the Mini toolbar, click the **Font Color arrow**, and then under **Theme Colors**, click the first choice—**White, Background 1**. Compare your screen with **Figure 3**.

9. Click cell **A4**. On the **Home tab**, in the **Alignment group**, click the **Center** button to center the text. In the **Clipboard group**, click the **Format Painter** button one time, click cell **B4** to apply the center format, and then turn off the Format Painter.

10. Click cell **A10**, and then in the **Font group**, change the **Font Size** to **9**.

11. On the **File tab**, click **Print**, and then compare your screen with **Figure 4**.

    The Excel Print page is used in the same manner as the Word Print page. Here, you can preview the document, select your printer, and verify that the worksheet will print on a single page. By default, the gridlines do not print.

12. If you are printing your work for this project, print the worksheet. Otherwise, click the **Back** button to return to Normal view.

13. Click **Save**.

■ **You have completed Skill 8 of 10**

▶ In Office, the *copy* command places a copy of the selected text or object in the **Office Clipboard**—a temporary storage area that holds text or an object that has been cut or copied.

▶ The *paste* command inserts a copy of the text or object from the Office Clipboard.

1. In the Excel window, click the border of the chart to select the chart. Compare your screen with **Figure 1**.

   In Office, certain graphics such as charts and SmartArt display a thick border when they are selected.

2. Right-click a blank area of the chart, and then click the **Copy** button 📋 to place a copy of the chart into the Office Clipboard.

3. On the taskbar, click the **PowerPoint** button 📊 to return to the **Last_First_cf01_RetailSlides** presentation.

4. With **Slide 1** as the active slide, on the **Home tab**, in the **Clipboard group**, click the **Paste** button to insert the copied Excel chart. If you accidentally clicked the Paste arrow to display the Paste Options, click the Paste button that is above it. Click a blank area of the slide, and then compare your screen with **Figure 2**.

5. Click the **Design tab**, and then in the **Themes group**, click the **More** button ⬇. Point to the thumbnails to preview their formatting, and then under Office, click the seventh choice—**Retrospect**.

   In PowerPoint, themes are sets of colors, fonts, and effects optimized for viewing in a large room with the presentation projected onto a screen in front of the audience.

■ **Continue to the next page to complete the skill** ➤

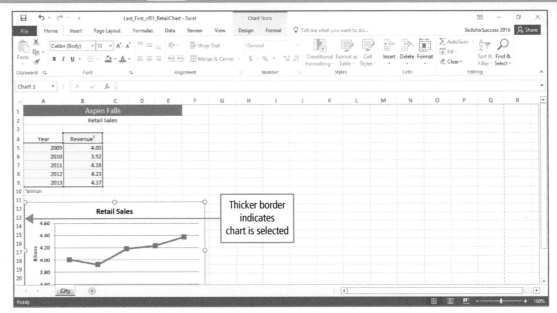

Figure 1

Excel 2016, Windows 10, Microsoft Corporation

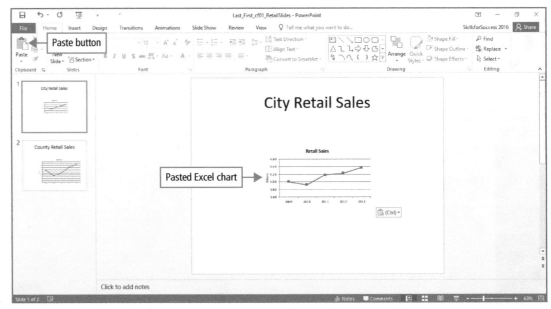

Figure 2

PowerPoint 2016, Windows 10, Microsoft Corporation

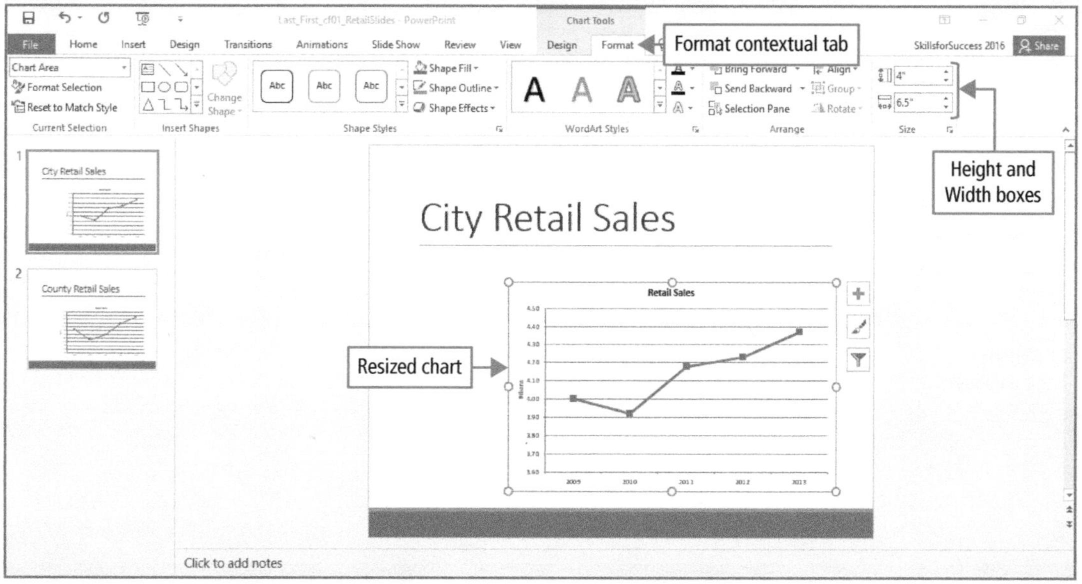

PowerPoint 2016, Windows 10, Microsoft Corporation

Figure 3

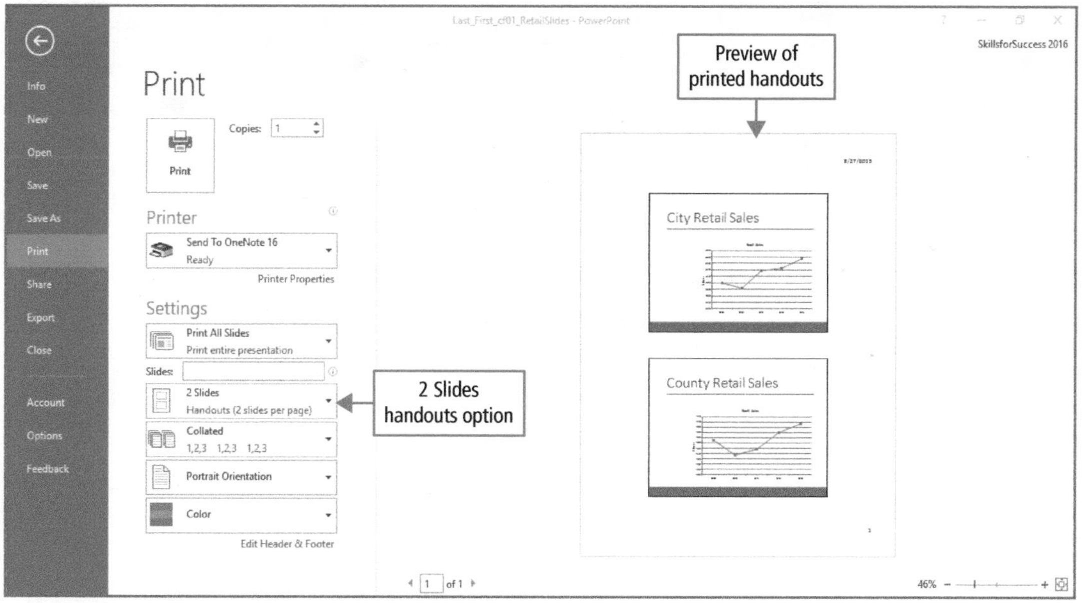

PowerPoint 2016, Windows 10, Microsoft Corporation

Figure 4

6. Drag to select the slide title text *City Retail Sales*. On the **Home tab**, in the **Font group**, click the **Font Size arrow**, and then click **60**. Alternatively, right-click the selected text, and then use the Mini toolbar to change the font size.
7. Click any area in the chart, and then click the border of the chart so that only the chart is selected.
8. Click the **Chart Tools Format tab**, and then in the **Size group**, click the **Shape Height arrow** until the value is **4**". Repeat this technique to change the **Width** value to **6.5**", and then compare your screen with **Figure 3**.

   The Format tab is a ***contextual tab***—a tab that displays on the ribbon only when a related object such as a graphic or chart is selected.
9. On the **File tab**, click **Print**. On the **Print** page, under **Settings**, click the **Full Page Slides** button. In the gallery, under **Handouts**, click **2 Slides**. Compare your screen with **Figure 4**.
10. If you are printing your work, click **Print** to print the handout. Otherwise, click **Save** to return to Normal view. **Close** [X] PowerPoint.
11. On the taskbar, click the **Excel** button, and then **Close** [X] Excel. If a message displays asking you to save changes, click Save.

■ **You have completed Skill 9 of 10**

▶ Access *reports* are database objects that present tables or query results in a way that is optimized for onscreen viewing or printing.

1. Start **Access 2016** , and then on the Start screen, click **Open Other Files**. On the **Open** page, click **Browse**.

2. In the **Open** dialog box, navigate to the student data files for this chapter. In the **Open** dialog box, select **cf01_RetailData**, and then click the **Open** button. If necessary, enable the content.

3. Take a few moments to familiarize yourself with the Access objects in the Navigation Pane as shown in **Figure 1**.

    Database files contain several different types of objects such as tables, queries, forms, and reports. Each object has a special purpose summarized in the table in **Figure 2**.

4. On the **File tab**, click **Save As**. With **Save Database As** selected, click the **Save As** button.

5. In the **Save As** dialog box, navigate to your **Common Features Chapter** folder. In the **File name** box, name the file Last_First_cf01_RetailData and then click **Save**. If a security message displays, click the Enable Content button.

    Malicious persons sometimes place objects in database files that could harm your computer. For this reason, the security message may display when you open a database that you did not create. You should click the Enable Content button only when you know the file is from a trusted source.

■ Continue to the next page to complete the skill ▶

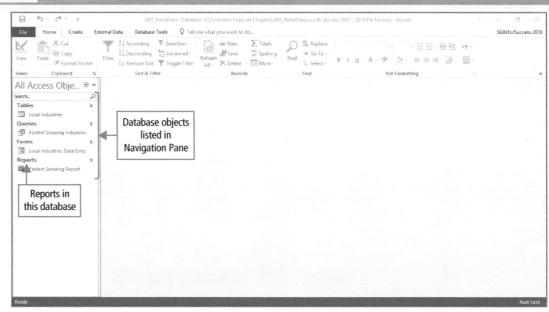

Figure 1

Access 2016, Windows 10, Microsoft Corporation

Common Database Objects	
Object	**Description**
Table	Stores the database data so that records are in rows and fields are in columns.
Query	Displays a subset of data in response to a question.
Form	Used to find, update, and add table records.
Report	Presents tables or query results optimized for onscreen viewing or printing.

Figure 2

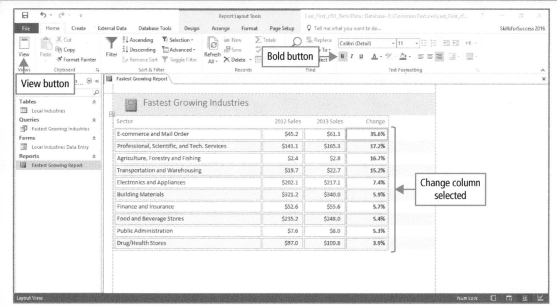

Access 2016, Windows 10, Microsoft Corporation

Figure 3

Access 2016, Windows 10, Microsoft Corporation

Figure 4

6. In the **Navigation Pane**, under **Reports**, double-click **Fastest Growing Report**.

7. On the **Home tab**, in the **Views group**, click the **View** button one time to switch to Layout view.

8. On the **Design tab**, in the **Themes group**, click **Themes**, and then click the seventh thumbnail—**Retrospect**.

9. Near the top of the **Change** column, click the first value—*35.6%*—to select all the values in the column.

10. Click the **Home tab**, and then in the **Text Formatting group**, click the **Bold** button. Compare your screen with **Figure 3**.

11. On the **Home tab**, click the **View arrow**, and then click **Print Preview**. Compare your screen with **Figure 4**. If necessary, in the Zoom group, click the One Page button to zoom to 100%.

12. If your instructor asked you to print your work, click the **Print** button, and then print the report.

13. **Save** 🔲 the formatting changes, and then **Close** ✕ the report.

> Objects such as reports are opened and closed without closing the Access application itself.

14. **Close** ✕ Access, and then submit your printouts or files for this chapter as directed by your instructor.

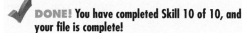

DONE! You have completed Skill 10 of 10, and your file is complete!

More Skills 11

Store Files Online

To complete this project, you will need the following files:

- cf01_MS11Memo (Word)
- cf01_MS11Chart (Excel)
- cf01_MS11Slide (PowerPoint)

You will save your files as:

- Last_First_cf01_MS11Memo (Word)
- Last_First_cf01_MS11Chart (Excel)
- Last_First_cf01_MS11Slide (PowerPoint)
- Last_First_cf01_MS11Snip

▶ *The Cloud*—an Internet technology used to store files and to work with programs that are stored in a central location.

▶ *Microsoft account*—personal account that you use to access your files, settings, and online services from devices connected to the Internet.

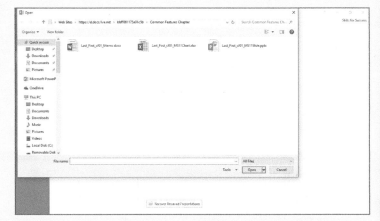

Figure 1   Office 2016, Windows 10, Microsoft Corporation

1. Start **Word 2016**. Open the student data file **cf01_MS11Memo**. In the upper right corner of the Word window, check to see if your Microsoft account name displays. If your account name displays, skip to step 3; otherwise, click **Sign In**.

2. In the dialog box, type your e-mail address. Click **Next**. In the **Sign in** screen, type your password. Click **Sign in**. If you don't have a Microsoft account, click **Sign up now**. Follow the onscreen directions to create an account.

3. On the **File tab**, click **Account**. If you are using an operating system other than Windows, this option is not available, skip to step 4. If your OneDrive is not listed as a connected service, click **Add a service**, point to **Storage**, and then click **OneDrive**.

4. Click **Save As**, and then double-click **OneDrive - Personal** connected to your Microsoft account. In the **Save As** dialog box, click **New folder**. Save the folder as Common Features Chapter Press [Enter] two times. Save the file as Last_First_cf01_MS11Memo

5. Replace the text *Your Name* with your First and Last names. **Save** 🖫 the file. Notice the green arrow on the save button. This indicates the file is syncing to OneDrive.

6. Start **Excel 2016**, and then open the student data file **cf01_MS11Chart**. Click the **File tab**, click **Save As**, and then double-click **OneDrive-Personal**. In the dialog box, double-click the **Common Features Chapter** folder. Save the file as Last_First_cf01_MS11Chart

7. Repeat the technique previously practiced to save the student data file **cf01_MS11Slides** to your OneDrive folder as Last_First_cf01_MS11Slide

8. On the **File tab**, click **Open**. Click **Browse**. In the dialog box, click the **File Type arrow**, and then click **All Files** to view the three files in the OneDrive folder. Compare your screen with **Figure 1**. Take a full-screen snip. Save the snip to your chapter folder as Last_First_cf01_MS11Snip

9. **Close** ✕ all open files. Submit the file as directed by your instructor.

■ **You have completed More Skills 11**

More Skills 12

Share Office Files

To complete this project, you will need the following file:

- cf01_MS12Rates

You will save your files as:

- Last_First_cf01_MS12Rates
- Last_First_cf01_MS12Share

▶ If you are working on a team project, you can share files, and provide others with editing or viewing privileges.

▶ You can share files instead of sending them as an e-mail attachment.

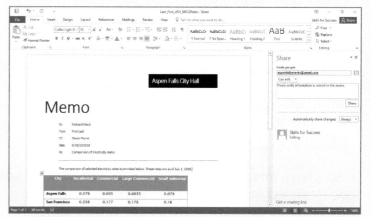

Word 2016, Windows 10, Microsoft Corporation

Figure 1

1. Start **Word 2016**. Open the student data file **cf01_MS12Rates**. Replace the *From:* placeholder text in the memo with your First and Last names.

2. In the upper right corner of the window, click the **Share** button. In the **Share** pane, click the **Save to Cloud** button.

3. If you are signed in to your Microsoft account, skip to step 4. If your computer does not show your Microsoft account, then click **Add a Place**. In the **Add a Place** page, click **OneDrive**. In the dialog box, type your e-mail address. Click **Next**. In the **Sign in** screen, type your password. Click **Sign in**. If you don't have a Microsoft account, click **Sign up now**. Follow the onscreen directions to create an account.

4. Click **OneDrive - Personal** connected to your Microsoft account. If you completed the More Skills 11 project, then skip to step 5; otherwise, double-click **OneDrive - Personal** to open your online folders. Click **New folder**, and then rename the folder as Common Features Chapter

5. Double-click the **Common Features Chapter** folder to open it. Save the file as Last_First_cf01_MS12Rates

6. In the **Share** pane, type the e-mail address as directed by your instructor in the **Invite people** box. Verify that *Can edit* is displayed, and then type the message Please verify information is correct in the memo. Click the **arrow** to **Automatically share changes**, and then click **Always**. Compare your screen with Figure 1.

An e-mail is sent to the owner of the e-mail address with a link. Saving files to the cloud ensures a link is created to the file and revisions are updated in one location. Sharing options allow shared files to be edited or viewed. If changes are allowed, options for sharing changes can be set.

7. Click the **Share** button below the message to share the file. Once the share is processed, the account associated with the e-mail address you shared the file with displays at the bottom of the Share pane.

8. Press ⊞, and type Snip Open the **Snipping Tool**, and then take a full-screen snip. Save the snip to your chapter folder as Last_First_cf01_MS12Share

9. **Save** 🖫 the file, and then **Close** ✖ Word. Submit the file as directed by your instructor.

■ **You have completed More Skills 12**

More Skills (13)

Install Office Add-ins

To complete this project, you will need the following file:

- cf01_MS13Skills

You will save your files as:

- Last_First_cf01_MS13Skills
- Last_First_cf01_MS13Cloud

▶ **Office Add-ins** are plugins that add extra features or custom commands to Office programs.

---

1. Start **Word 2016**, and then open the student data file **cf01_MS13Skills**. Save the file in your chapter folder as Last_First_cf01_MS13Skills

2. Click the **File tab**, and then replace the *Author* with your First and Last names. Click the **Back arrow**, and then click the **Insert tab**. In the **Header & Footer group**, click the **Header arrow**, and then click **Edit Header**. On the **Header & Footer Tools Design tab**, in the **Insert group**, click the **Document Info** button. Click **Author** to insert the Author's name in the header.

   Word inserts the author's name found in the document properties. Since you revised this property in step 2, your name will display.

3. Click **Close Header and Footer**. Starting with the text *Desktop Applications*, drag to select both columns through the text *Clipboard*.

4. Click the **Insert tab**, and then in the **Add-ins group**, click the **Store** button. Compare your screen with Figure 1.

   The Office add-ins available for Word display in the window. When you open other Office applications, add-ins associated with those applications will display.

5. Use the scroll bar on the right side of the Office Add-ins window to review the Add-ins. Notice there are also categories on the left of the window that provide several additional choices. If you have clicked any of the categories, click the Back arrow until the *Finalize and Polish Your Documents* category displays.

6. Click **Pro Word Cloud**. In the **Office Add-ins** window, click **Trust It**.

7. In the **Pro Word Cloud** pane, click the **Font arrow**, scroll down, and then click **Silentina Movie**. Click the **Colors arrow**, and then click **Sun Set**. Click the **Layout arrow**, and then click **Half And Half**. Verify the **Remove common words** check box is selected, and then click the **Create Word Cloud** button.

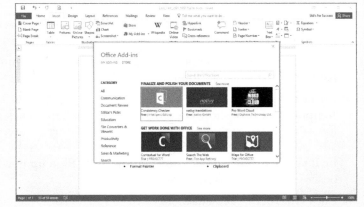

Figure 1   Word 2016, Windows 10, Microsoft Corporation

8. The word *cloud* will display in the top of the pane. Right-click the word **cloud**, and then click **Save Picture As**. Navigate to the folder for this chapter, and then save the file as Last_First_cf01_MS13Cloud

9. Close the **Pro Word Cloud** pane. **Save** 🖫, and then **Close** ✕ the file. Submit the files as directed by your instructor.

■ **You have completed More Skills 13**

More Skills 14

Customize the Ribbon and Options

To complete this project, you will need the following file:

- cf01_MS14Slide

You will save your file as:

- Last_First_cf01_MS14Ribbon

▶ The **Ribbon** contains commands placed in groups that are organized by tabs so that you can quickly find the tools you need.

1. Start **PowerPoint 2016**, and then open the student data file **cf01_MS14Slide**. Click the **Insert tab**. In the **Text group**, click the **Header & Footer** button. On the **Slide tab**, click the *Footer* check box. In the box, type your First and Last names, and then click **Apply**.

2. Click the **File tab**, and then click **Options**. Review the list, and then on the left, click **Save**. Under *Save presentations*, click the **arrow** to change **Save AutoRecover information every** to **5** minutes.

3. In the **PowerPoint Options** list, click **Customize Ribbon**. Compare your screen to Figure 1.

   Two panes display. In the left pane are the commands available to add to the ribbon. In the right pane are tabs and groups already added to the ribbon.

4. At the bottom of the right pane, click the **New Tab** button. Click **New Tab (Custom)**, and then click the **Rename** button. Type Common Features and then click **OK**. Click **New Group (Custom)**, click the **Rename** button, type Editing and then click **OK**.

5. In the left pane, click **Copy**, and then click the **Add** button. Notice the copy command appears in the *Editing (Custom)* group. Repeat this technique to add the commands **Cut, Font, Font Color, Font Size**, and **Format Painter**.

6. Click **Common Features (Custom),** and then click the **New Group** button. Click the **Rename** button, type Objects and click **OK**.

7. Repeat the technique previously practiced to add the commands **Add Table, Format Object, Insert Pictures**, and **Insert Text Box**. Click **OK** to close the Options window.

8. Review the tabs available, and then click the **Common Features tab** to view your new ribbon, groups, and commands.

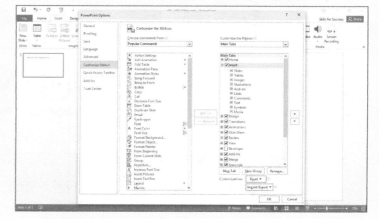

Access 2016, Windows 10, Microsoft Corporation

Figure 1

9. Press ⊞, and then type Snip Open the **Snipping Tool**, and then take a full-screen snip. Save the snip to your chapter folder as Last_First_cf01_MS14Ribbon

10. Click the **File tab**, click **Options**, and then click **Customize Ribbon**. At the bottom of the right pane, click the **Reset arrow**, click **Reset all customizations**, and then click **Yes** to delete the customizations. Click **OK** to close the Options window. Notice the tab is removed from the ribbon.

11. **Close** ⊠ PowerPoint without saving the file. Submit the file as directed by your instructor.

■ **You have completed More Skills 14**

Review

The following table summarizes the **SKILLS AND PROCEDURES** covered in this chapter.

Skills Number	Task	Step	Icon	Keyboard Shortcut
1	Start Office applications	Display Start menu or screen, and then type application name	⊞	⊞
2	Create a new folder while saving	Save As dialog box toolbar → New folder		
2	Save	Quick Access Toolbar → Save		Ctrl + S
2	Open a file	File tab → Open		Ctrl + O
2	Save a file with new name and location	File tab → Save As		F12
3	Apply bold	Home tab → Text Formatting group → Bold	B	Ctrl + B
3	Preview the printed page	File tab → Print		Alt + Ctrl + I
4	Change a font	Home tab → Font group → Font arrow		Ctrl + Shift + F
4	Change font size	Home tab → Font group → Font Size arrow	11 ▾	Ctrl + < Ctrl + >
5	Apply italic	Select text → Mini toolbar → Italic	I	Ctrl + I
5	Change font color	Home tab → Font group → Font Color arrow	A ▾	
5	Apply a theme	Design tab → Themes		
6	Change document properties	File tab → Options		
7	Insert online picture	Insert tab → Illustrations group → Online Pictures → Bing Image Search		
8	Fill Color	Mini toolbar → Fill Color arrow	abc	
8	Center align text	Select text → Mini toolbar → Center	☰ ▾	Ctrl + E
9	Copy	Select text or object → Right-click → Copy	✂	Ctrl + C
9	Paste	Home tab → Clipboard group → Paste		Ctrl + V
9	Save	File tab → Save		
10	Change report view	Home tab → View arrow		
MS11	Save files to OneDrive	File tab → OneDrive - Personal → Save		
MS11	View files in OneDrive	File tab → Open → Browse → All Files		
MS12	Share Office files	Share button → Sign in → Share		
MS13	Install Office Add-ins	Insert tab → Add-ins group → Store		
MS14	Customize Ribbon	File tab → Customize Ribbon		

Project Summary Chart

Project	Project Type	Project Location
Skills Review	Review	In Book & MIL MyITLab® Grader
Skills Assessment 1	Review	In Book & MIL MyITLab® Grader
Skills Assessment 2	Review	Book
My Skills	Problem Solving	Book
Visual Skills Check	Problem Solving	Book
Skills Challenge 1	Critical Thinking	Book
Skills Challenge 2	Critical Thinking	Book
More Skills Assessment	Review	In Book & MIL MyITLab® Grader
Collaborating with Google	Critical Thinking	Book

Key Terms

Matching

Match each term in the second column with its correct definition in the first column by writing the letter of the term on the blank line in front of the correct definition.

___ **1.** An individual page in a presentation that can contain text, pictures, or other objects.

___ **2.** The tool used to copy formatting from selected text and apply it to other text in the document, worksheet, or slide.

___ **3.** A menu with options such as Copy or Paste, available after selected text is right-clicked.

___ **4.** To insert, delete, or replace text in an Office document, spreadsheet, or presentation.

___ **5.** A prebuilt set of unified formatting choices including colors, fonts, and effects.

___ **6.** To change the appearance of text.

___ **7.** A set of characters with the same design and shape.

___ **8.** A feature that displays the result of a formatting change if you select it.

___ **9.** A view applied to documents downloaded from the Internet that allows you to decide if the content is safe before working with the document.

___ **10.** A command that moves a copy of the selected text or object to the Office Clipboard.

A Format Painter

B Copy

C Edit

D Font

E Format

F Live Preview

G Protected

H Slide

I Shortcut Menu

J Theme

Multiple Choice MyITLab®

Choose the correct answer.

1. The flashing vertical line that indicates where text will be inserted when you start typing.
   A. Cell reference
   B. Insertion point
   C. KeyTip

2. A reserved, formatted space into which you enter your own text or object.
   A. Gallery
   B. Placeholder
   C. Title

3. Until you save a document, the document is stored here.
   A. Office Clipboard
   B. Live Preview
   C. RAM

4. A collection of options on the File tab used to open, save, print, and perform other file management tasks.
   A. Backstage view
   B. Page Layout view
   C. File gallery

5. A temporary storage area that holds text or an object that has been cut or copied.
   A. Office Clipboard
   B. Dialog box
   C. Live Preview

6. A toolbar with common formatting buttons that displays after you select text.
   A. Gallery toolbar
   B. Mini toolbar
   C. Taskbar toolbar

7. A command that inserts a copy of the text or object from the Office Clipboard.
   A. Copy
   B. Insert
   C. Paste

8. A visual display of choices—typically thumbnails—from which you can choose.
   A. Gallery
   B. Options menu
   C. Shortcut menu

9. A tab that displays on the ribbon only when a related object such as a graphic or chart is selected.
   A. Contextual tab
   B. File tab
   C. Page Layout tab

10. A database object that presents tables or query results in a way that is optimized for onscreen viewing or printing.
    A. Form
    B. Report
    C. Table

Topics for Discussion

1. You have briefly worked with four Microsoft Office programs: Word, Excel, PowerPoint, and Access. Based on your experience, describe the overall purpose of each program.

2. Many believe that computers enable offices to go paperless—that is, to share files electronically instead of printing and then distributing them. What are the advantages of sharing files electronically, and in what situations is it best to print documents?

Skills Review

To complete this project, you will need the following files:

- **cf01_SRData (Access)**
- **cf01_SRChart (Excel)**
- **cf01_SRSlide (PowerPoint)**
- **cf01_SRMemo (Word)**

You will save your files as:

- **Last_First_cf01_SRData (Access)**
- **Last_First_cf01_SRChart (Excel)**
- **Last_First_cf01_SRSlide (PowerPoint)**
- **Last_First_cf01_SRMemo (Word)**

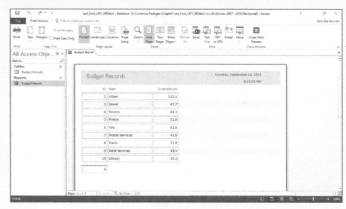

Figure 1   Access 2016, Windows 10, Microsoft Corporation

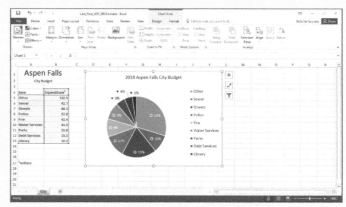

Figure 2   Excel 2016, Windows 10, Microsoft Corporation

1. Start **Access 2016**, and then click **Open Other Files**. Click **Browse**. In the **Open** dialog box, navigate to the student data files for this chapter and open **cf01_SRData**.

2. On the **File tab**, click **Save As**, and then click the **Save As** button. In the **Save As** dialog box, navigate to your chapter folder, and then save the file as Last_First_cf01_SRData Click **Save**. If necessary, enable the content.

3. In the **Navigation Pane**, double-click **Budget Report**, and then click the **View** button to switch to Layout view. On the **Design tab**, click **Themes**, and then click **Retrospect**.

4 Click the **View arrow**, click **Print Preview**, and then compare your screen with **Figure 1**. If you are printing this project, print the report.

5. Click **Save**, **Close** the report, and then **Close** Access.

6. Start **Excel 2016**, and then click **Open Other Workbooks**. Use the **Open** page to locate and open the student data file **cf01_SRChart**.

7. Navigate to your chapter folder, and then save the file as Last_First_cf01_SRChart

8. With **A1** selected, on the **Home tab**, in the **Font group**, click the **Font Size arrow**, and then click **24**.

9. On the **Page Layout tab**, click **Themes**, and then click **Retrospect**.

10. Click cell **B7**, and then type 84.3 Press Enter , and then click **Save**.

11. Click the border of the chart, and then compare your screen with **Figure 2**.

■ Continue to the next page to complete this Skills Review ➡

12. On the **Home tab**, in the **Clipboard group**, click the **Copy** button.

13. Start **PowerPoint 2016**. Click **Open Other Presentations**, and then open the student data file **cf01_SRSlide**.

14. On the **File tab**, click **Save As**. Click **Browse**, and then save the file in your chapter folder as Last_First_cf01_SRSlide

15. On the **Home tab**, in the **Clipboard group**, click **Paste** to insert the chart.

16. On the **Design tab**, in the **Themes group**, click the **More** button, and then click the seventh choice—**Retrospect**. Compare your screen with Figure 3.

17. If you are printing this project, on the **File tab**, click **Print**, change the **Settings** to **Handouts**, **1 Slide**, and then print the handout.

18. Click **Save**, and then **Close** PowerPoint.

19. Click cell **A4**. In the **Clipboard group**, click the **Format Painter**, and then click cell **B4**.

20. Click **Save**, and then **Close** Excel.

21. Start **Word 2016**, and then click **Open Other Documents**. Use the **Open** page to locate and open the student data file **cf01_SRMemo**.

22. On the **File tab**, click **Save As**. Click **Browse**, and then save the file in your chapter folder as Last_First_cf01_SRMemo

23. Click *[RECIPIENT NAME]*, and then type Janet Neal

24. Change *[YOUR NAME]* to your own name, and then change *[SUBJECT]* to City Budget

25. Change *[CLICK TO SELECT DATE]* to the current date, and then change *[NAME]* to Maria Martinez

26. Change *[Type your memo text here]* to the following: I am pleased to tell you that the city budget items that you requested are ready. I will send you the Access report and PowerPoint slide today.

27. Click to the left of *INTEROFFICE*, and then press Delete as needed to delete the word and the space following it.

28. On the **Design tab**, click the **Themes** button, and then click **Retrospect**.

29. Double-click the word *MEMORANDUM* to select it. On the Mini toolbar, click the **Font Color arrow**, and then click the fifth color—**Orange, Accent 1**.

30. With *MEMORANDUM* still selected, on the Mini toolbar, click the **Bold** button one time to remove the bold formatting from the selection, and then change the **Font Size** to **24**.

31. Click **Save**, and then compare your screen with Figure 4.

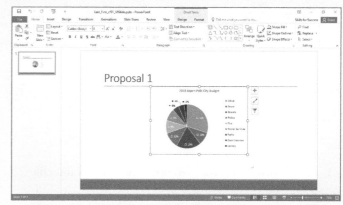

Access 2016, Windows 10, Microsoft Corporation

Figure 3

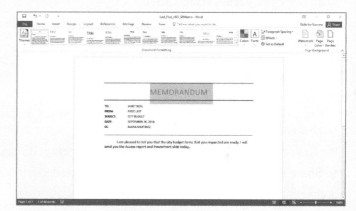

Word 2016, Windows 10, Microsoft Corporation

Figure 4

32. Click the **File tab**, and then click **Options**. Replace the User name with your First and Last names. Close the dialog box to save the change.

33. If you are printing your work, print the memo. Click **Save**, and then **Close** Word. Submit your printouts or files as directed by your instructor.

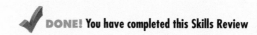 **DONE! You have completed this Skills Review**

More Skills Assessment

MyITLab®
Grader

To complete this project, you will need the following file:

- cf01_MSAEvents

You will save your file as:

- Last_First_cf01_MSASnip

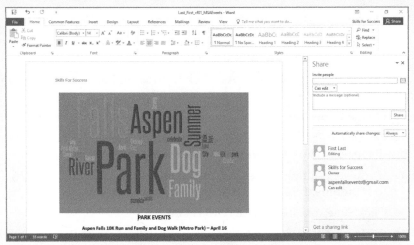

Figure 1
Word 2016, Windows 10, Microsoft Corporation

1. Start **Word 2016**, and then open the student data file **cf01_MSAEvents**.

2. Starting with the text *Park Events*, drag to select the text through *October 2*.

3. Using **My Add-ins**, insert the **Pro Word Cloud** add-in.

4. Create a word cloud using the **Steelfish** font and **Bluebell Glade** colors. Click **Create Word Cloud**.

5. Right-click the word cloud image, and then paste it to the top of the document. Close the **Pro Word Cloud** pane.

6. Open **Word Options**, and then replace the User name with your First and Last names.

7. Create a new tab, and then rename the tab Common Features and the group Tasks Add the *Popular Commands* **Copy**, **Cut**, **Delete**, and **Format Painter** to the *Tasks* group.

8. Open the new tab, and then view the commands in the group.

9. **Share** the file with the e-mail address as directed by your instructor, and then **Save** the file as Last_First_cf01_MSAEvents to **OneDrive - Personal** linked to your account in the **Common Features Chapter** folder.

10. Set the share options to **Can edit**, and then type the message I've created the word cloud for the events flyer.

11. Edit the **Author** property, and then insert your First and Last names. Insert the **Document Info** property **Author** as the header, and then **Close** the header. Compare your screen with **Figure 1**.

12. Click the **Common Features tab**, and then use the **Snipping Tool** to take a **Full-screen Snip** of your screen. **Save** the file as Last_First_cf01_MSASnip

13. **Close** the Snipping Tool window. **Save** the file, and then **Close** Word. Submit the file as directed by your instructor.

DONE! You have completed More Skills Assessment

Collaborating with Google

To complete this project, you will need a Google account (refer to the Common Features chapter) and the following files:

- cf01_GPParks
- cf01_GPImage

You will save your file as:

- Last_First_cf01_GPParks

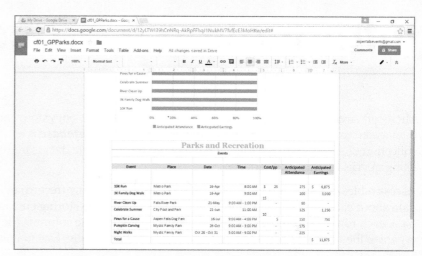

Google; Word 2016, Windows 10, Microsoft Corporation   Figure 1

1. Open the **Google Chrome**  web browser. If you already have a Google account, skip to step 2. In the upper right corner, click **Gmail**. In the next window, click **Create an account**. Follow the onscreen directions to create an account.

2. Log into your Google account, and then click the **Apps** button. Click **Drive** to open Google Drive.

3. Click **NEW**, and then click **File upload**. Navigate to the student data files, and then open **cf01_GPParks**.

4. Select the **cf01_GPParks** file in **Google Drive**. Click **More actions**, point to **Open with**, and then click **Google Docs**.

5. Position the insertion point after the title in the document. Click **Insert** on the menu, and then click **Image**. In the **Insert image** window, ensure **Upload** is selected. Click **Choose an Image to upload**, and then navigate to the student data files, click **cf01_GPImage**, and then click **Open**. Click the image, and then drag the lower middle sizing handle up until the image height is resized about 1 inch.

6. Drag to select the title text above image. On the toolbar, click the **Font arrow**, and then click **Georgia**. Click the **Font size arrow**, and then click **18**. Click **Text color**, and then click the third option in the second row—**orange**.

7. With the title text selected, click **Paint format**. Scroll down to the *Events* table. Drag to select the text *Parks and Recreation*, and then apply the **title format**.

8. In the first column, drag to select the text *Event*. Click the **Font size arrow**, and then click **10**. Double-click **Paint format**, and then copy the format to the other column titles. Drag to select all of the column titles, and then click **Center**. Compare your screen with Figure 1.

9. Click the **File tab**, point to **Download as**, and then click **Microsoft Word (.docx)**. Open the downloaded file, click **Enable Editing**, and then save the file in the chapter folder as Last_First_cf01_GPParks

10. Close all windows, and then submit your file as directed by your instructor.

DONE! You have completed Collaborating with Google

Introduction to Access

Microsoft Access is a ***database system***—a program used to both store and manage large amounts of data. In a database system, the ***database*** is a collection of structured tables designed to store the data. The data is managed using queries, forms, and reports.

Access tables organize data into rows and columns. Each row (record) stores data about each item in a collection. For example, in a table storing customer data, each row would represent an individual customer. The columns (fields) organize the types of data being collected, such as First Name, Last Name, Street, or City.

You can build a database from scratch or use one of the prebuilt templates provided by Microsoft. You can also add prebuilt tables, fields, and forms to an existing database.

After designing the tables, you are ready to enter data. Forms are built so that others can type the data quickly and accurately. You can also import data from other programs.

Queries are used to answer questions about the data. They filter and sort the data to display the information that answers these questions. Reports can be based on either tables or queries and are created to display information effectively.

Access has several wizards and views that you can use to build your tables, forms, queries, and reports quickly. You can format these objects using techniques similar to other Office programs.

Table field captions

Shelters

Shelter ID	Shelter Name	Park	Click to Add
1	Group Area A	Wiyot	
2	Central Picnic Area	Silver Lake	
3	Shelter East	Sunset Meadows	
4	Group Area A	Roosevelt	
5	Observation Point	Kellermann	
6	Willow Shelter	Aspen Falls Lake	
7	Franklin Shelter	Roosevelt	
8	Shelter in the Woods	Cedar Creek	
9	Aspen Shelter	Aspen Falls Lake	Table record
10	Shelter North	Silver Lake	
11	Veteran's Picnic Area	Sunset Meadows	
12	Poplar Shelter	Aspen Falls Lake	
13	Manor Picnic Area	Squires Lake	
14	Eleanor Shelter	Roosevelt	
15	Group Area A	Cedar Creek	
16	Upriver Shelter	Yurok	
17	Group Area B	Wiyot	
18	Downriver Shelter	Yurok	
19	Shelter South	Silver Lake	
20	Group Area B	Cedar Creek	
21	Group Area C	Roosevelt	
22	Shelter West	Silver Lake	

Shelter Reservations   Access form

CITY HALL Shelter Reservations

Shelter ID	1
Shelter Name	Group Area A
Park	Wiyot

Reservation ID ▾	Customer ID ▾	Date ▾	Group Size ▾	Fee ▾
27	5739776	4/27/2018	91	$45.50
* (New)				

Record: I◄ ◄ 1 of 1 ► ►I ►⊞ 🔾 No Filter   Search

Record: I◄ ◄ 1 of 28 ► ►I ►⊞ 🔾 No Filter   Search

Create Database Tables

- ▶ Microsoft Office Access is an application used to store and organize data, and access and display that data as meaningful information.

- ▶ A single Access file contains many objects including tables, forms, queries, and reports. Tables are used to store the data. The other objects are used to access the data stored in those tables.

- ▶ When you create a database, you first determine the purpose of the database. You can then plan how to organize the data into tables. Each row in the table represents one record, and each column represents common characteristics of the data, such as city, state, or zip code.

- ▶ When you create tables, you assign properties that match the data you intend to enter into the database tables.

- ▶ After creating tables, you establish the relationships between them and then test those relationships by adding sample data.

- ▶ After the table relationships are tested, you are ready to enter all the data and add other database objects such as forms, queries, and reports.

© Franck Boston / Fotolia.com

Aspen Falls City Hall

In this project, you will help Sadye Cassiano, Director of the Building Services Department of Aspen Falls City Hall, add two tables to the database that the department uses to track building permits. You will use Access to design and test prototypes of two related database tables that will be added to the city database.

The data stored in database tables is used in many ways. In Aspen Falls, building permits are considered public records, and the database will be used to publish permits on the city website. Internally, the city will use the data to adjust yearly property assessments, track city construction, track payments of fees, and contact the person filing a building permit. All of these tasks can be accomplished by accessing two tables in the database in different ways. Thus, the tables are the foundation of a database.

In this project, you will create a new database and then create one table in Datasheet view and a second table in Design view. In both tables you will add fields and assign properties to those fields, and create a relationship between the two tables. You will add data to one table by typing the data and add data to the second table by importing it from an Excel spreadsheet. Finally, you will use Datasheet view to filter, sort, format, and print the tables.

Time to complete all 10 skills — 60 to 90 minutes

Outcome

Using the skills in this chapter, you will be able create a database, create tables and fields, edit field properties, import data into tables, filter and sort table records, and create table relationships.

Objectives

1.1 Create tables in different database views

1.2 Relate tables in a database

1.3 Manipulate data in tables

1.4 Format and import data in a database

> **Student data file needed for this chapter:**
>
> acc01_PermitsData (Excel)
>
> **You will save your files as:**
>
> Last_First_acc01_Permits (Access)
> Last_First_acc01_PermitsData (Excel)

SKILLS

Skills 1-10 Training

At the end of this chapter you will be able to:

Skill 1 Create Databases

Skill 2 Create Tables in Datasheet View

Skill 3 Enter Data into Datasheets

Skill 4 Create Tables in Design View

Skill 5 Relate Tables

Skill 6 Enter Data in Related Tables

Skill 7 Import Data into Tables

Skill 8 Filter and Sort Datasheets

Skill 9 Format Datasheets

Skill 10 Preview and Print Datasheets

MORE SKILLS

Skill 11 Compact and Repair Databases

Skill 12 Work with the Long Text Data Type

Skill 13 Work with the Attachment Data Type

Skill 14 Work with the Hyperlink and Yes/No Data Types

Permit Number	Start Date	Project Title	Location	Fee	Click to Add
B8756215ELEC	7/24/2017	REMODEL MALASKY RESIDENCE	4863 S Biltmore Av	$54.23	
B5666375ELEC	7/24/2017	ADDITION JAPP RESIDENCE	8493 N Bannock St	$44.20	
B3680115ELEC	7/24/2017	REMODEL AHRENDES RESIDENCE	3858 S Glenn Brook Pl	$51.79	
B1684124ELEC	7/24/2017	REMODEL HARTNETT RESIDENCE	8147 S 5Th St	$49.32	
B3849977ELEC	7/29/2017	ADDITION BRANDL RESIDENCE	6031 S Hinsdale Ct	$53.79	
B1090716ELEC	7/29/2017	REMODEL CUBIT RESIDENCE	3674 W Teabrook Av	$74.50	
B9568069ELEC	8/1/2017	ADDITION TRIEU RESIDENCE	8668 E Hopkirk Av	$55.06	
B4824848ELEC	8/1/2017	REMODEL MIYAGAWA RESIDENCE	515 E Birch	$64.67	
*				$0.00	

Permits

Access 2016, Windows 10, Microsoft Corporation

▶ When you start Access, the start screen displays so that you can either open an existing database or create a new blank database.

▶ Before you create a new database, you assign a name and location for the database file.

1. Start **Access 2016**, and then compare your screen with **Figure 1**.

    On the Access start screen, you can create a database from a template, open a recent database, or create a blank database.

2. On the Access start page, click **Blank desktop database**. In the **Blank desktop database** dialog box, using your own name, replace the suggested **File Name** with Last_First_acc01_Permits

3. To the right of the **File Name** box, click the **Browse** button 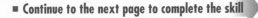 to open the File New Database dialog box.

4. In the **File New Database** dialog box, navigate to the location where you will be saving your work for this chapter.

5. In the **File New Database** dialog box, click **New folder**, and then type Access Chapter 1 Press [Enter] two times to create and open the new folder. Compare your screen with **Figure 2**.

    The Microsoft Access 2007 - 2016 file format is the default file format for Access 2016.

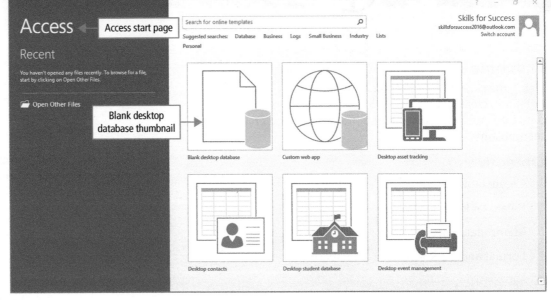

Figure 1

Access 2016, Windows 10, Microsoft Corporation

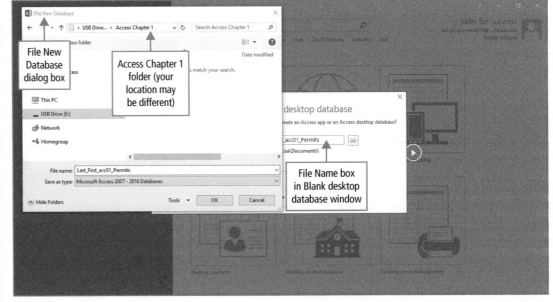

Figure 2

Access 2016, Windows 10, Microsoft Corporation

■ **Continue to the next page to complete the skill**

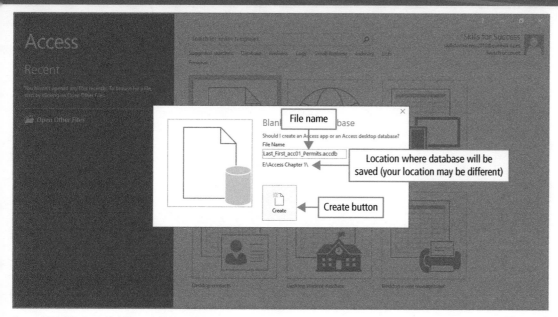

Access 2016, Windows 10, Microsoft Corporation

Figure 3

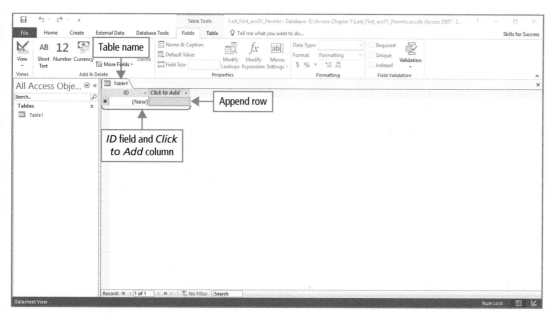

Access 2016, Windows 10, Microsoft Corporation

Figure 4

6. Click **OK** to accept the changes and close the **File New Database** dialog box.

7. Compare your screen with Figure 3, and then click the **Create** button.

8. Take a few moments to familiarize yourself with the Access window as described below and in Figure 4.

> When you create a blank database, a new table is automatically generated. The name *Table1* is temporarily assigned to the table, and the first column—*ID*—is the name of a ***field***—a common characteristic of the data that the table will describe, such as city, state, or postal code.
>
> Database ***tables*** are objects that store data by organizing it into rows and columns and are displayed in ***datasheets***. In a datasheet, each row is a ***record***—a collection of related data such as the contact information for a person. Each column is a field that each record will store such as city, state, or postal code.
>
> *Table1* currently displays in ***Datasheet view***—a view that features the data but also has contextual tabs on the Ribbon so that you can change the table's design. In Datasheet view, the last row of the table is the ***append row***—the last row of a datasheet into which a new record is entered. *Table1* currently has no data.

9. Leave the table open for the next skill.

■ **You have completed Skill 1 of 10**

▶ When you design a table, you add field names and their properties.

▶ **Data type** is a field property that specifies the type of information that a field will contain; for example, text, number, date, or currency.

MOS
Obj 2.1.1

1. In **Table1**, click the **ID** column header. On the **Fields tab**, in the **Properties group**, click **Name & Caption**. Replace the **Name** box value with ContractorID and then in the **Caption** box, type Contractor ID (include a space between the two words).

2. Compare your screen with **Figure 1**, and then click **OK**.

> *Contractor ID*—the field's caption—displays at the top of the column and is slightly truncated. You will widen the column in a later step. *Captions* determine what displays in all datasheet, form, and report labels. Actual field names should not contain spaces, but changing the caption to include spaces improves readability of forms, datasheets, and reports.

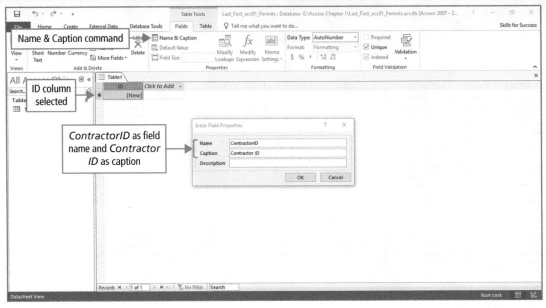

Figure 1   Access 2016, Windows 10, Microsoft Corporation

MOS
Obj 2.4.1

3. In the second column, click the text **Click to Add**, and then from the list of data types, click **Short Text**. Type CompanyName and then press Enter to move to the next column.

> The **Short Text data type** stores up to 255 characters of text.

4. On the **Fields tab**, in the **Add & Delete group**, click the **More Fields** button. Scroll to the last list of data types, click **Name**, and then compare your screen with **Figure 2**.

> **Quick Start fields** are a set of fields that can be added with a single click. For example, the Name Quick Start data type inserts the LastName and FirstName fields, assigns the Text data type, and adds a caption with a space between the two words.

■ **Continue to the next page to complete the skill**

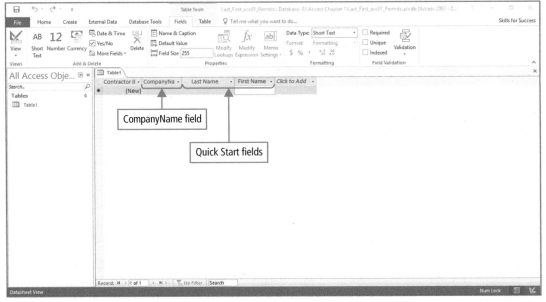

Figure 2   Access 2016, Windows 10, Microsoft Corporation

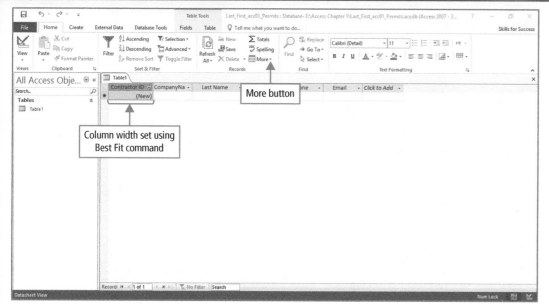

Column width set using Best Fit command

More button

Access 2016, Windows 10, Microsoft Corporation

Figure 3

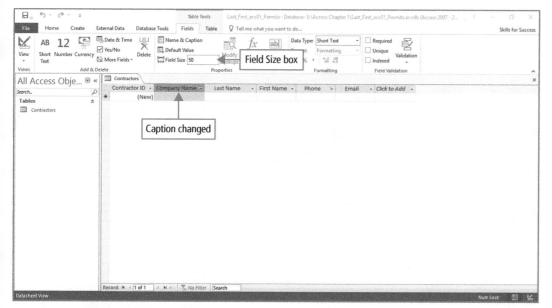

Field Size box

Caption changed

Access 2016, Windows 10, Microsoft Corporation

Figure 4

5. Click in the last column—*Click to Add*, and then click **Short Text**. Type Phone and then press Enter.

6. Repeat the technique just practiced to add a field name Email with the **Short Text** data type.

7. In the header row, click in the **Contractor ID** column. Click the **Home tab**. In the **Records group**, click **More**, and then click **Field Width**. In the **Column Width** dialog box, click **Best Fit**. Compare your screen with Figure 3.

   Column widths can be changed to match the width of their contents. As you add data, the widths may need to be adjusted.

8. Repeat the technique just practiced to adjust the **CompanyName** column width.

9. If necessary, click **CompanyName** to select the column, and then click the **Fields tab**. In the **Properties group**, change the **Field Size** value to 50

   Field size limits the number of characters that can be typed into a text or number field.

10. Click **Save**. In the **Save As** dialog box, type Contractors and then click **OK**.

    When you save a table that you have added or changed, its name displays in the Navigation Pane, and it becomes part of the database file.

11. With the CompanyName field selected, in the **Properties group**, click **Name & Caption**. Type the **Caption** Company Name and then click **OK**. Compare your screen with Figure 4.

12. Repeat the technique just practiced to change the **Field Size** property of the **Last Name**, **First Name**, **Phone**, and **Email** fields to 50 and then click **Save**.

MOS
Obj 2.4.4

MOS
Obj 2.4.3

■ **You have completed Skill 2 of 10**

▶ When you are designing and building database tables, it is a good idea to enter some of the data that they will store. In this way, the design can be tested and adjusted if needed.

1. In the **Contractors** table datasheet, in the append row, click the first empty **Company Name** cell, and then type Front Poarch Construction Compare your screen with **Figure 1**.

As soon as you enter data in the append row, it becomes a record, and the append row displays below the new record.

2. Press [Enter] to accept the data entry and move to the next column. Type Poarch Press [Enter], and then in the **First Name** column, type Ken

3. Continue in this manner to enter the **Phone** number, (805) 555-7721 and the **Email** address, poarch.ken@poarchcontractors.com

4. Press [Enter] to finish the record and move the insertion point to the append row. Compare your screen with **Figure 2**.

When you move to a different record or append row, the new or changed data is automatically saved to the database file on your storage device.

▪ **Continue to the next page to complete the skill** ➤

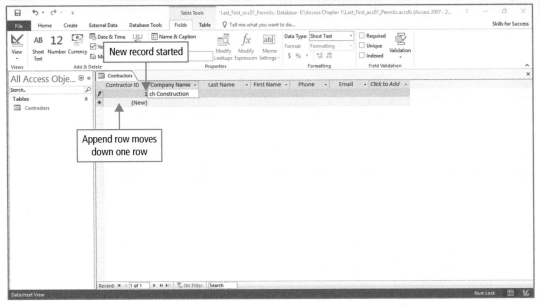

Figure 1

Access 2016, Windows 10, Microsoft Corporation

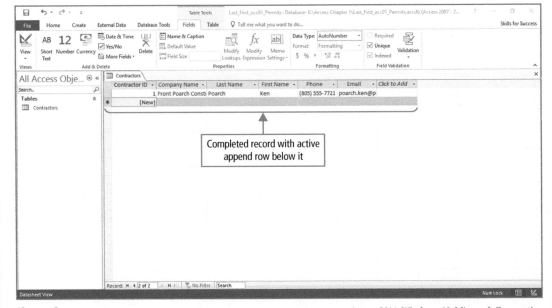

Figure 2

Access 2016, Windows 10, Microsoft Corporation

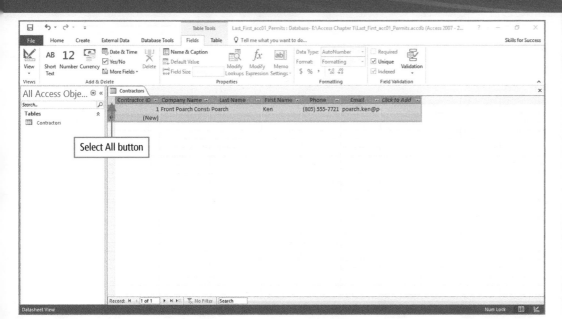

Access 2016, Windows 10, Microsoft Corporation

Figure 3

5. To the left of the **Contractor ID** column heading, click the **Select All** button ☐. Compare your screen with Figure 3.

> ContractorID is the table's ***primary key***—a field that uniquely identifies each record in a table. Primary key field names often include *ID* to help you identify them.

6. With all the cells still selected, repeat the technique practiced previously to apply **Best Fit** to the column widths.

> By selecting the entire datasheet, you can adjust column widths quickly. If your window is sized smaller than the datasheet, columns that are not in view will not be adjusted. You can adjust them by first maximizing the Access window or by scrolling to display them.

7. Starting with *Mikrot Construction*, add the records shown in the table in Figure 4. For the **Contractor ID**, accept the AutoNumber values.

> The ContractorID data type is ***AutoNumber***—a field that automatically enters a unique, numeric value when a record is created. Once an AutoNumber value has been assigned, it cannot be changed. If your AutoNumber values differ from the ones shown in this chapter's figures, you do not need to change them.

8. Click **Save** 💾, and then **Close** ☒ the table.

> When you close a database table, the database does not close. If you accidentally close the database, reopen it to continue.

▪ **You have completed Skill 3 of 10**

CompanyName	Last Name	First Name	Phone	Email
Front Poarch Construction	*Poarch*	*Ken*	*(805) 555-7721*	*poarch.ken@ poarchconstruction.com*
Mikrot Construction	Mikrot	Kim	(805) 555-6795	kmikrot@mikrot .com
Sobata Contractors	Sobata	Jeri	(805) 555-4789	jeri@sobatacon .com
(leave blank)	Jestis	Mee	(805) 555-8506	mee.jestis@ jestisandsons.com
Degasparre Remodelers	Degasparre	Artur	(805) 555-0770	artur@degasparre .com

Figure 4

▶ An alternate method for creating a table is to create it in **Table Design view**—a view that features table fields and their properties.

1. Click the **Create tab**, and then in the **Tables group**, click the **Table Design** button.

2. With the insertion point in the **Field Name** column's first row, type PermitID and then press [Enter] to automatically assign the Short Text data type.

MOS
Obj 1.2.2

3. On the **Design tab**, in the **Tools group**, click **Primary Key**.

4. In the **Field Properties** pane, change the **Field Size** value to 50 and the **Caption** to Permit Number Compare your screen with **Figure 1**.

> When working with a table in Design view, the Field Name, Data Type, and Description data are entered in rows. Other field properties are entered in the Field Properties pane.

5. Click in the next blank **Field Name** box, and then type StartDate

6. Press [Enter], click the **Data Type arrow**, and then click **Date/Time**. In the **Field Properties** pane, click the **Format** box, click the **Format arrow** that displays, and then click **Short Date**. Add the **Caption** property Start Date and then compare your screen with **Figure 2**.

> The **Date/Time data type** stores serial numbers that are converted and formatted as dates or times.

7. Add a third field named ProjectTitle with the **Short Text** data type and the **Caption** property Project Title

8. Add a fourth field named Location with the **Short Text** data type.

■ **Continue to the next page to complete the skill** ▶

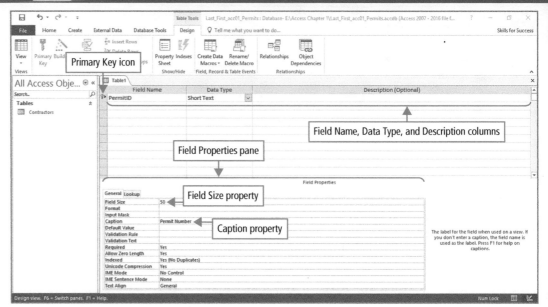

Figure 1   Access 2016, Windows 10, Microsoft Corporation

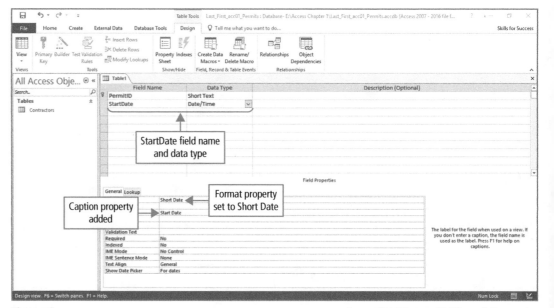

Figure 2   Access 2016, Windows 10, Microsoft Corporation

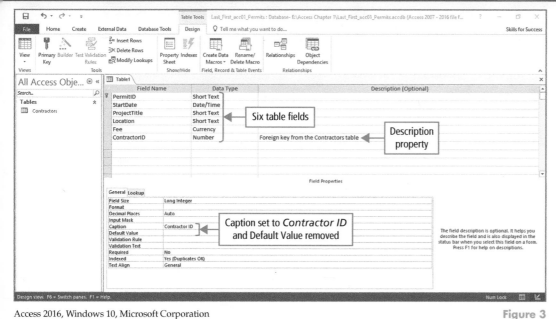

Access 2016, Windows 10, Microsoft Corporation

Figure 3

9. Add a fifth field named Fee with the **Currency** data type. Do not change any other field properties.

> The ***Currency data type*** stores numbers formatted as monetary values.

10. Add a sixth field named ContractorID with the **Number** data type and the caption Contractor ID In the **Default Value** box, delete the *0*.

> The ***Number data type*** stores numeric values.

11. In the **ContractorID Description** box, type Foreign key from the Contractors table Compare your screen with **Figure 3**.

> A ***foreign key*** is a field that is used to relate records in a second related table. The foreign key field is often the second table's primary key. Here, ContractorID is the primary key of the Contractors table. The ContractorID field will be used to join this table to the Contractors table.
>
> When you join tables, the common fields must share the same data type. Because the Contractors table automatically assigns a number in the ContractorID field, the foreign key field should be assigned the Number data type.

12. Click **Save**. In the **Save As** dialog box, type Permits and then click **OK**.

13. On the **Design tab**, in the **Views group**, click the **View** button to switch to Datasheet view. Click the **Select All** button, and then adjust the column widths to **Best Fit**. Compare your screen with **Figure 4**.

14. **Save** and then **Close** the table.

■ **You have completed Skill 4 of 10**

Access 2016, Windows 10, Microsoft Corporation

Figure 4

▶ Records in two tables can be related by placing the same field in both tables and then creating a relationship between the common fields.

MOS
Obj 1.2.5

1. Click the **Database Tools tab**, and then in the **Relationships group**, click the **Relationships** button to display the Relationships tab and Show Table dialog box.

   If the Show Table dialog box does not display, you can open it by clicking the Show Table button in the Relationships group.

2. In the **Show Table** dialog box, double-click **Permits** to add it to the Relationships tab. In the **Show Table** dialog box, double-click **Contractors**. Alternately, you can add tables to the Relationships tab by dragging them from the Navigation Pane.

3. Compare your screen with **Figure 1**, and then close the Show Table dialog box.

MOS
Obj 1.2.1

4. From the **Permits** table, drag the **ContractorID** field to the **ContractorID** field in the **Contractors** table. When the Access Relationship pointer displays, as shown in **Figure 2**, release the mouse button.

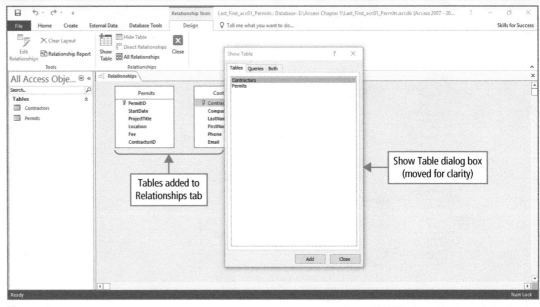

Figure 1

Access 2016, Windows 10, Microsoft Corporation

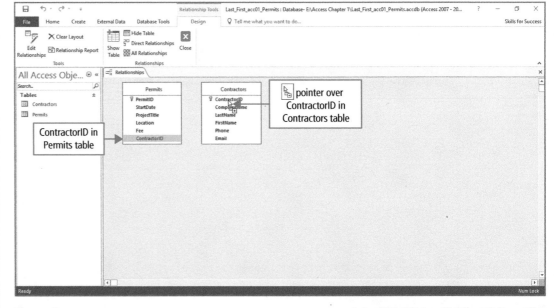

Figure 2

Access 2016, Windows 10, Microsoft Corporation

 ■ **Continue to the next page to complete the skill**

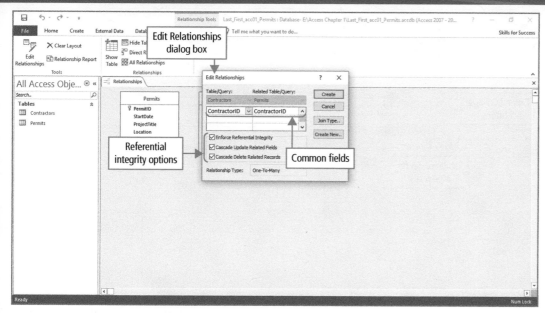

Access 2016, Windows 10, Microsoft Corporation

Figure 3

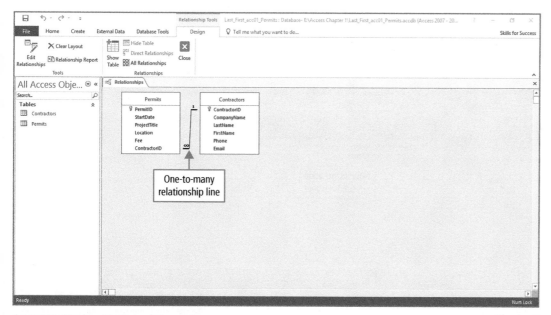

Access 2016, Windows 10, Microsoft Corporation

Figure 4

5. In the **Edit Relationships** dialog box, select the **Enforce Referential Integrity** check box. Select the **Cascade Update Related Fields** and **Cascade Delete Related Records** check boxes, and then compare your screen with **Figure 3**.

> Tables are typically joined in a ***one-to-many relationship***—a relationship in which a record in the first table can have many associated records in the second table.
>
> ***Referential integrity*** is a rule that keeps related values synchronized. For example, the foreign key value must be present in the related table. This option must be selected to create a one-to-many relationship.
>
> With a ***cascading update***, if you edit the primary key values in a table, all the related records in the other table will update accordingly.
>
> With a ***cascading delete***, you can delete a record on the *one* side of the relationship, and all the related records on the *many* side will also be deleted.

6. Click **Create**, and then compare your screen with **Figure 4**.

7. Click **Save** 🖫. On the **Design tab**, in the **Tools group**, click the **Relationship Report** button to create a report showing the database relationships.

8. If your instructor asks you to print your work for this chapter, print the report.

9. Click **Save** 🖫, and then click **OK**. **Close** ☒ the report, and then **Close** ☒ the Relationships tab.

■ **You have completed Skill 5 of 10**

- When you enter data in related tables, referential integrity rules are applied. For example, a foreign key value must have a matching value in the related table.

- A *subdatasheet* displays related records from another table by matching the values in the field that relates the two tables. For example, all the permits issued to each contractor can be listed by matching the ContractorID value assigned to that permit.

1. In the **Navigation Pane**, double-click **Contractors** to open its datasheet.

2. Locate the record for Mee Jestis (Jestis, Mee), click the **Expand** button ⊞, and then compare your screen with **Figure 1**.

   When a table is on the *one* side of a relationship, a subdatasheet is available. Here, no permits have been issued to this contractor.

3. In the subdatasheet append row, under **Permit Number**, type B1018504RFSW

4. In the same record, under **Start Date**, click the cell, and then click the **Date Picker** button 📅 that displays. In the **Date Picker**, click the **Today** button.

   Fields that have been assigned the Date/Time data type display a Date Picker when they are selected.

5. In the same record, enter a **Project Title** of REMODEL CHITTESTER RESIDENCE a **Location** of 6088 W Devon Way and a **Fee** of $217.71 Compare your screen with **Figure 2**.

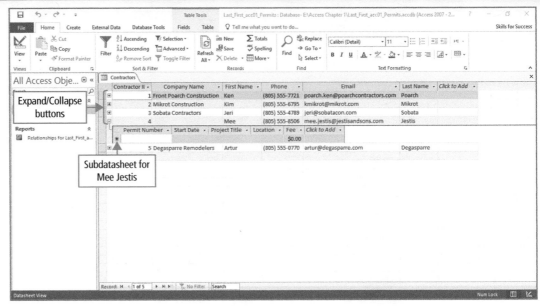

Figure 1   Access 2016, Windows 10, Microsoft Corporation

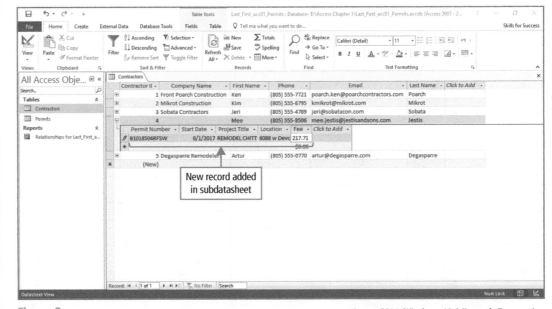

Figure 2   Access 2016, Windows 10, Microsoft Corporation

■ **Continue to the next page to complete the skill**

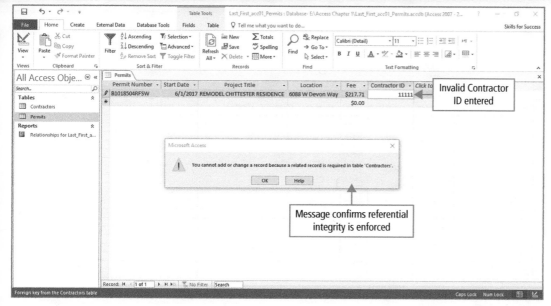

Access 2016, Windows 10, Microsoft Corporation

Figure 3

6. **Close** ☒ the table. In the **Navigation Pane**, under **Tables**, double-click **Permits** to open its datasheet.

7. Adjust the column widths to **Best Fit** to display all the data you previously entered in the subdatasheet.

   In this manner, records in a one-to-many relationship can be entered using a subdatasheet. Here, a new building permit record has been created, and the Contractor has been assigned.

8. In the first record, change the **Contractor ID** to 11111 Click in the append row, and then compare your screen with **Figure 3**.

   It is a good idea to test referential integrity. Here, referential integrity is working correctly. You are not allowed to enter a Contractor ID that does not exist in the related Contractors table.

9. Read the message, click **OK**, and then press [Esc] to cancel the change and return to the correct Contractor ID.

10. In the table, repeat the techniques just practiced to add the three records shown in **Figure 4**. For all records, use the same Contractor ID used in the first record.

11. If necessary, adjust the column widths to fit the contents. **Save** 🖫 and then **Close** ☒ the table.

■ **You have completed Skill 6 of 10**

Permit Number	Start Date	Project Title	Location	Fee
B1018504RFSW	Your date	REMODEL CHITTESTER RESIDENCE	6088 W Devon Way	217.71
B1052521RFSW	7/21/2017	ROOF ABADIE RESIDENCE	5943 S Balivi Ln	208.65
B1090716ELEC	7/29/2017	REMODEL CUBIT RESIDENCE	3674 W Teabrook Av	74.50
B1071316PLMB	8/19/2017	REMODEL LAA RESIDENCE	5901 S Farnyville Ln	58.00

Figure 4

▶ When Excel tables are arranged as a datasheet, the data can be imported into Access tables.

1. Start **Excel 2016**, and then on the Excel start page, click **Open Other Workbooks**. On the **Open** page, click **Browse**. In the **Open** dialog box, navigate to the student data files for this chapter, and then open the Excel file **acc01_PermitsData**.

2. On the **File tab**, click **Save As**, and then click **Browse**. In the **Save As** dialog box, navigate to your chapter folder. Name the file Last_First_acc01_PermitsData and then click **Save**.

3. Click cell **A1**, type PermitID and then press Tab. Continue in this manner to enter the column labels in this order: StartDate | ProjectTitle | Location | Fee Compare your screen with **Figure 1**.

> When you import data from Excel, it is best practice to insert the table's field names in the spreadsheet's header row. In this project, you will not import any ContractorID data.

4. Click **Save** 🖫, and then **Close** ✕ Excel.

5. In **Access**, click the **External Data tab**, and then in the **Import & Link group**, click **Excel**.

6. In the **Get External Data - Excel Spreadsheet** dialog box, click the **Browse** button. In the **File Open** dialog box, navigate to your **Access Chapter 1** folder, select **Last_First_acc01_PermitsData**, and then click **Open**.

7. Click the **Append a copy of the records to the table** option button, click the **arrow**, and then select the **Permits** table as shown in **Figure 2**.

▪ **Continue to the next page to complete the skill**

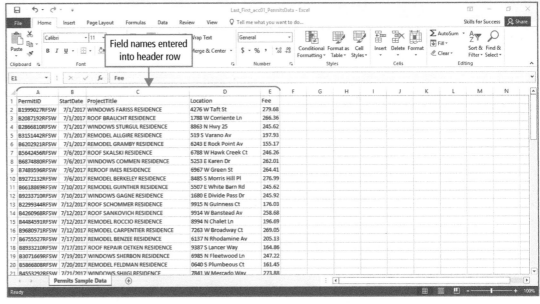

Figure 1

Access 2016, Windows 10, Microsoft Corporation

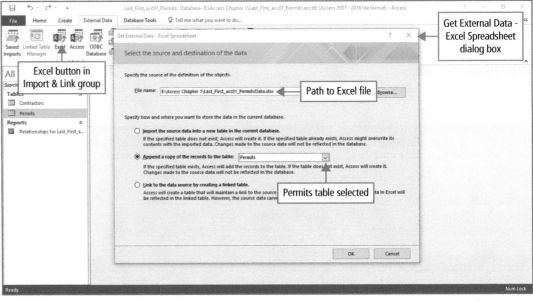

Figure 2

Access 2016, Windows 10, Microsoft Corporation

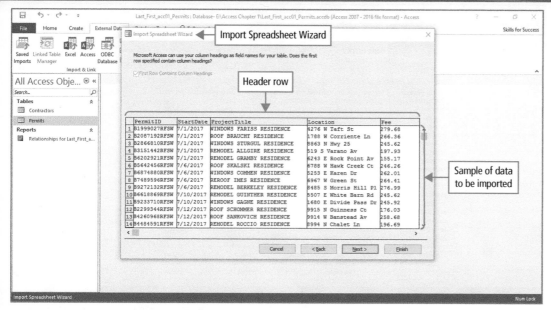

Access 2016, Windows 10, Microsoft Corporation

Figure 3

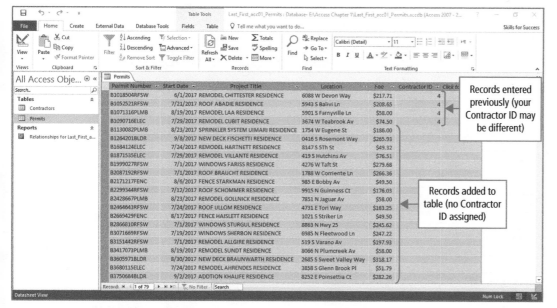

Access 2016, Windows 10, Microsoft Corporation

Figure 4

8. In the dialog box, click **OK** to open the **Import Spreadsheet Wizard** dialog box.

Because a workbook can contain multiple worksheets, you are asked to select the worksheet that contains the data you wish to import.

9. In the first screen of the **Import Spreadsheet Wizard**, verify that the **Permits Sample Data** worksheet is selected, and then click **Next**. Compare your screen with Figure 3.

In the wizard, it is recommended that you view the sample data and verify that it matches the field names in the header row. Here, the header that you previously inserted matches the field names in the Access table.

10. Click **Next** to display the last screen in the **Import Spreadsheet Wizard**. Verify that the **Import to Table** box displays the text *Permits*, and that the **I would like a wizard...** check box is cleared. Click **Finish** to complete the import.

11. In the **Save Import Steps** screen, verify that the **Save import steps** check box is cleared, and then click **Close**.

12. Open the **Permits** table in **Datasheet view**. Adjust the column widths to **Best Fit**, and then compare your screen with Figure 4.

The records are added to the table and then sorted by the primary key—*Permit Number*. The Contractor ID is blank because these permits were issued to homeowners who are completing the work themselves.

13. Click **Save** 💾, and then leave the table open for the next skill.

■ **You have completed Skill 7 of 10**

► Datasheets can be sorted and filtered to make the information more meaningful and useful.

MOS
Obj 2.3.6

1. With the **Permits** table open in **Datasheet view**, click anywhere in the **Start Date** column. On the **Home tab**, in the **Sort & Filter group**, click the **Ascending** button. Compare your screen with **Figure 1**.

   By default, tables are sorted by their primary key field. Here, the Start Date column arrow changes to a sort arrow to indicate that the records have been sorted in ascending order by date.

MOS
Obj 2.3.7

2. In the **Fee** column, click the **Fee arrow**. In the **Filter** menu that displays, clear the **(Select All)** check box, and then select the **$58.00** check box.

3. Compare your screen with **Figure 2**, and then click **OK** to view the eight records that result.

   In this manner, the Filter menu can be used to select records with the values you choose.

4. Click the **Fee arrow**, and then click **Clear filter from Fee**.

5. Click the **Fee arrow**, point to **Number Filters**, and then click **Less Than**. In the **Custom Filter** dialog box, type 75 and then click **OK** to display 31 records.

■ **Continue to the next page to complete the skill**

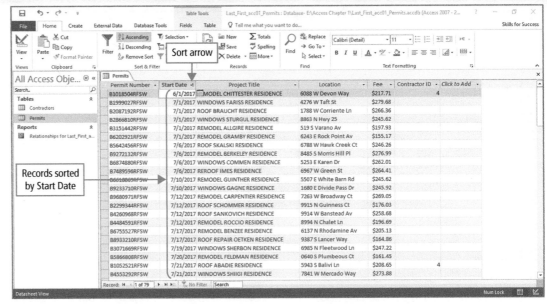

Figure 1

Access 2016, Windows 10, Microsoft Corporation

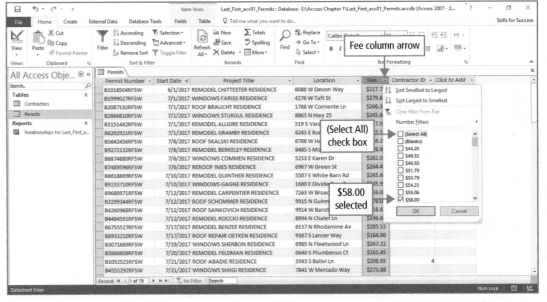

Figure 2

Access 2016, Windows 10, Microsoft Corporation

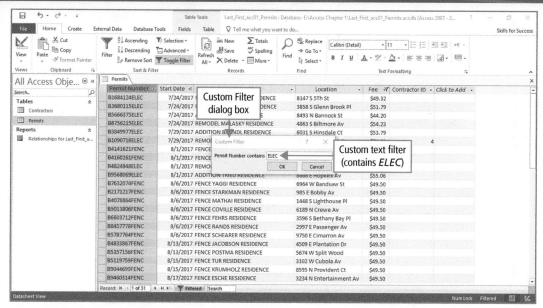

Access 2016, Windows 10, Microsoft Corporation

Figure 3

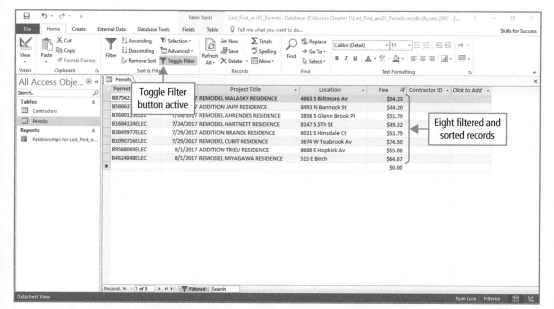

Access 2016, Windows 10, Microsoft Corporation

Figure 4

6. Click the **Permit Number arrow**. From the **Filter** menu, point to **Text Filters**, and then click **Contains**. In the **Custom Filter** dialog box, type ELEC

7. Compare your screen with **Figure 3**, and then click **OK** to display eight records.

In this manner you can display records that contain the text or numbers you specify. Here, only the permits with permit numbers ending with ELEC and with fees less than $75 display.

8. Click **Save** 🖫, and then **Close** ⊠ the table.

9. In the **Navigation Pane**, double-click **Permits** and notice that the 79 records are sorted by **Start Date** but the filters are not applied.

10. On the **Home tab**, in the **Sort & Filter group**, click **Toggle Filter** to reapply the filter. Compare your screen with **Figure 4**.

The sort order and filter that you create in a datasheet are saved as part of the table's design. When you open a table, it sorts in the order you specified, but the filter is not applied.

11. Leave the table open for the next skill.

■ **You have completed Skill 8 of 10**

▶ Datasheets can be formatted to make the data easier to read.

1. If necessary, open the Permits table, and then toggle the filter on.

2. On the **Home tab**, in the **Text Formatting group**, click the **Font Size arrow** [11 ▾], and then click **10**.

3. In the **Text Formatting group**, click the **Font arrow** [Calibri (Detail) ▾]. Scroll through the list of fonts as needed, and then click **Verdana**. Compare your screen with **Figure 1**.

> When you change the font size or font, the changes are applied to the entire datasheet.

4. Click the **Select All** button [ ], and then apply the **Best Fit** column width.

5. With all the cells still selected, on the **Home tab**, in the **Records group**, click **More**, and then click **Row Height**.

6. In the **Row Height** dialog box, replace the existing **Row Height** value with 15 and then click **OK**.

MOS
Obj 2.2.1

7. Click anywhere in the **Contractor ID** column. On the **Home tab**, in the **Records group**, click **More**, and then click **Hide Fields**. Compare your screen with **Figure 2**.

Figure 1

Access 2016, Windows 10, Microsoft Corporation

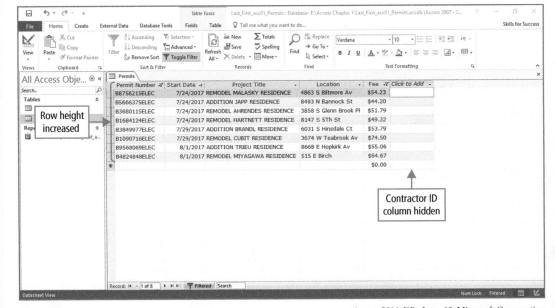

Figure 2

Access 2016, Windows 10, Microsoft Corporation

■ **Continue to the next page to complete the skill**

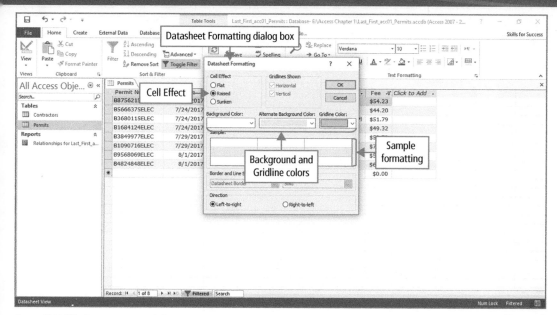

Access 2016, Windows 10, Microsoft Corporation

Figure 3

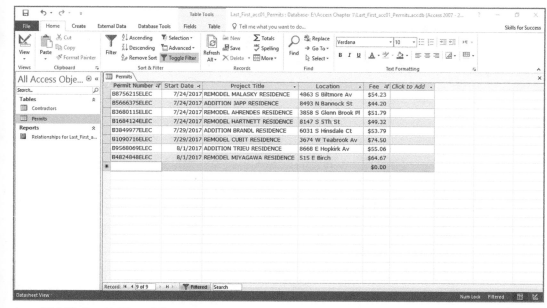

Access 2016, Windows 10, Microsoft Corporation

Figure 4

8. In the **Text Formatting group**, click the **Datasheet Formatting Dialog Box Launcher** ⌟.

9. In the **Datasheet Formatting** dialog box, under **Cell Effect**, select the **Raised** option button.

10. Click the **Background Color arrow**. In the gallery, click **Automatic**.

11. Click the **Alternate Background Color arrow**. In the gallery, under **Theme Colors**, click the sixth color in the second row—**Orange, Accent 2, Lighter 80%**.

12. Click the **Gridline Color arrow**. In the gallery, under **Theme Colors**, click the eighth color in the first row—**Gold, Accent 4**. Compare your screen with Figure 3.

   In the Datasheet Formatting dialog box, a sample of the selected formatting displays.

13. Click **OK** to apply the changes and to close the dialog box. Click in the append row, and then compare your screen with Figure 4.

14. **Save** 🖫 the table design changes, and leave the table open for the next skill.

■ **You have completed Skill 9 of 10**

► Before printing, it is a good idea to preview the printed page(s) and make adjustments if necessary.

1. With the **Permits** table open in **Datasheet view**, click the **File tab**, and then click **Print**. Compare your screen with Figure 1.

   The **Quick Print** command prints the object directly. You cannot make any adjustments to the object, choose a different printer, or change the printer settings.

   The **Print** command opens the Print dialog box so you can select a different printer or different print options.

   The **Print Preview** command opens a preview of the table with Ribbon commands that you can use to make adjustments to the object you are printing.

Figure 1   Access 2016, Windows 10, Microsoft Corporation

2. On the **Print** page, click **Print Preview**. In the **Zoom group**, click the **Zoom arrow**, and then click **Zoom 100%**. Compare your screen with Figure 2. If necessary, scroll to the top of the page.

   The last column—Fee—will not print on page one. Tools in the navigation bar at the bottom of the preview are used to view the other printed pages.

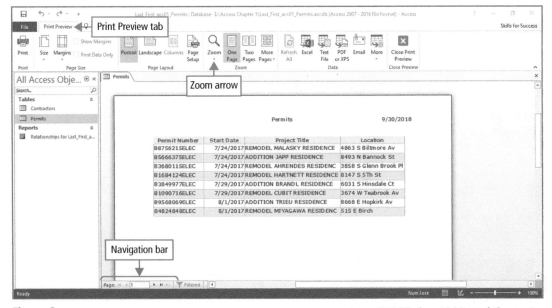

Figure 2   Access 2016, Windows 10, Microsoft Corporation

■ Continue to the next page to complete the skill ➤

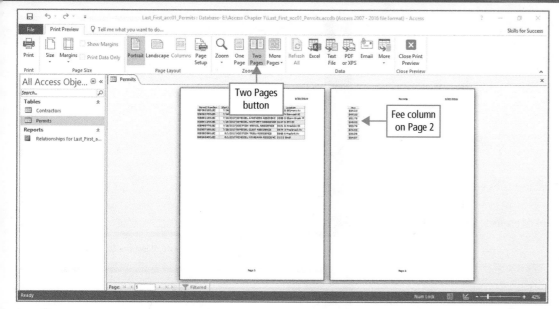

Access 2016, Windows 10, Microsoft Corporation

Figure 3

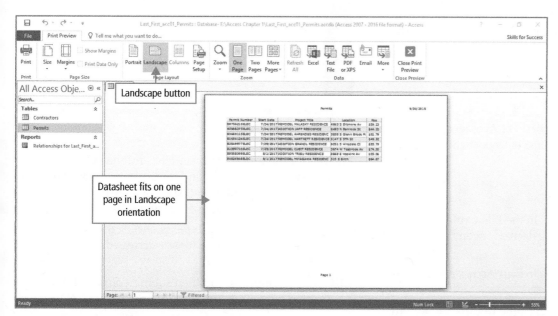

Access 2016, Windows 10, Microsoft Corporation

Figure 4

3. In the **Zoom group**, click **Two Pages**, and then compare your screen with Figure 3.

4. In the **Page Layout group**, click **Landscape**.

> By default, tables print in ***Portrait***—taller than wide. You can change the layout to ***Landscape***—wider than tall—to accommodate a wider table with few records.

5. In the **Zoom group**, click **One Page**, and then compare your screen with Figure 4.

> The buttons on the navigation bar are dimmed because the table now fits on one page.

6. If you are printing your work for this project, click the **Print** button, note the printer listed in the **Print** dialog box, and then click **OK**.

7. **Close** ☒ the table.

> A table's page layout settings cannot be saved. The next time the table is opened, the default Portrait view will be applied. Typically, when you want to print data from a table, an Access report is created. Report layout settings can be saved.

8. If you are printing your work for this project, use the technique just practiced to print the **Contractors** table with the portrait orientation.

9. With all tables closed, **Close** ☒ Access. Submit your work as directed by your instructor.

> All of the data and database objects are saved as you work with them, so you do not need to click Save before quitting Access.

✓ **DONE! You have completed Skill 10 of 10 and your databases are complete!**

More Skills ⑪
Compact and Repair Databases

To complete this project, you will need the following file:

- acc01_MS11Triathlon

You will save your file as:

- Last_First_acc01_MS11Triathlon

▶ The ***Compact and Repair*** process rebuilds database files so that data and database objects are stored more efficiently.

▶ Applying the Compact and Repair Database tool decreases the size of a database file.

Figure 1   Access 2016, Windows 10, Microsoft Corporation

1. Start **Access 2016**, and then open the student data file **acc01_MS11Triathlon**.

2. On the **File tab**, click **Save As**, and then click the **Save As** button. In the **Save As** dialog box, navigate to your **Access Chapter 1** folder, and then **Save** the database as Last_First_acc01_MS11Triathlon If necessary, enable the content.

3. **Close** the Access window. Start **File Explorer** 🖿, and then navigate to your **Access Chapter 1** folder.

4. Click one time to select the file **Last_First_acc01_MS11Triathlon**, and then compare your screen with **Figure 1**.

   The size of the database file is approximately 952 KB. Your computer may display a different file size.

5. Double-click **Last_First_acc01_MS11Triathlon** to open the database.

6. In the **Navigation Pane**, under **Queries**, click **Bracket Averages** to select it. Press and hold ⇧Shift while clicking **Bracket Averages Report** one time, and then release ⇧Shift.

7. With the four queries, one form, and three reports selected, press ⎀Delete. Read the displayed message, and then click **Yes.**

8. **Close** ✕ the database, and then **Close** Access. In the **File Explorer** window, notice that the file size for the database did not decrease even though several database objects were deleted.

9. Double-click **Last_First_acc01_MS11Triathlon** to start Access and open the database.

MOS
Obj 1.4.1

MOS
Obj 1.4.2

10. Click the **File tab**, and then on the **Info** page, click the **Compact & Repair Database** button.

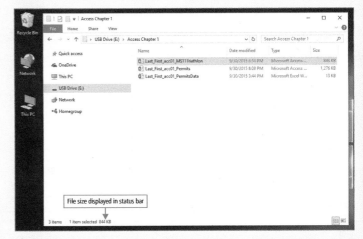

Figure 2   Access 2016, Windows 10, Microsoft Corporation

11. Wait for the process to complete, and then **Close** ✕ the database. **Close** Access. In **File Explorer**, click **Last_First_acc01_MS11Triathlon** to display its size in the status bar, and then compare your screen with **Figure 2**.

   The Compact and Repair process rebuilt the database file more efficiently, and the file size decreased to approximately 844 kB. Your computer may display a slightly different size.

12. Close all windows, and then submit your work as directed by your instructor.

■ **You have completed More Skills 11**

More Skills 12

Work with the Long Text Data Type

To complete this project, you will need the following file:

- acc01_MS12Classes

You will save your file as:

- Last_First_acc01_MS12Classes

▶ Recall that the Short Text data type can store up to 255 characters per record. When you need to store more characters, you can use the ***Long Text data type***—a data type that can store up to 65,535 characters in each record.

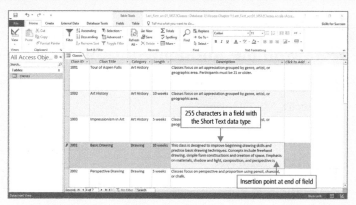

Access 2016, Windows 10, Microsoft Corporation   **Figure 1**

1. Start **Access 2016**, and then open the student data file **acc01_MS12Classes**.

2. On the **File tab**, click **Save As**, and then click the **Save As** button. In the **Save As** dialog box, navigate to your **Access Chapter 1** folder, and then **Save** the database as Last_First_acc01_MS12Classes If necessary, enable the content.

3. Open the **Classes** table in Datasheet view. In the **Description** field of the fourth record—*Basic Drawing*—click to the right of the period in the sentence ending *creation of space*.

4. Add to the record by adding a space and then typing the following:
   Emphasis on materials, shadow and light, composition, and perspective is

5. Add a space, and then attempt to type the word also Compare your screen with **Figure 1**.

   A short text field contains 255 characters, so no more characters can be added to the field. Here, the Description field has reached its upper limit and the rest of the sentence cannot be entered.

6. In the **Description** column, click in a different row to complete the data entry in the *Basic Drawing* record. You will type the rest of the sentence in a later step.

7. With a **Description** field still active, click the **Fields tab**. In the **Formatting** group, click the **Data Type arrow**, and then click **Long Text**. **MOS** Obj 2.4.5

8. In the fourth record—*Basic Drawing*—click at the end of the **Description** text, and then complete the sentence by typing also included. Compare your screen with **Figure 2**.

   With the data type changed to Long Text, more than 255 characters can be entered, and the sentence can be completed. If you changed a Long Text field to a Short Text field, all extra characters would be permanently removed from the database.

Access 2016, Windows 10, Microsoft Corporation   **Figure 2**

9. Save 🖫 the table design changes, **Close** ✕ the database, and then **Close** Access. Submit the database file as directed by your instructor.

■ **You have completed More Skills 12**

More Skills 13

Work with the Attachment Data Type

To complete this project, you will need the following files:

- acc01_MS13Outings
- acc01_MS13Pic1
- acc01_MS13Pic2
- acc01_MS13Flyer

You will save your file as:

- Last_First_acc01_MS13Outings

▶ The **Attachment data type** is used to store files such as Word documents or digital photo files.

▶ Attached files can be opened and viewed in the application in which they were created.

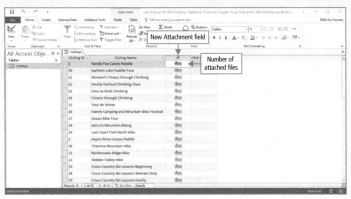

Figure 1   Access 2016, Windows 10, Microsoft Corporation

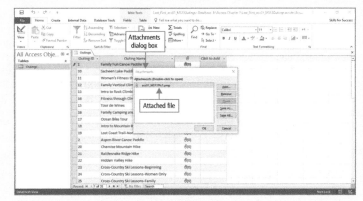

Figure 2   Access 2016, Windows 10, Microsoft Corporation

1. Start **Access 2016**, and then open the student data file **acc01_MS13Outings**.

2. On the **File tab**, click **Save**. In the **Save As** dialog box, navigate to your **Access Chapter 1** folder, and then **Save** the database as Last_First_acc01_MS13Outings If necessary, enable the content.

3. In the **Navigation Pane**, double-click **Outings** to open the table in Datasheet view.

4. In the datasheet's last column, click the **Click to Add arrow**, and then click **Attachment**. Compare your screen with **Figure 1**.

   The number in the parentheses indicates the number of files currently attached to each record.

5. In the record for **Family Fun Canoe Paddle**, double-click the **Paper Clip** icon. In the **Attachments** dialog box, click the **Add** button.

6. In the **Choose File** dialog box, navigate to the student files that came with this project. Click **acc01_MS13Pic1**, and then click **Open**. Compare your screen with **Figure 2**.

   The Attachments dialog box lists all files currently attached to the Family Fun Canoe Paddle record.

7. In the **Attachments** dialog box, click the **Add** button. In the **Choose File** dialog box, click **acc01_MS13Pic2**, and then click **Open**. Click **OK** to close the Attachments dialog box.

8. In the record for **Sacheen Lake Paddle Tour**, repeat the technique just practiced to attach the student data file **acc01_MS13Flyer**

   The numbers next to the Attachment icon indicate the number of files attached.

9. In the record for **Sacheen Lake Paddle Tour**, double-click the **Attachment** icon. In the **Attachments** dialog box, select **acc01_MS13Flyer.docx**, and then click **Open**.

   When you view an attached file, it is opened in the program associated with that file type.

10. **Close** ⊠ the Word document, **Close** ⊠ the Attachments dialog box, **Close** ⊠ the database, and then **Close** Access.

11. Submit the database file as directed by your instructor.

- **You have completed More Skills 13**

More Skills 14

Work with the Hyperlink and Yes/No Data Types

To complete this project, you will need the following file:

- acc01_MS14Sponsors

You will save your file as:

- Last_First_acc01_MS14Sponsors

▶ The **Hyperlink data type** stores links to websites or files located on your computer.

▶ The **Yes/No data type** stores variables that can have one of two possible values—for example, yes or no, or true or false.

Access 2016, Windows 10, Microsoft Corporation   Figure 1

1. Start **Access 2016**, and then open the student data file **acc01_MS14Sponsors**.

2. On the **File tab**, click **Save As**, and then click the **Save As** button. In the **Save As** dialog box, navigate to your **Access Chapter 1** folder, and then **Save** the database as Last_First_acc01_MS14Sponsors If necessary, enable the content.

3. In the **Navigation Pane**, double-click **Sponsors : Table** to open the datasheet.

4. Click the **Click to Add arrow**, and then click **Hyperlink**. With the new field name selected, type Web Site and then press [Enter].

5. Click **Web Site** two times to make it the active column. Click the **Fields tab**, and then compare your screen with Figure 1.

6. Click **Save** 🔲. Click in the **Web Site** field for the first record, *National Park Service*, type www.nps.gov and then press [Enter].

7. Place the pointer over the hyperlink just typed, but do not click it. Compare your screen with Figure 2.

   The Link Select pointer displays to indicate that clicking the hyperlink will open a website or file. For several seconds, a ScreenTip displays the web address for the hyperlink.

8. Click the hyperlink *www.nps.gov* to open your computer's default web browser and navigate to the home page for the National Park Service.

9. **Close** ☒ the web browser window.

10. In **Access**, in the first blank column, click the **Click to Add arrow**, and then click **Yes/No**. Type Auto Renew and then press [Enter].

Access 2016, Windows 10, Microsoft Corporation   Figure 2

11. In the first record, select the **Auto Renew** check box to set the value to *Yes*.

    Yes/No fields display a check box in each record so that each field's value can be set to Yes or No by checking or clearing its check box.

12. If your instructor asks you to print this project, print the datasheet.

13. **Save** 🔲 the table design changes, **Close** ☒ the database, and then **Close** Access. Submit the database file as directed by your instructor.

■ **You have completed More Skills 14**

The following table summarizes the **SKILLS AND PROCEDURES** covered in this chapter.

Skills Number	Task	Step	Icon
1	Create desktop databases	From the Access start screen, click Blank desktop database	
2	Create fields	Click the Click to Add column, and select the desired data type (Datasheet view)	
2	Insert Quick Start fields	Fields tab → Add & Delete group → More Fields	
2, 4	Set field properties	Click the field and use Fields tab commands Click the field and use Field Properties pane (Design view)	
2	Set Best Fit column widths	Home tab → Records group → More → Field Width	
3	Create new records in Datasheet view	Click append row, and type record data	
4	Define primary keys (Design view)	Design tab → Tools group → Primary Key	
4	Set data types (Design view)	Click Data Type arrow	
5	Add tables to Relationships tab	Database Tools → Relationships → Show Table	
5	Create a one-to-many relationship	Drag the primary key field from the table to the related field in the other table and select the Enforce Referential Integrity check box	
6	Display subdatasheets	Click the Expand button	⊞
7	Import Excel data	External Data → Import & Link → Excel	
8	Sort datasheets	Home tab → Sort & Filter group → Ascending (or Descending)	
8	Filter datasheets	Click column Filter arrow	
8	Disable or enable filters	Home tab → Sort & Filter group → Toggle Filter	
9	Change datasheet fonts and font sizes	Home tab → Text Formatting group	
9	Set datasheet row height	Home tab → Records group → More → Row Height	
9	Hide datasheet fields	Home tab → Records group → More → Hide Fields	
9	Apply alternate row shading	Home tab → Datasheet Formatting Dialog Box Launcher	⌐▫
10	Preview a printed table	File tab → Print → Print Preview	
10	Change orientation	Print Preview tab → Page Layout group	

Project Summary Chart

Project	Project Type	Project Location
Skills Review	Review	In Book & MIL MyITLab® Grader
Skills Assessment 1	Review	In Book & MIL MyITLab® Grader
Skills Assessment 2	Review	Book
My Skills	Problem Solving	Book
Visual Skills Check	Problem Solving	Book
Skills Challenge 1	Critical Thinking	Book
Skills Challenge 2	Critical Thinking	Book
More Skills Assessment	Review	In Book & MIL MyITLab® Grader
Collaborating with Google	Critical Thinking	Book

MOS Objectives Covered (Quiz in MyITLab®)

1.1.1 Create a blank desktop database	2.2.1 Hide fields in tables
1.2.1 Create and modifying relationships	2.3.2 Add records
1.2.2 Set primary key field	2.3.4 Append records from external data
1.2.3 Enforce referential integrity	2.3.6 Sort records
1.2.4 Set foreign keys	2.3.7 Filter records
1.2.5 View Relationships	2.4.1 Add fields to tables
1.4.1 Compact databases	2.4.3 Change field captions
1.4.2 Repair databases	2.4.4 Changing field sizes
2.1.1 Create a table	2.4.5 Change field data types
2.1.2 Import data into tables	2.4.6 Configure fields to auto-increment

Key Terms

BizSkills Video

1. Is there anything you would change about Theo's behavior at his performance evaluation? Why or why not?

2. How important do you think it is to set career development goals for yourself? Why?

Online Help Skills

1. Start **Access 2016**, and then in the upper-right corner of the Access start page, click the **Microsoft Access Help (F1)** button ?.

2. In the **Access Help** window **Search help** box, type table relationships and then press Enter.

3. In the search result list, click **Introduction to tables**. Compare your screen with **Figure 1**.

4. Read the article to the answer to the following question: Why create table relationships?

Figure 1   Access 2016, Windows 10, Microsoft Corporation

Matching

Match each term in the second column with its correct definition in the first column by writing the letter of the term on the blank line in front of the correct definition.

___ **1.** The object that stores the data by organizing it into rows and columns.

___ **2.** The collection of related information that displays in a single row of a database table.

___ **3.** This specifies the kind of information that a field will hold; for example, text or numbers.

___ **4.** A field property that determines what displays in datasheets, forms, and report labels.

___ **5.** A data type that automatically assigns a unique numeric value to a field.

___ **6.** A field that uniquely identifies each record in a table.

___ **7.** A data type that stores numbers formatted as monetary values.

___ **8.** A set of fields that can be added with a single click. For example, the Address data type inserts five fields for storing postal addresses.

___ **9.** An Access view that features table fields and their properties.

___ **10.** A field on the *many* side of a relationship used to relate to the table on the *one* side of the relationship.

A AutoNumber

B Caption

C Currency

D Data type

E Foreign key

F Primary key

G Quick Start

H Record

I Table

J Table Design

Multiple Choice (MyITLab®)

Choose the correct answer.

1. An Access view that displays records in rows and fields in columns.
   - A. Database
   - B. Data grid
   - C. Datasheet

2. Each individual characteristic in a record that displays as a single column in a datasheet.
   - A. Field
   - B. Record
   - C. Subset

3. A data type that stores up to 255 characters of text.
   - A. Currency
   - B. Number
   - C. Short Text

4. The blank row at the end of a datasheet used to add records to a table.
   - A. Append
   - B. Data entry
   - C. New record

5. An Access field property that limits the number of characters that can be typed into a text or number field.
   - A. Character limit
   - B. Character size
   - C. Field size

6. A relationship in which a record in the first table can have many associated records in the second table.
   - A. Cascading
   - B. One-to-one
   - C. One-to-many

7. A referential integrity option in which you can edit the primary key values in a table, and all the related records in the other table will update accordingly.
   - A. Cascading delete
   - B. Cascading update
   - C. One-to-many relationship

8. A rule that keeps related values synchronized.
   - A. Data duplication
   - B. Data redundancy
   - C. Referential integrity

9. A command that opens the Print dialog box so that you can select a different printer or different print options.
   - A. Quick Print
   - B. Print
   - C. Print Preview

10. An orientation of the printed page that makes it wider than it is tall.
    - A. Print Preview
    - B. Landscape
    - C. Portrait

Topics for Discussion

1. What kind of information do you think a small business or organization would organize into a database?

2. Each database object has a special purpose. For example, a query is used to filter and sort records.

Why do you think the filter and sort tools are also available when you work with tables, forms, and reports?

Skills Review

To complete this project, you will need the following file:

- acc01_SREmployees

You will save your file as:

- Last_First_acc01_SRDepartments

1. Start **Access 2016**, and then click **Blank desktop database**. Replace the **File Name** with Last_First_acc01_SRDepartments Click **Browse**, navigate to your chapter folder, and then click **OK**. Finish the process by clicking the **Create** button.

2. In **Table1**, select the **ID** column. On the **Fields tab**, in the **Properties group**, click **Name & Caption**. Change the **Name** to EmployeeID and the **Caption** to Employee ID and then click **OK**.

3. Click the **Click to Add** column. In the **Add & Delete group**, click **More Fields**, scroll down, and then click **Name**.

4. Click the **Click to Add** column, click **Date & Time**, and then type DateHired Press **Enter**, and then repeat to add a **Short Text** field named DeptID

5. With the **DeptID** field selected, in the **Properties group**, click in the **Field Size** box, and then type 50

6. Click **Save**, type Employees and then click **OK**. Compare your screen with **Figure 1**, and then **Close** the table.

7. On the **External Data tab**, in the **Import & Link group**, click **Excel**. In the **Get External Data - Excel Spreadsheet** dialog box, click the **Browse** button. In the **File Open** dialog box, navigate to and select the student data file **acc01_SREmployees**, and then click **Open**. Click the **Append a copy of the records to the table** option button, and then click **OK**. In the first screen of the **Import Spreadsheet Wizard**, click **Finish**, and then click **Close** to complete the import process.

8. Double-click **Employees** to open the table in **Datasheet view**. Set the column widths to **Best Fit**.

9. Click the **DateHired** column, and then on the **Home tab**, in the **Sort & Filter group**, click **Ascending**.

10. Click the **DeptID arrow**, and then in the Filter list, clear the **(Select All)** check box. Select the **HR** check box, click **OK**, and then compare your screen with **Figure 2**.

Figure 1   Access 2016, Windows 10, Microsoft Corporation

Figure 2   Access 2016, Windows 10, Microsoft Corporation

■ Continue to the next page to complete this Skills Review ➤

11. On the **Home tab**, in the **Text Formatting group**, change the font size to **10** and the font to **Verdana**.

12. In the **Text Formatting group**, click the **Datasheet Formatting Dialog Box Launcher**, and then in the dialog box, select the **Raised** cell effect. Click the **Background Color arrow**, and then click **Automatic**. Click the **Gridline Color arrow**, and then click the fifth color—**Blue, Accent 1**. Click **OK** to close the dialog box.

13. On the **File tab**, click **Print**, and then click **Print Preview**. In the **Page Layout group**, click **Landscape**. If you are printing this project, click **Print**. Otherwise, click the **Close Print Preview button**. **Save**, and then close the table.

14. On the **Create tab**, in the **Tables group**, click the **Table Design** button. Name the first field DeptID and then press Enter to assign the **Short Text** data type. On the **Design tab**, in the **Tools group**, click **Primary Key**.

15. With the **DeptID** field still selected, in the **Field Properties** pane, change the **Field Size** value to 50 and the **Caption** to Department ID

16. Add a second field named Department with the **Short Text** data type.

17. Click **Save**, type Departments and then click **OK**.

18. Click the **View** button to switch to **Datasheet view**, and then add the following departments:

Department ID	Department
BG	Buildings and Grounds
CD	Community Development
CI	Capital Improvement
F2	Fire
HR	Human Resources
PR	Parks and Recreation

19. Set the column widths to **Best Fit**, and then compare your screen with Figure 3.

20. **Save**, and then **Close** the table. On the **Database Tools tab**, click the **Relationships** button. In the **Show Table** dialog box, add **Employees**, add **Departments**, and then click **Close**.

21. Drag the **DeptID** field from the **Employees** table, point to **DeptID** in the **Departments** table, and then release the left mouse button.

22. In the **Edit Relationships** dialog box, select the **Enforce Referential Integrity** check box, and then click **Create**. If you receive a message, open the Departments table and carefully check your typing.

Figure 3   Access 2016, Windows 10, Microsoft Corporation

Figure 4   Access 2016, Windows 10, Microsoft Corporation

23. In the **Tools group**, click **Relationship Report**. Compare your screen with Figure 4. If you are printing this project, print the report.

24. Click **Save**, click **OK** to accept default name, and then **Close** the report.

25. **Save** and **Close** all open objects, and then **Close** Access. Submit your database files as directed by your instructor.

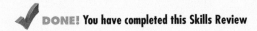

DONE! You have completed this Skills Review

Skills Assessment 1

MyITLab®
Grader

To complete this project, you will need the following file:

- acc01_SA1UtilityData

You will save your file as:

- Last_First_acc01_SA1Utilities

Access 2016,
Windows 10,
Microsoft
Corporation

Figure 1

1. Create a blank desktop database. Name the file Last_First_acc01_SA1Utilities and then save it in your chapter folder.

2. In **Table1**, rename the **ID** field BillingID In the second column, add a **Short Text** field named AccountNumber

3. In the third column, add a **Date & Time** field with the name BillingDate In the fourth column, add a **Currency** field with the name Charge and then save the table as Billings **Close** the table.

4. Import the records in the **Electricity** worksheet from the student data file **acc01_SA1UtilityData**. Append the records to the **Billings** table.

5. Sort the **Billings** datasheet by the **Charge** column in descending order, and then filter the datasheet to display only the records from **Account Number** 2610-408376.

6. Change the font to **Verdana**, the font size to **10**, and then set column widths to **Best Fit**.

7. Change the cell effect to **Raised**, the background color to **Automatic**, and the gridline color to **Blue-Gray, Text 2**. Compare your screen with Figure 1.

8. If you are printing this project, print the datasheet in Landscape orientation. **Save** and then close the table.

9. Create a new table in **Design view**. Name the first field AccountNumber Set the field as the table's primary key, assign the **Short Text** data type, and set its caption to Account Number

10. **Save** the table as Residents and then switch to **Datasheet view**. In the second and third columns, add the **Name Quick Start** fields. In the fourth column, add a **Short Text** field named Street

11. Add the following records to the table:

Account Number	Last Name	First Name	Street
1673-467266	Alloway	Dorris	56553 S Paddington Way
2610-408376	Klasen	Franklin	99721 E Powder River Dr

Access 2016,
Windows 10,
Microsoft
Corporation

Figure 2

Account Number	Last Name	First Name	Street
2790-748496	Cavagnaro	Crystle	72343 N Riverford Pl
3794-907351	Carie	Ryann	45340 N Gurdon Dr

12. Set the column widths to **Best Fit**, and then compare your screen with Figure 2. **Save** and **Close** the table.

13. Add the **Billings** and then the **Residents** table to the **Relationships** tab. Create a one-to-many relationship using the **AccountNumber** field as the common field. Do not select the cascade update or delete options.

14. Create a relationship report. **Save** the report using the name suggested in the **Save As** dialog box. **Close** the report. **Save** and then **Close** the Relationships tab.

15. **Close** the Access window. Submit your work as directed by your instructor.

 DONE! You have completed Skills Assessment 1

Skills Assessment 2

To complete this project, you will need the following file:

- acc01_SA2ClassData

You will save your file as:

- Last_First_acc01_SA2Interns

---

1. Create a blank desktop database. Name the file Last_First_acc01_SA2Interns and then save it in your chapter folder.

2. In **Table1**, rename the **ID** field as InternID and then change its data type to **Number**. In the second and third columns, add the **Name Quick Start** fields. In the fourth column, add a **Short Text** field with the name Phone

3. Add the following records to the table:

InternID	LastName	FirstName	Phone
1	Yerigan	Kenton	(805) 555-7928
2	Mostowy	Clarice	(805) 555-3107
3	Hemstreet	Caroline	(805) 555-5548
4	Marcantel	Almeda	(805) 555-7000
5	Shriver	Cheyenne	(805) 555-6991

4. Set the column widths to **Best Fit**, and then **Save** the table as Interns Compare your screen with **Figure 1**, and then **Save** and close the table.

5. Create a new table in **Design view**. Name the first field ClassID Set the field as the table's primary key, assign the **AutoNumber** data type, and then set its caption to Class ID

6. Add a **Short Text** field named Class as the second field. As the third field, add a **Date/Time** field named StartDate and then set its caption to Start Date

7. In the fourth row, add a **Number** data type named InternID and then set its caption to Intern ID **Save** the table as Sections and then close the table.

8. Add both tables to the **Relationships** tab. Create a one-to-many relationship using the **InternID** field as the common field. Do not select the cascade update or delete options.

9. Create a relationship report. **Save** the report using the name suggested in the **Save As** dialog box. **Close** the report. **Save** and then close the Relationships tab.

Access 2016, Windows 10, Microsoft Corporation

Figure 1

Access 2016, Windows 10, Microsoft Corporation

Figure 2

10. Import the records in the **Sections** worksheet from the Excel student data file **acc01_SA2ClassData**. Append the records to the **Sections** table.

11. Sort the **Sections** datasheet by the **InternID** column in ascending order, and then filter the datasheet to display only the records for the **Introduction to Windows** class.

12. Change the font to **Cambria**, the font size to **12**, and then set column widths to **Best Fit**.

13. Change the cell effect to **Raised**, the background color to **Automatic**, and the gridline color to **Blue-Gray, Text 2**. Compare your screen with **Figure 2**.

14. If you are printing this project, print the datasheet in Landscape orientation. **Save** and then close the table. **Close** Access.

15. Submit the database file as directed by your instructor.

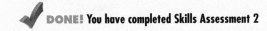 **DONE! You have completed Skills Assessment 2**

My Skills

To complete this project, you will need the following file:

- acc01_MYAddresses

You will save your file as:

- Last_First_acc01_MYContacts

Access 2016, Windows 10, Microsoft Corporation   **Figure 1**

Access 2016, Windows 10, Microsoft Corporation   **Figure 2**

1. Create a blank desktop database. Name the file Last_First_acc01_MYContacts and then save it in your chapter folder.

2. In **Table1**, rename the **ID** field as ContactID and then add a caption of Contact ID

3. In columns two and three, add the Quick Start **Name** fields.

4. In columns four through eight, add the Quick Start **Address** fields.

5. In columns nine through twelve, add the Quick Start **Phone** fields.

6. Delete the **Fax Number** and **Business Phone** fields.

7. Save the table as Contacts and then set the column widths to **Best Fit**. Compare your screen with **Figure 1**.

8. Complete the first record by inserting your own contact information, and then **Save** and close the table.

9. Import the contacts from the Excel student data file **acc01_MYAddresses**. Use the **Contacts** worksheet and append the data to the **Contacts** table.

10. Change the font to **Verdana** and the font size to **10**.

11. In the **Navigation Pane**, click the **Shutter Bar Open/Close Button** « to close the pane. Set the column widths to **Best Fit**.

12. Change the cell effect to **Raised**, the background color to **Automatic**, and the gridline color to **Blue-Gray, Text 2**.

13. Select the **Contact ID** column, and then on the **Home tab**, in the **Records group**, click **More**, and then click **Hide Fields**. **Save** the table changes.

14. Click the **Shutter Bar Open/Close Button** one time to display the Navigation Pane. Click in the append row, and then compare your screen with **Figure 2**.

15. If you are printing this project, print the datasheet in Landscape orientation. **Save** and then close the table.

16. **Close** Access. Submit your work as directed by your instructor.

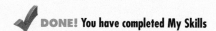 **DONE! You have completed My Skills**

Visual Skills Check

To complete this project, you will need the following file:

- acc01_VSAssessments

You will save your file as:

- Last_First_acc01_VSAssessments

Open the student data file **acc01_ VSAssessments**. On the **File tab**, click **Save As**, and then under **Save Database As**, click **Save As**. Use the **Save As** dialog box to save the file in your chapter folder with the name Last_First_acc01_VSAssessments Sort, filter, and format the **Assessments** table datasheet as shown in **Figure 1**. The table is sorted by the **Parcel** column and filtered by the **AssessorID** column. The font is **Verdana** size **10**, the columns are set to **Best Fit**, and the row height is **15**. The cell effect is **Raised**, the background color is **Automatic**, and the gridline color is **Blue, Accent 1, Darker 50%**.

Set the table to print in the Landscape orientation, and then submit your database file as directed by your instructor.

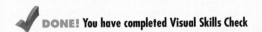 **DONE! You have completed Visual Skills Check**

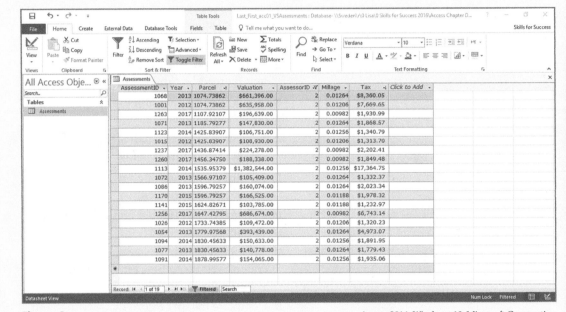

Figure 1

Access 2016, Windows 10, Microsoft Corporation

Skills Challenge 1

To complete this project, you will need the following file:

- acc01_SC1ZonesData

You will save your files as:

- Last_First_acc01_SC1ZonesData (Excel)
- Last_First_acc01_SC1Zones (Access)

Open the student data file **acc01_SC1ZonesData** in Excel, and then save it in your chapter folder as Last_First_acc01_SC1ZonesData View the data stored in the spreadsheet, which describes the zones used in Aspen Falls. Label each column with a label that describes the column and can be used as database field names, and then close the spreadsheet.

Create a new database named Last_First_acc01_SC1Zones and save it in your chapter folder. Create a table to store the data in the Excel spreadsheet. Assign field names, data types, and captions using the practices in this chapter's projects. Assign a

primary key to the field that will uniquely identify each record. Name the table Zones and then import the Excel data into the table you just created. Set the field widths to Best Fit, and then close the table.

Set the table to print in the Landscape orientation, and then submit your database file as directed by your instructor.

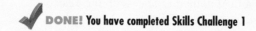 **DONE! You have completed Skills Challenge 1**

Skills Challenge 2

To complete this project, you will need the following file:

- acc01_SC2Plants

You will save your file as:

- Last_First_acc01_SC2Plants

Open the student data file **acc01_SC2Plants**, and then save the file in your chapter folder with the name Last_First_acc01_SC2Plants View the **Relationships** tab, and notice that each plant is assigned a scientific name but the plant may have many common names—a one-to-many relationship. Open the Plants table, and then expand the subdatasheet for *Asarum caudatum* to display three of its common names. Use the subdatasheets for the other nine plants to enter the

common names for each. To locate the common names, search the Internet using the plant's scientific name as the key term. For each plant, enter between one and three common names based on the information you find.

Submit your database file as directed by your instructor.

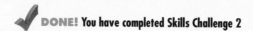 **DONE! You have completed Skills Challenge 2**

More Skills Assessment

MyITLab®
Grader

To complete this project, you will need the following files:

- acc01_MSAMuseum (Access)
- acc01_MSADonor (Word)

You will save your file as:

- Last_First_acc01_MSAMuseum

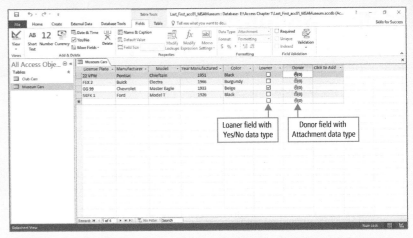

Figure 1   Access 2016, Windows 10, Microsoft Corporation

1. Start **Access 2016**, and **Open** the **acc01_MSAMuseum** file and then save it in your chapter folder as Last_First_acc01_MSAMuseum.

2. **Compact and Repair** the database.

3. In the **Museum Cars** table, add a field named Loaner with the **Yes/ No** data type. Place a checkmark in the *Buick Electra* and *Chevrolet Master Eagle* **Loaner** fields.

4. Add a field named Donor with the **Attachment** data type. Change the **caption** of this field to Donor Compare your screen with **Figure 1**.

5. Attach the **acc01_MSADonor.docx** file to the **Chevrolet Master Eagle Donor** field.

6. Open the **Club Cars** table, and then change the **Notes** field to the **Long Text** data type.

7. At the end of the **Note** for the **Lincoln Sport Touring**, add the following text: This car will not be included in the 6/1/2018 car show. Compare your screen with **Figure 2**.

8. Change the field width of the **Club Cars** table to **Best Fit**.

9. In the **Museum Cars** table, add a field with the **Hyperlink** data type. Change the field name to MuseumWebsite and then adjust the field width to **Best Fit**.

10. In the Pontiac Chieftain record, change the MuseumWebsite to: www.aspenfalls.org

11. **Save** and **Close** any open objects, and then **Close** Access. Submit the file as directed by your instructor.

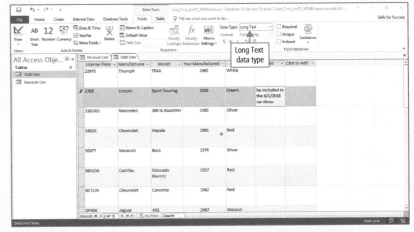

Figure 2   Access 2016, Windows 10, Microsoft Corporation

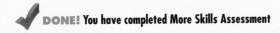

DONE! You have completed More Skills Assessment

Collaborating with Google

To complete this project, you will need a Google account (refer to the Common Features chapter)

You will save your file as:

- **Last_First_acc01_GPSnip**

1. Open the Google Chrome web browser. Log into your Google account, and then click the **Apps** button.

2. Click the **Drive** button to open Google Drive. If you receive a pop-up message, read the message, and then click **Next**. Read each message, and then close the dialog box.

3. Click the **NEW** button, and then click **Google Sheets** to open a blank spreadsheet.

4. Click cell **A1**, type CustomerID and then press Tab. Continue in this manner to enter the column labels in this order: LastName | FirstName | Address | City | Zip | Phone | Email Compare your screen with **Figure 1**.

5. Click the spreadsheet title, *Untitled spreadsheet*. In the dialog box, type CustomerTable as the name of the spreadsheet, and then press **Enter**.

   If you are using a different web browser, you may need to click **File**, and then click **Rename**.

6. Click the **Share** button, and in the **Share with others** dialog box, type AspenFallsEvents@gmail.com to share the sheet with another user.

7. In the **Add a note** text box, type Please add the customer information to this spreadsheet. Once all the records are added I will import the information into the database. and then compare your screen with **Figure 2**.

8. Click **Send**. Click the **Share** button, and then click **Advanced**.

9. Press ⊞, type snip and then press Enter to start the **Snipping Tool**. Click the **New arrow**, and then click **Full-screen Snip**.

10. In the **Snipping Tool** mark-up window, click the **Save Snip** button 💾. In the **Save As** dialog box, navigate to your Access Chapter 1 folder. Be sure the **Save as type** box displays **JPEG file**. Name the

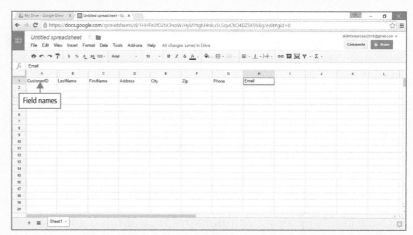

Figure 1

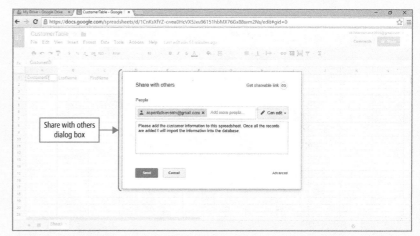

Figure 2

   file Last_First_acc01_GPSnip and then press Enter. **Close** ✕ the Snipping Tool mark-up window.

11. Close all windows, and then submit your work as directed by your instructor.

DONE! You have completed Collaborating with Google

CHAPTER 2

Create Select Queries

- ▶ Databases typically store thousands of records in multiple, related tables. Queries answer questions about the data stored in tables by selecting and presenting the records and fields with the information you need.

- ▶ In a query, you select the fields with the data you want, and then add criteria that filter the records.

- ▶ Criteria test to see if conditions are true or false, and then select only those records in which the results of those tests are true.

- ▶ When you run a select query, a datasheet is created with just the records and fields you selected. The data in the underlying tables is not changed or deleted.

- ▶ You can create new fields by calculating values derived from existing fields. These types of fields can be added to both tables and queries.

- ▶ Query results can also be grouped by one or more fields so that statistics such as totals and averages for each group can be calculated.

Arinahabich/Fotolia

Aspen Falls City Hall

In this chapter, you will create database queries for Aspen Falls City Hall, which provides essential services for the citizens and visitors of Aspen Falls, California. In this project, you will assist Diane Payne, Public Works Director, to answer several questions about the Water Utility monthly billing cycles.

For each monthly billing cycle, the Public Works Department needs to calculate charges—an amount that is derived from each resident's water usage and that month's rate for water. As payments are recorded in the database, the amount due should be automatically adjusted. You will complete both of these tasks by adding calculated fields to a table.

The Public Works Department needs to find records for specific residents by searching for their account number, name, or meter number. You will create select queries that can perform these searches. The department also needs to know which residents are late in their payments and add a late fee when appropriate. To do this, you will add a calculated field to a query.

Finally, the city needs to analyze water usage statistics. To do this, you will add grouping to a query, and then provide summary statistics such as count, average, and total. Throughout the project, you will test your queries using a small sample of the city database used to track resident utility bills.

Time to complete all 10 skills — 60 to 90 minutes

Outcome

Using the skills in this chapter, you will be able to create queries, add calculated fields to tables and queries, add comparison operators and date and time criteria to queries, group queries, and use logical operators and wildcards in queries.

Objectives

2.1 Create queries in a variety of views

2.2 Construct queries using logical operators and wildcards

2.3 Apply calculated fields to tables and queries

2.4 Adjust and add criteria to queries

Student data file needed for this chapter:

acc02_Water

You will save your file as:

Last_First_acc02_Water

SKILLS

Skills 1-10 Training

At the end of this chapter you will be able to:

Skill 1   Create Queries with the Simple Query Wizard

Skill 2   Add Text Criteria

Skill 3   Add Calculated Fields to Tables

Skill 4   Create Queries in Design View

Skill 5   Add Comparison Operators

Skill 6   Add Date and Time Criteria

Skill 7   Group and Total Queries

Skill 8   Add Calculated Fields to Queries

Skill 9   Work with Logical Operators

Skill 10   Add Wildcards to Query Criteria

MORE SKILLS

Skill 11   Export Queries to Excel

Skill 12   Export Queries as Web Pages

Skill 13   Link to External Data Sources

Skill 14   Create Crosstab Queries

Billing Date	Billing Count	Average Usage	Total Billing	Total Due
31-Jan-17	50	67.7	$778.09	($18.27)
28-Feb-17	55	68.4	$865.72	$0.00
31-Mar-17	60	78.8	$1,069.96	($1.00)
30-Apr-17	65	76.9	$1,149.54	$51.18
31-May-17	69	89.4	$1,541.50	$0.00
30-Jun-17	71	113.0	$2,006.00	$24.75
31-Jul-17	74	126.7	$2,312.25	$0.45
31-Aug-17	79	126.7	$2,702.43	$87.21
30-Sep-17	80	128.1	$2,743.20	$55.58
31-Oct-17	82	112.7	$2,279.00	$73.00
30-Nov-17	84	83.9	$1,761.00	$8.00
31-Dec-17	83	61.3	$1,170.24	$17.02
31-Jan-18	84	46.8	$903.67	$0.00
28-Feb-18	83	37.8	$753.60	$2.94
31-Mar-18	83	50.1	$1,039.75	$18.75
30-Apr-18	83	53.3	$1,312.22	($17.08)
31-May-18	82	73.7	$1,993.20	($32.01)
30-Jun-18	80	94.4	$2,643.90	$6.30
31-Jul-18	80	138.1	$4,199.38	$4,199.38

Statistics

Access 2016, Windows 10, Microsoft Corporation

▶ **Queries** are used to ask questions about—query—the data stored in database tables. **Select queries** select and display the records that answer the question, without having to change the data in the underlying table or tables.

1. Start **Access 2016**. On the **Recent** page, click **Open Other Files**. On the **Open** page, click **This PC**, and then click **Browse**. In the **Open** dialog box, navigate to the student data files for this chapter, select **acc02_Water**, and then click the **Open** button.

2. On the **File tab**, click **Save As**. With **Save Database As** selected, click the **Save As** button. In the **Save As** dialog box, navigate to the location you are saving your files for this project. Click **New folder**, type Access Chapter 2 and then press ⎡Enter⎤ two times. Name the file Last_First_acc02_Water Compare your screen with **Figure 1**, and then click **Save**.

3. If the security warning message displays, click Enable Content.

4. In the **Navigation Pane**, under **Tables,** select **Residents**.

5. Click the **Create tab**, and then in the **Queries group**, click the **Query Wizard** button. In the **New Query** dialog box, with **Simple Query Wizard** selected, click **OK** to start the Simple Query Wizard. Compare your screen with **Figure 2.**

   The Simple Query Wizard's first screen is used to select the fields you want to display as columns in the query result. You can choose fields from any table or query, but they should be from tables that are related. Including unrelated tables will result in too many records in the query results.

■ **Continue to the next page to complete the skill**

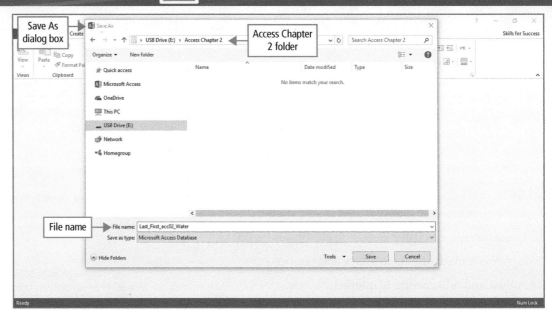

Figure 1

Access 2016, Windows 10, Microsoft Corporation

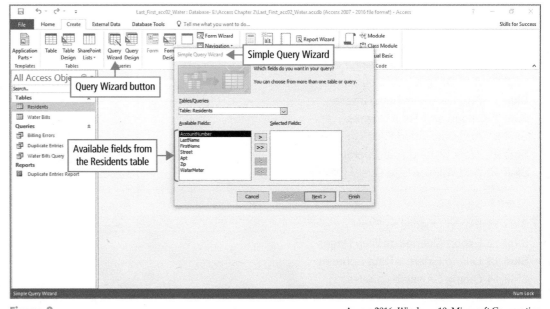

Figure 2

Access 2016, Windows 10, Microsoft Corporation

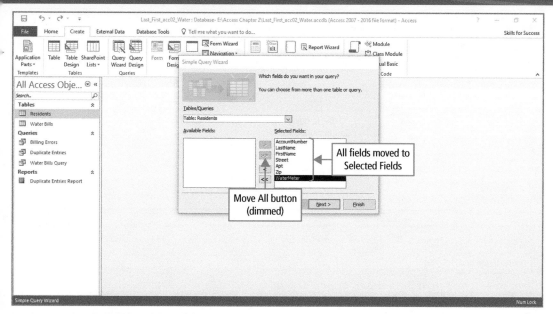

Access 2016, Windows 10, Microsoft Corporation

Figure 3

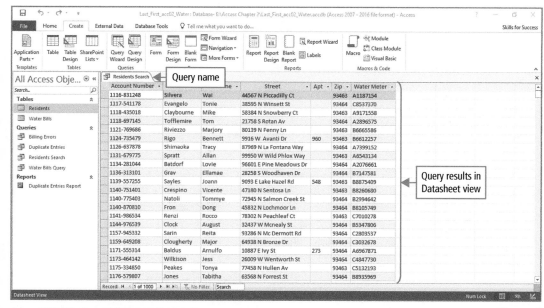

Access 2016, Windows 10, Microsoft Corporation

Figure 4

6. Click the **Move** button `>` one time, to move the **AccountNumber** field into Selected Fields.

7. Click the **Move All** button `>>` to move all the table's fields into Selected Fields. Compare your screen with Figure 3, and then click **Next**.

8. In the **What title do you want for your query** box, replace the existing text—*Residents Query*—with Residents Search

 In the last screen of the Simple Query Wizard, you type the name that will be given to the query and choose to either run the query or open it in Design view.

9. Click **Finish**, and then compare your screen with Figure 4.

 In this manner, the Simple Query Wizard quickly adds fields to a new query. When the query is run, the results display in Datasheet view. Here, all the records and fields from the Residents table have been selected and display. When the Run button is clicked, the query is automatically saved.

10. Leave the query open for the next skill.

■ **You have completed Skill 1 of 10**

▶ **Criteria** are conditions in a query used to select the records that answer the query's question.

1. With the **Residents Search** query open in Datasheet view, click the **Home tab**. In the **Views group**, click the **View** button to switch to Design view. Alternatively, in the lower right corner of the window, click the Design View button ![icon]. Compare your screen with **Figure 1**.

    Query Design view has two panes. The *query design workspace* displays the tables that the query will search. The *query design grid* displays the fields the query will display and the query settings that will be applied to each field.

2. If the table name—*Residents*—does not display under each field name in the design grid, on the Design tab, in the Show/Hide group, click Table Names so that it is selected.

3. In the intersection of the **LastName** column and **Criteria** row—the **LastName** column **Criteria** cell—type the letter h and then compare your screen with **Figure 2**.

    As you type in a criteria cell, *IntelliSense*—Quick Info, ScreenTips, and AutoComplete boxes—displays guidelines for the feature you are typing. *AutoComplete* is a menu of commands that match the characters you type. The *Quick Info* message explains the purpose of the selected AutoComplete command.

■ **Continue to the next page to complete the skill** ▶

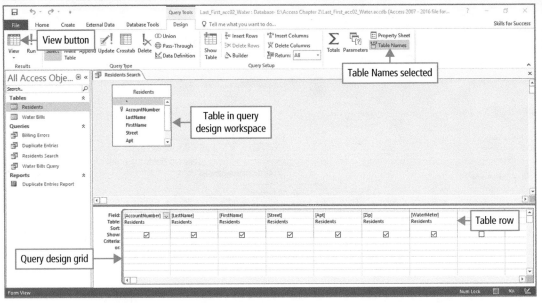

Figure 1   Access 2016, Windows 10, Microsoft Corporation

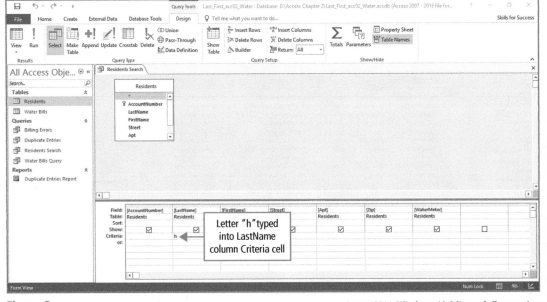

Figure 2   Access 2016, Windows 10, Microsoft Corporation

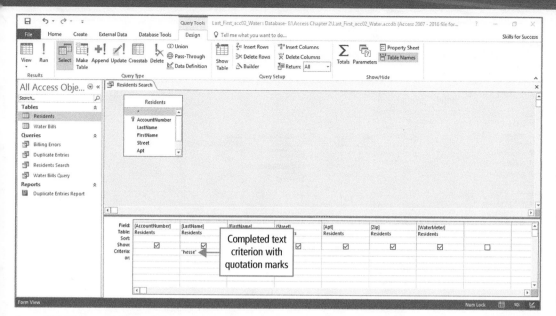

Access 2016, Windows 10, Microsoft Corporation

Figure 3

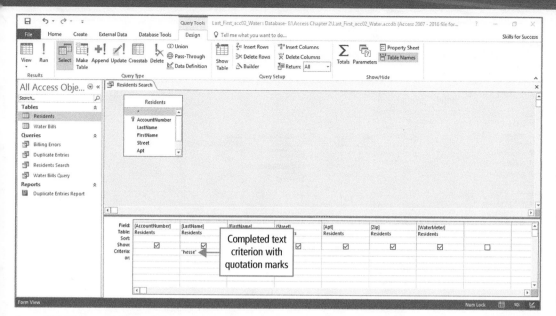

Access 2016, Windows 10, Microsoft Corporation

Figure 4

4. In the **LastName** column **Criteria** cell, complete the entry hesse Press ⎯Tab⎯, and then compare your screen with Figure 3.

> Criteria that contain text must be surrounded by quotation marks. If you do not type the quotation marks, they will be automatically inserted before the query is run.

5. On the **Design tab**, in the **Results group**, click the **Run** button to display the three records that result.

> In this manner, criteria filter the data. Here, the query answers the question, *Which residents have a last name of Hesse?* By default, criteria are not case sensitive. Here, the criterion *hesse* matched the value *Hesse*.

6. On the **Home tab**, in the **Views group**, click the **View** button to return to Design view.

7. In the **LastName** column **Criteria** cell, delete the quotation marks and text *"hesse"*.

8. In the **WaterMeter** column **Criteria** cell, type the quotation marks and text *"C7112526"*

> When you include the quotation marks around criteria, the AutoComplete and Quick Info messages do not display.

9. On the **Design tab**, in the **Results group**, click the **Run** button, and then compare your screen with Figure 4.

> The query answers the following questions, *Who owns meter C7112526, and what is the address?*

10. If you are printing your work for this project, print the datasheet in Landscape orientation.

11. Click **Save** 🔲, and then **Close** ⊠ the query.

■ **You have completed Skill 2 of 10**

▶ A **calculated field** is a field in a table or query that derives its values from other fields in the table or query.

1. In the **Navigation Pane**, under **Tables**, double-click **Water Bills** to open the datasheet.

2. Click anywhere in the **Usage** column to make it the active column.

3. Click the **Fields tab**, and then in the **Add & Delete group**, click **More Fields**. Near the bottom of the field list, point to **Calculated Field**, and then in the submenu that displays, click **Currency**.

4. In the **Expression Builder** dialog box, under **Expression Categories**, double-click **Rate** to insert it into the expression.

> An **expression** is a combination of fields, mathematical operators, and prebuilt functions that calculates values in tables, forms, queries, and reports. In expressions, field names are enclosed between left and right square brackets.

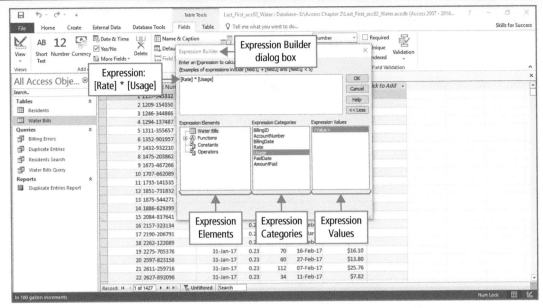

Figure 1

Access 2016, Windows 10, Microsoft Corporation

5. Under **Expression Elements**, click **Operators**, and then under **Expression Categories**, click **Arithmetic**.

6. Under **Expression Values**, double-click the multiplication operator—the asterisk (*)—to insert it into the expression.

7. Under **Expression Elements**, click **Water Bills**, and then under **Expression Categories**, double-click **Usage**.

8. Compare your screen with **Figure 1**, and then click **OK**.

9. In the datasheet, with the text *Field1* still selected, type Billing Press Tab, and then compare your screen with **Figure 2**.

> The Billing column displays the result of multiplying each record's Rate by its Usage.

■ **Continue to the next page to complete the skill** ▶

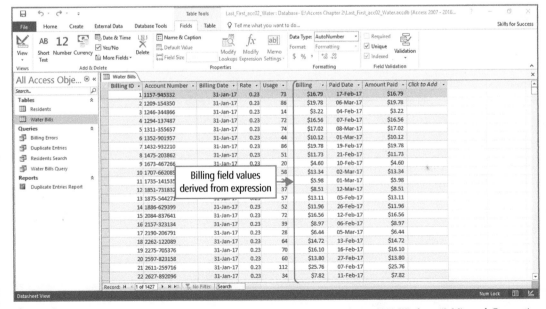

Figure 2

Access 2016, Windows 10, Microsoft Corporation

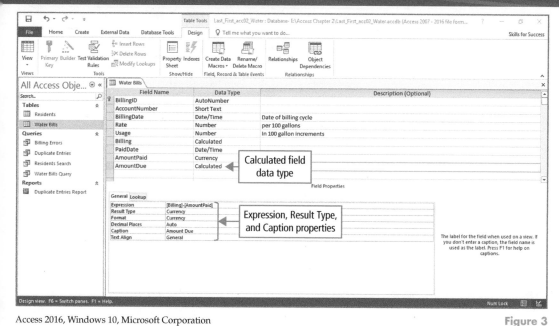

Access 2016, Windows 10, Microsoft Corporation

Figure 3

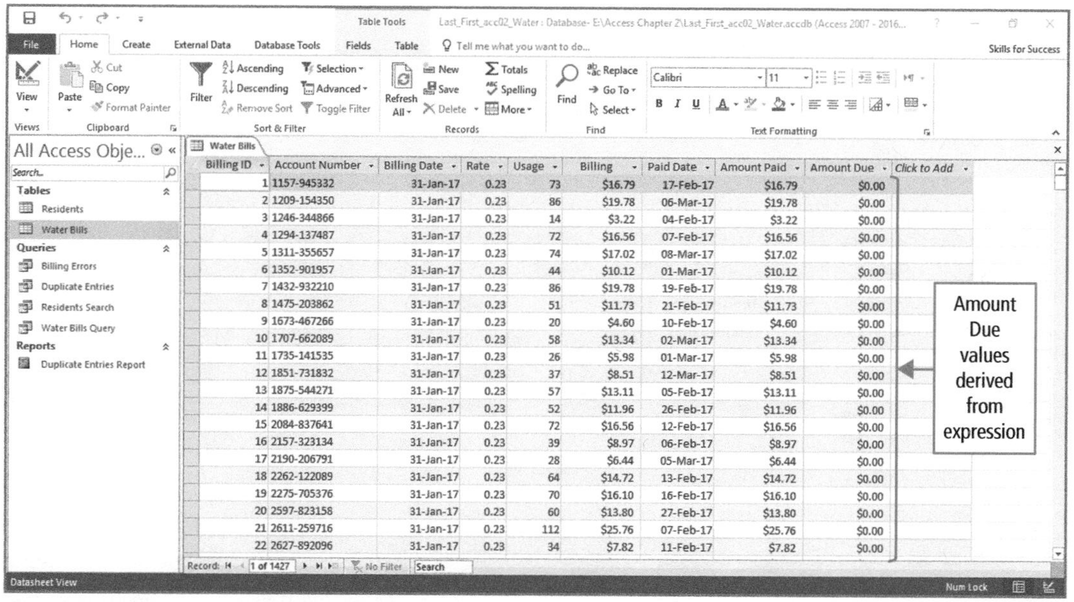

Access 2016, Windows 10, Microsoft Corporation

Figure 4

10. Click **Save** 🖫. On the **Home tab**, in the **Views group**, click **View** to switch to Design view.

11. In the **Field Name** column, click in the first empty cell, and then type AmountDue In the same row, display and click the **Data Type arrow**, and then click **Calculated** to open the Expression Builder.

12. In the **Expression Builder**, repeat the technique just practiced or type the following expression: [Billing] - [AmountPaid] and then click **OK**.

13. With the **AmountDue** field still active, in the **Field Properties** pane, click **Result Type**, click the **Result Type arrow**, and then click **Currency**.

> A calculated field can be assigned any of the data types other fields are assigned. Here, the Currency data type is the most appropriate data type.

14. In the **Field Properties** pane, click in the **Caption** cell, and then type Amount Due Compare your screen with **Figure 3**.

15. Click **Save** 🖫, and then switch to Datasheet view. Set the **Amount Due** column width to **Best Fit**, and then compare your screen with **Figure 4**.

> It is best practice to exclude spaces from field names. Labels, however, can display spaces. Here, the *Amount Due* caption displays at the top of the last column instead of the field name—*AmountDue*.

16. Click **Save** 🖫, and then **Close** ⊠ the table.

■ **You have completed Skill 3 of 10**

▶ To create a query in Design view, first add the necessary tables to the query design workspace. Then add the fields you want to use to the design grid.

1. Click the **Create tab**, and then in the **Queries group**, click the **Query Design** button.

2. In the **Show Table** dialog box, double-click **Residents** to add the table to the query design workspace. Alternately, select the table in the dialog box, and then click the Add button.

3. Repeat the technique just practiced to add the **Water Bills** table. Compare your screen with **Figure 1**.

   Tables can be added to the query design workspace using the Show Table dialog box or by dragging them from the Navigation Pane.

4. **Close** the **Show Table** dialog box, and then compare your screen with **Figure 2**.

   This query needs to answer these questions: *What are the names of the customers who have an overdue balance, what are those balances, and from what time periods?* To answer these questions, fields from two tables are needed.

   When a query selects fields from multiple tables, the tables need to be related. By default, queries follow the relationship rules defined in the Relationships tab. Here, the two tables are joined in a one-to-many relationship using AccountNumber as the common field. A resident can have many water billing cycles.

■ Continue to the next page to complete the skill

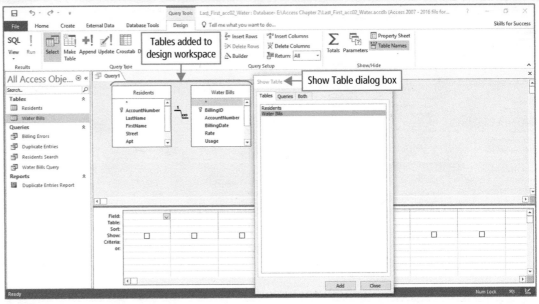

Figure 1

Access 2016, Windows 10, Microsoft Corporation

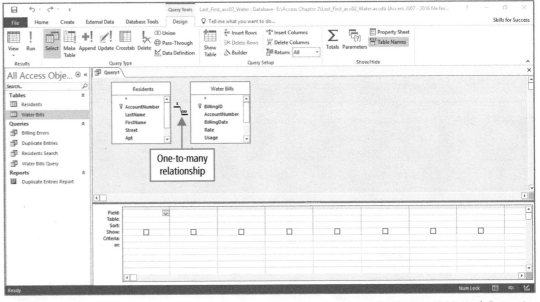

Figure 2

Access 2016, Windows 10, Microsoft Corporation

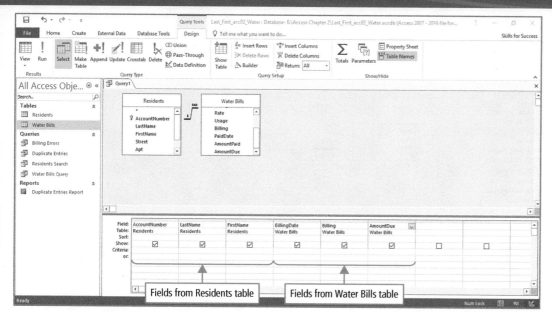

Access 2016, Windows 10, Microsoft Corporation

Figure 3

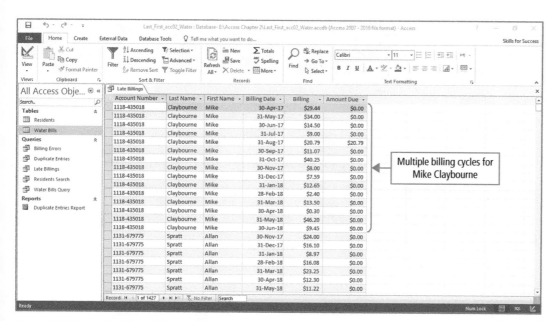

Access 2016, Windows 10, Microsoft Corporation

Figure 4

5. In the query design workspace, in the **Residents** table, double-click the **AccountNumber** field to add it to the first column of the design grid. Alternatively, drag the field into the first column Field cell.

6. Repeat the technique just practiced to add the **LastName** and **FirstName** fields to the second and third column of the design grid.

7. Scroll down the **Water Bills** table list as needed and add the following fields in this order: **BillingDate**, **Billing**, and **AmountDue**. Compare your screen with **Figure 3**.

MOS
Obj 3.2.2

8. Click **Save** 💾. In the **Save As** dialog box, type Late Billings and then press Enter.

MOS
Obj 3.1.6

9. On the **Design tab**, in the **Results group**, click **Run**. Compare your screen with **Figure 4**.

    Before adding criteria, it is a good idea to run the query to verify that it displays the fields you need. Here, you can see each billing cycle sorted by customer.

10. On the status bar, click the **Design View** button 📐, and then leave the query open for the next skill.

■ **You have completed Skill 4 of 10**

▶ In query criteria, numbers are typically combined with **comparison operators**—operators that compare two values including operators such as > (greater than) or < (less than).

1. If necessary, open the Late Billings query in Design view.

2. In the **Billing** column **Criteria** cell, type >80 Compare your screen with **Figure 1**.

3. On the **Design tab**, in the **Results group**, click the **Run** button to display the 15 records that answer the question, *Which billings are larger than 80?*

4. On the **Home tab**, click the **View** button to return to Design view.

5. In the **Billing** column **Criteria** cell, delete the criterion.

6. In the **Amount Due** column **Criteria** cell, type <0 and then **Run** the query to display the 12 records that answer the question, *Which customers have a negative balance?*

7. Switch to Design view. In the **Amount Due** column **Criteria** cell, replace the criteria with 0 **Run** the query to display the 1,314 records that answer the question, *Which billings have a balance of zero?*

When a value is to match exactly, simply type the value. The equals (=) operator is not needed. The commonly used comparison operators are summarized in the table in **Figure 2**.

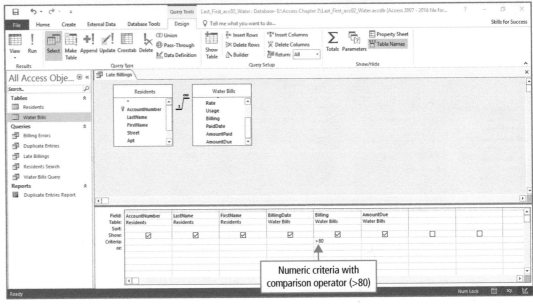

Figure 1

Numeric criteria with comparison operator (>80)

Access 2016, Windows 10, Microsoft Corporation

Common Comparison Operators	
Operator	**Purpose**
=	Is true when the field's value is equal to the specified value
<>	Is true when the field's value does not equal the specified value
<	Is true when the field's value is less than the specified value
<=	Is true when the field's value is less than or equal to the specified value
>	Is true when the field's value is greater than the specified value
>=	Is true when the field's value is greater than or equal to the specified value

Figure 2

■ Continue to the next page to complete the skill ▶

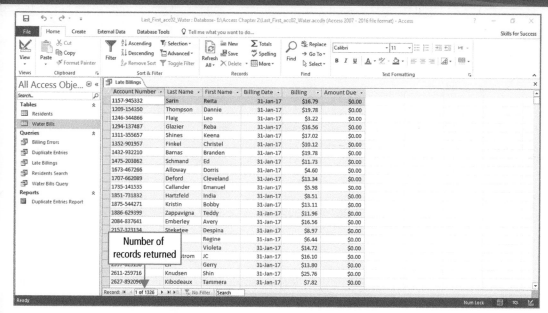

Access 2016, Windows 10, Microsoft Corporation

Figure 3

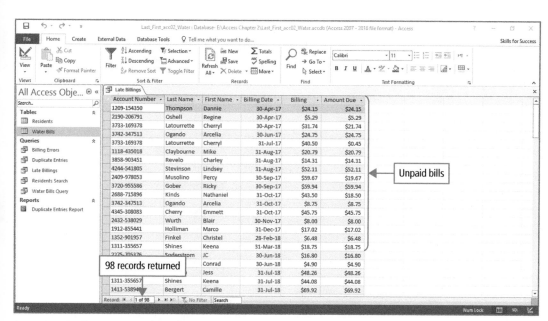

Access 2016, Windows 10, Microsoft Corporation

Figure 4

8. Switch to Design view. In the **Amount Due** column **Criteria** cell, replace the criteria with <=0 **Run** the query, and then compare your screen with Figure 3.

   The query returns records for which the amount due is zero and the records for which the amount due is negative. In this manner, the <= operator returns records that are equal to or less than the number following the criterion.

9. Switch to Design view. In the **Amount Due** column **Criteria** cell, replace the criteria with > 0 **Run** the query, and then compare your screen with Figure 4. Scroll down the datasheet to view the last records in the results.

   The query answers the question, *Which billings have a balance due?* An additional criterion is needed to return only those records for which the amount due is late.

10. Click **Save** 🔲, return to Design View, and leave the query open for the next skill.

■ **You have completed Skill 5 of 10**

▶ In Access, dates and times are stored as numbers. The underlying numbers display as dates in database objects. For example, the number 37979 displays as *12/24/2003* if the Short Date format is assigned to the Date/Time field.

▶ When you add criteria to more than one query column, both criteria must be true if the record is to be included in the results.

1. With the **Late Billings** query open in Design view, click in the **BillingDate** column **Criteria** cell, and then type <7/1/2018 Press Tab, and then compare your screen with **Figure 1**.

   Years can be typed with four digits (2018) or two digits (18). When a year is entered as two digits, it will be converted to four digits when you press Tab. Dates are stored as serial numbers, so you can include arithmetic and comparison operators in your criteria.

   When dates are used as query criteria, they are enclosed in number signs (#). If you do not include them, they will be inserted when the query is run or when you press Tab.

2. On the **Design tab**, in the **Results group**, click the **Run** button, and then compare your screen with **Figure 2**.

   This query answers the question, *Which billings before July 1, 2018 still have a balance due?* In this manner, both the billing date and amount due comparisons must be true for the record to be included in the query results.

■ Continue to the next page to complete the skill ▶

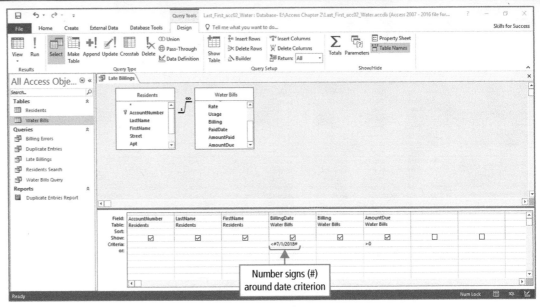

Figure 1

Access 2016, Windows 10, Microsoft Corporation

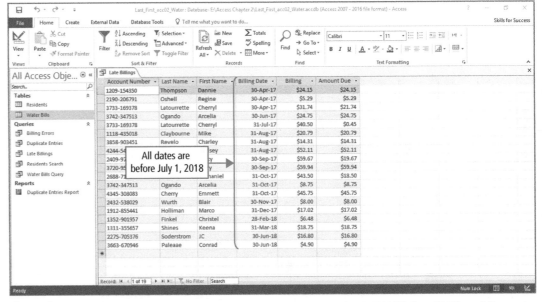

Figure 2

Access 2016, Windows 10, Microsoft Corporation

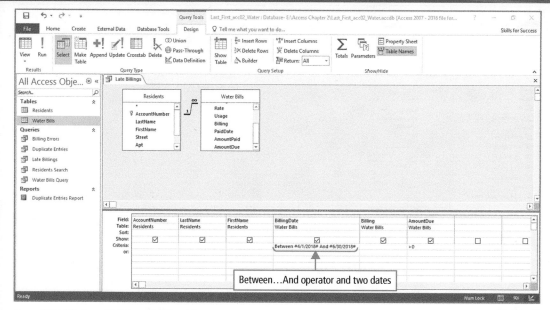

Between...And operator and two dates

Access 2016, Windows 10, Microsoft Corporation

Figure 3

3. Switch to Design view. In the **BillingDate** column **Criteria** cell, replace the criteria with >=4/1/2018 **Run** the query to display the 81 billings with balances due that occurred on or after April 1, 2018.

4. Switch to Design view. In the **BillingDate** column **Criteria** cell, replace the existing criterion with Between 4/1/2018 And 6/30/2018

5. Click an empty cell, and then with the ⊹ pointer, increase the width of the **BillingDate** column to display all its criteria, and then compare your screen with Figure 3.

   The ***Between . . . And operator*** is a comparison operator that finds all numbers or dates between and including two values. Here, the billing cycle must be between April 1 and June 30, 2018, to display in the query.

   When you widen a query column in the design grid, the column will return to its original width when the query is closed.

6. **Run** the query, and then compare your screen with Figure 4.

   The query answers the question, *Which billings from the second quarter of 2018 have a balance due?*

7. Click **Save** 🖫. If you are printing this project, print the datasheet in Landscape view. **Close** ☒ the query.

■ **You have completed Skill 6 of 10**

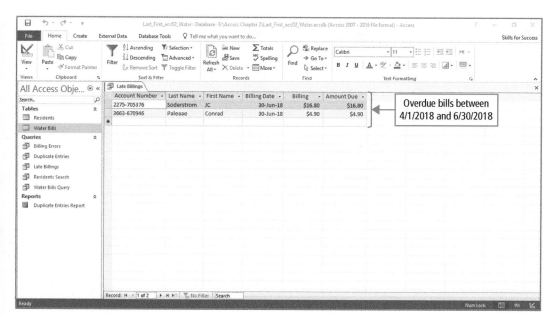

Overdue bills between 4/1/2018 and 6/30/2018

Access 2016, Windows 10, Microsoft Corporation

Figure 4

▶ The Total row is added to queries when you need *summary statistics*—calculations for groups of data such as totals, averages, or counts.

1. On the **Create tab**, in the **Queries group**, click the **Query Design** button. In the **Show Table** dialog box, add the **Water Bills** table, and then **Close** the dialog box.

2. On the **Design tab**, in the **Show/Hide group**, click **Totals**. Add **BillingDate** to the first column, and then compare your screen with **Figure 1**.

   The Total row is used to determine how queries should be grouped and summarized. By default, each column is set to Group By. The *Group By* operator designates which query column contains the group of values to summarize as a single record, one for each set. Here, totals will be calculated for each month.

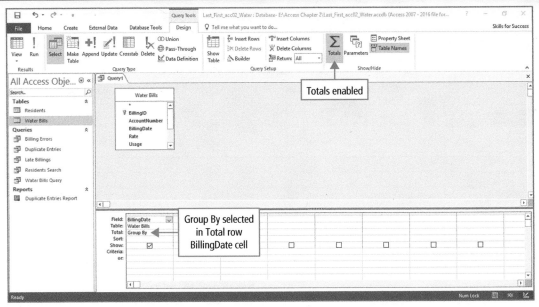

Figure 1

Access 2016, Windows 10, Microsoft Corporation

3. In the **Water Bills** list of fields, double-click **BillingDate** to add the field to the second column. Click the **BillingDate** column **Total** cell to display its arrow. Click the cell's **Total arrow**, and then from the menu, click **Count**.

   The *Count* operator calculates the number of records in each group. Here, the number of billings for each month will be calculated.

4. Repeat the technique just practiced to add the **Usage** field to the third column, and then change its **Total** cell value to **Avg**. Compare your screen with **Figure 2**.

   The *Avg* operator calculates the average of the values in each group.

■ Continue to the next page to complete the skill ▶

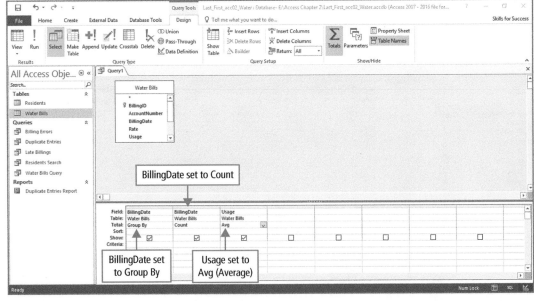

Figure 2

Access 2016, Windows 10, Microsoft Corporation

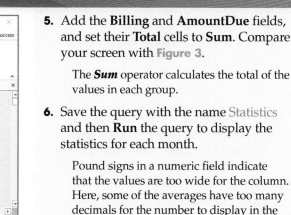
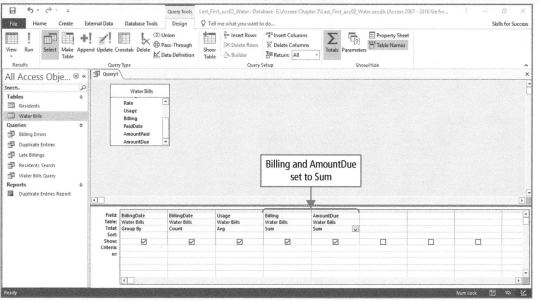

Access 2016, Windows 10, Microsoft Corporation

Figure 3

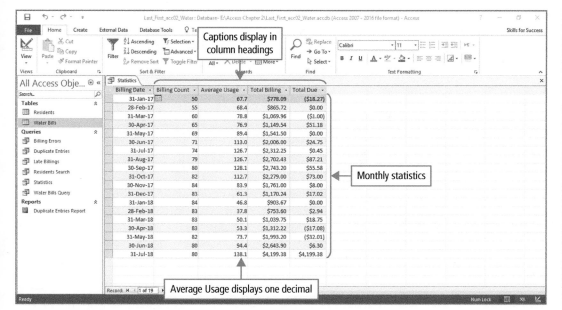

Access 2016, Windows 10, Microsoft Corporation

Figure 4

5. Add the **Billing** and **AmountDue** fields, and set their **Total** cells to **Sum**. Compare your screen with Figure 3.

   The **Sum** operator calculates the total of the values in each group.

6. Save the query with the name Statistics and then **Run** the query to display the statistics for each month.

   Pound signs in a numeric field indicate that the values are too wide for the column. Here, some of the averages have too many decimals for the number to display in the given column width.

7. Switch to Design view. Click in the **Usage** column to make it active, and then on the **Design tab**, in the **Show/Hide group**, click **Property Sheet**.

8. In the **Property Sheet**, click **Format**, click the **Format arrow** that displays, and then click **Fixed**. Display and click the **Decimal Places arrow**, and then click **1**. Click in the **Caption** cell, and then type Average Usage

9. Repeat the technique just practiced to change the caption of the second **BillingDate** to Billing Count Change the **Billing** caption to Total Billing and the **AmountDue** caption to Total Due

10. **Close** ☒ the Property Sheet. **Run** the query, set the column widths to **Best Fit**, and then compare your screen with Figure 4.

    The captions that were set previously in the property sheet display in the datasheet header row.

11. **Save** 🖫 the query. If you are printing this project, print the datasheet in Landscape orientation.

12. **Close** ☒ the query.

■ **You have completed Skill 7 of 10**

▶ You can insert calculated fields into queries. In queries, calculated fields need an *alias*—a descriptive label used to identify a field in expressions, datasheets, forms, and reports.

1. Click the **Create tab**, and then in the **Queries group**, click the **Query Design** button. In the **Show Table** dialog box, add the **Residents** table, add the **Water Bills** table, and then **Close** the dialog box.

2. From the **Residents** table, add the **AccountNumber**, **LastName**, and **FirstName** fields to the design grid.

3. From the **Water Bills** table, add **BillingDate**, and then in the **BillingDate** column **Criteria** cell, type <4/1/18 and then press Tab.

MOS
Obj 3.3.5
4. From the **Water Bills** table, add **AmountDue**, and then in the **AmountDue** column **Criteria** cell, type >0 **Run** the query, and then compare your screen with **Figure 1**.

5. Click **Save** 🖫, and then in the **Save As** dialog box, type Late Fees and then click **OK**.

MOS
Obj 3.2.4
6. Switch to Design view. In the **AmountDue** column, clear the **Show** cell check box so that the column will not display in the datasheet.

7. Click in the first blank column **Field** row. On the **Design tab**, in the **Query Setup group**, click the **Builder** button.

8. In the **Expression Builder** dialog box, type the following expression Penalty:[AmountDue]*0.25 taking care to include the colon. Compare your screen with **Figure 2**.

> The alias in a calculated field ends with a colon. Here, *Penalty* will be the alias.

■ **Continue to the next page to complete the skill**

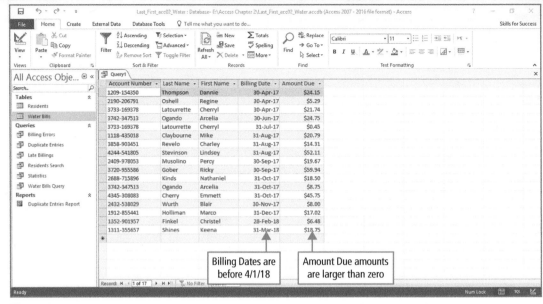

Billing Dates are before 4/1/18

Amount Due amounts are larger than zero

Figure 1

Access 2016, Windows 10, Microsoft Corporation

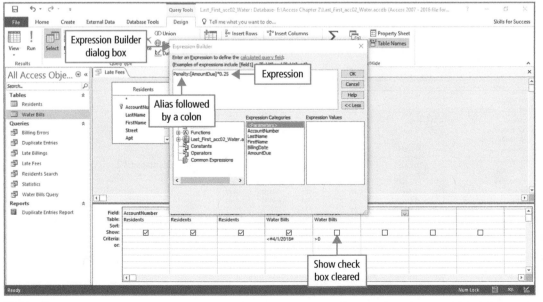

Expression Builder dialog box

Expression

Alias followed by a colon

Show check box cleared

Figure 2

Access 2016, Windows 10, Microsoft Corporation

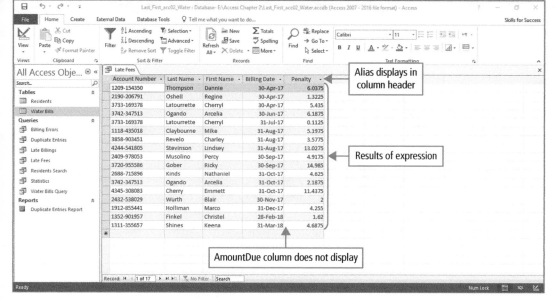

Access 2016, Windows 10, Microsoft Corporation

Figure 3

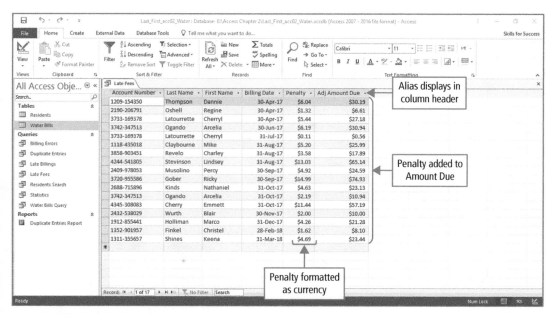

Access 2016, Windows 10, Microsoft Corporation

Figure 4

9. Click **OK** to close the Expression Builder and insert the expression.

10. **Run** the query, and then compare your screen with **Figure 3**. If the Enter Parameter dialog box displays, click Cancel, and then repeat steps 6 through 8, carefully checking your typing.

> In the last column, the alias *Penalty* displays in the header row. The result of the expression displays in each record. Here, a 25% penalty is derived by multiplying 0.25 by the amount due.

11. Click **Save** 🔲, and then switch to Design view. If necessary, click in the Penalty column to make it active.

12. Click the **Property Sheet** button to open it. In the **Property Sheet**, display and click the **Format arrow**, and then click **Currency**. **Close** ☒ the Property Sheet.

Obj 3.2.6

13. Click the first blank column **Field** cell, and then in the **Query Setup group**, click **Builder**.

14. In the **Expression Builder** dialog box, type the following alias and expression:
    Adj Amount Due:[AmountDue]+ [Penalty]

> Because an alias represents a field name, when an alias is used in an expression, it is enclosed in square brackets. Here, the Penalty alias is used to add the penalty to the original amount due.

15. Click **OK**, and then **Run** the query. Set the column widths to **Best Fit**, and then compare your screen with **Figure 4**.

16. Click **Save** 🔲. If you are printing this project, print the datasheet in Landscape orientation.

17. **Close** ☒ the query.

■ **You have completed Skill 8 of 10**

▶ When criteria are in more than one column, the placement of the criteria in the design grid rows determines whether one or both of the criteria must be true for the record to display.

1. In the **Navigation Pane**, under **Queries**, right-click **Billing Errors**, and then from the shortcut menu, click **Design View**.

2. In the **Usage** column, click the **Sort** cell, click the **arrow** that displays, and then click **Ascending**.

3. **Run** the query, and notice that the **Usage** values that are empty or negative are listed first.

4. Switch to Design view. In the **Usage** column **Criteria** cell, type Is Null Below the value just typed, in the **Usage** column or cell, type <0 Compare your screen with **Figure 1**.

    The **Is Null** and **Is Not Null** operators test if a field is empty or not empty.

5. **Run** the query to display only the records for which the **Usage** value is empty or less than 0.

6. **Save** 🖫, and then **Close** ☒ the query. In the **Navigation Pane**, right-click **Billing Errors**, and then click **Design View**. Compare your screen with **Figure 2**.

    When two criteria are placed in *different* rows in the design grid, the ***Or logical operator***—a logical comparison of two criteria that is true if either of the criteria outcomes is true—applies. Because the two criteria in this query can be combined into a single row, they were automatically combined with the Or operator separating them.

■ Continue to the next page to complete the skill

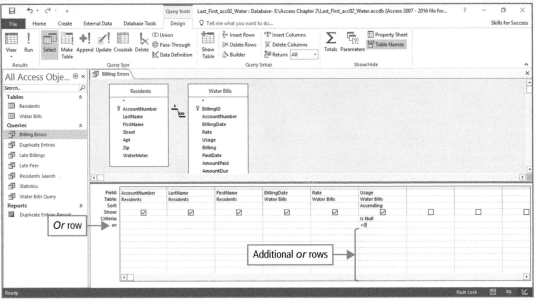

Figure 1   Access 2016, Windows 10, Microsoft Corporation

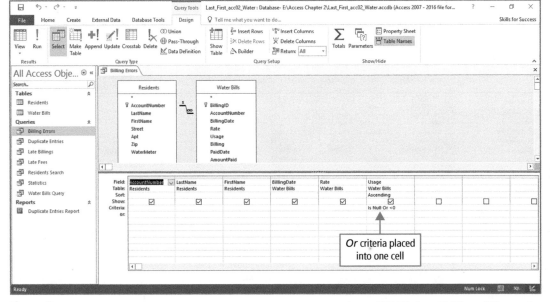

Figure 2   Access 2016, Windows 10, Microsoft Corporation

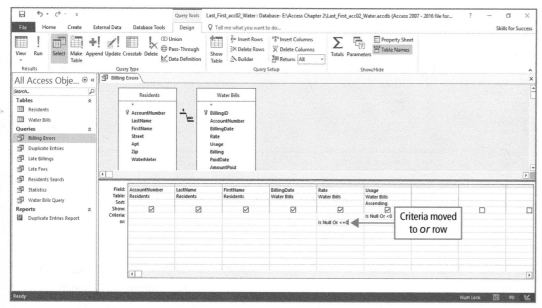

Access 2016, Windows 10, Microsoft Corporation

Figure 3

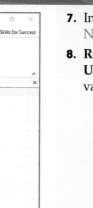

7. In the **Rate** column **Criteria** cell, type Is Null Or <=0

8. **Run** the query, and notice that both the **Usage** and **Rate** columns contain errant values as shown in Figure 3.

> When two criteria are placed in the same row, the **And logical operator**—a logical comparison of two criteria that is true only when both criteria outcomes are true— applies. Here, records are selected only where the Usage and Rate columns both have errors.

9. Switch to Design view. In the **Rate** column **Criteria** row, delete the criteria. In the **Rate** column **or** row (the row below the Criteria row), type Is Null Or <=0 and then compare your screen with Figure 4.

> Here, records are selected if either the Usage or Rate column has errors.

10. **Run** the query to display six records that match the criteria. If you are printing your work for this project, print the datasheet.

11. **Save** 🗗, and then **Close** ☒ the query.

■ **You have completed Skill 9 of 10**

Access 2016, Windows 10, Microsoft Corporation

Figure 4

► A ***wildcard*** is a special character, such as an asterisk, used in query criteria to allow matches for any combination of letters or characters.

► Using wildcards, you can expand your search criteria to find a more accurate subset of the data.

1. In the **Navigation Pane**, under **Queries**, right-click **Duplicate Entries**, and then, from the shortcut menu, click **Design View**.

2. In the **LastName** column **Criteria** cell, type Jones In the **FirstName** column **Criteria** cell, type William and then **Run** the query to display the record for William Jones.

> William Jones reports that he receives three bills each month. However, with the current criteria, his record is listed one time.

3. Switch to Design view. In the **FirstName** column **Criteria** cell, replace the existing criterion with Will* **Run** the query, and then compare your screen with **Figure 1**.

> The ***asterisk (*) wildcard*** character matches any combination of characters. Here, the two first names begin with *Will* but end differently.

4. Switch to Design view, and then compare your screen with **Figure 2**.

> When you include wildcards, the criterion needs to start with the Like operator. If you don't type the Like operator, it will be inserted automatically when the query is run.

■ **Continue to the next page to complete the skill** ➤

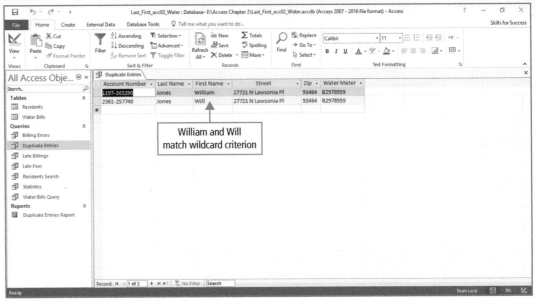

Figure 1

Access 2016, Windows 10, Microsoft Corporation

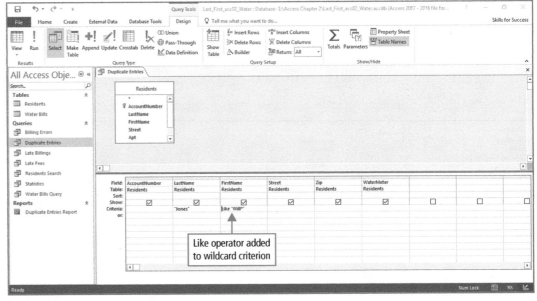

Figure 2

Access 2016, Windows 10, Microsoft Corporation

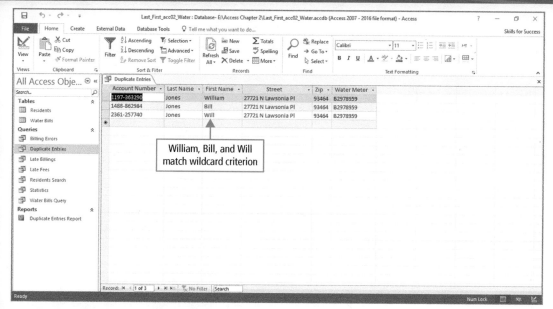

Access 2016, Windows 10, Microsoft Corporation

Figure 3

William, Bill, and Will match wildcard criterion

5. In the **FirstName** column **Criteria** cell, replace the existing criterion with Like "?ill*" **Run** the query to display the three duplicate records for William Jones. Compare your screen with Figure 3.

> The *question mark (?) wildcard* character matches any single character. Common wildcard characters supported by Access are summarized in the table in Figure 4.

6. **Save** , and then **Close** the query.

7. In the **Navigation Pane**, under **Reports**, double-click **Duplicate Entries Report**. If you are printing this project, print the report.

> Recall that reports are often used to display the results of queries. Here, the report displays the results of the Duplicate Entries query.

8. **Close** the report.

> Because you did not make any design changes to the report, you do not need to save it.

9. **Close** Access. Submit your printouts or file as directed by your instructor.

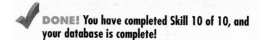

DONE! You have completed Skill 10 of 10, and your database is complete!

Common Access Wildcard Characters		
Character	**Description**	**Example**
*	Matches any number of characters.	Don* matches Don and Donna, but not Adonna.
?	Matches any single alphabetic character.	D?n matches Don and Dan, but not Dean.
[ ]	Matches any single character in the brackets.	D[ao]n matches Don and Dan, but not Den.
#	Matches any single numeric character.	C-#PO matches C-3PO, but not C-DPO.

Figure 4

More Skills 11

Export Queries to Excel

To complete this project, you will need the following file:

- acc02_MS11Results

You will save your files as:

- Last_First_acc02_MS11Results
- Last_First_acc02_MS11Excel

▶ Data from a table or query can be exported into file formats that are opened with other applications such as Excel and Word.

▶ In Excel, you can analyze the query results by adding summary statistics and charts.

---

1. Start **Access 2016**, and then open the student data file **acc02_MS11Results**. Save the database in your **Access Chapter 2** folder as Last_First_acc02_ MS11Results If necessary, enable the content.

2. Open the **2018 DNF** query datasheet, and then replace the first and last names of the first racer *Lavette* and *Hoyle* with your own first and last names.

3. Switch to Design view. In the **Year** column **Criteria** cell, type 2018 In the **RunTime** column **Criteria** cell, type Is Null Compare your screen with **Figure 1**.

4. **Save** 🖫, and then **Run** the query to display the 19 racers who did not finish—DNF. **Close** the query.

5. In the **Navigation Pane**, be sure that the **2018 DNF** query is still selected. Click the **External Data tab**, and then in the **Export group,** click the **Excel** button.

6. In the **Export - Excel Spreadsheet** dialog box, click the **File format arrow**.

   You can save a query in different Excel file formats.

7. Press Esc to close the menu, and then click the **Browse** button. In the **File Save** dialog box, navigate to your **Access Chapter 2** folder, name the file Last_First_acc02_MS11Excel and then click **Save**.

8. In the **Export - Excel Spreadsheet** dialog box, select the **Export data with formatting and layout** check box, and then select the **Open the destination file after the export operation is complete** check box, as shown in **Figure 2**.

9. Click **OK**. Wait a few moments for the data to display in Excel.

   When you export a table or query to Excel, the field names are included as column labels in the spreadsheet. In the taskbar, the Access button will flash to remind you to return to Access and close the dialog box that is open.

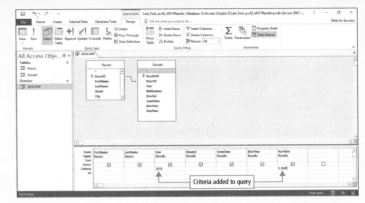

Figure 1   Access 2016, Windows 10, Microsoft Corporation

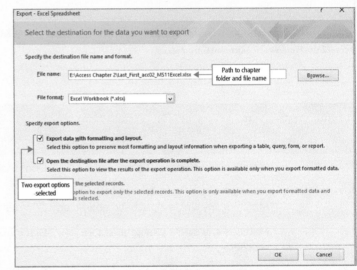

Figure 2   Access 2016, Windows 10, Microsoft Corporation

10. If your instructor asks you to print your work, print the worksheet.

11. **Close** ☒ Excel. In the **Export - Excel Spreadsheet** dialog box, click the **Close** button.

12. **Close** ☒ Access. Submit your files as directed by your instructor.

■ **You have completed More Skills 11**

More Skills ⑫

Export Queries as Web Pages

To complete this project, you will need the following file:

- acc02_MS12Females

You will save your files as:

- Last_First_acc02_MS12Females
- Last_First_acc02_MS12HTML

▶ By exporting a query as a web page, the file can be placed on a web server to make the results available on the web.

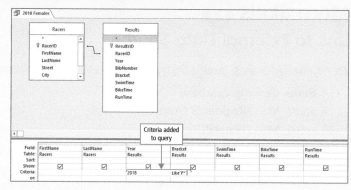

Access 2016, Windows 10, Microsoft Corporation   Figure 1

1. Start **Access 2016**, and then open the student data file **acc02_MS12Females**. Save the database in your **Access Chapter 2** folder as Last_First_acc02_MS12Females If necessary, enable the content.

2. Open the **2018 Females** query datasheet, and then replace the first and last names of the first racer *Lavette* and *Hoyle* with your own first and last names.

3. Switch to Design view. In the **Year** column **Criteria** box, type 2018 In the **Bracket** column **Criteria** cell, type Like "F*" Compare your screen with **Figure 1**.

   As you type *2018* IntelliSense will suggest *2018 Females* as an option. When you add a criterion, be careful to enter the correct data and not to accidentally select an IntelliSense suggestion that you do not want.

4. **Save** 🖫, and then **Run** the query to display 158 records. **Close** ⊠ the query.

5. In the **Navigation Pane**, be sure that the **2018 Females** query is still selected. On the **External Data tab**, in the **Export group**, click the **More** button. In the list of file types, click **HTML Document**.

   An **HTML document** is a text file with instructions for displaying its content in a web browser. When the file is placed on a web server, the web page can be viewed on the Internet.

6. In the **Export - HTML Document** dialog box, click the **Browse** button. In the **File Save** dialog box, navigate to your **Access Chapter 2** folder. Name the file Last_First_acc02_MS12HTML and then click **Save**.

7. In the **Export - HTML Document** dialog box, select the **Export data with formatting and layout** check box. Select the **Open the destination file after the export operation is complete** check box, and then click **OK**. Compare your screen with **Figure 2**.

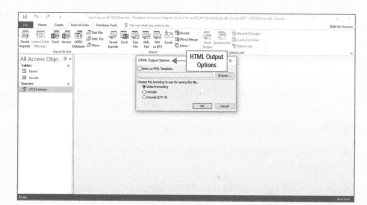

Access 2016, Windows 10, Microsoft Corporation   Figure 2

8. In the displayed **HTML Output Options** dialog box, click **OK** to accept the default settings and open the exported HTML file in a web browser. If necessary, select your browser on the toolbar to view the HTML file.

9. If your instructor asks you to print your work, print the web page.

10. **Close** ⊠ the web browser. Close the **Export - HTML Document** dialog box, and then **Close** ⊠ Access. Submit your files as directed by your instructor.

■ **You have completed More Skills 12**

More Skills 13

Link to External Data Sources

To complete this project, you will need the following files:

- Blank desktop database
- acc02_MS13Residents (Access)
- acc02_MS13WaterBills (Excel)

You will save your file as:

- Last_First_acc02_MS13Bills

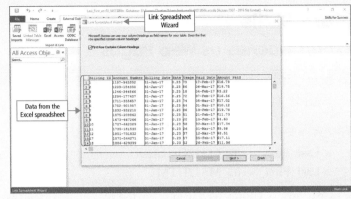

Figure 1   Access 2016, Windows 10, Microsoft Corporation

▶ Access can use data stored in a ***linked table***—a table that exists in a different file created by an application such as Access or Excel.

▶ Once a linked table is inserted, it can be used to create queries and reports. To update the data, the file must be opened in the application that created it.

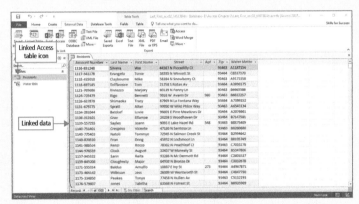

Figure 2   Access 2016, Windows 10, Microsoft Corporation

1. Start **Access 2016**, and then create a **Blank desktop database**. Save the database in your **Access Chapter 2** folder as Last_First_acc02_MS13Bills

2. **Close** ☒ Table1 without saving it.

3. Click the **External Data tab**, and then in the **Import & Link group**, click the **Excel** button.

4. In the **Get External Data - Excel Spreadsheet** dialog box, click the **Browse** button.

5. In the **File Open** dialog box, navigate to the student data files for this chapter. Click **acc02_MS13WaterBills**, and then click **Open**.

6. In the **Get External Data - Excel Spreadsheet** dialog box, select the **Link to the data source by creating a linked table** option button.

7. Click **OK** to start the Link Spreadsheet Wizard, compare your screen with **Figure 1**, and then click **Finish**. Read the message, and then click **OK**.

8. Double-click to open the **Water Bills** table. Set column widths to **Best Fit**.

    In the Navigation Pane, an arrow indicates that the data is linked, and the external application's icon displays.

9. **Save** ☐, and then **Close** ☒ the table. On the **External Data tab**, in the **Import & Link group**, click the **Access** button.

10. In the **Get External Data - Access Database** dialog box, click the **Browse** button.

11. In the **File Open** dialog box, navigate to the student data files. Click **acc02_MS13Residents**, and then click **Open**.

12. In the **Get External Data - Access Database** dialog box, select the **Link to the data source by creating a linked table** option button.

13. Click **OK**, and then in the **Link Tables** dialog box, click the **Residents** table. Click **OK** to link the table. **Close** the **Save Import Steps** dialog box.

14. Double-click to open the **Residents** table, and then compare your screen with **Figure 2**.

15. **Close** ☒ the table. **Close** ☒ Access, and then submit your file as directed by your instructor.

■ **You have completed More Skills 13**

More Skills 14

Create Crosstab Queries

To complete this project, you will need the following file:

- acc02_MS14Brackets

You will save your file as:

- Last_First_acc02_MS14Brackets

▶ A *crosstab query* is a select query that calculates a sum, an average, or a similar statistic and then groups the results by two sets of values.

▶ A crosstab query displays one group down the side of the datasheet and the other group across the top of the datasheet. For example, you could display racers' names on the left and race results at the top.

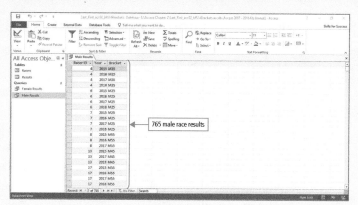

Access 2016, Windows 10, Microsoft Corporation   **Figure 1**

1. Start **Access 2016**, and then open the student data file **acc02_MS14Brackets**. Save the database in your **Access Chapter 2** folder as Last_First_acc02_MS14Brackets If necessary, enable the content.

2. In the **Navigation Pane**, under **Queries**, double-click **Male Results**. Be sure that the results for all males display as shown in Figure 1, and then **Close** ⊠ the query.

3. Click the **Create tab**, and then in the **Queries group**, click the **Query Wizard** button.

4. In the **New Query** dialog box, select **Crosstab Query Wizard**, and then click **OK**.

5. In the **Crosstab Query Wizard**, under **View**, select the **Queries** option button. Click **Query: Male Results**.

    A query can be built from another query. In this case, the crosstab query will use the data from the Male Results query.

6. Click **Next**, and then **Move** `>` **Year** into the **Selected Fields** list.

7. Click **Next**, and then, in the list of column headings, click **Bracket**.

    The column headings display at the top of each column in a crosstab query.

8. Click **Next**. Under **Functions**, click **Count**, and then compare your screen with Figure 2.

    The query will count the number of male racers for each year within each bracket. With the **Yes, include row sums** check box selected, the total count for each year will also be calculated.

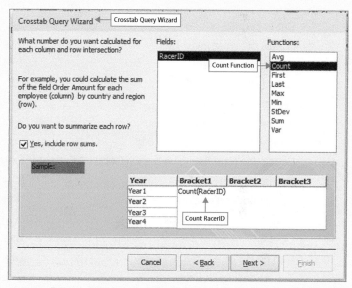

Access 2016, Windows 10, Microsoft Corporation   **Figure 2**

9. Click **Next**, and then under **What do you want to name your query**, replace the text *Male Results_Crosstab* with Male Counts by Year

10. Click **Finish**.

11. Click **Save** 🖫, **Close** ⊠ the query, and then **Close** ⊠ Access. Submit your file as directed by your instructor.

- **You have completed More Skills 14**

The following table summarizes the **SKILLS AND PROCEDURES** covered in this chapter.

Skills Number	Task	Step
1	Create queries (Simple Query Wizard)	Create tab → Queries group → Query Wizard
2	Add query criteria	In the Criteria row, type the criteria in the column(s) with the values you wish to filter
3	Add calculated fields to tables (Datasheet view)	Fields tab → Add & Delete group → More Fields → Calculated Field → click the desired data type
3	Add calculated fields to tables (Design view)	Data Type arrow → Calculated
4	Create queries (Design view)	Create tab → Queries group → Query Design
4	Add tables to queries in Design view	Design tab → Query Setup group → Show Table
7	Group and total queries	Design tab → Show/Hide group → Totals Group first column(s), set Totals row to statistic for other column(s)
	Criteria:	
2	Equals the word *five*	"five"
5	Equals the number 5	5
5	Greater than 5	>5
5	Less than or equal to 5	<=5
6	Is after July 5, 2018	>#7/5/2018#
6	Is between July 5 and 10, 2018	Between #7/5/2018# And #7/10/2018#
8	Equals the *Rate* field plus 5 and is labeled *Extra*	Extra: [Rate]+5
9	Cell is empty	Is Null
9	One or both criteria are true	"Will" Or "Bill"
9	Both criteria must be true	"Will" And "Bill"
10	Contains the word *five*	Like "*five*"
10	Can be *Bill* or *Will* but not *Cerill*	Like "?ill"
MS11	Export queries to Excel	External Data tab → Export group → Excel button
MS12	Export queries as web pages	External Data tab → Export group → More button → HTML
MS13	Link to external sources	External Data tab → Import & Link group → Select external source
MS14	Create a crosstab query	Create tab → Queries group → Query Wizard → Crosstab Query Wizard

Project Summary Chart

Project	Project Type	Project Location
Skills Review	Review	In Book & MIL MyITLab Grader
Skills Assessment 1	Review	In Book & MIL MyITLab Grader
Skills Assessment 2	Review	Book
My Skills	Problem Solving	Book
Visual Skills Check	Problem Solving	Book
Skills Challenge 1	Critical Thinking	Book
Skills Challenge 2	Critical Thinking	Book
More Skills Assessment	Review	In Book & MIL MyITLab Grader
Collaborating with Google	Critical Thinking	Book

MOS Objectives Covered (Quiz in MyITLab)

1.3.5 Change views of objects	3.2.4 Hide fields
2.1.3 Create linked tables from external sources	3.2.5 Sort data within queries
3.1.1 Run a query	3.2.6 Format fields within queries
3.1.2 Create a Crosstab Query	3.3.1 Add calculated fields
3.1.5 Create multi-table queries	3.3.3 Group and summarize data
3.1.6 Save a query	3.3.4 Group data by using comparison operators
3.2.2 Add fields	3.3.5 Group data by using arithmetic and logical operators

Key Terms

BizSkills
Video

1. If you could apply just one of the tips provided in this video to help manage your current priorities, which one would you choose? Why?

2. What techniques do you currently use to set a plan for your day? What other techniques could help you do this better?

Online Help Skills

1. Start **Access 2016**, and then in the upper right corner of the start page, click the **Help** button ? .

2. In the **Access Help** window **Search help** box, type query criteria and then press Enter .

3. In the search result list, click **Create an expression**, and then compare your screen with Figure 1.

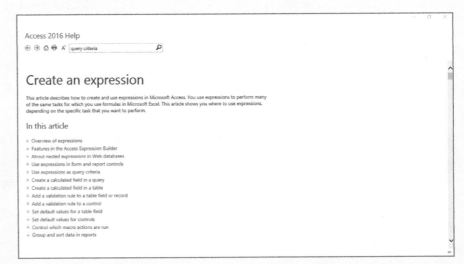

Figure 1   Access 2016, Windows 10, Microsoft Corporation

4. Read the article and answer the following question: Why would you set default values for controls?

Matching

Match each term in the second column with its correct definition in the first column by writing the letter of the term on the blank line in front of the correct definition.

___ **1.** A database object used to ask questions about the data stored in database tables.

___ **2.** Conditions in a query used to select the records that answer the query's question.

___ **3.** A field in a table or query that derives its values from other fields in the table or query.

___ **4.** Less than (<) and greater than (>) are examples of this type of operator.

___ **5** In the query design grid, two criteria placed in the same row use this logical operator.

___ **6.** To add summary statistics to a query, this row must be added to the query.

___ **7.** When two criteria are placed in different rows in the query design grid, this logical operator will be applied.

___ **8.** An operator that tests if a field is empty.

___ **9.** This wildcard character can represent any combination of characters.

___ **10.** This wildcard character can represent any single character.

A And

B Asterisk (*)

C Calculated

D Comparison

E Criteria

F Or

G Query

H Question mark (?)

I Is Null

J Total

Multiple Choice

Choose the correct answer.

1. A query that displays records without changing the data in a table.
   A. Select
   B. Simple
   C. View

2. In a query, criteria are added in this view.
   A. Datasheet
   B. Design
   C. Workspace

3. An IntelliSense box that explains the purpose of the selected AutoComplete.
   A. Balloon
   B. Quick Info
   C. ScreenTip

4. In a query, results are displayed in this view.
   A. Datasheet
   B. Design
   C. Design grid

5. A combination of fields, mathematical operators, and prebuilt functions that calculates values.
   A. Comparison operator
   B. Expression
   C. Quick Info

6. In query criteria, dates are surrounded by this character.
   A. >
   B. !
   C. #

7. A calculation for a group of data such as a total, an average, or a count.
   A. Calculated column
   B. Group formula
   C. Summary statistic

8. An operator that finds all numbers or dates between and including two values.
   A. And…Between
   B. Between…And
   C. In…Between

9. A descriptive label used to identify a field in expressions, datasheets, or forms and reports.
   A. Alias
   B. Label
   C. Name

10. The operator that is placed at the beginning of criteria that contain wildcards.
    A. Like
    B. Similar
    C. Wildcard

Topics for Discussion

1. You have created queries using the Simple Query Wizard and using Design view. Which method do you prefer, and why? What situations may be better suited to using the Simple Query Wizard? What situations may be better suited to using Design view?

2. Data that can be calculated from existing fields can be entered manually into its own field, or it can be included as a calculated field in a table or query. Which method would produce the most accurate results, and why?

Skills Review

To complete this project, you will need the following file:

- acc02_SRElectricity

You will save your file as:

- Last_First_acc02_SRElectricity

1. Start **Access 2016**, and then open the student data file **acc02_SRElectricity**. Save the file in your **Access Chapter 2** folder with the name Last_First_acc02_ SRElectricity If necessary, enable the content.

2. Open the **Billing Cycles** table in Datasheet view. In the last column, click the **Click to Add arrow**, point to **Calculated Field**, and then from the submenu, click **Currency**.

3. In the **Expression Builder**, add the following expression:
   [UsageFee] - [AmountPaid]

4. Click **OK**, and then replace the selected text *Field1* with BalanceDue

5. Compare your screen with **Figure 1**, and then **Save** and **Close** the table.

6. On the **Create tab**, in the **Queries group**, click **Query Design**. **Add** both tables to the query workspace, and then **Close** the Show Table dialog box.

7. From the **Residents** table, add the **AccountNumber**, **LastName**, and **FirstName** fields to the design grid.

8. From the **Billing Cycles** table, add the **CycleDate**, **UsageFee**, and **BalanceDue** fields to the design grid.

9. In the **CycleDate** column **Criteria** cell, type Between 6/1/2018 And 6/30/2018

10. In the **BalanceDue** column **Criteria** cell, type > 1 Or Is Null

11. Click **Save**, type Penalties Query and then click **OK**.

12. Click the first blank **Field** cell, and then in the **Query Setup group**, click **Builder**. In the **Expression Builder**, add the following expression: Penalty: [BalanceDue] * 0.2 Click **OK**. In the **Show/Hide group**, click **Property Sheet**, and then change the calculated field's **Format** to **Currency**. **Close** the Property Sheet.

13. Run the query, compare your screen with **Figure 2**, and then **Save** and **Close** the query.

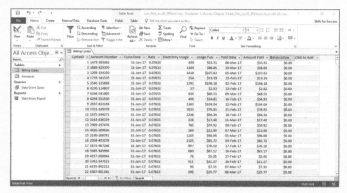

Access 2016, Windows 10, Microsoft Corporation   **Figure 1**

Access 2016, Windows 10, Microsoft Corporation   **Figure 2**

■ Continue to the next page to complete this Skills Review ▶

14. On the **Create tab**, in the **Queries group**, click **Query Wizard**, and then in the **New Query** dialog box, click **OK**.

15. In the **Simple Query Wizard**, click the **Tables/Queries arrow**, and then click **Table: Residents**.

16. Click **AccountNumber**, and then click the **Move** button. Repeat the procedure to move **LastName** and **FirstName**.

17. Click the **Tables/Queries arrow**, and then click **Table: Billing Cycles**. Move **CycleDate** and **UsageFee** into **Selected Fields**, and then click **Next** two times. In the **Wizard** dialog box, change the query name to Resident Statistics and then click **Finish**.

18. Switch to Design view, and then in the **LastName** column **Sort** cell, set the value to **Ascending**.

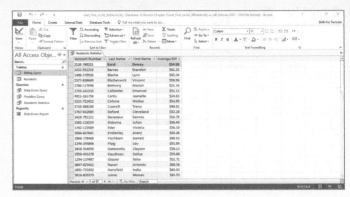

Figure 3   Access 2016, Windows 10, Microsoft Corporation

19. On the **Design tab**, in the **Show/Hide group**, click **Totals**. Change the **LastName**, **FirstName**, and **CycleDate** columns **Total** cells to **First**. Change the **UsageFee** column **Total** cell to **Avg**.

20. Click in the **LastName** column, and then open the **Property Sheet**. In the **Property Sheet Caption** box, type Last Name Click the **FirstName** column, and then change the **Caption** property to First Name

21. Click the **UsageFee** column. In the **Property Sheet**, change the **Format** to **Currency**, the **Caption** to Average Bill and then **Close** the property sheet.

22. In the **CycleDate** column **Criteria** cell, type <1/1/2018 Clear the **CycleDate** column **Show** cell check box, and then **Run** the query.

23. Compare your screen with Figure 3, and then **Save** and **Close** the query.

24. Open **Data Errors Query**, and then switch to Design view. In the **LastName** column **Criteria** cell, type Like Thomps?n

25. In the **FirstName** column **Criteria** cell, type Ralph

Figure 4   Access 2016, Windows 10, Microsoft Corporation

26. In the **ElectricityUsage** column **or** cell, type Is Null

27. **Run** the query, and then compare your screen with Figure 4. **Save** and then **Close** the query.

28. Open **Data Errors Report**. If you are printing your work, print the report.

29. **Close** the report, and then **Close** Access. Submit your file as directed by your instructor.

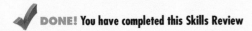

DONE! You have completed this Skills Review

Skills Assessment 1

To complete this project, you will need the following file:

- acc02_SA1Properties

You will save your file as:

- Last_First_acc02_SA1Properties

1. Start **Access 2016**, and then open the student data file **acc02_SA1Properties**. Save the file in your chapter folder as Last_First_acc02_SA1Properties

2. In the last column of the **Parcels** table datasheet, add a **Currency** calculated field that is derived by multiplying the **Value** field by 0.01206 Name the field Taxes and then **Save** and **Close** the table.

3. Use the **Simple Query Wizard** to start a query with the **Owner** field from the **Parcels** table and the **ZoneName** field from the **Zones** table. Name the query Tax Payments and then **Finish** the wizard.

4. In the **Tax Payments** query, add text criteria with a wildcard so that only records with *Residential* in their zone name result.

5. In the **Tax Payments** query, set the **ZoneName** column so that it does not show when the query is run.

6. Add a calculated field with the alias Payments that divides the **Taxes** field by two (Taxes/2). Set the field's **Format** property to **Currency**. **Run** the query, and then compare your results with **Figure 1**. **Save** and **Close** the query.

7. Create a new query in Design view, and then add the **Zones** and **Parcels** tables.

8. From the **Zones** table, add the **ZoneName** field, and then from the **Parcels** table, add the **Value** field three times.

9. Add the **Totals** row, and then group the query by **ZoneName**.

10. Set the first **Value** column summary statistic to **Count** each group, and then change its **Caption** property to Number of Parcels

11. Set the second **Value** column summary statistic to **Sum** each group, and then change its **Caption** property to Total Value

12. Set the third **Value** column summary statistic to average (**Avg**) each group, and then change its **Caption** property to Average Value

13. Set the third **Value** column **Sort** order to **Descending**.

14. **Save** the query with the name Zone Values and then **Run** the query. Set the datasheet column widths to **Best Fit**, and then

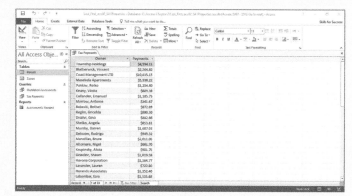

Access 2016, Windows 10, Microsoft Corporation   **Figure 1**

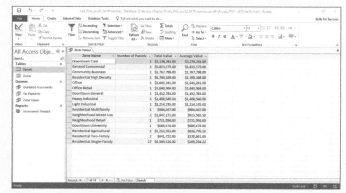

Access 2016, Windows 10, Microsoft Corporation   **Figure 2**

compare your results with **Figure 2**. **Save**, and then **Close** the query.

15. Open the **Outdated Assessments** query in Design view. In the **LastAssessed** column, add criteria so that values that are either before 1/1/2017 *or* are empty (Null) will display in the query datasheet. Run the query, and verify that 24 records result. **Save** and **Close** the query.

16. Open the **Assessments Needed** report to view the 24 records from the Outdated Assessments query. If you are printing your work, print the report.

17. **Close** the report, and then **Close** Access. Submit your file as directed by your instructor.

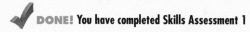 **DONE! You have completed Skills Assessment 1**

Skills Assessment 2

To complete this project, you will need the following file:

- acc02_SA2Fleet

You will save your file as:

- Last_First_acc02_SA2Fleet

---

1. Start **Access 2016**, and then open the student data file **acc02_SA2Fleet**. Save the database in your chapter folder as Last_First_acc02_SA2Fleet

2. In the last column of the **Fleet Services** table, add a calculated field that is derived from the product of the **Miles** and **MileageRate** fields (Miles * MileageRate). Name the field MileageFee assign it the **Currency** result type, and then add the caption Mileage Fee **Save** and **Close** the table.

3. Use the **Simple Query Wizard** to start a query with the **Department** field from the **Departments** table and the **StartDate** field from the **Fleet Services** table. Name the query Police and Fire Travel and then accept all other wizard defaults.

4. In the **Police and Fire Travel** query, add text criteria so that the **Department** can be from the Fire or Police department. Run the query, verify that 29 records result, and then **Save**.

5. In Design view, set the query to sort in ascending order by **StartDate**. Add criteria so that only records with a **StartDate** between 1/1/2018 and 7/31/2018 result.

6. Add a calculated field with the alias Charge that adds the BaseFee and MileageFee columns (BaseFee + MileageFee). **Run** the query, and then compare your results with **Figure 1**. **Save** and **Close** the query.

7. Create a new query in Design view, and then add the **Departments**, **Employees**, and **Fleet Services** tables.

8. From the **Departments** table, add the **Department** field, and then from the **Fleet Services** table, add the **ServiceID** field, and then add the **Miles** field two times.

9. Group the query by **Department**, and then **Count** the **ServiceID** in each group. Set the first **Miles** column to total each group and the second **Miles** column to average each group.

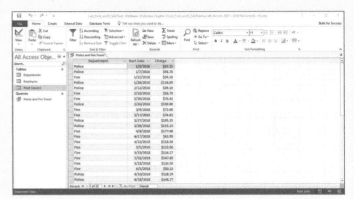

Figure 1   Access 2016, Windows 10, Microsoft Corporation

Figure 2   Access 2016, Windows 10, Microsoft Corporation

10. Set the **ServiceID** column **Caption** property to Trips and the first **Miles** column **Caption** property to Total Miles.

11. Set the second **Miles** column properties so that the datasheet displays no decimals and the column's caption will be Average Trip Length

12. **Save** the query with the name Department Travel and then **Run** the query. Set the datasheet column widths to **Best Fit**, and then compare your results with **Figure 2**. **Save** and then **Close** the query.

13. **Close** Access, and then submit your file as directed by your instructor.

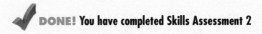 **DONE! You have completed Skills Assessment 2**

My Skills

To complete this project, you will need the following file:

- acc02_MYBaseball

You will save your file as:

- Last_First_acc02_MYBaseball

Access 2016, Windows 10, Microsoft Corporation   **Figure 1**

Access 2016, Windows 10, Microsoft Corporation   **Figure 2**

1. Start **Access 2016**, and then open the student data file **acc02_MYBaseball**. Save the database in your chapter folder as Last_First_acc02_MYBaseball

2. In the **League Statistics** table datasheet, click the **At Bats (AB)** column, and then add a **Number** calculated field. For the expression, divide the Hits field by the AtBats field. Name the field Batting Average You will format the numbers in a later step.

3. **Save** the table, and then switch to Design view. In the **BattingAverage Description (Optional)** cell, type Hits divided by AtBats

4. In the **BattingAverage** field properties, change the **Result Type** to **Single**, the **Format** to **Fixed**, and the **Decimal Places** to 3. Add Batting Average (BA) as the field's caption.

5. In the first available row, add a new calculated field named ERA For the expression, multiply the EarnedRuns field by 9, and then divide by the InningsPitched field (EarnedRuns * 9 / InningsPitched).

6. In the **ERA Description (Optional)** cell, type Earned run average (EarnedRuns * 9 / InningsPitched)

7. In the **ERA** field properties, change the **Result Type** to **Single**, the **Format** to **Fixed**, and the **Decimal Places** to 1.

8. **Save** the table, and then switch to Datasheet view. Set the column widths to **Best Fit**, and then compare your screen with Figure 1. **Save** and **Close** the table.

9. Create a new query in Design view that includes every field in the **League Statistics** table *except for* PlayerID, LastName, and FirstName. **Save** the query with the name Team Stats

10. Change the query to calculate the averages for each team.

11. Change the **Hits** column properties so that one decimal displays and the column heading displays as Avg Team Hits

12. Change the **AtBats** column properties so that one decimal displays and the column heading displays as Avg Team AB

13. Change the **BattingAverage** column properties so that three decimals display and the column heading displays as Team BA

14. Change the **EarnedRuns** column properties so that one decimal displays and the column heading displays as Avg Team ER

15. Change the **InningsPitched** column properties so that one decimal displays and the column heading displays as Avg Team IP

16. Change the **ERA** column properties so that one decimal displays and the column heading displays as Avg Team ERA

17. Run the query, set the column widths to **Best Fit**, and then compare your screen with Figure 2.

18. **Save** the query, and then **Close** Access. Submit your file as directed by your instructor.

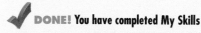 **DONE! You have completed My Skills**

Visual Skills Check

To complete this project, you will need the following file:

- acc02_VSPermits

You will save your file as:

- Last_First_acc02_VSPermits

Open the student data file **acc02_VSPermits**. Save the database in your chapter folder as Last_First_acc02_VSPermits

Create a query with the results shown in Figure 1. Name the query Fence Permits Due and add the columns as shown. Add a calculated field with the alias Balance and then add criteria that answer the question, *Which fencing projects have balances due?* Six records should result.

Submit your file as directed by your instructor.

Record	Start Date	Project Title	Work Location	Fee	Paid to Date	Balance
B4078864FENC	8/6/2018	FENCE MATHAI RESIDENCE	1448 S Lighthouse Pl	$49.50	$0.00	$49.50
B4141621FENC	8/1/2018	JOBS RESIDENCE FENCE	4069 S Shaffer Meadow Ln	$49.50	$0.00	$49.50
B5119759FENC	8/15/2018	FENCE TUR RESIDENCE	3102 W Cubola Av	$49.50	$0.00	$49.50
B5357156FENC	8/13/2018	POSTMA RESIDENCE	5674 W Split Wood	$49.50	$25.00	$24.50
B6603712FENC	8/6/2018	FENCE FEHRS RESIDENCE	3596 S Bethany Bay Pl	$49.50	$15.00	$34.50
B9460314FENC	8/17/2018	FENCE ESCHE RESIDENCE	3234 N Entertainment Av	$49.50	$0.00	$49.50
*					$0.00	

Figure 1

Access 2016, Windows 10, Microsoft Corporation

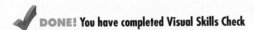

DONE! You have completed Visual Skills Check

Skills Challenge 1

To complete this project, you will need the following file:

- acc02_SC1Classes

You will save your file as:

- **Last_First_acc02_SC1Classes**

Open the student data file **acc02_SC1Classes**, and then save the file in your chapter folder as Last_First_acc02_SC1Classes Open the Instructor Class Counts query, and then add a column so that each instructor's first name is included after the last name field and the two interns with the last name of *Shriver* have an accurate count. Cheyenne Shriver should have a total of one, and Kenton Shriver should have a total of five.

Open the Intern Contacts List query, and then fix the query so that each intern is listed only once. To do this, you do not need to add any criteria, change any properties, use the Total row, or

apply any filters to the datasheet. You will need to delete a table from the query to ensure each intern is only listed once.

Open the Word Classes query, and then fix the criteria and add columns so that it answers the question, *Where are all the Word classes offered, and what are their start dates and times?*

Submit your file as directed by your instructor.

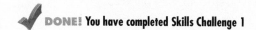 **DONE! You have completed Skills Challenge 1**

Skills Challenge 2

To complete this project, you will need the following file:

- acc02_SC2Rentals

You will save your file as:

- **Last_First_acc02_SC2Rentals**

Open student data file **acc02_SC2Rentals**, and then save the file in your chapter folder as Last_First_acc02_SC2Rentals Create a query named Refunds that answers the following question: *Which July renters of community center rooms get a refund?* Identify the renters by including the RenterID field. Display the date and hours each room was rented and the refund amount.

To calculate the balance due, subtract the deposit from the rental fee. The rental fee can be determined by multiplying the number of hours rented by the room's hourly rate. Define the calculated field's alias as Balance and format the column

to display as currency. (The currency format encloses negative numbers—refunds—in parentheses instead of using a negative sign.) Be sure to limit the query results to July 2018 and only to those receiving a refund.

Submit your file as directed by your instructor.

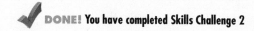 **DONE! You have completed Skills Challenge 2**

More Skills Assessment

MyITLab®
Grader

To complete this project, you will need the following files:

- acc02_MSARacers
- acc02_MSAVolunteers (Excel)

You will save your files as:

- Last_First_acc02_MSARacers
- Last_First_acc02_MSAVolunteers (Excel)
- Last_First_acc02_MSARacers (Excel)
- Last_First_acc02_MSAResults (HTML)

1. Start **Access 2016**, and then open the student data file **acc02_MSARacers**. **Save** the database in your chapter folder as Last_First_acc02_MSARacers

2. Open the **Racers** table in Datasheet view. **Export the data with formatting and layout** to an **Excel Workbook**. **Save** the file as Last_First_acc02_MSARacers **Close** the **Export - Excel Spreadsheet** dialog box, and then **Close** the **Racers** table.

3. Open the **Results** table, and then **Export the data with formatting and layout** to an **HTML** file format. Save the file as Last_First_acc02_MSAResults Compare your screen with **Figure 1**, and then **Close** the **HTML Output Options** dialog box.

4. Navigate to your student data files and open the **acc02_MSAVolunteers** Excel file. **Save** the file as Last_First_acc02_MSAVolunteers Review the content, and then close the spreadsheet.

5. Return to Access, and in the **Import & Link group**, select **Link to the data source by creating a linked table** to link to the Volunteers Excel spreadsheet.

6. If necessary, select the **First Row Contains Column Headings** checkbox. Accept the remaining default settings.

7. Create a **Crosstabs Query** that uses the **Queries** view in the **Crosstab Query Wizard**.

8. In the **Crosstab Query Wizard**, select the **Query: 2018 Females** query.

9. Move the **Year** into the **Selected Fields**.

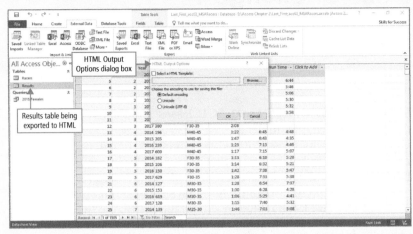

Figure 1   Access 2016, Windows 10, Microsoft Corporation

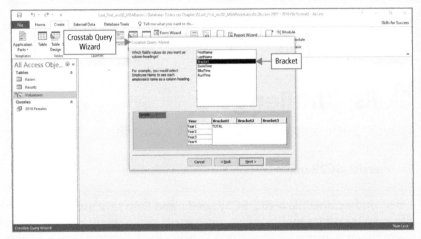

Figure 2   Access 2016, Windows 10, Microsoft Corporation

10. In **Which field's values do you want as column headings?** select **Bracket**, and then compare your screen to **Figure 2**.

11. Name the query 2018 Females_Crosstab

12. **Save** and **Close** the query.

13. **Close** Access, and submit the files as directed by your instructor.

DONE! You have completed More Skills Assessment

Collaborating with Google

To complete this project, you will need a Google account (refer to the Common Features chapter) and the following file:

- acc02_GPMembers (Excel)

You will save your file as:

- Last_First_acc02_GPSnip

1. Open Google Chrome web browser. Log into your Google account, and then click the **Apps** button.

2. Click the **Drive** button to open Google Drive. If you receive a pop-up message, read the message, and then click **Next**. Read each message, and then close the dialog box.

3. Click the **New** button, and then click **Google Sheets** to open a blank spreadsheet.

4. Click the spreadsheet title, **Untitled spreadsheet**. In the dialog box, type Members as the name of the spreadsheet, and then click **OK**. Double-click the **Sheet1** worksheet tab. Rename the *Sheet1* worksheet tab as Members

5. Open the student data file **acc02_GPMembers**. Copy the range **A1:H80** from the *Members* worksheet and paste in cell **A1** of the blank Google worksheet.

6. Right-click the row 10 heading to display the shortcut menu, and then compare your screen with **Figure 1**.

7. Click **Delete Row** to delete the entire row and its contents.

8. In the second row, replace the existing **FirstName** and **LastName** with your first and last names.

9. In the fourth row, replace the existing **ZipCode** with the value 93463

10. Select the range **A1:H1**, and then click the **Bold** button to remove the Bold formatting.

11. Select cell **I1**, and then type Email

12. Press **Enter**.

13. Click the **Share** button, and in the **Share with others** dialog box, type AspenFallsEvents@gmail.com to share the sheet with another user.

14. In the **Add a note** text box, type Please review the contact information, and add email addresses as available. If any

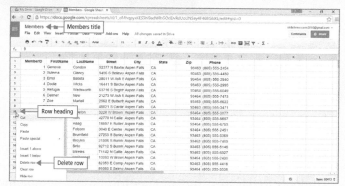

Figure 1

Figure 2

information is incorrect, please correct it. Compare your screen with **Figure 2**, and then click **Send**.

15. Press [⊞], type snip and then press [Enter] to start the **Snipping Tool**. Click the **New arrow**, and then click **Window Snip**. Point to the Google Chrome Browser, and when a red border displays around the window, click one time.

16. In the **Snipping Tool** mark-up window, click the **Save Snip** button [💾]. In the **Save As** dialog box, navigate to your Access Chapter 2 folder. Be sure the **Save as type** box displays **JPEG file**. Name the file Last_First_acc02_GPSnip and then press [Enter]. **Close** [×] the Snipping Tool mark-up window.

17. Close all windows, and then submit your file as directed by your instructor.

 DONE! You have completed Collaborating with Google

CHAPTER 3

Create Forms

- Forms are used to edit, delete, and add records stored in database tables and are designed to make data entry quick and accurate.
- Forms are often designed for entering data for the specific needs of the database. For example, a college database may provide one form for entering new students, another form for registering students for classes, and another form for assigning instructors to teach those classes.
- Forms are designed to be viewed on a computer screen and are rarely printed. Instead, reports are typically used when data needs to be printed.
- Forms show one record at a time so that you can work with just that data.

- Forms can take advantage of one-to-many relationships. The main form shows one record at a time from the first table, and below that, all the related records in the other table display in a subform.
- There are several methods for creating forms, including the Form Wizard and the Form Tool.
- Forms can be arranged in Word-like tables so that you can quickly position labels and text in cells to create a custom layout for your form.
- Forms can be based on queries so that you can work with a subset of the data.
- Some forms have buttons that open other database objects—tables, queries, other forms, and reports. These forms can be built quickly using the Navigation Form command.

Goodluz/Fotolia

Aspen Falls City Hall

In this chapter, you will create forms for Aspen Falls Utilities. You will work under the supervision of Diane Payne, Public Works Director, to design forms for entering records about city residents and their water bills. You will also build a form that data entry personnel will use to open and close the database forms.

There are several methods for creating forms in Access. The method you choose depends on the type of form you need and personal preference. No matter which method you choose, all forms need to provide a way to locate and update records quickly and accurately. Most forms also provide a way to add new records. The form's header displays information about the form's purpose, and the detail area displays labels and text boxes with values from the underlying table.

Some forms are used to open and close other forms and reports. These forms provide a way to navigate the database and can be set up in a way that hides the Navigation Pane. Using this method, you can provide a custom database interface based on the needs of the individuals who will use it.

To complete this project, you will create a form using a wizard and then format that form. You will use the form to edit records. You will create another form using the Form Tool that displays records from two related tables on the same screen and then enter new records using this form. You will also build a form based on a select query. Finally, you will create a Navigation Form that opens the other three forms, and then set up the form to hide the Navigation Pane when the form is in use.

Outcome

Using the skills in this chapter, you will be able to create various types of forms, add conditional formatting and controls to forms, work with tabular layouts, utilize input masks, validate fields, create databases in older formats, and backup databases.

Objectives

3.1 Create forms using various methods

3.2 Modify data within forms

3.3 Construct forms that use controls and conditional formatting

3.4 Generate forms that use input masks

Student data files needed for this chapter:

acc03_Water
acc03_WaterLogo

You will save your files as:

Last_First_acc03_Water
Last_First_acc03_WaterSnip (1 – 4)

SKILLS MyITLab®
Skills 1-10 Training

At the end of this chapter you will be able to:

Skill 1   Use the Form Wizard
Skill 2   Use Forms to Modify Data
Skill 3   Format Forms in Layout View
Skill 4   Add Controls and Conditional Formatting
Skill 5   Use the Form Tool
Skill 6   Work with Tabular Layouts
Skill 7   Add Input Masks
Skill 8   Change Data in One-to-Many Forms
Skill 9   Create Forms from Queries
Skill 10 Create Navigation Forms

MORE SKILLS

Skill 11 Validate Fields
Skill 12 Create Databases from Templates
Skill 13 Import Objects from Other Databases
Skill 14 Back Up Databases

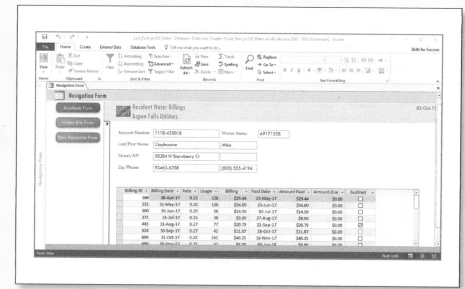

Access 2016, Windows 10, Microsoft Corporation

▶ Access has several tools for creating forms. The Form Wizard is an efficient method to create a form when you do not need to include all the fields from a table.

1. Start **Access 2016**, and then open the student data file **acc03_Water**. On the **File tab**, click **Save As**. With **Save Database As** selected, click the **Save As** button. In the **Save As** dialog box, navigate to the location where you are saving your files for this project. Click **New folder**, type Access Chapter 3 and then press [Enter] two times. Name the file Last_First_ acc03_Water and then click **Save.**

2. If the Security Warning message displays, click the Enable Content button.

^{MOS}
Obj 4.1.1

3. On the **Create tab**, in the **Forms group**, click the **Form Wizard** button. Click the **Tables/Queries arrow**, and then click **Table: Water Bills**. Compare your screen with Figure 1.

> By default, the table or query that is selected in the Navigation Pane will be selected in the first screen of the Form Wizard.

^{MOS}
Obj 4.2.2

4. Under **Available Fields**, double-click **BillingID** so that the field will be included in the form.

5. With **AccountNumber** selected, click the **Add Field** button [>] to place it into **Selected Fields**.

6. Use either technique just practiced to move the following fields into **Selected Fields** in this order: **BillingDate**, **Rate**, **Usage**, **Billing**, **PaidDate**, **AmountPaid**, and **AmountDue**. Do *not* move the Audited field. Compare your screen with **Figure 2.**

■ Continue to the next page to complete the skill ▶

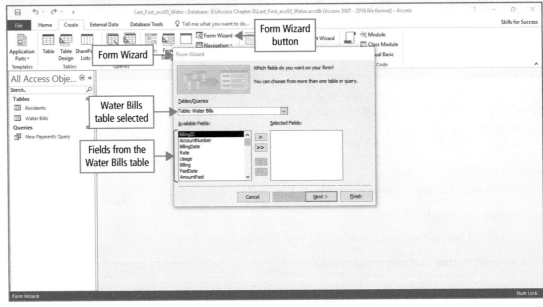

Figure 1   Access 2016, Windows 10, Microsoft Corporation

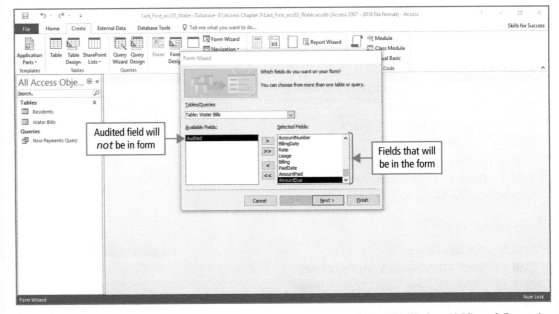

Figure 2   Access 2016, Windows 10, Microsoft Corporation

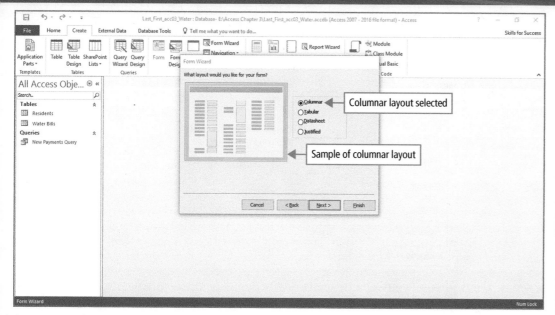

Access 2016, Windows 10, Microsoft Corporation

Figure 3

7. In the **Form Wizard**, click **Next**, and then compare your screen with **Figure 3**.

> You can use the Form Wizard to pick different layouts for your form. A *layout* determines how data and labels are arranged in a form or report. For example, the *columnar layout* places labels in the first column and data in the second column.

8. With **Columnar layout** selected, click **Next**. Under **What title do you want for your form**, change *Water Bills* to Water Bills Forms

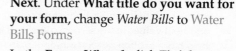

9. In the **Forms Wizard**, click **Finish** to create the form and open it in **Form view**. Compare your screen with **Figure 4**.

> The title that you type in the last screen of the Form Wizard becomes the name of the form in the Navigation Pane, and the theme last used in the database is applied to the form.

10. Leave the form open for the next skill.

■ **You have completed Skill 1 of 10**

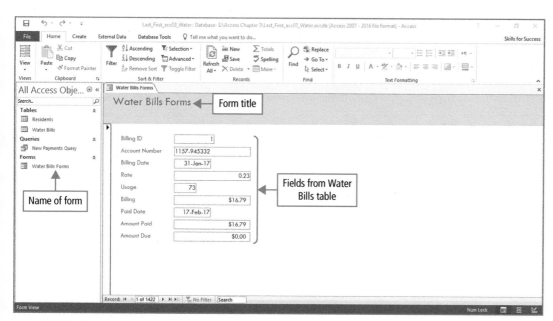

Access 2016, Windows 10, Microsoft Corporation

Figure 4

▶ Recall that forms are designed to input data into tables. When you edit data or add records, the changes are stored automatically in the underlying table.

1. Take a few moments to familiarize yourself with the **Water Bills Form**, as shown in Figure 1.

    Most forms display in **Single Form view**—a view that displays one record at a time with field names in the first column and field values in the second column. If a field has a caption property assigned, that value will display in the label. For example, the *BillingID* field displays as *Billing ID*.

    At the bottom of the form, the Navigation bar shows how many records are in the underlying table and has buttons for moving from one record to another.

2. On the Navigation bar, click the **Next record** button ▶ to display record 2 of 1422—*Billing ID* 2.

3. Click the **Paid Date** box, and then type the date 06-Feb-17 Press [Enter] to move to the next field, **Amount Paid**, and then type 19.78 Watch the **Amount Due** value automatically update as you press [Enter], and then compare your screen with Figure 2.

    The Amount Due field is a calculated field that automatically updates when the Rate, Usage, or AmountPaid fields are changed. The change you made to the AmountPaid field was changed in the table, and the AmountDue box updated to display the new value. In this manner, forms can be used to edit table data while viewing one record at a time.

■ **Continue to the next page to complete the skill** ▶

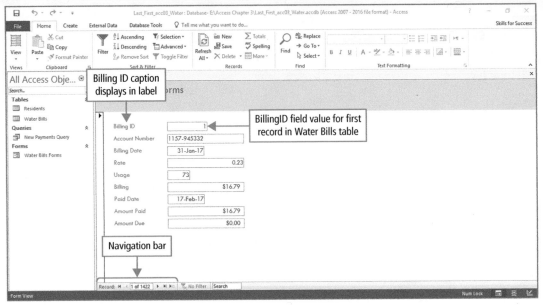

Figure 1   Access 2016, Windows 10, Microsoft Corporation

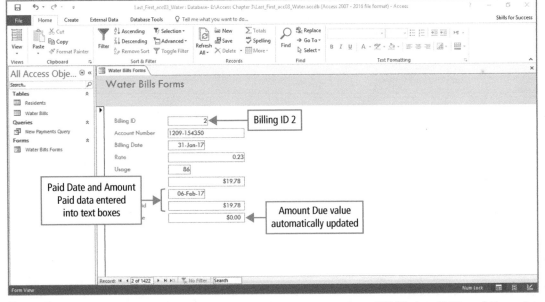

Figure 2   Access 2016, Windows 10, Microsoft Corporation

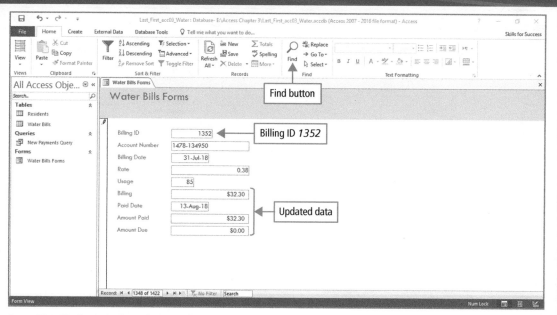

Find button

Billing ID 1352

Updated data

Access 2016, Windows 10, Microsoft Corporation

Figure 3

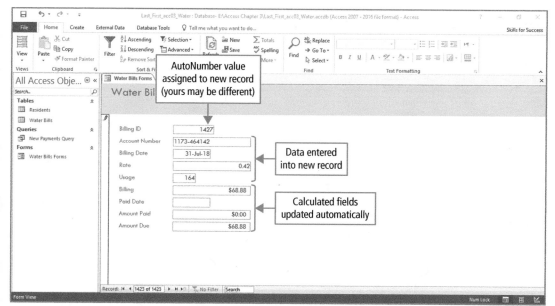

AutoNumber value assigned to new record (yours may be different)

Data entered into new record

Calculated fields updated automatically

Access 2016, Windows 10, Microsoft Corporation

Figure 4

4. Press Enter to move to the next record—*Billing ID 3*. With **Billing ID** active, on the **Home tab**, in the **Find group**, click the **Find** button.

5. In the **Find and Replace** dialog box **Find What** box, type 1352 Press Enter , and then **Close** ✕ the dialog box.

MOS
Obj 1.3.1

6. In the record for *Billing ID 1352*, enter a **Paid Date** of 13-Aug-18 and an **Amount Paid** of 32.30 Press Enter to update the record. Compare your screen with **Figure 3**.

7. On the Navigation bar, click the **New (blank) record** button ▸. Press Enter two times to move the insertion point to the **Account Number** box. Type 1173-464142 and then press Enter .

> You can move to the next field in a form by pressing Enter or Tab . In this way, you can continue typing values without having to use the mouse. Keeping your hands over the keyboard speeds data entry and increases accuracy.

8. In the **Billing Date** box, type 31-Jul-18 and then press Enter . In the **Rate** box, type 0.42 and then press Enter .

9. In the **Usage** box, type 164 Watch the **Billing** and **Amount Due** values update automatically as you press Enter , and then compare your screen with **Figure 4**.

> In the Water Bills table, the Billing field is a calculated field that multiplies the Rate value by the Usage value. Here, the July billing for this account is $68.88.

10. Leave the table open for the next skill.

> You do not need to save any changes because the data was automatically saved as you entered it.

■ **You have completed Skill 2 of 10**

▶ *Layout view* is used to format a form or report while you are viewing a sample of the data.

1. With the **Water Bills Form** open, on the **Home tab**, in the **Views group**, click the **View** button to switch to Layout view. If the Field List pane displays, **Close** ☒ the pane.

2. On the **Design tab**, in the **Tools group**, click the **Property Sheet** button as needed to open the property sheet.

3. On the Navigation bar, click the **First record** button ⏮. Click the **Account Number** text box, and then compare your screen with **Figure 1**.

In Layout view, you can select individual *controls*—objects in a form or report such as labels and text boxes—and format them. A *label* is a control in a form or report that describes other objects in the report or form. A *text box* is a control in a form or report that displays the data from a field in a table or query. Here, the label displays the caption *Account Number*, and the AccountNumber text box displays the value *1157-945332*.

4. With the **Account Number** text box control still selected, click the Ribbon **Format tab**. In the **Font group**, click the **Align Right** button.

5. Click the **Billing ID** text box to select it. Press and hold Shift while clicking the eight other text boxes with the 🖟 pointer. Release the Shift key, and then compare your screen with **Figure 2**.

■ Continue to the next page to complete the skill ▶

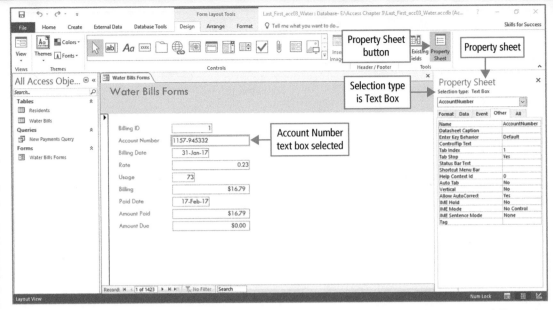

Figure 1

Access 2016, Windows 10, Microsoft Corporation

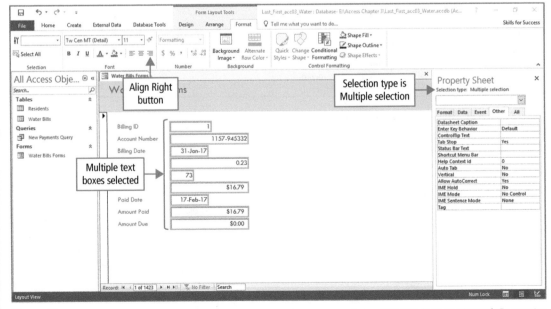

Figure 2

Access 2016, Windows 10, Microsoft Corporation

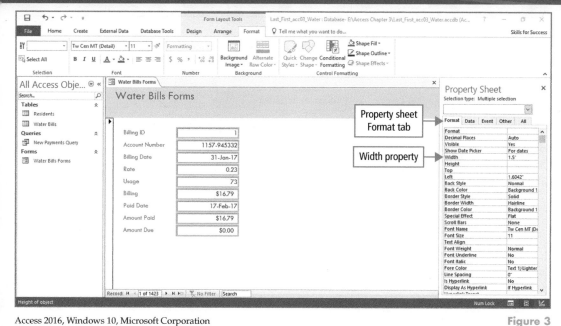

Access 2016, Windows 10, Microsoft Corporation

Figure 3

6. On the Property Sheet **Format tab**, click in the **Width** box, type 1.5" and then press Enter to simultaneously set the width of all nine text boxes. Compare your screen with **Figure 3**.

In this manner, you can select multiple controls and then format them at the same time.

7. On the **Format tab**, in the **Selection group**, click **Select All** to select all the form controls. In the **Font group**, click the **Font arrow**. Scroll down the list of fonts, and then click **Calibri**.

8. With all the controls still selected, press and hold Ctrl while clicking the **Title** control with the text *Water Bills Form* to remove it from the current selection, and then release the Ctrl key.

9. On the **Format tab**, in the **Font group**, click the **Font size arrow** 11 ▼ , and then click **12** to increase the font size by one point. Compare your screen with **Figure 4**.

10. Click **Save** 💾 to save the design changes, and then leave the form open for the next skill.

When you make changes to the form's design, you need to save those changes. Here, the form's design was changed; however, none of the data was changed.

■ **You have completed Skill 3 of 10**

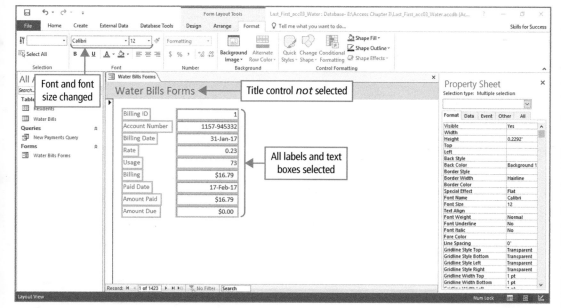

Access 2016, Windows 10, Microsoft Corporation

Figure 4

WATCH SKILL 3.4

▸ Controls such as logos and titles can be added to forms to identify a company and the purpose of the form.

▸ You can format values so that when a condition is true, the value will be formatted differently than when the condition is false.

1. If it is not already open, open the Water Bills Form in Layout view.

2. In the form header, click the **Title** control with the text *Water Bills Form*. Be careful to select the control and not the text in the control—an orange border should surround the control as shown in **Figure 1**.

3. Press **Delete** to remove the Title control.

MOS
Obj 4.3.8

4. On the **Design tab**, in the **Header / Footer group**, click the **Logo** button. In the **Insert Picture** dialog box, navigate to the student data files for this project. Select **acc03_WaterLogo**, and then click **OK** to insert the control.

5. On the **Design tab**, in the **Header / Footer group**, click the **Title** button, and then type Monthly Billings

6. Click the **Amount Due** text box. Click the **Format tab**, and then in the **Control Formatting group**, click the **Conditional Formatting** button.

7. In the **Conditional Formatting Rules Manager** dialog box, click the **New Rule** button. In the **New Formatting Rule** dialog box, under **Format only cells where the**, click the second **arrow**. Compare your screen with **Figure 2**.

The second box contains a drop-down list of *comparison operators*—operators such as greater than and less than that compare two values.

■ **Continue to the next page to complete the skill**

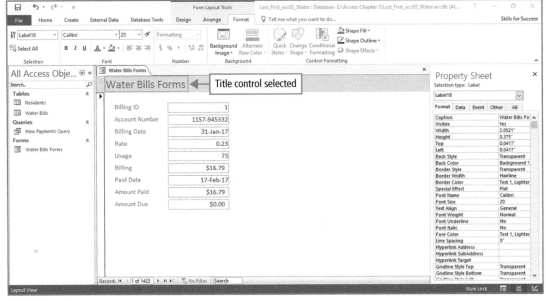

Figure 1

Access 2016, Windows 10, Microsoft Corporation

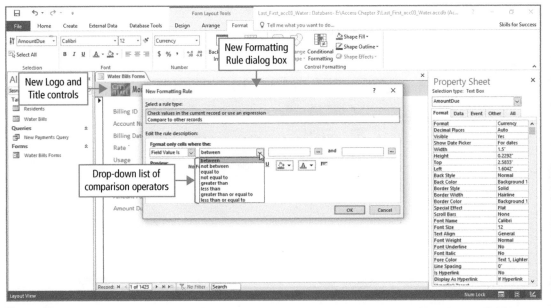

Figure 2

Access 2016, Windows 10, Microsoft Corporation

8. In the conditions list, click **less than**. Click in the third box, and then type 0

9. In the **New Formatting Rule** dialog box, click the **Font color arrow** [A ▾], and then click the second color in the last row—**Red**.

10. In the dialog box, click the **Bold** button [B], and then preview the conditional formatting, as shown in **Figure 3.**

11. Click **OK** two times to accept the changes, and **Close** the two dialog boxes. Click **Save** [🖫], and then on the **Home tab**, click the **View** button to switch to Form view. Alternatively, on the status bar, click the Form View button [▦].

12. On the Navigation bar, click the **Last record** button [▮]. In the **Paid Date** field, type 13-Aug-18 Press [Enter], and then in the **Amount Paid** box, type 70 Press [Enter], click in the **Amount Due** box to deselect the text, and then compare your screen with **Figure 4.**

13. Press [⊞], type snip and then press [Enter] to start the **Snipping Tool**. In the **Snipping Tool** window, click the **New arrow**, and then click **Full-screen Snip**.

14. Click the **Save Snip** button [🖫]. In the **Save As** dialog box, navigate to your **Access Chapter 3** folder, **Save** the snip as Last_First_acc03_WaterSnip1 and then **Close** [✕] the Snipping Tool window.

15. **Save** [🖫] the design changes, and then **Close** the form.

■ **You have completed Skill 4 of 10**

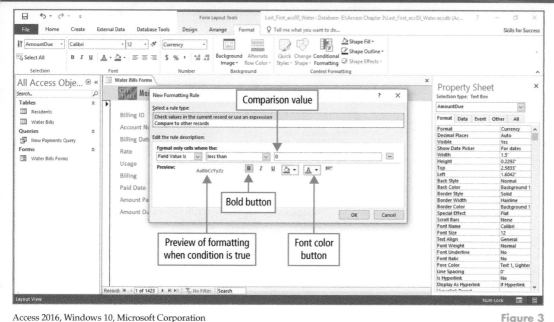

Access 2016, Windows 10, Microsoft Corporation

Figure 3

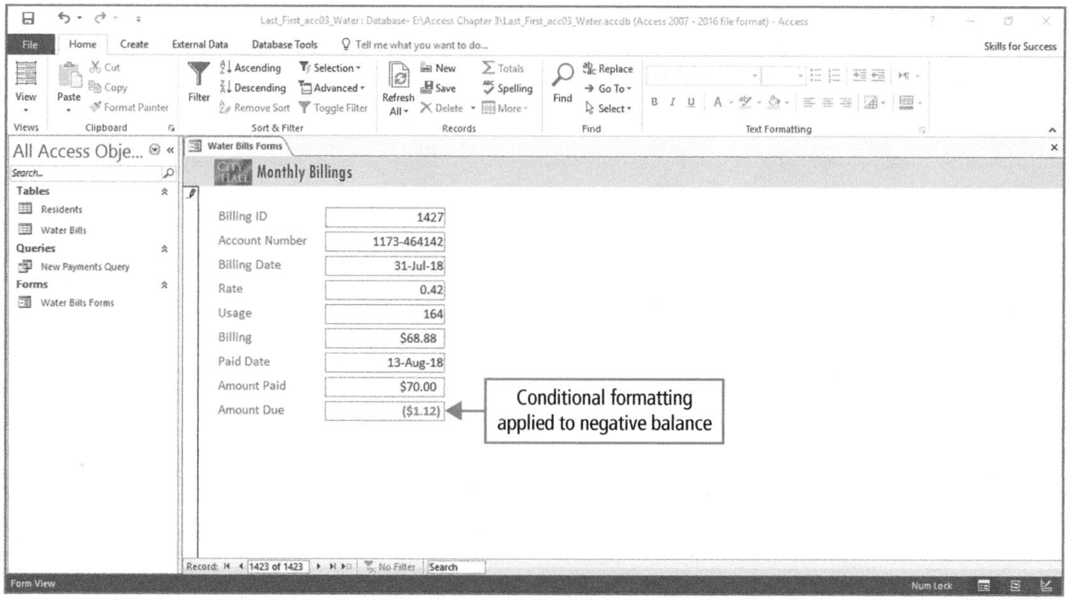

Figure 4

Access 2016, Windows 10, Microsoft Corporation

▶ You can use the Form Tool to quickly create a form for any table or query that is selected in the Navigation Pane.

1. Click the **Database Tools tab**, and then click the **Relationships** button. Drag the **AccountNumber** field from the **Residents** table, point to the **AccountNumber** field in the **Water Bills** table, and then when the 🖳 displays, release the left mouse button.

2. In the **Edit Relationships** dialog box, select the **Enforce Referential Integrity** check box. Compare your screen with **Figure 1**, and then click **Create**.

   The Residents and Water Bills tables need to have a one-to-many relationship so that each resident's account information can be linked to their monthly water bills.

3. **Close** ☒ the Relationships tab.

4. In the **Navigation Pane**, select the **Residents** table. Click the **Create tab**, and then in the **Forms group**, click the **Form** button to create a one-to-many form. If necessary, **Close** ☒ the property sheet. Compare your screen with **Figure 2**.

   When a one-to-many relationship exists, a main form and subform will be created when you use the Form Tool. In a *one-to-many form*, the main form displays in Single Form view, and the related records display in a subform in Datasheet view. Here, a single resident displays in the main form, and that resident's monthly billings display in the subform.

■ Continue to the next page to complete the skill

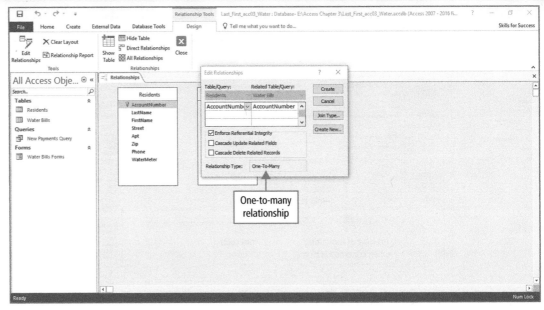

One-to-many relationship

Figure 1

Access 2016, Windows 10, Microsoft Corporation

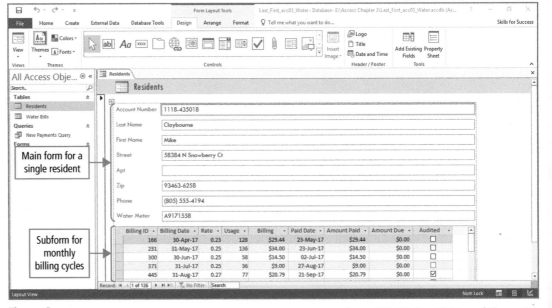

Main form for a single resident

Subform for monthly billing cycles

Figure 2

Access 2016, Windows 10, Microsoft Corporation

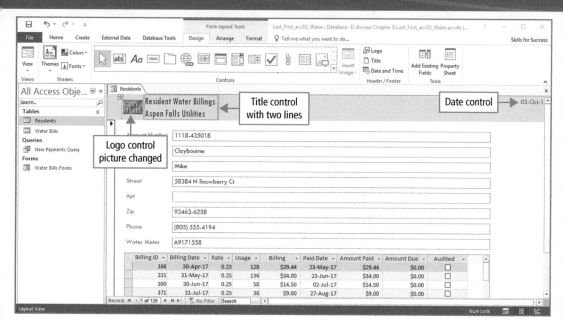

Access 2016, Windows 10, Microsoft Corporation

Figure 3

5. On the **Design tab**, in the **Header / Footer group**, click the **Logo** button, and then use the **Insert Picture** dialog box to insert **acc03_WaterLogo** as the form's logo.

6. In the **Header / Footer group**, click the **Date and Time** button. In the **Date and Time** dialog box, select the middle date—**dd-mmm-yy**—option button, clear the **Include Time** check box, and then click **OK**.

7. In the **Header / Footer group**, click the **Title** button to select the text in the form's **Title** control. Type Resident Water Billings and then press [Ctrl] + [Enter] to insert a new line in the control. Type Aspen Falls Utilities press [Enter] to finish editing the text, and then compare your screen with **Figure 3**.

> To change text in a control, you need to be in edit mode. *Edit mode* is a mode that selects the text inside a control, not the control itself. As you type in edit mode, the Title control adjusts its size to fit the new text.

8. With the **Title** control still selected, click the **Format tab**. In the **Font group**, click the **Font Color arrow** [A ▾], and then click the last color in the first row—**Teal, Accent 6**.

9. In the header, click a blank area to the right of the form title to select the entire header. On the **Format tab**, in the **Font group**, click the **Background Color arrow** [⬧ ▾], and then click the last color in the second row—**Teal, Accent 6, Lighter 80%**. Compare your screen with **Figure 4**.

10. Click **Save** [💾]. In the **Save As** dialog box, type Residents Form and then press [Enter]. Leave the form open for the next skill.

■ **You have completed Skill 5 of 10**

Access 2016, Windows 10, Microsoft Corporation

Figure 4

► Forms created with the Form Tool use a *tabular layout*—a layout in which the controls are positioned as table cells in rows and columns. You can insert, delete, and merge columns and then position controls within these tables as needed.

1. With **Residents Form** open in Layout view, click the **Account Number** text box to select the control.

2. Point to the selected control's right border to display the ⟷ pointer. Drag the right border to the left. When the column is aligned with the **Usage** column in the subform as shown in **Figure 1**, release the left mouse button to resize the entire column. (You will resize the subform later in this skill.)

3. With the **Account Number** text box still selected, click the **Arrange tab**. In the **Rows & Columns group**, click the **Insert Right** button two times to insert two new columns.

MOS
Obj 4.2.6

4. Point to the label with the text *Water Meter*, and then with the ⟨⬚⟩ pointer, drag and drop the label into the first cell in the first blank column.

5. Repeat the previous technique to move the **WaterMeter** text box—*A9171558*— into the blank cell to the right of the **Water Meter** label. Compare your screen with **Figure 2**.

MOS
Obj 4.2.1

6. Move the **First Name** text box—*Mike*— into the blank cell to the right of the **Last Name** text box.

7. Double-click the **Last Name** label, change the label text to Last / First Name and then press [Enter].

■ **Continue to the next page to complete the skill** ▶

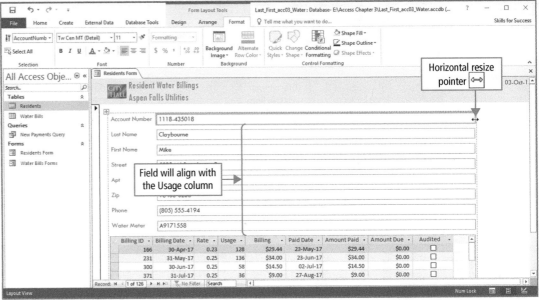

Figure 1   Access 2016, Windows 10, Microsoft Corporation

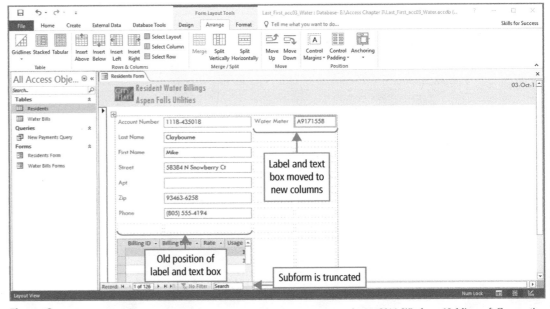

Figure 2   Access 2016, Windows 10, Microsoft Corporation

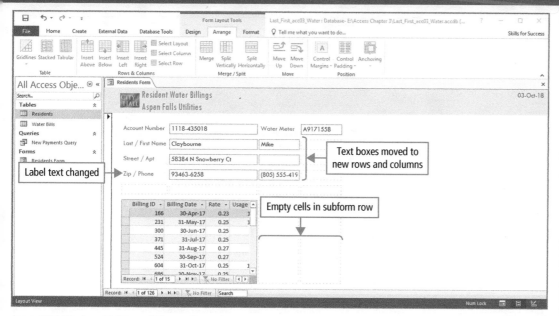

Access 2016, Windows 10, Microsoft Corporation

Figure 3

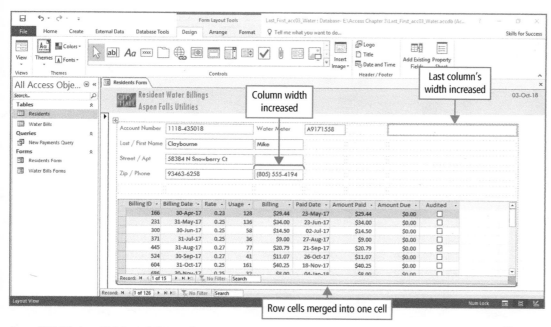

Access 2016, Windows 10, Microsoft Corporation

Figure 4

8. In the fifth row, click to select the **Apt** text box—it has a blank value. Drag to move the control into the empty cell to the right of the **Street** text box. In the first column of the same row, change the **Street** label text to Street / Apt

9. Move the **Phone** text box to the right of the **Zip** text box, and then change the **Zip** label text to Zip / Phone

10. In the third row, click the **First Name** label. On the **Arrange tab**, in the **Rows & Columns group**, click **Select Row**. With the row selected, press Delete to remove the unused row from the table.

MOS
Obj 4.2.4

11. Repeat the technique just practiced to delete the unused **Apt** and **Phone** rows. Compare your screen with **Figure 3**.

12. In the row with the subform, click in the last empty cell on the right, and then in the **Rows & Columns group**, click the **Insert Right** button two times to add two new columns. Click the **Select Row** button, and then with the five cells selected, in the **Merge / Split group**, click the **Merge** button.

13. In the main form, click the **PhoneNumber** text box to select it. On the **Design tab**, in the **Tools group**, click the **Property Sheet** button, and then change the **Width** value to 1.2"

14. Click in a blank cell in the last column, and then in the property sheet, change the **Width** value to 3.2" **Close** ☒ the property sheet, and then compare your screen with **Figure 4**.

15. Click **Save** 🖫, and leave the form open for the next skill.

■ **You have completed Skill 6 of 10**

▶ An **input mask** is a set of special characters that control what can and cannot be entered in a field.

1. With **Residents Form** open in Layout view, click the **Phone** text box. On the **Design tab**, in the **Tools group**, click the **Property Sheet** button.

2. On the property sheet **Data tab**, click **Input Mask**, and then click the **Build** button ⋯ that displays in the box. Compare your screen with **Figure 1**.

3. With **Phone Number** selected in the **Input Mask Wizard** dialog box, click **Next**. Click the **Placeholder character arrow**, and then click the number sign (#). Click in the **Try It** box, and then compare your screen with **Figure 2**.

   The Try It box displays a sample of the input mask in which you can try entering sample data. **Placeholder characters** are the symbols in an input mask that are replaced as you type data into the field. Here, the parentheses, space, and hyphen are in place, and number signs display where each number can be typed.

4. In the **Try It** box, click the first number sign, and then watch the box as you type ten digits—any digit can be typed in this preview.

■ **Continue to the next page to complete the skill** ➤

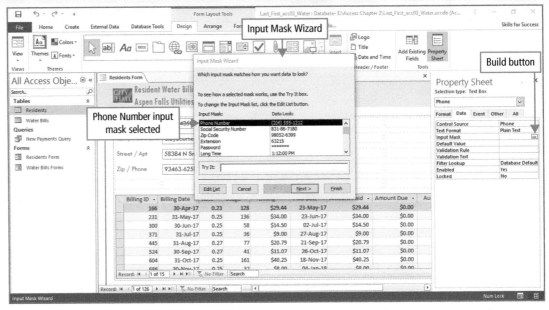

Figure 1

Access 2016, Windows 10, Microsoft Corporation

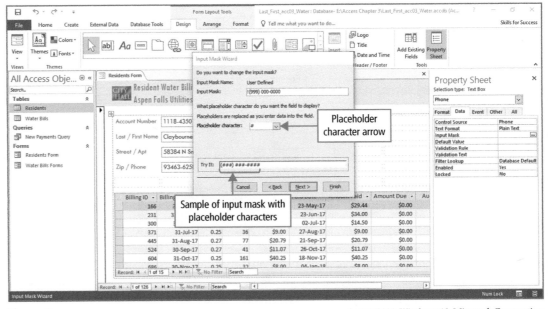

Figure 2

Access 2016, Windows 10, Microsoft Corporation

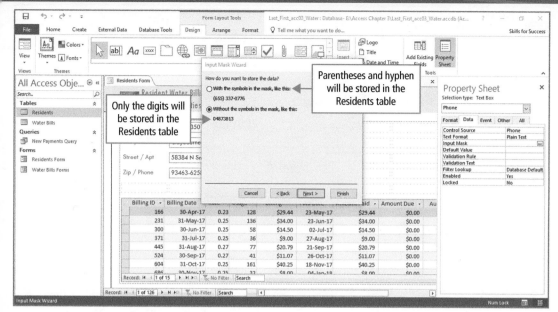

Access 2016, Windows 10, Microsoft Corporation

Figure 3

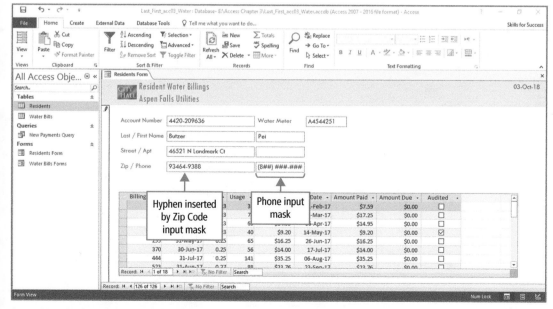

Access 2016, Windows 10, Microsoft Corporation

Figure 4

5. Click **Next**, and then compare your screen with **Figure 3**.

> The Phone Number input mask has one option that stores the number, parentheses, space, and hyphen in the table; the other option stores only the digits in the phone number.

6. Select the **With the symbols in the mask** option button, click **Next**, and then click **Finish**.

> In the property sheet Input Mask box, special characters have been inserted. These characters are needed for the input mask to perform correctly.

7. Select the **Zip** text box, and then use the property sheet to start the Input Mask Wizard. In the **Input Mask Wizard**, click **Zip Code**, and then accept the wizard defaults by clicking **Finish**.

8. **Close** ⊠ the property sheet, and then **Save** 🖫 the form.

9. Click the **View** button to switch to Form view. In the main form's Navigation bar—the lower Navigation bar—click the **Last record** ▶ button. Click in the left side of the **Zip** box, and then watch as you type 934649388

10. Press Enter to move to the **Phone** box, type 8 and then compare your screen with **Figure 4**.

11. Watch the **Phone** field as you type the rest of the phone number: 045556894

> The input mask converts the digits to *(804) 555-6894* and stores that value in the table.

12. Leave the form open for the next skill.

■ **You have completed Skill 7 of 10**

▶ In a one-to-many form, you can work with the data from two tables on a single screen.

1. If necessary, open **Residents Form** in Form view.

2. Using the technique practiced in a previous skill, use the **Find and Replace** dialog box to navigate to the record for **Account Number** 4367-618513 and then **Close** the dialog box.

3. In the subform datasheet for Lizzette Middents, click in the third record's **Paid Date** cell, and then type 13-Aug-18

4. Press Enter, and then in the **Amount Paid** cell, type 7.98 Press Enter, and then compare your screen with **Figure 1**.

> A payment from Lizzette Middents has just been recorded in the Water Bills table.

5. In the main form's Navigation bar, click the **Next Record** button ▶. In the subform Navigation bar for Pei Butzer, click the **New (blank) record** button ▶* to scroll to the bottom of the datasheet and create a new record.

6. Press Enter, and then in the **Billing Date** cell, type 31-Jul-18 Press Enter, and type 0.38 as the **Rate**. Press Enter, and then type 83 as the **Usage**. Press Enter to update the **Billing** and **Amount Due** columns, and leave the rest of the row blank. Compare your screen with **Figure 2**.

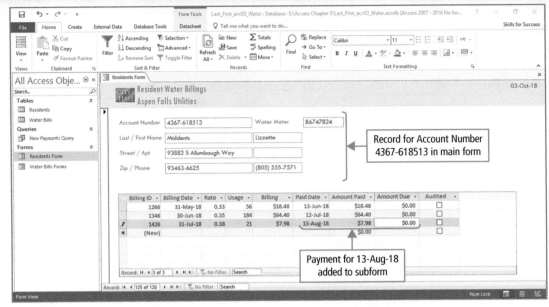

Figure 1

Access 2016, Windows 10, Microsoft Corporation

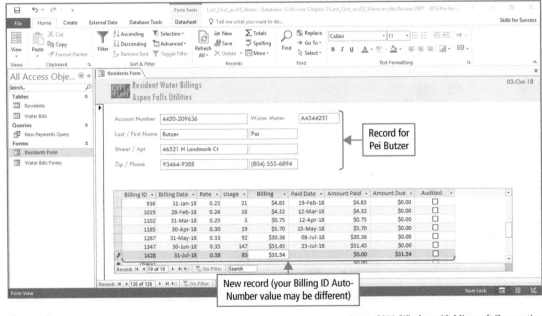

Figure 2

Access 2016, Windows 10, Microsoft Corporation

■ Continue to the next page to complete the skill

Account Number	4421-879567	Water Meter	C4847198
Last Name	Bransom	First Name	Alfred
Street	12133 S Azure Ln	Apt	A110
Zip	93464-5635	Phone	(805) 555-2685

Figure 3

7. In the main form's Navigation bar, click the **New (blank) record** button ▶* to create a new Resident record.

8. In the main form, enter the data shown in **Figure 3**, pressing Enter to move to each text box.

9. In the subform for **Alfred Bransom**, click in the first row **Billing Date** cell. Type 31-Jul-18 and then press Enter. In the **Rate** cell, enter 0.38 and then in the **Usage** cell, enter 27 Press Enter, and then compare your screen with **Figure 4**.

   In this manner, a one-to-many form can add records to two tables. Here, a new resident was added to the Residents table, and then the first billing for that resident was added to the Water Bills table.

10. Repeat the skills practiced in a previous skill to start the **Snipping Tool** and create a **Full-screen Snip**. **Save** the snip in your chapter folder with the name Last_First_acc03_WaterSnip2 and then **Close** ✕ the Snipping Tool window.

11. **Close** ✕ the form.

■ **You have completed Skill 8 of 10**

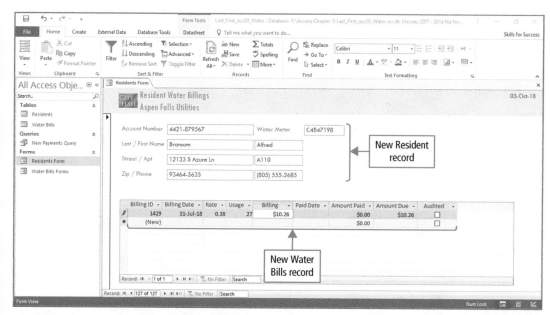

Access 2016, Windows 10, Microsoft Corporation

Figure 4

- ▶ When you need to edit data for a specific subset of data, you can base the form on a query.

- ▶ A form based on a query displays only the records returned by the query's criteria.

1. In the **Navigation Pane**, under **Queries**, right-click **New Payments Query**, and then from the shortcut menu, click **Design View**. If the property sheet displays, **Close** ☒ it.

2. In the **AmountDue** column **Criteria** cell, type >0 and then compare your screen with **Figure 1**.

   In the New Payments Query, fields from two related tables are selected. The criteria will filter only those records for which an amount is due.

3. Click **Save** 🖫. On the **Design tab**, in the **Results group**, click **Run** to display 50 records. **Close** ☒ the query.

4. Under **Queries**, verify that **New Payments Query** is selected. Click the **Create tab**, and then in the **Forms group**, click the **Form** button. Compare your screen with **Figure 2**.

   The form displays all the fields from the select query. In this manner, you can build forms with fields from related tables in Single Form view or filter data by adding criteria to the query.

■ Continue to the next page to complete the skill ▶

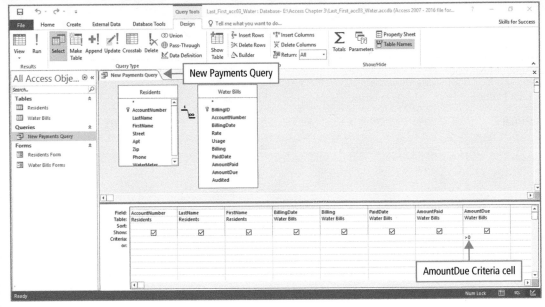

Figure 1   Access 2016, Windows 10, Microsoft Corporation

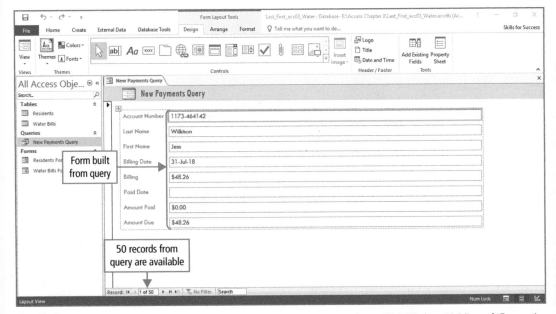

Figure 2   Access 2016, Windows 10, Microsoft Corporation

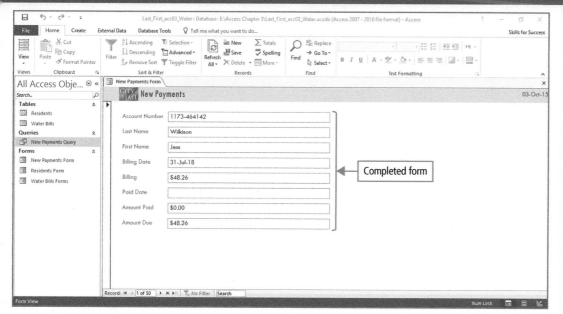

Access 2016, Windows 10, Microsoft Corporation

Figure 3

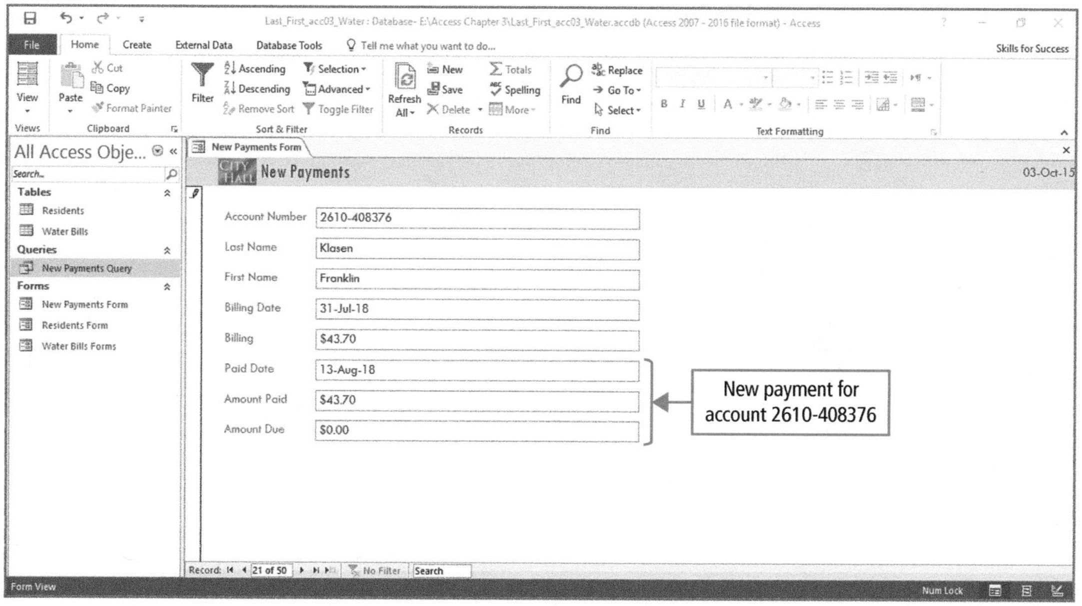

Access 2016, Windows 10, Microsoft Corporation

Figure 4

5. On the **Design tab**, in the **Tools group**, click the **Property Sheet** button to open the sheet. Verify that the first text box is selected, and then on the property sheet **Format tab**, change the **Width** value to 4" **Close** ☒ the property sheet.

MOS
Obj 4.2.5

6. Repeat the technique practiced previously to insert the **acc03_WaterLogo** file as the form's logo, and then change the **Title** control's text to New Payments

7. Insert a **Date and Time** control with the middle date—**dd-mmm-yy**—option button selected and the **Include Time** check box cleared.

8. Click **Save** ☐. In the **Save As** box, type New Payments Form and then press Enter.

9. Click the **View** button to switch to Form view, and then compare your screen with **Figure 3**.

10. **Find** the record for **Account Number** 2610-408376 In the **Paid Date** text box, enter 13-Aug-18 and then press Enter. In the **Amount Paid** field, enter 43.70 Press Enter, and then compare your screen with **Figure 4**.

11. Create a **Full-screen Snip**, **Save** the snip in your chapter folder as Last_First_ acc03_WaterSnip3 and then **Close** ☒ the Snipping Tool window.

12. **Close** ☒ the form.

■ **You have completed Skill 9 of 10**

▶ **Navigation forms** are forms that contain a Navigation Control with tabs that you can use to quickly open forms and reports.

1. On the **Create tab**, in the **Forms group**, click the **Navigation** button, and then compare your screen with **Figure 1**.

    The gallery provides a visual summary of the several layouts available in a Navigation form.

2. In the **Navigation Form** gallery, click **Vertical Tabs, Left** to create the form.

3. Near the top left corner of the new form, click to select the **[AddNew]** button, and then click the **Format tab**. In the **Control Formatting group**, click the **Quick Styles** button, and then click the last style in the last row—**Intense Effect – Teal, Accent 6**.

4. With the button still selected, in the **Control Formatting group**, click the **Change Shape** button, and then click the third shape—**Rounded Rectangle**.

5. Drag **Residents Form** from the **Navigation Pane** to the **[Add New]** button in the Navigation form, and then release the left mouse button. Repeat this technique to add **Water Bills Form** and then **New Payments Form** to the Navigation form. Compare your screen with **Figure 2**. If the Field List list displays, **Close** ☒ it.

6. Click the **Design tab**, and then click the **Property Sheet** button. In the property sheet, below **Selection type**, click the **arrow**, and then click **Form** to display the form's properties.

■ Continue to the next page to complete the skill ▶

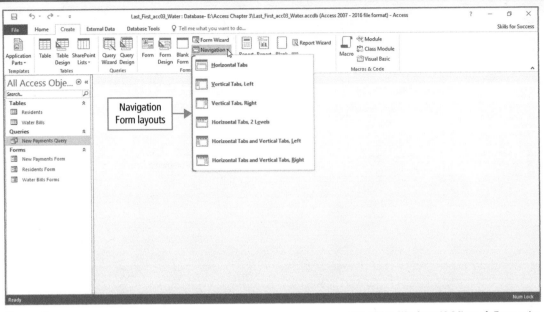

Figure 1   Access 2016, Windows 10, Microsoft Corporation

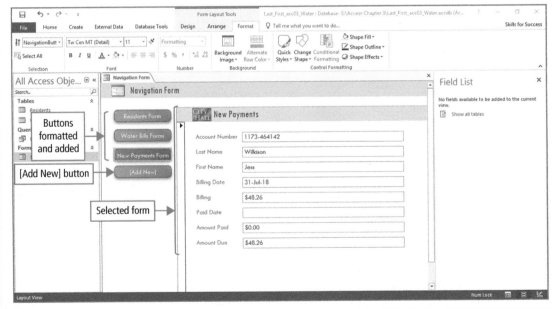

Figure 2   Access 2016, Windows 10, Microsoft Corporation

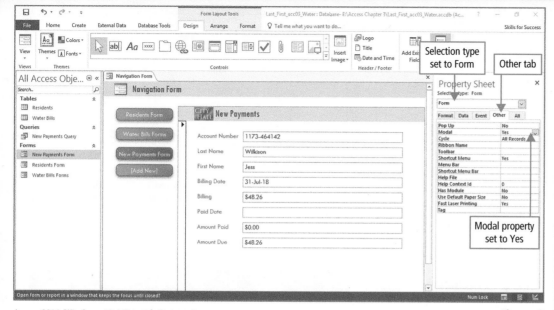

Access 2016, Windows 10, Microsoft Corporation

Figure 3

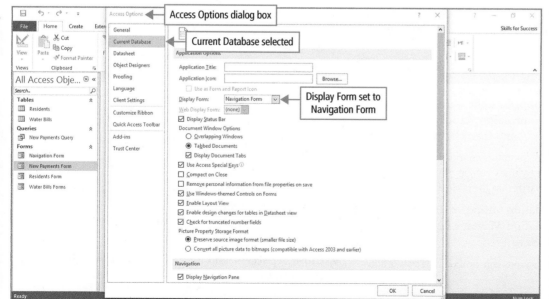
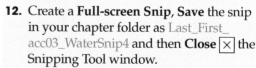

Access 2016, Windows 10, Microsoft Corporation

Figure 4

7. On the property sheet, click the **Other tab**, and then click **Modal**. Click the **Modal arrow**, and then click **Yes**. Compare your screen with **Figure 3**.

> When a form's **Modal** property is set to Yes, the Navigation Pane will collapse when the form is opened. When the form is closed, the Navigation Pane will display.

8. Click **Save** 🖫, and then click **OK** to accept the default name for the form. **Close** ✕ the property sheet, and then **Close** ✕ the form.

9. Click the **File tab**, and then click **Options**. On the left side of the **Access Options** dialog box, click **Current Database**. Click the **Display Form arrow** to display a list of all the database forms, and then click **Navigation Form**. Compare your screen with **Figure 4**.

> In the Application Options dialog box, you can pick one form that opens automatically when the database is opened.

10. Click **OK**, read the message that displays, and then click **OK**.

11. **Close** ✕ and then reopen the database to verify that Navigation Form opens as a modal form.

12. Create a **Full-screen Snip**, **Save** the snip in your chapter folder as Last_First_acc03_WaterSnip4 and then **Close** ✕ the Snipping Tool window.

13. **Close** ✕ the form to display the Navigation Pane, and then **Close** ✕ Access.

14. If you are printing this project, open the snips and then print them. Otherwise, submit the files as directed by your instructor.

 DONE! You have completed Skill 10 of 10, and your database is complete!

More Skills 11

Validate Fields

To complete this project, you will need the following file:

- acc03_MS11Employees

You will save your file as:

- Last_First_acc03_MS11Employees

▶ A ***validation rule*** is a field property that requires that specific values be entered into a field.

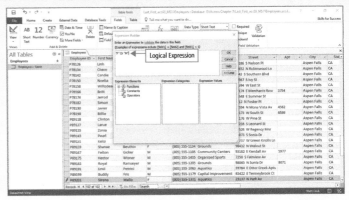

Figure 1   Access 2016, Windows 10, Microsoft Corporation

1. Start **Access 2016**, and then open the student data file **acc03_MS11Employees**. **Save** the file in your **Access Chapter 3** folder as Last_First_acc03_MS11Employees

2. Open the **Employees** table in Datasheet view. In the Navigation bar, click the **Last record** navigation button [▶|].

3. In the record for Buddy Fris, change **Gender** to M and then, in the record for Sirena Wallo, change **Gender** to F

4. With a **Gender** field still active, click the **Fields tab**. In the **Properties group**, click in the **Field Size** box, type 1 and then press [Enter]. Read the message that displays, and then click **Yes**.

   This field size setting limits values to a single letter, but it will not prevent wrong letters from being entered into the field.

5. On the **Fields tab**, in the **Field Validation group**, click the **Validation** button, and then click **Field Validation Rule**. In the **Expression Builder**, type "F" Or "M" Compare your screen with **Figure 1**, and then click **OK**.

   Validation rules must be written precisely. Here, quotation marks indicate that the value can be the letter F or the letter M. No other values will be allowed during data entry. Common validation rules are summarized in the table in **Figure 2**.

6. In the **Field Validation group**, click the **Validation** button, and then click **Field Validation Message**. In the **Enter Validation Message** box, type Please enter an F or an M. Click **OK**, and then click **Save** [💾].

   A validation message is the text that displays in a message box when a validation rule is broken during data entry.

7. Click the **New (blank) record** navigation button [▶*]. In the first column of the append row, type P90021 and then press [Enter]. In the next two fields,

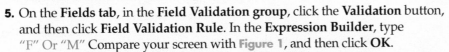

Common Validation Rules	
Validation Ruler	**Description**
>0	Value must be a number greater than zero.
BETWEEN 0 and 1	Value must be a number between zero and one.
< 01/01/2018	Value must be a date before 2018.
≥ 01/01/2018 And ≤ 12/31/2018	Value must be a date during the year 2018.
"Male" Or "Female"	Value must be the text *Male* or the text *Female*.
Like "(A-Z)*@ (A-Z).gov"	Value must be a government website.
(ShipDate) ≤ (OrderDate)+30	Value of the ShipDate field must be within 30 days of the value in the OrderDate field.
Len(PASSWORD)>7	Value in the Password field must have more than seven characters.

Figure 2

type your first and last name. Press [Enter], and then in the **Gender** field, type the letter q Press [Enter] to display the validation message.

8. In the displayed Access message, click **OK**. Press [Backspace], and then attempt to type male or female Notice that only one letter is allowed. Enter your gender as F or M and then **Close** [✕] the table.

9. **Close** [✕] Access, and then submit the file as directed by your instructor.

■ **You have completed More Skills 11**

More Skills 12

Create Databases from Templates

To complete this project, you will need the following file:

- Blank desktop database

You will save your file as:

- Last_First_acc03_MS12Tasks

▶ When you create a database, you can select a database from several prebuilt templates.

▶ Most database templates can provide all the tables, queries, forms, reports, and macros you need to begin entering data immediately after creating the database.

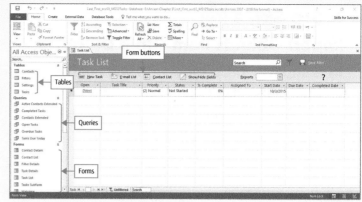

Access 2016, Windows 10, Microsoft Corporation   **Figure 1**

1. Start **Access 2016**. On the Access start screen, locate and then click the **Desktop task management** thumbnail. If necessary, type Desktop task management in the Search for online templates text box to locate the file.

   MOS Obj 1.1.2

2. In the **Desktop task management** preview, read the description, and then in the **File Name** box, replace the text with Last_First_acc03_MS12Tasks

3. Click the **Browse** button, and then in the **File New Database** dialog box, navigate to your **Access Chapter 3** folder. Click **OK**. Click the **Create** button to download and open the database file. If necessary, **Close** the **Getting Started with Tasks** dialog box.

4. Take a few moments to familiarize yourself with the database shown in **Figure 1**.

5. If necessary, in the security message, click **Enable Content** to display the Getting Started window.

6. **Close** ☒ the Getting Started with Tasks dialog box.

7. **Close** « the Navigation Pane. In the **Task List** buttons row, click **New Task** to open the Task Details form.

8. In the **Task Details** form, in the **Task Title** box, type Interview college interns

9. In the **Assigned To** box, type Cathy Story Press [Enter], read the message that displays, and then click **Yes**.

   The Task Details form's List Items Edit Form property is set to Contact Details so that if you assign a task to a contact who is not in the Contacts table, the Contact Details form will automatically open. You can use this form to add that contact's information into the Contacts table.

10. In the **Contact Details** form, enter the following data:

Access 2016, Windows 10, Microsoft Corporation   **Figure 2**

Company: IT Department
Job Title: IT Services Supervisor
Business Phone: (805) 555-1033
E-mail: cstory@aspenfalls.org

11. Click **Close** to return to the Task Details form.

12. In the **Task Details** form, click the **Status arrow**, and then click **In Progress**. Click in the **% Complete** box, and then replace the existing text with 50% Click **Close** to update the Task List.

13. In the **Task List** form header, click the **Reports arrow**, and then click **Active Tasks** to open the Active Tasks report. Compare your screen with **Figure 2**.

14. **Close** ☒ the Active Tasks report, and then **Close** ☒ Access. Submit the file as directed by your instructor.

- **You have completed More Skills 12**

More Skills 13

Import Objects from Other Databases

To complete this project, you will need the following files:

- acc03_MS13BackEnd
- acc03_MS13FrontEnd

You will save your file as:

- Last_First_acc03_MS13Camps

▶ You can build a database by importing objects from other Access databases.

▶ Commonly imported objects include tables, forms, queries, reports, and macros.

Figure 1   Access 2016, Windows 10, Microsoft Corporation

---

1. **Start Access 2016**, and then start a **Blank desktop database**. **Save** the database in your **Access Chapter 3** folder as Last_First_acc03_Camps

2. **Close** ⊠ Table1 without saving it. Click the **External Data tab**, and then in the **Import & Link group**, click **Access**.

3. In the **Get External Data – Access Database** dialog box, click **Browse**. In the **File Open** dialog box, navigate to the student data files that you downloaded for this project. Click **acc03_MS13BackEnd**, and then click **Open**, and then click **OK**.

   The Get External Data - Access Database dialog box can be used to import Access objects into a database. It can also be used to create links to tables in another database file.

4. In the **Import Objects** dialog box, click the **Select All** button. Compare your screen to **Figure 1**, and then click **OK**.

5. **Close** the **Get External Data - Access Database** dialog box to import the tables into the database.

   When tables are imported from other databases, the fields, field properties, data, and relationships with other tables are imported. Here, four related tables were imported.

6. On the **External Data tab**, in the **Import & Link group**, click **Access**. In the **Get External Data – Access Database** dialog box, click **Browse,** and then open the student data file **acc03_MS13FrontEnd**. Click **OK** to open the Import Objects dialog box.

7. In the **Import Objects** dialog box, click the **Queries tab**, and then click **Select All** to add them to the import.

Figure 2   Access 2016, Windows 10, Microsoft Corporation

8. In the **Import Objects** dialog box, click the **Forms tab**, and then click **Registration Form** to add it to the import. Compare your screen with **Figure 2**.

   The queries selected in the previous step are still selected and will be included in the import. The Camps Form is not selected and will not be imported.

9. In the **Import Objects** dialog box, click the **Reports tab**, and then click **Select All** to add all the reports to the import.

10. In the **Import Objects** dialog box, click **OK**. **Close** the Get External Data - Access Data dialog box to complete the import.

11. **Close** ⊠ Access. Submit the file as directed by your instructor.

■ **You have completed More Skills 13**

More Skills 14

Back Up Databases

To complete this project, you will need the following file:

- acc03_MS14Art

You will save your files as:

- Last_First_acc03_MS14Art
- Last_First_acc03_MS14Art_Backup

▶ You can save a database as a template and back up databases. Missing tables, queries, or reports from a database can be restored from a backup.

---

1. Start **Access 2016**, and then open the student data file **acc03_MS14Art**. **Save** the file in your **Access Chapter 3** folder as Last_First_acc03_MS14Art If necessary, enable the content.

2. Click the **File tab**, and then click **Save As**. In the **Save Database As group**, click **Template**, and then click **Save As**.

    The Create New Template from This Database dialog box displays.

3. In the **Name** text box, type Art Database Template Compare your screen with **Figure 1**, and then click **OK**.

4. Read the message, and then click **OK**.

5. Click the **File tab**, and then click **Save As**. In the **Save Database As group**, click **Back Up Database**. Compare your screen with **Figure 2**, and then click **Save As**.

6. In the **Save As** dialog box, type Last_First_acc03_MS14Art_Backup and then click **Save**.

7. **Close** Access.

8. Submit your files as directed by your instructor.

■ **You have completed More Skills 14**

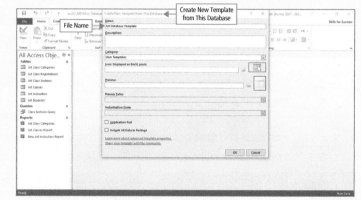

Access 2016, Windows 10, Microsoft Corporation   **Figure 1**

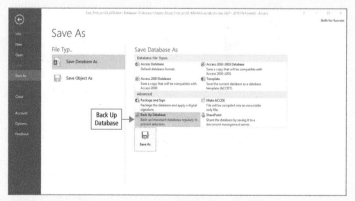

Access 2016, Windows 10, Microsoft Corporation   **Figure 2**

Review

Skills Number	Task	Step	Icon	Keyboard Shortcut
1	Create forms with the Form Wizard	Create tab → Forms group → Form Wizard		
2	Locate a record in a form	Click in the field to be searched. Then, Home → Find group → Find		Ctrl + F
2	Create new records	In the Navigation bar, click New (blank) record	▶	
3	Format form controls	Select the control(s) in Layout view, and then use the groups on the Format tab		
3	Set control widths and heights	On the property sheet Format tab, change the Width or Height property		F4
4	Apply conditional formatting	Format tab → Control Formatting group → Conditional Formatting → New Rule		
4	Add logos	Design tab → Header / Footer group → Logo		
5	Create forms with the Form Tool	Select table or query in Navigation Pane. Then, Create tab → Forms group → Form		
5	Create one-to-many forms	In the Navigation Pane, select the table that will be the main form. Then, Create tab → Forms group → Form		
5	Add date and time controls	Design tab → Header / Footer group → Date and Time		
6	Insert columns and rows	Arrange tab → Rows & Columns group		
6	Delete columns and rows	Arrange tab → Rows & Columns group → Select Column or Select Row. Then, press Delete		
6	Merge columns and rows	Select cells or Select Row. Then, Arrange tab → Merge / Split group → Merge		
6	Edit label control text	Double-click the label control		
7	Add input masks to form text box controls	Property sheet Data tab → Input Mask → Build button		F4
8	Edit data in one-to-many forms	Use the main form Navigation bar to locate the desired record. Change data in either the main form or the subform datasheet		
10	Create navigation forms	Create tab → Forms group → Navigation Form		
10	Automatically close the Navigation Pane when the form is open	Property sheet Other tab → Modal → Yes		F4
10	Automatically set a form to open when the database is first opened	File → Options → Current Database → Display Form		
10	Format button controls	Format tab → Control Formatting group → Quick Styles (and other commands in the group)		
MS11	Create Validation rule	Fields tab → Field Validation group → Validation button → Expression Builder		
MS12	Create a database from a template	Access start screen → Select template		
MS14	Save database as a backup	File tab → Save As → Save Database As → Select Back Up Database		

Project Summary Chart

Project	Project Type	Project Location
Skills Review	Review	In Book & MIL MyITLab Grader
Skills Assessment 1	Review	In Book & MIL MyITLab Grader
Skills Assessment 2	Review	Book
My Skills	Problem Solving	Book
Visual Skills Check	Problem Solving	Book
Skills Challenge 1	Critical Thinking	Book
Skills Challenge 2	Critical Thinking	Book
More Skills Assessment	Review	In Book & MIL MyITLab Grader
Collaborating with Google	Critical Thinking	Book

MOS Objectives Covered (Quiz in MyITLab)

1.1.2 Create a database from a template	4.1.3 Save a form
1.3.1 Navigate to specific records	4.2.1 Move form controls
1.3.2 Create and modify a navigation form	4.2.2 Add form controls
1.3.3 Set a form as the startup option	4.2.4 Remove form controls
1.4.3 Back up a database	4.2.5 Set form control properties
1.5.3 Save a database as a template	4.2.6 Manage labels
2.1.4 Import tables from other databases	4.2.7 Add subforms
2.4.2 Add validation rules to fields	4.3.7 Insert headers and footers
2.4.8 Use input masks	4.3.8 Insert images
4.1.1 Create a form	

Key Terms

BizSkills
Video

1. What do you think are the biggest sources of conflict in the meeting portrayed in the video?

2. What suggestions do you have to reduce the conflict in the group portrayed in the video?

Online Help Skills

1. Start **Access 2016**, and then in the upper right corner of the start page, click the **Help** button ? .

2. In the **Access Help** window **Search help** box, type form tool and then press Enter .

3. In the search result list, click **Create a form by using the Form Tool**, and then compare your screen with Figure 1.

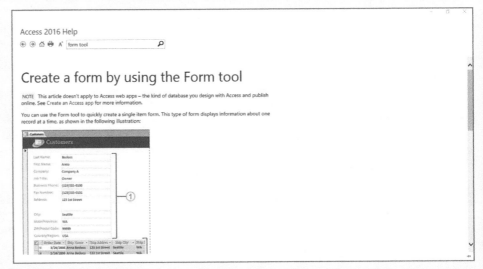

Figure 1   Access 2016, Windows 10, Microsoft Corporation

4. Read the article to see if you can answer the following questions: Under which circumstances would you use the Form Tool to create a form? Why would you use the Form Tool and not the Form Wizard?

Matching

Match each term in the second column with its correct definition in the first column by writing the letter of the term on the blank line in front of the correct definition.

____ **1.** A tool used to create a form that provides a way to select tables and fields before the form is created.

____ **2.** The arrangement of data and labels in a form or report—columnar or tabular, for example.

____ **3.** A form control that displays the name of a form by default; the actual text can be edited later.

____ **4.** A set of special characters that control what can and cannot be entered in a field.

____ **5.** A layout with cells arranged in rows and columns into which controls are placed.

____ **6.** By default, subforms display in this view.

____ **7.** By default, main forms display in this layout.

____ **8.** A type of form that has a subform that displays related records from another table.

____ **9.** A form that can be used to quickly switch between forms and reports in the database.

____ **10.** To set a form to open automatically when the database is opened, open the Access Options dialog box, and then display the options for this category.

A Current Database

B Datasheet view

C Form Wizard

D Input mask

E Layout

F Navigation Form

G One-to-many form

H Single Form view

I Tabular layout

J Title

Multiple Choice   MyITLab®

Choose the correct answer.

1. An Access view used to format a form or report while you are viewing a sample of the data.
   A. Design view
   B. Form view
   C. Layout view

2. A layout that places labels in the first column and data in the second column.
   A. Columnar
   B. Datasheet
   C. Tabular

3. Controls on a form or report that describe each field—often the field name—in the underlying table.
   A. IntelliSense Quick Info boxes
   B. Labels
   C. Text boxes

4. Controls on a form or report that display the data from each field in the underlying table or query.
   A. Labels
   B. Text boxes
   C. Titles

5. The property sheet tab that contains the Input Mask property.
   A. Data
   B. Format
   C. Other

6. The symbol in an input mask that is replaced as you type data into the field.
   A. Data character
   B. Input character
   C. Placeholder character

7. Formatting that evaluates the values in a field and formats that data according to the rules you specify; for example, only values over 1,000 will have bold applied.
   A. Conditional formatting
   B. Logical formatting
   C. Rules-based formatting

8. A form contained within another form that contains records related to the record displayed in the main form.
   A. Parent form
   B. Relationship form
   C. Subform

9. When you want to build a form for a subset of table data, you can base the form on this.
   A. Blank Form tool
   B. Filtered table
   C. Query

10. To automatically close the Navigation Pane whenever the form is open, this form property needs to be set to *Yes*.
    A. Full Width
    B. Modal
    C. Open Exclusive

Topics for Discussion

1. You have created forms using two different methods: the Form Tool and the Form Wizard. Which method do you prefer, and why? What are the primary advantages of each method?

2. Recall that forms are used to enter data into a database. Consider the types of data businesses might store in a database. For example, a school needs a class registration form to enter students into classes. What type of forms might other businesses need to enter data?

Skills Review

To complete this project, you will need the following files:

- acc03_SRElectricity
- acc03_SRLogo

You will save your file as:

- Last_First_acc03_SRElectricity

1. Start **Access 2016**, and then open the student data file **acc03_SRElectricity**. **Save** the file in your **Access Chapter 3** folder with the name Last_First_acc03_ SRElectricity If necessary, enable the content.

2. On the **Create tab**, in the **Forms group**, click the **Form Wizard** button. In the **Form Wizard** dialog box, select the **Billing Cycles** table, and then move **AccountNumber**, **CycleDate**, **Rate**, **ElectricityUsage**, and **UsageFee** into **Selected Fields**. Click **Next** two times, name the form Charges Form and then **Finish** the wizard.

3. On the **Home tab**, in the **Views group**, click **View** to switch to Layout view.

4. With the **Account Number** text box control selected, press and hold Ctrl, while clicking the other four text boxes. Click the **Format tab**, and then in the **Font group**, click the **Align Left** button.

5. Click the **Home tab**, and then click the **View** button to switch to Form view. In the Navigation bar, click **New (blank) record**, and then enter the following billing data: **Account Number** is 4420-209636, **Cycle Date** is 31-Jul-18, **Rate** is 0.07623, and **Electricity Usage** is 242. Click in the **Usage Fee** field, and then compare your screen with **Figure 1**.

6. **Save** and then **Close** the form. In the **Navigation Pane**, click **New Billings Query** one time to select it. Click the **Create tab**, and then in the **Forms group**, click the **Form** button.

7. Double-click the **Title** control, and then change the text to New Payments Form

8. Click the **Account Number** text box, and then click as needed to open the property sheet. On the property sheet **Format tab**, change the **Width** property to 4" and then compare your screen with **Figure 2**.

9. Click **Save**, type New Payments Form and then click **OK**. **Close** the form.

■ Continue to the next page to complete this Skills Review

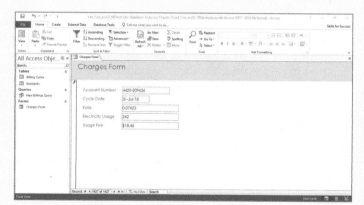

Access 2016, Windows 10, Microsoft Corporation   **Figure 1**

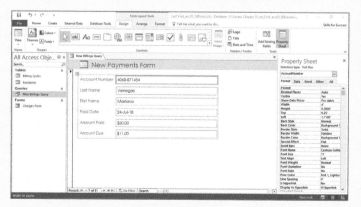

Access 2016, Windows 10, Microsoft Corporation   **Figure 2**

10. In the **Navigation Pane**, click the **Residents** table one time to select it. Click the **Create tab**, and then in the **Forms group**, click the **Form** button. Click **Save**, type Residents Form and then click **OK**.

11. On the **Design tab**, in the **Header / Footer group**, click **Logo**, and then use the **Insert Picture** dialog box to insert the file **acc03_SRLogo**.

12. Click the **Zip** text box, and then click the property sheet **Data tab**. Click the **Input Mask** box, and then click the displayed **Build** button. In the **Input Mask Wizard**, select **Zip Code**, and then click **Finish**.

13. Using the property sheet, set the width of the column of the **Account Number** text box to 4" With the column still active, click the **Arrange tab**, and then in the **Rows & Columns group**, click the **Insert Right** button three times.

14. Drag the **Electricity Meter** label to the first empty cell to the right of the **Account Number** text box. Drag the **Electricity Meter** text box control to the first empty cell to the right of the **Electricity Meter** label. Use the property sheet to set the width of the column with the **Electricity Meter** label to 1.5", and then **Close** the property sheet.

15. Click in the row with the subform. On the **Arrange tab**, in the **Rows & Columns group**, click **Select Row**. In the **Merge / Split group**, click **Merge**.

16. Click **Save**, and then switch to Form view. **Find** the record for **Account Number** 4420-209636 and then **Close** the Find and Replace dialog box.

17. In the subform, click the **Last Record** button, and then in the last record, record a **Paid Date** of 13-Aug-18 and an **Amount Paid** of 18.45 Compare your screen with **Figure 3**, and then **Close** the form.

18. On the **Create tab**, in the **Forms group**, click **Navigation**, and then click **Vertical Tabs, Left**.

19. Select the **[Add New]** button, and then click the **Format tab**. In the **Control Formatting group**, click the **Quick Styles** button, and then click the second style in the last row—**Intense Effect – Dark Red, Accent 1**.

20. Drag **Residents Form** to the **[Add New]** button. Repeat to add **Charges Form** and then **New Payments Form**.

21. Display the property sheet, and then under **Selection type**, select **Form**. On the property sheet **Other tab**, change the **Modal** property to **Yes**.

22. Click **Save**, click **OK**, and then switch to Form view. Compare your screen with **Figure 4**.

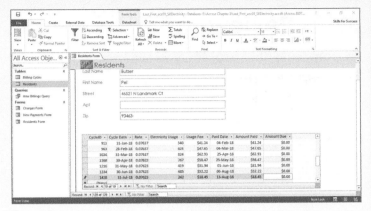

Figure 3   Access 2016, Windows 10, Microsoft Corporation

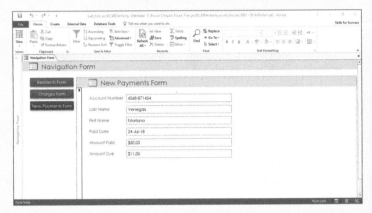

Figure 4   Access 2016, Windows 10, Microsoft Corporation

23. Close Access, and then submit the file as directed by your instructor.

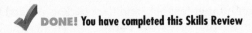 **DONE! You have completed this Skills Review**

Skills Assessment 1

MyITLab®
Grader

To complete this project, you will need the following files:

- acc03_SA1Classes
- acc03_SA1Logo

You will save your file as:

- Last_First_acc03_SA1Classes

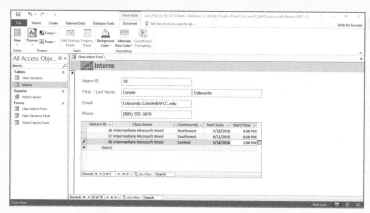

Access 2016, Windows 10, Microsoft Corporation   **Figure 1**

1. Start **Access 2016**, and then open the student data file **acc03_SA1Classes**. **Save** the file in your chapter folder with the name Last_First_acc03_SA1Classes If necessary, enable the content.

2. Use the **Form Wizard** to create a form with all the fields from the **Class Sessions** table *except* SessionID. Name the form Class Sessions Form and then accept all other wizard defaults.

3. Set the width of all the form's text boxes to 3" and their text alignment to left.

4. Use the form to add the following record: **Class Name** is Intermediate Microsoft Word **Community Center** is Central and **Intern ID** is 10 Leave the other fields blank. **Save** and then **Close** the form.

5. Use the **Form Tool** to create a form based on the **Word Classes** query. Change the **Title** control text to Word Classes Form **Save** the form as Word Classes Form and then **Close** the form.

6. Use the **Form Tool** to create a form with a main form based on the **Interns** table and with a subform based on the **Class Sessions** table. Change the form's logo using the file acc03_SA1Logo.

7. Add a **Phone Number** input mask to the **Phone** text box control that uses the number sign (#) as the placeholder character. Accept all other wizard defaults.

8. Add a column to the right of the table, and then move the **Last Name** text box control into the first cell to the right of the **First Name** text box.

9. Delete the unused row with the **Last Name** label, and then change the *First Name* label text to First / Last Name

10. Set the width of the table's first column to 1.5" and the width of the second and third columns to 2.6" In the subform row, merge all of the cells.

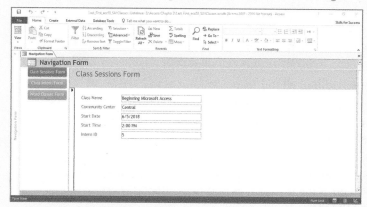

Access 2016, Windows 10, Microsoft Corporation   **Figure 2**

11. **Save** the form with the name Class Intern Form and then switch to Form view. Navigate to the last **Intern** record, and then in the subform for Connie Colasurado, complete the last record by adding a **Start Date** of 5/14/2018 and **Start Time** of 2:00 PM Compare your screen with **Figure 1**, and then **Close** the form.

12. Create a **Navigation Form** with the **Vertical Tabs, Left** layout. Apply the **Intense Effect – Green, Accent 1** Quick Style to the [Add New] button, and then add buttons in the following order: **Class Sessions Form**, **Class Intern Form**, and **Word Classes Form**.

13. Set the form's **Modal** property to **Yes**. Click **Save**, and then click **OK**. Reopen the form, and then compare your screen with **Figure 2**.

14. **Close** the form, **Close** Access, and then submit the file as directed by your instructor.

DONE! You have completed Skills Assessment 1

Skills Assessment 2

To complete this project, you will need the following files:

- acc03_SA2Rentals
- acc03_SA2Logo

You will save your file as:

- Last_First_acc03_SA2Rentals

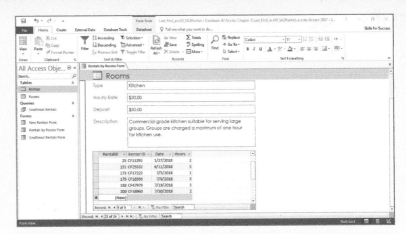

Figure 1　　　　　　　　Access 2016, Windows 10, Microsoft Corporation

1. Start **Access 2016**, and then open the student data file **acc03_SA2Rentals**. **Save** the file in your chapter folder with the name Last_First_acc03_SA2Rentals If necessary, enable the content.

2. Use the **Form Wizard** to create a form with fields from the **Rentals** table in this order: **RenterID**, **Date**, and **RoomNumber**. Name the form New Rentals Form and then accept all other wizard defaults.

3. Set the width of all the form's text boxes to 2".

4. Use the form to add the following record: **Renter ID** is CF38960 **Date** is 7/30/2018 and **Room Number** is SW115 **Save** and then **Close** the form.

5. Use the **Form Tool** to create a form based on the **Southeast Rentals** query. Change the form's logo using the student data file **acc03_SA2Logo**. **Save** the form as Southeast Rentals Form and then **Close** the form.

6. Use the **Form Tool** to create a form with a main form based on the **Rooms** table and with a subform based on the **Rentals** table.

7. For the **Deposit** text box control, create a new conditional formatting rule: If the field value is greater than 75 the font should be **Green** (column 6, last row) and **Bold**.

8. Use the property sheet to set the **Description** text box control's **Width** to 4.5" and the **Height** to 1"

9. **Save** the form with the name Rentals by Room Form and then switch to **Form view**. In the main form, navigate to **Room Number SW115**. In the subform for that room, complete the last record by entering 2 in the **Hours** field. Compare your screen with **Figure 1**, and then **Close** the form.

10. Create a **Navigation Form** with the **Horizontal Tabs** layout. Apply the **Colored Outline - Purple, Accent 6** Quick Style (column 7,

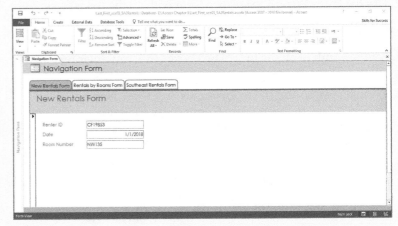

Figure 2　　　　　　　　Access 2016, Windows 10, Microsoft Corporation

row 1) to the [Add New] button, and then change its shape to **Round Same Side Corner Rectangle** (shape 5).

11. Add buttons in the following order: **New Rentals Form**, **Rentals by Room Form**, and **Southeast Rentals Form**.

12. Set the form's **Modal** property to **Yes**. Click **Save**, and then click **OK**. **Close** the form. Reopen the form, and then compare your screen with **Figure 2**.

13. **Close** the form, **Close** Access, and then submit the file as directed by your instructor.

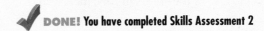

DONE! You have completed Skills Assessment 2

My Skills

To complete this project, you will need the following file:

- acc03_MYGrades

You will save your file as:

- Last_First_acc03_MYGrades

Access 2016, Windows 10, Microsoft Corporation   **Figure 1**

Access 2016, Windows 10, Microsoft Corporation   **Figure 2**

1. Start **Access 2016**, and then open the student data file **acc03_MYGrades**. **Save** the file in your chapter folder with the name Last_First_acc03_MYGrades If necessary, enable the content.

2. Use the **Form Wizard** to create a form with all of the fields from the **Scores** table *except* ScoreID. Name the form Scores Form and then accept all other wizard defaults.

3. Set the width of all the form's text boxes to 2.5" and their text alignment to left. **Save** and then **Close** the form.

4. Use the **Form Tool** to create a form based on the **Missing Scores** query. Change the **Title** control text to New Scores

5. Set the width of the text box controls to 3.5" **Save** the form as New Scores Entry Form and then **Close** the form.

6. Use the **Form Tool** to create a form with a main form based on the **Classes** table and with a subform based on the **Scores** table.

7. In the main form, change the **Title** control to My Classes Click a blank cell on the right side of the subform, and then use the property sheet to set the **Height** of the row to 3.2"

8. **Save** the form with the name My Classes Form and then switch to Form view. Compare your screen with **Figure 1**.

9. In the main form, create a new record using the data from the class that is assigning this project to you. In the subform, fill in the data for all of the assignments, quizzes, tests, or other grading opportunities that have been posted for your class. If you received scores on any of these, enter those scores. When you are done, **Close** the form.

10. Create a **Navigation Form** with the **Vertical Tabs, Left** layout. Apply the **Moderate Effect - Brown, Accent 4** Quick Style (column 5, row 5) to the [Add New] button.

11. Add buttons in the following order: **My Classes Form**, **Scores Form**, and **New Scores Entry Form**.

12. Set the form's **Modal** property to **Yes**. Click **Save**, and then click **OK**. **Close** the form. Reopen the form, and then compare your screen with **Figure 2**.

13. **Close** the form, **Close** Access, and then submit the file as directed by your instructor.

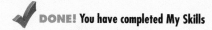 **DONE! You have completed My Skills**

Visual Skills Check

To complete this project, you will need the following files:

- acc03_VSArtCenter
- acc03_VSLogo

You will save your file as:

- Last_First_acc03_VSArtCenter

Open the student data file **acc03_VSArtCenter**, and then **Save** the file in your **Access Chapter 3** folder as Last_First_acc03_VSArtCenter

Open the **Students Form** in Layout view, and then arrange and format the label and text box controls as shown in Figure 1. The **First Name** and **Last Name** labels are bold, the **City** label text has been changed to City / State / Zip and unused rows have been deleted. Adjust the field widths to ensure all data displays.

Create the Navigation form shown in **Figure 1**. The form is named Navigation Form The title text has been changed to Art Classes Navigation Form and the logo was inserted from the student data file **acc03_VSLogo**. The buttons have been formatted with the **Subtle Effect - Dark Blue, Accent 1** Quick Style and the **Rounded Rectangle** shape, and the button text is bold. The form properties have been changed so that the Navigation Pane automatically closes whenever the form is open.

Submit the file as directed by your instructor.

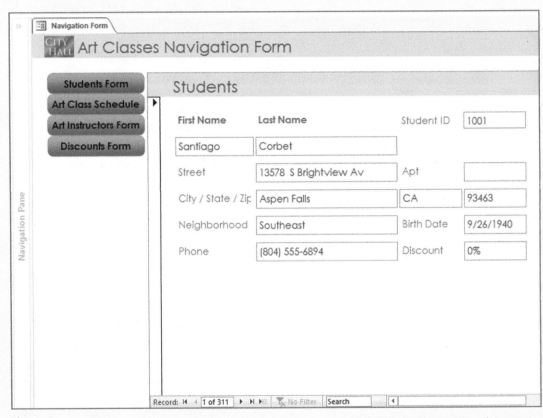

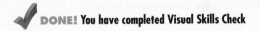 **DONE! You have completed Visual Skills Check**

Figure 1

Access 2016, Windows 10, Microsoft Corporation

Skills Challenge 1

To complete this project, you will need the following file:

- acc03_SC1Farms

You will save your file as:

- Last_First_acc03_SC1Farms

Open the student data file **acc03_SC1Farms**, and then save the file in your **Access Chapter 3** folder as Last_First_acc03_SC1Farms Use the Form Tool to create a form that displays all the records and fields from the Farms table. Using the techniques practiced in this chapter, arrange the labels and text boxes so that anyone who uses the form can fill in the data in a logical order. Add columns and rows and merge cells as needed, and resize them to better fit the data they contain. Delete any unused rows or columns. Update the label text so

that the labels clearly describe the data. For example, add spaces between words and, where appropriate, describe all the controls in a single row. Format the controls with the farm's name to so they stand out from the rest of the controls.

Submit the file as directed by your instructor.

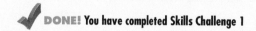 **DONE! You have completed Skills Challenge 1**

Skills Challenge 2

To complete this project, you will need the following file:

- acc03_SC2Wildlife

You will save your file as:

- Last_First_acc03_SC2Wildlife

Open the student data file **acc03_SC2Wildlife**, and then save the file as Last_First_acc03_SC2Wildlife Create a one-to-many form based on the Wildlife table in the main form and the Alternate Names table in the subform. Format the form to fit the data it will hold making sure to leave room for about five lines of text in the Description text box. Research each of the animals in the Wildlife table in order to complete the form. You can find the information you need at a website such as

Wikipedia. Using the information you find, fill in the form. The first record—Tule Elk—has been completed as an example. Place alternate names in the subform. If an alternate name cannot be found, leave the subform blank for that animal. Submit the file as directed by your instructor.

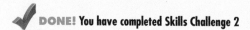 **DONE! You have completed Skills Challenge 2**

More Skills Assessment

MyITLab®
Grader

To complete this project, you will need the following files:

- Blank desktop database
- acc03_MSAResults

You will save your files as:

- Last_First_acc03_MSA
- Last_First_acc03_MSA_Backup

1. Start **Access 2016**, and then **Create** a **Desktop task management** database. **Save** the file in your **Access Chapter 3** folder as Last_First_acc03_MSA

2. Open the **Contacts** table in Datasheet view. Create a **Field Validation Rule** in the **Expression Builder** that verifies that either ND or SD is entered in the State/Province field. Compare your screen with **Figure 1**, and then click **OK** to close the **Expression Builder** dialog box.

3. Rename the **State/Province** field State and then test the field by typing MD in the **State** column. Enter the value ND in the **State** field in the first row.

4. **Save** the file as a **Back Up Database** with the file name Last_First_acc03_MSA_Backup

5. **Import** the **Racers** table from the **acc03_MSAResults** student data file, and then compare your screen to **Figure 2**.

6. **Close** the database, and then **Close** Access.

7. Submit your files as directed by your instructor.

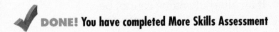
DONE! You have completed More Skills Assessment

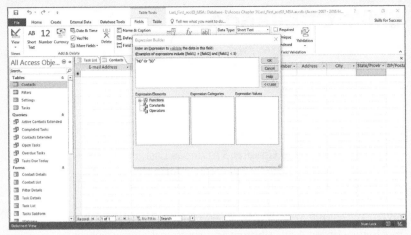

Figure 1   Access 2016, Windows 10, Microsoft Corporation

Figure 2   Access 2016, Windows 10, Microsoft Corporation

Collaborating with Google

To complete this project, you will need a Google account (refer to the Common Features chapter) and the following file:

- Blank Google form

You will save your file as:

- Last_First_acc03_GPSnip

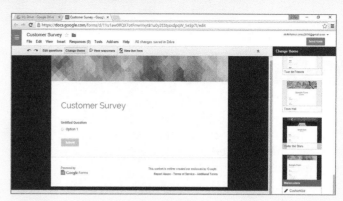

Figure 1

1. Open Google Chrome web browser. Log into your Google account, and then click the **Apps** button.

2. Click the **Drive** button to open Google Drive, and then click the **NEW** button. Click **More**, and then click **Google Forms** to open a blank form.

3. Read the message, and then click **Get started**.

4. At the top of the web page, click the **Title** label, *Untitled form*, and then rename the form Customer Survey

5. Click the **Change theme** button. In the **Change theme** pane, scroll down and click the **Watercolors** theme. Compare your screen with Figure 1, and then click the **Edit questions** button.

6. In the **Form Description** text box, type Your feedback is appreciated!

7. In the first **Question** title, add the text Overall how satisfied are you with the service you received?

8. Below the **Question Type**, click **Add Option** as needed, and then type the following text as the three answer options: Very satisfied | Satisfied | Not satisfied

9. If necessary, below the first question, click the Add item button, and then click Multiple Choice.

10. In the second question textbox, type Would you recommend our services to a friend? and then type the follow answer options: Definitely | Maybe | No

11. Click **Done**, and then at the top of the screen, click the **View live form** button. Compare your screen with Figure 2, and then return to the Google Survey tab in your browser.

12. Click the **Send form** button, and then in **Send form** via email, type AspenFallsEvents@gmail.com to send the form to a customer.

13. In the **Custom message** text box, type Please take our two question survey.

Figure 2

14. Click **Send**. If a confirmation page displays, click **OK**. Press, type snip and then press Enter to start the **Snipping Tool**. Click the **New arrow**, and then click **Window Snip**. Point to the Google Chrome window, and then when a red border displays around the window, click one time.

15. In the **Snipping Tool** mark-up window, click the **Save Snip** button. In the **Save As** dialog box, navigate to your Access Chapter 3 folder. Be sure the **Save as type** box displays **JPEG file**. Name the file Last_First_acc03_GPSnip and then press Enter. **Close** x the Snipping Tool mark-up window.

16. Click **Send**, read the message that displays, and then click **Create**. **Close** all windows, and then submit your file as directed by your instructor.

 DONE! You have completed Collaborating with Google

CHAPTER 4

Create Reports

- Access reports are designed to present information derived from tables and queries.

- You can use several methods to add fields to reports. You can then format and arrange the fields to make the information more meaningful.

- The records in reports can be grouped, sorted, and filtered to make the information more useful.

- You can build a report with fields from an entire table or fields that are selected when you run a query using the Report tool.

- To select certain fields from one or more tables, you can create a report using the Blank Report tool.

- When you need to print addresses on self-adhesive labels, you can create a labels report.

- As you work with reports, each view has a special purpose. You can modify reports in Layout view. Report view shows the report's screen version and Print Preview shows the report's printed version.

Auremar/Fotolia

Aspen Falls City Hall

In this chapter, you will create reports for Aspen Falls Utilities. You will work under the supervision of Diane Payne, Public Works Director, to build a report about water bills for city residents and create mailing labels using resident addresses. You will also build a report that provides statistics about monthly water usage.

Good reports filter and sort the data found in the database tables in a way that provides useful information. Many reports are started by first creating a query so that the query can provide the fields and criteria needed by the report. After a report is created, you can add additional grouping, sorting, and filters so that just the records and fields you need will be displayed.

Reports can be designed in Layout view, and then viewed in Report view or printed. Reports that will be printed typically need to be narrower than reports that are designed to be viewed on a computer screen. For this reason, it is a good practice to view reports in Print Layout view and then make adjustments as needed to present the report effectively on the printed page.

You will create reports using the Report Wizard, Blank Report tool, Report tool, and Labels tool. You will also format, group, sort, and filter reports to display the information more effectively. Finally, you will summarize report data by adding totals.

Introduction

Outcome

Using the skills in this chapter, you will be able to create and format reports; add totals; group, sort, and filter reports; and create label reports.

Objectives

4.1 Create reports in different database views

4.2 Devise reports that include totals, groups, and filters

4.3 Modify and format reports

4.4 Construct reports based on queries

Student data files needed for this chapter:

acc04_Water (Access)
acc04_WaterLogo (JPG)

You will save your file as:

Last_First_acc04_Water

 **SKILLS** MyITLab®
Skills 1-10 Training

At the end of this chapter you will be able to:

Skill 1   Build Queries for Reports
Skill 2   Create Reports Using the Report Tool
Skill 3   Format Reports
Skill 4   Add Totals to Reports
Skill 5   Preview and Print Reports
Skill 6   Create Reports with the Blank Report Tool
Skill 7   Group and Sort Reports
Skill 8   Modify Report Layouts
Skill 9   Filter Reports
Skill 10 Create Label Reports

MORE SKILLS

Skill 11 Change Report Sort Order and Orientation
Skill 12 Export Reports to Word
Skill 13 Save Reports as PDF Documents
Skill 14 Save Reports as Web Pages

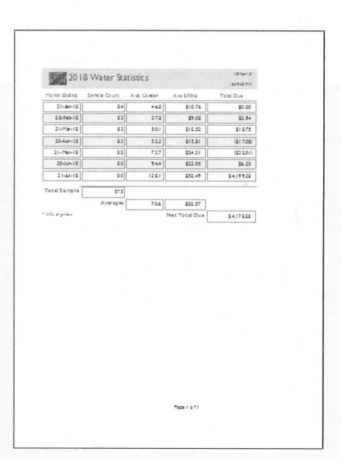

▸ Reports are often based on queries. You can create a query with fields, add criteria, and then build the report using the query as the data source.

1. Start **Access 2016**, and then open the student data file **acc04_Water**. On the **File tab**, click **Save As**. With **Save Database As** selected, click the **Save As** button. In the **Save As** dialog box, navigate to the location you are saving your files. Click **New folder**, type Access Chapter 4 and then press Enter two times. **Save** the file as Last_First_acc04_Water

2. If the Security Warning message displays, click the Enable Content button.

3. Click the **Create tab**, and then in the **Queries group**, click the **Query Wizard** button. In the **New Query** dialog box, verify that **Simple Query Wizard** is selected, and then click **OK**.

4. In the **Simple Query Wizard**, click the **Table/Queries arrow**, and then click **Table: Water Bills**.

5. Double-click the following fields to move them into **Selected Fields** in this order: **BillingDate**, **BillingID**, **Usage**, **Billing**, and **AmountDue**. Compare your screen with **Figure 1**, and then click **Finish**.

6. Click the **Home tab**, and then click the **View** button to switch to **Design view**. On the **Design tab**, in the **Show/Hide group**, click **Totals** to display the Total row. Compare your screen with **Figure 2**.

■ Continue to the next page to complete the skill ▸

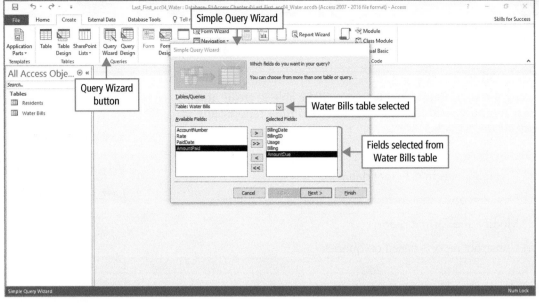

Figure 1

Access 2016, Windows 10, Microsoft Corporation

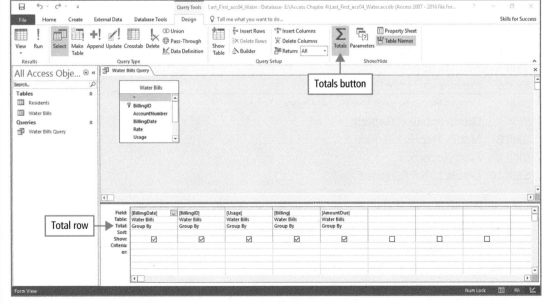

Figure 2

Access 2016, Windows 10, Microsoft Corporation

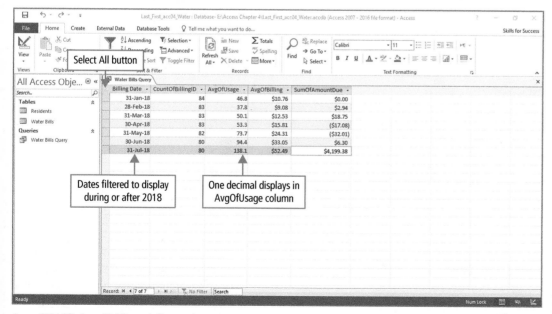

Access 2016, Windows 10, Microsoft Corporation

Figure 3

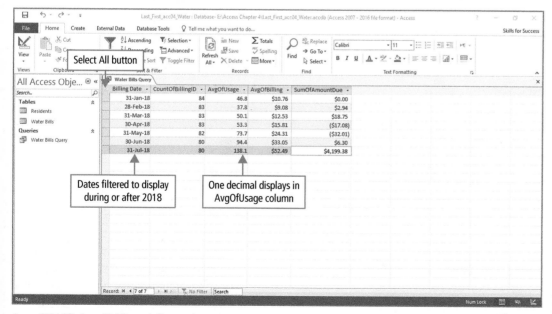

Access 2016, Windows 10, Microsoft Corporation

Figure 4

7. Click the **Total** cell for the **BillingID** column, click the arrow that displays, and then click **Count**.

8. Repeat the same technique to change the **Usage** column **Total** cell to **Avg**, the **Billing** column **Total** cell to **Avg**, and the **AmountDue** column **Total** cell to **Sum**.

9. In the **BillingDate** column **Criteria** cell, type >1/1/2018

10. Click in the **Usage** column **Criteria** cell, and then if necessary, in the Show/Hide group, click Property Sheet to open it. In the property sheet, change the **Format** to **Fixed** and the **Decimal Places** to **1**. Compare your screen with Figure 3.

11. **Close** ☒ the property sheet, and then **Run** the query.

12. In the upper left corner of the query datasheet, click the **Select All** button ☐ to select all the columns. On the **Home tab**, in the **Records group**, click the **More** button, and then click **Field Width**. In the **Column Width** dialog box, click **Best Fit**. Click a cell to deselect the columns, and then compare your screen with Figure 4.

    This query displays statistics about Aspen Falls water usage and bills for each month in 2018. This shows how a query can select the data that needs to be presented in a report.

13. Click **Save** ☐, and then **Close** ☒ the query.

■ **You have completed Skill 1 of 10**

▶ Reports can be created by selecting a table or query in the Navigation Pane and then clicking the Report button.

MOS
Obj 5.1.1

1. In the **Navigation Pane**, under **Queries**, click **Water Bills Query** one time to select it.

2. Click the **Create tab**, and then in the **Reports group**, click the **Report** button to create the report and open it in *Report Layout view*—a view that can be used to format a report while viewing the report's data.

3. Click the **Save** button 🔲. In the **Save As** dialog box, replace the suggested report name with 2018 Statistics and then click **OK**. Compare your screen with **Figure 1**.

> Access reports have three main sections: the header(s), details, and footer(s). In each section, text boxes display the data, and label controls identify the text boxes. In this report, the labels are above each column in a tabular layout.

MOS
Obj 5.3.8

4. On the **Design tab**, in the **Themes group**, click the **Themes** button, and then click the last thumbnail—**Wisp**.

5. In the **Themes group**, click the **Colors** button, and then in the **Colors** gallery, click **Marquee**.

6. In the **Themes group**, click the **Fonts** button, and then near the bottom of the **Fonts** gallery, click **Gill Sans MT**. Compare your screen with **Figure 2**.

> You can refine a theme by changing its colors to a different color theme and its fonts to a different fonts theme.

■ **Continue to the next page to complete the skill**

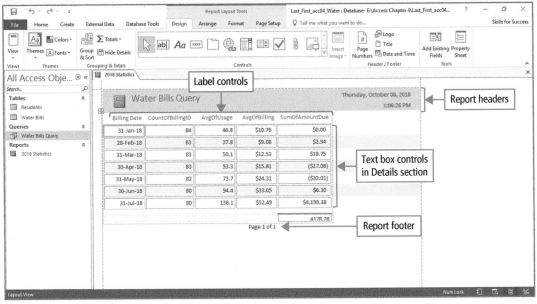

Figure 1

Access 2016, Windows 10, Microsoft Corporation

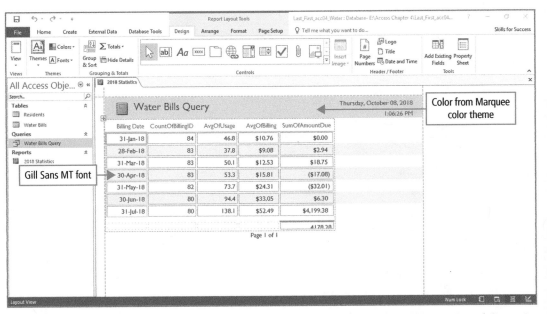

Figure 2

Access 2016, Windows 10, Microsoft Corporation

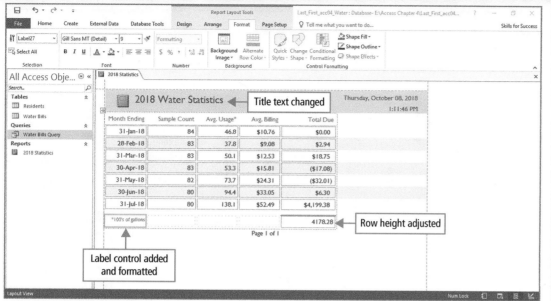

Access 2016, Windows 10, Microsoft Corporation

Figure 3

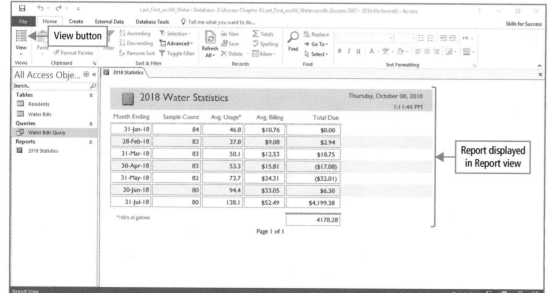

Access 2016, Windows 10, Microsoft Corporation

Figure 4

7. In the report header, double-click the title *Water Bills Query* to enter Edit mode, and then replace the text with 2018 Water Statistics

8. Double-click the **Billing Date** label control, change the label's text to Month Ending and then press Enter. Repeat this technique to change **CountOfBillingID** to Sample Count **AvgOfUsage** to Avg. Usage* **AvgOfBilling** to Avg. Billing and **SumOfAmountDue** to Total Due

9. Click the last cell—the cell with the value *4178.28*. Point to the cell's lower orange border to display the ↕ pointer, and then double-click to AutoSize the cell's height.

10. Click in the empty cell below the **Month Ending** column, and then type *100's of gallons Press Enter to complete the entry.

11. With the cell *100's of gallons selected, click the **Format tab**. In the **Font group**, click the **Font Size arrow**, and then click 9. Compare your screen with **Figure 3**.

12. Click the **Home tab**, and then in the **Views group**, click the **View button** to switch to Report view. Alternately, in the status bar, click the Report View button. Compare your screen with **Figure 4**.

  Report view is a view optimized for onscreen viewing of reports.

13. Click **Save** 🖫, and then leave the report open for the next skill.

■ **You have completed Skill 2 of 10**

▶ Report controls can be formatted using the property sheet and the commands on the Format tab.

1. With the **2018 Water Statistics** report open, on the **Home tab**, click the **View** button to switch to Layout view. Alternately, on the status bar, click the Layout View button.

2. On the **Design tab**, in the **Header / Footer group**, click the **Logo** button. In the **Insert Picture** dialog box, navigate to the student files, select **acc04_WaterLogo**, and then click **OK**.

3. Select the **Title** control, and then on the **Design tab**, in the **Tools group**, click **Property Sheet**.

4. In the property sheet **Format tab**, change the **Title** control's **Width** to 2.6" In the report header, select the **Date** control, and then in the property sheet, change its **Width** to 2.4" Compare your screen with **Figure 1**.

The Time control is in the same layout column as the Date control, so the width of both controls can be adjusted at the same time.

5. With the **Date** control still selected, click the Ribbon's **Format tab**. Change the **Font size** to 9, and then apply **Italic**.

6. In the **Font group**, click the **Format Painter** button, and then with the pointer, click the **Time** control to apply the formatting from the previous step. Compare your screen with **Figure 2**.

■ Continue to the next page to complete the skill

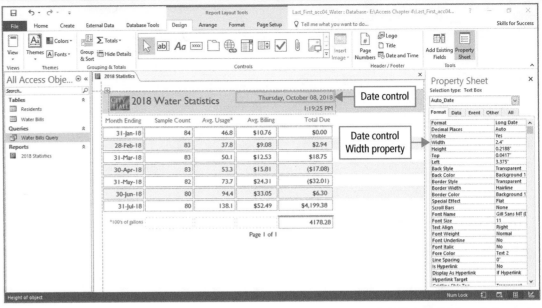

Figure 1

Access 2016, Windows 10, Microsoft Corporation

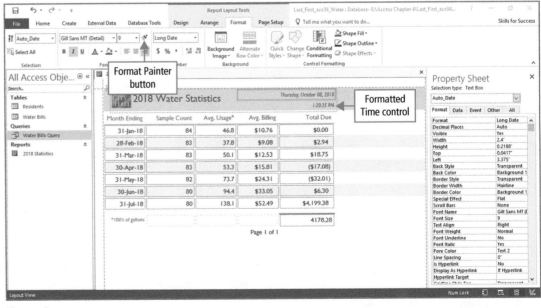

Figure 2

Access 2016, Windows 10, Microsoft Corporation

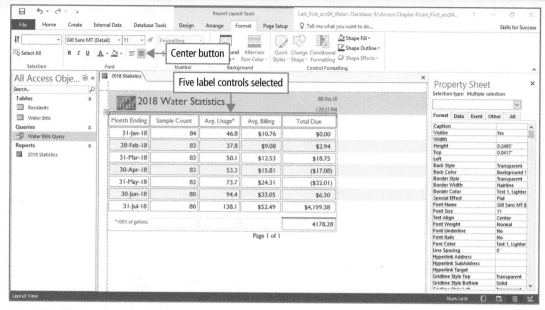

Access 2016, Windows 10, Microsoft Corporation

Figure 3

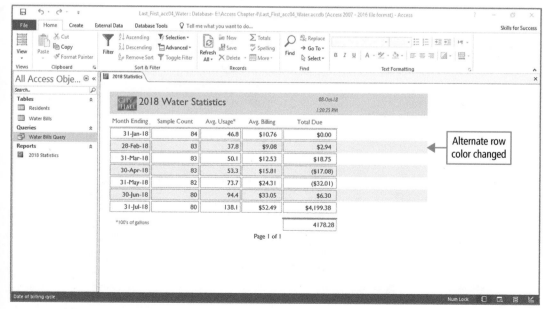

Access 2016, Windows 10, Microsoft Corporation

Figure 4

7. With the **Date** control still selected, on the Ribbon's **Format tab**, in the **Number group**, click the **Number Format arrow**, and then click **Medium Date**. Select the **Time** control, and then if necessary, change the **Number Format** to **Long Time**.

8. Above the first column, click the label control with the text *Month Ending*. Press and hold [Shift] while clicking the four other labels. Be careful not to move the mouse while clicking the left button.

9. With the five labels selected, on the **Format tab**, in the **Font group**, click the **Center** button ≡. Compare your screen with Figure 3.

10. On the **Format tab**, in the **Selection group**, click the **Selection arrow**, and then click **Detail**. On the **Format tab**, in the **Background group**, click the **Alternate Row Color arrow**, and then in the color gallery's second row, click the sixth color—**Green, Accent 2, Lighter 80%**.

    To change the color of banded rows, you need to select the ***Detail control***—the area of a report that repeats for each record in the table or query.

11. On the status bar, click the **Report View** button 🗐, and then compare your screen with Figure 4.

12. Click **Save** 🖫, and then leave the report open for the next skill.

- **You have completed Skill 3 of 10**

▶ You can add *summary statistics*—calculations for groups of data such as totals, averages, and counts—to report columns.

1. With the **2018 Water Statistics** report still open, switch to Layout view 🔲.

2. In the report's last row, click in a blank cell, and then click the **Arrange tab**. In the **Rows & Columns group**, click the **Insert Above** button two times to insert two blank rows.

3. Click in the first cell of the upper blank row just inserted, and then type Total Sample

MOS
Obj 5.3.2

4. Click a number in the **Sample Count** column to make it active, and then click the **Design tab**. In the **Grouping & Totals group**, click the **Totals** button, and then click **Sum** to add a total for the active column.

5. Click the **Sum** control just inserted, point to its lower border, and then double-click with the 🔼 pointer to AutoFit the row's height. Compare your screen with **Figure 1**.

6. Click a number in the **Avg. Usage** column to make it active. On the **Design tab**, in the **Grouping & Totals group**, click the **Totals** button, and then click **Average**. Repeat this technique to add an average for the **Avg. Billing** column. Compare your screen with **Figure 2**.

■ Continue to the next page to complete the skill

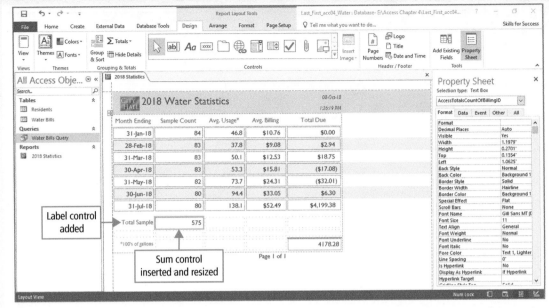

Figure 1

Access 2016, Windows 10, Microsoft Corporation

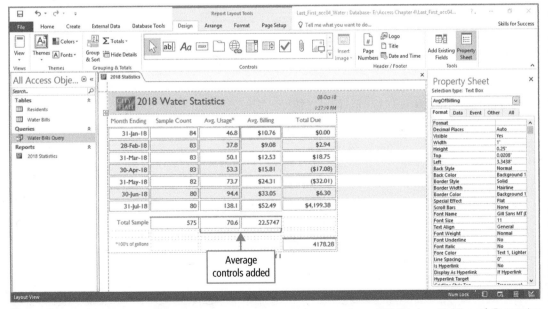

Figure 2

Access 2016, Windows 10, Microsoft Corporation

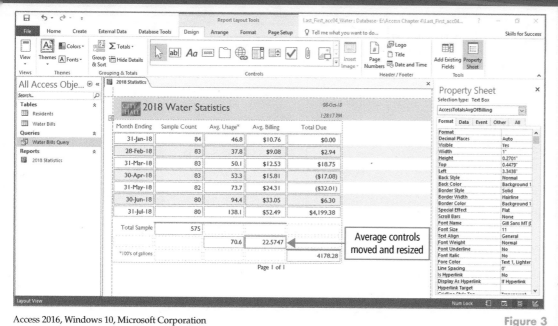

Access 2016, Windows 10, Microsoft Corporation

Figure 3

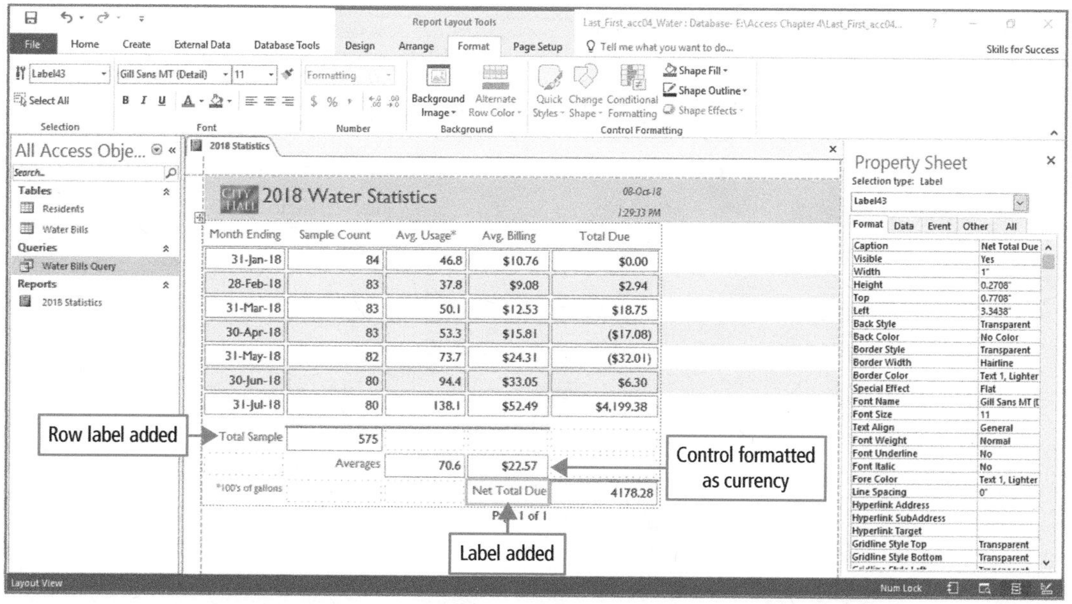

Access 2016, Windows 10, Microsoft Corporation

Figure 4

7. Point to the middle of the cell with the **Avg. Usage** column **Average** control—*70.6*. With the [+] pointer, drag the control down one cell. Repeat to move the **Average** control of the **Avg. Billing** column down one cell.

8. Point to the lower border of the selected Average control, and then double-click with the [↕] pointer to AutoFit the row's height. Compare your screen with **Figure 3**.

9. With the **Avg. Billing** column **Average** control still selected, click the Ribbon's **Format tab**, and then in in the **Number group**, click the **Apply Currency Format** button [$].

10. Click in the blank cell below the **Sample Count** column **Sum** control, and then type Averages

11. Click in the blank cell below the **Avg. Billing** column **Average** control, and then type Net Total Due Press [Enter]. Compare your screen with **Figure 4**.

12. Click **Save** [💾], and then leave the report open for the next skill.

■ **You have completed Skill 4 of 10**

▶ It is good practice to preview reports before printing them to see if they need any formatting adjustments.

1. With the **2018 Water Statistics** report still open, click the **Home tab**. In the **Views group**, click the **View arrow**, and then click **Print Preview**. If the entire page does not display, in the Zoom group, click the One Page button. Compare your screen with **Figure 1**.

    In Print Preview view, the Print Preview tab is the only Ribbon tab, and the report displays as it will print on paper. Here, the page number footer—*Page 1 of 1*—displays at the bottom of the printed page.

2. In the **Close Preview group**, click the **Close Print Preview** button to return to Layout view. If your report displays in a different view, on the status bar, click the Layout View button 🔲.

3. Click the **Format tab**. In the **Selection group**, click the **Selection arrow**, and then click **Report** to select the report and display its properties in the property sheet. If necessary, open the property sheet.

4. Near the middle of the property sheet **Format tab**, double-click the **Fit to Page** box to change the value to **No**. Change the **Width** property to 5.8" Press Enter, and then compare your screen with **Figure 2**.

    By default, a report is set to the width of a printed sheet of paper. By removing this setting, you can decrease the width of the report to fit the contents.

■ Continue to the next page to complete the skill ▶

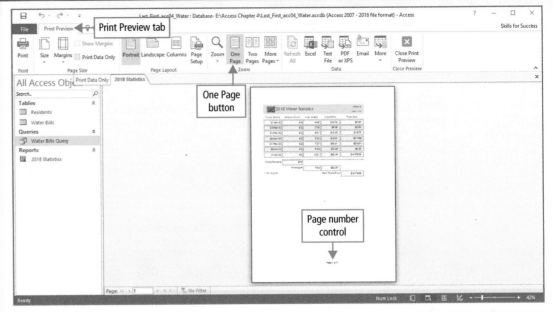

Figure 1   Access 2016, Windows 10, Microsoft Corporation

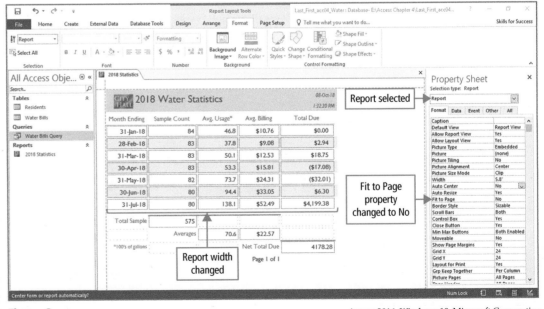

Figure 2   Access 2016, Windows 10, Microsoft Corporation

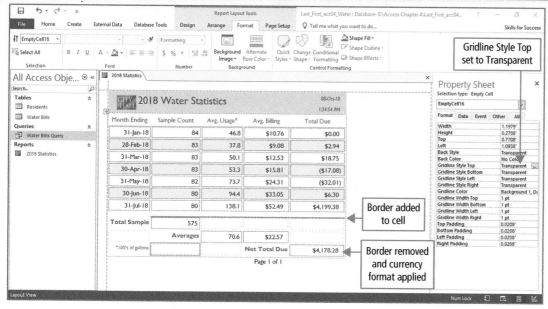

Access 2016, Windows 10, Microsoft Corporation

Figure 3

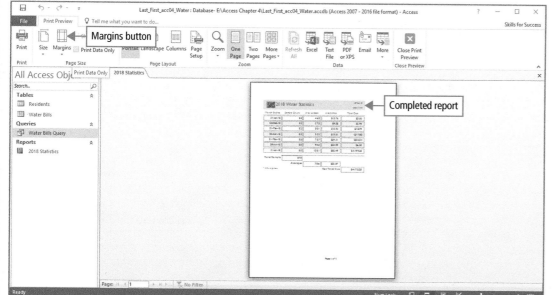

Access 2016, Windows 10, Microsoft Corporation

Figure 4

5. Below the **Month Ending** column, select the label with the text *Total Sample*. On the **Format tab**, in the **Font group**, click **Bold** B, and then click **Align Right** ☰. Double-click **Format Painter** 🖌, and then click the *Averages* and *Net Total Due* labels to apply the same formatting. Click the **Format Painter** button 🖌 so that it is no longer active.

6. Click the *Net Total Due* label control, point to its right border, and then with the ↔ pointer, double-click to AutoFit the column width.

7. Click in the first empty cell below *$4,199.38*. On the property sheet **Format tab**, double-click **Gridline Style Top** to change its value to **Solid**. Double-click **Gridline Width Top** to change its value to **2 pt**.

8. Click in the last cell—*$4,178.28*. On the property sheet **Format tab**, click **Gridline Style Top** one time, click the displayed **arrow**, and then click **Transparent**. On the **Format tab**, in the **Number group**, click **Apply Currency Format** $. Click in a blank cell in the report, and then compare your screen with **Figure 3**.

9. **Close** ✕ the property sheet. On the status bar, click the **Print Preview** button 🔍.

10. In the **Page Size group**, click the **Margins** button, and then click **Wide**. Click the **One Page** button. Compare your screen with **Figure 4**.
Obj 5.3.3

11. If you are printing this project, click **Print**, and then use the **Print** dialog box to print the report.
Obj 1.5.1

12. Click **Save** 💾, and then **Close** ✕ the report.

■ **You have completed Skill 5 of 10**

▶ The Blank Report tool is used to build a report by adding fields one at a time.

1. On the **Create tab**, in the **Reports group**, click the **Blank Report** button.

2. In the **Field List** pane, click **Show all tables**. In the **Field List**, to the left of **Residents**, click the **Expand** button ⊞.

3. In the **Field List**, double-click **AccountNumber** to add the field to the report. Compare your screen with **Figure 1**.

> As you add fields with the Blank Report tool, the other tables move to the lower sections of the Field List pane. Here, the Water Bills table is a related table because it contains the AccountNumber as a foreign key.

4. In the **Field List**, double-click **LastName** and **FirstName** to add them to the report.

5. In the **Field List**, under **Fields available in related tables**, **Expand** ⊞ the **Water Bills** table.

6. Double-click **BillingDate**, and then compare your screen with **Figure 2**.

> When you add a field from another table, that table moves to the upper pane of the Field List.

■ Continue to the next page to complete the skill ▶

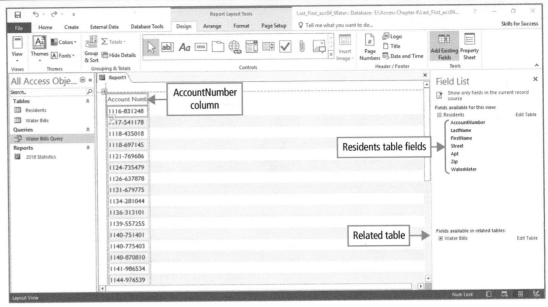

Figure 1

Access 2016, Windows 10, Microsoft Corporation

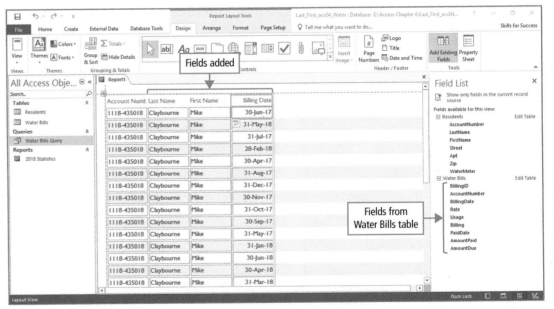

Figure 2

Access 2016, Windows 10, Microsoft Corporation

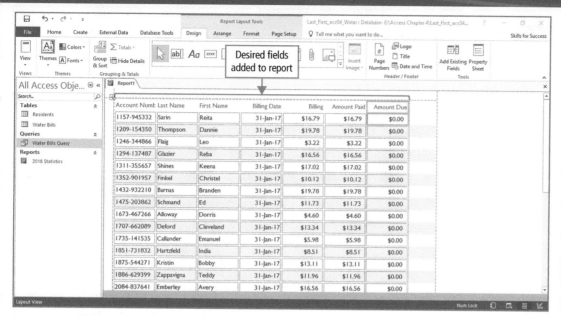

Access 2016, Windows 10, Microsoft Corporation

Figure 3

Access 2016, Windows 10, Microsoft Corporation

Figure 4

7. In the **Field List**, under **Water Bills**, double-click **Billing, AmountPaid,** and **AmountDue** to add the three fields to the report.

8. **Close** ☒ the Field List pane, and then compare your screen with **Figure 3**.

9. On the **Design tab**, in the **Header / Footer group**, click the **Logo** button. In the **Insert Picture** dialog box, navigate to the student files, select **acc04_WaterLogo,** and then click **OK** to create a report header and insert the logo.

10. In the **Header / Footer group,** click the **Title** button, type Billing History and then press Enter .

11. In the **Header / Footer group,** click the **Date and Time** button. In the **Date and Time** dialog box, under **Include Date,** select the middle option button—**dd-mmm-yy.** Under **Include Time,** click the middle option button—**hh:mm PM.** Compare your screen with **Figure 4,** and then click **OK.**

12. Click **Save** 🖫. In the **Save As** dialog box, type Billing History Report and then press Enter . Leave the report open for the next skill.

■ **You have completed Skill 6 of 10**

▶ Report data can be grouped and sorted to make the report information more useful.

▶ Reports created with the Blank Report tool lay out controls in a table. You can position controls by dragging them into other cells, and you can format text controls by selecting the cell's location.

1. If necessary, open the *Billing History Report* in Layout view. On the **Design tab**, in the **Grouping & Totals group**, click the **Group & Sort** button as needed to display the **Group, Sort, and Total** pane.

2. In the **Group, Sort, and Total** pane, click the **Add a group** button. In the list of fields, click **AccountNumber** to group the billings within each account.

3. In the report, click **Account Number** to select the label. Point to the right border, and then with the ⬍ pointer, double-click to AutoFit the label width. Compare your screen with **Figure 1**.

4. Click the first text box control with the text *Claybourne*, and then, with the ▯ pointer, drag the control into the empty cell below the *Last Name* label.

5. Repeat this technique to move the control with the text *Mike* into the empty cell below the *First Name* label. Compare your screen with **Figure 2**.

> The resident names do not change within each group of account numbers, so they can be in the same row as the Account Number. As a result, the names are not repeated in each billing row.

■ **Continue to the next page to complete the skill**

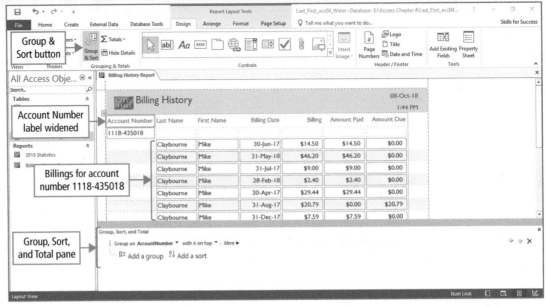

Figure 1

Access 2016, Windows 10, Microsoft Corporation

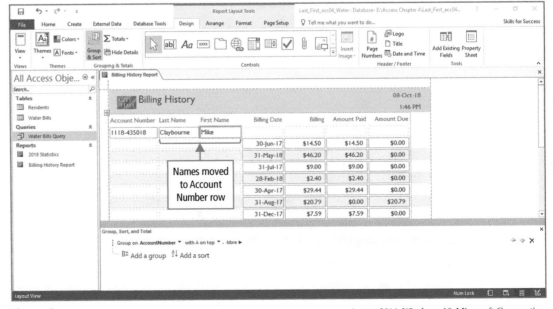

Figure 2

Access 2016, Windows 10, Microsoft Corporation

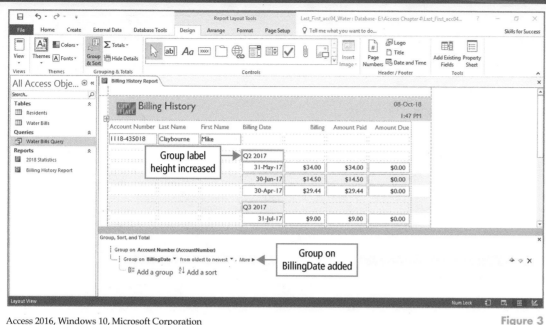

Access 2016, Windows 10, Microsoft Corporation

Figure 3

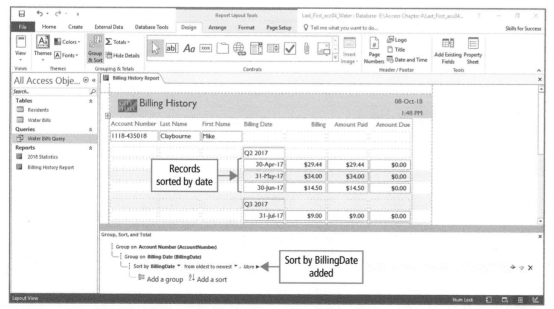

Access 2016, Windows 10, Microsoft Corporation

Figure 4

6. In the **Group, Sort, and Total** pane, click the **Add a group** button, and then in the list of fields, click **BillingDate** to group the Billing Cycles by quarter.

7. Click the first quarter label with the text *Q2 2017*. Point to the lower border, and then with the ⬍ pointer, double-click to AutoFit the row height. Compare your screen with **Figure 3**.

   Fields that contain dates can be grouped by several time intervals including days, months, quarters, and years. By default, they are grouped into yearly quarters with the oldest quarters displayed first.

8. In the **Group, Sort, and Total** pane, click the **Add a sort** button, and then in the list of fields, click **BillingDate** to sort by month within each yearly quarter. Compare your screen with **Figure 4**.

MOS
Obj 5.2.

9. On the **Design tab**, in the **Grouping & Totals group**, click the **Group & Sort** button to close the pane.

10. **Save** 💾 the report, and then leave it open for the next skill.

■ **You have completed Skill 7 of 10**

▶ **WATCH** SKILL 4.8

▶ In a tabular layout, you can insert and delete rows and columns and then move controls so that they better communicate the report's information.

1. If necessary, open the *Billing History Report* in Layout view. Point to the cell with the text *Q2 2017*. With the pointer, drag the control into the first empty cell below the cell with the text *Claybourne*.

2. Click in the first **Billing Date** cell with the text *30-Apr-17*. Press and hold Shift while clicking the **Amount Due** cell in the same row. Compare your screen with **Figure 1**.

MOS
Obj 5.3.1

3. With the four cells selected, point to the cell with the text *30-Apr-17*, and then drag the cell into the empty cell below the **Q2 2017** control. Compare your screen with **Figure 2**.

4. Below the report header, click the **Billing Date** label, and then press Delete to remove the label from the report.

5. Repeat the techniques practiced in this skill to move the **Billing** label to the empty cell to the right of the **Q2 2017** control.

6. Move the **Amount Paid** label to the empty cell to the right of the **Billing** label.

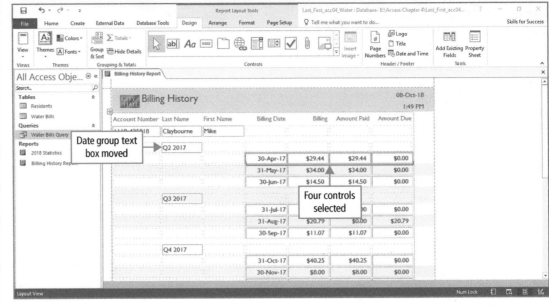

Figure 1

Access 2016, Windows 10, Microsoft Corporation

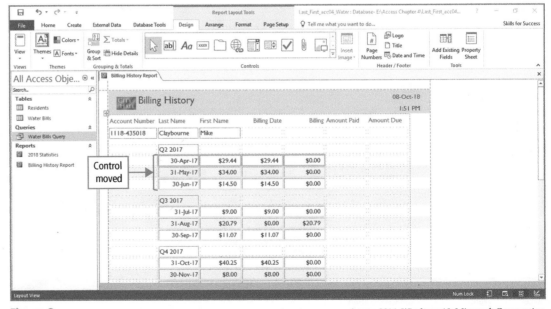

■ **Continue to the next page to complete the skill**

Figure 2

Access 2016, Windows 10, Microsoft Corporation

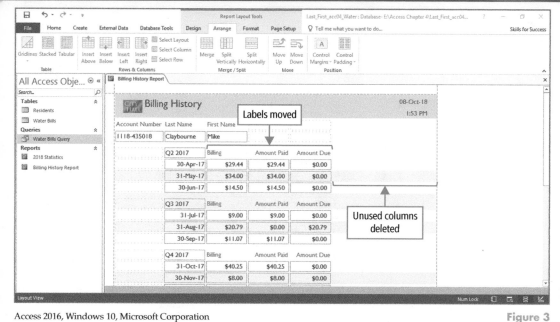

Access 2016, Windows 10, Microsoft Corporation

Figure 3

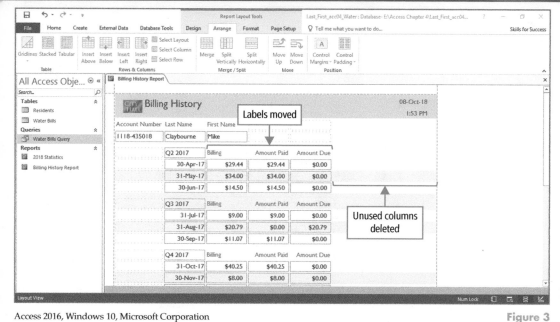

Access 2016, Windows 10, Microsoft Corporation

Figure 4

7. Move the **Amount Due** label to the empty cell to the right of the **Amount Paid** label.

8. Click in one of the blank columns on the right side of the report. Click the **Arrange tab**, and then in the **Rows & Columns group**, click **Select Column**. Press `Delete` to remove the column from the report. Repeat to this technique to delete the other blank column, and then compare your screen with **Figure 3**.

9. Use the Shift-click technique to select these labels: **Billing**, **Amount Paid**, and **Amount Due**. Click the **Format tab**, and then in the **Font group**, click the **Center** button ☰.

10. Click in any cell below the **Billing** label to make the column active. Click the **Design tab**. In the **Grouping & Totals group**, click the **Totals** button, and then click **Sum** to add a summary statistic for each quarter.

11. Repeat the technique just practiced to insert the **Sum** total to the **Amount Paid** and **Amount Due** columns.

12. Click one of the cells with a Sum control that was inserted in the previous step. Point to the lower border, and then with the ↕ pointer, double-click to AutoFit the row's height. Compare your screen with **Figure 4**.

13. Click **Save** 🖫, and then leave the report open for the next skill.

■ **You have completed Skill 8 of 10**

▶ WATCH SKILL 4.9

▶ Reports can be filtered in a variety of ways so that you can view just the information you need.

1. With the **Billing Report** open in Layout view, switch to Report view 🔲.

2. Click in the text box with the last name *Claybourne*. Click the **Home tab**. In the **Sort & Filter group**, click the **Filter** button. In the **Filter** list, point to **Text Filters**, and then click **Equals**.

3. In the **Custom Filter** dialog box, type *swickard* and then click **OK**. Compare your screen with **Figure 1**.

   When you apply a filter, only the subset of records that match the filter criteria display and the Toggle Filter button is active. Here, only the billing history for Evie Swickard displays.

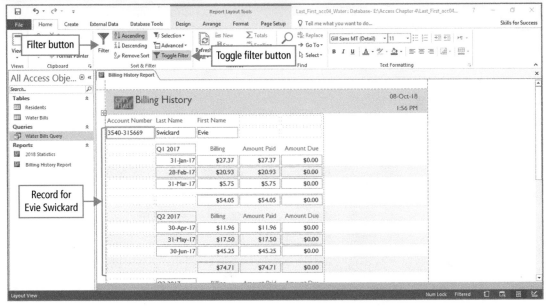

Figure 1

Access 2016, Windows 10, Microsoft Corporation

4. In the report, click in a control that displays a **Billing Date** value. On the **Home tab**, in the **Sort & Filter group**, click the **Filter** button. In the **Filter** list, point to **Date Filters**, and then click **Between**.

5. In the **Between Dates** dialog box, in the **Oldest** box, type 7/1/17 In the **Newest** box, type 9/30/17 Click **OK**, and then compare your screen with **Figure 2**.

   When you add filters, the previous filters remain in effect. Here, only the records for Evie Swickard in the third quarter of 2017 display. At the end of this report, three rows of totals display: one for the quarter, the account number, and the entire report.

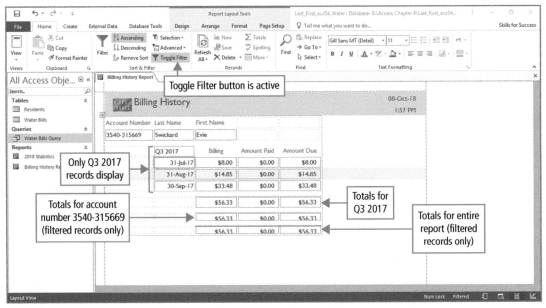

Figure 2

Access 2016, Windows 10, Microsoft Corporation

■ Continue to the next page to complete the skill ▶

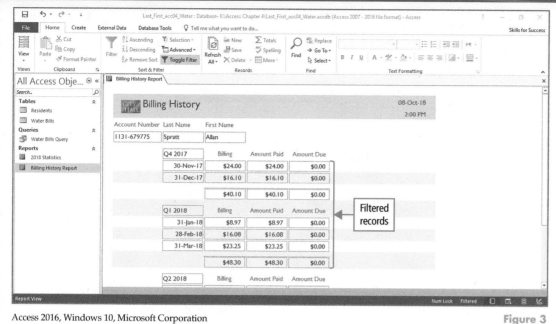

Access 2016, Windows 10, Microsoft Corporation

Figure 3

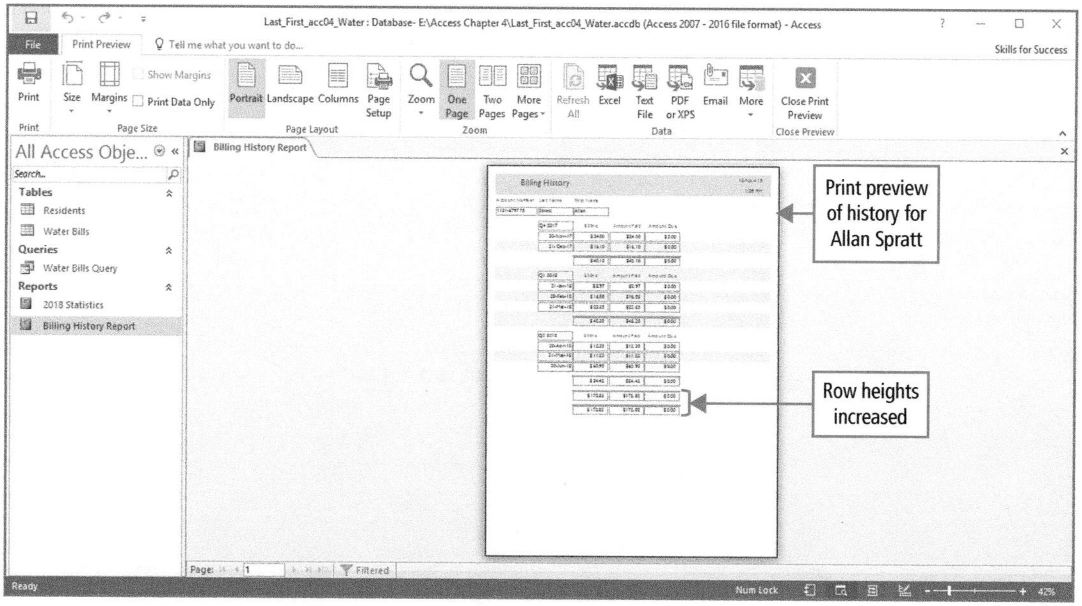

6. **Save** 🖫, and then **Close** ✕ the report. In the **Navigation Pane**, double-click **Billing History Report** to open it in Report view. In the **Sort & Filter group**, click the **Toggle Filter** button to reapply the filter previously created.

> By default, any filters saved in a report are not active when you open the report.

7. In the **Sort & Filter group**, click **Advanced**, and then click **Clear All Filters**.

> The Clear All Filters command removes all filters from the report. Once the filter is cleared, it can no longer be enabled by clicking the Toggle Filter button.

8. Scroll down to the second account to display the history for *Allan Spratt*. Click in the text box with the text *Spratt*. On the **Home tab**, in the **Sort & Filter group**, click the **Selection** button, and then click **Equals "Spratt"**. Compare your screen with **Figure 3**.

9. On the status bar, click the **Layout View** button 🖳. Using the technique practiced previously, AutoFit the height of the last two rows—the rows with the Sum controls.

10. On the status bar, click the **Print Preview** button 🔍. If necessary, in the Zoom group, click One Page to display the entire page, and then compare your screen with **Figure 4**.

11. If you are printing your work, print the report.

12. Click **Save** 🖫, and then **Close** ✕ the report.

■ **You have completed Skill 9 of 10**

Access 2016, Windows 10, Microsoft Corporation

Figure 4

▶ A *label report* is a report formatted so that the data can be printed on a sheet of labels.

1. In the **Navigation Pane**, under **Tables**, click **Residents** one time to select the table.

2. On the **Create tab**, in the **Reports group**, click the **Labels** button.

MOS
Obj 5.1.3

3. In the **Label Wizard**, be sure that the **Filter by manufacturer** box displays the text **Avery**. Under **What label size would you like**, select the label size where **Product number** is **C2160**, as shown in **Figure 1**.

   Each manufacturer identifies its label sheets using a product number. Access formats the report to match the dimensions of the selected sheet size.

4. Click **Next**. If necessary, change the **Font name** to Arial, and the **Font weight** to Light. Change the **Font size** to **10**.

5. Click **Next**. Under **Available fields**, click **FirstName**, and then click the **Add Field** button ▸ to add the field to the **Prototype label**.

6. With the insertion point in the **Prototype label** and to the right of *{FirstName}*, add a space, and then **Add Field** ▸ the **LastName** field into the first line of the **Prototype label**.

7. Press Enter, and then **Add Field** ▸ the **Street** field into the second line of the **Prototype label**. Compare your screen with **Figure 2**.

■ Continue to the next page to complete the skill ▶

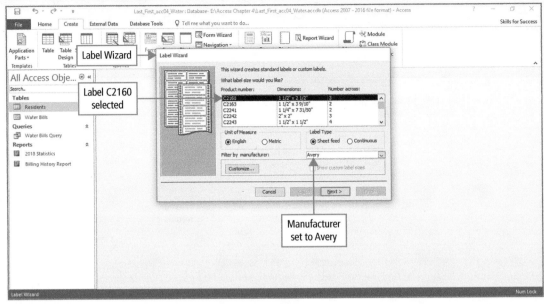

Figure 1   Access 2016, Windows 10, Microsoft Corporation

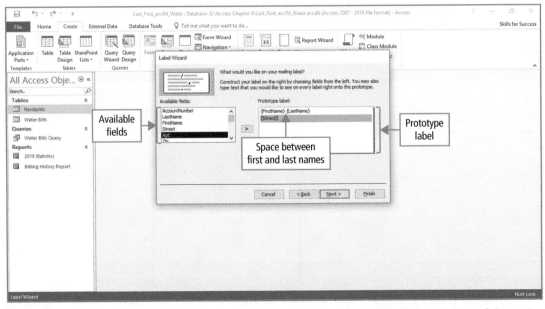

Figure 2   Access 2016, Windows 10, Microsoft Corporation

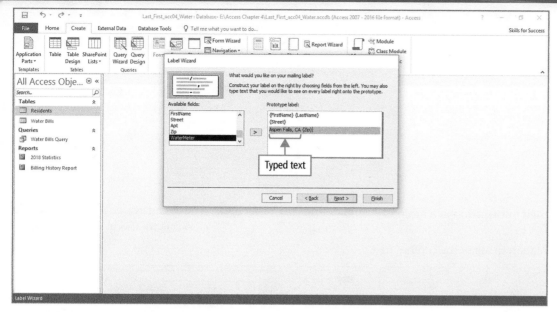

Access 2016, Windows 10, Microsoft Corporation

Figure 3

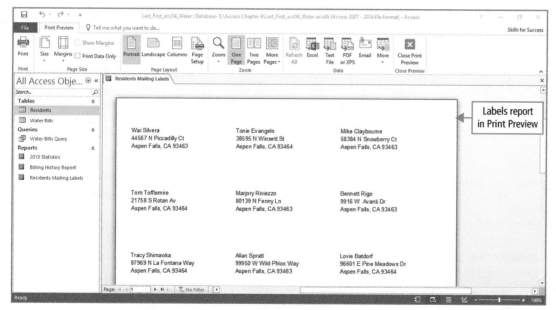

Access 2016, Windows 10, Microsoft Corporation

Figure 4

8. Press `Enter`, and then type Aspen Falls, CA Add a space, and then **Add Field** `>` the **Zip** field. Compare your screen with Figure 3.

> You can create labels using a combination of typed characters and fields from a table or query.

9. Click **Next** two times. Under **What name would you like for your report**, replace the existing name with Residents Mailing Labels

10. Click **Finish** to open the report in Print Preview. Compare your screen with Figure 4.

11. If you are printing your work for this project, print the first page of labels by setting the **From** and **To** values in the **Print** dialog box to *1*.

> When printing a label report, your printer may require additional steps. Most printers will not print until a sheet of labels or sheet of paper is placed in the manual feed tray. If you are working in a computer lab, check with your lab technician or instructor for what is required in your situation.

12. **Close** ⊠ the report, and then **Close** ⊠ Access. Submit your file as directed by your instructor.

 DONE! You have completed Skill 10 of 10, and your file is complete!

More Skills 11

Change Report Sort Order and Orientation

To complete this project, you will need the following file:

- acc04_MS11Results

You will save your files as:

- Last_First_acc04_MS11Results
- Last_First_acc04_MS11Snip

▶ You can change the sort order of a report to present information in a more meaningful manner.

▶ Reports can be set to landscape or portrait orientation to allow the content to fit within the report page margins.

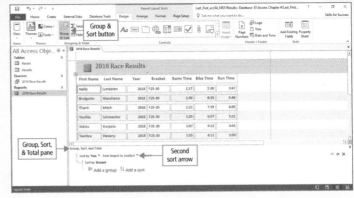

Figure 1   Access 2016, Windows 10, Microsoft Corporation

1. Start **Access 2016**, and then open the student data file **acc04_MS11Results**. **Save** the file in your **Access Chapter 4** folder as Last_First_acc04_MS11Results If necessary, enable the content.

2. Open the **2018 Race Results** report in Layout view. If necessary, on the **Design tab**, in the **Grouping & Totals group**, click the **Group & Sort** button to view the report's current sorting method.

MOS
Obj 5.3.6

3. In the **Group, Sort, and Totals** pane, click the second arrow, and then click **from largest to smallest**. Compare your screen with **Figure 1**.

4. Click **Add a sort**, and then click **Bracket**.

    The report is now sorted by date, with a secondary sort based on the racer's bracket.

MOS
Obj 5.3.5

5. Switch to Print Preview. In the **Page Layout group**, click **Landscape**. Read the message, and then click **OK**.

6. In the **Zoom group**, click the **One Page** button to view the report in landscape orientation.

    The report does not fit properly in landscape orientation. There is too much blank space on the right side of the report.

7. Press , type snip and then press Enter to start the Snipping Tool. Click the **New arrow**, and then click **Window Snip**. Point to the Access window, and when a red border displays around the window, click one time.

8. In the **Snipping Tool** window, click the **Save Snip** button 💾. In the **Save As** dialog box, navigate to your Access Chapter 4 folder. Be sure the **Save as**

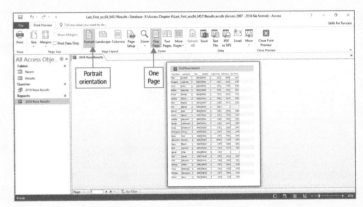

Figure 2   Access 2016, Windows 10, Microsoft Corporation

type box displays **JPEG file**. Name the file Last_First_acc04_MS11Snip and then press Enter . **Close** ✕ the Snipping Tool mark-up window.

9. Click the **Portrait** button to return the report to portrait orientation. Compare your screen with **Figure 2**.

10. **Save**, and then **Close** ✕ the report.

11. **Close** ✕ Access. Submit the files as directed by your instructor.

■ **You have completed More Skills 11**

More Skills 12

Export Reports to Word

To complete this project, you will need the following file:

- acc04_MS12Reservations

You will save your file as:

- Last_First_acc04_MS12Reservations (Word)

▶ You can export reports to other file formats so that you can work with the data in other applications.

▶ When you export a report to Word, the report is saved as a ***Rich Text Format file***—a document file format designed to work with many different types of programs.

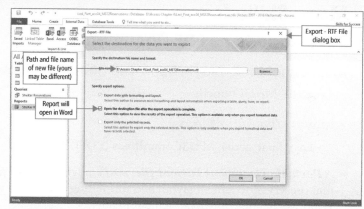

Access 2016, Windows 10, Microsoft Corporation   Figure 1

1. Start **Access 2016**, and then open the student data file **acc04_ MS12Reservations**. If necessary, enable the content.

2. In the **Navigation Pane**, right-click **Shelter Reservations Report**, and then click **Print Preview**. If necessary, set the Zoom to **Zoom 100%**.

3. **Close** ☒ the report. In the **Navigation Pane**, be sure that **Shelter Reservations Report** is selected.

4. On the **External Data tab**, in the **Export group**, click the **More** button, and then click **Word**.

5. In the **Export - RTF File** dialog box, click the **Browse** button. In the **File Save** dialog box, open your **Access Chapter 4** folder. In the **File name** box, type Last_First_acc04_MS12Reservations and then click **Save**.

6. Select the **Open the destination file after the export operation is complete** check box. Compare your screen with **Figure 1**.

    Rich Text Format is often referred to as ***RTF***.

7. Click **OK**. Wait a few moments for the report to open in Word. In the **Word** window, click the **File tab**, and then click **Print**. Compare your screen with **Figure 2**.

    When you open an RTF file in Word 2013, it opens in ***Compatibility mode***—a mode that limits formatting and features to those supported in earlier versions of Office.

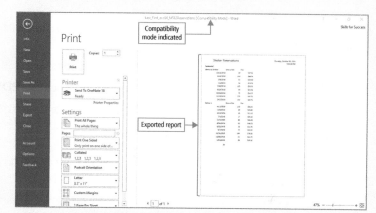

Access 2016, Windows 10, Microsoft Corporation   Figure 2

8. If you are printing this project, print the Word document.

9. **Close** ☒ Word. In Access, in the **Export - RTF File** dialog box, click the **Save export steps** checkbox, and then click **Save Export**.

10. **Close** ☒ Access, and then submit the file as directed by your instructor.

■ **You have completed More Skills 12**

More Skills 13

Save Reports as PDF Documents

To complete this project, you will need the following file:

- acc04_MS13Councils

You will save your file as:

- Last_First_acc04_MS13Committees (PDF)

▶ A *Portable Document Format file*, also known as a *PDF file*, is a file format that preserves document layout and formatting and can be viewed in Word, Windows Reader, or Adobe Acrobat Reader.

---

1. Start **Access 2016**, and then open the student data file **acc04_MS13Councils**. If necessary, enable the content.

2. In the **Navigation Pane**, click the **Committee List** report.

MOS
Obj 1.5.4

3. On the **External Data tab**, in the **Export group**, click the **PDF or XPS** button.

4. In the **Publish as PDF or XPS** dialog box, navigate to your Access Chapter 4 folder. In the **File name** box, type Last_First_acc04_MS13Committees Compare your screen with **Figure 1**.

5. If necessary, select the **Open file after publishing** check box, and then to the right of **Optimize for**, select the **Standard** option button.

> When you export a report as a PDF file, it is a good idea to open it in a PDF reader application to verify the report looks as intended. The Standard option provides the best quality, but the file size may be larger than when the Minimum size option is used.

6. Click **Publish**, and then wait a few moments for the report to open in your computer's default reader application.

7. **Close** the PDF file. In Access, in the **Export - PDF** dialog box, click the **Save export steps** checkbox, and then click **Save Export**.

8. **Close** ⊠ Access, and then submit the file as directed by your instructor.

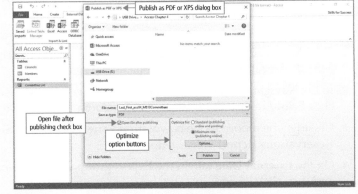

Figure 1   Access 2016, Windows 10, Microsoft Corporation

- **You have completed More Skills 13**

More Skills 14

Save Reports as Web Pages

To complete this project, you will need the following file:

- acc04_MS14Rosters

You will save your files as:

- Last_First_acc04_MS14Rosters (Access)
- Last_First_acc04_MS14Rosters (HTML file)

▶ You can export reports so that they can be opened in a web browser.

▶ A *Hypertext Markup Language document* (*HTML document*) is a text file with instructions for displaying its content in a web browser.

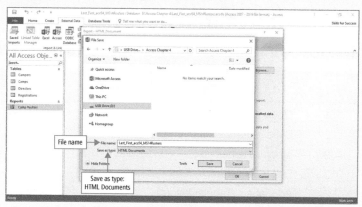

Access 2016, Windows 10, Microsoft Corporation

Figure 1

---

1. Start **Access 2016**, and then open the student data file **acc04_MS14Rosters**. **Save** the file in your **Access Chapter 4** folder as Last_First_acc04_MS14Rosters If necessary, enable the content.

2. In the **Navigation Pane**, select the **Camp Rosters** report.

3. On the **External Data tab**, in the **Export group**, click the **More** button, and then click **HTML Document**.

4. In the **Export - HTML Document** dialog box, click the **Browse** button. In the **File Save** dialog box, navigate to your Access Chapter 4 folder. In the **File name** box, type Last_First_acc04_MS14Rosters Compare your screen with Figure 1, and then click **Save**.

5. Select the **Open the destination file after the export operation is complete** check box.

6. Click **OK**. In the **HTML Output Options** dialog box, under **Choose the encoding to use for saving this file**, select the **Unicode (UTF-8)** option button, and then compare your screen with Figure 2. Click **OK**. Wait a few moments for the report to open in your web browser.

    Unicode (UTF-8) is a system for representing a large variety of text characters and symbols. It is used often in HTML documents.

7. If you are printing this project, print the web page. **Close** ⊠ the web browser window.

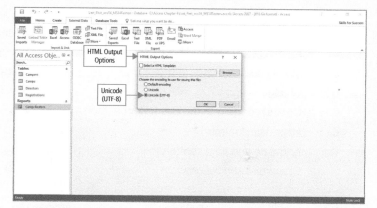

Access 2016, Windows 10, Microsoft Corporation

Figure 2

8. In Access, in the **Export - HTML Document** dialog box, select the **Save export steps**, and then click **Save Export**.

9. **Close** ⊠ Access, and then submit the files as directed by your instructor.

■ **You have completed More Skills 14**

Chapter Summary

The following table summarizes the **SKILLS AND PROCEDURES** covered in this chapter.

Skills Number	Task	Step
1	Open the property sheet	Design tab → Tools group → Property Sheet
2	Build reports from queries	With the query selected in the Navigation Pane, Create tab → Reports group → Report
2	Modify themes	Design tab → Themes group → Colors or Fonts
2	Edit label text	Double-click the label control to enter Edit mode
2	Add labels (Tabular layout)	Click in a blank table cell. Type the label text.
3	Format labels and text boxes	With the control selected, Format tab → Font group
3	Insert logos	Design tab → Header / Footer group → Logo
3	Select a specific control	Format tab → Selection group → Selection arrow
3	Change alternate row colors	Select Detail control, and then Format tab → Background group → Alternate Row Color
4	Change number formats	Format tab → Number group → Number Format arrow
4	Add totals to reports	Click in column, and then Design tab → Grouping & Totals group → Totals
4	AutoFit labels and text boxes	With the control selected, double-click a selection border
5	Modify cell borders	In the property sheet, on the Format tab, change Gridline Style properties
5	Change margins	Print Preview tab → Page Size group → Margins
6	Create reports with the Blank Report Tool	Create tab → Reports group → Blank Report. In the Field List, double-click or drag to add fields to the report.
6	Insert title controls	Design tab → Header / Footer group → Title
6	Add date and time controls	Design tab → Header / Footer group → Date and Time
7	Group and sort reports	Design tab → Grouping & Totals group → Group & Sort → Group, Sort, and Total pane → Add a group or Add a sort
8	Delete rows and columns	Arrange tab → Rows & Columns group → Select Column or Select Row → press Delete
9	Apply custom text and date filters	With field selected, Home tab → Sort & Filter group → Filter button → Text Filters or Date Filters
9	Remove filters	Home tab → Sort & Filter group → Advanced → Clear All Filters
9	Toggle filter on	Home tab → Sort & Filter group → Toggle Filter
9	Filter by selection	Click in field with desired value, Home tab → Sort & Filter group → Selection
10	Create label reports	Create tab → Reports group → Labels
MS11	Change sort order	Design tab → Grouping & Totals group → Group & Sort → Group, Sort, and Total Pane → Sort arrow
MS11	Change orientation	Print Preview → Page Layout group → select orientation
MS12	Export report to Word	External Data tab → Export group → More button → Word
MS13	Export report to PDF	External Data tab → Export group → PDF or XPS button
MS14	Export report to HTML	External Data tab → Export group → More button → HTML document

Project Summary Chart

Project	Project Type	Project Location
Skills Review	Review	In Book & MIL MyITLab Grader
Skills Assessment 1	Review	In Book & MIL MyITLab Grader
Skills Assessment 2	Review	Book
My Skills	Problem Solving	Book
Visual Skills Check	Problem Solving	Book
Skills Challenge 1	Critical Thinking	Book
Skills Challenge 2	Critical Thinking	Book
More Skills Assessment	Review	In Book & MIL MyITLab Grader
Collaborating with Google	Critical Thinking	Book

MOS Objectives Covered (Quiz in MyITLab)

1.5.1 Print reports	5.3.1 Format reports into multiple columns
1.5.3 Save a database as a template	5.3.2 Add calculated fields
1.5.4 Export objects to alternative formats	5.3.3 Control report positioning
5.1.1 Create a report	5.3.4 Format report elements
5.1.3 Create a report by using a wizard	5.3.5 Change report orientation
5.2.1 Group and sort fields	5.3.6 Insert header and footer information
5.2.3 Add report controls	5.3.7 Insert images
5.2.4 Add and modify labels	5.3.8 Apply a theme

Key Terms

BizSkills
Video

1. What are some examples of good e-mail etiquette?

2. What are some things to avoid when e-mailing co-workers?

Online Help Skills

1. Start **Access 2016**, and then in the upper right corner of the start page, click the **Help** button .

2. In the **Access Help** window **Search help** box, type conditional formatting and then press ⌗Enter⌗.

3. In the search result list, click **Introduction to reports in Access**. Scroll down the article and click **Highlight data with conditional formatting**, **Maximize** the Help window, and then compare your screen with **Figure 1**.

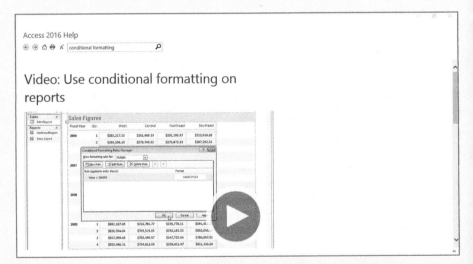

Figure 1   Access 2016, Windows 10, Microsoft Corporation

4. Read the article to answer the following question: How does adding conditional formatting add meaning to report data?

Matching

Match each term in the second column with its correct definition in the first column by writing the letter of the term on the blank line in front of the correct definition.

____ **1.** To change a theme, Colors theme, or Fonts theme, use this tab.

____ **2.** The Font group is located on this tab.

____ **3.** This is used when you want to build a report by adding fields one at a time or arrange them in a different layout.

____ **4.** A small picture that can be added to a report header, typically to the left of the title.

____ **5.** To set the width of a report control to a precise dimension in Layout view, this pane can be used.

____ **6.** An area at the beginning of a report that contains labels, text boxes, and other controls.

____ **7.** The Format Painter button can be found in this group.

____ **8.** To change the alternate row color, this report control should be selected.

____ **9.** To display a subset of records on a report that matches a given criterion.

____ **10.** This button creates and applies a filter automatically using the value in the active field.

A Blank Report tool

B Design

C Detail

D Filter

E Font

F Format

G Logo

H Property sheet

I Report header

J Selection

Multiple Choice

Choose the correct answer.

1. A tool that can create a report with a single click.
   - A. Blank Report tool
   - B. Report tool
   - C. Report Wizard

2. The method used to edit text in a label control in Layout view.
   - A. Double-click the control
   - B. Right-click the control, then click Edit
   - C. Click the control, and then on the Design tab, click Edit

3. A method used to add a label control in Layout view.
   - A. On the Design tab, in the Controls group, click Text Box
   - B. Click in an empty cell and type the label text
   - C. On the Insert tab, in the Labels group, click Add

4. This pane is used to add fields to a report in Layout view.
   - A. Add Fields
   - B. Blank Report
   - C. Field List

5. Buttons to insert logo, title, and date and time controls are found in this group on the Design tab.
   - A. Controls
   - B. Header / Footer
   - C. Tools

6. This pane is used to group and sort reports.
   - A. Group pane
   - B. Group and Sort pane
   - C. Group, Sort, and Total pane

7. To delete a report column in Layout view, this method can be used.
   - A. Click in the row, and then press Delete
   - B. Click in the column, and then on the Arrange tab, click Delete Column
   - C. Click in the column. On the Arrange tab, click Select Column, and then press Delete

8. To apply a custom filter, this method can be used.
   - A. Click in the field, and then on the Home tab, click the Filter button
   - B. Click in the field, and then on the Home tab, click the Custom button
   - C. Click in the field, and then on the Home tab, click the Selection button

9. When a report is closed that has a filter applied, the following describes what happens when the report is opened the next time.
   - A. The filter created previously was deleted
   - B. The filter was saved, but it is not enabled
   - C. The filter was saved, and it is enabled

10. A report formatted so that the data can be printed on a sheet of labels.
    - A. Label report
    - B. Mail report
    - C. Merge report

Topics for Discussion

1. You have created reports using two different methods: the Report tool and the Blank Report tool. Which method do you prefer, and why? What are the primary advantages of each method?

2. You have filtered reports using two different methods: One method added criteria to a query and then built the report from the query. The other method added filters after the report was finished. Which method do you prefer, and why? What are the primary advantages of each method?

Skills Review

MyITLab®
Grader

To complete this project, you will need the following files:

- acc04_SRElectricity (Access)
- acc04_SRLogo (JPG)

You will save your file as:

- Last_First_acc04_SRElectricity

1. Start **Access 2016**, and then open the student data file **acc04_SRElectricity**. **Save** the file in your **Access Chapter 4** folder as Last_First_acc04_SRElectricity If necessary, enable the content.

2. Click the **Create tab**, and then in the **Reports group**, click **Blank Report**. In the **Field List**, click **Show all tables**, and then expand the **Residents** table. Double-click to add these fields in the following order: **Account**, **LastName**, and **FirstName**.

3. In the **Field List**, expand the **Billing Cycles** table, and then double-click **CycleDate** and **Usage** to add them to the report.

4. Click **Save**, type Resident Usage Report and then click **OK**. **Close** the Field List, and then compare your screen with **Figure 1**.

5. On the **Design tab**, in the **Header / Footer group**, click **Title**, type Electricity Usage by Resident and then press Enter.

6. On the **Design tab**, in the **Grouping & Totals group**, click **Group & Sort**. In the **Group, Sort, and Total** pane, click **Add a group**, and then click **Account**. **Close** the Group, Sort, and Total pane.

7. Drag the field with the value *Claybourne* into the blank cell below the **Last Name** label. Drag the field with the value *Mike* into the blank cell below the **First Name** label.

8. Click the field displaying **Account** *1118-435018*, and then click the **Home tab**. In the **Sort & Filter group**, click **Selection**, and then click **Equals "1118-435018"**.

9. On the **Design tab**, in the **Views group**, click the **View arrow**, and then click **Print Preview**. Compare your screen with **Figure 2**. If you are printing this project, print the report. Click **Save**, **Close Print Preview**, and then **Close** the report.

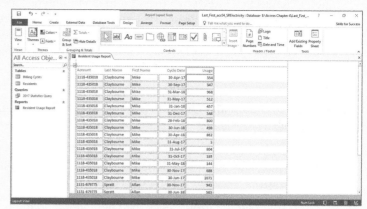

Access 2016, Windows 10, Microsoft Corporation

Figure 1

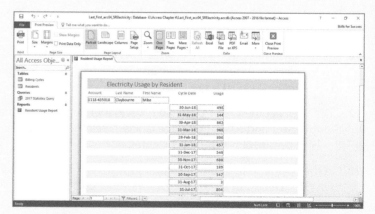

Access 2016, Windows 10, Microsoft Corporation

Figure 2

10. In the **Navigation Pane**, select the **Residents** table. Click the **Create tab**, and then in the **Reports group**, click the **Labels** button.

■ Continue to the next page to complete this Skills Review

11. In the **Label Wizard**, verify **Avery C2160** is selected, and then click **Next** two times. Double-click **FirstName** to add it to the Prototype label. Add a space, and then add **LastName**. Press [Enter], and then add **Street**. Press [Enter], type Aspen Falls, CA add a space, and then add the **Zip** field. Compare your screen with Figure 3, and then click **Finish**. If you are printing your work, print the first page of the report. **Close Print Preview**, and then **Close** the report.

12. Open the **2017 Statistics Query** in Design view. In the **CycleDate** column **Criteria** cell, type <1/1/2018 Click **Save**, and then **Close** the query.

13. If necessary, in the Navigation Pane, select the 2017 Statistics Query. Click the **Create tab**, and then in the **Reports group**, click the **Report** button. Click **Save**, type 2017 Usage Report and then click **OK**.

14. In the **Header / Footer group**, click the **Logo** button. In the **Insert Picture** dialog box, navigate to the student files for this chapter, click **acc04_SRLogo**, and then click **OK**.

15. In the **Header / Footer group**, click the **Title** button, type 2017 Electricity Usage and then press [Enter].

16. Double-click the **CountOfCycleID** label control, and then double-click the text to select it. Type Sample Size and then press [Enter]. Repeat this technique to change the **AvgOfUsage** label text to Average Usage

17. Click to select the **Cycle Date** label. Press and hold [Shift] while clicking the **Sample Size** and **Average Usage** labels. Click the **Format tab**, and then in the **Font group**, click **Bold** and **Center**.

18. On the **Format tab**, in the **Selection group**, click the **Selection arrow**, and then click **Detail**. In the **Background group**, click the **Alternate Row Color arrow**, and then click **No Color**.

19. Click a field in the **Sample Size** column, and then click the **Design tab**. In the **Grouping & Totals group**, click **Totals**, and then click **Sum**. Repeat this technique to add an **Average** total to the **Average Usage** column.

20. Below the **Sample Size** values, click the cell with the value *852*. Point to the top border, and then double-click to AutoFit the row. Click the total cell with the value *12*, and then press [Delete] to remove the control.

21. Compare your screen with Figure 4. If you are printing this project, print the report.

Figure 3 Access 2016, Windows 10, Microsoft Corporation

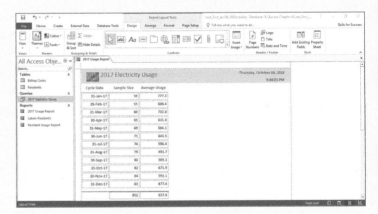

Figure 4 Access 2016, Windows 10, Microsoft Corporation

22. Click **Save**, **Close** the report, and then **Close** Access. Submit the file as directed by your instructor.

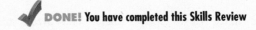 **DONE! You have completed this Skills Review**

Skills Assessment 1

To complete this project, you will need the following files:

- acc04_SA1Parcels (Access)
- acc04_SA1Logo (JPG)

You will save your file as:

- Last_First_acc04_SA1Parcels

1. Start **Access 2016**, and then open the student data file **acc04_SA1Parcels**. **Save** the file in your **Access Chapter 4** folder as Last_First_acc04_SA1Parcels If necessary, enable the content.

2. Use the **Blank Report** tool to create a report with these fields in the following order: **Owner**, **Value**, **Assessed**, and **Zone**. Save the report as Assessments

3. Apply the **Organic** theme, and then add a **Title** control with the text Assessments by Quarter

4. Group the report by the **Assessed** field, and then if necessary, sort the Assessed field within each group in oldest to newest order. AutoFit the control height of the quarter label controls.

5. Use the property sheet to set the width of the **Owner** column to **2"** and the width of the **Zone** column to **2"**. Change the alignment of the **Value** label to **Align Left**.

6. For the **Detail** control, change the **Alternate Row Color** to **Orange, Accent 5, Lighter 80%** (row 2, column 9).

7. Create a custom **Text Filter** to display only the records in which the **Zone** contains the word Residential

8. Switch to **Print Preview**, and then compare your screen with Figure 1. If you are printing this project, print the report. **Save**, and then **Close** the report.

9. Create a **Labels** report based on the **Parcels** table. In the **Label Wizard**, verify **Avery C2160** is selected, and then accept the default label format settings. In the first line of the **Prototype** label, add the **Owner** field. In the second line, add the **Street** field. In the third line, type Aspen Falls, CA add a space, and then add the **Zip** field. Accept all other wizard defaults, and then **Close** the report.

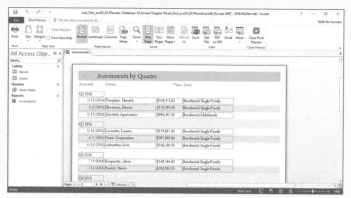

Access 2016, Windows 10, Microsoft Corporation — **Figure 1**

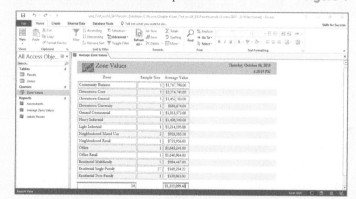

Access 2016, Windows 10, Microsoft Corporation — **Figure 2**

10. Modify the **Zone Values** query so that the second **Value** column computes an average for the group. **Save**, and then **Close** the query.

11. Use the **Report** tool to create a report based on the **Zone Values** query. **Save** the report as Average Zone Values

12. Add a logo using the file **acc04_SA1Logo**. Select the three column labels, and then apply **Bold** and **Center**.

13. Change the **AvgOfValue** label control text to Average Value and then add a control that calculates the column's average. Format the calculated control as **Currency**, and then AutoFit its height.

14. Switch to Report view, and then compare your screen with Figure 2. If you are printing this project, print the report.

15. Click **Save**, **Close** the report, and then **Close** Access. Submit the file as directed by your instructor.

 DONE! You have completed Skills Assessment 1

Skills Assessment 2

To complete this project, you will need the following file:

- acc04_SA2Rentals

You will save your file as:

- Last_First_acc04_SA2Rentals

---

1. Start **Access 2016**, and then open the student data file **acc04_SA2Rentals**. **Save** the file in your **Access Chapter 4** folder as Last_First_acc04_SA2Rentals If necessary, enable the content.

2. Use the **Blank Report** tool to create a report with these fields in the following order: **Center** and **Room Number** from the **Rooms** table; and **Date** and **Hours** from the **Rentals** table. Save the report as Rentals Report

3. Apply the **Facet** theme, and then add a **Title** control with the text Community Center Rentals

4. Group the report by **Center**, and then group it again by **RoomNumber**. Sort by **Date** from oldest to newest.

5. Below the **Hours** column, add a control that calculates the column's total.

6. For the **Detail** control, change the **Alternate Row Color** to **Orange, Accent 4, Lighter 80%** (row 2, column 8).

7. Use filter by **Selection** to display only the rentals for Room CE110. AutoFit the height of the three summary controls in the **Hours** column.

8. Switch to Print Preview, and then compare your screen with **Figure 1**. If you are printing this project, print the report. **Save**, and then **Close** the report.

9. Create a **Labels** report based on the **Renters** table. In the **Label Wizard**, verify **Avery C2160** is selected, and then accept the default label format settings. In the **Prototype** label, add fields and spaces to create labels in the following format:

   FirstName LastName
   Street
   City, State Zip
   Accept all other wizard defaults. If you are printing this project, print the first page of the report. **Close** the report.

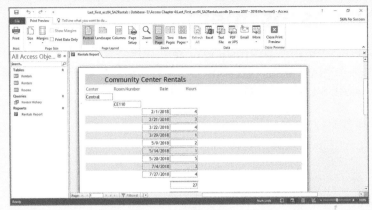

Figure 1 Access 2016, Windows 10, Microsoft Corporation

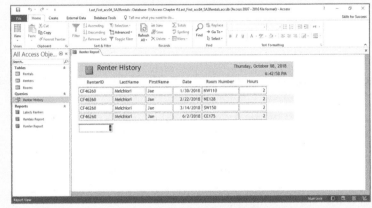

Figure 2 Access 2016, Windows 10, Microsoft Corporation

10. Modify the **Renter History** query to display only the records with **RenterID** CF46260 **Save**, and then **Close** the query.

11. Use the **Report** tool to create a report based on the **Renter History** query. **Save** the report as Renter Report

12. Resize the column widths so that the report is one page wide, and then delete the page number control.

13. Select the six column labels, and then apply **Bold** and **Center**. AutoFit the height of the **Count** control in the **RenterID** column.

14. Switch to Report view, and then compare your screen with **Figure 2**. If you are printing this project, print the report.

15. Click **Save**, **Close** the report, and then **Close** Access. Submit the file as directed by your instructor.

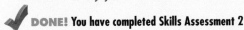

DONE! You have completed Skills Assessment 2

My Skills

To complete this project, you will need the following file:

- acc04_MYBaseball

You will save your file as:

- Last_First_acc04_MYBaseball

Access 2016, Windows 10, Microsoft Corporation   **Figure 1**

Access 2016, Windows 10, Microsoft Corporation   **Figure 2**

1. Start **Access 2016**, and then open the student data file **acc04_MYBaseball**. **Save** the file in your **Access Chapter 4** folder as Last_First_acc04_MYBaseball If necessary, enable the content.

2. Use the **Blank Report** tool to create a report with these fields from the **League Statistics** table in the following order: **Team, FirstName, LastName, Hits (H), AtBats (AB)**, and **BattingAverage (BA)**. Save the report as Batting Averages

3. Apply the **Integral** theme, and then add a **Title** control with the text Batting Averages

4. Group the report by **Team**, and then below the **Batting Average (BA)** column, add a control that calculates the column's averages.

5. For the **Detail** control, change the **Alternate Row Color** to **Teal, Accent 6, Lighter 80%** (row 2, last column).

6. Use filter by **Selection** to display only statistics for the *Golden Rays* team. Autofit the height of the two summary controls in the **Batting Average (BA)** column.

7. Switch to Print Preview, and then compare your screen with Figure 1. If you are printing this project, print the report. **Save**, and then **Close** the report.

8. Create a **Labels** report based on the **Coaches** table. In the **Label Wizard**, verify **Avery C2160** is selected, and then accept the default label format settings. In the

Prototype label, add fields and spaces to create labels in the following format:

FirstName LastName
Street
City, State Zip

Accept all other wizard defaults. If you are printing this project, print the first page of the report. **Close** the report.

9. Modify the **Pitching Stats** query so that the **ERA** column calculates the average for each team. **Save**, and then **Close** the query.

10. Use the **Report** tool to create a report based on the **Pitching Stats** query. **Save** the report as Team Pitching

11. Change the **Title** control text to Team Pitching Statistics For the four column labels, apply **Bold** and **Center**.

12. Add a sort so that the **Team ERA** *(AvgOfERA)* column is ordered from smallest to largest. Delete the **Count** control in the **Team** column.

13. Switch to Report view, and then compare your screen with Figure 2. If you are printing this project, print the report.

14. Click **Save**, **Close** the report, and then **Close** Access. Submit the file as directed by your instructor.

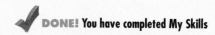

DONE! You have completed My Skills

Visual Skills Check

To complete this project, you will need the following files:

- acc04_VSPhones (Access)
- acc04_VSLogo (JPG)

You will save your file as:

- Last_First_acc04_VSPhones

Open the student data file **acc04_VSPhones**, and then save the file in your **Access Chapter 4** folder as Last_First_acc04_VSPhones

Use the Blank Report tool to create the report shown in Figure 1. In the report header, add the title, date, and time controls as shown. The logo is from the file **acc04_VSLogo**. Group the report by *Department* and sort it by *LastName*. Position, size, and delete controls as shown in Figure 1. Set the *Department* label control to size **14**, **Bold**, and merge cells so that the label spans the first two columns. Set the alternate row color of the group header row to **No Color**. Delete any unnecessary labels or rows, as needed.

Save the report as Phone List Print the report if needed. **Close** the report, **Close** Access, and then submit the file as directed by your instructor.

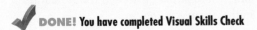 **DONE! You have completed Visual Skills Check**

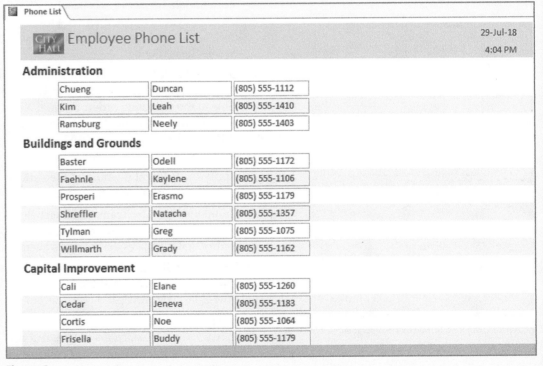

Phone List			
CITY HALL Employee Phone List			29-Jul-18 4:04 PM

Administration

Chueng	Duncan	(805) 555-1112
Kim	Leah	(805) 555-1410
Ramsburg	Neely	(805) 555-1403

Buildings and Grounds

Baster	Odell	(805) 555-1172
Faehnle	Kaylene	(805) 555-1106
Prosperi	Erasmo	(805) 555-1179
Shreffler	Natacha	(805) 555-1357
Tylman	Greg	(805) 555-1075
Willmarth	Grady	(805) 555-1162

Capital Improvement

Cali	Elane	(805) 555-1260
Cedar	Jeneva	(805) 555-1183
Cortis	Noe	(805) 555-1064
Frisella	Buddy	(805) 555-1179

Figure 1

Skills Challenge 1

To complete this project, you will need the following file:

- acc04_SC1Reviews

You will save your file as:

- Last_First_acc04_SC1Reviews

Open the student data file **acc04_SC1Reviews**, and then save the file in your **Access Chapter 4** folder as Last_First_acc04_SC1Reviews Open Employee Evaluations in layout view, and then add grouping so that each employee's evaluations display under his or her name. Position and sort the fields and labels to make the report easier to understand. Add Totals to the Attendance and Customer Relations columns that calculate the average values for each column and format the numbers to display two decimals. Format the report to make it easier

to read, and adjust the column widths and heights to fit the content each needs to display. Add a title control that describes the purpose of the report, and then filter the report to display the evaluations for Jack Hooley.

Print the report if needed. Close the report, Close Access, and then submit the file as directed by your instructor.

 DONE! You have completed Skills Challenge 1

Skills Challenge 2

To complete this project, you will need the following file:

- acc04_SC2Students

You will save your file as:

- Last_First_acc04_SC2Students

Open the student data file **acc04_SC2Students**, and then save the file in your **Access Chapter 4** folder as Last_First_acc04_SC2Students Create a query that can be used to create a mailing labels report. In the query, include the necessary name and address fields from the Students table, and then filter the query so that only participants from the Central neighborhood display. Save the query as Central Students Query. Use the Label Wizard to create a label report. Arrange the fields in the standard mailing address format. Include

spacing and punctuation where appropriate. Do not include the Neighborhood field in the label. Accept all other default wizard settings.

Print the report if needed. Close the report, Close Access, and then submit the file as directed by your instructor.

 DONE! You have completed Skills Challenge 2

More Skills Assessment

To complete this project, you will need the following file:

- acc04_MSAClasses

You will save your files as:

- Last_First_acc04_MSAClasses (Access)
- Last_First_acc04_MSARTF (Rich Text Format)
- Last_First_acc04_MSAPDF (PDF)
- Last_First_acc04_MSAHTML (HTML)

1. Start **Access 2016**, and then open the student data file **acc04_MSAClasses**. **Save** the file in your **Access Chapter 4** folder as Last_First_acc04_MSAClasses

2. Open the **Sessions Report** in Layout view. Change the **Sort by Community Center** to **with Z on top**. Compare your screen with **Figure 1**, and then **Close** the **Group, Sort, and Total** dialog box. **Save**, and then **Close** the report.

3. Verify the Sessions Report is selected, and then export the report as a **Word** file. **Save** the Word file as Last_First_acc04_MSARTF in your **Access Chapter 4** folder. In the Access **Export - RTF File** dialog box, save the export steps as acc04_MSASessionsWord

4. With the Sessions Report still selected, export the report as a **PDF** file. During the export process, select **Optimize for Standard (publishing online and printing)**. **Save** the PDF file as Last_First_acc04_MSAPDF in your **Access Chapter 4** folder. In the Access **Export - PDF File** dialog box, save the export steps as acc04_MSASessionsPDF

5. With the Sessions Report still selected, export the report as an **HTML document** file. **Save** the HTML file as Last_First_acc04_MSAHTML in your **Access Chapter 4** folder. During the export process, **Choose the encoding to use for saving this file: Unicode (UTF-8)**. In the Access **Export - HTML File** dialog box, save the export steps as acc04_MSASessionsHTML

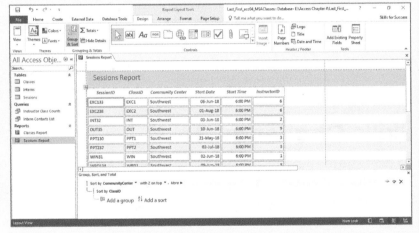

Figure 1   Access 2016, Windows 10, Microsoft Corporation

6. **Close** Access.

7. Submit the files as directed by your instructor.

 **DONE! You have completed More Skills Assessment**

Collaborating with Google

To complete this project, you will need a Google account (refer to the Common Features chapter) and the following file:

- acc04_GPOutings

You will save your files as:

- Last_First_acc04_GPReport (Word)
- Last_First_acc04_GPDownload (Word)

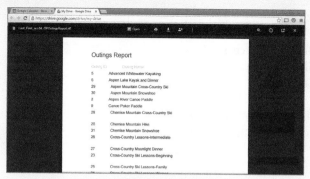

Figure 1

1. Start **Access 2016**, and then open the student data file **acc04_GPOutings**.

2. In the **Navigation Pane**, select the **Outings Report**. On the **External Data tab**, in the **Export group**, click **More**, and then click **Word**. **Save** the Word file as Last_First_acc04_GPReport in your **Access Chapter 4** folder. During the export process, in the **Export - RTF File** dialog box, select **Open the designation file after the export operation is complete**.

3. When the Word file opens, switch to Access, **Close** the dialog box, and then **Close** Access. **Close** Word.

4. Open the Google Chrome web browser. Log into your Google account, and then click the **Apps** button. Click the **Drive** button to open Google Drive, and then click the **NEW** button. Click **File upload**.

5. Navigate to your Access Chapter 4 folder, and then double-click the **Last_First_GPReport** file.

6. In the bottom right portion of your browser, in the **Uploads completed** dialog box, click the **Last_First_acc04_GPReport** file. Compare your screen with Figure 1, and then click the **Open with Google Docs** button.

7. With your insertion point before the **Outings Report** title, if necessary, click the **More** button, and then click the **Center** button to center the title.

8. Select the title text **Outings Report**, and then change the font size to **24**.

9. Select the text **Outing ID** and **Outing Name**, click **Format**, and then click **Underline**.

10. Scroll down to view the second page of the document.

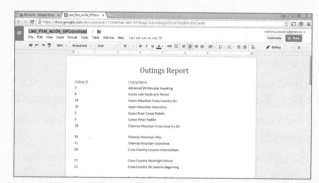

Figure 2

11. Select the text **Outing ID** and **Outing Name**, and then on the formatting toolbar, click **Underline**.

12. At the top of the browser, double-click the name of the document file.

13. Rename the document Last_First_acc04_GPDownload Compare your screen to Figure 2, and then click **OK**.

14. Click the **File tab**, and then point to **Download as**. In the submenu, click **Microsoft Word (.docx)**.

15. In the download bar, click the **arrow** next to the downloaded file, and then click **Open**. After the file opens in Microsoft Word, if necessary, Enable Editing, click the **File tab**, click **Save As**, and then save the file in your Access Chapter 4 folder.

16. **Close** both Word files, and then close Chrome. Submit the files as directed by your instructor.

 **DONE! You have completed Collaborating with Google**

CAPSTONE PROJECT

Student data files needed for this project:

acc_CSShelters (Access)
acc_CSShelterData (Excel)
acc_CSLogo (JPG)

MyITLab®
Grader

You will save your file as:

Last_First_acc_CSShelters (Access)

---

1. Start **Access 2016**, and then open the student data file, **acc_CSShelters**. Use the **Save As** dialog box to save the file to your chapter folder as Last_First_ acc_CSShelters If necessary, enable the content.

2. Create a new table in Design view. Add a field named ShelterID with the **AutoNumber** data type. Set the field as the table's primary key, and then change the field's **Caption** property to Shelter ID

3. Add a field named ShelterName with the **Short Text** data type. Change the field's **Field Size** property to 50 and its **Caption** property to Shelter Name

4. Add a field named Park with the **Short Text** data type, and then change the field's **Field Size** property to 50

5. **Save** the table with the name Shelters and then **Close** the table.

6. Import the data from the Excel file **acc_CSShelterData** by appending the data to the **Shelters** table.

7. Open the **Shelters** table, set the column widths to **Best Fit**, and then compare your screen with **Figure 1**. **Save**, and then **Close** the table.

8. Relate the database's two tables in a one-to-many relationship by enforcing referential integrity between the **ShelterID** fields. For the relationship, select both cascading options. **Save**, and then **Close** the Relationships tab.

9. Create a query in Design view, add both database tables, and then add the following fields: **ShelterName**, **ReservationDate**, **GroupSize**, and **Fee**. Add criteria so that only reservations for the month of July 2018 display. **Save** the query with the name July Reservations

10. **Run** the query. Compare your screen with **Figure 2**, and then **Close** the query.

Figure 1   Access 2016, Windows 10, Microsoft Corporation

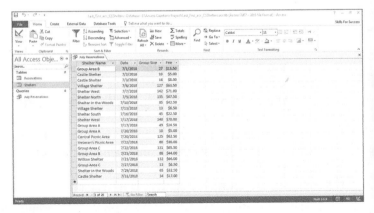

Figure 2   Access 2016, Windows 10, Microsoft Corporation

■ **Continue to the next page to complete the project**

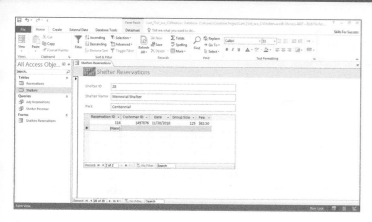

Access 2016, Windows 10, Microsoft Corporation

Figure 3

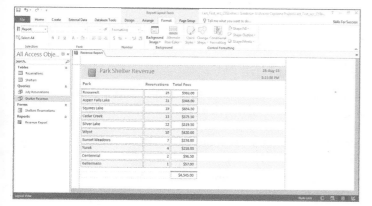

Access 2016, Windows 10, Microsoft Corporation

Figure 4

11. Create a query in Design view, add both database tables, and then add the following fields: **Park**, **ReservationDate**, and **Fee**. **Save** the query with the name Shelter Revenue

12. Group the **Shelter Revenue** query by **Park**. In the **ReservationDate** column, add a **Count** total, and then in the **Fee** column, add a **Sum** total.

13. **Save**, and then **Run** the query. Verify that 10 records display, and then **Close** the query.

14. Use the **Form** tool to create a form and subform with the main form based on the **Shelters** table. **Save** the form with the name Shelter Reservations

15. Apply the **Retrospect** theme, insert the logo from the file **acc_CSLogo**, and then change the form's title text to Shelter Reservations

16. Use the property sheet to change the width of the **Shelter ID** text box control to 4.8" and then **Close** the property sheet.

17. In the main form, add a new record with Memorial Shelter as the shelter name and Centennial as the park name. In the subform, add a reservation with a **Customer ID** of 1497076 The date is 11/30/2018 and the **Group Size** is 125

18. Compare your screen with **Figure 3**. **Save** all tables and forms, and then **Close** the form.

19. Use the **Report** tool to create a report based on the **Shelter Revenue** query. **Save** the report as Revenue Report

20. Change the report title to Park Shelter Revenue and then change the Date control's **Number Format** to **Medium Date**.

21. Add a sort that orders the **CountOfReservationDate** column from largest to smallest.

22. Change the second column label to Reservations and the third column label to Total Fees

23. For all three column labels, change the font size to **12**, apply **Bold**, and apply **Align Left**. **AutoFit** the second column's width.

24. Below the **Total Fees** column, **AutoFit** the height of the Total control, and then change the control's **Number Format** to **Currency**.

25. **Close** the Group, Sort, and Total pane, and then delete the control with the page number. Compare your screen with **Figure 4**.

26. **Save**, and then **Close** the report. **Close** Access, and then submit the file as directed by your instructor.

 DONE! You have completed Access Capstone Project

Create OneNote Notebooks

- ▶ **OneNote** is a program used to collect notes, drawings, and media from multiple participants.
- ▶ A OneNote document is a loose structure of digital pages called a **notebook**.
- ▶ Notebooks can be shared by saving them to OneDrive and using OneNote Office Online to edit them.

- ▶ OneNote notebooks are divided into sections, and each section can have multiple pages.
- ▶ In a OneNote notebook, participants enter text, graphics, or audio anywhere on a page. In this manner, notebooks collect and foster ideas that can be published in a more formal format later.

© 3ddock / Fotolia

Aspen Falls City Hall

In this project, you will create documents for the Aspen Falls City Hall, which provides essential services for the citizens and visitors of Aspen Falls, California. Using OneNote Office Online, you will assist City Manager Maria Martinez to create a OneNote notebook for the city council.

To create a shared notebook, you save it to OneDrive. You can then invite others to work on the notebook. Those who you invite can add text, pictures, tables, or other objects to the notebook in the web browser. You are able to track the changes each author makes and return the page to a previous version if you do not want the changes they have made. In this way, an online notebook helps teams collaborate from any computer connected to the Internet. When all the OneNote features are needed, the notebook can be opened in the Desktop OneNote.

In this project, you will use OneDrive and OneNote Office Online to create a notebook. You will add sections and pages and add text, graphics, and other objects to the pages in the notebook.

Outcome

Using the skills in this project, you will be able to create a
OneNote notebook on OneDrive, add notebook sections and
tables, add text and pictures to pages, and share notebooks.

Objectives

1 Construct a OneNote notebook

2 Produce notebook content

Student data file needed for this project:

acc_OPPhoto

You will save your files as:

City Council Notebook (OneDrive)
Last_First_acc_OPSnip1
Last_First_acc_OPSnip2

SKILLS

At the end of this project, you will be able to:

▶ Create a OneNote notebook on OneDrive

▶ Name notebook sections and pages

▶ Add notebook sections and pages

▶ Add text, tables, and pictures to pages

▶ Display pages in Reading view

▶ Show authors and share notebooks

Access 2016, Windows 10, Microsoft Corporation

1. Start **Microsoft Edge**, navigate to onedrive.live.com and then log on to your Microsoft account. If you do not have an account, follow the links and directions on the page to create one.

2. After logging in, navigate as needed to display your **OneDrive** page. Compare your screen with Figure 1.

   OneDrive and Office Online technologies are accessed through web pages that can change often, and the formatting and layout of some pages may often be different than the figures in this book. You may need to adapt the steps to complete the actions they describe.

3. On the toolbar, click **New**, and then click **OneNote notebook**. In the **OneNote notebook** dialog box, name the file City Council Notebook and then click the **Create** button to save the document to your OneDrive and start OneNote Online.

4. With the insertion point in the blank page title, type Maria Martinez Compare your screen with Figure 2.

   In OneNote, notes are organized in notebooks. Each notebook is divided into sections, and each section can have multiple pages. Here, the notebook is named City Council Notebook, the section is untitled, and the first page is titled Maria Martinez.

   The changes you make in OneNote Online are automatically saved. For this reason, there is no save button.

■ **Continue to the next page to complete the skill**

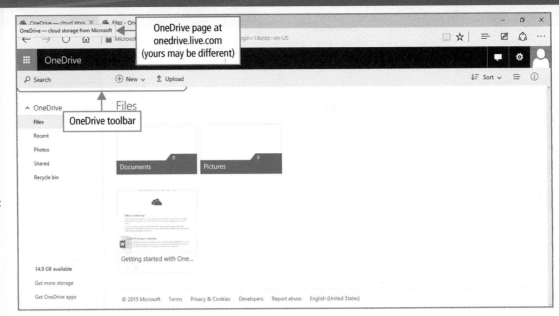

Figure 1

Access 2016, Windows 10, Microsoft Corporation

Figure 2

Access 2016, Windows 10, Microsoft Corporation

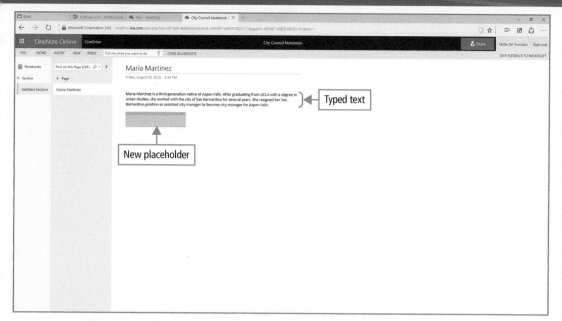

Access 2016, Windows 10, Microsoft Corporation

Figure 3

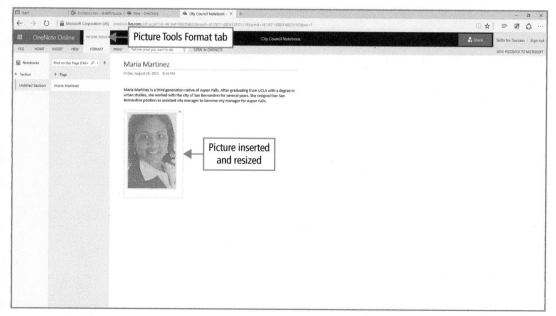

Access 2016, Windows 10, Microsoft Corporation

Figure 4

5. Press `Tab` to move the insertion point into the page, and then type the following: Maria Martinez is a third generation native of Aspen Falls. After graduating from UCLA with a degree in urban studies, she worked with the city of San Bernardino for several years. She resigned her San Bernardino position as assistant city manager to become city manager for Aspen Falls.

6. Click in a blank area in the middle of the page to create a new placeholder. Point to the title bar of the new placeholder, and then with the 🔄 pointer, drag to position the placeholder below the text typed previously similar to the position shown in Figure 3.

> An object can be inserted anywhere on the page. It can then be moved by dragging its placeholder.

7. Click in the new placeholder positioned in the previous step. Click the **INSERT tab**, and then in the **Pictures group**, click **Picture**.

8. In the **Choose File to Upload** dialog box, navigate to the student data files that you downloaded for this project. Click **acc_OPPhoto**, and then click **Open**.

9. Wait a few moments for the picture to upload and display. Click the picture to select it and display the Picture Tools Format tab.

10. Click the **FORMAT tab**, and then in the **Image Size group**, select the value in the **Scale** box. Type 50% press `Enter`, and then compare your screen with Figure 4.

■ Continue to the next page to complete the skill ➤

11. Click in the page to deselect the picture. In the left pane, right-click **Untitled Section**, and then from the shortcut menu, click **Rename**. In the **Section Name** dialog box, name the section Biographies and then click **OK**.

12. To the right of *Biographies*, click the **+ Page** button, and then type Donald Norris

13. Press Tab to move the insertion point into the page, and then type Donald, you need to post your bio. Thanks. **Compare** your screen with **Figure 5**.

14. Click the **INSERT tab**, and then in the **Notebook group**, click **New Section**. In the **Section Name** dialog box, type Agendas and then click **OK**.

15. With the insertion point in the title of the new Untitled Page, type April Meeting to title the page.

16. Press Tab to move the insertion point to the first line of the page. Click the **INSERT tab**, and then in the **Tables group**, click the **Table** button. In the **Table** gallery, click the second cell in the third row to insert a **2x3 Table**.

17. In the six table cells, type the following:

Item	Presenter
Aspen Falls Lake Flood Mitigation	Donald Norris
Community College Internships	Evelyn Stone and George Gato

18. Using the ⟨┼⟩ pointer, drag the columns to the right until each cell's content fits on one line. Compare your screen with **Figure 6**.

➤ Continue to the next page to complete the skill

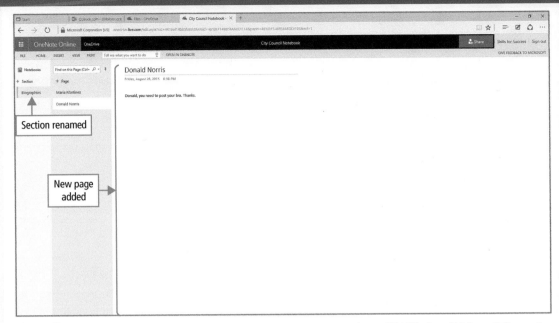

Figure 5

Access 2016, Windows 10, Microsoft Corporation

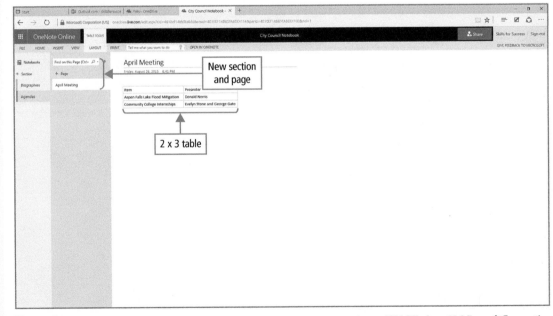

Figure 6

Access 2016, Windows 10, Microsoft Corporation

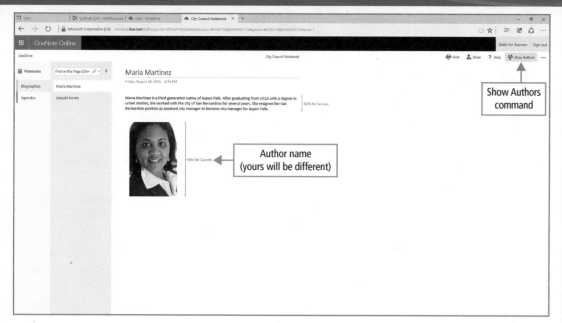

Access 2016, Windows 10, Microsoft Corporation

Figure 7

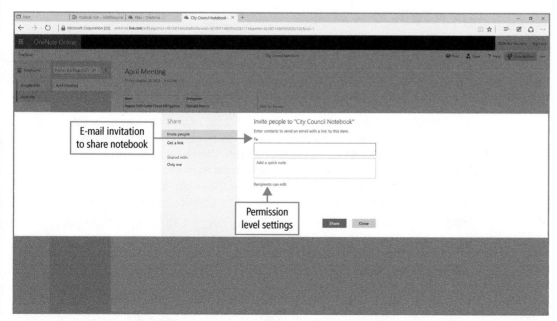

Access 2016, Windows 10, Microsoft Corporation

Figure 8

19. Click the **VIEW tab**, and then in the **Notebook Views group**, click **Reading View**. In the left pane, click **Biographies** to display the page. If necessary, click the **More** button, and then click **Show Authors**. Compare your screen with Figure 7.

   When you display the authors, each author's contributions are marked so that you can track each author's contributions to the notebook.

20. In the **Search** text box, type snip and then press [Enter] to start the Snipping Tool. Create a **Full-screen Snip**. Save 🖫 the snip as Last_First_acc_OPSnip1 and then **Close** ✕ the Snipping Tool mark-up window.

21. In the left pane, click **Agendas** to display the page. Create a **Full-screen Snip** named Last_First_acc_OPSnip2 and then **Close** ✕ the Snipping Tool mark-up window.

22. Click the **Share** button, then compare your screen with Figure 8.

   In Reading view, you can click Share to invite others view the notebook. You can allow them to make changes as authors or limit them only to Reading view.

23. If your instructor has asked you to share the notebook, enter the e-mail address of the person you are to share with, and then click **Share**. Otherwise, click **Close**.

24. Click the **Sign out** link, and then **Close** ✕ your browser window. Submit the files as directed by your instructor.

 **DONE!** You have completed Online Project 4

CHAPTER 5

Design Databases

- When you create a database, you should begin by determining the purpose of the database and the tables needed.
- Tables can be created in Datasheet view or Design view. Tables can also be created during the import process and from templates.
- To populate tables with data, you can import the data from several file formats such as Excel, XML, or text files.
- Data from other files often must be modified to ensure compatibility before it can be imported into the database.

- Table field properties can be changed to improve accuracy and efficiency during the data entry process.
- In addition to one-to-many relationships, you can also relate tables in a many-to-many relationship or a one-to-one relationship.
- After a database is created or modified, you can use Access tools to create documentation describing the tables, relationships, and properties of the database.

Darrinhenry | Dreamtime.com

Aspen Falls City Hall

In this project, you will assist Jack Ruiz, Community Services Director of Aspen Falls City Hall, to create a database that assigns volunteers from local businesses to city projects. Businesses supply a list of volunteers, and those individuals are assigned tasks available from city projects. You will use Access to create and populate the tables used in the database.

Jack needs a database that can organize a list of volunteers and a list of tasks from city projects. Tasks and Volunteers tables need to be joined in a relationship that allows a volunteer to be assigned to more than one task, and a task to be assigned to more than one volunteer, creating a many-to-many relationship. Jack will use the assignments table to create the many-to-many relationship. The volunteers and logons tables will be joined in a one-to-one relationship.

Initially the volunteer data was kept in an Excel file, but this method became inefficient and difficult to use. The Excel files will be used to create some of the tables in the database. The Logons table will be created using data imported from a mainframe database.

In this project, you will modify a table that tracks volunteers and imports records into it. You will create another table using a template, and after preparing data in Excel, you will create a third table during the import data process. Finally, you will create database documentation.

Time to complete all 10 skills — 45 to 60 minutes

Introduction

Outcome

Using the skills in this chapter, you will be able to design a database, import data from text files, create tables from application parts and by importing data, create many-to-many relationships, prepare Excel data, and document databases. You will also add Lookup fields, create custom input masks, and search and replace data in datasheets and forms.

Objectives

5.1 Construct and design a database

5.2 Create many-to-many relationships

5.3 Create tables by importing data

5.4 Identify unmatched records

5.5 Generate database documentation

Student data files needed for this chapter:

acc05_Volunteers (Access)
acc05_VolunteerLogons (XML text file)
acc05_VolunteersData (Excel)
acc05_VolunteersText (Text)
acc05_VolunteerXSD (XSD text file)

You will save your files as:

Last_First_acc05_Volunteers (Access)
Last_First_acc05_VolunteersText (Text)
Last_First_acc05_VolunteersData (Excel)
Last_First_acc05_VolunteerDocs (PDF)

SKILLS

Skills 1-10 Training

At the end of this chapter you will be able to:

Skill 1 Design Databases and Modify Field Properties
Skill 2 Import Data from Text Files
Skill 3 Create Tables Using Application Parts and Add Rich Text Fields
Skill 4 Create Many-to-Many Relationships
Skill 5 Prepare Excel Data for Importing
Skill 6 Create Tables by Importing Data
Skill 7 Add Lookup Fields
Skill 8 Import XML Data
Skill 9 Find Unmatched Records and Create One-to-One Relationships
Skill 10 Document Databases

MORE SKILLS

Skill 11 Create Custom Input Masks
Skill 12 Search and Replace Data in Datasheets and Forms
Skill 13 Export XML Data
Skill 14 Make Tables from Queries

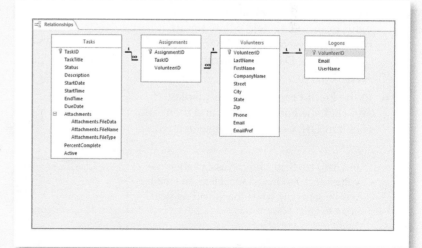

 **WATCH** SKILL 5.1

- Database designers often sketch a database, and then they follow that plan to create tables.
- Assigning field properties can increase accuracy and efficiency. For example, making a field required ensures that the field will not be left empty during data entry.

1. Take a few moments to study the entity relationship diagram in **Figure 1**.

    An *entity relationship diagram*, or **ERD**, is a visual model used to plan a database. An ERD shows the tables and their fields. Each field's data type is also displayed. The lines between the tables show how each table will be related. The ERD in the figure is the plan for the database you will build in this project.

2. Start **Access 2016**, and then open the student data file **acc05_Volunteers**. Use the **Save As** dialog box to create a **New folder** named Access Chapter 5 Save the database in the new folder as Last_First_acc05_Volunteers If necessary, enable the content.

3. Open the **Volunteers** table in Design view. In the blank field below **Email**, type EmailPref as the field name. Press Tab , click the **Data Type arrow**, and then select **Yes/No**.

4. In the **Field Properties** pane, display and click the **Format arrow**, and then click **On/Off**. Compare your screen with **Figure 2**.

    In a Yes/No field, you can assign alternate values such as On and Off. Here, an email will be sent only when the EmailPref field is set to On.

■ **Continue to the next page to complete the skill**

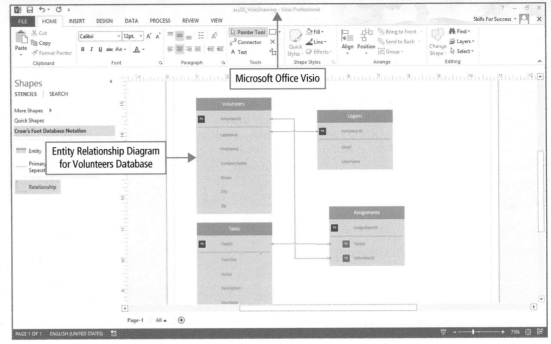

Figure 1

Visio 2016, Windows 10, Microsoft Corporation

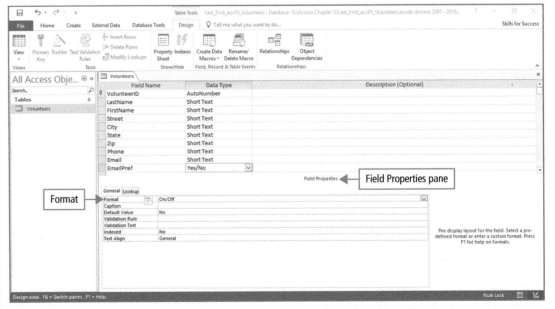

Figure 2

Access 2016, Windows 10, Microsoft Corporation

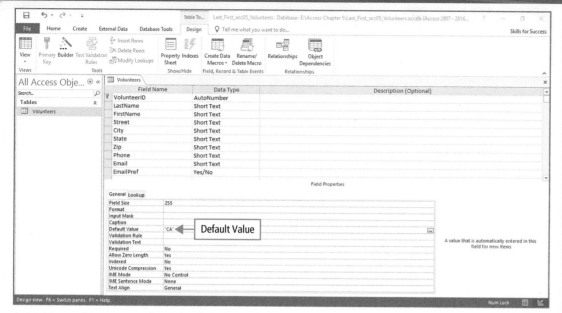

Access 2016, Windows 10, Microsoft Corporation

Figure 3

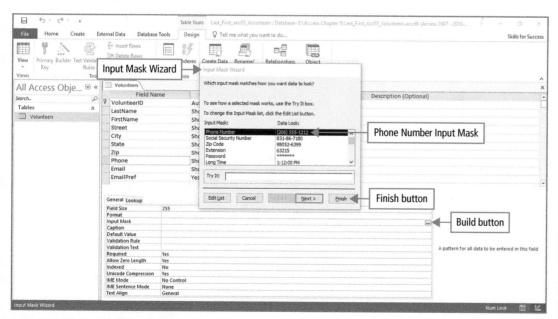

Access 2016, Windows 10, Microsoft Corporation

Figure 4

5. In the **Field Properties** pane, click **Default Value**, and then double-click *No*. Type Yes and then press [Enter].

6. Click the **LastName** row, and then in the **Field Properties** pane, click **Indexed**. Click the **Indexed arrow**, and then click **Yes (Duplicates OK)**.

   An *index* stores the locations of all records for a given field in the same way that a book's index stores each location of a word in the book. Here, the LastName field is indexed to improve database performance when records are searched by last name.

7. In the **Field Properties** pane, display and click the **Required arrow**, and then click **Yes**. Repeat this technique to set the **FirstName** and **Phone** fields as required.

   When a field is required, data must be entered into the field when adding a record.

8. Click the **City** row. In the **Field Properties** pane, click in the **Default Value** box, and then type Aspen Falls

   Default values save time and increase accuracy during data entry. Here, *Aspen Falls* will automatically appear in the City field during data entry.

9. Click the **State** row, and then change the **Default Value** to CA Compare your screen with Figure 3, and then click **Save** 🖫.

10. Click the **Phone** row. In the **Field Properties** pane, click **Input Mask**, and then click the **Build** button ⊡. In the **Input Mask Wizard**, if necessary, click **Phone Number**. Compare your screen with Figure 4.

11. Click **Finish** to close the Input Mask Wizard. Click **Save**, and then **Close** the table.

■ **You have completed Skill 1 of 10**

▶ **Text files** store text characters, but not formatting, tables, or graphics. They are often used to move data from Excel into Access databases.

▶ Information can be imported into Access from a **delimited text file**—a text file in which columns are separated by a special character such as a space, comma, or tab. When used this way, these characters are called **delimiters**.

1. On the taskbar, click **File Explorer** 📁. In the folder window, navigate to the student files for this chapter. Right-click **acc05_VolunteersText**. From the shortcut menu, point to **Open with**, and then click **Notepad**. Maximize □ the Notepad window, and then compare your screen with Figure 1.

Text files use delimiters to indicate columns of data. Delimiters can be tabs, commas, semicolons, spaces, or other characters. Here, the data columns are separated by tabs. Your file may appear different.

2. In the first row, select the word *Email*, and then type EmailPref Compare your screen with Figure 2.

3. Click **File**, and then click **Save as**. In the **Save As** dialog box, navigate to your **Access Chapter 5** folder. Name the file Last_First_acc05_VolunteersText and then click **Save**.

The names of each field are displayed in the first row of the text file. The names need to match the names of the fields in the Access table that will receive the imported data.

4. **Close** × Notepad. If necessary, on the taskbar, click the **Access** button 🗗 to make it the active window.

■ **Continue to the next page to complete the skill** ➤

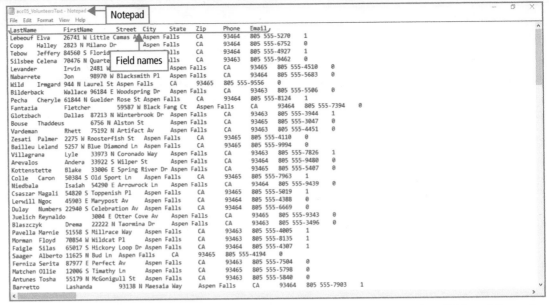

Figure 1

Notepad 2016, Windows 10, Microsoft Corporation

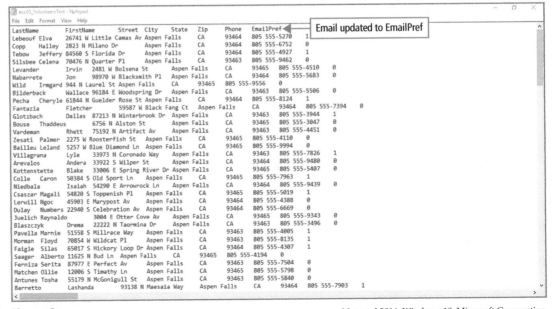

Figure 2

Notepad 2016, Windows 10, Microsoft Corporation

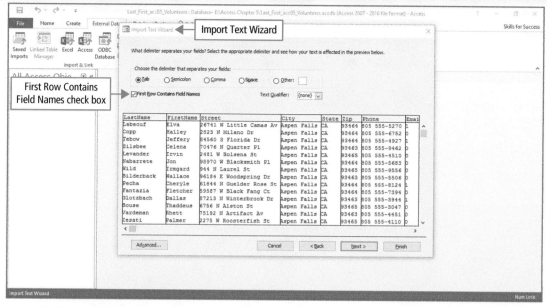

Access 2016, Windows 10, Microsoft Corporation

Figure 3

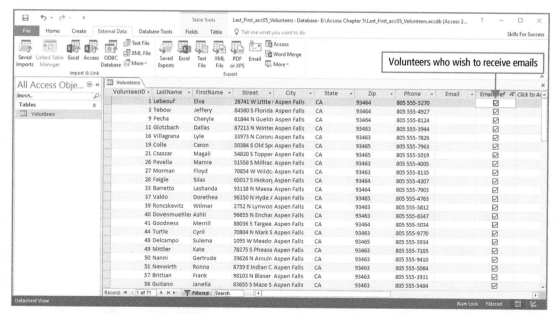

Access 2016, Windows 10, Microsoft Corporation

Figure 4

5. On the **External Data tab**, in the **Import & Link group**, click **Text File**. In the **Get External Data - Text File** dialog box, click **Browse**, and then navigate to your **Access Chapter 5** folder. Select the **Last_First_acc05_VolunteersText** text file, and then click **Open**.

6. Select the **Append a copy of the records to the table** option button, and then click **OK** to start the Import Text Wizard.

    Data from the text file will be added to the Volunteers table without replacing existing records in the table.

7. In the **Import Text Wizard**, verify the **Delimited - Characters such as comma or tab separate each field** button is selected, and then click **Next**.

8. In the **Choose the delimiter that separates your fields** pane, verify the **Tab** button is selected.

9. Select the **First Row Contains Field Names** check box, compare your screen with Figure 3, and then click **Next**.

10. Click **Finish**, and then click **Close**. Open the **Volunteers** table in Datasheet view.

11. Click the **EmailPref arrow**, and then in the **Filter** list, clear the **Off** check box. Click **OK**, and then compare your screen with Figure 4.

    A volunteer who wants to be contacted by email has the On value selected on EmailPref. The On value is selected during data entry by selecting the EmailPref check box. Only volunteers with the On value display when the Off value is cleared in the filtered list.

12. Click **Save** 🖫, and then **Close** ☒ the table.

■ **You have completed Skill 2 of 10**

▶ *Application Parts* are tables, forms, and other objects created from templates.

▶ *Quick Start tables* are tables created from templates.

MOS
Obj 2.1.5

1. On the **Create tab**, in the **Templates group**, click **Application Parts**, and then compare your screen with **Figure 1**.

2. In the **Application Parts** gallery, under **Quick Start**, click **Tasks**.

3. In the **Create Relationship** dialog box, select the **There is no relationship** option button, and then click **Create** to add the Tasks table and two related forms to the database.

4. Open the **Tasks** table in Datasheet view. Double-click the **ID** field, and then type TaskID to rename the field. Press [Enter].

MOS
Obj 2.4.9

5. Click **Priority**. Click the **Fields tab**, and then in the **Add & Delete group**, click **Delete** to remove the field.

6. Click the **Description** field. In the **Properties group**, click the **Memo Settings** button, and then click **Rich Text**. Read the message that displays, and then click **Yes** to convert the column to Rich Text. Compare your screen with **Figure 2**.

> Rich Text format provides the ability to format fonts using HTML coding, which can be displayed on reports or queries. The Long Text data type is used to store memos, lists, or notes that require more characters than Short Text such as a first name.

■ **Continue to the next page to complete the skill**

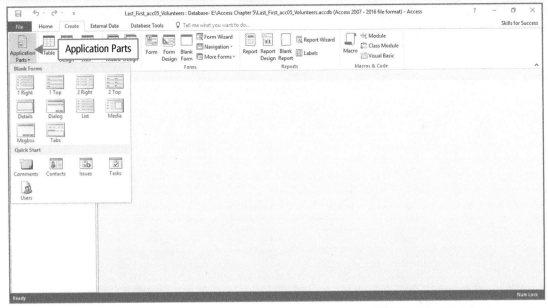

Figure 1

Access 2016, Windows 10, Microsoft Corporation

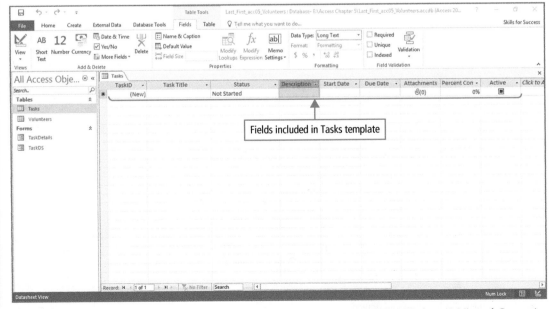

Figure 2

Access 2016, Windows 10, Microsoft Corporation

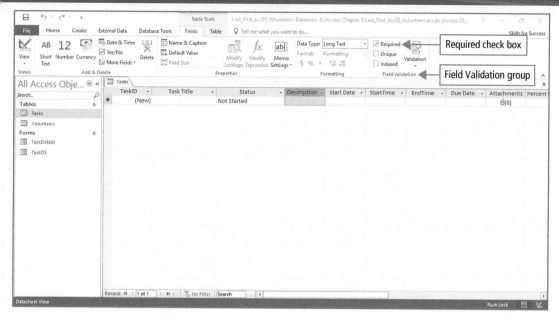

Access 2016, Windows 10, Microsoft Corporation

Figure 3

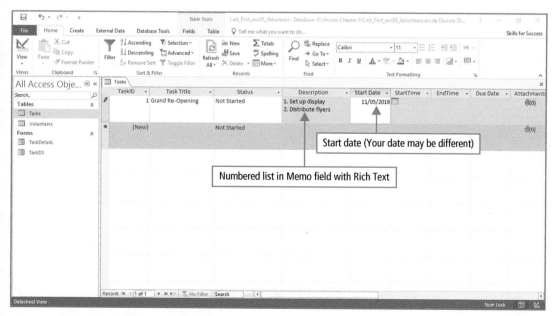

Access 2016, Windows 10, Microsoft Corporation

Figure 4

7. Click the **Start Date** field. In the **Add & Delete group**, click the **More Fields arrow**, and then click **Time am/pm**. Name the field StartTime Repeat this technique to add a **Time am/pm** field named EndTime to the right of the StartTime column.

8. Click the **Description** field. In the **Field Validation group**, select the **Required** checkbox. Compare your screen with **Figure 3**, and then click **Save** 🖫.

9. Click the **Home tab**. In the **Records group**, click **More**, and then click **Row Height**. In the **Row Height** box, type 45 and then click **OK**.

10. In the append row, in the **Task Title** cell, type Grand Re-Opening and then press [Tab] two times. Type Set up display

11. On the **Home tab**, in the **Text Formatting group**, click the **Numbering** button 📊. Press [Ctrl] + [Enter], type Distribute flyers and then press [Tab]. Right-click the **Description** field name, and then click **Field Width**. Type 20 and then click **OK**.

12. In the **Start Date** field, enter today's date, and then compare your screen with **Figure 4**.

13. Click **Save** 🖫, and then **Close** ☒ the **Tasks** table.

■ **You have completed Skill 3 of 10**

▶ A *many-to-many relationship* is a relationship in which one record in either table can have many associated records in the other table. For example, a person can volunteer for many tasks, and a task can have many volunteers assigned to it.

▶ Many-to-many relationships are created by associating primary keys from outer tables in a junction table.

---

1. Click the **Create tab**, and then in the **Tables group**, click **Table**. Click **Save** 🖫, name the table Assignments and then click **OK**.

2. Double-click the **ID** field name, type AssignmentID and then press Enter.

   Using meaningful field names provides users with a clear indication of each field's purpose. This is especially important when the database is used by multiple individuals or when the database creator transfers the database to a new administrator.

3. If necessary, click the **Click to Add** menu, click **Number**, and then type TaskID to name the field.

4. Click **Click to Add**, click **Number**, and then type VolunteerID to name the field. Compare your screen with **Figure 1**.

5. Click **Save** 🖫, and then **Close** ✕ the **Assignments** table.

6. Click the **Database Tools tab**, and then in the **Relationships** group, click **Relationships**. In the **Show Table** dialog box, add the tables in this order: **Tasks**, **Assignments**, and then **Volunteers**. **Close** the dialog box, and then compare your screen with **Figure 2**.

■ **Continue to the next page to complete the skill** ▶

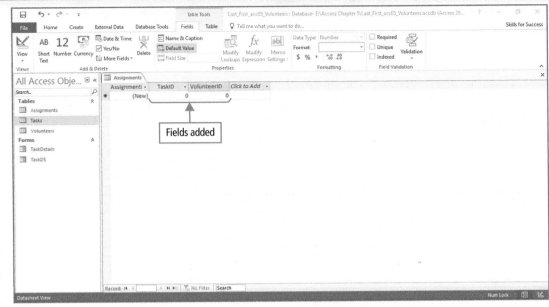

Figure 1

Access 2016, Windows 10, Microsoft Corporation

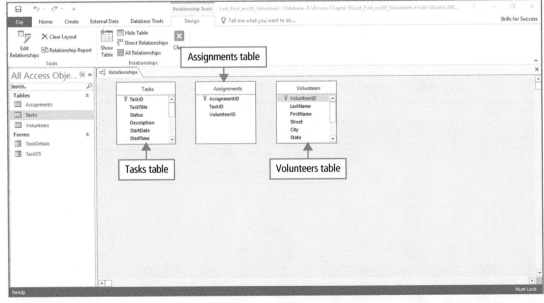

Figure 2

Access 2016, Windows 10, Microsoft Corporation

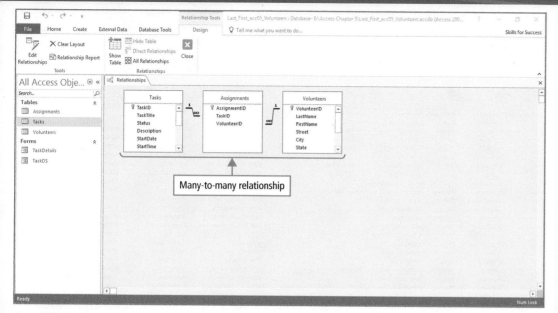

Many-to-many relationship

Access 2016, Windows 10, Microsoft Corporation

Figure 3

7. Drag the **TaskID** field from the **Tasks** table to the **TaskID** field in the **Assignments** table to open the **Edit Relationships** dialog box. Select the **Enforce Referential Integrity** check box, and then click **Create**.

> Many-to-many relationships consist of two one-to-many relationships. In many-to-many relationships, one record in either of the outer tables can have many associated records in the other outer table.

8. Drag and drop the primary key **VolunteerID** from the **Volunteers** table to the **VolunteerID** in the **Assignments** table.

9. Select the **Enforce Referential Integrity** check box, and then click **Create**. Compare your screen with Figure 3, click **Save** ⊞, and then **Close** ⊠ the **Relationships tab**.

10. Open the **Assignments** table in Datasheet view. In the append row, in the **TaskID** field, type 1 and then press Tab. In the **VolunteerID** field, type 16 and then press Tab.

> In this record, the Grand Re-Opening task—TaskID 1—has been assigned to Lyle Villagrana—who has a VolunteerID of 16.

11. In the append row, in the **TaskID** field, type 1 and then press Tab. In the **VolunteerID** field, type 4 and then press Tab. Compare your screen with Figure 4.

> A single task has now been assigned to two volunteers. This is a one-to-many relationship.

12. **Close** ⊠ the **Assignments** table.

■ **You have completed Skill 4 of 10**

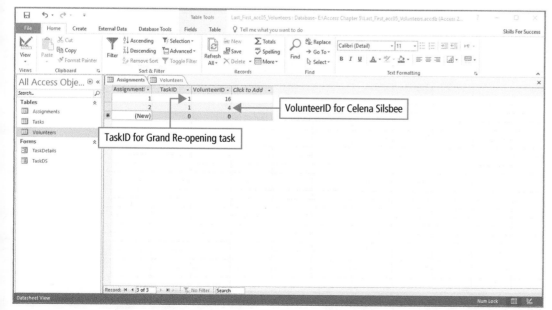

VolunteerID for Celena Silsbee

TaskID for Grand Re-opening task

Access 2016, Windows 10, Microsoft Corporation

Figure 4

 **WATCH** SKILL 5.5

▶ Excel data is commonly used to update or download information from databases. Frequently, Excel data needs to be formatted to work properly with the database.

▶ Deleting and adding columns, removing duplicate records, and filling columns with data are techniques commonly used to prepare data being uploaded to a database.

1. Click the Start button on the taskbar, type Excel and then press [Enter]. On the Excel Start screen, click **Open Other Workbooks**. Navigate to the student data files for this chapter, and then open **acc05_VolunteersData**. Use **Save As** to save the file in your **Access Chapter 5** folder as Last_First_acc05_VolunteersData.

2. Point to the top of column **A**. When the [↓] pointer displays, drag to the right to select columns **A:D**. Press and hold the [Ctrl] key, and use the same technique to select columns **F:K**. Do not select the *Company* column. Compare your screen with **Figure 1**.

3. On the **Home tab**, in the **Cells group**, click the **Delete arrow**, and then click **Delete Sheet Columns**.

4. Click **A** to select column **A**, and then click the **Data tab**. In the **Data Tools group**, click **Remove Duplicates**.

   Removing duplicates ensures that only one record is created for each company.

5. In the **Remove Duplicates** dialog box, select the **My data has headers** check box, and then verify the **Company** check box is selected. Compare your screen with **Figure 2**, and then click **OK**.

■ Continue to the next page to complete the skill

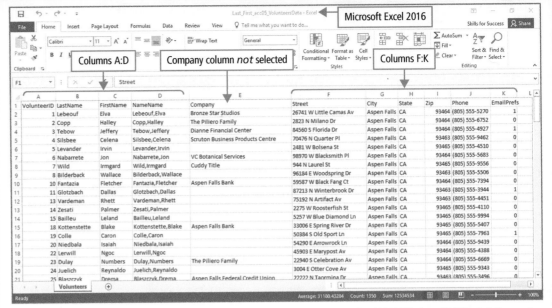

Figure 1

Excel 2016, Windows 10, Microsoft Corporation

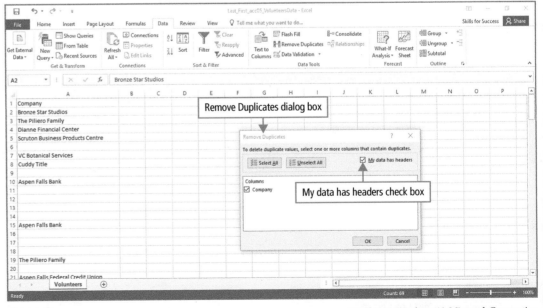

Figure 2

Excel 2016, Windows 10, Microsoft Corporation

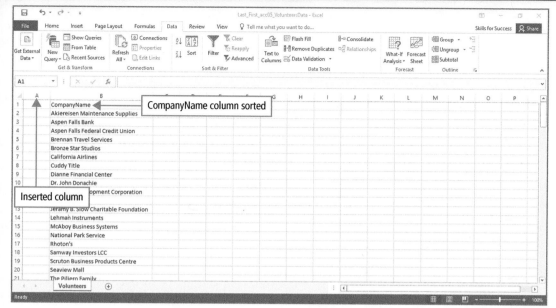

CompanyName column sorted

Inserted column

Excel 2016, Windows 10, Microsoft Corporation

Figure 3

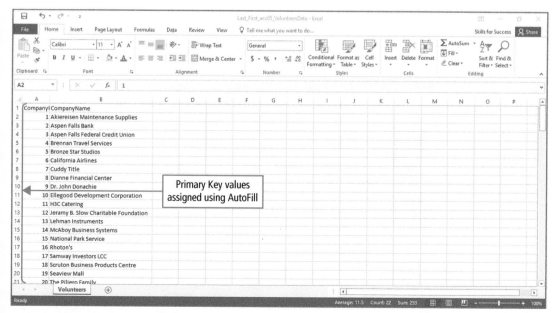

Primary Key values assigned using AutoFill

Excel 2016, Windows 10, Microsoft Corporation

Figure 4

6. Read the message and then click **OK**.

   Duplicate company names were removed from the column, leaving 23 unique values.

7. With the ➡ pointer, click to select row **6**, and then on the **Home tab**, in the **Cells group**, click **Delete**.

8. Click cell **A1**, type CompanyName and then press Enter. Drag to select the range **A2** to **A23**, and then click the **Data tab**. In the **Sort & Filter group**, click the **Sort A to Z** button.

9. Right-click column **A**, and then click **Insert**. Compare your screen with Figure 3.

10. Click cell **A1**, type CompanyID and then press Enter. In cell **A2**, type 1 and then press Enter. In cell **A3**, type 2 and then press Enter.

11. Drag to select the range **A2** to **A23**, and then click the **Home tab**. In the **Editing group**, click **Fill**, and then click **Series**. In the **Series** dialog box, click **OK** to fill the **CompanyID** column. Compare your screen with Figure 4.

    AutoFill is an Excel tool that quickly adds consecutive values to cells. These values can be numbers or certain types of words such as days and months. Here, the CompanyID values were created for use as the primary key in the Companies table that will be created when the data is imported.

12. Click **Save**, and then **Close** the file.

■ **You have completed Skill 5 of 10**

▶ Tables can be created automatically during the data import process. The information contained in the data file is used to assign field names and properties.

▶ After creating a table by importing data, it is a good idea to review and adjust the table's properties.

1. Ensure the **Last_First_acc05_Volunteers** Access file is active.

2. Click the **External Data tab**, and then in the **Import & Link group**, click **Excel**. In the **Get External Data - Excel Spreadsheet** dialog box, click **Browse**. In the **File Open** dialog box, navigate to your **Access Chapter 5** folder, select **Last_First_VolunteersData**, and then click **Open**.

3. In the **Get External Data - Excel Spreadsheet** dialog box, verify the **Import the source data into a new table in the current database** option button is selected. Compare your screen with **Figure 1**, and then click **OK**.

4. In the **Import Spreadsheet Wizard** dialog box, verify that the **First Row Contains Column Headings** check box is selected, and then click **Next**. Under **Field Options**, with **CompanyID** selected as the **Field Name**, click the **Data Type**, and then click **Long Integer**.

5. Click **Next**. Select the **Choose my own primary key** option button, and then verify that **CompanyID** is selected. Compare your screen with **Figure 2**, and then click **Next**.

If you do not choose a field to be the primary key, an AutoNumber primary key will automatically be created.

■ **Continue to the next page to complete the skill** ➤

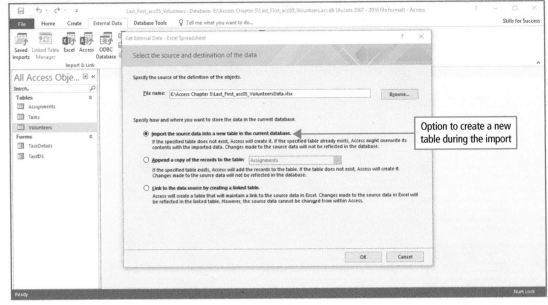

Figure 1

Access 2016, Windows 10, Microsoft Corporation

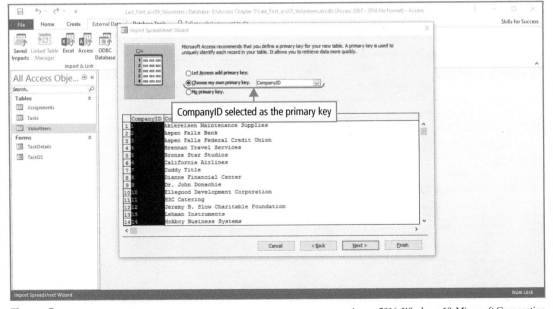

Figure 2

Access 2016, Windows 10, Microsoft Corporation

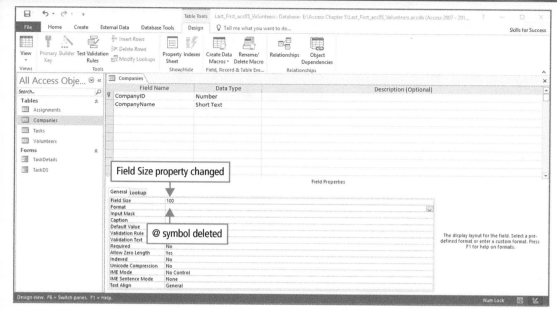

Field Size property changed

@ symbol deleted

Access 2016, Windows 10, Microsoft Corporation

Figure 3

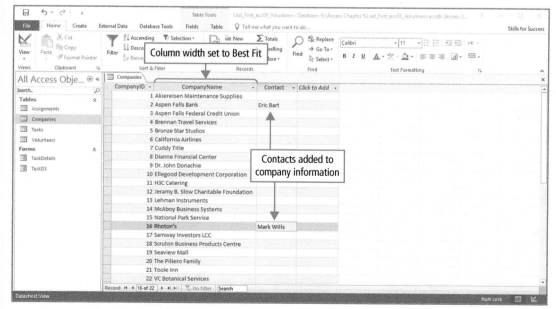

Column width set to Best Fit

Contacts added to company information

Access 2016, Windows 10, Microsoft Corporation

Figure 4

6. In the **Import to Table** box, replace the text with Companies and then click **Finish** to create the table. **Close** the **Save Import Steps** dialog box.

7. Open the **Companies** table, and then switch to Design view.

8. Click the **CompanyName** cell, and then in the **Field Properties** pane, change the **Field Size** to 100 In the **Format** box, delete the @ symbol. Compare your screen with **Figure 3**.

> Recall that the @ symbol indicates the formatting from the original Excel file may not have been imported.

9. Click **Save** 🖫, read the message, and then click **Yes**.

> Reducing the field size to 100 allows for fewer characters in the CompanyName field.

10. Switch to Datasheet view. Select the CompanyName column. On the **Home tab**, in the **Records group**, click **More**, and then click **Field Width**. In the **Column Width** dialog box, click **Best Fit**.

11. Click **Click to Add**, and then click **Short Text**. Type Contact and then press Enter to name the field.

12. Click the **Contact** field for *Aspen Falls Bank*, type Eric Bart and then press Enter. Click the **Contact** field for *Rhoton's*, and then type Mark Wills Compare your screen with **Figure 4**.

13. Click **Save** 🖫, and then **Close** ✕ the table.

■ **You have completed Skill 6 of 10**

▶ A **Lookup field** is a field in which values are obtained from another table or from a list.

▶ Lookups increase data entry efficiency and reduce errors by providing defined options to choose from during the data entry process.

1. Open the **Volunteers** table in Datasheet view. Click the **FirstName** field name, and then click the **Table Tools Fields tab**. In the **Add & Delete group**, click the **More Fields** button, and then click **Lookup & Relationship** to start the Lookup Wizard.

2. In the **Lookup Wizard**, verify that the **I want the lookup field to get the values from another table or query** option button is selected, and then click **Next**.

3. Click **Table: Companies**, compare your screen with **Figure 1**, and then click **Next**.

4. Under **Available Fields**, click **CompanyName**, and then click the **Add Field** button ▷. Click **Next**.

   Adding a lookup for CompanyName allows users to quickly select from a list of companies. Here, the values will be selected from values stored in the Companies table.

5. Click the **arrow** to the left of the **Ascending** button, and then click **CompanyName**. Click **Next**, compare your screen to **Figure 2**, and then click **Next**.

■ Continue to the next page to complete the skill ▶

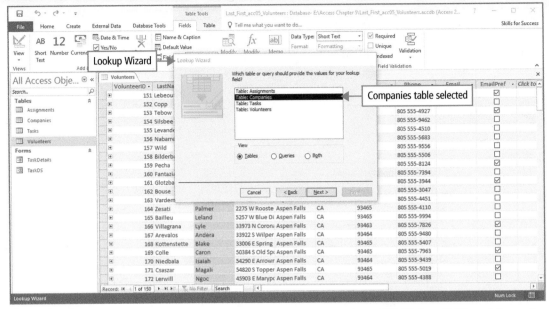

Figure 1

Access 2016, Windows 10, Microsoft Corporation

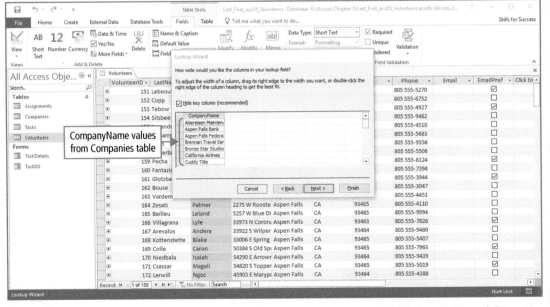

Figure 2

Access 2016, Windows 10, Microsoft Corporation

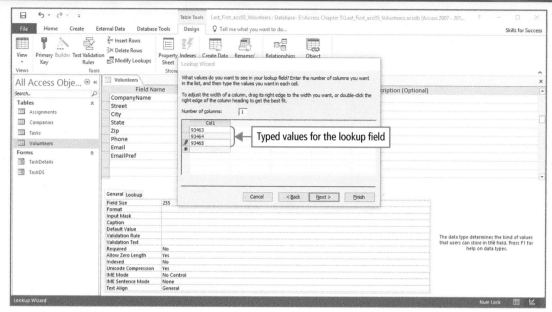

Access 2016, Windows 10, Microsoft Corporation

Figure 3

6. Under **What label would you like for your lookup** field, type CompanyName and then click **Finish**.

7. Switch to Design view. Click the **Zip** field, click the **Data Type arrow**, and then click **Lookup Wizard**.

8. In the **Lookup Wizard**, select the **I will type in the values that I want** option button, and then click **Next**.

9. In the first three rows, type these zip codes in the following order: 93463 | 93464 | 93465 Compare your screen with **Figure 3**.

In this lookup, the values that you type in the Wizard will be used for the lookup data.

10. Accept the remaining wizard defaults by clicking **Finish**, and then click **Save** 🖫. Switch to Datasheet view.

If you create a lookup for the wrong field, you can delete the lookup in the Field Properties pane Lookup tab.

11. In the first record, click the **Zip** field, click the **Zip field arrow**, and then click **93463**. Compare your screen with **Figure 4**.

12. Click the **CompanyName** field, and then if necessary, click the **Home tab**. In the **Records group**, click **More**, and then click **Row Height**. In the **Row Height** box, type 32 and then click **OK**.

13. In the second record, display and click the **CompanyName** arrow. Select **Bronze Star Studios**.

14. Click **Save** 🖫, and then **Close** ⊠ the table.

■ **You have completed Skill 7 of 10**

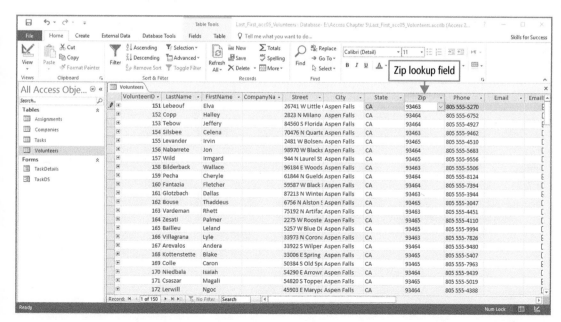

Access 2016, Windows 10, Microsoft Corporation

Figure 4

▸ **Extensible Markup Language (XML)** is a standard that uses text characters to define the meaning, structure, and appearance of data.

▸ XML stores data in text files and is a common method for storing database, application, and operating system data.

1. On the taskbar, click **File Explorer**, and then navigate to the student files for this chapter. Right-click **acc05_VolunteerLogons**. From the shortcut menu, point to **Open with**, and then click **Notepad. Maximize** □ the Notepad window and compare your screen with **Figure 1**.

> The text between the < and > characters is called a **tag. Data elements** consist of an opening tag, the actual data, and a closing tag.
>
> The xsd file acc05_VolunteerXSD included with the student data files contains instructions about how the xml file should be interpreted.

2. Close **Notepad** without saving changes. In Access, click the **External Data tab**, and then in the **Import & Link group**, click **XML File**.

3. In the **Get External Data - XML File** dialog box, click **Browse**, and navigate to your student files. Click **acc05_VolunteerLogons**, and then click **Open**. In the **Get External Data-XML File** dialog box, click **OK**.

4. In the **Import XML** dialog box, expand **Logons**, and then verify that the **Structure and Data** option button is selected. Compare your screen with **Figure 2**, and then click **OK**.

5. In the **Get External Data - XML File** dialog box, select the **Save import steps** check box.

■ **Continue to the next page to complete the skill**

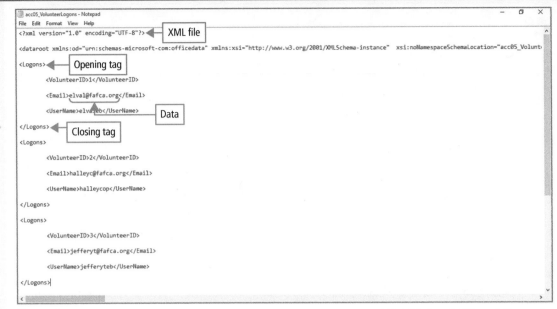

Figure 1   Notepad 2016, Windows 10, Microsoft Corporation

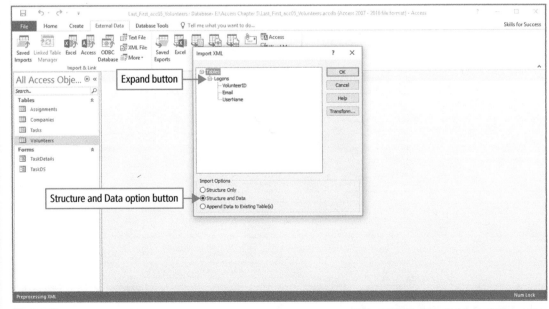

Figure 2   Access 2016, Windows 10, Microsoft Corporation

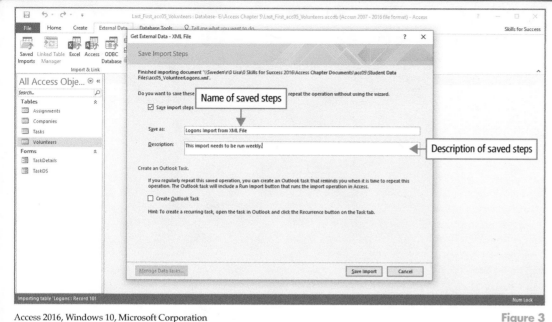

Access 2016, Windows 10, Microsoft Corporation

Figure 3

Access 2016, Windows 10, Microsoft Corporation

Figure 4

6. In the **Save as** box, select the text *import-acc05_VolunteerLogons*, and then type Logons Import from XML File

7. In the **Description** box, type This import needs to be run weekly. Compare your screen with **Figure 3**, and then click **Save Import**.

   When imported data files will be used to update existing tables frequently, you can save time by saving the imported steps. Here, logon data can be imported again by clicking the saved imported steps instead of opening the Import Wizard.

   You can check the Create Outlook Task check box and a reminder will be added to your Outlook tasks. The reminder will include a button that will run the import process in Access.

8. Open the **Logons** table in Design view. If necessary, click the **VolunteerID** field. In the **Field Properties** pane, display and click the **Field Size arrow**, and then click **Long Integer**. Click the **View** button, read the message that displays, and then click **Yes** to save the change.

9. Read the next message, and then click **Yes**. Verify that the XML data was imported, as shown in **Figure 4**.

10. Switch to Design view. Click the **Email** field, and then in the **Field Properties** pane, remove the @ symbol from the **Format** property. Repeat the technique to remove the @ symbol from the **UserName** field **Format** property.

11. **Save** [📷], and then **Close** [✕] the table.

■ **You have completed Skill 8 of 10**

▶ **Unmatched records** occur when the data contained in one field does not have a corresponding value in a related table. In this skill, some logons do not have corresponding values in the Volunteers table.

▶ In a **one-to-one relationship**, each record in one table can have only one corresponding record in the other table.

1. Click the **Create tab**, and then in the **Queries group**, click the **Query Wizard** button.

2. In the **New Query** dialog box, click **Find Unmatched Query Wizard**. Read the information displayed on the left side of the **New Query** dialog box. Compare your screen with **Figure 1**, and then click **OK**.

3. At the top of the **Find Unmatched Query Wizard**, read the information that displays, and then select **Table: Logons**. Click **Next**, click **Table: Volunteers**, and then click **Next**.

4. Compare your screen with **Figure 2**, and then click **Next**.

    Each logon record should have a matching volunteer record. The query will search for volunteer IDs that appear in the Logons table, but not the Volunteers table.

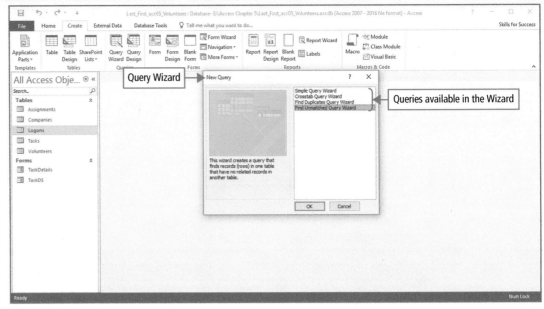

Figure 1

Access 2016, Windows 10, Microsoft Corporation

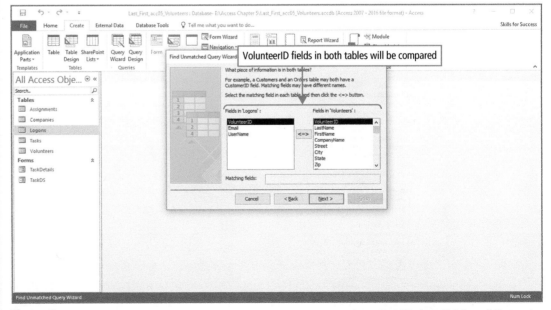

Figure 2

Access 2016, Windows 10, Microsoft Corporation

■ Continue to the next page to complete the skill

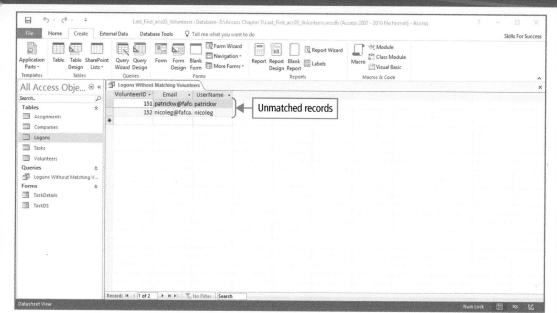

Access 2016, Windows 10, Microsoft Corporation

Figure 3

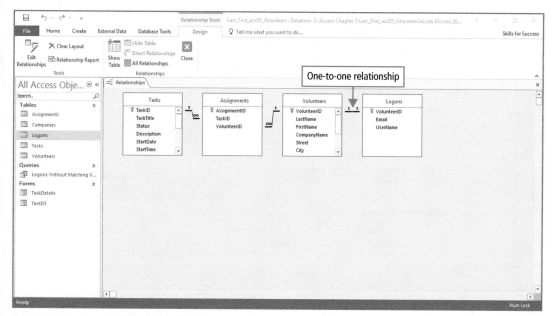

Access 2016, Windows 10, Microsoft Corporation

Figure 4

5. Move **All** available fields into **Selected fields**. Click **Next**, and then click **Finish** to open the **Logons Without Matching Volunteers** query datasheet. Compare your screen with Figure 3.

6. With the first record active, click the **Home tab**. In the **Records group**, click the **Delete arrow**, and then click **Delete Record**. Read the message that displays, and then click **Yes**. Repeat the technique just practiced to delete the other unmatched record.

MOS
Obj 2.3.3

7. **Close** ⊠ the query.

8. Click the **Database Tools tab**, and then in the **Relationships** group, click **Relationships**. In the **Relationships group**, click **Show Table**.

9. Select the **Logons** table, click **Add**, and then **Close** the **Show Table** dialog box.

10. Drag the **VolunteerID** from the **Volunteers** table to the **VolunteerID** in the **Logons** table to open the **Edit Relationships** dialog box.

11. In the **Edit Relationships** dialog box, click **Enforce Referential Integrity**, click **Create**, and then compare your screen with Figure 4.

   Each volunteer can have only one logon, and each logon can be associated with only one volunteer.

12. Click **Save** 🖫, and then **Close** ⊠ the **Relationships** tab.

■ **You have completed Skill 9 of 10**

▶ *Database documentation* is information about object properties, relationships, and permissions in a database.

▶ *Database Documenter* is an Access tool that creates database documentation.

1. Click the **Database Tools tab**, and then in the **Analyze group**, click **Database Documenter**.

2. In the **Documenter** dialog box, if necessary, click the **Tables tab**, and then select the **Assignments**, **Companies**, **Logons**, **Tasks**, and **Volunteers** check boxes. Compare your screen with **Figure 1**, and then click **OK** to create the **Object Definition** report.

3. In the Navigation bar, click the **Next Page** button ▶ one time to view Page 2.

4. In the **Zoom group**, click the **Zoom arrow**, and then click **150%**.

5. **Close** « the Navigation Pane, and then scroll down to view the **Relationships** section. Compare your screen with **Figure 2**.

Database documentation lists tables, field properties, relationships between tables, and permissions. This information is used by database administrators for reference and planning purposes. Here, information about the Assignments table primary key displays.

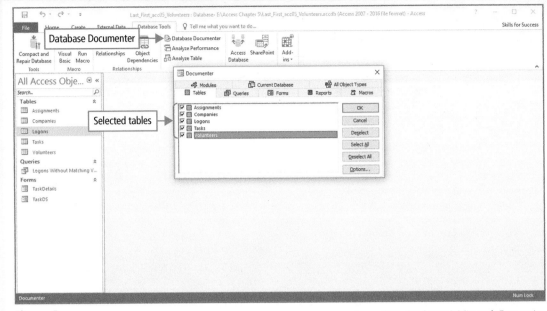

Figure 1

Access 2016, Windows 10, Microsoft Corporation

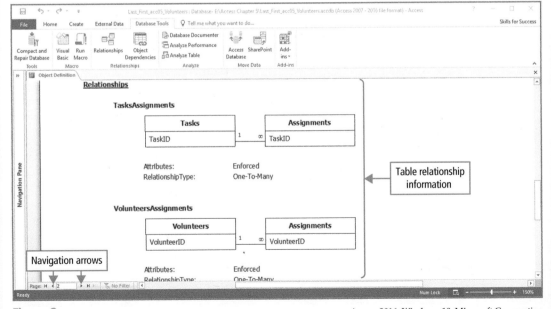

Figure 2

Access 2016, Windows 10, Microsoft Corporation

■ Continue to the next page to complete the skill

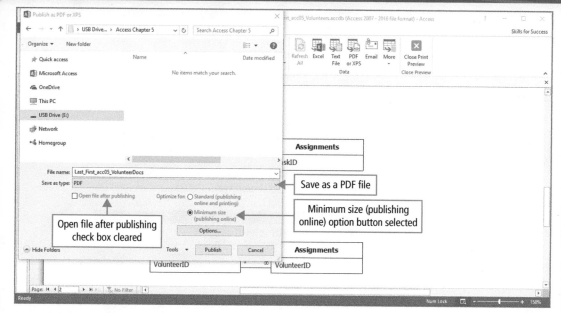

Access 2016, Windows 10, Microsoft Corporation

Figure 3

6. On the Print Preview tab, in the **Data group**, click **PDF or XPS**. In the **Publish as PDF or XPS** dialog box, navigate to your **Access Chapter 5** folder, and then in the **File name:** text box, type Last_First_acc05_VolunteerDocs

7. Verify that **PDF** is selected as the **Save as type**, and then if necessary, clear the **Open file after publishing** check box.

8. If necessary, select the **Minimum size (publishing online)** option button. Compare your screen to **Figure 3**, and then click **Publish**.

   Database documentation is frequently stored on an organization's shared drives. As the database is altered, new documentation is created and uploaded to the drive. Previous records are maintained so a history of the database is documented.

9. **Close** the **Export - PDF** window.

10. Click the **First Page** |◄| button, and then scroll to the top of the page to display the **Properties** section.

11. Compare your screen to **Figure 4**, and then in the **Close Preview group**, click **Close Print Preview**.

12. **Open** |»| the Navigation Pane, and then **Close** |×| Access. Submit the files as directed by your instructor.

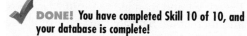
DONE! You have completed Skill 10 of 10, and your database is complete!

Access 2016, Windows 10, Microsoft Corporation

Figure 4

More Skills 11

Create Custom Input Masks

To complete this project, you will need the following file:

- acc05_MS11Highways

You will save your file as:

- Last_First_acc05_MS11Highways

▶ **Custom Input Masks** are input masks created to meet specific needs such as the number of characters entered into a field.

▶ Input masks are used to control how users enter data into a field in order to maintain consistency with data entry.

▶ When you need to enter data that does not follow one of the input masks provided in the Input Mask wizard, you can customize the input mask to accommodate the data you need.

---

1. Start **Access 2016**, and then open the student data file **acc05_ MS11Highways**. **Save** the file in your **Access Chapter 5** folder as Last_First_ acc05_MS11Highways If necessary, enable the content.

2. Open the **Sponsors** table in Design view.

3. Click anywhere in the **State** row. In the **Field Properties** pane, click **Input Mask**, and then click the **Build** button ⋯.

4. In the **Input Mask Wizard**, click **Edit list**. Compare your screen with Figure 1.

   The Customize Input Mask Wizard dialog box is used to create new input masks.

5. In the **Customize Input Mask Wizard** dialog box, click the **New (blank) record** button ▶. In the **Description** box, type State

6. Press Tab, and then in the **Input Mask** box, type >LL Press Tab two times, and then in the **Sample Data** box, type ca and then **Close** the **Customize Input Mask Wizard** dialog box.

   In the Input Mask box, the wizard placed special characters that control how the input mask will function. For example, the L character indicates that a letter is required. The > character converts any lowercase letters to capital letters.

7. In the **Input Mask Wizard**, under **Input Mask**, click **State**. Click **Finish**.

   Common input mask characters are summarized in Figure 2.

8. **Save** 🖫 the table, and then switch to Datasheet view.

9. In the first record, replace the value in the **Contact Name** field with your First and Last names.

Figure 1   Access 2016, Windows 10, Microsoft Corporation

Character	Usage
0	User must enter a number from 0 to 9.
9	User can enter a number from 0 to 9.
#	User can enter a digit, space, plus, or minus sign.
L	User must enter a letter.
?	User can enter a letter.
A	User must enter a number or letter.
A	User can enter a number or letter.
&	User must enter either a character or a space.
C	User can enter either character or spaces.
. , : ; - /	These are decimal, thousands, placeholders, date and time separators.
>	All characters will be changed to uppercase.
<	All characters will be changed to lowercase.
!	The input mask will fill from left to right.
\	Characters immediately following will be displayed literally.
" "	Characters enclosed in double quotation marks will be displayed literally.

Figure 2   Access 2016, Windows 10, Microsoft Corporation

10. Press Tab, and then type ca

11. In the **State** field for the second record—The Piliero Family—type CAL.

    The input mask prevents you from entering any more characters into the field. During data entry, input masks improve accuracy by reducing mistakes.

12. Press Tab four times, and then in the **State** field, type the number 4

    The input mask prevents you from entering any numbers into the field.

13. Type OR as the State.

14. **Close** the **Sponsors** table, and then **Close** Access.

15. Submit the file as directed by your instructor.

- **You have completed More Skills 11**

More Skills 12

Search and Replace Data in Datasheets and Forms

To complete this project, you will need the following file:

- acc05_MS12Cars

You will save your file as:

- Last_First_acc05_MS12Cars

▶ The Find and Replace tool provides an easy way to locate text and replace it with more appropriate wording.

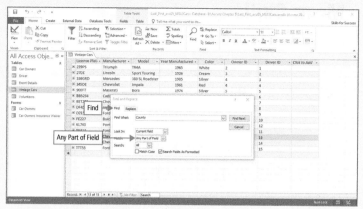

Access 2016, Windows 10, Microsoft Corporation

Figure 1

1. Start **Access 2016**, and then open the student data file **acc05_MS12Cars**. **Save** the file in your **Access Chapter 5** folder as Last_First_acc05_MS12Cars If necessary, enable the content.

2. Open the **Vintage Cars** table in Datasheet view, and then click the **Model** column. On the **Home tab**, in the **Find group**, click **Find**.

3. In the **Find and Replace** dialog box, in the **Find What** text box, type County 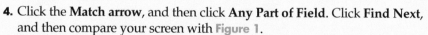 **Obj 2.3.5**

4. Click the **Match arrow**, and then click **Any Part of Field**. Click **Find Next**, and then compare your screen with **Figure 1**.

    The field containing the text is highlighted.

5. In the **Find and Replace** dialog box, click the **Replace tab**, and then in the **Replace With** text box, type Country

6. Click **Replace**. **Close** the **Find and Replace** dialog box, and then compare your screen with **Figure 2**.

7. **Close** the **Vintage Cars** table.

8. Open the **Car Owners** form in Form view, and then on the **Home tab**, in the **Find group**, click **Find**.

9. In the **Find and Replace** dialog box, in the **Find What** text box, type Nomee Click the **Look In arrow**, and then click **Current Document**. Click **Find Next**.

10. In the **Find and Replace** dialog box, click the **Replace tab**. In the **Replace With** text box, type Nomen and then click **Replace**.

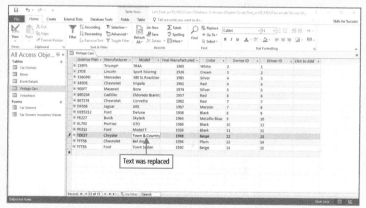

Access 2016, Windows 10, Microsoft Corporation

Figure 2

11. **Close** the **Find and Replace** dialog box, and then **Close** the **Car Owners** form.

12. **Close** ☒ Access. Submit the file as directed by your instructor.

- **You have completed More Skills 12**

More Skills 13

Export XML Data

To complete this project, you will need the following file:

- acc05_MS13Rentals

You will save your file as:

- Last_First_acc05_MS13Renters

▶ Access tables can be exported as XML text files.

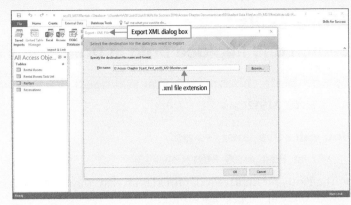

Figure 1   Access 2016, Windows 10, Microsoft Corporation

1. Start **Access 2016**, and then open the student data file **acc05_MS13Rentals**. If necessary, enable the content.

2. In the **Navigation Pane**, click the **Renters** table to select it. Click the **External Data tab**, and then in the **Export group**, click **XML File**.

3. In the **Export - XML File** dialog box, click **Browse**. In the **File Save** dialog box, navigate to your **Access Chapter 5** folder. In the **File Name** box, replace *Renters* with Last_First_acc05_MS13Renters and then click **Save**. Compare your screen with Figure 1.

   XML text files are assigned the.xml file extension.

4. In the **Export - XML File** dialog box, click **OK**.

   The Export XML dialog box can export the data—XML, the table field properties—XSD, and/or the table formatting—XSL.

5. In the **Export XML** dialog box, verify the **Data (XML)** check box and the **Schema of the data (XSD)** check box are selected. Click **OK**. **Close** the **Export - XML File** dialog box.

6. On the taskbar, click **File Explorer** 📁. In the displayed folder window, navigate to your **Access Chapter 5** folder.

7. Right-click **Last_First_acc05_MS13Renters**. From the shortcut menu, point to **Open with**, and then click **Notepad**. Compare your screen with Figure 2.

   During the export process, each record was converted into a Renters XML element, and XML tags for the field names within each record were created.

8. In the first line of the XML document, click to the right of "*UTF-8*"?>, and then press [Enter]. Using your own name, type the following XML comment: <!-- Exported by First Last -->

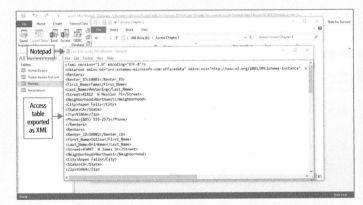

Figure 2   Access 2016, Windows 10, Microsoft Corporation

9. From the **File** menu click **Save**, and then **Close** Notepad.

10. **Close** Access. Submit the file as directed by your instructor.

- **You have completed More Skills 13**

More Skills 14

Make Tables from Queries

To complete this project, you will need the following file:

- acc05_MS14Museum

You will save your file as:

- Last_First_acc05_MS14Museum

▶ A **Make Table Query** is used to create a new table from the results of the query.

▶ Tables are made from queries when migrating data to a new database or to capture and store data at a specific point in time.

---

1. Start **Access 2016**, and then open the student data file **acc05_MS14Museum**. **Save** the file in your **Access Chapter 5** folder as Last_First_acc05_MS14Museum If necessary, enable the content.

2. On the **Create tab**, in the **Queries group**, click **Query Design**.

3. Add the **Museum Cars** table to the Design grid. **Close** the **Show Table** dialog box, and then double-click each of the **Museum Cars** fields to add them to the query columns.

4. **Run** the query and verify that four records display. In the **Loanable?** column, notice that two cars cannot be loaned. Compare your screen with **Figure 1**.

   Before creating a new table, it is good practice to first view the results using a select query. You can verify that you are adding the desired records to the new table. Here, the two cars that are not loanable are the data needed to be used to create the new table.

5. Switch to Design view. In the **Loanable?** column **Criteria** box, type No **Run** the query, and then compare your screen with **Figure 2**.

6. Switch to Design view. Click **Save**, type Cars Not Loaned and then click **OK**.

7. On the **Design tab**, in the **Query Type group**, click **Make Table**. In the **Make Table** dialog box, type Cars Not Loaned to name the table that will be created. Click **OK**.

   In the Make Table dialog box, you specify the name of the new table that will contain the records from the query.

8. **Run** the query. Read the message, and then click **Yes**. Read the next message, and then click **Yes**. Click **Close**, and then click **Yes** two times to save the query.

   In the Navigation Pane, the query has an icon indicating it is a make table query. Each time you run a make table query, a message will display warning that the last table created from this query will be deleted before the query is run.

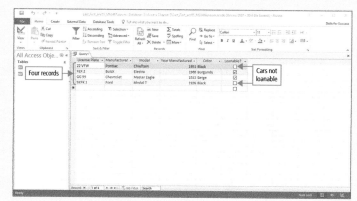

Access 2016, Windows 10, Microsoft Corporation   Figure 1

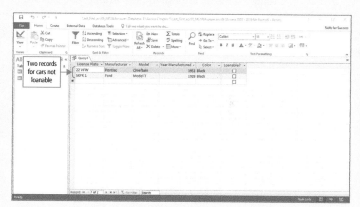

Access 2016, Windows 10, Microsoft Corporation   Figure 2

9. In the **Navigation Pane**, double-click to open the **Cars Not Loaned** table, which has two records.

10. **Close** the **Cars Not Loaned** table, and then **Close** Access.

11. Submit the file as directed by your instructor.

■ **You have completed More Skills 14**

The following table summarizes the **SKILLS AND PROCEDURES** covered in this chapter.

Skill	Task	Step
1	Index fields	Design view → click the field → field property pane → Indexed property
1	Set fields as required	Design view → click the field → field property pane → Required property
1	Change the Yes/No data type format	Design view → click the field name → Data Type arrow → Yes/No
1	Add Input Masks to fields	Design view → Field Properties → Input Mask
2	Import data from text files	External Data → Import & Link → Text File
3	Create tables from Application Parts	Create tab → Templates group → Application Parts → Quick Start
3	Adjust row heights	Home tab → Records group → More → Row Height
3	Set column widths	Right-click field name → Field Width
3	Add Rich Text fields	Fields tab → Properties groups → Memo Settings → Rich Text
4	Create many-to-many relationships	Database Tools tab → Relationships → Show Table → Drag keys to tables → Select Enforce Referential Integrity
5	Remove duplicate records in Excel	Data tab → Data Tools group → Remove Duplicates
5	Assign primary key values in Excel	Highlight cells → Home tab → Editing group → Fill → Series → OK
6	Create tables by importing data from Excel files	External Data tab → Import & Link → Excel → Import the source data into a new table in the current database
7	Create Lookup fields	Click field name, from Fields tab in the Add & Delete group, click More Fields. Click Lookup & Relationship
7	Create Lookup from a typed list	Design view → Select field → Data Type arrow → Lookup Wizard → I will type in the values that I want → Next → Type values
7	Create Lookup from another table	Fields tab → Add & Delete group → More Fields → Lookup & Relationship → Select the I want the lookup field to get the values from another table or query option button
8	View XML files in Notepad	Right-click file, click Open with, and then click Notepad
8	Import XML data	External Data tab → Import & Link → XML File
9	Find unmatched records	Create tab → Queries group → Query Wizard → Find Unmatched Query
9	Create one-to-one relationships	Enforce referential integrity using a foreign key that is also a primary key for its table. The foreign key can also be any field that is indexed with no duplicates.
10	Create database documentation	Database Tools tab → Analyze group → Database Documenter
10	Export database documentation as PDF files	With the database documentation open in Print Preview, in the Data group, click PDF
MS11	Create Custom Input Mask	Field property selected → Input Mask build button → Edit list → New blank record
MS12	Find and Replace	Home tab → Find group → Find → Find What
MS13	Export XML data	External Data tab → Export group → XML File
MS14	Make Table query	Design tab → Query Type group → Make Table

Project Summary Chart

Project	Project Type	Project Location
Skills Review	Review	In Book and MIL MyITLab® Grader
Skills Assessment 1	Review	In Book and MIL MyITLab® Grader
Skills Assessment 2	Review	Book
My Skills	Problem Solving	Book
Visual Skills Check	Problem Solving	Book
Skills Challenge 1	Critical Thinking	Book
Skills Challenge 2	Critical Thinking	Book
More Skills Assessment	Review	In Book and MIL MyITLab® Grader
Collaborating with Google	Critical Thinking	Book

MOS Objectives Covered (Quiz in MyITLab®)

1.1.3 Create a database by using import objects or data from other sources	2.3.5 Find and replace data
2.1.5 Create a table from a template with application parts	2.4.7 Set default values
2.3.1 Update records	2.4.9 Delete field
2.3.3 Delete records	

Key Terms

Online Help Skills

1. Start **Access 2016**, and then in the upper right corner of the start page, click the **Help** button [?].

2. In the **Access Help** window **Search help** box, type edit a table relationship and then press [Enter].

3. In the search result list, click **Create, edit or delete a relationship**. **Maximize** the window, and then compare your screen with Figure 1.

Figure 1   Access 2016, Windows 10, Microsoft Corporation

4. Read the article to answer the following question: What is a join type, and how is join type used in Access queries?

Matching

Match each term in the second column with its correct definition in the first column by writing the letter of the term on the blank line in front of the correct definition.

___ **1.** Files that store text characters, but not formatting, tables, or graphics.

___ **2.** A text file where columns are separated by a special character such as a space, comma, or tab.

___ **3.** Tables created from templates.

___ **4.** A relationship where one record in either table can have many associated records in the other table.

___ **5.** Tables, forms, and other objects created from templates.

___ **6.** A standard that uses text characters to define the meaning, structure, and appearance of data.

___ **7.** Data contained in a field that does not have corresponding values in a related table.

___ **8.** A relationship where each record in one table can have only one corresponding record in the other table.

___ **9.** An Access tool that creates database documentation.

___ **10.** Information about object properties, relationships, and permissions within a database.

A Database documentation

B Database Documenter

C Delimited text file

D Extensible Markup Language

E Application Parts

F Many-to-many relationship

G One-to-one relationship

H Quick Start table

I Text file

J Unmatched record

Multiple Choice (MyITLab®)

Choose the correct answer.

1. A visual model used to plan a database.
   - A. Database Documenter
   - B. Entity relationship diagram
   - C. Database documentation

2. A directory that stores the locations of all records for a given field in the same way that a book's index stores each location of a word in the book.
   - A. Index
   - B. Database Documenter
   - C. Field properties

3. A property setting that saves time and increases accuracy during the data entry process.
   - A. Field properties
   - B. Input mask
   - C. Default value

4. Characters in text files that indicate columns of data.
   - A. Delimiters
   - B. Parameters
   - C. Indexes

5. A file format that provides the ability to format fonts.
   - A. XML format
   - B. Rich text format
   - C. Delimited format

6. A relationship consisting of two one-to-many relationships.
   - A. One-to-one
   - B. One-to-many
   - C. Many-to-many

7. An Excel tool that adds consecutive values quickly to cells.
   - A. AutoComplete
   - B. AutoFill
   - C. AutoFinish

8. A field property that provides defined values to choose from during the data entry process.
   - A. AutoFill
   - B. Lookup
   - C. Input Mask

9. Stores data in text files and is a common method for storing database, application, and operating system data.
   - A. HTML
   - B. DOC
   - C. XML

10. Documentation that displays table relationship information.
   - A. Database documentation
   - B. Delimited files
   - C. Extensible Markup Language

Topics for Discussion

1. When designing a database, is it best to create an entity relationship diagram first, or is it better to create tables throughout the process? State the reasons for your answer.

2. When creating a table, which method would be best—using an Application Part or creating a table in Datasheet view? State the reasons for your answer.

Skills Review

MyITLab®
Grader

To complete this project, you will need the following files:

- acc05_SRData (Excel)
- acc05_SRMembers (Text)
- acc05_SRLogons (XML)
- acc05_SRUsers (XSD)
- acc05_SRCommittees (Access)

You will save your files as:

- Last_First_acc05_SRCommittees
- Last_First_acc05_SRData
- Last_First_acc05_SRDocs

1. Start **Access 2016**. Open the student data file **acc05_SRCommittees**, and then save the file in your **Access Chapter 5** folder as Last_First_acc05_SRCommittees If necessary, enable the content.

2. Open the **Members** table in Datasheet view. Click the **LastName** column, and then click the **Table Tools Fields tab**. In the **Field Validation group**, select the **Required** and **Indexed** check boxes.

3. Click the **Street** column. In the **Properties group**, click the **Memo Settings arrow**, and then click **Rich Text**. In the message that displays, click **Yes**.

4. Switch to Design view. Click the **Zip** field, click the **Data Type arrow**, and then click **Lookup Wizard**. Select the **I will type in the values that I want** option button, and then click **Next**. In **Col1**, type the following values: 93463 | 93464 | 93465 Compare your screen with **Figure 1**, and then click **Finish**.

5. **Save** and **Close** the **Members** table.

6. Click the **External Data tab**, and then in the **Import & Link group**, click **Text File**. In the **Import Wizard**, click **Browse**, and then locate and double-click **acc05_SRMembers**. In the wizard, select the **Append a copy of the records to the table** option button, and then verify the **Members** table is selected. Compare your screen with **Figure 2**, and then click **OK**.

7. In the **Import Text Wizard**, click **Next**, and then select the **First Row Contains Field Names** check box. Click **Finish**, and then click **Close**.

8. Click the **Create tab**. In the **Templates group**, click **Application Parts**, and then click **Users**.

Access 2016, Windows 10, Microsoft Corporation   **Figure 1**

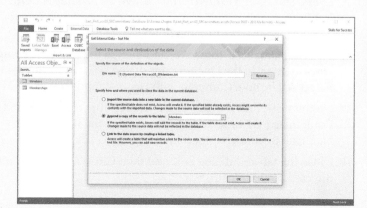

Access 2016, Windows 10, Microsoft Corporation   **Figure 2**

■ Continue to the next page to complete this Skills Review

9. In the **Create Relationship** dialog box, select the **There is no relationship** option button, and then click **Create**.

10. On the **External Data tab**, in the **Import & Link group**, click **XML File**. In the **Import Wizard**, click **Browse**, and then locate and double-click **acc05_SRLogons**. Click **OK**. In the **Import XML** dialog box, select the **Append Data to Existing Table(s)** option button. Click **OK**, and then click **Close**.

11. Start **Excel 2016**, and then open **acc05_SRData**. In cell **A1**, type CommitteeName Select column **B**, and then on the **Home tab**, in the **Cells group**, click **Delete**. Save the file in your chapter folder as Last_First_acc05_SRData and then **Close** Excel.

12. Switch to Access. On the **External Data tab**, in the **Import & Link group**, click **Excel**. Click **Browse**, and then locate and double-click **Last_First_acc05_SRData**. Click **OK** to start the **Import Spreadsheet Wizard**. Select the **First Row Contains Column Headings** check box, click **Finish**, and then click **Close**.

13. Click the **Database Tools tab**, and then in the **Relationships group**, click **Relationships**.

14. Relate the **Committees** table to the **Memberships** table by joining the **ID** field to the **CommitteeID** field. For the relationship, enforce referential integrity. Relate the **Members** table to the **Memberships** table by using the **MemberID** fields. For the relationship, enforce referential integrity. Compare with Figure 3, and then **Save** and **Close** the **Relationships tab**.

15. On the **Create tab**, in the **Queries group**, click **Query Wizard**. Click **Find Unmatched Query Wizard**, and then click **OK**. In the **Find Unmatched Query Wizard**, select **Table: Members**, and then click **Next**. Select the **Table: Users**, and click **Next** two times. **Move all Available fields** into **Selected fields**, and then click **Finish**. In the query results, **Delete** the one record that displays, and then **Close** the query.

16. Click the **Database Tools tab**, and then in the **Analyze group**, click **Database Documenter**. In the **Documenter** dialog box, on the **Tables tab**, click the **Select All** button. Compare with Figure 4, and then click **OK**.

17. On the **Print Preview** tab, in the **Data group**, click **PDF or XPS**. In the **Publish as PDF or XPS** dialog box, name the file Last_First_acc05_SRDocs Navigate to your chapter folder, and then click **Publish**.

18. **Close** the tab and dialog box, and then **Close** Access. Submit the files as directed by your instructor.

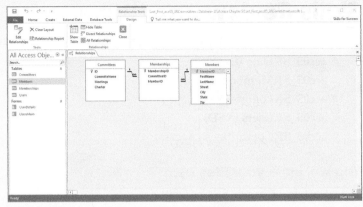

Figure 3   Access 2016, Windows 10, Microsoft Corporation

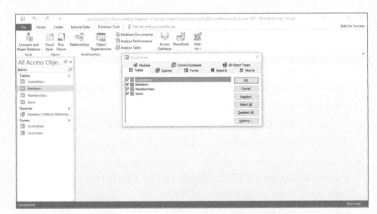

Figure 4   Access 2016, Windows 10, Microsoft Corporation

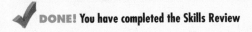

DONE! You have completed the Skills Review

Skills Assessment 1

MyITLab®
Grader

To complete this project, you will need the following files:

- acc05_SA1CheckOut (Access)
- acc05_SA1Acct (XML)
- acc05_SA1Accounts (XSD)
- acc05_SA1Equipment (Excel)
- acc05_SA1Employees (Text)

You will save your files as:

- Last_First_acc05_SA1CheckOut
- Last_First_acc05_SA1Equipment

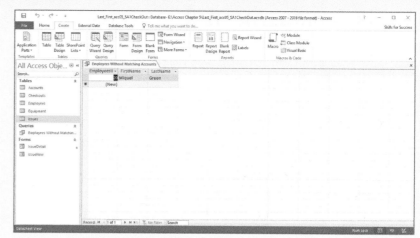

Access 2016, Windows 10, Microsoft Corporation

Figure 1

1. Start **Access 2016**, and then open the student data file **acc05_SA1CheckOut**. **Save** the file in your **Access Chapter 5** folder as Last_First_acc05_SA1CheckOut

2. Create a new table by importing the XML file **acc05_SA1Acct**. Use the *Save Import Steps* dialog box to save the import with the name Accounts Import from XML File and a **Description** of This import needs to be run every other day.

3. In the **Checkouts** table, change the **Checkout** field name to CheckoutDate

4. For the **CheckoutDate** field, add the **Short Date** input mask. **Save** and **Close** the **Checkouts** table.

5. Prepare the Excel file **acc05_SA1Equipment** by deleting the **Warranty** column and using **Fill Series** to populate the **EquipmentID** field. Save the file in your chapter folder as Last_First_acc05_SA1Equipment **Close** Excel.

6. Create a new table named Equipment by importing the Excel file **Last_First_acc05_SA1Equipment**. Make the primary key **EquipmentID**, and then change the field's data type to **Long Integer**.

7. Add a Lookup field as the last field in the **Equipment** table, named Garage For the lookup, use a list you type with the following values: 1|2|3

8. Change the **Equipment** field size to 200 **Save** and **Close** the **Equipment** table.

9. Import the text file **acc05_SA1Employees** so that records are appended to the **Employees** table.

10. In the **Employees** table, set the **FirstName** and **LastName** to **Required**. **Save** and **Close** the table.

11. Using **Application Parts**, create an **Issues** table with no relationship to other tables. Rename the primary key IssuesID

12. In the **Issues** table, add the field CheckoutsID in the last column, and then change the **CheckoutsID** field data type to **Number**. **Save** and **Close** the table.

13. Open the **Relationships tab**. Create a one-to-one relationship between the **Employees** and **Accounts** tables.

14. Create a many-to-many relationship by dragging the **Employees** table **EmployeesID** to the **Checkouts** table **EmployeesID**. Select **Enforce Referential Integrity**, and then click **Create**. Drag the **Equipment** table **EquipmentID** to the **Checkouts** table **EquipmentID**, select **Enforce Referential Integrity**, and then click **Create**.

15. On the **Create tab**, in the **Queries group**, run the **Find Unmatched Query Wizard** to find **Employees** without matching **Accounts**. Compare your screen with **Figure 1**, and then delete the unmatched record.

16. **Close** Access. Submit your files as directed by your instructor.

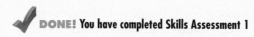 **DONE! You have completed Skills Assessment 1**

Skills Assessment 2

To complete this project, you will need the following files:

- acc05_SA2Park (Access)
- acc05_SA2Employees (Text)
- acc05_SA2Supplies (Excel)

You will save your files as:

- Last_First_acc05_SA2Park
- Last_First_acc05_SA2Supplies
- Last_First_acc05_SA2ParkDocs

Figure 1   Access 2016, Windows 10, Microsoft Corporation

1. Start **Access 2016**, and then open the student data file **acc05_ SA2Park**. **Save** the file in your **Access Chapter 5** folder as Last_First_acc05_SA2Park

2. Using **Application Parts**, create a **Tasks** table with no relationship to other tables. For the **Tasks** table, rename the primary key TaskID and then **Save** and **Close** the table.

3. In the **Employees** table, set the **FirstName** and **LastName** as required, and then index both fields. In the **Phone** field, add the default Phone Number input mask property. **Save** and **Close** the table.

4. Import the text file **acc05_SA2Employees** so that records are appended to the **Employees** table.

5. Prepare the Excel file **acc05_SA2Supplies** for import by deleting the **Cost** column and removing records with duplicate **Supplies** values. **Save** the file as Last_First_acc05_SA2Supplies and then **Close** Excel.

6. Create a Supplies table using **SupplyID** as the primary key by importing the data in the **Excel** file **Last_First_acc05_SA2Supplies**.

7. Create an Assignments table with the following fields: AssignmentsID, EmployeeID, and TaskID Set the **AssignmentsID** as AutoNumber and the primary key. Change the data type of the other two fields to **Number** with the **Long Integer** field size. Compare your screen with **Figure 1**.

8. Add a Lookup field as the last field in the **Assignments** table, named Supplies The Supplies field should access the supply description from the **Supplies** table and be sorted in ascending order.

9. Create a many-to-many relationship by dragging the **Employees** table **EmployeeID** to the **Assignments** table **EmployeeID**. Select

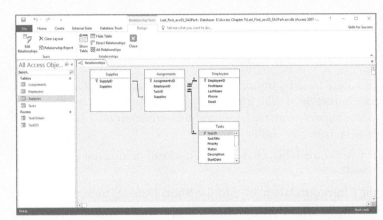

Figure 2   Access 2016, Windows 10, Microsoft Corporation

Enforce Referential Integrity, and then click **Create**. Drag the **Tasks** table **TaskID** to the **Assignments** table **TaskID**, select **Enforce Referential Integrity**, and then click **Create**. Compare your screen with **Figure 2**.

10. Use the **Database Documenter** to create database documentation for the four tables. Save the documentation as a PDF file named Last_First_acc05_SA2ParkDocs

11. **Save** and then **Close** the tables. **Close** Access, and then submit the files as directed by your instructor.

DONE! You have completed Skills Assessment 2

My Skills

To complete this project, you will need the following files:

- acc05_MYMaintenance (Access)
- acc05_MYVehicles (Excel)

You will save your files as:

- Last_First_acc05_MYMaintenance
- Last_First_acc05_MYVehicles

---

1. Start **Access 2016**, and then open the student data file **acc05_MYMaintenance**. **Save** the file in your **Access Chapter 5** folder as Last_First_acc05_MYMaintenance

2. Open the **RepairShops** table in Design view. Add an index with no duplicates to the **ShopName** field, and then set the shop **Phone** field as required.

3. In the **RepairShops** table, create a **Zip** field lookup that uses a typed list of values with at least five zip codes in your local area. **Save** and **Close** the table.

4. Open the **Maintenances** table in Datasheet view, and then change the row height to 45

5. In the **Maintenances** table, add a field named RepairShopID with the **Number** data type and **Long Integer** field size. Add another field named VehicleID field with the **Number** data type and **Long Integer** field size.

6. Create a many-to-many relationship by dragging the **RepairShops** table **RepairShopID** to the **Maintenances** table **RepairShopID**. Select **Enforce Referential Integrity**, and then click **Create**. Drag the **Vehicles** table **VehicleID** to the **Maintenances** table **VehicleID**, select **Enforce Referential Integrity** and then click **Create**.

7. Start **Excel 2016**, and then open **acc05_MYVehicles**. Save the file in your **Access Chapter 5** folder as Last_First_acc05_MSVehicles

8. In the first blank row, type a vehicle model, make, and year of a car you have taken to a shop. If applicable, list up to three additional vehicles in subsequent rows.

9. If you entered more than one vehicle, using **AutoFill**, populate the **VehicleID** starting with the number 1 **Save** and **Close** the file.

10. From the **External Data tab**, import the **Last_First_acc05_MSVehicles** file into the **Vehicles** table.

11. Populate at least two rows of the **RepairShops** table with information about repair shops in your area.

12. Create database documentation, selecting all of the tables using the Database Documenter. Save a copy of the database documentation in PDF format. Compare your screen with **Figure 1**. **Save** and **Close** the tables, and then **Close** Access. Submit your files as directed by your instructor.

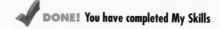 **DONE! You have completed My Skills**

Z:\00 Lisa\0 Lisa\0 Skills for Success 2016\Access Chapter Documents\acc05\Solution Files\acc05_MYMaintenance_solution.accdb

Table: Maintenances

Monday, February 29, 2017

Page: 1

Properties

AlternateBackShade:	95	AlternateBackThemeColorIn	1
AlternateBackTint:	100	BackShade:	100
BackTint:	100	DatasheetForeThemeColorIn	0
DatasheetGridlinesThemeCol	3	DateCreated:	12/15/2012 4:42:21 PM
DefaultView:	2	DisplayViewsOnSharePointSi	1
FilterOnLoad:	False	GUID:	{guid {283F8812-A255-4DB0-BAED-5211598555F1}}
HideNewField:	False	LastUpdated:	3/10/2013 1:03:52 PM
NameMap:	Long binary data	OrderByOn:	False
OrderByOnLoad:	True	Orientation:	Left-to-Right
PublishToWeb:	1	ReadOnlyWhenDisconnected	False
RecordCount:	0	RowHeight:	900
ThemeFontIndex:	1	TotalsRow:	False
Updatable:	True		

Columns

Name	Type	Size
MaintenanceID	Long Integer	4
AggregateType: -1		
AllowZeroLength: False		
AppendOnly: False		
Attributes: Fixed Size, Auto-Increment		
CollatingOrder: General		
ColumnHidden: False		
ColumnOrder: 1		
ColumnWidth: Default		
CurrencyLCID: 0		
DataUpdatable: False		
GUID: {guid {D02B5748-82B1-4391-9C2A-69D5C005B1B7}}		
OrdinalPosition: 0		
Required: False		
ResultType: 0		
SourceField: MaintenanceID		
SourceTable: Maintenances		
TextAlign: General		
Maintenance	Short Text	255
AggregateType: -1		
AllowZeroLength: True		
AppendOnly: False		
Attributes: Variable Length		
CollatingOrder: General		
ColumnHidden: False		
ColumnOrder: 2		
ColumnWidth: 1845		
CurrencyLCID: 0		
DataUpdatable: False		
DisplayControl: Text Box		
GUID: {guid {77F91B48-FA9C-4347-9023-7E9CAD854B53}}		
IMEMode: 0		

Access 2016, Windows 10, Microsoft Corporation   **Figure 1**

Visual Skills Check

To complete this project, you will need the following file:

- acc05_VSDonations

You will save your file as:

- Last_First_acc05_VSDonations

Open the student data file **acc05_VSDonations**, and then save the file in your **Access Chapter 5** folder as Last_First_acc05_VSDonations

Create the tables as shown in **Figure 1**. For each table, assign the primary key as indicated with the **AutoNumber** data type and field size **Long Integer**. Add the fields shown. In the **Projects** table, set the **Goal** data type to **Currency**. In the **Contributors** table, set the **Zip** input mask to **Zip Code**, and the **Phone** field input mask to **Phone Number**. In the **Receipts** table, create a **Donation** field and set the data type to **Currency**. In the **Receipts** table, create **ContributorsID** and **ProjectsID** fields and set the data types to **Number** with a **Field Size** of **Long Integer**. Create a many-to-many relationship, enforcing referential integrity, between the **Projects** and **Contributors** tables. Close Access, and then submit the file as directed by your instructor.

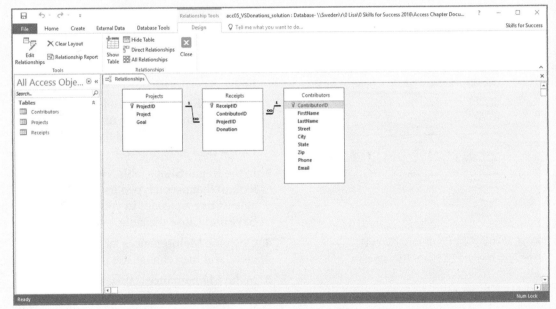

Figure 1

Access 2016, Windows 10, Microsoft Corporation

✓ **DONE! You have completed Visual Skills Check**

Skills Challenge 1

To complete this project, you will need the following files:

- acc05_SC1Rentals (Access)
- acc05_SC1Customers (Excel)

You will save your file as:

- Last_First_acc05_SC1Rentals

Open the student data file **acc05_SC1Rentals**, and then save the file in your **Access Chapter 5** folder as Last_First_acc05_SC1Rentals In the **Boats** table, change the data type of the **BoatType** field to **Rich Text**. Create a table named Customers by importing the data in the Excel file **acc05_SC1Customers** and assigning the **CustomerID** field as the primary key. In the **Customers** table, change the field size of the **CustomerID** field to **Long Integer**. Set the appropriate fields to required or indexed, and select the appropriate input masks. Create

a many-to-many relationship between the **Customers** and **Boats** tables using the **Receipts** table as a junction table. In all relationships, enforce referential integrity and select both cascading options. Close Access, and then submit the file as directed by your instructor.

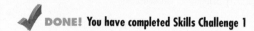 **DONE!** You have completed Skills Challenge 1

Skills Challenge 2

To complete this project, you will need the following files:

- acc05_SC2FarmersMarket (Access)
- acc05_SC2Products (Excel)

You will save your files as:

- Last_First_acc05_SC2FarmersMarket
- Last_First_acc05_SC2Products

Open the student data file **acc05_SC2FarmersMarket**, and then save the file in your **Access Chapter 5** folder as Last_First_acc05_SC2FarmersMarket Open the **acc05_SC2Products** Excel file. Using the Internet, research other products sold at farmers markets and add five items to the Excel list. Save the file as Last_First_acc05_SC2Products In Access, create a **Products** table by importing the Excel file, **Last_First_acc05_SC2Products**, assigning the **ProductID** as the primary key and the data type as **Long Integer**. Create a third table named

FarmOfferings that lists the products available from each farm. Create a many-to-many relationship by creating a one-to-many relationship between the **Farms** and **FarmOfferings** tables and between the **Products** and **FarmOfferings** tables. Close Access, and then submit the files as directed by your instructor.

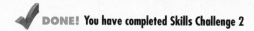 **DONE!** You have completed Skills Challenge 2

More Skills Assessment

MyITLab® Grader

To complete this project, you will need the following file:

- acc05_MSAArt

You will save your files as:

- Last_First_acc05_MSAArt
- Last_First_acc05_MSAInstructors(XML)

1. Start **Access 2016**. Open the student data file **acc05_MSAArt**, and then save the file in your Access Chapter 5 folder as Last_First_acc05_MSAArt

2. In the **Art Instructors** table, create an Input Mask in the **State** field that will convert lowercase letters to capital letters and restrict input to two characters. In the State Input Mask, type CA as the Sample data.

3. In the **Art Instructors** table, type CA in the records for *Loretta Shane* and *Mitchell Screen*.

4. In the **Art Class Categories** table, use **Find and Replace** to find the word *sorted* and replace it with grouped

5. Create a query using **Query Design** that includes all the fields from the **Art Class Sections** table. Include a criterion in the **Fee** field so only records with fees greater than $54 will display. Compare your screen with **Figure 1**.

6. Save the query as Premium Art Classes

7. Use the **Make Table** query to create a table named Premium Art Classes from the *Premium Art Classes* query.

8. Export the Art Instructors table as an XML file named Last_First_acc05_MSAInstructors During the export, verify the **Data (XML)** and **Schema of the data (XSD)** check boxes are selected. Save the export steps with the default settings.

9. **Close** Access. Submit the files as directed by your instructor.

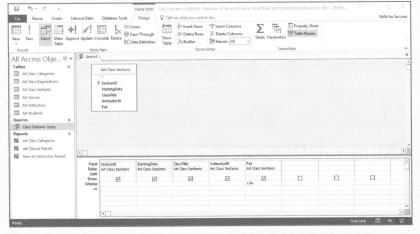

Figure 1

Access 2016, Windows 10, Microsoft Corporation

DONE! You have completed the More Skills Assessment

Collaborating with Google

To complete this project, you will need a Google account (refer to the Common Features chapter) and the following file:

- acc05_GPStudentData (Excel)

You will save your files as:

- Last_First_acc05_GPStudentData (Excel)
- Last_First_acc05_GPStudent (Access)

1. Open the Google Chrome web browser. Log into your Google account, and then click the **Apps** button.

2. Click **Drive** to open Google Drive.

3. Click the **NEW** button, and then click **File upload**. Navigate to the student data files and open **acc05_GPStudentData**

4. Right-click the **acc05_GPStudentData** in **Google Drive**. Click **Open With**, and then click **Google Sheets**.

5. On the *Students* sheet, select column **F**, and then press Delete.

6. Click cell **F1**, type Email and then press Enter.

7. Click **File**, point to **Download as**, and then click **Microsoft Excel (.xlsx)**.

8. After the download opens, save it in your chapter folder as Last_First_acc05_GPStudentData and then **Close** Excel. Replace the text in the first row with your first and last name.

9. **Open** a Blank database in Access, and then save the file as Last_First_acc05_GPStudents in your **Access Chapter 5** folder.

10. Click the **External Data tab**, and then in the **Import & Link group**, click **Excel**. In the **Get External Data - Excel Spreadsheet** dialog box, click **Browse**. In the **File Open** dialog box, navigate to your **Access Chapter 5** folder, select **Last_First_ acc05_GPStudentData**, and then click **Open**.

11. In the **Get External Data - Excel Spreadsheet** dialog box, verify the **Import the source data into a new table in the current database** option button is selected. Compare your screen with Figure 1, and then click **OK**.

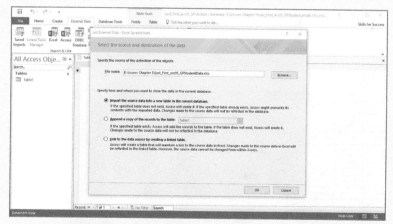

Access 2016, Windows 10, Microsoft Corporation

Figure 1

12. Verify that the **First Row Contains Column Headings** check box is selected, and then accept all other defaults. Click **Finish**.

13. **Close** the dialog box, and then close Table 1.

14. **Close** Access, and then submit the files as directed by your instructor.

DONE! You have completed Collaborating with Google

CHAPTER 6

Create Advanced Queries

- ► Access has many types of queries other than select queries. These queries can be used to create new tables or change data in existing tables.

- ► You can use the Find Duplicates Query Wizard to locate and delete duplicate records.

- ► When you use the query work space, the SQL commands needed to execute the query are written as you modify the query. In SQL view, you can write and edit SQL commands directly.

- ► Update queries can change the data stored in a field using the instructions that you provide in the query.

- ► You can write queries that add records to a table or delete them from a table.

- ► You can write expressions that join fields into one query column.

- ► When you need to provide multiple reports for similar data, you can add parameters to a query and then base the report on that query. The records that display depend on the input provided by the person opening the report.

igor/Fotolia

Aspen Falls City Hall

In this chapter, you will use queries to modify the Aspen Falls Water Utilities database. You will work under the supervision of Diane Payne, Public Works Director, to build several queries to improve database tables. You will also write several advanced queries to display information needed by the utility.

When a database contains a large amount of records, queries are essential tools for finding the information you need. In addition to selecting data, queries can also be used to create tables, add records to tables, and delete records. You can also write queries that modify field values.

Writing queries that ask the user for input enables you to use a single query that provides custom sets of data in response to the user's input. For example, you could ask the user for a range of dates when the query is run. Only the records that match the parameters typed by the user are displayed.

In this project, you will create several types of advanced queries. Some will select data, some will change data, and some will be used to improve the design of the Water Utilities database.

Outcome

Using the skills in this chapter, you will be able to find duplicate records; modify queries in SQL view; make tables from queries; create update, append, delete, and parameter queries; concatenate fields; modify queries; and create reports from parameter queries.

Objectives

6.1 Create update, append, delete, and parameter queries

6.2 Modify queries in SQL view

6.3 Construct reports from parameter queries

6.4 Generate tables from queries

Student data file needed for this chapter:

acc06_Water

You will save your file as:

Last_First_acc06_Water

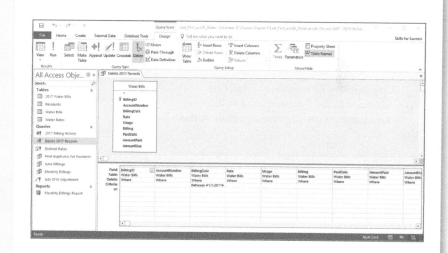

Access 2016, Windows 10, Microsoft Corporation

▶ As a database is used over time, a table can become quite large and eventually contain duplicate data.

▶ A **find duplicates query** searches a field and then displays records that contain duplicate values. The query can then be used to remove the duplicate values.

1. Start **Access 2016**, and then open the student data file **acc06_Water**. Use the **Save As** dialog box to create a **New folder** named Access Chapter 6 Save the database in the new folder as Last_First_acc06_Water

2. If the Security Warning message displays, click the Enable Content button.

3. In the **Navigation Pane**, right-click the **Residents** table, and then click **Design View**. ·

4. With the **AccountNumber** row active, on the **Design tab**, in the **Tools group**, click the **Primary Key** button so that it is selected. Compare your screen with **Figure 1**.

5. Click **Save** 🖫, and then compare your screen with **Figure 2**.

> The primary key property cannot be assigned to the AccountNumber field because there are duplicated values in the field.

6. Read the message that displays, and then click **OK**. Read the next message that displays, and then click **OK**.

7. **Close** ☒ the table without saving changes.

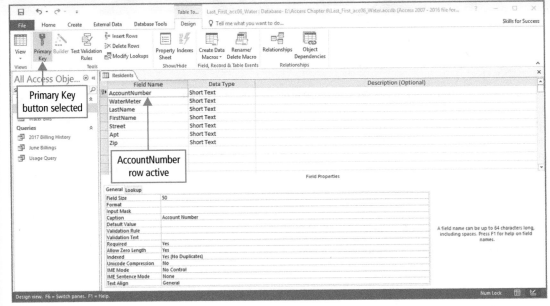

Figure 1　　　　　　　　　　　　　　　Access 2016, Windows 10, Microsoft Corporation

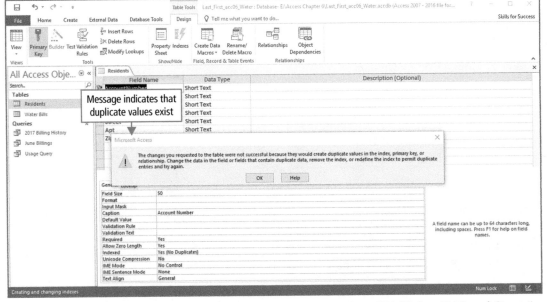

Figure 2　　　　　　　　　　　　　　　Access 2016, Windows 10, Microsoft Corporation

■ Continue to the next page to complete the skill

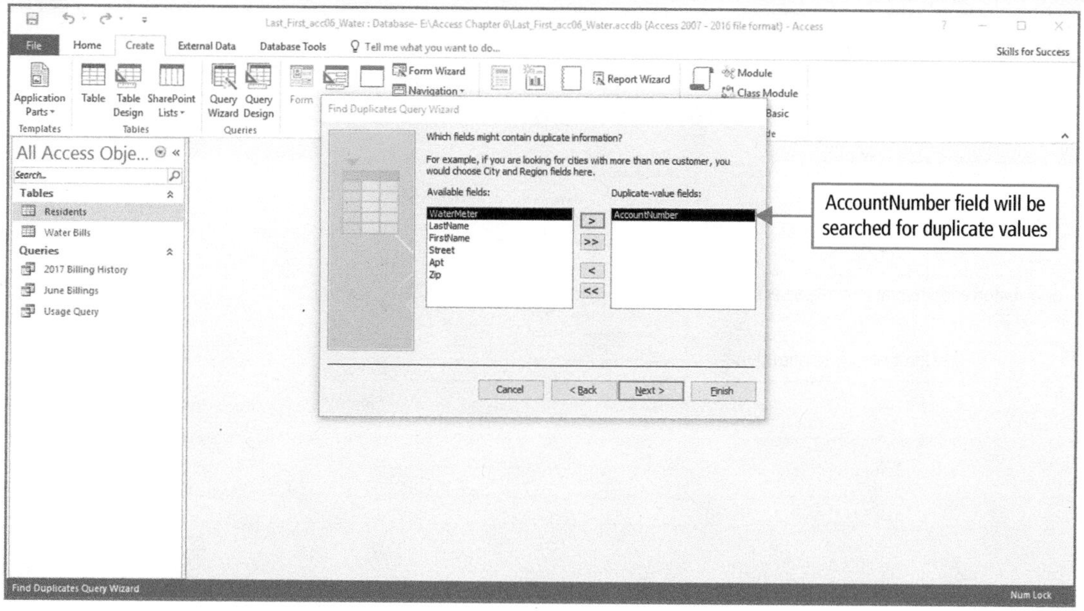

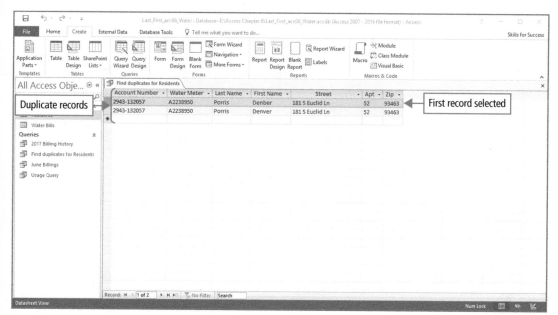

Access 2016, Windows 10, Microsoft Corporation

Figure 3

8. Click the **Create tab**, and then in the **Queries group**, click **Query Wizard**. In the **New Query** dialog box, click **Find Duplicates Query Wizard**, and then click **OK**.

9. In the **Find Duplicates Query Wizard** dialog box, verify that **Table: Residents** is selected, and then click **Next**.

10. Under **Available fields**, verify that **AccountNumber** is selected, and then click the **Move** button > one time to move the field to **Duplicate-value fields**. Compare your screen with **Figure 3**, and then click **Next**.

11. Click the **Move All** button >> to add all the remaining fields as **Additional query fields**, and then click **Finish** to create, save, and run the query.

12. In the query datasheet, select the record with the first name value *Denber*. Compare your screen with **Figure 4**.

13. With the record still selected, press Delete. Read the message that displays, and then click **Yes. Close** ✕ the query.

14. Open the **Residents** table in Design view, and then for the **AccountNumber** field, assign the **Primary Key** property.

15. Click **Save** 🖫, and then **Close** ✕ the table.

> With the duplicate AccountNumber record deleted, the primary key property can now be assigned.

■ **You have completed Skill 1 of 10**

Access 2016, Windows 10, Microsoft Corporation

Figure 4

▸ *Structured Query Language—SQL—*is a language used to query database tables.

▸ In Access, all queries are written in SQL, and the SQL statements can be viewed and edited in SQL view.

1. Click the **Database Tools tab**, in the **Relationships group,** click the **Relationships** button. Drag **AccountNumber** from the **Residents** table to the **AccountNumber** field in the **Water Bills** table.

2. In the **Edit Relationships** dialog box, select the **Enforce Referential Integrity** check box. Compare your screen with **Figure 1**, and then click **Create.**

3. **Close** ☒ the Relationships tab. In the **Navigation Pane,** under **Queries,** double-click **June Billings** to open the datasheet.

4. Notice that 80 billing records currently display, and then switch to *Design View.* On the **Design tab,** in the **Query Setup group,** click the **Return arrow,** and then from the list, click **25.**

5. In the Usage Column, click the **Sort** property. Click the **Sort arrow,** and then click **Descending.** Compare your screen with **Figure 2.**

6. In the **Results group,** click the **Run** button to display the top 25 water users for June 2018.

■ **Continue to the next page to complete the skill** ➤

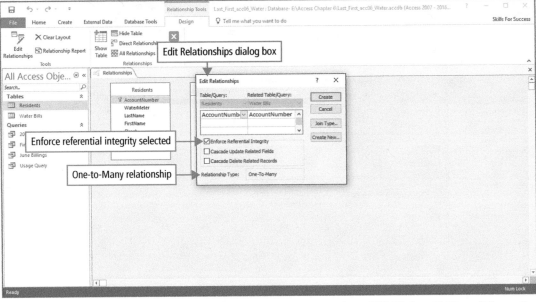

Figure 1

Access 2016, Windows 10, Microsoft Corporation

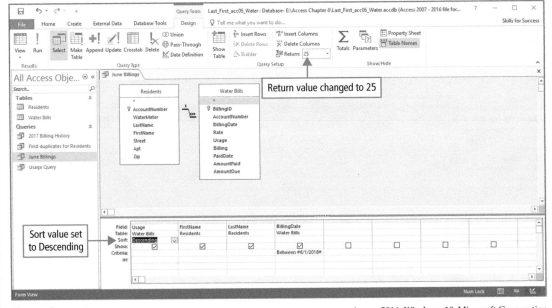

Figure 2

Access 2016, Windows 10, Microsoft Corporation

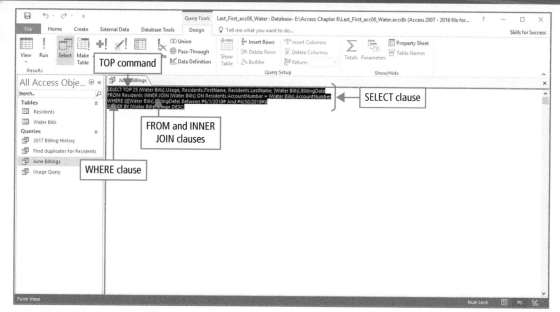

Access 2016, Windows 10, Microsoft Corporation

Figure 3

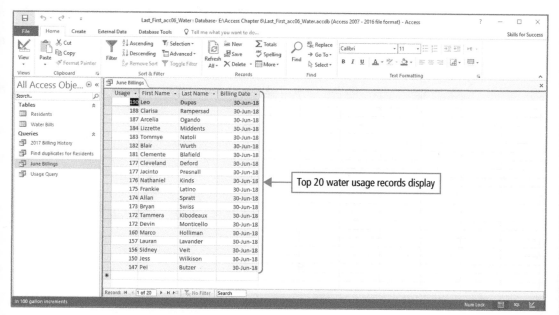

Access 2016, Windows 10, Microsoft Corporation

Figure 4

7. On the **Home tab**, in the **Views** group, click the **View arrow**, and then click **SQL View**. Compare your screen with Figure 3.

In SQL view, the query's underlying SQL statement displays. SQL statements consist of one or more clauses. Here, the *SELECT* clause lists the fields the query should display. This type of query is called a select query.

The *TOP* clause selects the highest values of the next field listed in the SELECT clause. The number of values to display is determined by the number that follows it.

The *FROM* clause lists the table or tables the query fields are from. In the FROM clause, the *INNER JOIN* clause defines how fields from related tables should be joined.

The *WHERE* clause identifies the query criteria. In SQL, when two tables have a field with the same name, the field name must be preceded by the table name and a period. When table or field names have spaces, they must be enclosed in brackets ([ ]).

The *ORDER BY* clause is used to sort a field. The sort order can be changed from ascending by including the *DESC* command.

8. In the *SELECT* clause, and to the right of the *TOP* command, change the *25* value to 20

9. Click **Save** 🖫, and then **Run** the query. Compare your screen with Figure 4.

In this manner, SQL statements can be viewed, modified, or written in SQL view before a query is run.

10. **Close** ☒ the query.

■ **You have completed Skill 2 of 10**

- You can make a new table by running a query called a **make table query**.

- In a make table query, the records and fields that display in the query become the data and fields in the new table.

- Make table queries are useful when you need to save data at a certain point in time or when you need to design database tables.

1. Click the **Create tab**, and then in the **Queries group**, click **Query Design**. In the **Show Table** dialog box, double-click **Water Bills**, and then **Close** the dialog box.

2. Double-click the **Rate** field to add it to the query. Click **Save** 🖫, type Distinct Rates and then press [Enter]. Compare your screen with **Figure 1**.

3. **Run** the query to verify that 1427 records result.

4. On the **Home tab**, click the **View button arrow**, and then click **SQL View**.

5. To the right of the *SELECT* command, add a space, and then type DISTINCT Compare your screen with **Figure 2**.

   DISTINCT is an SQL command that removes duplicate data from query results. Here, each unique rate value will be listed only once.

6. **Save** 🖫, and then **Run** the query to display the eight unique rates.

   Before running a make table query, it is a good practice to verify the data wanted will be added to the new table.

7. Switch to Design view. On the **Design tab**, in the **Query Type group**, click the **Make Table** button.

8. In the **Make Table** dialog box, name the table Water Rates

■ **Continue to the next page to complete the skill**

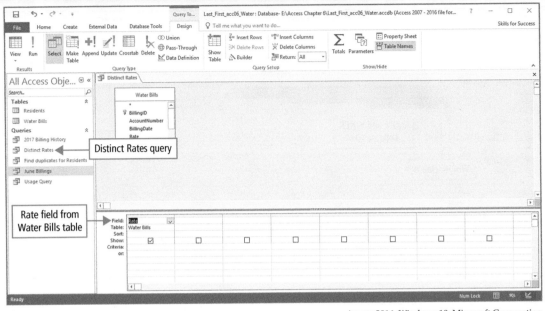

Distinct Rates query

Rate field from Water Bills table

Figure 1

Access 2016, Windows 10, Microsoft Corporation

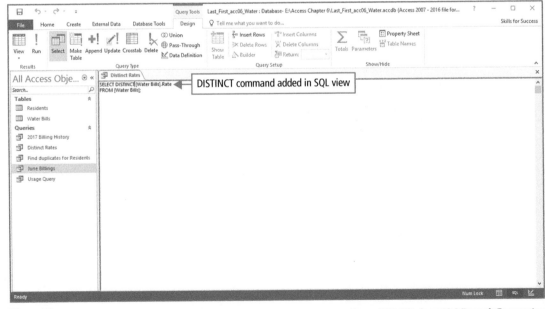

DISTINCT command added in SQL view

Figure 2

Access 2016, Windows 10, Microsoft Corporation

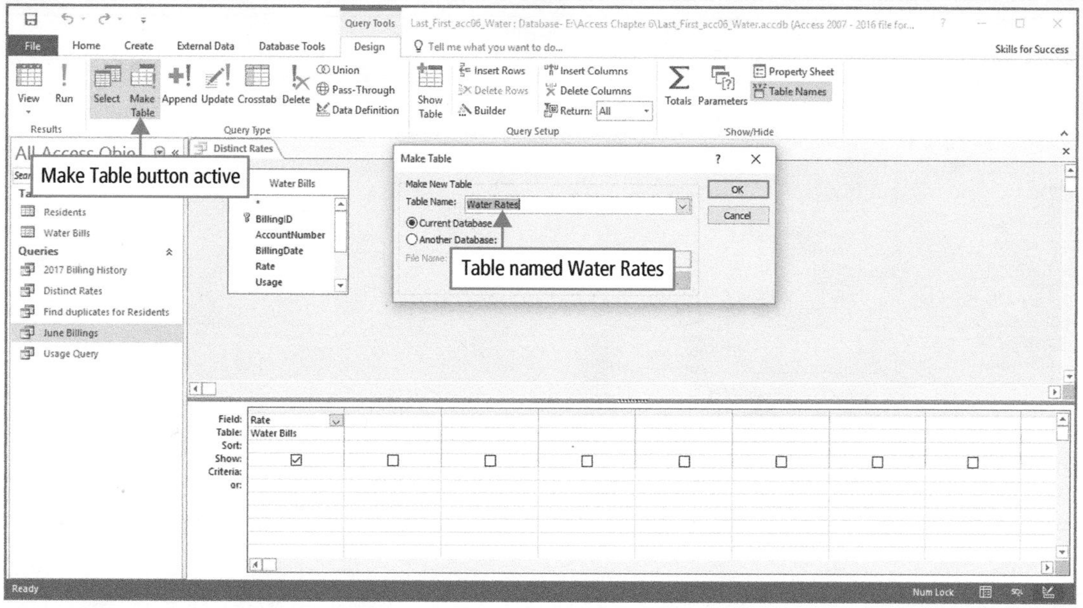

Access 2016, Windows 10, Microsoft Corporation

Figure 3

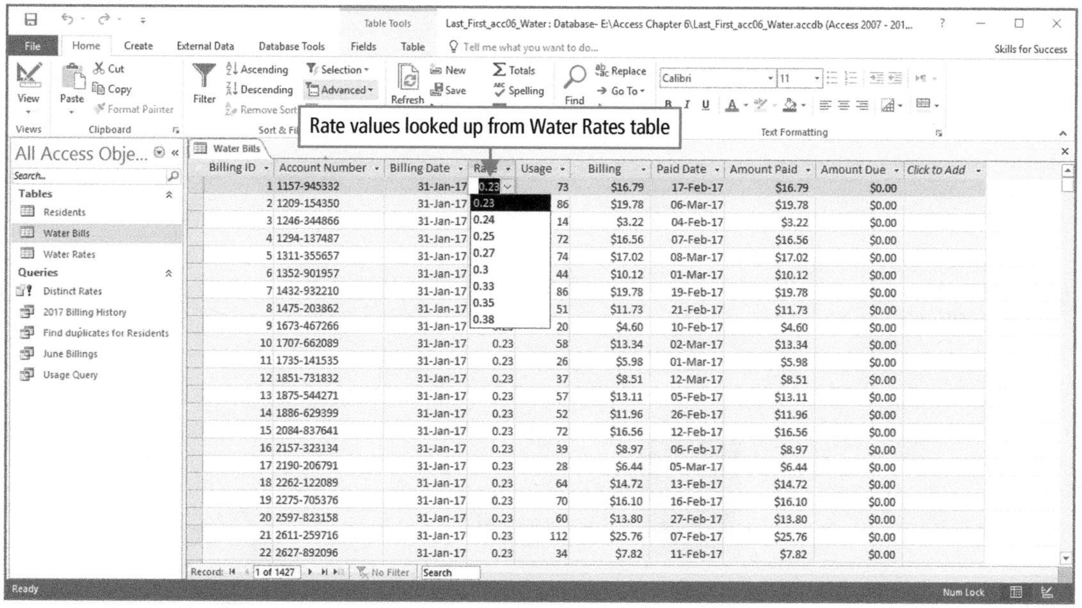

Access 2016, Windows 10, Microsoft Corporation

Figure 4

9. Compare your screen with **Figure 3**, and then click **OK**.

In the Query Type group, the Make Table button is active and the Select button is no longer active to indicate the query is now a make table query.

10. Click the **Run** button, read the message that displays, and then click **Yes**.

11. **Save** [💾], and then **Close** [✕] the query.

In the Navigation Pane, make table queries display a different icon than select queries.

12. In the **Navigation Pane**, right-click the **Water Bills** table, and then click **Design View**. Click in the **Rate** row, click the selected row's **Data Type arrow**, and then click **Lookup Wizard**.

13. In the **Lookup Wizard**, verify the first option button is selected, and then click **Next**. Select **Table: Water Rates**, and then click **Next**.

14. **Move** [>] the **Rate** field from **Available Fields** to **Selected Fields**, and then click **Next**.

15. To the left of the **Ascending** button, click the **arrow**, and then click **Rate**.

16. Click **Next** to see a sample of the lookup values, and then click **Finish**. Read the message that displays, and then click **Yes**.

17. Switch to Datasheet view, click the arrow in the first record's Rate field, and then compare your screen with **Figure 4**.

The list box displays the values from the Water Rates table—the table created by running the Distinct Rates make table query.

18. **Close** [✕] the table.

■ **You have completed Skill 3 of 10**

▶ You can repurpose existing queries by adding and removing fields and tables, editing criteria, or changing the order of the columns.

1. In the **Navigation Pane**, under **Queries**, double-click the **Usage Query** to run the query.

   Before modifying a query, it is a good idea to first view the datasheet to see what changes need to be made.

2. Switch to Design view. Point to the top of the **AccountNumber** column, and then compare your screen with Figure 1.

3. With the ↓ pointer above the **AccountNumber** column, click one time to select the column. Press Delete to remove the field and column from the query.

4. Repeat the technique just practiced to delete the **FirstName** and **LastName** columns from the query.

5. In the query workspace, right-click the title bar of the **Residents** table. From the shortcut menu that displays, click **Remove Table**.

   To avoid errors in the query results, tables that do not have any fields in the query design grid must be removed from the query workspace.

6. Select the Usage column. With the ⬚ pointer, point to the upper edge of the Usage column, above the field name *Usage*. Press and hold the left mouse button, and then compare your screen with Figure 2.

■ **Continue to the next page to complete the skill**

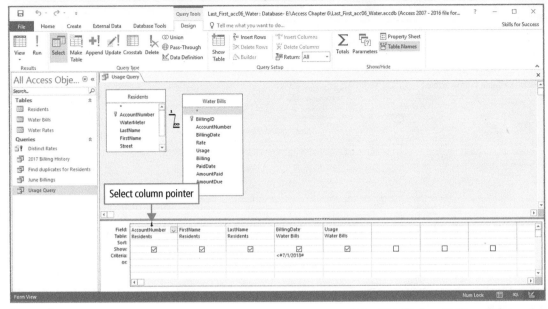

Figure 1

Access 2016, Windows 10, Microsoft Corporation

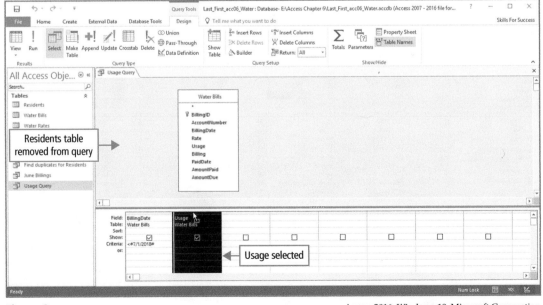

Figure 2

Access 2016, Windows 10, Microsoft Corporation

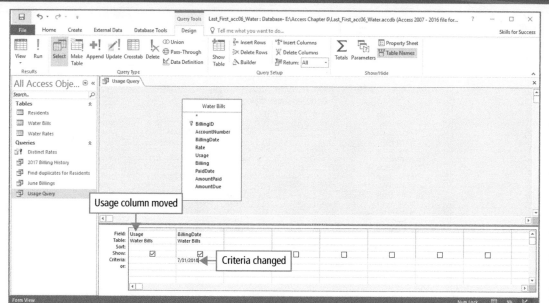

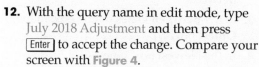

Access 2016, Windows 10, Microsoft Corporation

Figure 3

7. With the pointer, drag the **Usage** column to the left. When a black vertical line displays to the left of the **BillingDate** column, release the left mouse button.

8. In the **BillingDate** field **Criteria** row, select the existing criteria.

9. With the criteria selected, type 7/31/2018 to replace the criteria value. Compare your screen with **Figure 3**.

10. **Run** the query to display 77 records that meet the new criteria. **Save** 🖫, and then **Close** ☒ the query.

11. In the **Navigation Pane**, under **Queries**, right-click **Usage Query**, and then click **Rename**.

12. With the query name in edit mode, type July 2018 Adjustment and then press ⌷Enter⌷ to accept the change. Compare your screen with **Figure 4**.

> When you change the purpose of the query, it is a good practice to also rename the query.

■ **You have completed Skill 4 of 10**

Access 2016, Windows 10, Microsoft Corporation

Figure 4

▶ WATCH SKILL 6.5

- An *update query* is a query that can add, delete, or modify records.

- In Access, update queries are typically used to change data stored in tables. The query criteria are used to apply the changes only to the records you need.

- Update queries are useful when you need to modify large amounts of data quickly and accurately.

1. In the **Navigation Pane**, under **Tables**, double-click the **Water Bills** table.

2. In the datasheet, click the **Billing Date arrow** to display the filter list. In the filter list, point to **Date Filters**, and then click **Between**.

MOS
Obj 3.3.2

3. In the **Between Dates** dialog box, in the **Oldest** box, type 7/1/2018

4. In the **Newest** box, type 7/31/2018 Compare your screen with **Figure 1**.

5. Click **OK**, and then compare your screen with **Figure 2**.

Before changing data using an update query, it is a good idea to analyze the data you will be changing. The company is aware that a water leak occurred between the July 15 and July 31 billings. To remedy overcharging residents, the utility needs to reduce usage by 10 percent for all July 31, 2018 records.

6. **Save** 🖫, and then **Close** ✕ the table.

7. In the **Navigation Pane**, under **Queries**, right-click **July 2018 Adjustment**, and then click **Design View**.

MOS
Obj 3.1.4

8. Click the **Design tab**. In the **Query Type group**, click the **Update** button.

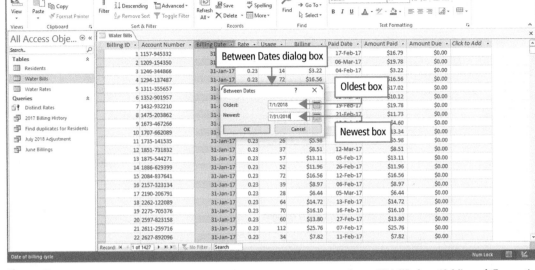

Figure 1

Access 2016, Windows 10, Microsoft Corporation

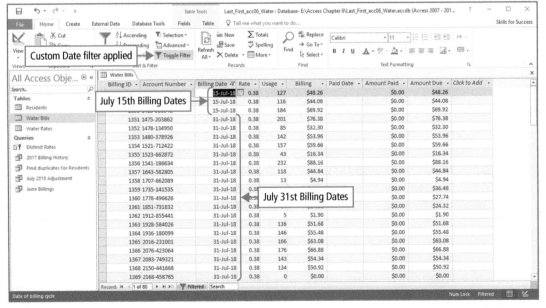

Figure 2

Access 2016, Windows 10, Microsoft Corporation

■ **Continue to the next page to complete the skill**

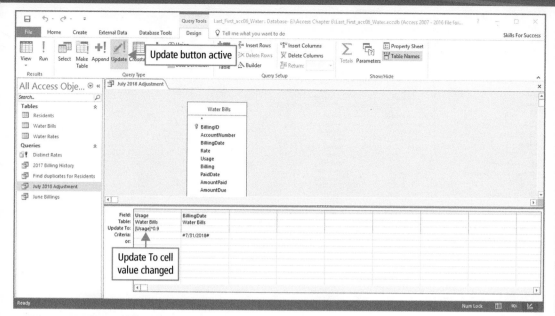

Access 2016, Windows 10, Microsoft Corporation

Figure 3

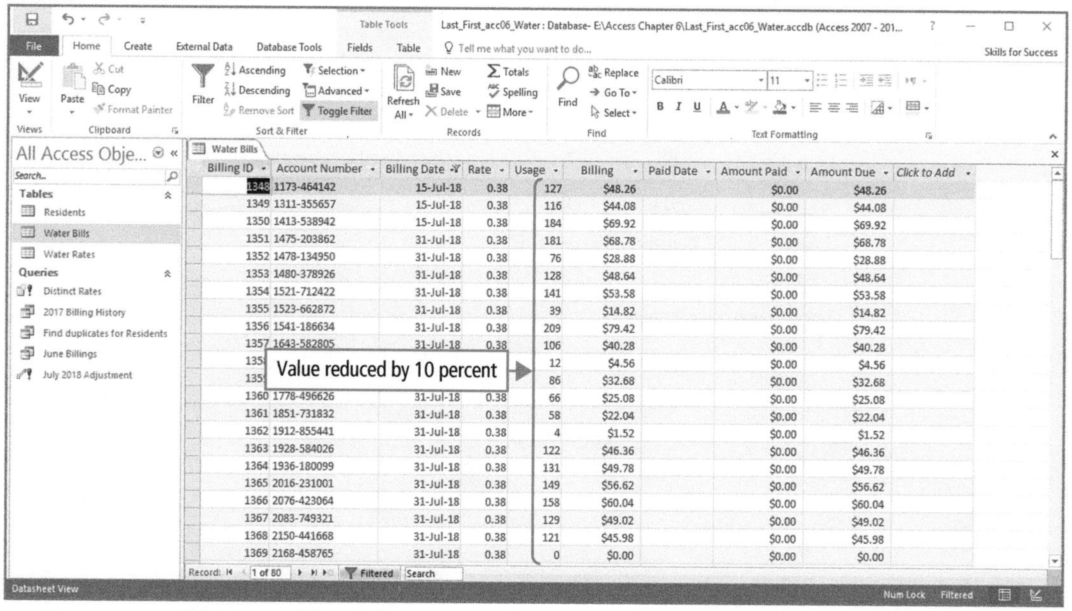

Access 2016, Windows 10, Microsoft Corporation

Figure 4

9. In the **Usage** column **Update To** row, type [Usage]*0.9 Compare your screen with **Figure 3**.

> In an Access update query, the Update To row provides instructions on how to modify the values in the corresponding table field. Additional columns can be added to further modify or filter the records.

> It is a good practice to carefully analyze the query before running it. Here, by multiplying the current Usage values by 0.9, a 10 percent reduction will be applied. Only the records in which the billing date is 7/31/2018 will be affected.

10. Click **Save** 💾, and then click **Run**. Read the message that displays, and then click **Yes**. **Save** 💾, and then **Close** ✕ the query. Be careful to *not* run the query additional times.

> Each time an update query is run, the changes are applied again. Running the July 2018 Adjustment query a second time would result in an additional 10 percent reduction in Usage values for July 31, 2018.

11. In the **Navigation Pane**, double-click the **Water Bills** table.

12. On the **Home tab**, in the **Sort & Filter group**, click the **Toggle Filter** button to reapply the custom date filter created previously. Compare your screen with **Figure 4**.

> In the fourth record, the Usage value is 181, which is a 10 percent reduction from 201— the value previous to running the update query.

13. **Close** ✕ the table.

■ **You have completed Skill 5 of 10**

▶ **Concatenate** is the process of combining two or more values to create one single value.

1. Click the **Create tab**, and then in the **Queries group**, click the **Query Design** button.

2. In the **Show Table** dialog box, double-click to add the **Residents** and **Water Bills** tables, and then **Close** the dialog box.

3. In the **Residents** table, double-click to add the **AccountNumber** field, and then double-click to add the **Street** field.

4. With the 1 pointer, drag the Water Bills table's lower border down to display all the table's fields.

5. In **Water Bills** table, double-click to add the **AmountDue** field, and then the **BillingDate** field.

6. Click **Save** 🖫, type Monthly Billings and then press Enter . Compare your screen with **Figure 1**.

7. **Run** the query, verify that 1427 records display, and then switch to Design view.

8. Right-click the first empty column in the **Field** row, and then from the shortcut menu that displays, click **Zoom**.

9. In the **Zoom** dialog box, type the following expression: FullName:[FirstName] + " " + [LastName] Between the two quotation marks, be sure to type a space. Compare your screen with **Figure 2**.

   To concatenate values in an expression, the plus operator (+) is inserted. Recall that in an expression, field names are enclosed in square brackets and text is enclosed in quotation marks. Here, the expression will display the FirstName value from the Residents table, a space, and then the LastName value. The text *FullName* names the calculated column.

■ **Continue to the next page to complete the skill** ➤

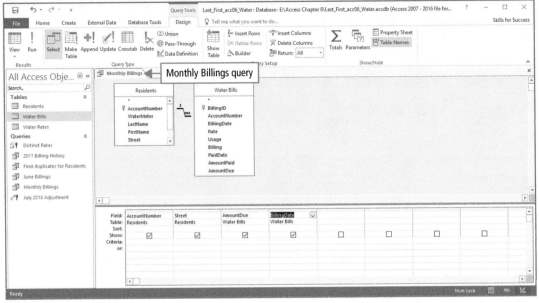

Figure 1

Access 2016, Windows 10, Microsoft Corporation

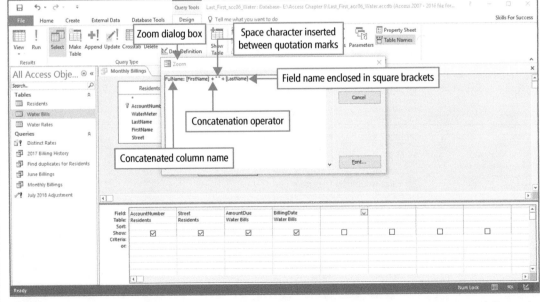

Figure 2

Access 2016, Windows 10, Microsoft Corporation

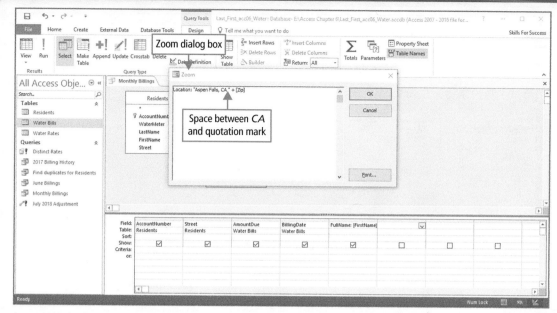

Access 2016, Windows 10, Microsoft Corporation

Figure 3

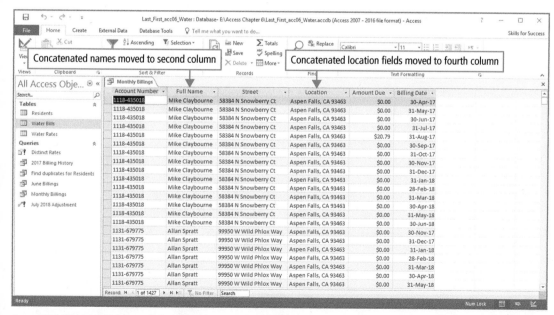

Access 2016, Windows 10, Microsoft Corporation

Figure 4

10. In the **Zoom** dialog box, click **OK**. If an error message displays, repeat the previous step carefully checking your typing.

11. **Save**, and then **Run** the query. Set the *FullName* column to **Best Fit**, and then verify the name values were concatenated correctly. Switch to Design view.

12. Right-click the first empty column in the **Field** row, and then from the shortcut menu that displays, click **Zoom**. In the **Zoom** dialog box, type the following expression: Location: "Aspen Falls, CA " + [Zip] Be sure to include a space after *CA*. Compare your screen with **Figure 3**, and then click **OK**.

13. Drag the **FullName** column so that it is the second column in the query. Repeat this technique so that the **Location** column is the fourth column in the query.

14. **Save**, and the **Run** the query. Set all columns to **Best Fit**, and then compare your screen with **Figure 4**. If necessary, repeat the previous steps to correct any errors.

15. Leave the query open for the next skill.

■ **You have completed Skill 6 of 10**

▶ A ***parameter query*** is a query that displays an input box that asks for criteria each time the query is run.

▶ Parameter queries return a subset of the data based on the values that are typed in the Enter Parameter Value input box.

1. With the **Monthly Billings** query datasheet open, switch to Design view

2. In the **BillingDate** column **Criteria** row, type Between 7/1/2018 And 7/31/2018 and then compare your screen with Figure 1.

3. **Save** 🖫, and then **Run** the query. Verify that 80 records display, and then switch to Design view.

4. In the last column, right-click the **BillingDate Criteria** row, and then click **Zoom**.

MOS
Obj 3.1.3

5. In the **Zoom** dialog box, replace the existing criteria with Between [Enter Beginning Date] And [Enter Ending Date] Compare your screen with Figure 2.

> Recall that in query criteria, field names are enclosed in square brackets. When those brackets enclose values that are not field names, Access displays a dialog box asking the user to type the criteria manually. Here, two dialog boxes will display. The first will determine the starting date value, and the second will determine the ending date value.

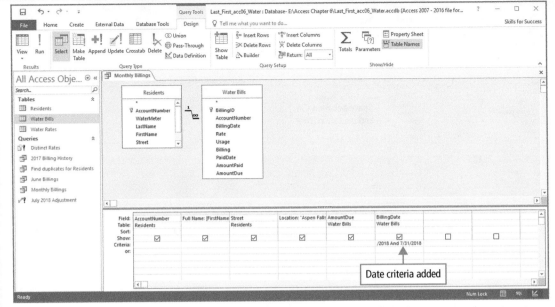

Figure 1

Access 2016, Windows 10, Microsoft Corporation

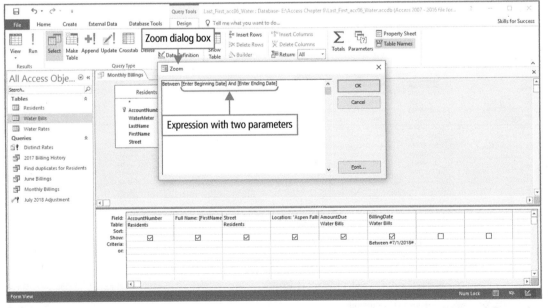

Figure 2

Access 2016, Windows 10, Microsoft Corporation

■ **Continue to the next page to complete the skill**

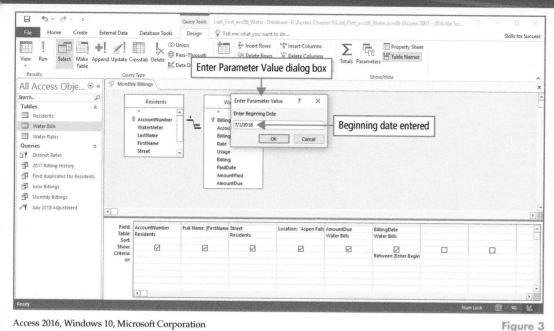

Access 2016, Windows 10, Microsoft Corporation

Figure 3

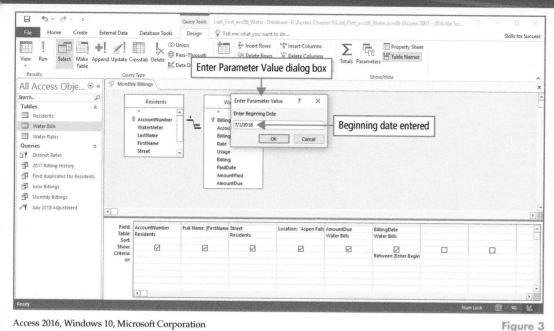

Access 2016, Windows 10, Microsoft Corporation

Figure 4

6. Click **OK** to close the **Zoom** dialog box. Click **Save** 🔲, and then **Run** the query.

7. In the **Enter Parameter Value** dialog box, type 7/1/2018 and then compare your screen with **Figure 3**.

   In the Enter Parameter Value dialog box, the criteria text that is enclosed in square brackets displays as a prompt. Here, *Enter Beginning Date*—the value you typed previously—is the prompt.

8. In the **Enter Parameter Value** dialog box, click **OK**. For the second prompt—**Enter Ending Date**—type 7/31/2018

9. Click **OK** to run the query and display the 80 values that match the criteria you typed previously.

10. On the **Home tab**, in the **Records group**, click the **Refresh All** button.

11. In the **Enter Parameter Value** dialog box, for the first prompt—**Enter Beginning Date**—type 6/1/2018 and then press ⏎. In the second prompt—**Enter Ending Date**—type 6/30/2018 Press ⏎ to run the query, and then compare your screen with **Figure 4**.

   In this manner, a single query can return varied results depending on the parameters entered by the user. Using a parameter query eliminates the need to create separate queries with different criteria for each month in the billing year.

12. Leave the query open for the next skill.

■ **You have completed Skill 7 of 10**

▶ Reports based on parameter queries can display a variety of results without having to create multiple queries and reports.

1. With the **Monthly Billings** query datasheet open, switch to Design view

2. In the **BillingDate** column, clear the **Show** check box, and then compare your screen with **Figure 1**.

   The report that will be based on this query will not need to display the BillingDate values.

3. **Save** 🖫, and then **Close** ✕ the query.

4. In the **Navigation Pane**, under **Queries**, ensure the **Monthly Billings** query is selected.

5. Click the **Create tab**, and then in the **Reports group**, click the **Report** button to create a report based on the query.

6. In the **Enter Parameter Value** dialog box, type 7/1/2018 and then press Enter . For the **Enter Ending Date** prompt, type 7/15/2018 and then press Enter .

7. Click **Save** 🖫, name the report Monthly Billings Report and then press Enter . Compare your screen with **Figure 2**.

   When a report is created from a parameter query, the report asks for input each time the report is opened or refreshed. Here, the first prompt—*Enter Beginning Date*—displays in the Enter Parameter Value dialog box.

8. Switch to Design view. On the **Design tab**, in the **Tools group**, click the **Property Sheet** button. If it is not already selected, click the property sheet **Selection Type arrow**, and then click **AccountNumber**.

■ Continue to the next page to complete the skill

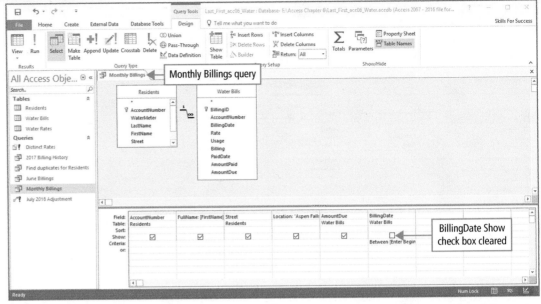

Figure 1

Access 2016, Windows 10, Microsoft Corporation

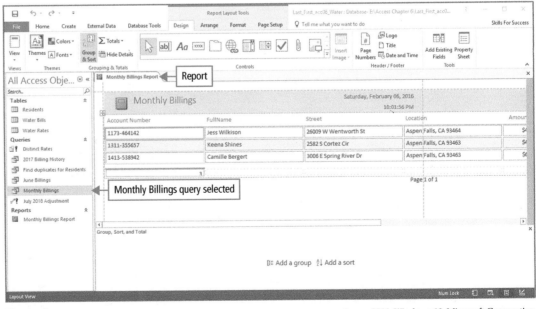

Figure 2

Access 2016, Windows 10, Microsoft Corporation

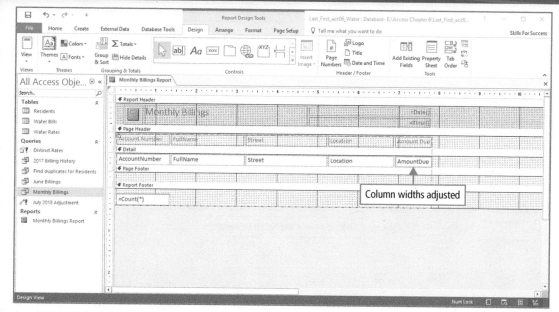

Access 2016, Windows 10, Microsoft Corporation

Figure 3

9. With the **AccountNumber** text box selected in the Property Sheet pane, ensure the **All tab** is selected. Select the **Width** value, type 1.3" and then press Enter .

10. Click the property sheet **Selection Type arrow**, and then click **FullName**. Change the **Width** value to 1.8" and then press Enter .

11. Click the property sheet **Selection Type arrow**, and then click **Street**. Change the **Width** value to 2" and then press Enter .

12. Using the previous technique, change the **Location** text box **Width** value to 1.6" and the **AmountDue** text box **Width** value to 0.9"

13. **Close** ☒ the property sheet, and then compare your screen with Figure 3.

14. In the **Page Footer** section, click the control that displays the page number information, and then press Delete to remove the control from the report. Scroll to the right and drag the right edge of the report left, to the 8 inch horizontal gridline.

15. In the **Report Footer** section, click the control that displays the record count. Point to the selected control's upper border, and then with the ↕ pointer, double-click to AutoSize the control's height.

16. Click the **Home tab**, click the **View button arrow**, and then click **Print Preview**. Type 7/1/2018 as the Beginning Date and 7/15/2018 as the Ending Date. Compare your screen with Figure 4.

17. Click **Save** ☐, and then **Close** ☒ the report.

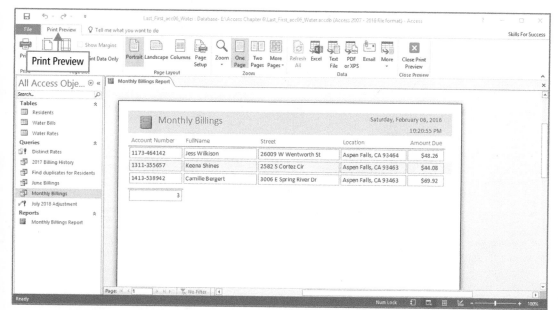

Access 2016, Windows 10, Microsoft Corporation

Figure 4

■ **You have completed Skill 8 of 10**

 **WATCH** SKILL 6.9

▶ An **append query** adds the results of a query to an existing table.

1. In the **Navigation Pane**, under **Tables**, click **Water Bills**. On the **Home tab**, in the **Clipboard group**, click **Copy**. In the **Clipboard group**, click the **Paste** button.

2. In the **Paste Table As** dialog box, replace the **Table Name** text with 2017 Water Bills Under **Paste Options**, select the **Structure Only** option button, and then click **OK**.

3. In the **Navigation Pane**, right-click **2017 Water Bills**, and then click **Design View**.

4. In the Field Name column, click the first blank row, and then type TimeStamp

5. Change the **TimeStamp** field's data type to **Date/Time**.

6. With the **TimeStamp** row still active, in the **Field Properties** pane, click in the **Default Value** box. Type the expression NOW() and then compare your screen with **Figure 1**.

> By using the NOW() expression as the default value, the date and time will automatically be inserted when each record in the table is created.

7. **Save** the table, and then switch to Datasheet view. Set the **TimeStamp** column width to **Best Fit**, and then **Save** and **Close** the table.

8. In the **Navigation Pane**, under **Queries**, double-click to open the **2017 Billing History** table datasheet. Compare your screen with **Figure 2**.

> Before appending records, it is a good practice to first view the query as a select query. Here, all the bills from the year 2017 are selected.

■ **Continue to the next page to complete the skill**

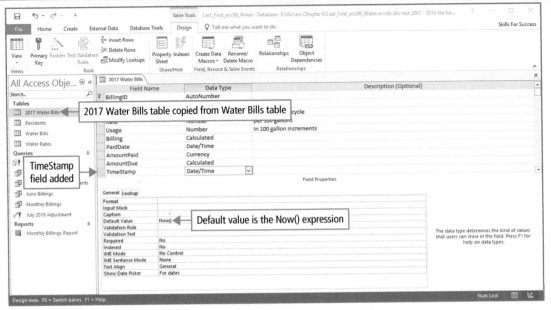

Figure 1

Access 2016, Windows 10, Microsoft Corporation

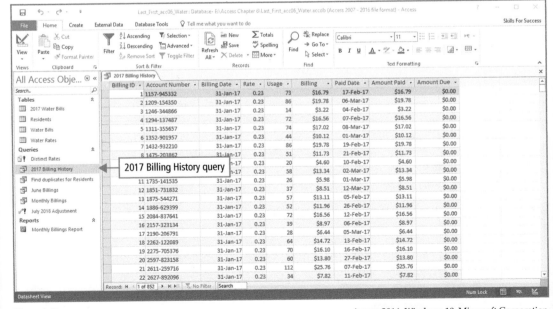

Figure 2

Access 2016, Windows 10, Microsoft Corporation

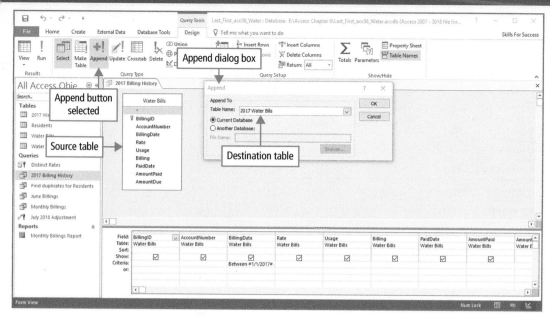

Access 2016, Windows 10, Microsoft Corporation

Figure 3

9. Switch to Design view. On the **Design tab**, in the **Query Type group**, click the **Append** button.

10. In the **Append** dialog box, click the **Table Name arrow**, and then click **2017 Water Bills**. Compare your screen with **Figure 3**.

> When you append records, the fields and data types from the source table must match the destination table. Here, the query selects all the fields from the Water Bills table. Because you copied and pasted this table to make the destination table—2017 Water Bills—all the fields and data types match.

11. Click **OK** to close the **Append** dialog box and insert the *Append To* row into the query design grid.

12. Click the **Run** button, read the message that displays, and then click **Yes**.

13. **Save** 🖫, and then **Close** ✕ the query.

14. In the **Navigation Pane**, open the **2017 Water Bills** in Datasheet View. Compare your screen with **Figure 4**.

> The 852 records from 2017 were added—appended—to the 2017 Water Bills table, and the original records are still stored in the Water Bills table. The TimeStamp values were added for each new record.

15. **Close** ✕ the table.

■ **You have completed Skill 9 of 10**

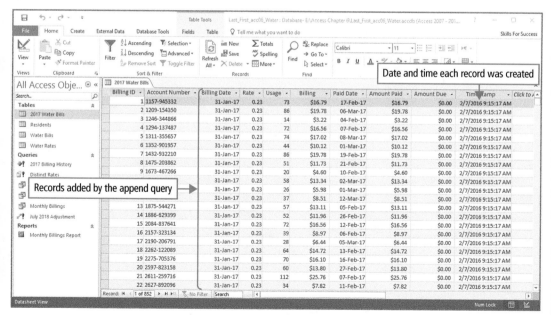

Access 2016, Windows 10, Microsoft Corporation

Figure 4

▶ A *delete query* is a query that deletes records from a table. The records selected by the query criteria are deleted when the query is run.

1. In the **Navigation Pane**, under **Tables**, double-click the **Water Bills** table.

2. In the datasheet, click the **Billing Date arrow**, point to **Date Filters**, and then click **Between**. In the **Between Dates** dialog box, set the **Oldest** value to 1/1/2017 and the **Newest** value to 12/31/2017 and then click **OK** to display the 852 records from the year 2017.

3. **Save** 🖫, and then **Close** ☒ the table.

4. In the **Navigation Pane**, under **Queries**, click the **2017 Billing History** query to select it.

5. On the **Home tab**, in the **Clipboard group**, click **Copy**. In the **Clipboard group**, click the **Paste** button.

6. In the **Paste Query As** dialog box, replace the **Query Name** value with Delete 2017 Records Compare your screen with **Figure 1**, and then click **OK**.

MOS
Obj 3.2.3

7. In the **Navigation Pane**, under **Queries**, right-click **Delete 2017 Records**, and then click **Design View**.

   In this manner, a query can be opened and modified without running the query.

8. On the **Design tab**, in the **Query Type group**, click **Delete**, and then compare your screen with **Figure 2**.

Figure 1   Access 2016, Windows 10, Microsoft Corporation

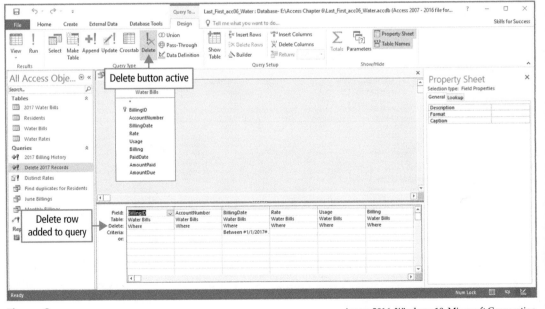

Figure 2   Access 2016, Windows 10, Microsoft Corporation

■ **Continue to the next page to complete the skill**

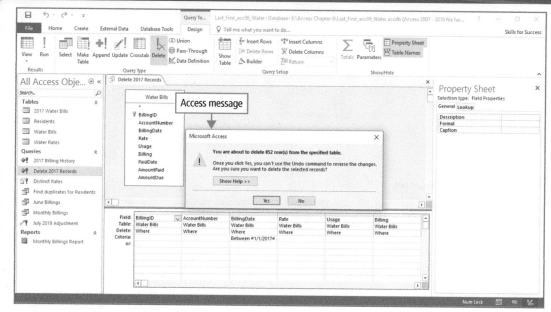

Access 2016, Windows 10, Microsoft Corporation

Figure 3

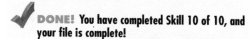

Access 2016, Windows 10, Microsoft Corporation

Figure 4

9. Click **Run**, and then compare your screen with **Figure 3**.

> The message warns that all the records selected by the query will be deleted from the underlying table—Water Bills. Because the actions taken by a delete query cannot be reversed using the Undo command, care should be taken before running a delete query. Here, we verified that the correct records would be selected in a previous step.

10. Read the displayed message, and then click **Yes**. **Save** 🖫, and then **Close** ☒ the query.

11. Double-click to open the **Water Bills** table datasheet. On the **Home tab**, in the **Sort & Filter group**, click the **Toggle Filter** button, and then compare your screen with **Figure 4**.

> Applying the filter results in no records because all the records from the year 2017 were deleted when the delete query was run.

12. Click the **Toggle Filter** so that it is no longer active, and then **Close** ☒ the table.

13. **Close** ☒ Access. Submit the file as directed by your instructor.

✔ **DONE! You have completed Skill 10 of 10, and your file is complete!**

More Skills 11

Create Union Queries

To complete this project, you will need the following file:

- acc06_MS11Utilities

You will save your file as:

- Last_First_acc06_MS11Utilities

Figure 1   Access 2016, Windows 10, Microsoft Corporation

▶ A **union query** combines the results of two or more similar select queries.

▶ When combining queries in a union query, both queries must have matching fields that share the same data type.

---

1. **Start Access 2016**, and then open the student data file **acc06_MS11Utilities**. **Save** the file in your **Access Chapter 6** folder as Last_First_acc06_MS11Utilities

2. If necessary, enable the content.

3. In the **Navigation Pane**, under **Queries**, double-click the **Hedspeth Electricity Bills** query. Leave the query open.

4. In the **Navigation Pane**, under **Queries**, double-click the **Hedspeth Water Bills** query. Leave the query open.

5. Click the **Create tab**, and then in the **Queries group**, click the **Query Design** button. **Close** the **Show Table** dialog box without adding any tables.

6. With the blank query open in Design view, on the **Design tab**, in the **Query Type group**, click the **Union** button.

   Union queries must be written in SQL view. When the Union button is clicked, a blank query displays in SQL view.

7. Click the **Hedspeth Electricity Bills tab** to display the datasheet. On the **Home tab**, click the **View arrow**, and then click **SQL View**.

8. With the entire SQL SELECT statement selected, click the **Home tab**, and then in the **Clipboard group**, click **Copy**. **Close** ☒ the Hedspeth Electricity Bills query.

9. Ensure the **Query1 tab** is selected. On the **Home tab**, in the **Clipboard group**, click the **Paste** button.

10. Switch to the **Hedspeth Water Bills** query datasheet, and then switch to SQL view. With the entire SQL SELECT statement selected, click the **Home tab**, and then in the **Clipboard group**, click **Copy**.

11. **Close** ☒ the Hedspeth Water Bills query.

12. With the insertion point in the **Query1 tab**, press ⏎ Enter two times, and then type UNION

    The **UNION** clause is used to combine one or more queries in a union query.

13. Press ⏎ Enter two more times, and then on the **Home tab**, click the **Paste** button.

14. Click the **Design tab**, and then click the **Run** button. Compare your screen with **Figure 1**.

15. Click **Save** 🖫, name the query All Hedspeth Bills and then press ⏎ Enter.

16. **Close** ☒ the query, and then **Close** ☒ Access. Submit the file as directed by your instructor.

■ **You have completed More Skills 11**

More Skills (12)

Base Queries on Other Queries Part 1

To complete this project, you will need the following file:

- acc06_MS12Bills

You will save your file as:

- Last_First_acc06_MS12Bills

▶ Complex and powerful queries can be built by using queries as their data source.

---

1. Start **Access 2016**, and then from the student data files for this project, open **acc06_MS12Bills**.

2. Use the **Save As** dialog box to save the database in your **Access Chapter 6** folder with the name Last_First_acc06_MS12Bills

3. If necessary, enable the content.

4. Click the **Create tab**, and then in the **Queries group**, click **Query Design**. In the **Show Table** dialog box, click **Add**, and then **Close** the dialog box.

5. Double-click the Bills table fields in the following order: **BillingDate**, **AccountNumber**, **Rate**, and then **Usage**.

6. On the **Design tab**, in the **Show/Hide group**, click the **Totals** button.

7. Click the **AccountNumber** column **Total** field to display the **arrow**, and then change the value from **Group By** to **Count**.

8. Repeat the technique just practiced to change the **Rate** column **Total** row to **Avg**. Change the **Usage** column **Total** row to **Sum**. Compare your screen with **Figure 1**.

9. **Run** the query. Set the datasheet field widths to **Best Fit**, and then compare your screen with **Figure 2**.

   Data that has been summarize often needs to be formatted. You will format the data in this query in the second query.

10. Click **Save** 🖫, name the query Billing Summary Data and then press ⌈Enter⌋. **Close** ✕ the query.

11. **Close** ✕ Access, and then submit the file as directed by your instructor.

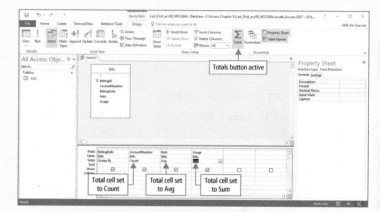

Access 2016, Windows 10, Microsoft Corporation   **Figure 1**

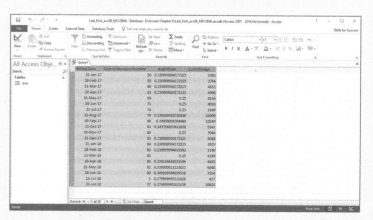

Access 2016, Windows 10, Microsoft Corporation   **Figure 2**

■ **You have completed More Skills 12**

More Skills (13)

Base Queries on Other Queries Part 2

To complete this project, you will need the following file:

- acc06_MS13Billings

You will save your file as:

- Last_First_acc06_MS13Billings

▶ Building a query from a summary query enables you to add calculated fields based on the data created in the summary query.

1. Start **Access 2016**, and then from the student data files for this project, open **acc06_MS13Billings**.

2. Use the **Save As** dialog box to save the database in your **Access Chapter 6** folder with the name Last_First_acc06_MS13Billings

3. If necessary, enable the content.

4. Click the **Create tab**, and then in **Queries group**, click **Query Design**.

5. In the **Show Table** dialog box, click the **Queries tab**, and then click **Add**.

6. **Close** the Show Table dialog box. Add these fields in the following order: **BillingDate**, **AccountNumber**, **Rate**, and then **Usage**.

7. Click in the **AccountNumber** column, and then on the **Design tab**, in the **Show/Hide group**, click **Property Sheet**.

8. In the property sheet, click in the **Caption** box, and then type Account Number Compare your screen with **Figure 1**.

9. Click in the **BillingDate** column, and then repeat the technique just practice to set the **Caption** property to Billing Date

10. Click the **Rate** column. In the property sheet, click **Format**, and then click the **Format arrow**. From the list, click **Fixed**.

11. Set the **Rate** column **Decimal Places** property to **2**.

12. Click in the first blank column in the **Field** row, and then type the following expression: TotalBill:[Rate]*[Usage]

13. With the calculated column still active, change the column's **Format** property to **Currency**, and the **Caption** property to Total Bill **Close** ⊠ the property sheet.

Figure 1   Access 2016, Windows 10, Microsoft Corporation

14. Click **Save** ⊞, name the query Monthly Billings and then press [Enter].

15. **Run** the query, and then set the datasheet field widths to **Best Fit**.

16. **Save** ⊞, and then **Close** ⊠ the query. **Close** ⊠ Access, and then submit the file as directed by your instructor.

■ **You have completed More Skills 13**

More Skills (14)

Use Subqueries as Criteria

To complete this project, you will need the following file:

- acc06_MS14Outings

You will save your file as:

- Last_First_acc06_MS14Outings

▶ *Subqueries* are queries nested within another query.

▶ Subqueries are useful when need to simplify complex criteria. For example, multiple OR criteria can be eliminated by inserting a subquery.

1. Start **Access 2016**, and then from the student data files for this project, open **acc06_MS14Outings**.

2. Use the **Save As** dialog box to save the database in your **Access Chapter 6** folder with the name Last_First_acc06_MS14Outings

3. If necessary, enable the content.

4. In the **Navigation Pane**, under **Queries**, double-click **Discounted Fees**.

   The eight outings are listed with their discounted fee amounts displayed in the last column.

5. Switch to Design view, and leave the query open.

6. In the **Navigation Pane**, under **Tables**, double-click **Discounted Outings**.

7. In the **Discounted Outings** column, click the first record's **arrow**.

8. **Close** ☒ the table without making any changes.

9. In the **Discounted Fees** query, right-click the **Outing ID** column **Criteria** row, and then from the shortcut menu, click **Zoom**.

10. Replace the existing text with the following subquery: IN (SELECT * FROM [Discounted Outings])

   The *IN* operator is used to select records from a list of acceptable values. The arguments in the parenthesis after the IN operator define the list of acceptable values. The *asterisk (*)* is used to select all the fields from the table(s) listed in the FROM statement. Here, any Outing ID that matches the Outing IDs listed in the Discounted Outings table will be acceptable values for the main query's criteria.

11. Click **OK** to close the Zoom dialog box, and then **Run** the query to display the six discounted queries as listed in the Discount Outings table.

12. Leave the query open, and then open the **Discounted Outings** table in Datasheet view.

13. Click in the **Append** row **Discounted Outings** field to display the combo box arrow, and then click the **arrow**. In the combo box, click **47 | Intro to Mountain Biking** to add it to the list. **Close** ☒ the table.

14. With the **Discounted Fees** query open, on the **Home tab**, in the **Records group**, click the **Refresh All** button to run the query again.

15. **Save** ☐, and then **Close** ☒ the query.

16. **Close** ☒ Access. Submit the file as directed by your instructor.

■ **You have completed More Skills 14**

Review

The following table summarizes the **SKILLS AND PROCEDURES** covered in this chapter.

Skill	Task	Step
1	Find duplicate records	Create tab → Queries group → Query Wizard → Find Duplicate Queries Wizard
2	Switch to SQL view	Home tab → Views group → View arrow → SQL View
2	Change TOP command	Switch to SQL view, and then type a new value to the right of the *TOP* command
3	Create make table queries	Design tab → Query Types group → Make Table button
3	Find unique records	Switch to SQL view, and then in the SELECT clause, insert the word DISTINCT before the field
4	Rename queries	Right-click the query → Rename
4	Remove query tables	Right-click the table title bar → Remove Table
4	Remove query columns	Select the column, and then press Delete
4	Move query columns	Drag and drop the query column
5	Create update queries	Design tab → Query Types group → Update button
6	Concatenate query fields	Create an expression following this syntax: ColumnName: [FieldName] + "Text"
7	Create parameter queries	In place of criteria, write a prompt following this syntax: [Enter the starting date]
8	Create reports from parameter queries	Select the query in the Navigation Pane, and then click the Report button
9	Enter time stamp automatically	For field's Default Value property, enter NOW()
9	Copy tables	Select the table in the Navigation Pane, then click Copy; click Paste, and name table
9	Create append queries	Design tab → Query Types group → Append button
10	Copy queries	Select the query in the Navigation Pane, then click Copy; click Paste, and name query
10	Create delete queries	Design tab → Query Types group → Delete button
MS11	Create Union queries	Design tab → Query Type group → Union button
MS12	Group by count	Total row → display arrow → click Count

Project Summary Chart

Project	Project Type	Project Location
Skills Review	Review	In Book & MIL MyITLab Grader
Skills Assessment 1	Review	In Book & MIL MyITLab Grader
Skills Assessment 2	Review	Book
My Skills	Problem Solving	Book
Visual Skills Check	Problem Solving	Book
Skills Challenge 1	Critical Thinking	Book
Skills Challenge 2	Critical Thinking	Book
More Skills Assessment	Review	In Book & MIL MyITLab Grader
Collaborating with Google	Critical Thinking	Book

MOS Objectives Covered (Quiz in MyITLab)

3.1.3 Create a parameter query	3.2.3 Remove fields
3.1.4 Create an action query	3.3.2 Set filtering criteria
3.2.1 Rename a query	

Key Terms

Online Help Skills

1. Start **Access 2016**, and then in the upper right corner of the start page, click the **Help** button.

2. In the **Access Help** window **Search help** box, type append query and then press Enter .

3. In the search result list, click **Common errors when you run an append query**. **Maximize** the window, and then compare your screen with **Figure 1**.

Access 2016 Help

append query

Common errors when you run an append query

When you run an append query in an Access desktop database, you may receive an error message that says, "Microsoft Access can't append all the records in the append query."

This error message can appear for one of the following reasons:

Type conversion failures   You may be trying to append data of one type into a field of another type. For example, appending text into a field whose data type is set to Number will cause the error to appear. Check the data types of fields in the destination table, and then make sure you're appending the correct type of data into each one.

Key violations   You may be trying to append data into one or more fields that are part of the table's primary key, such as the ID field. Check the design of the destination table to see if the primary key (or any index) has the No Duplicates property set to Yes. Then, check the data you are appending to make sure it doesn't violate the rules of the destination table.

Lock violations   If the destination table is open in Design view or open by another user on the network, this could result in record locks that would prevent the query from being able to append records. Make sure everyone's closed out of the database.

Validation rule violations   Check the design of the destination table to see what validation rules exist. For example, if a field is required and your query doesn't provide data for it, you'll get the error. Also, check the destination table for any Text fields where the Allow Zero Length property is set to No. If your query doesn't append any characters into such a field, you'll get the error. Other validation rules may also be causing the problem—for example, you may have the following validation rule for the Quantity field:

Figure 1   Access 2016, Windows 10, Microsoft Corporation

4. Read the article to answer the following question: How can duplicate keys result in an error message?

Matching

Match each term in the second column with its correct definition in the first column by writing the letter of the term on the blank line in front of the correct definition.

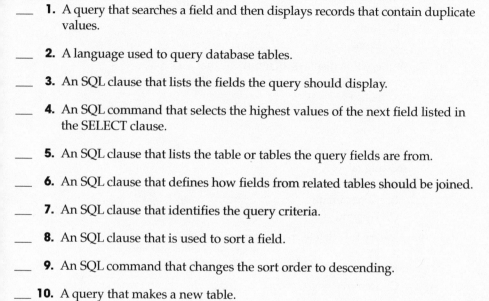

____ **1.** A query that searches a field and then displays records that contain duplicate values.

____ **2.** A language used to query database tables.

____ **3.** An SQL clause that lists the fields the query should display.

____ **4.** An SQL command that selects the highest values of the next field listed in the SELECT clause.

____ **5.** An SQL clause that lists the table or tables the query fields are from.

____ **6.** An SQL clause that defines how fields from related tables should be joined.

____ **7.** An SQL clause that identifies the query criteria.

____ **8.** An SQL clause that is used to sort a field.

____ **9.** An SQL command that changes the sort order to descending.

____ **10.** A query that makes a new table.

A DESC

B Find duplicates query

C FROM

D INNER JOIN

E Make table query

F ORDER BY

G SELECT

H Structured Query Language

I TOP

J WHERE

Multiple Choice

Choose the correct answer.

1. Under what circumstances can a primary key not be assigned to a field?
   A. When duplicate values exist in the field
   B. When a similar field in another table is used as a primary key
   C. When the field only contains unique values

2. All Access queries are written using which type of statements?
   A. Edit
   B. Question
   C. SQL

3. Which type of query is useful when you need to save data at a certain point in time?
   A. Make table
   B. Time query
   C. Append

4. A query that can add, delete, or modify records.
   A. Delete
   B. Change
   C. Update

5. Which type of query is useful when you need to modify large amounts of data quickly and accurately?
   A. Change
   B. Update
   C. Modify

6. The criteria used to join two or more values to create one single value.
   A. Concatenate
   B. Join
   C. From

7. A query that displays an input box that asks for criteria each time the query is run.
   A. Select
   B. Append
   C. Parameter

8. A query that adds the results of the query to an existing table.
   A. Parameter
   B. Concatenate
   C. Append

9. A query that deletes records from a table.
   A. Delete
   B. From
   C. Remove

10. How can the results from a delete query be reversed?
    A. Click undo
    B. Run the reverse query
    C. The delete query cannot be reversed

Topics for Discussion

1. What is the difference between an update query and an append query? Under which circumstances would you use each type of query?

2. You have concatenated two fields in a query. Why would you choose to concatenate two fields in a query instead of storing the data in one field in the original table? Why would storing information such as first and last names in the same field create issues when trying to store or retrieve data?

Skills Review

MyITLab®
Grader

To complete this project, you will need the following file:

- acc06_SRElectricity

You will save your file as:

- Last_First_acc06_SRElectricity

1. Start **Access 2016**, and then open the student data file **acc06_SRElectricity**. Save the database in your **Access Chapter 6** folder with the name Last_First_ acc06_SRElectricity If necessary, enable the content.

2. Click the **Create tab**, and then in the **Queries group**, click **Query Wizard**. In the **New Query** dialog box, click **Find Duplicates Query Wizard**, and then click **OK**.

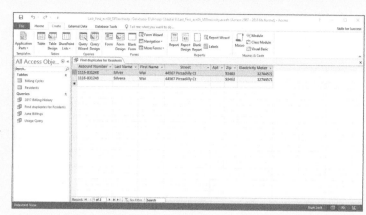

Access 2016, Windows 10, Microsoft Corporation   **Figure 1**

3. In the **Find Duplicates Query Wizard** dialog box, click **Table:Residents**, and then click **Next**. Click the **Move** button, and then click **Next**. Click the **Move All** button, and then click **Finish**. Select the first record, compare with Figure 1, and then press Delete . Click **Yes** to delete the record.

4. Close the **Find duplicates for Residents** query. Open the **Residents** table in Design view, and then assign the **Primary Key** to the **AccountNumber** field. **Save** and **Close** the table. Click the **Database Tools tab**, and then click the **Relationships** button. Drag the **AccountNumber** from the **Residents** table to the **AccountNumber** in the **Billing Cycles** table. Select the **Enforce Referential Integrity** check box, and then click **Create**. **Save** and **Close** the **Relationships tab**.

5. Open the **June Billings** query in Design view. On the **Design tab**, in the **Query Setup group**, click the **Return arrow**, and then click **25**. Switch to SQL view. To the right of the *TOP* command, change the *25* value to *20* **Save**, **Run**, and then **Close** the query.

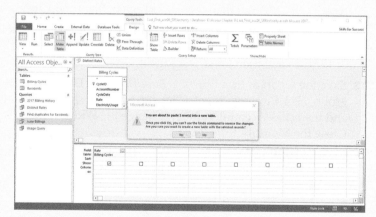

Access 2016, Windows 10, Microsoft Corporation   **Figure 2**

6. Click the **Create tab**, and then in the **Queries group**, click **Query Design**. Click to show **Billing Cycles**, and then **Close** the dialog box. Double-click the **Rate** field. Click **Save**, type Distinct Rates press Enter , and then click **Run**. Switch to SQL view. After the *SELECT* command, add a space, and then type DISTINCT Click **Save**, and then switch to Design view. In the **Query Type** group, click **Make Table**, type Electric Rates and then click **OK**. Click **Run**, compare with Figure 2, and then click **Yes**.

■ Continue to the next page to complete this Skills Review

7. **Save** and **Close** the query. Open the **Usage Query** in Design view. Select the **LastName** field and drag it to the left of the **FirstName** field. Click **Save**, compare with Figure 3, and then **Close** the query.

8. Open the **June Billings** query in Design view. In the **Query Type group**, click **Update**. In the **ElectricityUsage** column **Update To** row, type [ElectricityUsage]*0.9 **Save** and **Run** the query. Click **Yes**, and then **Close** the query.

9. Click the **Create tab**, and then click **Query Design**. Double-click to add the **Residents** and **Billing Cycles** tables. **Close** the dialog box. From the **Residents** table, add the **AccountNumber** and **Street** fields. From the **Billing Cycles** table, add **UsageFee** and **PaidDate**. Right-click the first empty column in the **Field** row, and then click **Zoom**. Type FullName: [FirstName]+" "+[LastName] and then click **OK**.

10. **Save** the query as Monthly Bills and then click **Run**.

11. In Design view, right-click the **PaidDate** column **Criteria** row. Click **Zoom**, and then type Between [Enter Beginning Date] And [Enter Ending Date] Click **OK**, and then **Save** and **Run** the query. Type 7/1/2018 press Enter, type 7/31/2018 and then press Enter again. **Save** and **Close** the query.

12. In the **Navigation Pane**, select the **Monthly Bills** query. Click the **Create tab**. In the **Reports group**, click **Report**. Type 7/1/2018 press Enter, type 7/15/2018 and then press Enter again.

13. **Save** the report as Monthly Bills Report On the **Design tab**, in the **Tools** group, click **Property Sheet**. Click the property sheet **Selection Type arrow**, and then click **AccountNumber**. Change the **Width** value to 1.2" **Save** and **Close** the **Monthly Bills Report**.

14. Click the **Billing Cycles** table. On the **Home tab**, in the **Clipboard group**, click **Copy**, and then click **Paste**. In the **Paste Table As** dialog box, type 2017 Electric Bills Select the **Structure Only** option, and then click **OK**.

15. Open the **2017 Billing History** query in Design view. In the **Query Type group**, click **Append**. In the **Append** dialog box, click the **Table Name arrow**, and then click **2017 Electric Bills**. Click **OK**, and then click **Run**. Click **Yes**. **Save** and **Close** the query.

16. In the **Navigation Pane**, click the **2017 Billing History** query. On the **Home tab**, click **Copy**, and then click **Paste**. In the **Paste As** dialog box, type Delete 2017 Records and then click **OK**. Compare your screen with Figure 4.

17. Open the **Delete 2017 Records** query in Design view. On the **Design tab**, in the **Query Type group**, click **Delete**. Click **Run**.

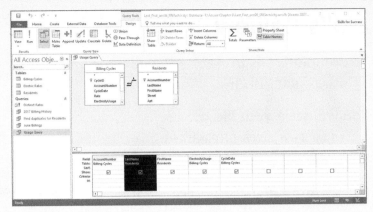

Figure 3   Access 2016, Windows 10, Microsoft Corporation

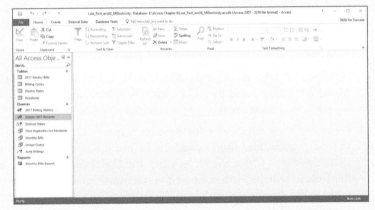

Figure 4   Access 2016, Windows 10, Microsoft Corporation

18. Click **Yes**. **Save** and **Close** the query. **Close** Access. Submit the file as directed by your instructor.

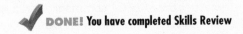

DONE! You have completed Skills Review

Skills Assessment 1

To complete this project, you will need the following file:

- acc06_SA1Outings

You will save your file as:

- Last_First_acc06_SA1Outings

1. Start **Access 2016**, and then open the student data file **acc06_SA1Outings**. Save the database in your **Access Chapter 6** folder with the name Last_First_acc06_SA1Outings If necessary, enable the content.

2. Use the **Query Wizard** to find duplicate records in the **Outing Leader Contact Listing** table. Use the **E-mail Address** field to identify duplicates. Move the **Leader ID** and **Outing Leader** fields as additional query fields. Delete the record with a **Leader ID** value of **26**.

3. In SQL view, change the **Outings Query** *TOP* command value to 5

4. Create a Volunteers Query that displays the **VolunteerID** from the **Volunteers** table, and a FullName concatenated field, which combines the **FirstName** and **LastName** of each volunteer.

5. Create a parameter query named Scheduled Outings Parameter Query displaying the **Schedule ID**, **Outing Date**, **Start Time**, **End Time**, **Outing ID**, and **Leader** from the **Scheduled Outings** table. In the **Outing Date** column **Criteria**, type Between [Enter Beginning Date] And [Enter Ending Date]

6. In the **Scheduled Outings Parameter Query**, sort the **Outing Date** field as **Ascending**.

7. Create a Scheduled Outings Report using the **Scheduled Outings Parameter Query**. Use 6/1/2018 as the **Beginning Date** and 8/31/2018 as the **Ending Date**. From the **Property Sheet**, change the width of the **Schedule ID** to 1" and the width of the **Outing Date** to 2"

8. In the **Outings Query**, add the **Ages** and **Fee** fields from the **Outings** table. Add the **Category** field from the **Outing Categories** table, and then compare with Figure 1. **Save** and **Close** the **Outings Query**.

9. Create a copy of the **Scheduled Outings Parameter Query** named Make Table Scheduled Outings Query and then change it to a Make Table query. Using the **Make Table Scheduled Outings Query**, make a new Summer Outings table including outings from 6/1/2018 through 8/31/2018 **Save** and **Close** the query.

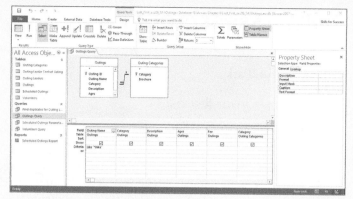

Access 2016, Windows 10, Microsoft Corporation   **Figure 1**

Access 2016, Windows 10, Microsoft Corporation   **Figure 2**

10. Create a Fee Update Query including the **Outing ID** and **Fee** fields from the **Outings** table. In the **Fee** column **Update To** field, type [Fee] - 1 to reduce the fee for each outing. Run the query.

11. Copy the **Volunteers Query** as Delete Volunteer Query Change it to a Delete query, and then under the **VolunteerID** column **Criteria**, type [VolunteerID] = 9 Compare with Figure 2.

12. **Run, Save,** and **Close** the query.

13. In the **Volunteers** table, add the field **SignUpDate** with the **Data Type** Date/Time and a **Default** value of Now()

14. Click **Save, Close** the table, and then **Close** Access. Submit the file as directed by your instructor.

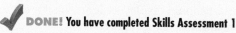

DONE! You have completed Skills Assessment 1

Skills Assessment 2

To complete this project, you will need the following file:

- acc06_SA2Park

You will save your file as:

- Last_First_acc06_SA2Park

---

1. Start **Access 2016**, and then open the student data file **acc06_SA2Park**. Save the database in your **Access Chapter 6** folder with the name Last_First_acc06_SA2Park If necessary, enable the content.

2. Use the **Query Wizard** tool to create a query that locates duplicate employee records in the **Employees** table, using the **Phone** field to identify duplicate records. Delete the record with the **EmployeeID** value of **5**. **Save** the query using the default query name.

3. Add an **AssignmentDate** field to the **Assignments table**. Change the data type to **Date/Time**. Set the field width to **Best Fit**. Add a new row to the *Assignments* table using the following values: **AssignmentID: 7 EmployeeID:** 11 **Supplies:** Extended Kit

4. Change the **Return** on the **Assignments Query** to **25**. From SQL view, change the value after the *TOP* command to 10, and then compare your screen with **Figure 1**.

5. Concatenate the **FirstName** and **LastName** fields on the **Assignments Query** to create a new field named FullName Delete the **FirstName** and **LastName** fields from the query. Add the **AssignmentDate** field from the **Assignments** table as the last field in the query.

6. In the **Assignments** table, add the following as the **AssignmentDate** field values in the first six rows: 6/11/2018 | 6/13/2018 | 6/15/2018 | 7/11/2018 | 7/11/2018 | 7/12/2018 | 7/15/2018

7. Create a Beginning Date and Ending Date criteria to the **AssignmentDate** field of the **Assignments Query**. **Save** and **Close** the query.

8. Create a copy of the **Assignments Query** named Make Table Assignments Query Using the **Make Table Assignments Query**, make a new table named July Assignments that includes all assignments during July 2018. **Save** and **Close** the query.

9. Create a report named June Assignments from the **Assignments Query**. The report should display assignments for the month of June 2018. **Save** and **Close** the report.

Figure 1

Access 2016, Windows 10, Microsoft Corporation

Figure 2

Access 2016, Windows 10, Microsoft Corporation

10. Create a copy of the **Assignments Query** named AssignmentDate Update Query Delete the AssignmentDate parameter criteria. Delete all fields except AssignmentDate. In the Update To row in AssignmentDate, type [AssignmentDate] +1

11. Run the AssignmentDate Update Query. **Save** and **Close** the query.

12. Open the Assignments table, and then compare your screen with Figure 2.

13. Click **Save**, **Close** the table, and then **Close** Access. Submit the file as directed by your instructor.

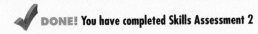 **DONE! You have completed Skills Assessment 2**

My Skills

To complete this project, you will need the following file:

- acc06_MyMaintenance

You will save your file as:

- Last_First_acc06_MyMaintenance

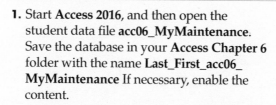

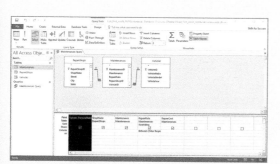

Access 2016, Windows 10, Microsoft Corporation **Figure 1**

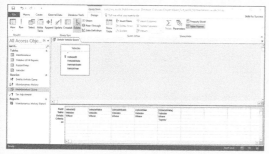

Access 2016, Windows 10, Microsoft Corporation **Figure 2**

1. Start **Access 2016**, and then open the student data file **acc06_MyMaintenance**. Save the database in your **Access Chapter 6** folder with the name **Last_First_acc06_MyMaintenance** If necessary, enable the content.

2. Use the **Relationships** tool to create a relationship between the **RepairShops** and **Maintenances** tables using the **RepairShopsID**, and between the **Maintenances** and **Vehicles** tables using the **VehiclesID**. Enforce Referential Integrity with both relationships.

3. Open the **Maintenances** table, and then add at least three repair records to the table, including **RepairCosts**. Ensure all repair dates are in October 2018.

4. Use the **Query Design** tool to create a Maintenances Query The query should include the **VehicleModel**, **ShopName**, **Maintenance**, **RepairDate**, and the **RepairCost**. Sort the records in **Ascending** order according to **RepairDate**. Set the query to return **5** records.

5. Switch to SQL view, and then change the *TOP* command to return the first 3 records.

6. Switch to Design view. In the **RepairDate** column **Criteria** row, type Between [Enter Beginning Date] And [Enter Ending Date]

7. Right-click the first empty column in the **Field** row, and then click **Zoom**. Type Vehicle:[VehicleMake] + " " +[VehicleModel] and then click **OK**.

8. Delete the **VehicleModel** column, drag the **Vehicle** column to the left of the **ShopName**, and then compare your screen with **Figure 1**.

9. **Save** and **Run** the query. Use the **Make Table** tool to create an October 2018 Repairs table using the parameters 10/1/2018 and 10/31/2018

10. Create a copy of the **Maintenances Query** called Maintenances History and then open the query in Design view. Click **Select Query**, and then **Save** the query. Create a Maintenances History Report using the parameters 10/1/2018 and 10/31/2018

11. Create a Tax Adjustment query that includes the **MaintenanceID**, **Maintenance**, and **RepairCost** fields from the **Maintenances** table. In the **RepairCost** column **Update To** row, type [RepairCost] * 1.06 Run the query.

12. Create a Delete Vehicle Query that includes all fields from the **Vehicles** table. In the **VehicleMake** column **Criteria** row, type [VehicleMake] = Toyota Compare your screen with **Figure 2**, and then **Run** the query to delete the vehicle from the **Vehicles** table.

13. **Save** and **Close** all queries, tables, and the report. **Close** Access. Submit the file as directed by your instructor.

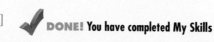

DONE! You have completed My Skills

Visual Skills Check

To complete this project, you will need the following file:

- acc06_VSDonations

You will save your file as:

- Last_First_acc06_VSDonations

Open the student data file **acc06_VSDonations**, and then save the file in your **Access Chapter 6** folder as Last_First_acc06_VSDonations

Use the Query Design tool to create the query shown in **Figure 1**. Use the Show Tables dialog box to add the tables shown. Include the fields shown and save the query as Donations Query In the DonationsDate column Criteria row, include the following criteria: Between [Enter Beginning Date] And [Enter Ending Date] Run the query using 1/1/2018 as the Beginning Date and 12/31/2018 as the Ending Date. Change the width of all columns to Best Fit.

Submit the file as directed by your instructor.

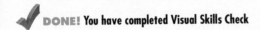

DONE! You have completed Visual Skills Check

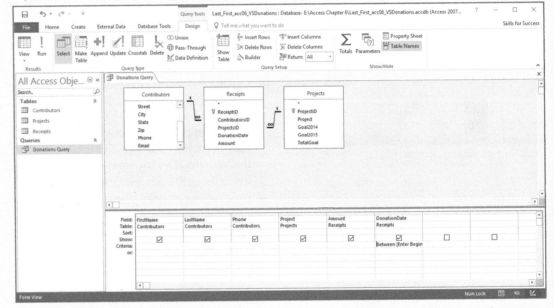

Figure 1

Access 2016, Windows 10, Microsoft Corporation

Skills Challenge 1

To complete this project, you will need the following file:

- acc06_SC1Rentals

You will save your file as:

- Last_First_acc06_SC1Rentals

Open the student data file **acc06_SC1Rentals**, and then save the file in your **Access Chapter 6** folder as Last_First_acc06_ SC1Rentals Create a query that displays the type of boat rented by each customer between specific dates. In the query, include the necessary customer name, boat name, and date fields from the **Customers**, **Boats**, and **Receipts** tables. Include a criterion that allows users to enter specific Checkout dates to query. Save the query as Boat Rentals Between Specific Dates

and change the width of all displayed fields to Best Fit. Run the query to view boats rented between 7/4/2018 and 7/6/2018.

Submit the file as directed by your instructor.

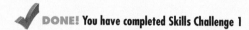 **DONE! You have completed Skills Challenge 1**

Skills Challenge 2

To complete this project, you will need the following file:

- acc06_SC2FarmersMarket

You will save your file as:

- Last_First_acc06_SC2 FarmersMarket

Open the student data file **acc06_SC2FarmersMarket**, and then save the file in your **Access Chapter 6** folder as Last_First_ acc06_SC2FarmersMarket Create a query that can be used to create a Farm Offerings report. In the query, include the necessary farm name field from the **Farms** table, description name from the **Products** table, and products ID from the **Farm Offerings** table. Save the query as Farm Offerings Query Sort the description names in Ascending order. Create a Farm

Offerings Report Change the width of the **Farm** text box to 2" and the width of the **Description** text box to 1.5"

Submit the file as directed by your instructor.

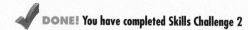 **DONE! You have completed Skills Challenge 2**

More Skills Assessment

To complete this project, you will need the following file:

- acc06_MSAWater

You will save your file as:

- Last_First_acc06_MSAWater

---

1. Start **Access 2016**. Open the file **acc06_MSAWater**, and then save the file in your chapter folder as Last_First_acc06_MSAWater

2. Create a Union query that combines the 2017 *Billing History* and the 2018 *Billing History* queries.

3. Save the query as 2017-2018 Billing History

4. Change the 2017 Billing Summary Data query to include a Total row. Adjust **Group By** to **Count** *AccountNumber*, **Avg** the *Rate*, and **Sum** the *Usage*.

5. Change the AccountNumber Caption to Customer Count the Rate Caption to Average Rate and the Usage Caption to Total Usage Compare your screen with **Figure 1**.

6. In the first blank **Field** column, type the expression: TotalBill:[Rate]*[Usage] Set the *Total Bill* **Format** property to **Currency**, and then **Save** the query.

7. In the Usage Query, type IN (SELECT [AccountNumber] FROM [Residents]) in the *AccountNumber* **Criteria** row.

8. **Save** and **Close** the query.

9. **Close** Access. Submit the file as directed by your instructor.

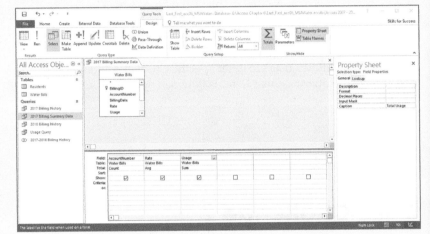

Figure 1

Access 2016, Windows 10, Microsoft Corporation

 **DONE!** You have completed the More Skills Assessment

Collaborating with Google

To complete this project, you will need a Google account (refer to the Common Features chapter) and the following file:

- acc06_GPRentals (Excel)

You will save your file as:

- Last_First_acc06_GPRentals (Excel)

---

1. Open the Google Chrome web browser. Log into your Google account, and then click the **Apps** button.

2. Click **Drive** to open Google Drive.

3. Click the **New** button, and then click **File upload**. Navigate to the student data files, and then open **acc06_GPRentals**.

4. Right-click the **acc06_GPRentals** in **Google Drive**. Click **Open With**, and then click **Google Sheets**.

5. On the *Rentals* sheet, click cell **F1**, and then type Renters of Room CE150 Press Enter .

6. In cell **F2**, type the expression =Query(Rentals!A2:E201, "select B where D CONTAINS 'CE150'") and then press Enter .

   The statement asks Google Sheets to conduct a query. The *Rentals!* tells Google Sheets to select the Rental sheet to locate data. *A2:E201* requests data from that cell range. The *select B where D CONTAINS 'CE150'* states that the query is to return the RenterID of any renter who has rented Room Number CE150.

7. Point to the line between columns **F** and **G** to display the pointer, and then double-click to set column F to Best Fit.

8. Click cell **E1**. Click **Paint format**, and then click cell **F1**. Compare your screen with **Figure 1**, and then click cell **F2**.

9. Press , type snip and then press Enter to start the **Snipping Tool**. Click the **New arrow**, and then click **Window Snip**. Point to the Google Chrome browser, and when a red border displays around the window, click one time.

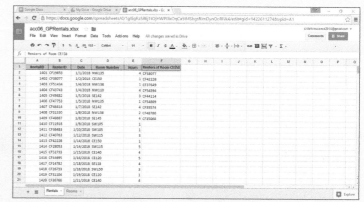

Figure 1

10. In the **Snipping Tool** mark-up window, click the **Save Snip** button . In the **Save As** dialog box, navigate to your Access Chapter 6 folder. Be sure the **Save as type** box displays **JPEG file**. Name the file Last_First_acc06_GPRentalsSnip and then press Enter . **Close** the Snipping Tool mark-up window.

11. Close all windows, and then submit your file as directed by your instructor.

DONE! You have completed Collaborating with Google

CHAPTER 7

Add Advanced Form Features

- ▸ A form provides a convenient way of entering data into a table. In Access 2016, controls can be easily moved in Layout and Design view.
- ▸ Form controls can be modified to produce a customized layout.
- ▸ You can add background images or logos to forms.

- ▸ Once opened, a pop up form remains on top, even when it is not the active form.
- ▸ Functional buttons can be added to allow records to be printed, to advance to the next record, or to open another form.

bradcalkins/Fotolia

Aspen Falls City Hall

In this project, you will assist Amado Pettinelli, Outdoor Recreation Supervisor of Aspen Falls, to create forms to enter race entrants, results, and sponsors into the Triathlon database. Each year Aspen Falls holds a triathlon and entrants are added to the database. Sponsors contribute money for prizes, and after the triathlon, the race results are recorded.

A Prize Sponsorships form will be created using Application Parts to expedite the creation process. This form will be added as a subform in the Sponsors form. As Amado calls potential sponsors, she will use the Sponsors form to enter donation information into the database. For this reason, the Sponsors form will be changed to a pop up to ensure it remains on top of all open database components.

Amado also needs other forms to make entering data into the database more efficient and accurate. These forms need customized features such as combo boxes, lookup fields, and conditional formatting.

In this project, you will create a form to enter race results and another form to enter sponsors into the database. You will create a form using Application Parts, add button controls to forms, create a pop up form and a subform, and modify forms to enhance usability and design.

Outcome

Using the skills in this chapter, you will be able to create forms and position controls, create pop up forms and add button controls, apply conditional formatting to form controls, create hyperlinks and subforms, and improve usability and design of forms.

Objectives

7.1 Create pop up forms and forms from Application Parts

7.2 Modify forms to include hyperlinks and button controls

7.3 Apply conditional formatting to form controls

7.4 Create subforms, use lookup fields, and improve form usability and design

Student data files needed for this chapter:

acc07_Triathlon
acc07_Triathlon_Logo
acc07_Triathlon_Background
acc07_Triathlon_PrivacyPolicy

You will save your file as:

Last_First_acc07_Triathlon

SKILLS

Skills 1–10 Training

At the end of this chapter you will be able to:

Skill 1 Create Forms in Design View

Skill 2 Position Form Controls

Skill 3 Use Lookup Fields in Forms

Skill 4 Create Pop Up Forms

Skill 5 Add Button Controls

Skill 6 Apply Conditional Formatting to Form Controls

Skill 7 Create Forms from Application Parts

Skill 8 Add Hyperlinks to Forms

Skill 9 Create Subforms

Skill 10 Improve Form Usability and Design

MORE SKILLS

Skill 11 Add Option Groups to Forms

Skill 12 Add Combo Boxes to Forms

Skill 13 Create Multiple Item Forms

Skill 14 Set Tab Order

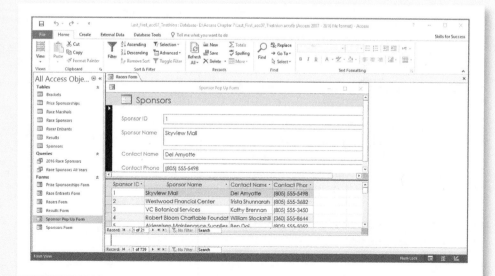

Access 2016, Windows 10, Microsoft Corporation

- You can use the Blank Form tool to create forms with just the fields you need and in the order you need for data entry.
- Form Design view provides tools and commands not available in other views.

1. Start **Access 2016**, and then open the student data file **acc07_Triathlon**. Use the **Save As** dialog box to create a **New folder** named Access Chapter 7 Save the database in the new folder as Last_First_ acc07_Triathlon If necessary, enable the content.

2. On the **Create tab**, in the **Forms group**, click the **Blank Form** button.

3. Click **Show all tables**. In the **Field List**, expand ⊞ the **Racers** table. Double-click to add these fields in the following order: **Racer ID**, **First Name**, **Last Name**, **Street**, **City**, **State**, and **Zip**. Compare your screen with **Figure 1**.

   When you add fields using the Blank Form tool, they are added in a *stacked layout*—a layout in which labels display the field names in the left column, and text boxes display the corresponding field values in the right column.

4. Click **Save** 🖫, and then in the **Save As** dialog box, type Racers Form Click **OK**.

5. In the layout's left column, click the **First Name** label. Point to the control's right border, and then when the ↔ pointer displays, double-click to set the control's width to Best Fit. Compare your screen with **Figure 2**.

6. **Close** ✕ the **Field List** pane, and then click the **State** text box.

- Continue to the next page to complete the skill

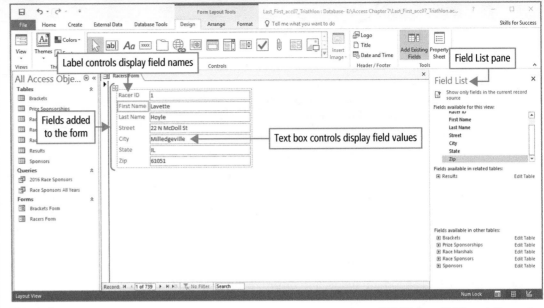

Figure 1

Access 2016, Windows 10, Microsoft Corporation

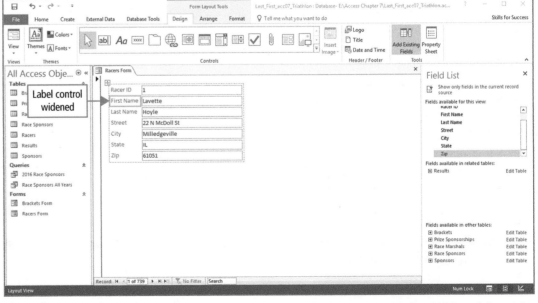

Figure 2

Access 2016, Windows 10, Microsoft Corporation

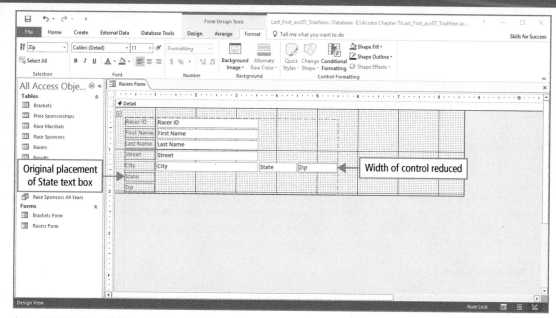

Access 2016, Windows 10, Microsoft Corporation

Figure 3

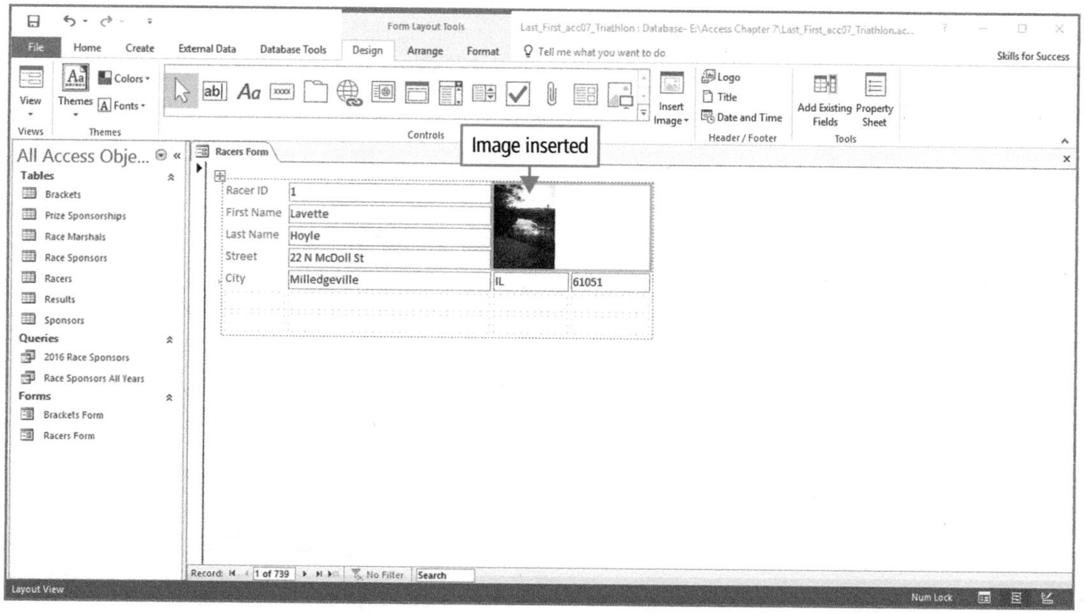

Access 2016, Windows 10, Microsoft Corporation

Figure 4

7. Point to the field, and when the ![pointer] pointer displays, drag the **State** text box to the right of the **City** text box just before the dotted line. When a vertical orange line displays to the right of the **City** text box, release the left mouse button.

8. Click the **Zip** text box, and then drag the text box to the right of the **State** text box.

9. Switch to Design view. Click the **State** text box. With the ![pointer] pointer displayed, drag the right border of the **State** text box to the **4.5 inch** horizontal gridline. Repeat this technique to drag the right edge of the **Zip** text box to the **5.5 inch** horizontal gridline, and then compare your screen to **Figure 3**.

MOS
Obj 4.3.5

10. Click the **State** label. Press [Shift], and then click the **Zip** label. On the **Arrange tab**, in the **Rows & Columns group**, click **Select Row**, and then press **Delete**.

11. Click the empty cell to the right of the **Racer ID** text box. Press [Shift], and then select the remaining empty cells above the State and Zip text boxes.

12. On the **Arrange tab**, in the **Merge/Split group**, click **Merge**.

    The eight empty cells have been merged to create one cell.

13. Switch to Layout view and click inside the merged cells. On the **Design tab**, in the **Controls group**, click the **More** button ![button], and then click the last button—**Image**. With the ![pointer] pointer, click in the merged cell.

14. In the **Insert Picture** dialog box, navigate to the student data files for this chapter, and then click **acc07_Triathlon_Logo**. Click **OK**. Compare your screen with **Figure 4**.

15. Click **Save** ![save icon], and then **Close** ![close icon] the form.

■ **You have completed Skill 1 of 10**

 **WATCH** SKILL 7.2

▶ **Controls** are objects on forms or reports such as labels, text boxes, lines, and pictures.

▶ Positioning tools can be used to position controls with greater accuracy.

1. In the **Navigation Pane**, select the **Racers** table. On the **Create tab**, in the **Forms group**, click the **Form** button.

2. Click **Save** 🖫, type Race Entrants Form and then click **OK**.

3. If necessary, close the Field List pane. Switch to Design view, and then click the **Table.Results** subform. Compare your screen with **Figure 1**, and then press Delete.

> The Results table was automatically added as a subform because it is related to the Racers table. The Race Entrants Form does not need a subform.

4. In the **Detail** section, click the **Racer ID** text box. Press **Shift**, and then click the **First Name**, **Last Name**, **Street**, **City**, **State**, and **Zip** text boxes.

5. Point to the right border of one of the selected text boxes. Using the ↔ pointer, drag to the left until the right border reaches the **3 inch** horizontal gridline. Compare your screen with **Figure 2**.

6. Click the **Arrange tab**, and then in the **Table group**, click **Remove Layout**.

> The stacked control layout is removed, and each control can now be positioned independently.

■ **Continue to the next page to complete the skill** ▶

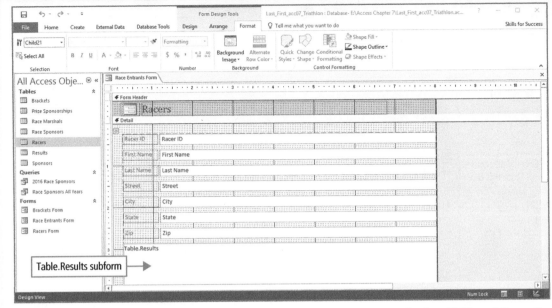

Figure 1

Access 2016, Windows 10, Microsoft Corporation

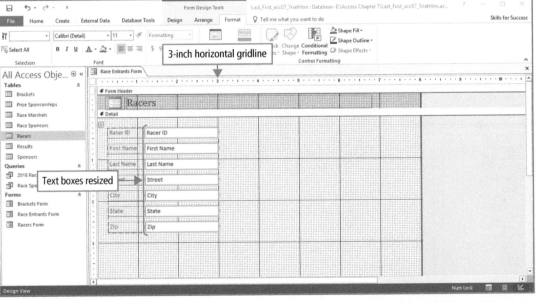

Figure 2

Access 2016, Windows 10, Microsoft Corporation

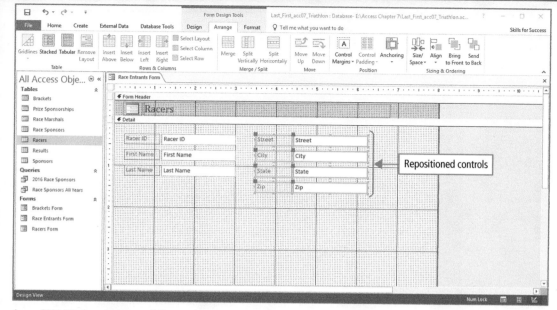

Access 2016, Windows 10, Microsoft Corporation

Figure 3

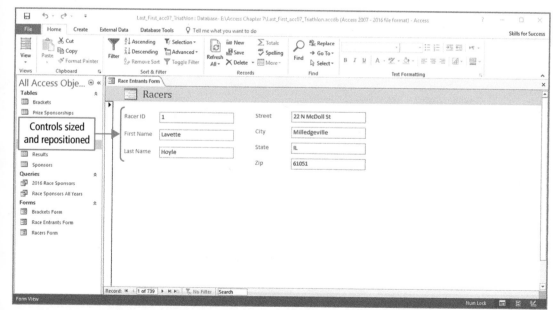

Access 2016, Windows 10, Microsoft Corporation

Figure 4

7. Click a blank area of the form so no controls are selected. Click the **Street** label, press [Shift], and then click the **Street** text box. Repeat this technique to select the labels and text boxes for the **City**, **State**, and **Zip**.

8. Point to the **City** label, and then when the pointer displays, drag all the controls and labels up and to the right so the controls are placed on the **3.5 inch** horizontal gridline and the top edge of the **Street** controls are vertically aligned with the top edge of the **Racer ID** controls. Compare your screen with Figure 3.

9. Repeat the technique just practiced to select labels and text boxes for **Racer ID**, **First Name**, and **Last Name**.

10. With the six controls selected, click the **Arrange tab**, and then in the **Sizing & Ordering group**, click **Size/Space**. From the list, click **Increase Vertical** one time.

11. With the six controls still selected, on the **Arrange tab**, in the **Sizing & Ordering group**, click **Align**, and then click **To Grid**.

12. Switch to Form view, and then compare your screen with Figure 4.

13. Save, and then **Close** the form.

■ **You have completed Skill 2 of 10**

▶ A **lookup field** is a field whose values are retrieved from another table.

▶ The Lookup Wizard simplifies the steps for creating a lookup field.

1. Open the **Results** table in Datasheet view, and then click the **Click to Add arrow**.

2. Click **Lookup & Relationship** to start the Lookup Wizard. Compare your screen to **Figure 1**.

3. Verify the **I want the lookup field to get the values from another table or query** option button is selected, and then click **Next**.

4. In the list of available tables, verify the **Table: Brackets** is selected, and then click **Next**.

5. In the list of **Available Fields**, verify that the **Bracket ID** is selected, and then click the **Move** button ▷ .

6. Click **Next** three times. In the **What label would you like for your lookup field** box, type Bracket Compare your screen with **Figure 2**, and then click **Finish**.

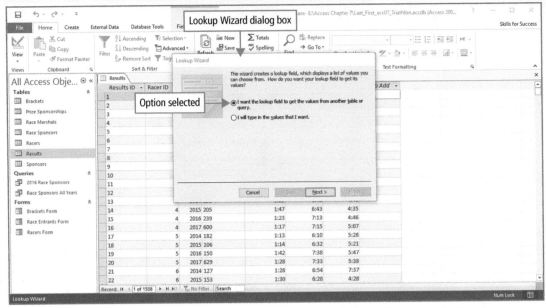

Figure 1

Access 2016, Windows 10, Microsoft Corporation

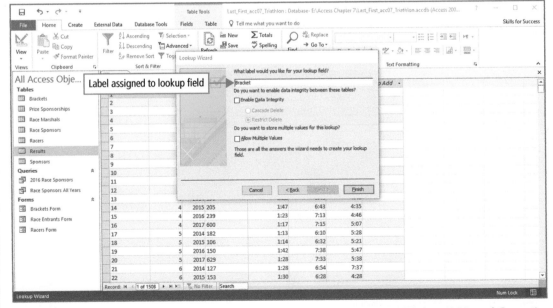

Figure 2

Access 2016, Windows 10, Microsoft Corporation

■ Continue to the next page to complete the skill

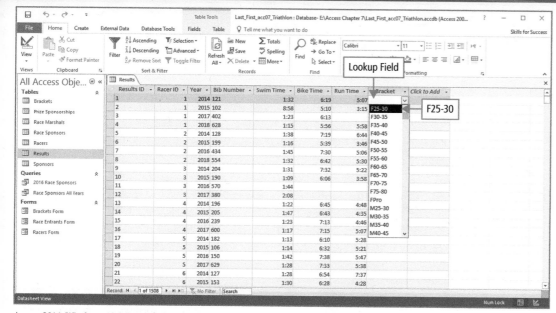

Access 2016, Windows 10, Microsoft Corporation

Figure 3

7. Click **Save** 🖫. Click the Bracket field in the first record to select it. Click the displayed **Bracket arrow**. Compare your screen with **Figure 3**, and then from the displayed list, click **F25-30**.

> The values from the Brackets table display in a ***combo box***, a text box and a list that is hidden until you click its arrow. Lookup fields display as combo boxes in datasheets and forms.

8. In the second record, click the **Bracket** field. Type fp and notice that the first choice in the combo box list that starts with the letters *FP* displays. Press Tab to assign *FPRO* to the Bracket field.

9. **Close** ✕ the **Results** table. With the **Results** table selected in the **Navigation Pane**, on the **Create tab**, in the **Forms group**, click **Form**.

10. In the **Views group**, click the **View arrow**, and then click **Form View**. In the **Navigation bar**, click the **Next record** button two times.

11. Click the **Bracket arrow**, compare your screen with **Figure 4**, and then click **FPro**.

12. Click **Save** 🖫, type Results Form, and then press Enter.

13. **Close** ✕ the form.

■ **You have completed Skill 3 of 10**

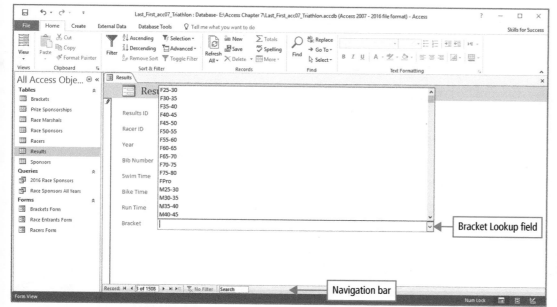

Access 2016, Windows 10, Microsoft Corporation

Figure 4

▶ A **pop up form** is a form that when opened remains on top, even when it is not the active form.

1. In the **Navigation Pane**, select the **Sponsors** table. On the **Create tab**, in the **Forms group**, click **More Forms**, and then click **Split Form**.

   A **split form** displays two synchronized views of the same form. By default, a split form displays in Form view in the top half of the form and in Datasheet view in the lower half of the form.

2. Click **Save** 🖫. In the **Save As** dialog box, type Sponsor Pop Up Form and then click **OK**.

3. Switch to Design view. On the **Design tab**, in the **Tools group**, click **Property Sheet**. In the **Property Sheet**, click the **Selection type** arrow, and then if necessary, click **Form**. On the **Property Sheet Other tab**, click the **Pop Up arrow**, and then click **Yes**. Compare your screen with **Figure 1**.

4. Switch to Form view. In the **Navigation Pane**, double-click the **Racers Form**, and then compare your screen with **Figure 2**.

   Notice the pop up form remains over the active Racers Form. You can reduce the size of the pop up form so the active form is partially visible.

5. Move the pointer over the lower right corner of the pop up form until the ↖ pointer displays. Drag the edge of the form up and to the left until the form is approximately two-thirds its original size and the subform is no longer visible.

■ **Continue to the next page to complete the skill**

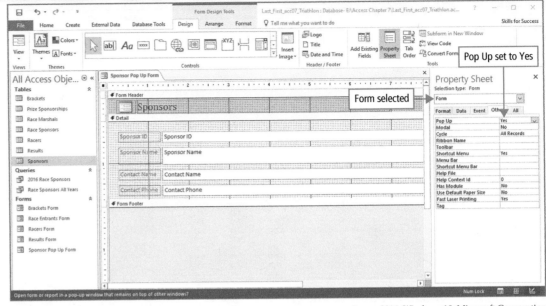

Figure 1

Access 2016, Windows 10, Microsoft Corporation

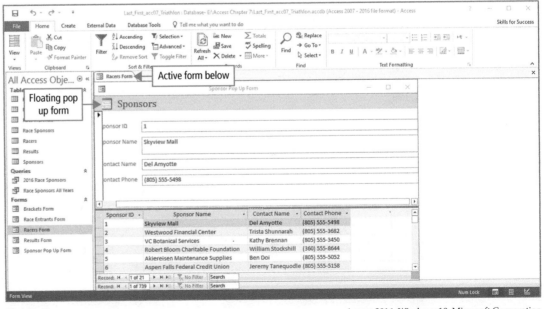

Figure 2

Access 2016, Windows 10, Microsoft Corporation

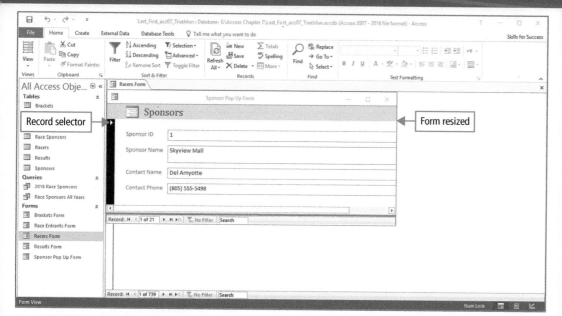

Access 2016, Windows 10, Microsoft Corporation

Record selector

Form resized

Figure 3

6. On the pop up form, click the **Record Selector** to display the **Sponsor Pop Up Form** fields, and then compare your screen with Figure 3.

7. Click **Close** ☒, and then click **Yes** to save the *Sponsor Pop Up Form*.

8. In the **Navigation Pane**, select the **Sponsor Pop Up Form**. Right-click, and then click **Design View**.

9. On the **Design tab**, in the **Themes group**, click **Themes**. From the displayed gallery, click **Slice**—the first choice in the third row. Click the **Sponsor ID label**. Press ⇧ Shift, and then click the remaining form labels. Point to the control's right border, and then when the ↔ pointer displays, double-click to set the control's width to Best Fit.

MOS
Obj 4.3.4

10. Switch to Form view, click the **Record Selector arrow**, and then compare your screen with Figure 4.

    The form has been resized back to its original size.

11. Click **Save** 🖫, and then **Close** ☒ the **Sponsor Pop Up Form** and the **Racers Form**.

■ **You have completed Skill 4 of 10**

Slice Theme applied

Access 2016, Windows 10, Microsoft Corporation

Figure 4

- A *command button* is a control that performs an action or sequence of actions when it is clicked.

- Buttons can perform a variety of tasks when clicked such as opening other objects or starting the printing process.

1. In the **Navigation Pane**, select the **Sponsors** table. On the **Create tab**, in the **Forms group**, click the **Form** button. If necessary, close the Property Sheet.

2. Click **Save** 💾, type Sponsors Form and then click **OK**.

3. Switch to Design view, click the **Table. Race Sponsors** subform control, and then press **Delete**. Compare your screen with **Figure 1**.

4. On the **Design tab**, in the **Controls group**, click the **Button** button.

5. In the **Detail** area, position the pointer at the intersection of the **2 inch** vertical gridline and the **2 inch** horizontal gridline, and then click one time.

    A button displays in the Detail section, and the Command Button Wizard displays a list of actions that the button can perform when clicked in Form view.

6. In the **Command Button Wizard**, under **Categories**, click **Form Operations**. Under **Actions**, click **Open Form**, and then compare your screen with **Figure 2**.

7. Click **Next**, and then under **What form would you like the command button to open**, click **Race Entrants Form**.

■ **Continue to the next page to complete the skill**

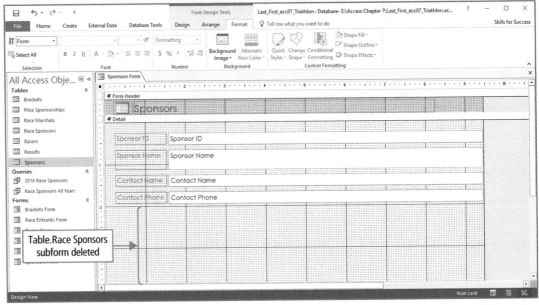

Figure 1

Access 2016, Windows 10, Microsoft Corporation

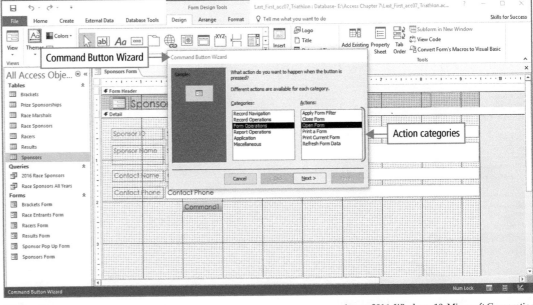

Figure 2

Access 2016, Windows 10, Microsoft Corporation

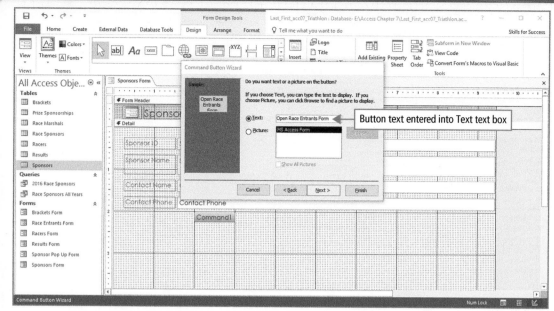

Access 2016, Windows 10, Microsoft Corporation

Figure 3

8. Click **Next** two times. Select the **Text** option button, and then in the **Text** text box, replace the existing value with Open Race Entrants Form. Compare your screen with **Figure 3**.

9. Click **Finish** to accept the remaining default settings.

10. With the button still selected, click the **Format tab**, and then in the **Control Formatting group**, click **Quick Styles**. In the gallery, click the second choice in the fourth row—**Subtle Effect – Dark Blue, Accent 1**.

> **Quick Styles** are prebuilt collections of formatting choices such as background colors, font colors, and shading that can be applied with one click.

11. Click **Save**. Switch to Form view, and then compare your screen to **Figure 4**.

> Button controls are edited in Design view, but clicked to perform actions in Form view.

12. Click the **Open Race Entrants Form** button. Verify that the **Race Entrants Form** displays, and then **Close** ☒ the Race Entrants Form and the Sponsors Form.

■ **You have completed Skill 5 of 10**

Access 2016, Windows 10, Microsoft Corporation

Figure 4

> ▶ *Conditional Formatting* changes the appearance of a control based on the display configuration related to the value that appears in a field.

> ▶ Values can be formatted so when a condition is true, the value will be formatted differently than when the condition is false.

1. Open the **Results Form** in **Layout** view.

2. Click the **Year** text box, and then click the **Format tab**. In the **Control Formatting group**, click the **Conditional Formatting** button.

3. In the **Conditional Formatting Rules Manager**, click the **New Rule** button. In the **New Formatting Rule** dialog box, under **Format only cells where the**, click the second **arrow**. Compare your screen to Figure 1.

4. In the list of conditions, click **greater than**. Click in the third text box, and then type 2017

5. Click the **Background Color arrow**, and then click the sixth color in the fourth row—**Maroon 3**. Compare your screen with Figure 2.

> All years greater than 2017 will appear with a maroon background color.

6. Click **OK** two times, and then **Save** 🖫 the form. Switch to Form view.

7. Click the **Results ID** text box. On the **Home tab**, in the **Find group**, click the **Find** button. In the **Find What** box, type 4 and then press Enter.

■ **Continue to the next page to complete the skill**

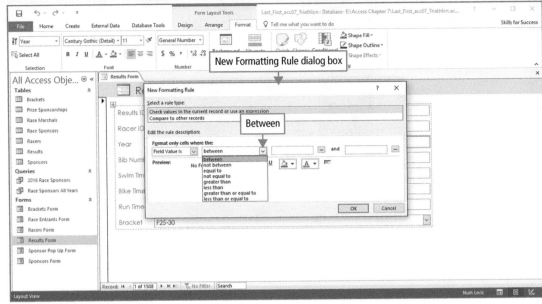

Figure 1

Access 2016, Windows 10, Microsoft Corporation

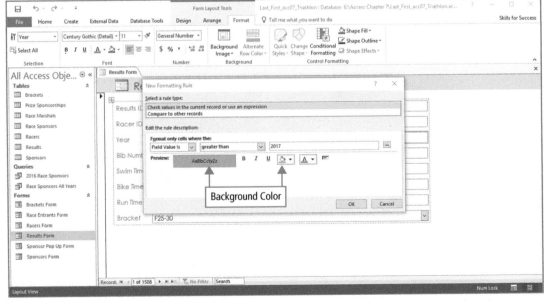

Figure 2

Access 2016, Windows 10, Microsoft Corporation

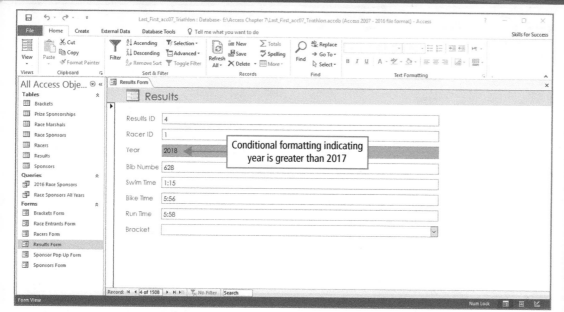

Access 2016, Windows 10, Microsoft Corporation

Figure 3

Access 2016, Windows 10, Microsoft Corporation

Figure 4

8. **Close** ⊠ the **Find and Replace** dialog box to view the conditional formatting. Compare your screen with Figure 3.

  The year in record 4 is 2018, so the background of the year field is maroon.

9. Switch to Design view. On the **Format tab**, in the **Background group**, click **Background Image**, and then click **Browse**. If necessary, change the file type to All Files. In the **Insert Picture** dialog box, navigate to the student data files, and then double-click **acc07_Triathlon_ Background**. Compare your screen with Figure 4.

  MOS
  Obj 4.3.6

10. On the **File tab**, click **Print**, and then click **Print Preview**. In the **Page Size group**, click the **Margins arrow**, and then click **Wide**.

  MOS
  Obj 4.3.2

11. In the **Page Layout group**, click **Landscape**. **Close** ⊠ the Print Preview.

12. Click the **Design tab**, and then in the **Header/Footer group**, click **Date and Time**. In the **Date and Time** dialog box, clear the **Include Time** check box, and then click **OK**.

13. **Save** 🖫, and then **Close** ⊠ the Results Form.

14. Click the **Brackets Form**, and then press **Delete**. Click **Yes** to confirm the deletion.

  MOS
  Obj 1.1.4

■ **You have completed Skill 6 of 10**

▶ ***Application Parts*** provide form templates that can be used to create forms quickly.

MOS
Obj 4.1.2

1. On the **Create tab**, in the **Templates group**, click the **Application Parts arrow**, and then click **1 Right** to add a form named SingleOneColumnRightLabels to the Navigation Pane.

2. In the **Navigation Pane**, right-click **SingleOneColumnRightLabels**, and then click **Design View**.

   This Application Parts template includes a Save, and a Save & Close button.

3. Click the **Field1** label, press and hold Shift, and then click the **Field2**, **Field3**, and **Field4** labels. Compare your screen with **Figure 1**, and then press **Delete**.

4. In the title, select the text *Form Title*, type Prize Sponsorships and then press Enter.

5. On the **Design tab**, in the **Tools group**, click **Add Existing Fields**. If necessary, click **Show all tables**. In the **Field List** pane, expand ⊞ the **Prize Sponsorships** table to view the table fields, and then compare your screen to **Figure 2**.

MOS
Obj 4.2.3

6. In the **Field List**, double-click **First Prize**, **Second Prize**, **Third Prize**, and **Race Year**. Click the **First Prize** label, press Shift, and then click the **Second Prize**, **Third Prize**, and **Race Year** labels. Point to the **First Prize** control's right border, and then when the ↔ pointer displays, double-click to set the control's width to Best Fit.

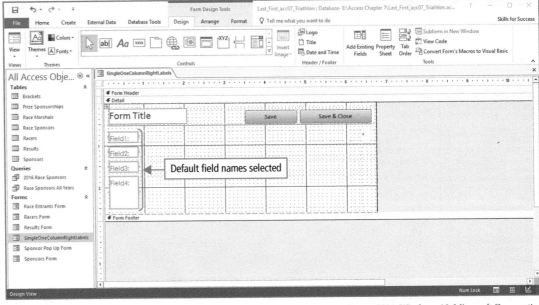

Figure 1

Access 2016, Windows 10, Microsoft Corporation

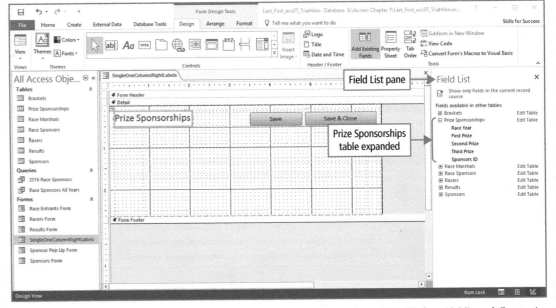

Figure 2

Access 2016, Windows 10, Microsoft Corporation

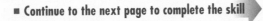

■ Continue to the next page to complete the skill

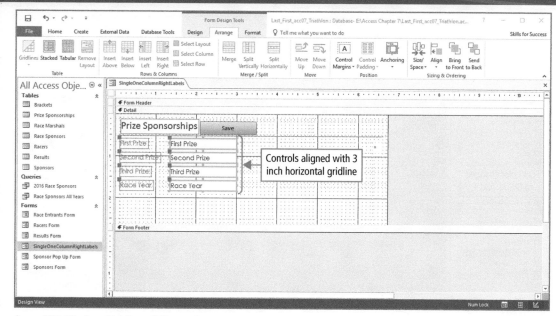

Controls aligned with 3 inch horizontal gridline

Access 2016, Windows 10, Microsoft Corporation

Figure 3

Expression Builder

Expression to calculate the prize totals

Access 2016, Windows 10, Microsoft Corporation

Figure 4

7. **Close** ☒ the Field List pane. Click the form's **Save** button to select it, and then drag the control into the cell to the right of the **Prize Sponsorships** form title. Click the **Save & Close** button, and then press Delete.

8. Click the **First Prize** text box, press Shift, and then click the remaining text boxes. Point to the **First Prize** text box control's right border, and then when the ↔ pointer displays, drag the right edge of the border to the **3 inch** horizontal gridline. Compare your screen with Figure 3.

9. Click the **View** button to return to Form view. **Save** 🖫, and then **Close** ☒ the form.

10. In the **Navigation Pane**, right-click the **SingleOneColumnRightLabels** form, and then click **Rename**. Type Prize Sponsorships Form and then press Enter.

11. Open the **Prize Sponsorships** table in Datasheet View. Click the **Click to Add arrow**, point to **Calculated Field**, and then click **Currency**.

12. In the Expression Builder dialog box, type [First Prize]+[Second Prize]+[Third Prize] to enter the expression. Compare your screen with Figure 4.

MOS
Obj 2.2.2

The **Expression Builder** is a tool used to create expressions used in controls and fields. An **expression** is a combination of fields, mathematical operators, and prebuilt functions that calculate values in tables, forms, queries, and reports. The Expression Builder autocompletes the field names when you begin typing them. Be careful not to press tab and accept a field you did not intend to use.

13. Click **OK**. Type Total Prizes and then press Enter. **Save** and **Close** the Prize Sponsorship table.

■ **You have completed Skill 7 of 10**

► **Hyperlinks** are text or other objects that display a document, location, or window when clicked.

► Hyperlinks and attached files such as terms of service and privacy notices can be added to forms to provide users with additional information.

1. Open the **Results Form** in Layout view. Select the first label. Press and hold Shift while clicking the remaining labels. Click the **Format tab**. In the **Font group**, click the **Font Color arrow**, and then click the second color in the first row—**Black, Text 1**. Compare your screen with **Figure 1**.

2. Point to the **Bib Number** label control's right border, and then when the ↔ pointer displays, double-click to set the control's width to Best Fit.

3. Repeat the technique just practiced to change the font color of the **Results** title label to **White, Background 1**. **Save** and **Close** ✕ the form.

4. Open the **Race Entrants Form** in Design view. On the **Design tab**, in the **Controls group**, click the **Hyperlink** button, and then compare your screen with **Figure 2**.

5. In the **Text to display** box, type Terms of Service In the **Address** box, type http://www.aspenfalls.org/ and then click **OK**.

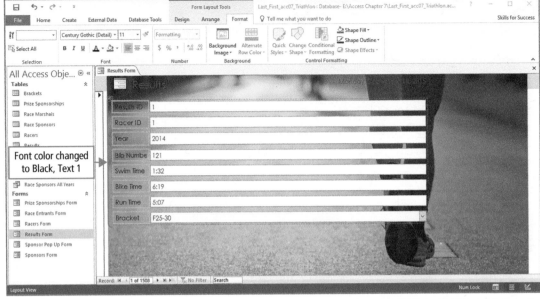

Figure 1

Access 2016, Windows 10, Microsoft Corporation

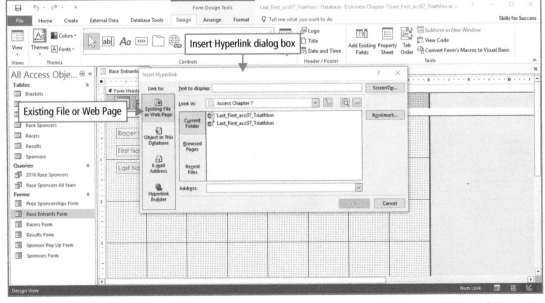

Figure 2

Access 2016, Windows 10, Microsoft Corporation

■ **Continue to the next page to complete the skill**

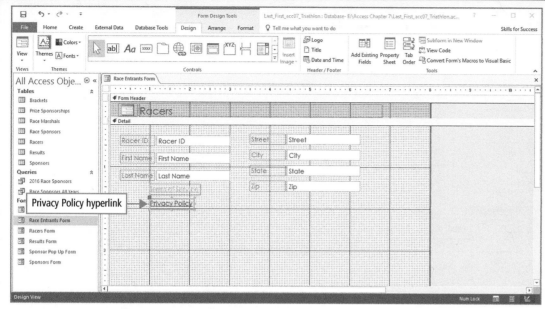

Access 2016, Windows 10, Microsoft Corporation

Figure 3

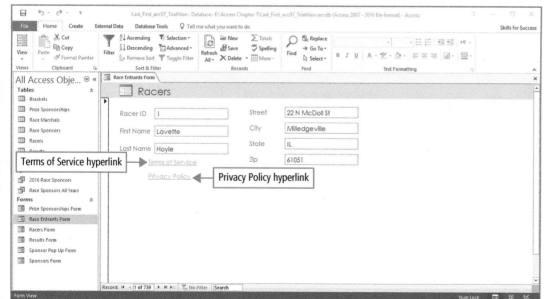

Access 2016, Windows 10, Microsoft Corporation

Figure 4

6. Using the pointer, drag the **Terms of Service** control to the **1 inch** horizontal gridline, two grid dots below the Last Name controls. Click the **Format tab**, and then in the **Font group**, click the **Font Color arrow**. In the Standard Colors, click **Maroon 3**, the sixth color in the fourth row.

7. On the **Design tab**, in the **Controls group**, click the **Hyperlink** button. In the **Text to display** box, type Privacy Policy Click the **Look in arrow**, navigate to the student data files for this chapter, and then click **acc07_Triathlon_ PrivacyPolicy**. Click **OK**. Compare your screen to Figure 3.

   Providing a file allows users to save the document for their own records.

8. Click the **Format tab**, and then in the **Font group**, click the **Font Color arrow**. In the Standard Colors, click **Maroon 3**, the sixth color in the fourth row.

9. On the **Home tab**, click the **View arrow**, and then click **Form View**. Compare your screen with Figure 4, and then **Save** and **Close** the form.

10. In the **Navigation Pane**, right click the **Racers** table, and then click **Rename**. Type Race Entrants and then press Enter.

MOS
Obj 2.2.4

■ **You have completed Skill 8 of 10**

▶ **Subforms** are forms within other forms. Subforms are often used when a one-to-many relationship exists between tables.

▶ When a form contains a subform, the main form typically contains data from the one side of the one-to-many table relationship. The subform contains data from the many side of the relationship.

1. Open the **Prize Sponsorships Form** in Design view. Click the cell below the **Race Year** label, press `Shift`, and then click the cell below the **Race Year** text box. Press `Delete`

2. On the **Design tab**, in the **Tools group**, click **Add Existing Fields**. If necessary, in the **Field List**, click **Show all tables**, and then expand the Prize Sponsorships table.

3. Double-click the **Sponsors ID** label. Drag the **Sponsors ID** controls to the **2 inch** vertical gridline two grid dots below the Race Year controls. Click a blank area in the form, and then click the **Sponsors ID** label. Double-click the right border of the label to set the control's width to Best Fit. Compare your screen to **Figure 1**.

4. **Close** ✕ the **Field List** pane. **Save** 💾 and **Close** ✕ the **Prize Sponsorship Form**.

5. In the **Navigation Pane**, right-click the **Sponsors Form**, and then click **Design View**.

6. On the **Design tab**, in the **Controls group**, click the **More arrow** 🔽. Compare your screen with **Figure 2**.

■ **Continue to the next page to complete the skill**

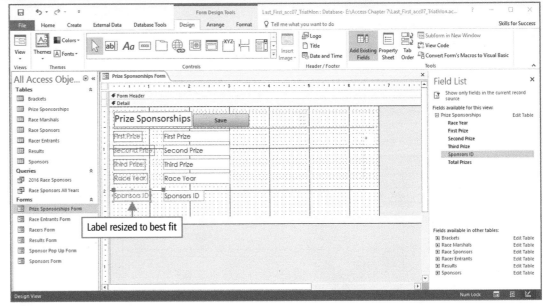

Figure 1   Access 2016, Windows 10, Microsoft Corporation

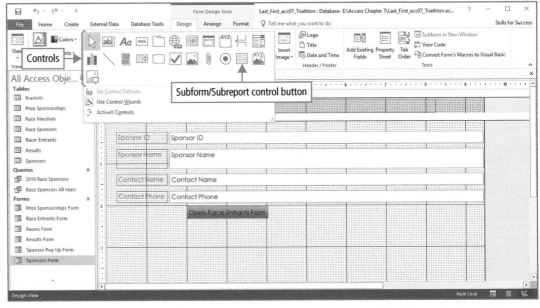

Figure 2   Access 2016, Windows 10, Microsoft Corporation

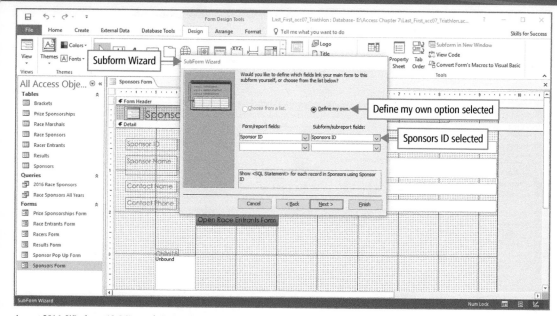

Access 2016, Windows 10, Microsoft Corporation

Figure 3

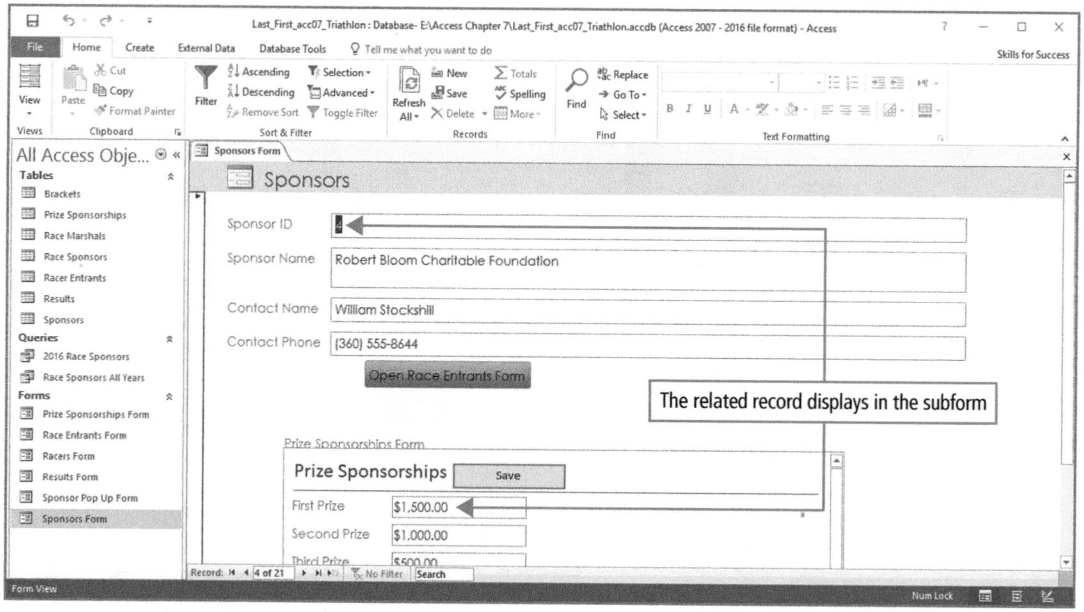

7. Click the **Subform/Subreport** button. Click at the intersection of the **3 inch** vertical and **1 inch** horizontal gridlines.

8. In the **Subform Wizard**, click the **Use an existing form** option button. Verify that the Prize Sponsorships Form is selected.

9. Click **Next**. Under the **Form/report fields:**, click the first selection arrow, and then click **Sponsor ID**. Under **Subform/subreport fields:**, click the first selection arrow, and then click **Sponsors ID**. Compare your screen with **Figure 3**.

10. Click **Next**.

   The Sponsor ID from the Sponsors Form has been linked to the Sponsors ID from the Prize Sponsorships Form.

11. Click **Finish**, and then switch to Form view.

   The first record in the Sponsors Form has no related record in the Prize Sponsorships Form, so no record displays in the subform.

12. In the **Sponsors Form**, click the **Next Record** button three times. Compare your screen with **Figure 4**.

   The fourth record in the Sponsors Form is related to a record in the Prize Sponsorships Form, so the record displays in the subform.

13. **Save** 🖫, and then **Close** ✕ the **Sponsors Form.**

■ **You have completed Skill 9 of 10**

Access 2016, Windows 10, Microsoft Corporation

Figure 4

▶ Controls added to forms can help users perform tasks such as printing records or navigating through records.

▶ Changing font colors, resizing text boxes, and resizing controls improve form usability.

1. Right-click the **Sponsors Form**, and then click **Design View**.

2. Click the **Sponsor ID** text box, and then with the ⊞ pointer, drag the right edge of the **Sponsor ID** control to the **5 inch** horizontal gridline. Compare your screen with **Figure 1**.

3. Above the subform, select the **Prize Sponsorships Form** label, and then press Delete . On the **Design tab**, in the **Controls group**, click the **Button** button.

4. Click at the **5 inch** horizontal and **2 inch** vertical gridline intersection. In the **Command Button Wizard** dialog box, below **Actions**, click **Go To Next Record**, and then click **Next**.

5. Select the **Text** option button, and then click **Next**. Name the button Next Record Compare your screen with **Figure 2**, and then click **Finish**.

> The Next Record button gives users a way to move to the next record without needing to use the Navigation bar.

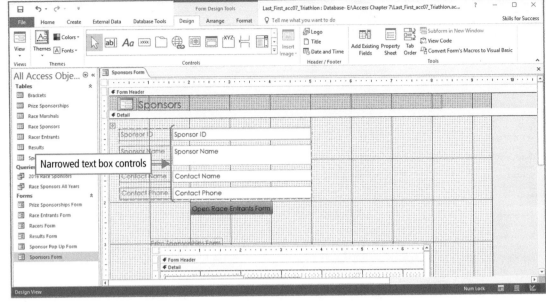

Figure 1

Access 2016, Windows 10, Microsoft Corporation

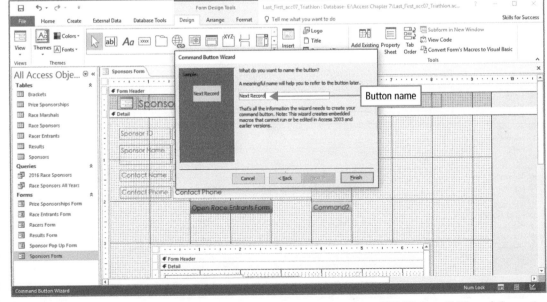

Figure 2

Access 2016, Windows 10, Microsoft Corporation

■ Continue to the next page to complete the skill ➤

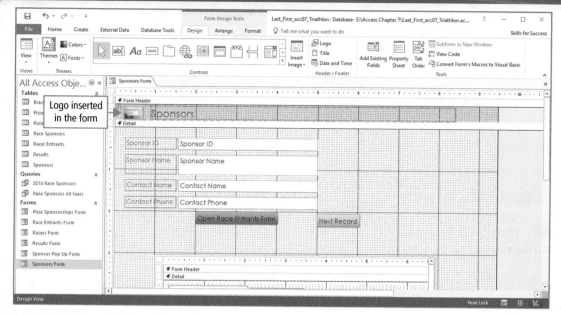

Access 2016, Windows 10, Microsoft Corporation

Figure 3

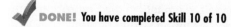

Access 2016, Windows 10, Microsoft Corporation

Figure 4

6. Click the **View** button to switch to Form view. Click the **Next Record** button three times.

   The subform displays the related record for Sponsor ID 4.

7. Click the **View arrow**, and then switch to Design view. On the **Design tab**, in the **Header/Footer group**, click **Logo**.

8. Navigate to the student data files, click **acc07_Triathlon_Logo**, and then click **OK**. Compare your screen to Figure 3.

9. In the **Controls group**, click the **Button** button, and then click at the **2 inch** vertical gridline with the left edge of the button aligning with the left edge of the Contact Phone label.

10. In the **Command Button Wizard**, below **Categories**, click **Record Operations**. Below **Action**, click **Print Record**, and then click **Next**.

11. Click the **Text** button, and then click **Next**. Type Print Record and then click **Finish**. Compare your screen to Figure 4.

12. Click **Save** [💾], and then **Close** [✕] the Sponsors form.

13. **Close** Access, and then submit the project as directed by your instructor.

✔ **DONE! You have completed Skill 10 of 10**

More Skills ⑪

Add Option Groups to Forms

To complete this project, you will need the following file:

- acc07_MS11Health

You will save your file as:

- Last_First_acc07_MS11Health

▶ An *option group* is a frame with a set of boxes, toggle buttons, or option buttons.

▶ Option groups can be bound or unbound to a field. When bound to a field, the option selected will be entered as a value into the underlying table.

---

1. Start **Access 2016**, and then open the student data file **acc07_MS11Health**. Save the file in your **Access Chapter 7** folder with the name Last_First_ acc07_MS11Health If necessary, enable the content.

2. On the **Create tab**, in the **Form group**, click **Blank Form**.

3. In the **Field List Pane**, click **Show all tables**, click the **Employees** expand button ⊞, and then double-click the following fields in this order: **Employee ID**, **First Name**, **Last Name**, and **HP_ID**. **Close** the **Field List**.

4. Click **Save**. In the **Save As** dialog box, type Employee Health Insurance Form and then click **OK**.

5. Switch to Design view, and then drag the form's lower edge down approximately 1 inch.

6. On the **Design tab**, in the **Controls group**, click the **More** button, and then click the **Option Group** button.

7. Position the pointer on the **1 inch** horizontal gridline two grid dots below the **HP_ID** control, click one time.

8. In the **Option Group Wizard**, in the **Label Names** column, type Plan A Press [Tab], and then type Plan B Press [Tab], and then type Plan C

   Plan A, Plan B, and Plan C are the three values that can be entered into the HP_ID field.

9. Click **Next**. Under **Do you want one option to be the default choice**, click the **arrow**, and then click **Plan B**.

10. Click **Next**.

    Each label corresponds to the primary key value in the Health Plan table for each of the three health plans.

11. Click **Next**. Under **What do you want to do with the value of a selected option**, select the **Store the value in this field** option button. Click the **Store the value in the field arrow**, and then click **HP_ID**.

12. Click **Next**. Under **What style would you like to use**, select the **Sunken** option button.

    In the **Sample** area, notice the option group displays the **Sunken** style.

13. Click **Next**. Under **What caption do you want for the option group**, type Health Insurance and then click **Finish**.

14. Switch to Form view, and then in the **Option group**, click the **Plan B** option button.

15. **Save** and **Close** the form. **Close** Access. Submit the file as directed by your instructor.

- **You have completed More Skills 11**

More Skills 12

Add Combo Boxes to Forms

To complete this project, you will need the following file:

- acc07_MS12Registrations

You will save your file as:

- Last_First_acc07_MS12Registrations

▶ A combo box is a control that has a text box and a list that is hidden until you click its arrow.

▶ Combo boxes can display values from a related table and are often added in forms to assist with data entry.

---

1. Start **Access 2016**, and then open the student data file **acc07_MS12Registrations**. Save the file in your **Access Chapter 7** folder with the name Last_First_acc07_MS12Registrations

2. In the **Navigation Pane**, double-click **Registration Form**.

   Registration Form has a form and a subform. The main form displays each scheduled class, and the subform is used to enter students into sections.

3. In the subform append row, click the **Student ID** text box, and then type 1188, which is the Student ID for Scotty Kats.

4. In Design view, in the subform, click the **Student ID** text box to select it, and then press **Delete** to remove the control and its label.

5. On the **Design tab**, in the **Controls group**, click the **More** button, and then click the **Combo Box** button. Place the pointer approximately two grid dots below the **Registration ID** label, and then click one time to insert the control and start the Combo Box Wizard.

6. In the **Combo Box Wizard**, verify the **I want the combo box to get the values from another table or query** option box is selected, and then click **Next**.

7. Under **Which table or query should provide the values for your combo box**, click **Table: Students**, and then click **Next**.

8. Move **Student ID**, **First Name**, and **Last Name** into **Selected Fields**.

9. Click **Next**. Under **What sort order do you want for the items in your list box**, click the **arrow**, and then click **Last Name**.

10. Click **Next**. Clear the **Hide key column** check box.

11. Click **Next**. Verify that under **Available Fields**, **Student ID** is selected, and then click **Next**. Select the **Store that value in this field** option button, click the **arrow**, and then click **Student ID**.

12. Click **Next**, and then under **What label would you like for your combo box**, type Student Click **Finish**, click **Save**, and then switch to Form view. In the subform append row, click the **Student** field, and then click the **Student combo box arrow** that displays.

13. In the list, click **Erik Lehmer**, and then notice that his Student ID is entered automatically into the form.

14. Click **Save**, and then **Close** the form. **Close** Access. Submit the file as directed by your instructor.

- **You have completed More Skills 12**

More Skills 13

Create Multiple Item Forms

To complete this project, you will need the following file:

- acc07_MS13Students

You will save your file as:

- Last_First_acc07_MS13Students

▶ A *multiple item form* displays records in rows and columns in the same manner as a datasheet.

▶ A multiple item form provides more formatting options than a datasheet.

---

1. Start **Access 2016**, and open the student data file **acc07_MS13Students**. Save the file in your **Access Chapter 7** folder with the name Last_First_acc07_MS13Students If necessary, enable the content.

2. In the **Navigation Pane**, double-click the **Students** table. On the **Create tab**, in the **Forms group**, click the **More Forms** button, and then click **Multiple Items** to create a multiple item form based on the Students table. Compare your screen with **Figure 1**.

3. Click **Save**, and then in the **Save As** dialog box, click **OK**. **Close** the **Navigation Pane**.

4. Click the **Design tab**. In the **Themes group**, click the **Themes** button, and then click the **Retrospect** theme.

5. If necessary, in the first record, click to select the **Student ID** field, and then in the **Tools group**, click the **Property Sheet** button.

6. Click the **Property Sheet Format tab**, and then change the **Width** property to 0.6 and the **Height** property to 0.3.

7. Click the **First Name** field to display its properties. In the **Property Sheet**, change the **Width** property to 1 and then press Enter . Repeat this technique to set the width of the **Last Name** column to 1

8. Set the **Street** column width to 2.5 the **Zip** column width to 1 and the **Home Phone** column width to 1.5

9. **Close** the **Property Sheet**.

Figure 1   Access 2016, Windows 10, Microsoft Corporation

10. Click **Save**. In the **Views group**, click the **View** button to switch to Form view. In the first record, change the **First Name** and **Last Name** values to your own name.

11. **Save** and **Close** the form and table, and then **Close** Access. Submit the file as directed by the instructor.

■ **You have completed More Skills 13**

More Skills 14

Set Tab Order

To complete this project, you will need the following file:

- acc07_MS14Geocaching

You will save your file as:

- Last_First_acc07_MS14Geocaching

▶ Setting a logical tab order can increase data entry efficiency.

▶ Tab order is important, especially if there are two or more columns of text boxes.

---

1. Start **Access 2016**, and then open the student data file **acc07_MS14Geocaching**. Save the file in your **Access Chapter 7** folder with the name Last_First_acc07_MS14Geocaching If necessary, enable the content.

2. In the **Navigation Pane**, double-click the **Geocache Event** form. Press Tab four times, and then compare your screen with **Figure 1**.

   Currently, the tab order switches between the left and right columns of text boxes. This tab order may be confusing and slow down data entry.

3. Switch to Design view. On the **Design tab**, in the **Tools group**, click **Tab Order**.

   Obj 4.3.1

4. In the **Tab Order** dialog box, to the left of the word *Description*, select the **Description** row by clicking the gray area.

5. Drag the **Description** row upward. When a dark gray line displays between the **Geocache** and **Event Date** rows, release the mouse button.

6. Repeat the technique just practiced to arrange the remaining rows in the following order: **Park ID**, **Event Date**, **Start Time**, **End Time**, **Outing Leader ID**, and **Fee**. Click **OK**.

7. Switch to Form view. Press Tab eight times to verify the new tab order.

8. Press Tab one time to view the next record.

9. Press Tab four times to select the **Event Date** text box.

10. Click the **Date Picker**, click **Thursday, June 07, 2018**, and then press Tab to view the date change.

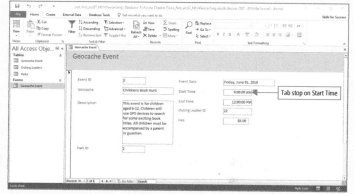

Access 2016, Windows 10, Microsoft Corporation

Figure 1

11. Click **Save**, **Close** the form, and then **Close** Access. Submit the file as directed by your instructor.

■ **You have completed More Skills 14**

Review

The following table summarizes the **SKILLS AND PROCEDURES** covered in this chapter.

Skill	Task	Step	Icon
1	Create a blank form	Create tab → Forms group → Blank Form	
1	Merge cells on a form	Arrange tab → Merge/Split group → Merge	
1	Add background images to forms	Design tab → Controls group → Image	
2	Remove stacked control layouts	Arrange tab → Tables group → Remove Layout	
2	Align controls to grid	Select controls → Arrange tab → Sizing & Ordering group → Align → To Grid	
3	Start Lookup Wizard in tables	Click the last column, click the Click to Add arrow, and then click Lookup & Relationship	
4	Create split forms	Create tab → Forms group → More Forms → Split Form	
4	Create pop up forms	Property sheet → Other tab → Pop Up arrow → Yes	
5	Add buttons to forms	Design tab → Controls group → Button button	
5	Format buttons	Format tab → Control Formatting group → Quick Styles	
6	Apply conditional formatting	Format tab → Control Formatting group → Conditional Formatting → Conditional Formatting Rules Manager → New Rule → New Formatting Rule	
6	Find records in forms	Home tab → Find group → Find	
6	Add background images to forms	Format tab → Background → Background Image	
7	Create forms from Application Parts	Create tab → Templates group → Application Parts → Forms	
7	Add Currency calculated field to a table	Click to Add arrow → Calculated Field → Currency → Expression Builder → Type expression	
8	Add hyperlinks	Design tab → Controls group → Hyperlink button → Address	
8	Add attachments	Design tab → Controls group → Hyperlink button → Navigate to attachment	
9	Add subforms	Design tab → Controls group → Subform/Subreport button	
10	Add logos	Design tab → Header/Footer group → Logo	

Project Summary Chart

Project	Project Type	Project Location
Skills Review	Review	In Book and MIL MyITLab Grader
Skills Assessment 1	Review	In Book and MIL MyITLab Grader
Skills Assessment 2	Review	Book
My Skills	Problem Solving	Book
Visual Skills Check	Problem Solving	Book
Skills Challenge 1	Critical Thinking	Book
Skills Challenge 2	Critical Thinking	Book
More Skills Assessment	Review	In Book and MIL MyITLab Grader
Collaborating with Google	Critical Thinking	Book

MOS Objectives Covered (Quiz in MyITLab)

1.1.4 Delete database objects	4.3.2 Configure print settings
2.2.2 Add total rows	4.3.3 sort records by form field
2.2.4 Rename tables	4.3.4 Apply a theme
4.1.2 create a for from a template with application parts	4.3.5 control form positioning
4.2.3 modify data sources	4.3.6 Insert backgrounds
4.3.1 Modify tab order	

Key Terms

Online Help Skills

1. Start **Access 2016**, and then in the upper right corner of the start page, click the **Help** button ⑦.

2. In the **Access Help** window **Search Online help** box, type Create an Access form and then press ⏎. In the search result list, click **Create a Form in Access**. **Maximize** the Access 2016 Help Window.

3. Scroll down, and then below **What do you want to do?**, click **Create a split form in Access**. Compare your screen with **Figure 1**.

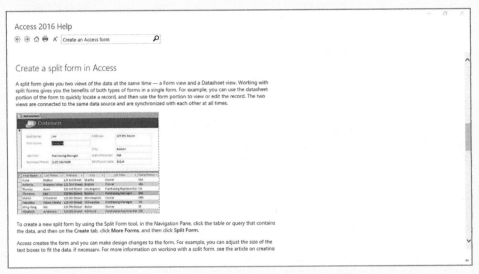

Figure 1   Access 2016, Windows 10, Microsoft Corporation

4. Read the article to answer the following question: What are the benefits of working with the Datasheet view portion of the form? What tasks are easier to perform in the form portion?

Matching

Match each term in the second column with its correct definition in the first column by writing the letter of the term on the blank line in front of the correct definition.

___ **1.** A form that when opened remains on top, even when it is not the active form.

___ **2.** Objects on forms or reports that can be used to complete actions.

___ **3.** Changes the appearance of a control based upon the display configuration related to the value that appears in a field.

___ **4.** A field whose values are retrieved from another table or form.

___ **5.** Forms within other forms.

___ **6.** Provides form templates that can be used to expedite form creation.

___ **7.** A control that performs an action or sequence of actions when it is clicked.

___ **8.** A combination of fields, mathematical operators, and prebuilt functions that calculate values in tables, forms, queries, and reports.

___ **9.** Text or other objects that display a document, location, or window when clicked.

___ **10.** A tool used to create expressions used in controls and fields.

A Application Parts

B Command button

C Conditional Formatting

D Control

E Expression

F Expression Builder

G Hyperlink

H Lookup field

I Pop up form

J Subform

Multiple Choice   MyITLab®

Choose the correct answer.

1. The Controls group can be found on which tab?
   A. Design
   B. Create
   C. Insert

2. In a lookup field, values can be chosen from which of the following?
   A. Another table or query
   B. Values you type
   C. Both A and B

3. Which tab contains tools for aligning controls?
   A. Format
   B. Design
   C. Arrange

4. A form can be set as a pop up form from which of the following?
   A. Navigation Pane
   B. Property sheet
   C. Format

5. Which tab contains the Conditional Formatting tools?
   A. Create
   B. Arrange
   C. Format

6. Controls can be added to a form from which tab?
   A. Create
   B. Design
   C. Database tools

7. Which dialog box displays after clicking the Conditional Formatting button in the Conditional Formatting group?
   A. New rule
   B. Rule manager
   C. Conditional Formatting Rules Manager

8. Which of the following can be created using Application Parts?
   A. Forms
   B. Queries
   C. Conditional Formatting

9. When clicked, a hyperlink can display which of the following?
   A. Document
   B. Web page
   C. Both A and B

10. When a form contains a subform, the main form typically contains data from which side of the one-to-many relationship?
    A. One
    B. Many
    C. Neither A nor B

Topics for Discussion

1. What are the advantages of using a subform? Are there any disadvantages to using a subform? State the reasons for your answers.

2. Under what circumstances could a hyperlink or attachment be useful in a form? State the reasons for your answer.

Skills Review

MyITLab®
Grader

To complete this project, you will need the following files:

- acc07_SRCommittees
- acc07_SR_Logo

You will save your file as:

- Last_First_acc07_SRCommittees

1. Start **Access 2016**. Open **acc07_SRCommittees**, and then save the database in your **Access Chapter 7** folder as Last_First_acc07_SRCommittees If necessary, enable the content.

2. Open the **Committees Form** in Design view, and then on the **Design tab**, in the **Controls group**, click the **Image** button.

3. In the **Detail** area, position the pointer at the **5 inch** horizontal gridline at the top of the Detail area, and then click one time. Navigate to your **Access Chapter 7** student data files, and then click **acc07_SR_Logo**.

4. Click the **CommitteeID** text box. Press `Shift`, and then click **CommitteeName**, **CommitteePurpose**, and **MeetingFrequency**. On the **Arrange tab**, in the **Sizing & Ordering group**, click **Size/Space**, and then click **Increase Vertical**. Compare your screen with Figure 1.

5. **Save** and **Close** the Committees form.

6. Select the **Members** table, and then on the **Create tab**, in the **Forms group**, click **Form**. Switch to Form view, and then in the **Navigation bar**, click the **Next record** button one time. Click the **Zip arrow**, and then click **93463**. Compare your screen with Figure 2.

7. **Save** and **Close** the **Members** form.

8. Select the **Locations** table. On the **Create tab**, in the **Forms group**, click **More Forms**, and then click **Split Form**. Switch to Design view.

9. Click the **Design tab**. In the **Tools group**, click **Property Sheet**. On the **Other tab**, click **Pop Up**, and then click **Yes**. Click **Save**, in the **Save as** dialog box, type Locations Pop Up Form and then click **OK**.

10. Close the **Property Sheet**. Click the **LocationsID** text box, press `Shift`, and then click the **Location** text box. Drag the right edge of the text boxes to the **4 inch** horizontal gridline.

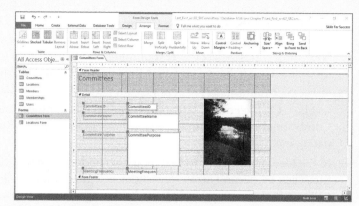
Access 2016, Windows 10, Microsoft Corporation
Figure 1

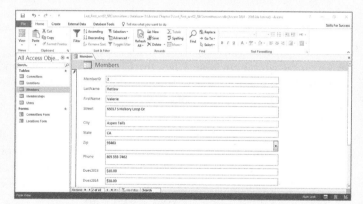
Access 2016, Windows 10, Microsoft Corporation
Figure 2

■ Continue to the next page to complete this Skills Review ▶

11. On the **Design tab**, in the **Control group**, click the **Button** button. Position the pointer at the **5 inch** horizontal gridline and the **1 inch** vertical gridline, and then click one time. In the **Command Button Wizard**, under **Categories**, click **Form Operations**, and then under **Actions**, click **Open Form**. Click **Next** three times. Select the **Text** option button, type Open Committees, and then click **Finish**. **Save** and **Close** the **Locations Pop Up Form**.

12. Open the **Committees Form** in **Design** view. Click the **MeetingFrequency** text box. On the **Format tab**, in the **Control Formatting group**, click **Conditional Formatting**. In the **Conditional Formatting Rules Manager** dialog box, click **New Rule**.

13. In the **New Formatting Rule** dialog box, under **Format only cells where the:**, click the second arrow, and then click **greater than**. Click in the third text box, and then type 1 Click the **Background color arrow**, and then click **Dark Blue**. Compare your screen with **Figure 3**, and then click **OK** two times.

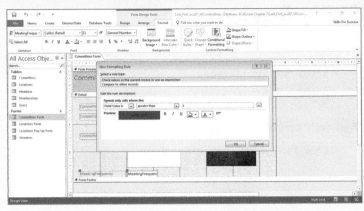

Figure 3   Access 2016, Windows 10, Microsoft Corporation

14. On the **Design tab**, in the **Controls group**, click the **Hyperlink** button. In the **Text to display:** box, type Privacy Policy and then in the **Address:** box, type http://www.aspenfalls.org Click **OK**. Using the selector, drag the Privacy Policy next to the **5 inch** horizontal gridline, two grid dots below the logo image. **Save** and **Close** the **Committees Form**.

15. Open the **Members** table. Click the **Click to Add arrow**, and then point to **Calculated Field**. Click **Currency**, and then in the **Expression Builder**, type [Dues2017]+[Dues2018] Click **OK**, and then type TotalDues **Save** and **Close** the Members table.

16. Open the **Locations Form** in Design view. On the **Design tab**, click the **Controls group arrow**, and then click the **Subform/Subreport** button. Click at the **1 inch** horizontal gridline four grid dots below the Location text box. In the **Subform Wizard**, select the **Use an existing form** option button, and then click **Finish**. Compare your screen with **Figure 4**.

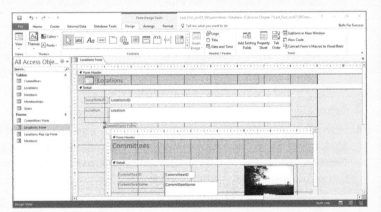

Figure 4   Access 2016, Windows 10, Microsoft Corporation

17. Open the **Members** form in Design view, and then drag the right edge of the form to the **9 inch** horizontal gridline. Select the **MemberID** text box, and then hold down Shift and select the remaining text boxes. Drag the right edge of the text boxes to the **4 inch** horizontal gridline. Click **Save**.

18. **Close** all forms and tables, and then **Close** Access. Submit the file as directed by your instructor.

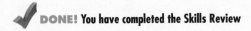

DONE! You have completed the Skills Review

Skills Assessment 1

To complete this project, you will need the following file:

- acc07_SA1CheckOut

You will save your file as:

- Last_First_acc07_SA1CheckOut

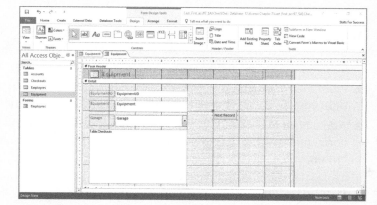

Access 2016, Windows 10, Microsoft Corporation

Figure 1

1. Start **Access 2016**, and then open **acc07_SA1CheckOut**. **Save** the file in your **Access Chapter 7** folder with the name Last_First_acc07_SA1CheckOut

2. Open the **Equipment** table, and then create a lookup field named Garage as the last field in the table using 1 2 and 3 as the possible values.

3. Using the **Forms tool**, create an Equipment Form and then drag the right edge of the text box controls to the **4 inch** horizontal gridline.

4. Add a **Next Record** button to the **Equipment Form** at the **5 inch** horizontal and **1 inch** vertical gridlines. Include the text Next Record on the button. Compare your screen with **Figure 1**.

5. Create a **Split Form** named Checkouts Pop Up Form From the Design view, change the **Pop Up** property to **Yes**. Drag the right edge of the text box controls to the **3 inch** horizontal gridline.

6. In the **Checkouts Pop Up Form**, apply **Conditional Formatting** to the **EquipmentID** text box. The **EquipmentID** should include the **Yellow** fill color for a value equal to **1**.

7. Add a Terms of Service **Hyperlink** to the *Checkouts Pop Up Form* using http://www.aspenfalls.org as the **Address**. Drag the hyperlink to the **4 inch** horizontal and **1 inch** vertical gridlines.

8. Create a Print Record button on the *Checkouts Pop Up Form*. Place the button three grid dots below the **Terms of Service** hyperlink at the **4 inch** gridline.

9. Using **Application Parts**, create a **1 Right** form named Accounts Form deleting the **Fields 1-4**. Add all of the existing fields from the **Accounts** table.

10. Open the **Employees Form**, and then from the **Design tab**, add a **Checkouts Pop Up Form** subform at the **1 inch** horizontal and **2 inch** vertical gridlines.

11. **Save** and then **Close** the forms and **Close** Access. Submit the file as directed by your instructor.

✔ **DONE! You have completed Skills Assessment 1**

Skills Assessment 2

To complete this project, you will need the following file:

- acc07_SA2Park

You will save your file as:

- Last_First_acc07_SA2Park

---

1. Start **Access 2016**, and then open the student data file **acc07_SA2Park**. Save the file in your **Access Chapter 7** folder with the name Last_First_acc07_SA2Park

2. From the **Forms group**, create a Supplies Form, and then drag the right edge of the text box controls to the **4 inch** horizontal gridline.

3. Add a **Next Record** button to the **Supplies** form at the **5 inch** horizontal and **1 inch** gridline. Include the text Next Record on the button.

4. Create a **Split Form** named Assignments Pop Up Form. From the Design view, change the **Pop Up** property to **Yes**. Drag the right edge of the text box controls to the **3 inch** horizontal gridline.

5. In the **Assignments Pop Up** form, apply **Conditional Formatting** to the **EmployeeID** text box. The **EmployeeID** should include the **Yellow Background color** for a value equal to **2**.

6. Add a Terms of Service **Hyperlink** to the **Assignments Pop Up** form using http://www.aspenfalls.org as the **Address**. Drag the hyperlink next to the **4 inch** horizontal and **1 inch** vertical gridlines.

7. On the **Employees** form, drag the right edge of the text box controls to the **4 inch** horizontal gridline. Create a Print Record button placed at the **5 inch** horizontal and **1 inch** vertical gridlines. Compare your screen with Figure 1.

8. On the **Employees Form**, from the **Design tab**, add an **Assignments Pop Up Form** subform. Place the subform at the **1 inch** horizontal and **3 inch** vertical gridlines.

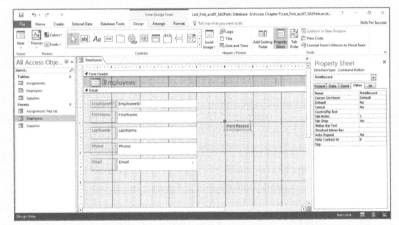

Figure 1   Access 2016, Windows 10, Microsoft Corporation

9. Create a Next Record button on the **Employees** form. Place the button three grid dots below the Print Record button at the **5 inch** horizontal gridline.

10. **Save** and then **Close** the forms and **Close** Access. Submit the file as directed by your instructor.

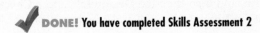 **DONE! You have completed Skills Assessment 2**

My Skills

To complete this project, you will need the following file:

- acc07_MYMaintenance

You will save your file as:

- Last_First_acc07_MYMaintenance

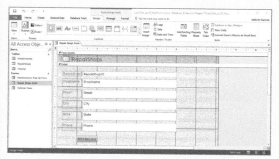

Access 2016, Windows 10, Microsoft Corporation **Figure 1**

1. Start **Access 2016**, and then open **acc07_MYMaintenance**. **Save** the file in your **Access Chapter 7** folder with the name Last_First_acc07_MYMaintenance

2. Open the **Repair Shops** table in Datasheet view. Create a Repair Shops Form by clicking the **Form** button. Delete the **Table.Maintenances** subform.

3. In the **Repair Shops Form**, drag the right edge of the text box controls to the **6 inch** horizontal gridline. **Save** the form as Repair Shops Form

4. Open the **Maintenances** table, and then on the **Create tab**, click **Split Form**. **Save** the form as Maintenances Pop Up Form Switch to Design view, and then on the **Design tab**, open the **Property Sheet**. On the **Other tab**, in the **Pop Up** field, select **Yes**.

5. In the **Maintenances Pop Up Form**, drag the bottom edge of the form down approximately 1 inch. In the **Command Button Wizard**, choose the **Form Operations** category and the **Open Form** action. Set the button to open the **Repair Shops Form**. Type Open Repair Shops Form as the text to display on the button.

6. Open the **Vehicles** table, and then create a Vehicles Form by clicking the **Form** button. Switch to Design view, and then delete the **Table.Maintenances** subform. **Save** the form as **Vehicles Form**.

7. On the **Format tab**, apply **Conditional Formatting** to the **Vehicle Model** text box, which applies a yellow background to your primary vehicle.

8. Apply the **Slice** theme to the **Vehicles Form**.

9. On the **Vehicles Form**, add a **Next Record** button with the text display of Next Record

10. Open the **Repair Shops Form**. On the **Design tab**, add a **Print Record** button. Compare your screen with **Figure 1**. **Save** and **Close** the tables, and then **Close** Access. Submit your file as directed by your instructor.

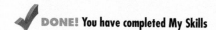 **DONE! You have completed My Skills**

Visual Skills Check

To complete this project, you will need the following file:

- acc07_VSDonations

You will save your file as:

- Last_First_acc07_VSDonations

Open the database **acc07_VSDonations**, and then save the database in your **Access Chapter 7** folder as Last_First_acc07_VSDonations

Create the form as shown in **Figure 1**. Apply the **Facet** Theme and a **Next Record** button to the **Projects Form**. Include a Privacy Policy hyperlink that links to http://www.aspenfalls .org Create a calculated field in the **Projects** table named TotalGoal that sums the **Goal2017** and **Goal2018** values. In the Projects Form, apply conditional formatting to **Goal2018**. The conditional formatting should highlight any amount more than $50,000 in the field, with the background color **Light Blue 3**. Submit the file as directed by your instructor.

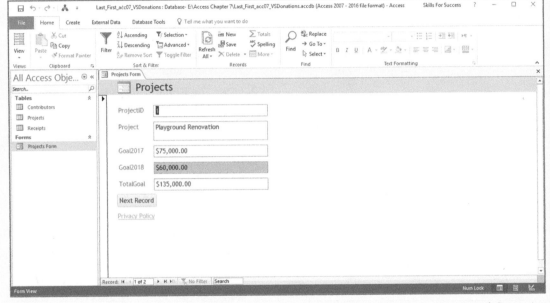

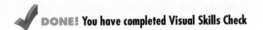

DONE! You have completed Visual Skills Check

Figure 1

Access 2016, Windows 10, Microsoft Corporation

Skills Challenge 1

To complete this project, you will need the following file:

- acc07_SC1Rentals

You will save your file as:

- Last_First_acc07_SC1Rentals

Open **acc07_SC1Rentals**, and then **Save** the database in your **Access Chapter 7** folder as Last_First_acc07_SC1Rentals In the **Boats Form**, add a **Next Record** button with the display text Next Record Create a Customers Form based on the **Customers** table. Add a Terms of Service hyperlink using http://www.aspenfalls.org as the address. In the **Boats Form** and **Customers Form**, delete the **Table.Receipts** subform. Add the **Slice** theme to the **Customers Form**. Position and format

the buttons and link so that the person using the form will be able to use them easily and effectively.

Submit the file as directed by your instructor.

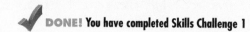 **DONE!** You have completed Skills Challenge 1

Skills Challenge 2

To complete this project, you will need the following file:

- acc07_SC2FarmersMarket

You will save your file as:

- Last_First_acc07_SC2FarmersMarket

Open **acc07_SC2FarmersMarket**, and then save the database in your **Access Chapter 7** folder as Last_First_acc07_SC2FarmersMarket Add a **Next Record** button with the text display Next Record to the **Products Form**. Change the theme of the **Products Form** to **Integral**. Open the **Farms** table, and then create a Farms Form Delete the **Table.Farm Offerings** subform from the **Farms Form**. On the **Farms Form**, add

conditional formatting to the **Zip** control that highlights all 93464 zip codes.

Submit the file as directed by your instructor.

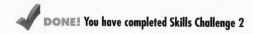 **DONE!** You have completed Skills Challenge 2

More Skills Assessment

MyITLab®
Grader

To complete this project, you will need the following file:

- acc07_MSAClasses

You will save your file as:

- Last_First_acc07_MSAClasses

1. Start **Access 2016**. Open the file **acc07_MSAClasses**, and then save the file in your chapter folder as Last_First_acc07_MSAClasses

2. Create a Session Form from a blank form. Include the following fields in the form: **Session ID**, **Community Center**, and **ClassID**.

3. Add an **Option Group** entered into the **Class ID** with the Label Names Excel | PowerPoint and Word Use the Sunken style, and Course as the Option group name. Save the form, and then switch to Form view. Compare your screen with Figure 1.

4. In the **Intern Contacts List** form, change the tab order to **Last Name**, **First name**, **Email**, **Phone**. Compare your screen with Figure 2.

5. Create a **Multiple Item Form** based on the **Interns** form. Name the form Interns Form

6. In the **Classes** form, on the Sessions subform, delete the existing **Session ID**. Create a **Combo Box** in place of the Session ID control.

7. Base the Combo Box on the **Sessions table** and include the following fields: **SessionID**, **CommunityCenter**, **StartDate**, and **StartTime**. Sort the field by **CommunityCenter** in **Ascending** order.

8. Do not **Hide key column** for the **Combo Box**, and then store the value in the **SessionID** field.

9. Save the **Combo Box** as Session

10. **Save** and **Close** the form, and then **Close** Access.

11. Submit the file as directed by your instructor.

DONE! You have completed the More Skills Assessment

Figure 1   Access 2016, Windows 10, Microsoft Corporation

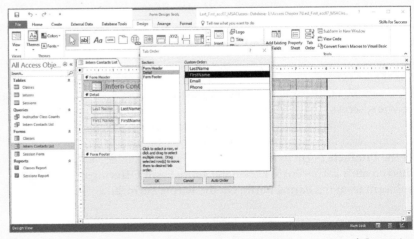

Figure 2   Access 2016, Windows 10, Microsoft Corporation

Collaborating with Google

To complete this project, you will need a Google account(refer to the Common Features chapter) and the following file:

- Blank Google form

You will save your file as:

- Last_First_acc07_GPSnip

1. Open the **Google Chrome** web browser. Log into your Google account, and then click the **Google apps** button.

2. Click **Drive** to open Google Drive, and then click the **NEW** button. Click **More**, and then click **Google Forms** to open a blank form.

3. At the top of the form, click the **Title** label, *Untitled form*, and then rename the form Interns

4. Under the Title, in the *Form Description* label, type Please complete this form to register as an intern.

5. Next to the *Question* text box, click the **Delete** button.

6. Click the **Add item arrow**, and then click **Text**. In the **Question Title** text box, type First Name and then click **Done**.

7. Repeat this technique to add the following **Text** items to the form: Last Name | Street | City | State | Zip | Email | Phone

8. Click the **Edit** button next to the *City* text box, and then click the **Question Type arrow**. Select **Choose from a list**, and then under Option 1, type Aspen Falls Click **Option 2 (Click to add option)**, and then compare your screen with **Figure 1**.

9. Type Curtis and then click **Option 3**. Type Jackson and then click **Done**.

10. Under the *phone* field, click the **Add item arrow**, and then click **Checkboxes**. In the **Question Title** text box, type How many hours can you work? Under **Option 1**, type 5-10 hours Under **Option 2**, type 10-15 hours and then under **Option 3**, type 15-20 hours

11. Click **Done**, and then at the top of the form, click **View live form**. Scroll down until you can see the bottom of the form.

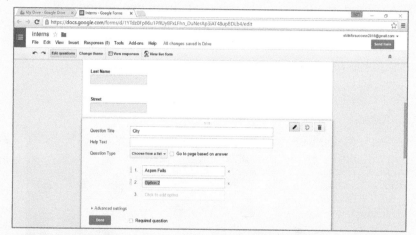

Figure 1

12. Open the **Snipping Tool,** click the **New arrow**, and then take a **Window Snip**. In the **Snipping Tool** mark-up window, click the **Save Snip** button. In the **Save As** dialog box, navigate to your Access Chapter 7 folder. Be sure the **Save as type** box displays **JPEG file**. Name the file Last_First_acc07_GPSnip and then press Enter. **Close** the Snipping Tool mark-up window.

13. Close all windows, and then submit the file as directed by your instructor.

 **DONE! You have completed the Collaborating with Google Project**

CHAPTER 8

Add Advanced Report Features

- ▶ Reports can be created using the Report Wizard or the Report Design tool.
- ▶ Reports can be based on queries or tables.
- ▶ A subreport allows you to view data from two related tables.

- ▶ You can format reports by adding background colors, page numbers, hyperlinks, conditional formatting, and calculated fields.
- ▶ Report information can be grouped and filtered.
- ▶ Reports can include charts and ActiveX controls.

nolonely/Fotolia

Aspen Falls City Hall

In this project, you will assist Carter Horikoshi, Art Center Supervisor of Aspen Falls, in creating reports to document art students, class categories, and class sections from the Art Class database. A variety of art classes are offered throughout the year. Instructors are assigned to teach courses and students sign up to take classes.

In this project, a grouped report will be created to display all class sections offered at the Art Center. This report will display classes grouped by class title and sorted by the course starting date. Another report will be created that uses a query inside the report.

Horikoshi also needs a report that includes a subreport, enabling him to view each art category and its related art classes. Another report will assist Horikoshi in viewing classes with fees greater than a specific amount. All of these reports need customized features such as calculated fields, conditional formatting, hyperlinks, and page breaks.

In this project, you will create a report to display categories of classes that are offered. Classes offered between specific dates will include conditional formatting, and another report will be needed to view art students listed in the database. You will create reports using a blank report tool, and you will modify existing reports. You will add controls, subreports, calculated fields, grouping, and other features to provide the most useful information and make the reports easier to read.

Outcome

Using the skills in this chapter, you will be able to group, sort, and filter reports; change layouts; apply conditional formatting; insert hyperlinks; add calculated fields; and create and format subreports.

Objectives

8.1 Construct reports from queries

8.2 Apply conditional formatting to reports

8.3 Generate reports that include hyperlinks, subreports, and calculated fields

8.4 Apply grouping, sorting, and filtering to reports

8.5 Modify subreports

Student data files needed for this chapter:

acc08_ArtCenter (Access)
acc08_ArtDescriptions (Word)

You will save your file as:

Last_First_acc08_ArtCenter

SKILLS

Skills 1–10 Training

At the end of this chapter you will be able to:

Skill 1 Create Reports from Queries

Skill 2 Group, Sort, and Filter Reports

Skill 3 Format Reports in Design View

Skill 4 Apply Conditional Formatting

Skill 5 Insert Page Breaks, Change Layouts, and Modify Reports

Skill 6 Modify Report Queries

Skill 7 Insert Hyperlink Controls

Skill 8 Add Calculated Fields

Skill 9 Create a Subreport Using a Wizard

Skill 10 Format Subreports

MORE SKILLS

Skill 11 Add Charts to Reports

Skill 12 Create Subreports Using Drag-and-Drop

Skill 13 Align Report Controls

Skill 14 Add ActiveX Controls to a Report

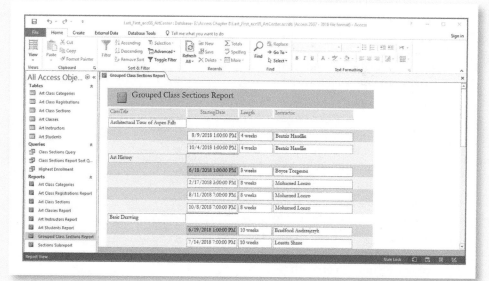

Access 2016, Windows 10, Microsoft Corporation

▶ You can create reports from existing queries.

▶ Controls can be resized, formatted, added to, or deleted from reports.

▶ *Print Preview* allows you to view how a document will look when it is printed.

1. Start **Access 2016**, and then open the student data file **acc08_ArtCenter**. Use the **Save As** dialog box to create a **New folder** named Access Chapter 8 Save the database in the new folder as Last_First_acc08_ArtCenter If necessary, enable the content.

2. In the **Navigation Pane**, select the **Class Sections Query**. Click the **Create tab**, and then in the **Reports group**, click the **Report** button.

3. Click **Save**, and then in the **Save As** dialog box, type Class Sections Report Click **OK**.

4. Switch to Design view. If necessary, open the Property Sheet pane. In the Property Sheet, click the **Selection type arrow**, and then click **Starting Date**. On the property sheet **Format tab**, change the **Width** value to 1.5" and then press [Enter]. Compare your screen with **Figure 1**.

5. Click the property sheet **Selection type arrow**, and then click **Length**. Change the **Width** value to 1" and then press [Enter]. Repeat this technique to change the **Instructor** column width to 2.38"

> Changing the size of the text boxes improves the appearance of the report and ensures it will fit on the printed page.

6. On the property sheet, change the **Selection type** to **Report**, and then compare your screen with **Figure 2**.

■ Continue to the next page to complete the skill

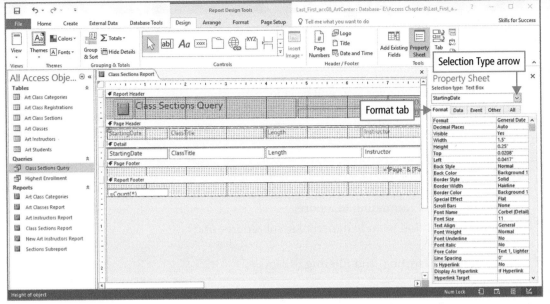

Figure 1

Access 2016, Windows 10, Microsoft Corporation

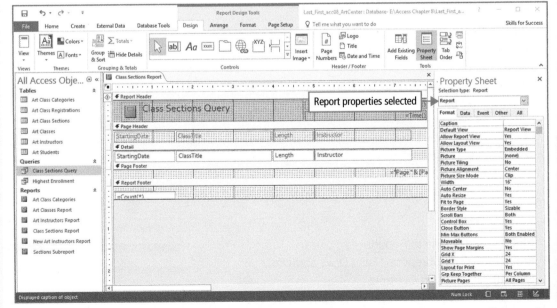

Figure 2

Access 2016, Windows 10, Microsoft Corporation

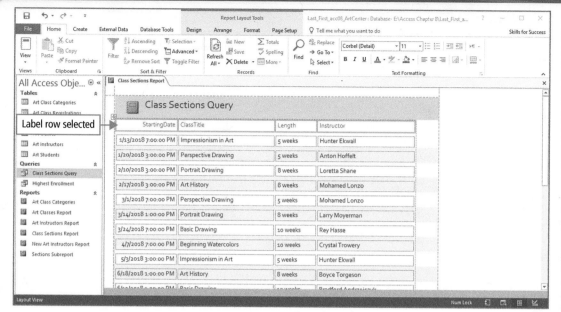

Access 2016, Windows 10, Microsoft Corporation

Figure 3

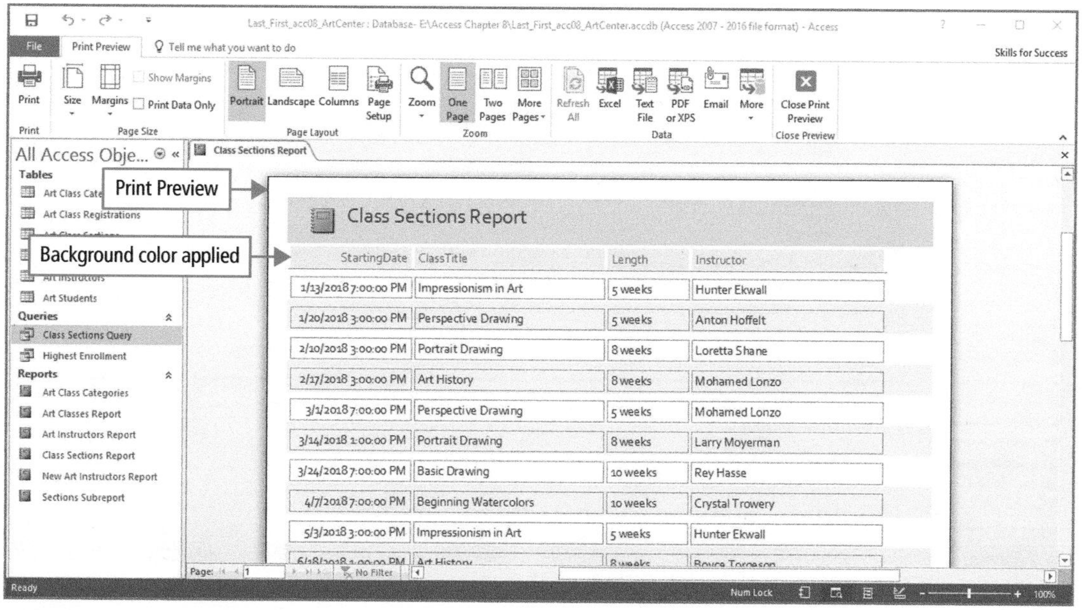

Access 2016, Windows 10, Microsoft Corporation

Figure 4

7. In the **Page Footer**, click the calculated control with the text =**"Page " & [Page] & " of" & [Pages]** to select it, and then press Delete.

8. On the Property Sheet, click the **Data tab**. In the **Order By** box, type StartingDate and then press Enter. On the **Format tab**, change the **Width** to 8

9. **Close** ☒ the Property Sheet, and then in the **Report Header**, click the **Date()** control. Hold down Shift, click the **Time()** control, and then press Delete.

10. Switch to Layout view. Click the **StartingDate** label. Using the pointer →, double-click the left border of the **StartingDate** label to select the entire row, and then compare your screen to Figure 3.

11. On the **Home tab**, in the **Text Formatting group**, click the **Background Color arrow**. Click the seventh color in the third row—**Olive Green, Accent 3, Lighter 60%**

12. Click the report header control to select it. On the **Home tab**, in the **Text Formatting group**, click the **Background Color arrow**, and then click the seventh color in the third row—**Olive Green, Accent 3, Lighter 80%**.

13. Double-click the report title label, select the word **Query**, and then type, Report Press Enter.

14. Click **Save** ☐. On the **Design tab**, in the **Views group**, click the **View arrow**, and then click **Print Preview**. Compare your screen with Figure 4, and then switch to Layout view.

    Before printing a report, view the document in Print Preview to ensure all text boxes fit properly on the page. Viewing documents in Print Preview can help avoid printing documents that do not fit on a single page horizontally.

■ **You have completed Skill 1 of 10**

▶ You can group, sort, and filter records to better organize report information.

▶ **Grouped records** a tool that combines records with identical values from a field in a report.

▶ You can apply **filters** in a report to view only the records that match the criteria you specify.

1. On the *Class Sections Report*, click the count control in the last row, and then press [Delete]. In the first row of the report, click the **StartingDate** label. On the **Home tab**, in the **Sort & Filter group**, click the **Descending** button.

2. In the **Sort & Filter group**, click the **Filter** button. Clear the **Select All** check box, select the four June dates, and then click **OK**. Compare your screen with **Figure 1**.

    Only classes with a StartingDate in June are displayed.

3. In the **Sort & Filter group**, click the **Toggle Filter** button.

    Each time the Toggle Filter button is clicked, the filter is applied or temporarily cleared. It does not delete the filter.

4. Click the **Toggle Filter** button again to reapply the filter. In the **Sort & Filter group**, click the **Advanced arrow**, and then click **Advanced Filter/Sort**.

5. In the **Class Sections ReportFilter1**, double click **Length**. In the **Length** column **Sort** cell, select **Descending**. Compare your screen with **Figure 2**.

6. In the **Sort & Filter group**, click the **Advanced arrow**, and then click **Apply Filter/Sort**.

    The classes that begin on 6/21/2018 are now sorted in descending order according to the course length.

■ Continue to the next page to complete the skill

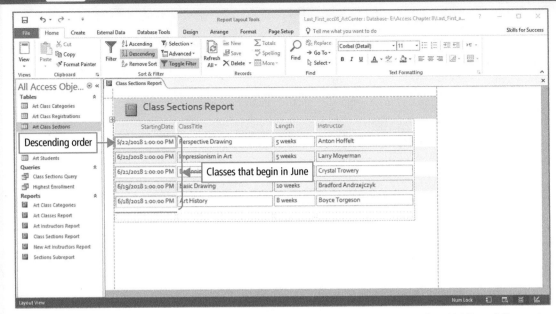

Figure 1

Access 2016, Windows 10, Microsoft Corporation

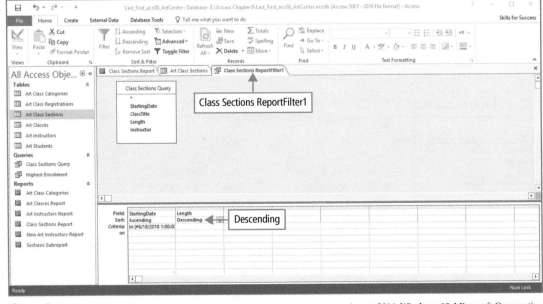

Figure 2

Access 2016, Windows 10, Microsoft Corporation

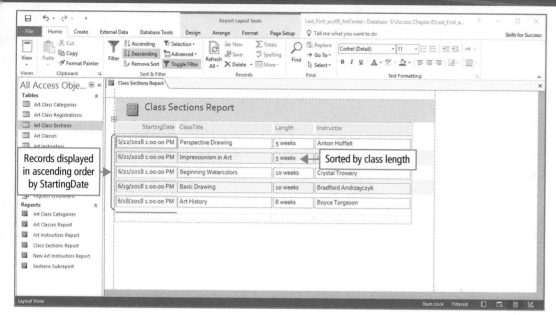

Figure 3

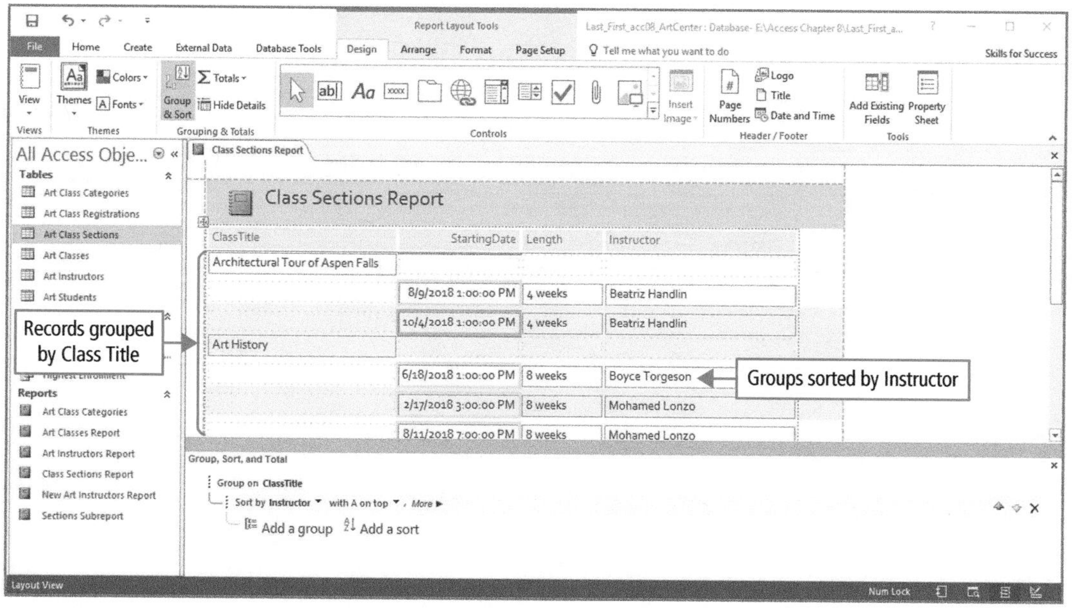

7. Click the **Class Sections ReportFilter1 tab**. Click **Save** 🖫, and then in the **Save As Query** dialog box, type Class Sections Report Sort Query Click **OK**, and then close the query.

8. Verify the Class Sections Report is in Layout view. Compare your screen with **Figure 3**, and then in the **Sort & Filter group**, click the **Toggle Filter** button.

9. On the **Design tab**, in the **Grouping & Totals group**, click **Group & Sort**. In the **Group, Sort, and Total** pane, delete ☒ the **Sort by StartingDate**. Click **Add a group**, and then from the list that displays, click **ClassTitle**.

10. In the **Group, Sort, and Total** pane, click **Add a sort**, and then click **Instructor**. Compare your screen with **Figure 4**.

    The Add a group option grouped records by Class Title. The Add a sort option sorted each group of classes alphabetically by instructor.

11. Close ☒ the **Group, Sort, and Total** pane.

12. **Save** 🖫, and then **Close** ☒ the report.

■ **You have completed Skill 2 of 10**

Figure 4

▶ When working with reports, Design view provides more tools and greater precision than Layout view.

▶ When a report is created, calculated controls that display dates, times, and page numbers are automatically placed in the report headers and footers.

▶ Changing the layout and applying theme colors can make the report more professional and presentable.

1. In the **Navigation Pane**, right-click the **Class Sections Report**, and then click **Rename**. Type Grouped Class Sections Report and then press Enter.

2. In the **Navigation Pane**, click the **New Art Instructors Report**, press Delete, and then click **Yes**.

3. On the **Create tab**, in the **Reports group**, click the **Blank Report** button.

4. In the **Field List** pane, click **Show all tables**, and then **Expand** ⊞ the **Art Class Sections** table. Compare your screen with Figure 1.

5. In the **Field List** pane, double-click the following fields in this order: **SectionID**, **StartingDate**, **ClassTitle**, **InstructorID**, and **Fee**.

   The fields from the table have now been added to the report.

MOS
Obj 5.1.2

6. Switch to Design view. In the **Page Header**, click the **SectionID** label. Press and hold Shift, while clicking the **StartingDate**, **ClassTitle**, **InstructorID**, and **Fee** controls. Compare your screen with Figure 2.

   The *page header* is located at the top of each printed page and can contain labels, text boxes, and other controls.

■ Continue to the next page to complete the skill

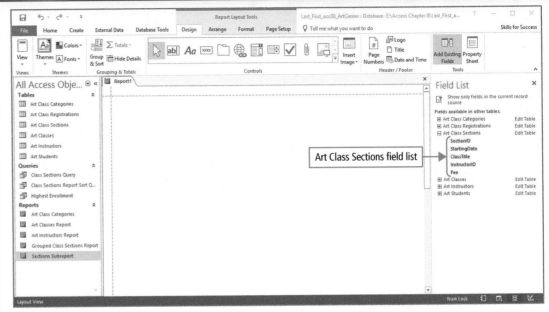

Art Class Sections field list

Figure 1

Access 2016, Windows 10, Microsoft Corporation

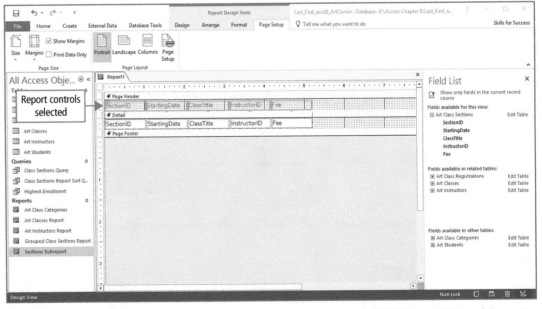

Report controls selected

Figure 2

Access 2016, Windows 10, Microsoft Corporation

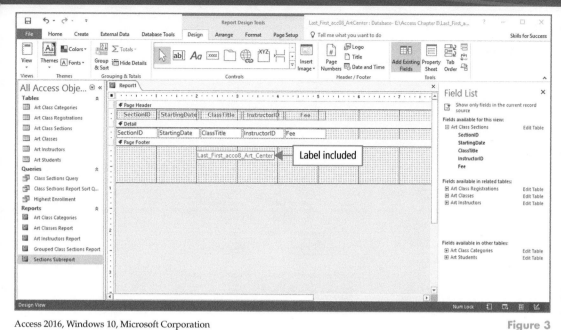

Access 2016, Windows 10, Microsoft Corporation

Figure 3

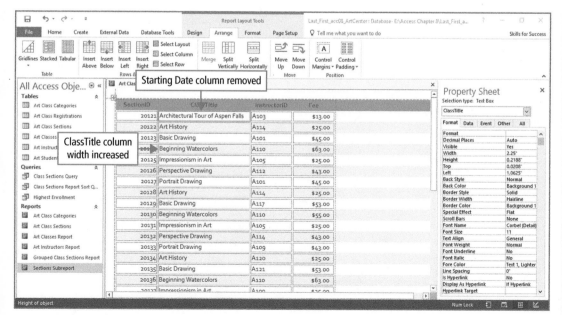

Access 2016, Windows 10, Microsoft Corporation

Figure 4

7. Click the **Format tab**. In the **Font group**, click the **Center** button ☰, and then click the **Bold** button B.

8. Point to the bottom of the **Page Footer** bar, and then using the pointer ↨, drag the pointer down approximately 1 inch to increase the size of the **Page Footer**.

9. Click the **Design tab**, and then in the **Controls group**, click the **Label** button *Aa*. Using the pointer ⁺A, click two grid dots below the top of the Page Footer and on the 2 inch horizontal gridline. Type Last_First_acc08_ArtCenter Compare your screen with **Figure 3**.

   The *page footer* is located at the bottom of each page and can contain labels, text boxes, and other controls.

10. Click the **Page Header** bar. On the **Design tab**, in the **Tools group**, click the **Property Sheet** button.

11. If necessary, click the Property Sheet **Format tab**. Click **Back Color**, click the **Back Color arrow**, and then click **Access Theme 5**.

12. Click **Save** 🖫. In the **Save As** dialog box, type Art Class Sections and then press Enter.

13. Switch to Layout view. Click the **StartingDate** column heading, and then click the **Arrange tab**. In the **Rows & Columns group**, click **Select Column**, and then press Delete.

14. Click any text box in the **ClassTitle** column. On the property sheet, change the **Width** to 2.25" Compare your screen with **Figure 4**.

15. **Close** ✕ the Property Sheet pane. **Save** 🖫 and **Close** ✕ the report.

■ **You have completed Skill 3 of 10**

 **WATCH** SKILL 8.4

▶ *Conditional formatting* changes the appearance of a control based on a display configuration related to the value that appears in a field.

▶ Using conditional formatting can help highlight information in a report such as values that fall above or below a certain criterion.

1. Open the **Grouped Class Sections Report** in Layout view. On the **Design tab**, in the **Header/Footer group**, click **Page Numbers**.

2. In the **Page Numbers** dialog box, under **Format**, verify that **Page N** is selected. Below **Position**, select the **Bottom of Page [Footer]** option button. Click the **Alignment arrow**, and then click **Right**. Compare your screen with **Figure 1**, and then click **OK**.

3. Scroll down to the bottom of the report to view the page number, and then scroll back to the top of the report.

4. In the first row of the **Architectural Tour of Aspen Falls group**, click the **StartingDate** value, *8/9/2018 1:00:00 PM*. Compare your screen with **Figure 2**.

5. Click the **Format tab**, and then in the **Control Formatting group**, click **Conditional Formatting**. In the **Conditional Formatting Rules Manager** dialog box, click the **New Rule** button.

6. In the **New Formatting Rule** dialog box, under **Select a rule type**, verify that **Check values in the current record or use an expression** is selected. Under **Format only cells where the:**, click the second **arrow**, and then if necessary, click **between**.

▪ **Continue to the next page to complete the skill**

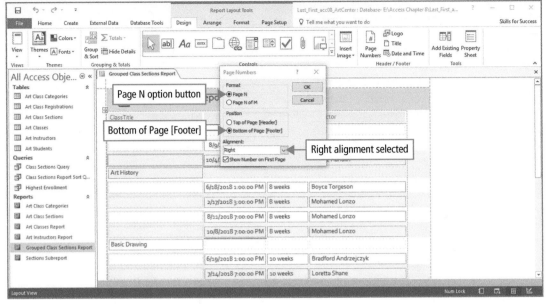

Figure 1   Access 2016, Windows 10, Microsoft Corporation

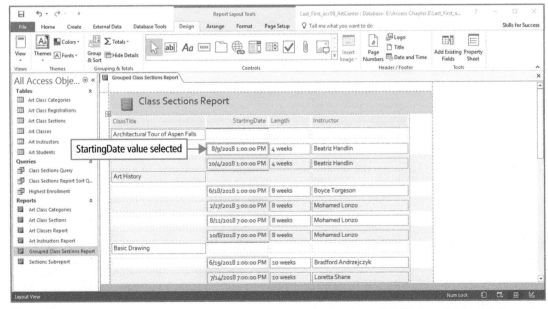

Figure 2   Access 2016, Windows 10, Microsoft Corporation

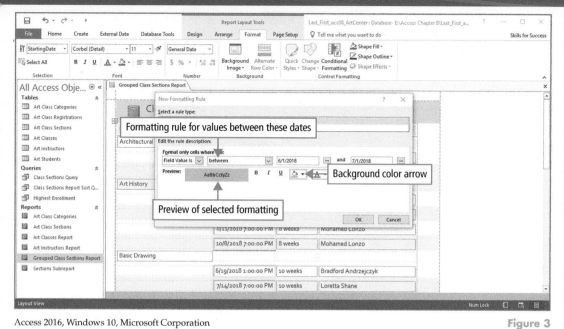

Access 2016, Windows 10, Microsoft Corporation

Figure 3

7. Under **Format only cells where the:**, click in the third box, and then type 6/1/2018 Press Tab two times, and then in the fourth box, type 7/1/2018

8. In the **New Formatting Rule** dialog box, click the **Background color arrow**, and then click the last color in the fifth row—**Brown 4**. Compare your screen with **Figure 3**, and then click **OK**.

9. In the **Conditional Formatting Rules Manager** dialog box, click **Apply**. Compare your screen with **Figure 4**, and then click **OK**.

> After clicking Apply, the formatting rule is applied to the report. Here, all classes with a starting date between 6/1/2018 and 7/1/2018 have a brown background color.

10. Switch to Design view. Click the **Detail** bar, and then click the **Home tab**. In the **Text Formatting group**, click the **Background Color arrow**, and then click the eighth color in the second row—**Purple, Accent 4, Lighter 80%**.

11. In the **Report Header** section, click the **Class Sections Report** label, and then select the title text. Type Grouped Class Sections Report Press Enter, and then switch to Report view.

12. Click **Save** 🖫, and then **Close** ✕ the report.

■ **You have completed Skill 4 of 10**

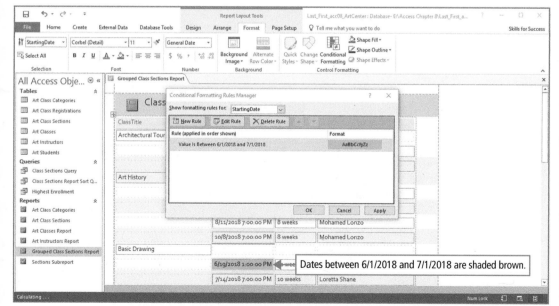

Access 2016, Windows 10, Microsoft Corporation

Figure 4

▶ For printed reports, inserting a page break below the Report Header will protect sensitive information by placing only the report title on the first page.

1. In the **Navigation Pane**, click the **Art Students** table. Click the **Create tab**, and then in the **Reports group**, click the **Report** button. On the **Design tab**, in the **Tools group**, click **Property Sheet**. Click the **Selection type arrow**, and then click **FirstName**. Change the **Width** to 1.5"

2. Repeat the technique just practiced to change the **LastName** field **Width** to 1.6" the **Neighborhood** field **Width to** 1.5" and the **Phone** field **Width** to 1.6"

MOS
Obj 5.2.2

3. On the **Design tab**, in the **Tools group**, click **Add Existing Fields**. **Expand** ⊞ the **Art Class Registrations** table, and then double-click the **SectionID** field. **Close** ⊠ the Field List pane, and then compare your screen with **Figure 1**.

> **Portrait layout** is the standard page orientation in which the page is taller than it is wide. Because the report orientation is in portrait layout, the SectionID field will not fit onto the printed page.

4. Click the **Page Setup tab**, and then in the **Page Layout group**, click **Landscape** so all fields fit into the width of a printed page.

> **Landscape layout** is when the page orientation is wider than it is tall.

5. Switch to **Design View**. Double-click the **Page Header** bar, and then in the Property Sheet, on the **Format tab**, change the **Height** to 0.45 and then compare your screen with **Figure 2**.

■ **Continue to the next page to complete the skill**

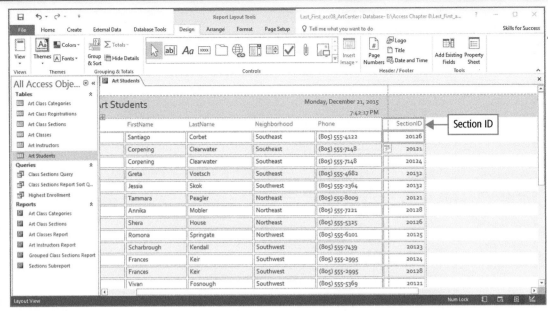

Figure 1

Section ID

Access 2016, Windows 10, Microsoft Corporation

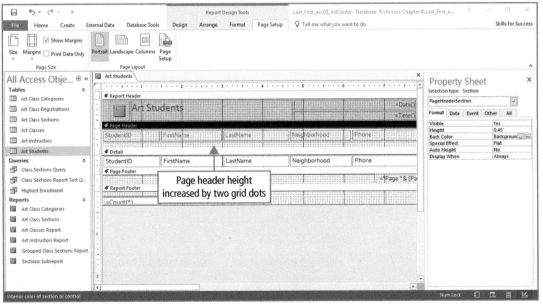

Figure 2

Page header height increased by two grid dots

Access 2016, Windows 10, Microsoft Corporation

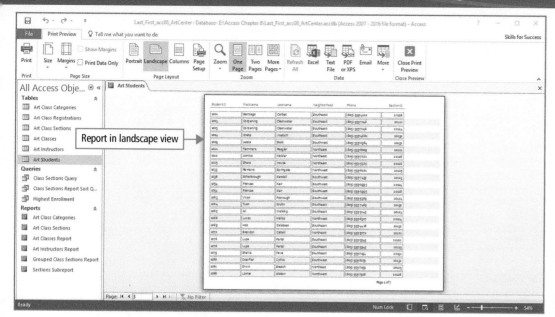

Access 2016, Windows 10, Microsoft Corporation

Figure 3

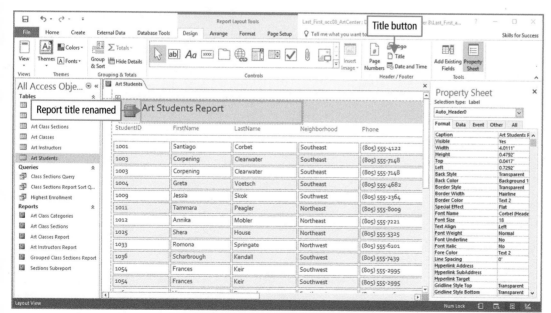

Access 2016, Windows 10, Microsoft Corporation

Figure 4

6. Click the **Report Header** bar, and then in the property sheet on the **Format tab**, click the **Force New Page arrow**, and then click **After Section**.

7. Click the text box with the text =*Time()*, press and hold down Shift , click the =*Date()* text box, and then press Delete .

8. Switch to Print Preview view. Click the center of the page to zoom to display one page, and then click the **Next Page** button to view the second page of the report. Compare your screen with **Figure 3**.

9. If required by your instructor, in the **Print group**, click the **Print** button. On the **Print Preview tab**, in the **Close Preview group**, click **Close Print Preview**.

   MOS
   Obj 1.5.2

10. On the **Design tab**, in the **Header/Footer group**, click the **Title** button, type Art Students Report and then press Enter . Compare your screen to **Figure 4**.

11. If necessary, open the **Property Sheet**. Click the **Selection type arrow**, and then click **AccessTotalsStudentID**. In the **Height** text box, type 0.25"

12. Click the **StudentID** label, hold down the Shift key, and then click the **FirstName**, **LastName**, **Neighborhood**, **Phone**, and **SectionID** labels. On the **Format tab**, in the **Font group**, click the **Bold** button B .

13. **Close** the Property Sheet pane, and then click **Save** 🖫 . In the **Save As** dialog box, type Art Students Report and then press Enter . **Close** ✕ the report.

■ **You have completed Skill 5 of 10**

▶ When creating a report that uses data from tables in a many-to-many relationship, it is helpful to create a query within the report to display the information.

▶ The ***Query Builder*** creates queries within database objects such as forms and reports.

1. Open the **Art Class Sections** report in Design view.

2. On the **Design tab**, in the **Tools group**, click **Property Sheet**. If necessary, click the Selection type arrow, and then click **Report**.

3. Click the property sheet **Data tab**, and then compare your screen with **Figure 1**.

4. Click the **Record Source Build** button [...].

5. In the **Fee** column **Criteria** cell, type >40 and then compare your screen with **Figure 2**.

The Query Builder tab displays with all of the fields from the Art Class Sections table.

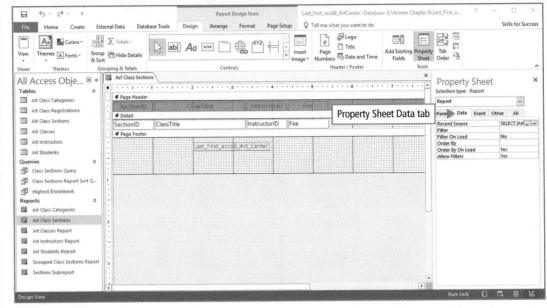

Figure 1

Access 2016, Windows 10, Microsoft Corporation

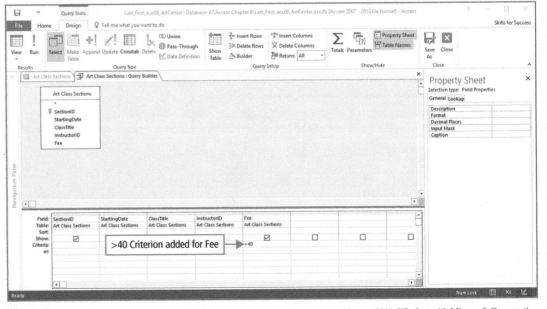

Figure 2

Access 2016, Windows 10, Microsoft Corporation

■ **Continue to the next page to complete the skill**

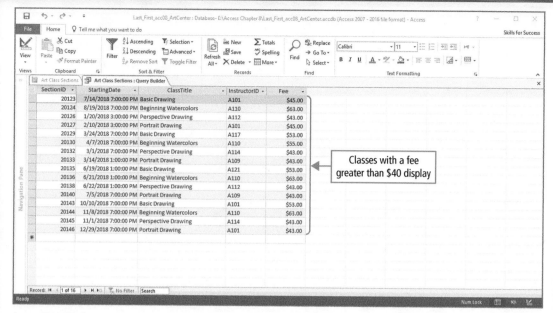

Classes with a fee greater than $40 display

Access 2016, Windows 10, Microsoft Corporation

Figure 3

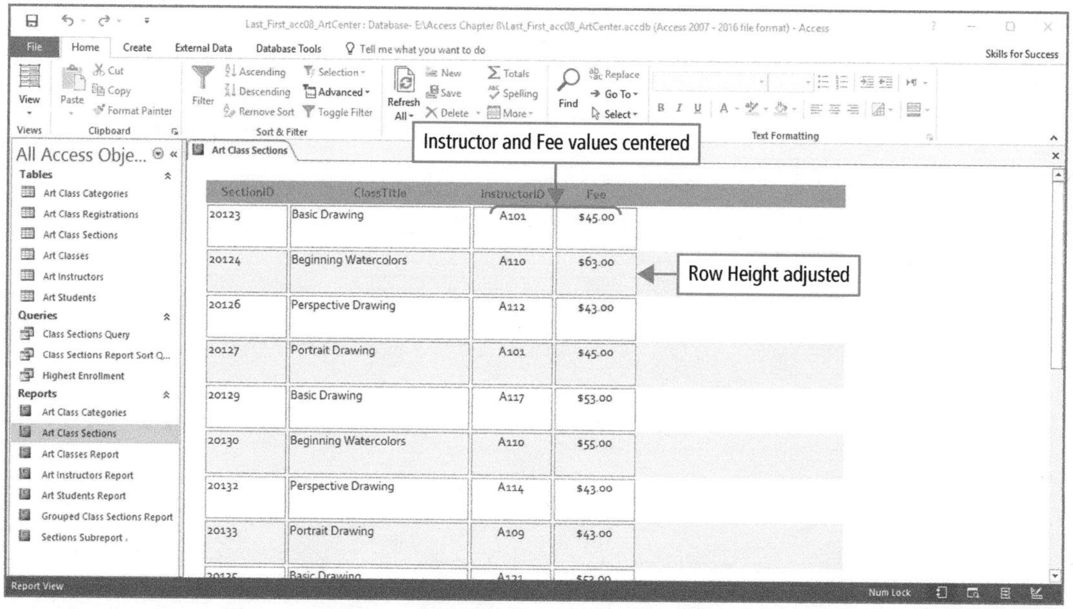

6. On the **Design tab**, in the **Results group**, click **Run**. Compare your screen with **Figure 3**.

   Sixteen records display in the query datasheet. Only the classes that have a fee greater than $40 are displayed.

7. Click **Save** 🖫, and then **Close** ☒ the Art Class Sections Report: Query Builder tab.

8. In the **Detail** section, click the **InstructorID** text box. Press and hold the ⇧Shift key, and then click the **Fee** text box. On the **Format tab**, in the **Font group**, click **Center** B .

9. If necessary, use the technique just practiced to set the **SectionID** text box to **Align Left**.

10. Click the property sheet **Selection type arrow**, and then click **ClassTitle**. Click the property sheet **Format tab**, and then change the **Height** to 0.5"and press Enter .

11. **Close** ☒ the **Property Sheet**. Click **Save** 🖫, and then switch to **Report** view. Compare your screen with **Figure 4**.

12. **Save** 🖫, and then **Close** ☒ the report.

■ **You have completed Skill 6 of 10**

Instructor and Fee values centered

Row Height adjusted

Access 2016, Windows 10, Microsoft Corporation

Figure 4

▶ A **hyperlink** is an electronic reference to another part of the same document or link to a different document or web page.

▶ Hyperlinks are an effective way to open related documents or web pages with a single click.

▶ You can insert hyperlinks in reports to open Word documents, other files, or web pages.

1. Open the **Grouped Class Sections Report** in Layout view. Scroll down to the bottom of the report. Compare your screen with **Figure 1**.

2. On the **Design tab**, in the **Controls group**, click the **Insert Hyperlink** button. Click in the last cell in the last row of the report.

   In the Insert Hyperlink dialog box, you can type the Uniform Resource Locator (URL) of a web page or browse to a file to create the hyperlink.

3. In the **Insert Hyperlink** dialog box, click in the **Text to display** box, and then type Class Descriptions

4. Click the **Look in arrow**, and then navigate to the student data files for this chapter. Click **acc08_ArtDescriptions**, and then click **OK**.

5. On the **Design tab**, in the **Controls group**, click the **Insert Hyperlink** button. Compare your screen to **Figure 2**.

■ Continue to the next page to complete the skill

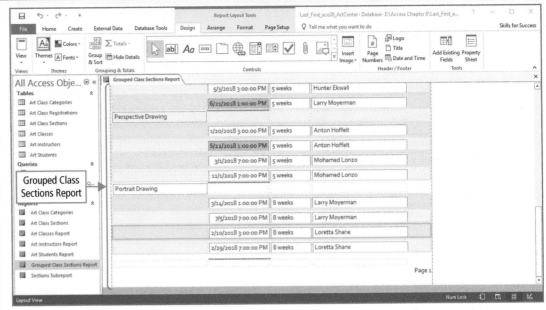

Figure 1

Access 2016, Windows 10, Microsoft Corporation

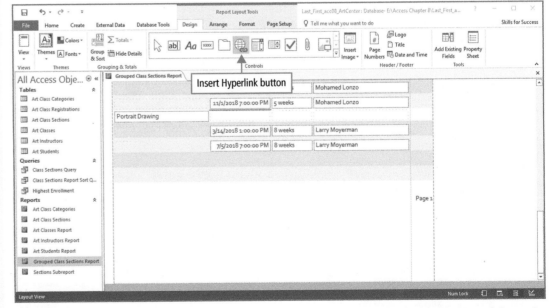

Figure 2

Access 2016, Windows 10, Microsoft Corporation

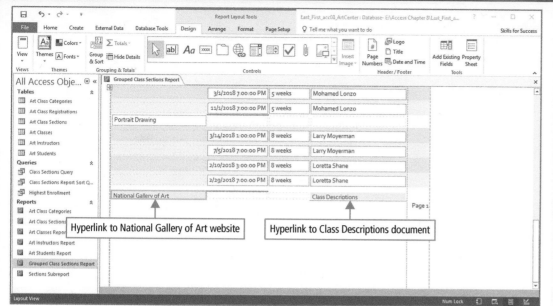

Access 2016, Windows 10, Microsoft Corporation

Figure 3

6. With the 🌐 pointer, click the first cell in the last row of the report. In the **Insert Hyperlink** dialog box, in the **Text to display** box, type National Gallery of Art

7. In the **Address** box, type http://www.nga.gov

8. Click **OK** to close the dialog box, and then compare your screen with **Figure 3**.

9. Switch to Report view, scroll to the bottom of the report, and then compare your screen with **Figure 4**.

10. Click the **National Gallery of Art** hyperlink.

> If you are connected to the Internet, your default web browser displays the home page for the National Gallery of Art.

11. **Close** ☒ the web browser. Scroll to the top of the report.

12. Switch to Layout view. Click the **StartingDate** label. On the **Format tab**, in the **Font group**, click the **Center** button ☰.

13. **Save** 🖫, and then **Close** ☒ the report.

■ **You have completed Skill 7 of 10**

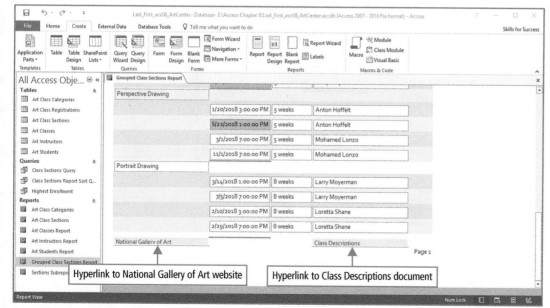

Access 2016, Windows 10, Microsoft Corporation

Figure 4

▶ A *calculated field* is a field added to queries, tables, or reports that derives its value from other fields.

▶ When you create a report from a query, a calculated field is automatically added to the bottom of the report. The added field counts the number of records in the report. You can include other calculated fields in a report.

1. Click the **Create tab**, and then in the **Reports group**, click **Report Wizard**. In the **Report Wizard** dialog box, click the **Tables/Queries arrow**, and then click **Table: Art Class Sections**.

2. Under **Available Fields**, click **ClassTitle**, and then click the **Move** button > . Repeat this technique to move the **Fee** field to the **Selected Fields**. Compare your screen with Figure 1.

3. Click the **Tables/Queries arrow**, and then click **Table: Art Class Registrations**. Move > the **StudentID** and **SectionID** fields from the **Available Fields** to the **Selected Fields**, and then click **Next**.

4. Click **by Art Class Registrations**, compare your screen with Figure 2, and then click **Next**.

5. With **ClassTitle** selected, click the **Move** button > to group the report by ClassTitle. Click **Next**, click the first sort order **arrow**, and then click **SectionID**.

■ Continue to the next page to complete the skill

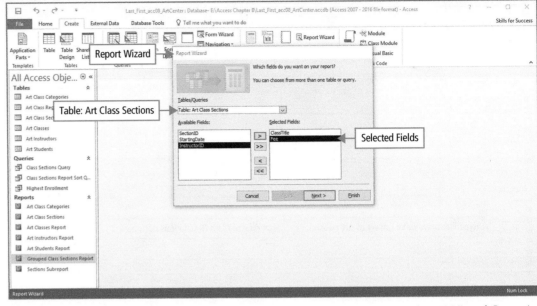

Figure 1

Access 2016, Windows 10, Microsoft Corporation

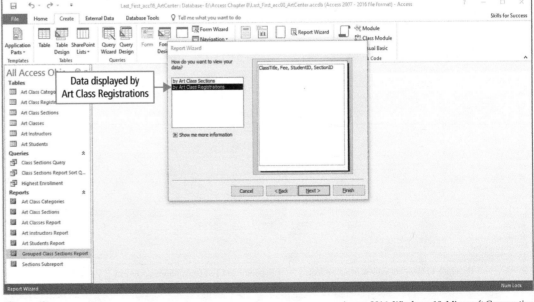

Figure 2

Access 2016, Windows 10, Microsoft Corporation

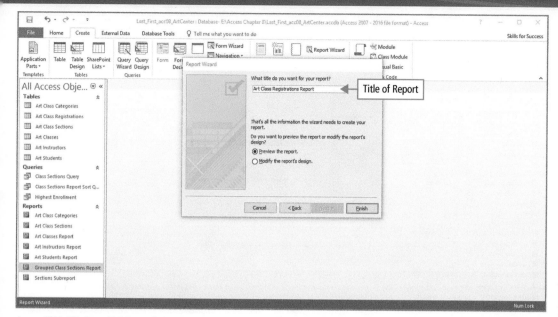

Title of Report

Access 2016, Windows 10, Microsoft Corporation

Figure 3

6. Click the **Summary Options** button. In the **Summary Options** dialog box, select the **Sum** check box, and then click **OK**.

7. Click **Next** two times. In the **What title do you want for your report?** text box, type Art Class Registrations Report Compare your screen to **Figure 3**, and then click **Finish**.

> The SectionID and Student ID text boxes are too close to be easily read.

8. Click the **Close Print Preview** button to switch to Design view.

9. In the **Detail** section, click the **SectionID** text box. Click the **Format tab**, and then in the **Font group**, click the **Align Left** button. In the **Page Header**, repeat this technique to align the **SectionID** label to the left.

> Changing the alignment of the label and text boxes will make the report easier to read.

10. Click **Save**, and then switch to Report view. Scroll down to display the **Art History** group. Compare your screen with **Figure 4**, and then **Close** the report.

> At the bottom of each group, the total fees collected for each class title are displayed. The classes are sorted by SectionID.

■ **You have completed Skill 8 of 10**

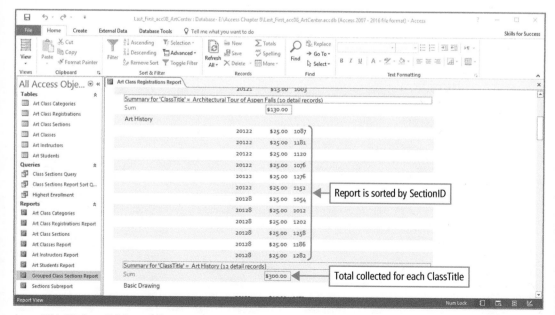

Report is sorted by SectionID

Total collected for each ClassTitle

Access 2016, Windows 10, Microsoft Corporation

Figure 4

▶ A *subreport* is a report that is inserted into another report.

▶ Main reports are linked to subreports using a common field.

▶ Reports and subreports are commonly used to show related records from tables in a one-to-many relationship.

1. Open the **Art Class Categories** report in Design view. On the **Design tab**, in the **Controls group**, click the **More** button. Verify the **Use Control Wizards** command is selected.

2. In the **Controls** gallery, click the **Subform/Subreport** button. Position the pointer in the upper left corner of the **Detail** section, one grid dot below the **Category** control, aligned with the left edge of the Category control, and then click the left mouse button.

3. In the **SubReport Wizard**, select the **Use an existing report or form** option button, and then click **Art Classes Report**. Click **Next**, and then compare your screen to **Figure 1**.

4. Verify that the **Choose from a list** radio button is selected, and then click **Finish**. Compare your screen with **Figure 2**.

5. In the **Detail** section of the main report, click the **Art Classes Report** label, and then press ⌷Delete⌷.

6. Click the **Design tab**, and then in the **Controls group**, click the **Label** button.

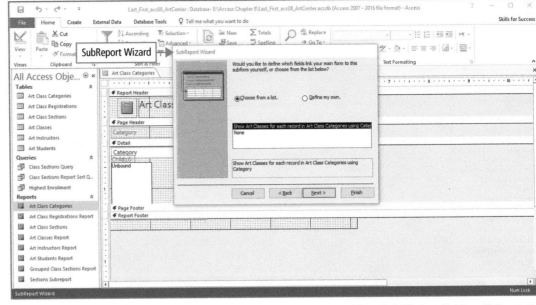

Figure 1

Access 2016, Windows 10, Microsoft Corporation

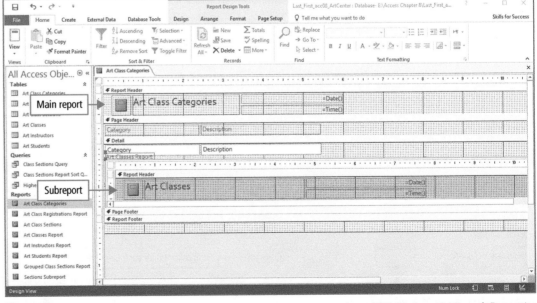

Figure 2

Access 2016, Windows 10, Microsoft Corporation

■ **Continue to the next page to complete the skill**

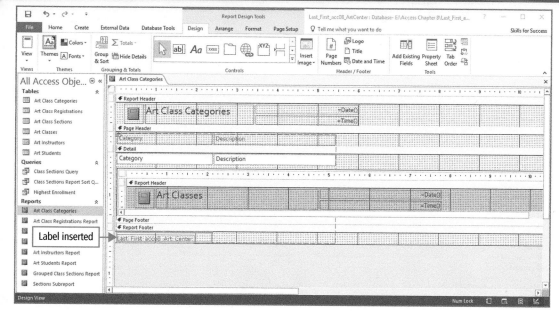

Access 2016, Windows 10, Microsoft Corporation

Figure 3

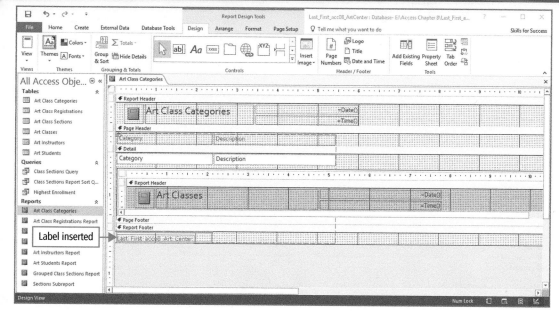

Access 2016, Windows 10, Microsoft Corporation

Figure 4

7. In the upper left corner of the **Report Footer**, one grid dot below the **Report Footer** bar, click to insert the label. Type Last_First_acc08_Art_Center Click outside the label to deselect it. Compare your screen with **Figure 3**.

8. On the **Design tab**, in the **Themes group**, click **Themes**, and then click **Organic**. In the **Tools group**, click **Property Sheet**.

9. On the Property Sheet, click the **Selection type arrow**, and then click **Art Classes Report**. Change the **Width** to 8.5" Click the **Selection type arrow**, and then click **Report**. Change the **Width** to 10" Compare your screen with **Figure 4**.

   The subform and main form are resized, reducing excess blank space on the report.

10. Click the **Page Setup tab**, and then in the **Page Layout group**, click **Landscape**.

11. **Save** 🖫, and then **Close** ✕ the report.

■ **You have completed Skill 9 of 10**

 **WATCH** SKILL 8.10

Formatting a subreport in its own window provides more options and control when designing the subreport.

1. In the **Navigation Pane**, double-click the **Sections Subreport**.

2. Switch to Design view, and then double-click the **Detail** bar. On the Property Sheet **Format tab**, change the **Height** to 1.5".

3. In the Report Header section, click the logo control, and then while holding down Shift, click **Title**, **Date**, and the **Time** controls. Press Delete Compare your screen with **Figure 1**.

4. In the **Page Header** section, select the **SectionID** text box, press and hold Shift, and then click the **StartingDate**, **ClassTitle**, **InstructorID**, and **Fee** text box controls. On the **Home tab**, in the **Text Formatting group**, click the **Font Size arrow**, and then click **10**. Click **Bold** B, and then compare your screen with **Figure 2**.

5. Switch to Layout view. Scroll to the bottom of the report. Click the last text box in the last row, displaying **$995.00**, and then press Delete. Repeat this technique to delete the text box displaying the text **Page 1 of 1**.

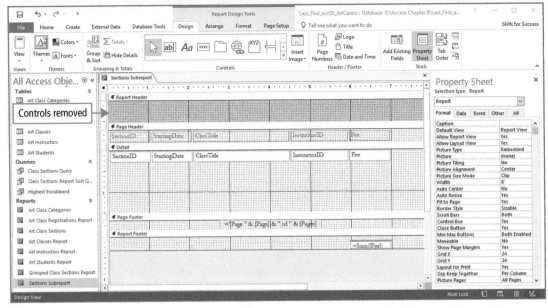

Figure 1

Access 2016, Windows 10, Microsoft Corporation

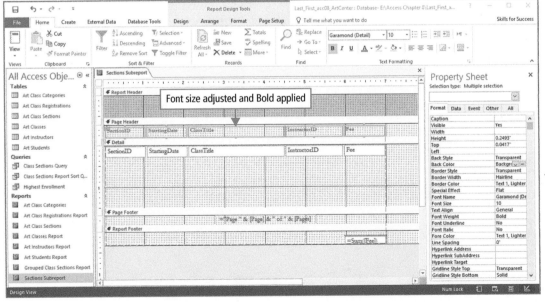

Figure 2

Access 2016, Windows 10, Microsoft Corporation

■ **Continue to the next page to complete the skill**

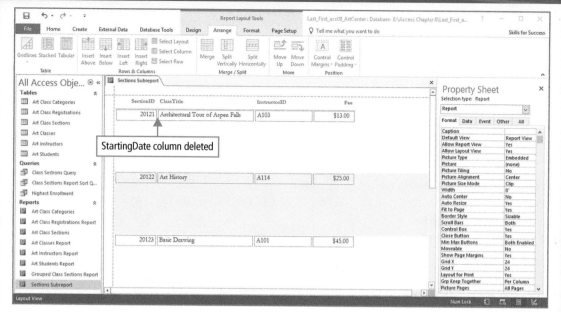

Access 2016, Windows 10, Microsoft Corporation

Figure 3

6. Click anywhere in the **StartingDate** column, and then click the **Arrange tab**. In the **Rows & Columns group**, click **Select Column**, and then press Delete. Compare your screen to **Figure 3**.

7. **Save** 🖫, and then **Close** ✕ the report.

8. Open the **Art Instructors Report** in Design view. In the **Detail** section, select the **FirstName** and **LastName** text boxes. Click the **Format tab**, and then in the **Font group**, click the **Bold** button B. Change the **Font Size** to **10**.

9. Switch to Layout view. In the first row, click the blank cell next to the last name, *Shane*. Scroll to the right. Hold down Shift, and then click the last blank cell in the first row. Press Delete.

10. Select the **FirstName** label, hold down Shift, and then click the **LastName** label. Click the **Format tab**. In the **Font group**, click the **Bold** button, change the **Font Size** to **12**, and then compare your screen to **Figure 4**.

11. Click **Save** 🖫, and then **Close** ✕ the report.

12. **Close** ✕ Access, and then submit the file as directed by your instructor.

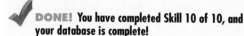

DONE! You have completed Skill 10 of 10, and your database is complete!

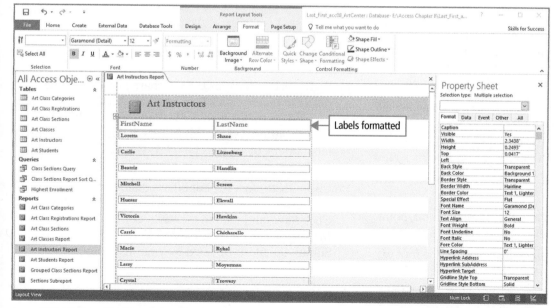

Access 2016, Windows 10, Microsoft Corporation

Figure 4

More Skills ⑪

Add Charts to Reports

To complete this project, you will need the following file:

- acc08_MS11Cars

You will save the file as:

- Last_First_acc08_MS11Cars

▶ Report charts are a method of visually displaying data in reports. Charts can display data from a table, a query, or both.

▶ The *plot area* is the area bound by the axes in a chart. This area can be enhanced by adding a pattern, changing colors, or inserting an image.

---

1. Start **Access 2016**, and then open the student data file **acc08_MS11Cars**. Save the file in your **Access Chapter 8** folder with the name Last_First_acc08_ MS11Cars If necessary, enable the content.

2. Click the **Create tab**, and then in the **Reports group**, click **Report Design**.

3. Drag the right edge of the **Detail** section to the **8** inch horizontal gridline.

4. In the **Controls group**, click the **More** button ⌄ , and then click the **Chart** button. Position the crosshairs of the pointer in the upper left corner of the **Detail** section, and then drag down and to the right so that the pointer is positioned at the **5 inch** vertical gridline and **8 inch** horizontal gridline.

5. In the **Chart Wizard**, under **Which table or query would you like to use to create your chart**, click **Table: Vintage Cars**, and then click **Next**.

6. Under **Available Fields**, click **Manufacturer**, and then click the **Move** button ▸ one time to move the field to the Fields for Chart pane, and then click **Next**.

7. Click the first chart in the last row—**Pie Chart**, and then click **Finish**. Switch to Report view to display the chart.

8. Switch to Design view. Right-click the chart. From the shortcut menu, point to **Chart Object**, and then click **Edit** to start Microsoft Graph.

9. Click the chart title, and then on the **Formatting** toolbar, change the font to **Times New Roman** with a font size of **8**.

10. Double-click the **Pie** area. In the **Format Data Series** dialog box, select the **Data Labels tab**, and then under **Label Contains**, select the **Percentage** check box. Click **OK**.

11. Right-click a blank area of the chart, and then in the displayed menu, click **Format Chart Area**. In the **Format Chart Area** dialog box, on the **Patterns tab**, click the **Fill Effects** button. On the **Fill Effects** dialog box **Gradient tab**, under **Colors**, select the **Preset** option button. Click the **Preset colors arrow**, and then select **Daybreak**.

12. Click **OK** to close the Fill Effects dialog box, and then click **OK** to close the Format Chart Area dialog box. Click **Save**, and then in the **Save As** dialog box, type Manufacturers Chart **Close** the report. **Close** Access. Submit the file as directed by your instructor.

■ **You have completed More Skills 11**

More Skills (12)

Create Subreports Using Drag-and-Drop

To complete this project, you will need the following file:

- acc08_MS12Museum

You will save your file as:

- Last_First_acc08_MS12Museum

▶ A report can be added to another report as a subreport by dragging the report from the Navigation Pane into the open report.

▶ Using the drag-and-drop method to add a subreport enables you to create and work with the subreport before adding it to the main report.

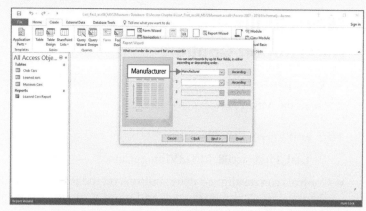

Access 2016, Windows 10, Microsoft Corporation   **Figure 1**

---

1. Start **Access 2016**, and then open the student data file **acc08_MS12Museum**. Save the file in your **Access Chapter 8** folder with the name Last_First_acc08_MS12Museum If necessary, enable the content.

2. Click the **Create tab**, and then in the **Reports group**, click **Report Wizard**.

3. In the **Report Wizard** dialog box, click the **Tables/Queries arrow**, and then click **Table: Museum Cars**. Move > the **Manufacturer, Model, Year Manufactured**, and **License Plate** to the **Selected Fields**, and then click **Next** two times.

4. Under **What sort order do you want for your records**, click the first **arrow**, and then click **Manufacturer**. Compare your screen with **Figure 1**, and then click **Next** two times.

   The records will be sorted in ascending order by manufacturer.

5. Under **What title do you want for your report**, type Museum Cars Report and then click **Finish**.

6. **Close** ⊠ the **Print Preview tab**. If necessary, **Close** the Field List pane. If necessary, open the report in Design view. In the **Page Header**, click the **Manufacturer** label. Press and hold down Shift, and then click the **Model, Year Manufactured**, and **License Plate** labels. On the **Arrange tab**, in the **Sizing & Ordering group**, click the **Size/Space arrow**, and then click **To Fit**. Compare your screen with **Figure 2**.

7. In the **Page Footer**, click the **Page Number** text box, and then press Delete. Repeat this technique to delete the **=Now()** text box.

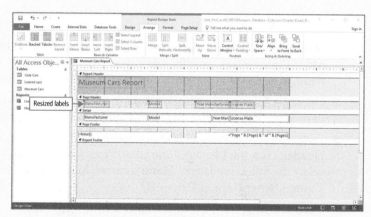

Access 2016, Windows 10, Microsoft Corporation   **Figure 2**

8. Drag the bottom edge of the Details area down 1 inch. From the **Navigation Pane**, drag **Loaned Cars Report** to the **Detail** section of the open report. Position the pointer about four grid dots below the left edge of the **Manufacturer** text box. Release the mouse button.

   The Cars Not Loaned Subreport becomes a subreport in the main report.

9. Switch to Report view to view the finished report. Click **Save** 🖫, and then **Close** ⊠ the report. Close **Access**. Submit the file as directed by your instructor.

■ **You have completed More Skills 12**

More Skills ⓭
Align Report Controls

To complete this project, you will need the following file:

- acc08_MS13VintageCars

You will save the file as:

- Last_First_acc08_MS13VintageCars

▶ Controls can be aligned using buttons on the Ribbon. Using the Ribbon's alignment tools can be quicker and more accurate than positioning controls using the mouse.

▶ *Padding* determines the space between controls in a report or form.

1. Start **Access 2016**, and then open the student data file **acc08_MS13VintageCars**. Save the file in your **Access Chapter 8** folder with the name Last_First_acc08_MS13VintageCars If necessary, enable the content.

2. Open the **Vintage Cars Report 2018** in Report view. Notice that the controls in both the Page Header and the Detail area are misaligned.

3. Switch to Design view, and then **Close** ⟪ the Navigation Pane. In the **Page Header**, click the **License Plate** label. Press and hold the Shift key, and then select the following labels: **Manufacturer**, **Model**, **Year Manufactured**, **Color**, **Owner ID**, and **Driver ID**.

4. On the **Arrange tab**, in the **Sizing & Ordering group**, click **Align**. From the gallery, click **Top**.

5. In the Detail section, click the **License Plate** text box. Press and hold the Shift key, and then select the following text boxes: **Manufacturer**, **Model**, **Year Manufactured**, **Color**, **Owner ID**, and **Driver ID**.

6. On the **Arrange tab**, in the **Sizing & Ordering group**, click **Align**. From the gallery, click **Top**.

7. With the seven labels still selected, press Ctrl + B.

8. In the **Page Header**, click the **Year Manufactured** control. Press Shift, and then in the **Detail** section, click the **Year Manufactured** text box. Position the ↔ pointer over the right handle of the control border, and then double-click to AutoSize its width.

9. Switch to Layout view. In the column heading, click the **License Plate** label. Press Shift, and then click the following labels: **Manufacturer**, **Model**, **Year Manufactured**, **Color**, **Owner ID**, and **Driver ID**. On the **Format tab**, in the **Control Formatting group**, click **Shape Fill**, and then from the gallery, click **Light Blue 3**.

10. On the **Format tab**, in the **Control Formatting group**, click **Shape Outline**, and then from the gallery, click **Dark Blue**.

11. Click any control in the **Year Manufactured** column. On the **Format tab**, in the **Font group**, click the **Center** button ≣.

12. Click the **Page Setup tab**, and then in the **Page Layout group**, click **Landscape**.

13. Switch to Report view. **Save** 🖫, and then **Close** ✕ the report.

14. **Open** ⟫ the Navigation Pane, and then select the **Car Owners** table. On the **Create tab**, in the **Reports group**, click **Report**.

15. Click the **Arrange tab**, and then in the **Position group**, click **Control Padding**. From the displayed list, click **Wide**. Click **Save** 🖫, and then press Enter to save the report with the default name. **Close** ✕ the report, and then **Close** ✕ Access. Submit the file as directed by your instructor.

■ **You have completed More Skills 13**

More Skills (14)

Add ActiveX Controls to a Report

To complete this project, you will need the following file:

- acc08_MS14Highways
- acc08_MS14AudioFile

You will save the file as:

- Last_First_acc08_MS14Highways

▶ ActiveX controls can be added to reports. ***ActiveX controls*** enable your active applications to interact with another application across the web.

▶ ActiveX controls can be used to embed tools from applications such as Adobe Acrobat, Microsoft Windows Media Player, or Microsoft Outlook.

▶ A Windows Media Player file could be used to provide information about the report or a tutorial.

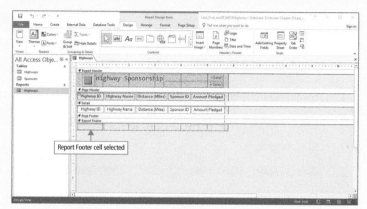

Access 2016, Windows 10, Microsoft Corporation   Figure 1

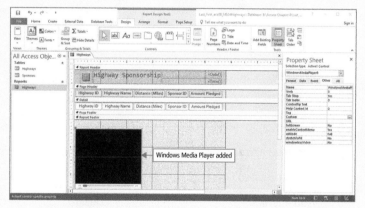

Access 2016, Windows 10, Microsoft Corporation   Figure 2

1. Start **Access 2016**, and open the student data file **acc08_MS14Highways**. Save the file in your **Access Chapter 8** folder with the name Last_First_acc08_MS14Highways If necessary, enable the content.

2. Open the **Highways** report in Design view.

3. Click in the upper left corner of the **Report Footer** to select the first empty cell, and then compare your screen with Figure 1.

4. On the **Design tab**, in the **Controls group**, click the **More** button, and then below the gallery, click **ActiveX Controls**.

    The Insert ActiveX Control dialog box displays with a list of ActiveX controls that can be added to the report.

5. In the **Insert ActiveX Control** dialog box, scroll to the bottom of the list, and then click **Windows Media Player**. Click **OK**.

6. With the **WindowsMediaPlayer8 ActiveX** control still selected, click the **Property Sheet** button. Click the property sheet **Other tab**, and then click in the **Custom box**.

7. Click the **Build** button [...].

8. In the **Windows Media Player Properties** dialog box, click the **Browse** button. In the **Open** dialog box, navigate to your **Student Data files** folder. Select the **acc08_MS14AudioFile**, and then click **Open**. Compare your screen with Figure 2.

9. In the **Windows Media Player Properties** dialog box, click **OK**.

10. Make sure the sound is enabled on your computer. Switch to Report view, and then scroll to the bottom of the report.

    The sound file will automatically play. To stop the sound from playing, close the report.

11. **Save** and the **Close** [×] the report. **Close** [×] Access. Submit the file as directed by your instructor.

■ **You have completed More Skills 14**

The following table summarizes the **SKILLS AND PROCEDURES** covered in this chapter.

Skill	Task	Step	Icon
1	Create a report from a query	Click query → Create tab → Reports group → Report	
1	Change control widths	Design tab → Tools group → Property Sheet → Selection Type → Format tab → Width	
1	Switch to Print Preview view	Design tab → Views group → View → Print Preview	
2	Filter records	Home tab → Sort and Filter group → Filter → Clear Select All → Select criteria	
2	Sort records	Design view → Sort cell arrow → Select sort order	
2	Group report information	Design tab → Grouping & Totals group → Group & Sort → Add a group → Add criteria	
3	Create reports from a blank report	Create tab → Report group → Blank Report	
3	Add label controls	Design tab → Controls group → Label → Click to place label	
4	Add page numbers	Design tab → Header/Footer group → Page Numbers button	
4	Apply conditional formatting	Format tab → Control Formatting group → Conditional Formatting Rules Manager → New Rule → New Formatting Rule	
5	Apply landscape orientation	Page Setup tab → Page Layout group → Landscape	
5	Insert a page break	Click Report Header → Property sheet → Format tab → Force New Page → After Section	
6	Center control text	Design view → Details section → Select control → Format tab → Font group → Center	
7	Add hyperlinks	Design tab → Controls group → Insert Hyperlink → Click on form to place link	
8	Add calculated field	Report Wizard → Summary Options button → Select Calculated field → OK	
9	Add subreport	Design tab → Controls group → More button → Subform/Subreport → Click to place subreport	
9	Resize report	Design view → Point to edge of report → Drag to desired size	
10	Delete subreport column	Arrange tab → Rows & Columns group → Select column → Press delete	

Project Summary Chart

Project	Project Type	Project Location	
Skills Review	Review	In Book and MIL	MyITLab® Grader
Skills Assessment 1	Review	In Book and MIL	MyITLab® Grader
Skills Assessment 2	Review	Book	
My Skills	Problem Solving	Book	
Visual Skills Check	Problem Solving	Book	
Skills Challenge 1	Critical Thinking	Book	
Skills Challenge 2	Critical Thinking	Book	
More Skills Assessment	Review	In Book and MIL	MyITLab® Grader
Collaborating with Google	Critical Thinking	Book	

MOS Objectives Covered (Quiz in MyITLab®)

1.5.2 Print records	5.2.2 Modify data sources
5.1.2 Create a report in Design view	

Review

Key Terms

Online Help Skills

1. Start **Access 2016**, and then in the upper right corner of the start page, click the **Help** button [?].

2. In the **Access Help** window **Search help** box, type Create an Access report and then press [Enter]. In the search result list, click **Create a grouped or summary report**. Maximize the Access 20016 Help window.

3. Scroll down, and then below **In this article**, click **Create a quick grouped or sorted report**. Compare your screen with **Figure 1**.

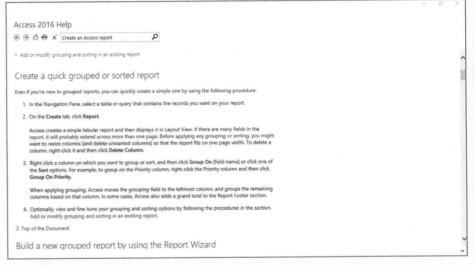

Figure 1   Access 2016, Windows 10, Microsoft Corporation

4. Read the article to answer the following questions: What are some of the methods you can use to ensure all columns needed in the report will fit on one page? When you apply grouping to a column, where is the column placed in the report? Would placing the grouped column in that location make it easier to understand the report?

Matching

Match each term in the second column with its correct definition in the first column by writing the letter of the term on the blank line in front of the correct definition.

_____ **1.** A view used to see how a document will look when it is printed.

_____ **2.** A tool used to combine records with identical values from a field in a report.

_____ **3.** A tool that displays report data containing only specified values, such as specific dates.

_____ **4.** A report area located at the top of each printed page that can contain labels, text boxes, and other controls.

_____ **5.** A report area located at the bottom of each printed page that can contain labels, text boxes, and other controls.

_____ **6.** This changes the appearance of a control based on the display configuration related to the value that appears in a field.

_____ **7.** The page orientation where the page is taller than it is wide.

_____ **8.** The page orientation where the page is wider than it is tall.

_____ **9.** A tool used to create queries within database objects such as forms and reports.

_____ **10.** An electronic reference to another part of the same document or link to a different document or web page.

A Conditional formatting

B Filter

C Grouped record

D Hyperlink

E Landscape orientation

F Page footer

G Page header

H Portrait orientation

I Print Preview

J Query Builder

Multiple Choice   (MyITLab®)

Choose the correct answer.

1. The Property Sheet pane can be found under which group?
   A. Tools
   B. Font
   C. Group & Sort

2. The Sort & Filter group can be found on which tab?
   A. Create
   B. Design
   C. Home

3. You can add a label to a report from which group?
   A. Controls
   B. Format
   C. Tools

4. What must be clicked to add a rule in the Conditional Formatting Rules Manager dialog box?
   A. Create rule
   B. Rule manager
   C. New rule

5. Which tab contains the Page Layout group?
   A. Create
   B. Page Setup
   C. Format

6. On the Design tab, which group contains the Run button?
   A. Results
   B. Manage
   C. Reports

7. Which group contains the Insert Hyperlink button?
   A. Buttons
   B. Controls
   C. Links

8. Which is a field added to queries, tables, or reports that derives its value from other fields?
   A. Conditional formatting
   B. Calculated field
   C. Page footer

9. Which is a report inserted into another report?
   A. Subreport
   B. Subform
   C. Both A and B

10. The Themes group is located on which tab?
    A. Create
    B. Design
    C. Neither A nor B

Topics for Discussion

1. What is the difference between grouping a report and filtering a report? Under which circumstances would you use each? State the reasons for your answers.

2. Under which circumstances could a hyperlink be useful in a report? State the reasons for your answer.

Skills Review

MyITLab®
Grader

To complete this project, you will need the following file:

- acc08_SRTriathlon

You will save your file as:

- Last_First_acc08_SRTriathlon

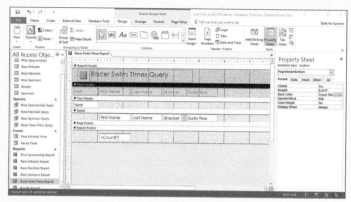

Access 2016, Windows 10, Microsoft Corporation

Figure 1

1. Open **acc08_SRTriathlon**, and then save the database in your **Access Chapter 8** folder as Last_First_acc08_SRTriathlon If necessary, enable the content.

2. In the **Navigation Pane**, click the **Prize Sponsorship Query**. On the **Create tab**, in the **Reports group**, click **Report**. On the **Design tab**, in the **Tools group**, click **Property Sheet**. Click the **Selection type arrow**, and then click **Race Year**. On the **Format tab**, change the **Width** to 1" and then close the Property Sheet pane. Click the **Page Number** text box, and then press [Delete]. **Save** the report as Prize Sponsorship Report and then close the report.

3. Open the **Racer Swim Times Report** in Layout view. On the **Design tab**, in the **Grouping & Totals group**, click **Group & Sort**. In the **Group, Sort, and Total** pane, click **Add a group**, and then click **Year**. Close the **Group, Sort, and Total** pane, and then switch to Design view.

4. In the **Page Header** section, click the **Year** label. On the **Format tab**, in the **Font group**, click **Left Align**. Click the **Page Header** bar. Click the **Design tab**, and then on the **Tools group**, click **Property Sheet**. On the **Format tab**, click **Back Color**, and then click **Access Theme 2**. Compare your screen with Figure 1.

5. Switch to Layout view, and then click the **Bracket** value in the first row of the **2014 group**. Click the **Format tab**, and then in the **Conditional Formatting group**, click **Conditional Formatting**. Click **New Rule**, click the second **arrow**, and then click **equal to**. Press [Tab], and then type M25-30 Click the **Background Color arrow**, click **Aqua Blue 3**, and then click **OK**. Click **Apply**, and then click **OK**. Click **Save**, and then **Close** .

Access 2016, Windows 10, Microsoft Corporation

Figure 2

6. Open the **Prize Sponsorship Report** in Design view. Click the **Page Setup tab**, and then in the **Page Layout group**, click **Landscape**. **Save** and **Close** the report.

7. Open the **Race Marshals Report** in Design view. On the **Design tab**, in the **Tools group**, click **Property Sheet**. On the **Data tab**, click the **Record Source** text box, and then click the **Build** button. In the **Year** column **Criteria** cell, type >2016 **Run** the query. Compare your screen with Figure 2. **Save**, and then **Close** the **Race Marshals Query: Query Builder**.

■ Continue to the next page to complete this Skills Review

8. Close the Property Sheet pane. In the **Report Footer**, click the cell to the right of =*Count(*)*. On the **Design tab**, in the **Controls group**, click the **Hyperlink** button. In the **Text to display** box, type Race Marshals Bios and then in the **Address** box, type http://www.aspenfalls.org Click **OK**. **Save** and **Close** the report.

9. Open the **Prize Sponsorship Report** in Design view. If necessary, close the **Property Sheet**. In the **Report Footer**, click the cell with the text =*Sum[ThirdPrize]*, and then press Delete . In the **Report Header**, click the **Prize Sponsorship Query** label, and then select the word **Query**. Type Report and then press Enter . **Save** and **Close** the report.

10. On the **Create tab**, in the **Reports group**, click **Report Wizard**. In the wizard, verify the **Tables/Queries** text box displays **Table: Race Entrants**, and then move the **RacerID**, **Bracket**, and **Fee** fields from the **Available Fields** to **Selected Fields**. Click **Next**.

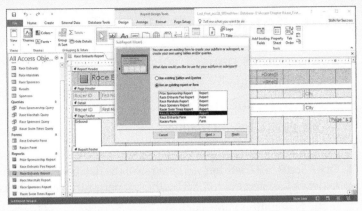

Figure 3

Access 2016, Windows 10, Microsoft Corporation

11. Under **Do you want to add any grouping levels**, click **Bracket**, and then click the **Move** button. Click **Next**, and then click **Summary Options**. In the **Summary Options** dialog box, select the **Fee** row **Sum** check box, and then click **OK**. Click **Next** two times, name the report Race Entrants Fee Report and then click **Finish**.

12. Close the **Print Preview tab**. Click **Save**, and then **Close** the report.

13. Open the **Race Entrants Report** in Design view. On the **Design tab**, in the **Controls group**, click the **More** button. From the gallery, click the **Subform/ Subreport** button. Directly under the **Page Footer** bar, click two grid dots from the left edge of the report. In the **SubReport Wizard**, click **Use an existing report or form**, and then click **Results Report**. Compare your screen with **Figure 3**, and then click **Next** two times. Name the subreport Results Subreport and then click **Finish**. **Save** and **Close** the report.

14. Open the **Results Report** in Design view. In the **Page Footer**, click the **Page Number** control, and then press Delete . In the **Report Footer**, repeat this technique to delete the **Count** control. On the **Design tab**, in the **Tools group**, click **Property Sheet**. In the **Page Header**, click the **Racer ID** label. On the property sheet **Format tab**, change the **Width** to 0.8" Compare your screen with **Figure 4**, and then **Save** and **Close** the report.

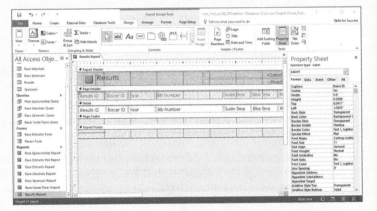

Figure 4

Access 2016, Windows 10, Microsoft Corporation

15. Close Access. Submit the file as directed by your instructor.

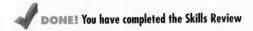

DONE! You have completed the Skills Review

Skills Assessment 1

To complete this database, you will need the following file:

- acc08_SA1Utilities

You will save your file as:

- Last_First_acc08_SA1Utilities

---

1. Start **Access 2016**, and then open **acc08_SA1Utilities**. **Save** 🖫 the file in your **Access Chapter 8** folder with the name Last_First_acc08_SA1Utilities

2. Create a Resident Report using the **Resident Query**. From the property sheet, change the text box widths as follows: **Account Number** to 1" **Last Name** to 1" **First Name** to 1.2" **Street** to 2" **Apt** to 0.5" **Zip** to 0.75" and **Water Meter** to 0.9"

3. Change the **Resident Report** to **Landscape** layout, and then change the title label to Resident Report

4. From Layout view, **Group** the **Water Bills Report** by **Usage**. Apply conditional formatting to the **Usage Fee** text boxes that changes the **Background Color** of fees greater than 30 to **Maroon 3**.

5. From Design view, double-click the **Page Header** bar, and then in the property sheet, change the **Back Color** to **Access Theme 2**.

6. From the Property Sheet **Data tab**, click the **Record Source Build** button. In the **UsageFee Criteria** cell, type >20 **Run** and **Save** the query. **Save** and **Close** the query and report.

7. Add a Terms of Service **Hyperlink** to the **Resident Report** using http://www.aspenfalls.org as the **Address**. Drag the hyperlink to the **8 inch** vertical gridline, one grid dot below the **Page Header** bar. **Save** the report as Resident Report and then **Close** the report.

8. Create a new report with the Report Wizard. Use the **Report Wizard** to add all of the fields from **Table: Electricity Bills** to the **Selected fields**. In the wizard, group the report by **BillingDate**, and then in **Summary Options**, in the **UsageFee** row, select **Sum**. In the wizard, choose the Landscape layout. Save the report as Electricity Bills Report

9. Switch the **Electricity Bills Report** to Design view. In the **Page Footer** area, delete the **=Now()** control. **Save** and **Close** the report.

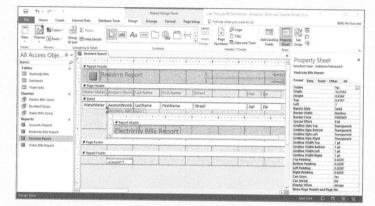

Access 2016, Windows 10, Microsoft Corporation

Figure 1

10. Open the **Resident Report** in Design view. Click the **Detail** bar, and then change the **Height** to 1 From the **Controls** group, use the **Subreport** button to add a subreport to the **Details** area, two grid dots below the **Account Number** control at the **1 inch** vertical gridline. In the **SubReport Wizard**, click to add the **Electricity Bills Report**, and then click **Finish** to accept the remaining defaults. Compare your screen with **Figure 1**. **Save** and **Close** the reports. Close **Access**. Submit the file as directed by your instructor.

 **DONE! You have completed Skills Assessment 1**

Skills Assessment 2

To complete this database, you will need the following file:

- acc08_SA2Electricity

You will save your file as:

- Last_First_acc08_SA2Electricity

---

1. Start **Access 2016**, and then open the student data file **acc08_SA2Electricity**. Save the file in your **Access Chapter 8** folder with the name Last_First_acc08_SA2Electricity

2. Create a Residents Report using the **Residents Query**. From the property sheet, change the text box widths as follows: **Account Number** to 1" **Last Name** to 1" **First Name** to 1" **Street** to 2" **Apt** to 0.5" **Zip** to 0.75" and **Electricity Meter** to 1.2"

3. Change the **Residents Report** to **Landscape** layout, and then change the title label to Residents Report **Save** the report as Residents Report

4. From Layout view, **Group** the **Residents Report** by **Zip**. **Sort** the report by **Last Name**.

5. From Design view, select the **Page Header**, and then in the property sheet, change the **Back Color** to **Access Theme 2**.

6. From the property sheet, change the **Selection type** to **Report**, and then on the **Data tab**, click the **Record Source Build** button. In the **ElectricityMeter Criteria** cell, type >24474865 **Run**, **Save**, and **Close** the query.

7. Add a Terms of Service **Hyperlink** to the **Residents Report** using http://www.aspenfalls.org as the **Address**. Place the hyperlink in the **Report Footer** at the **2 inch** vertical gridline, two dots below the **Report Footer** bar. Set the control to **Best Fit**. **Save** and **Close** the report.

8. Use the **Report Wizard** to add the **AccountNumber**, **CycleDate**, **Rate**, and **AmountPaid** from **Table: 2017 Electricity Bills** to the **Selected Fields**. In the wizard, group the report by **CycleDate**, and then in **Summary Options**, in the **AmountPaid** row, select **Sum**. In the wizard, choose the **Landscape** layout. Save the report as 2017 Electric Bills Report

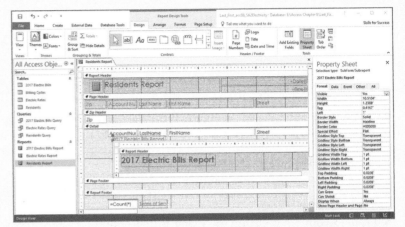

Figure 1   Access 2016, Windows 10, Microsoft Corporation

9. Switch the **2017 Electric Bills Report** to Design view. In the **Page Footer** area, delete the **=Now()** control. Select the label in the **Report Header**, and then from the **Home tab**, click **Bold**. **Save** and **Close** the report.

10. Open the **Residents Report** in Design view. Click the **Detail** bar, and then change the **Height** to 1" From the **Controls group**, use the **Subreport** button to add a subreport to the **Details** area, two grid dots below the **Account Number** control at the **1 inch** vertical gridline. In the **SubReport Wizard**, click to add the **2017 Electric Bills Report**, and then click **Finish** to accept the remaining defaults. Compare your screen with **Figure 1**.

11. **Save** and **Close** all reports. **Close** Access. Submit your file as directed by your instructor.

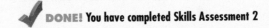 **DONE! You have completed Skills Assessment 2**

My Skills

To complete this database, you will need the following file:

- acc08_MYMaintenance

You will save your file as:

- Last_First_acc08_MYMaintenance

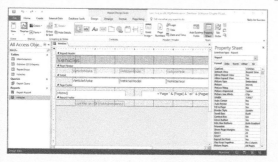

Access 2016, Windows 10, Microsoft Corporation   **Figure 1**

1. Start **Access 2016**, and then open **acc08_ MYMaintenance**. Save 💾 the file in your **Access Chapter 8** folder with the name Last_First_acc08_MYMaintenance

2. Click the **Repair Query**, and then on the **Create tab**, click **Report**. From the property sheet, change the **Width** of the following text boxes: **VehicleMake** and **VehicleModel** to 1.5" and **Maintenance** to 2 **Save** the report as Repair Report

3. On the **Repair Report**, in the last row, increase the **Height** of the total repair costs text box to 0.25" Change the title of the report to Repair Report

4. From the **Format tab**, add conditional formatting to the RepairCost controls. Apply the **Yellow** background color to any **RepairCost** greater than 50

5. From the **Design tab**, in the **Group, Sort, and Total** pane, click **Add a group**, and then group the report by **VehicleMake**.

6. From the **Home tab**, sort the report in **Descending** order by **RepairCost**.

7. From the **Page Setup tab**, change the page layout to **Landscape**. Save the report.

8. On the **Create tab**, click the **Report Wizard**, and then click the **Tables/Queries arrow** to select **Table:Vehicles**. Move all of the Vehicle table fields into the selected fields, and then click **Finish**. From the property sheet, change the **Width** of the **VehicleMake** and **VehicleModel** labels to 1.25"

9. From Design view, select the **VehicleID** label and text box, and then press Delete .

10. Open the **Vehicles** report in Design view. Double-click the **Report Footer** bar, and then in the property sheet, change the **Height** to 0.25" In the **Controls group**, click the **Label** button, and then click two grid dots below the **Report Footer** bar at the **1 inch** horizontal gridline. Type Last_ First_acc08_MyMaintenance and then press Enter . Compare your screen with Figure 1. **Save** and **Close** the reports, and then **Close** Access. Submit the file as directed by your instructor.

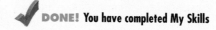
DONE! You have completed My Skills

Visual Skills Check

To complete this database, you will need the following file:

- acc08_VSDonations

You will save your file as:

- Last_First_acc08_VSDonations

Open the database **acc08_VSDonations**, and then save the database in your **Access Chapter 8** folder as Last_First_acc08_VSDonations

Create the report as shown in **Figure 1**. Apply the **Organic** Theme and change the **Project** text box width to 1.5" Increase the **Height** of the **AccessTotalGoals2018** text box to 0.25" Apply conditional formatting to the **Goal2018** column, which applies the **Dark Blue 1** background to Goal2018 text boxes that contain values greater than 10,000 Delete the **Time** control from the report header. Change the report to Landscape layout. Sort the records in **Descending** order according to **TotalGoal**. Change the title of the report to Projects Report Save the report as Projects Report Submit the file as directed by your instructor.

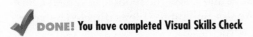

DONE! You have completed Visual Skills Check

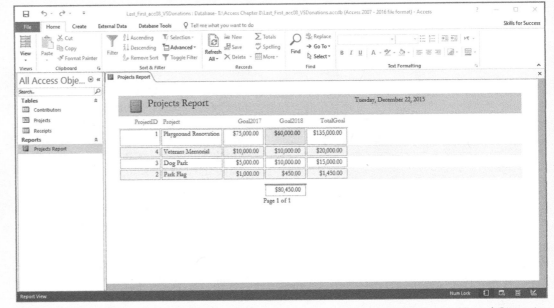

Figure 1

Access 2016, Windows 10, Microsoft Corporation

Skills Challenge 1

To complete this database, you will need the following file:

- acc08_SC1Water

You will save your file as:

- Last_First_acc08_SC1Water

Open **acc08_SC1Water**, and then save the database in your **Access Chapter 8** folder as Last_First_acc08_SC1Water Using the **Residents Query**, create a Residents Report On the Residents Report, resize the controls so a person reading the report can do so easily and effectively. Rename the title of the report with an appropriate title, and then change the layout to **Landscape**. Sort the Residents Report by Water Meter in Descending order. Using the **2017 Water Bills Query**, create a 2017 Water Bills Report selecting appropriate **Widths** for

all columns. In the **Amount Paid** control, apply conditional formatting that changes the background color to **Yellow** for any amounts greater than 15

Submit the file as directed by your instructor.

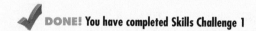 **DONE! You have completed Skills Challenge 1**

Skills Challenge 2

To complete this database, you will need the following file:

- acc08_SC2Outings

You will save your file as:

- Last_First_acc08_SC2Outings

Open **acc08_SC2Outings**, and then save the database in your **Access Chapter 8** folder as Last_First_acc08_SC2Outings Using the **Scheduled Outings Query**, create a Scheduled Outings Report Select an appropriate report title and suitable **Widths** for all columns. Group the report by **Outing Name**, and then **Sort** the report by **Outing Date** in **Descending** order. Filter the report to display outings that occur only during the months

of June, July, and August. In the **Fee** column, apply conditional formatting that changes the background color to **Yellow** for any fees greater than 30

Submit the file as directed by your instructor.

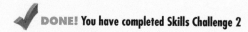 **DONE! You have completed Skills Challenge 2**

More Skills Assessment

MyITLab®
Grader

To complete this project, you will need the following file:

- acc08_MSARacers
- acc08_MSAAudioFile

You will save your file as:

- Last_First_acc08_MSARacers

---

1. Start **Access 2016**. Open the file **acc08_MSARacers**, and then save the file in your chapter folder as Last_First_acc08_MSARacers

2. Create a report using **Report Design**. Increase the width of the report to **8"**. Place a pie chart in the **8"** vertical and **5"** horizontal section of the details area of the report. Select the **Table: Racers** as the source for the chart, and then move **Zip** to the **Fields for Chart**. **Save** the report as Racer Location Report

3. Using drag-and-drop, drag the **Results** table to the details area of the **Racers** report. Accept all wizard defaults. Compare your screen with **Figure 1**.

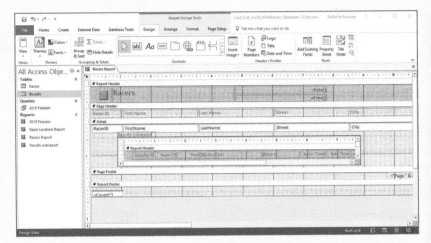

Figure 1   Access 2016, Windows 10, Microsoft Corporation

4. In the report footer section of the Racers report, select the blank cell to the right of the **=Count()** control. Insert the **ActiveX Windows Media Player** control. Using then **Custom** build button on the property sheet, add the **acc08_MSAAudioFile** to the control. Compare your screen with **Figure 2**.

5. On the **2018 Females** report, **Align** the labels in the **Page Header** to the **Top**.

6. **Save** and **Close** all reports, and then **Close** Access.

7. Submit the file as directed by your instructor.

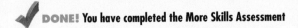
DONE! You have completed the More Skills Assessment

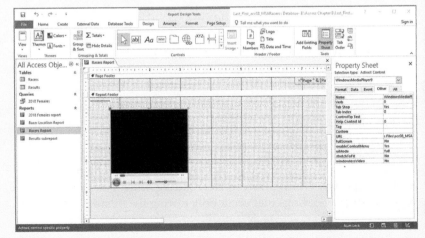

Figure 2   Access 2016, Windows 10, Microsoft Corporation

Collaborating with Google

To complete this project, you will need a Google account (refer to the **Common Features** chapter) and the following file:

- acc08_GP2017ElectricBillsReport

You will save your file as:

- Last_First_acc08_GPSnip

1. Open the **Google Chrome** web browser. Log into your Google account, and then click the **Apps** button.

2. Click **Drive** to open Google Drive, and then click the **New** button. Click **File upload**, navigate to the student data files, and then open **acc08_GP2017ElectricBillsReport**.

3. Select **acc08_GP2017ElectricBillsReport** in **Google Drive**. Click the **More actions** button, point to **Open with**, and then click **Google Docs**.

4. Select the report title, and then click the **Center** button. Click the **Styles arrow**, and then click **Title**. Click the **Text color arrow**, and then click **dark blue 2**.

5. Select the labels in the first row of the report, and then click the **Styles arrow**. Click **Heading 1**, and then click the **Underline** button.

6. With the first row still selected, click the **Font arrow**, and then click **Arial**.

7. Starting on Page 3 of the report, select the text from **February 2017** to the end of the document, and then press Delete.

8. Scroll to the top of the report, and then click before 2017. Type January and then compare your screen with **Figure 1**.

9. In the second row of the report, select the text **January 2017**, and then click **Bold**.

10. Open the **Snipping Tool**, click the **New arrow**, and then take a **Window Snip**. In the **Snipping Tool** mark-up window, click the **Save Snip** button. In the **Save As** dialog box, navigate to your

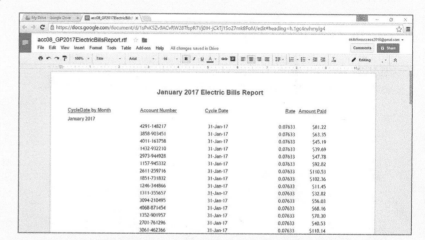

Figure 1

Access Chapter 8 folder. Be sure the **Save as type** box displays **JPEG file**. Name the file Last_First_acc08_GPSnip and then press Enter. **Close** [x] the Snipping Tool mark-up window.

11. Close all windows, and then submit the file as directed by your instructor.

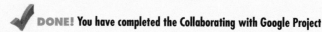

DONE! You have completed the Collaborating with Google Project

CHAPTER 9

Build Macros and Modify VBA Procedures

- ▶ Macros and Microsoft Visual Basic for Applications (VBA) are used to automate tasks such as opening and navigating forms or entering data.
- ▶ Macros perform built-in sets of instructions, and VBA programs perform instructions that you write yourself.
- ▶ You can automate tasks by storing actions in a macro. All the actions can then be performed by running the macro. For example, all of the tables in your database can be exported as

Excel workbooks by clicking a button on a form or a button added to the Quick Access Toolbar.

- ▶ Macros and VBA code can help you make decisions by testing conditions and then performing certain actions only when the conditions are true.
- ▶ While creating macros or VBA programs, you should frequently check that they perform as intended.

rangizzz / Fotolia

Aspen Falls City Hall

In this project, you will assist Amando Pettinelli, Outdoor Recreation Supervisor of Aspen Falls, to create macros and automate tasks using Visual Basic for Applications (VBA). Each year a triathlon is held and participants sign up to compete in the race. The fee to participate is $25.00 unless the racer lives in California. California residents only pay $15.00 to race in the triathlon.

Pettinelli wants to make macros that will automatically create an Excel file or HTML file that lists all triathlon participants and the fees collected from each racer. The macros must include comments so anyone using the database will know what each macro does and when the macro was written.

Using the Expression Builder, you will create a macro containing conditions. This macro will include message boxes that allow Pettinelli to choose which macros to run. The Export Racers table and the Fees query can be run at the same time, or Pettinelli can choose to run only the macro he needs.

In this project, you will create a button that will run a macro when clicked. You will also place conditions and comments in macros, and add Quick Access Toolbar buttons to macros. Macros will be converted to VBA, and you will create VBA procedures. Finally, you will debug VBA code, learn to work with statements and variables, and add conditions to VBA procedures. These customizations will allow Pettinelli to quickly download Excel or HTML files that contain the information he needs.

Outcome

Using the skills in this chapter, you will be able to build and test macros, add conditions and buttons to macros, test macros, create VBA procedures and edit the code, and add conditions to VBA procedures.

Objectives

9.1 Construct and test macros

9.2 Apply conditions and buttons to macros

9.3 Create VBA procedures and edit the code

9.4 Apply conditions to VBA procedures

Student data file needed for this chapter:

acc09_Races

You will save your files as:

Last_First_acc09_Races
Last_First_acc09_Fees_HTML
Last_First_acc09_Fees_Workbook
Last_First_acc09_Fees_Races_Snip

SKILLS

Skills 1–10 Training

At the end of this chapter, you will be able to:

Skill 1 Build and Test Client Macros

Skill 2 Add Comments and Reorder Macro Actions

Skill 3 Add Conditions to Macros

Skill 4 Test Macros with Conditions

Skill 5 Add Command Buttons That Run Macros

Skill 6 Add Quick Access Toolbar Buttons and Convert Macros to VBA

Skill 7 Create VBA Procedures

Skill 8 Edit VBA Code

Skill 9 Write VBA Statements and Work with Variables

Skill 10 Add Conditions to VBA Procedures

MORE SKILLS

Skill 11 Build Macros That Send Reports via E-Mail

Skill 12 Build Macros to Navigate Forms

Skill 13 Run Macros on Startup

Skill 14 Add Table Descriptions

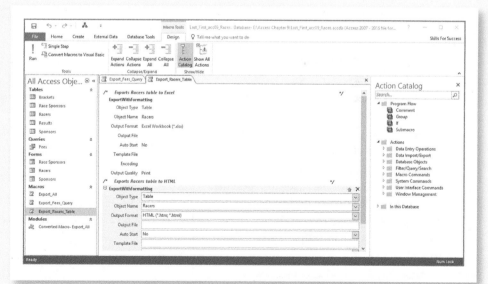

Access 2016, Windows 10, Microsoft Corporation

► A **macro** is an action or group of stored instructions used to automate tasks.

► A macro is created, saved, and named so that it can be used by any other database object for a repetitive task.

1. Start **Access 2016**, and then open the student data file **acc09_Races**. Use the **Save As** dialog box to create a **New folder** named Access Chapter 9 Save the database in the new folder as Last_First_acc09_ Races If necessary, enable the content.

2. On the **Create tab**, in the **Macros & Code group**, click the **Macro** button to display the **Macro Builder**.

3. In the **Action Catalog** pane, under **Actions**, expand **Data Import/Export**, and then double-click **ExportWithFormatting** to insert the action. Compare your screen with **Figure 1**.

> The ExportWithFomatting action displays a list of macro arguments needed to export database objects.

4. In the **ExportWithFormatting** action, click the **Object Type box arrow**, and then click **Query**.

5. Click the **Object Name box arrow**, and then click **Fees**.

6. Click the **Output Format box arrow**, and then click **Excel Workbook (*.xlsx)**.

> These macro arguments instruct the ExportWithFormatting action to export the Fees query as an Excel workbook.

7. Click **Save** 🔲, type Export_Fees_Query and then click **OK.** Compare your screen with **Figure 2**.

> After they are saved, client macros are listed in the Navigation Pane under Macros so that they can be accessed by other database objects.

■ Continue to the next page to complete the skill ▶

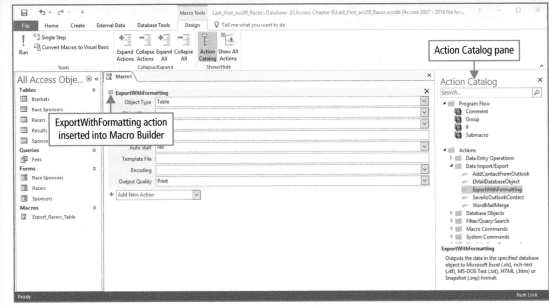

Figure 1

Access 2016, Windows 10, Microsoft Corporation

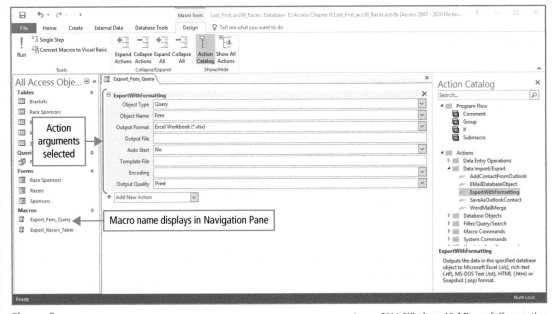

Figure 2

Access 2016, Windows 10, Microsoft Corporation

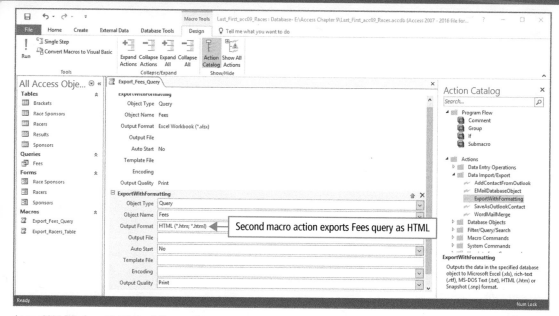

Access 2016, Windows 10, Microsoft Corporation

Figure 3

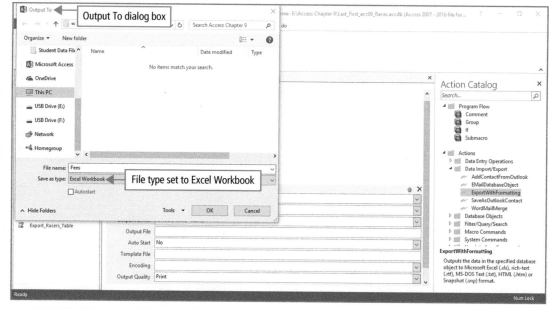

Access 2016, Windows 10, Microsoft Corporation

Figure 4

8. In the macro, click the **Add New Action arrow**, and then from the list, click **ExportWithFormatting** to insert a second query action.

   Macro actions can be selected from the Action Catalog pane or from the Add New Action box in the macro

9. In the second **ExportWithFormatting** action, repeat the techniques just practiced so that the action exports the **Query** named **Fees** as an **HTML (*.htm, *.html)** file. Compare your screen with Figure 3.

10. Click **Save** 🖫. On the **Design tab**, in the **Tools group**, click the **Run** button, and then compare your screen with Figure 4.

    If you receive an error message, click OK, and then carefully check that your macro actions and arguments match the previous steps.

    The Output To dialog box displays with the file type set to Excel Workbook, which indicates that the first macro action ran successfully.

11. In the **Output To** dialog box, click **Cancel** so that the query is not actually exported.

12. In the second **Output To** dialog box, verify that the **Save as type** is set to **HTML**, and then click **Cancel** so that the query is not actually exported.

    When building macros, it is a good idea to test early and often. This helps isolate and fix potential errors.

13. Keep the **Export_Fees_Query** open for the next skill.

■ **You have completed Skill 1 of 10**

▶ ***Comments*** are remarks added to a macro or VBA code to provide information to those writing or reviewing the macro or VBA code. ***Visual Basic for Applications (VBA)*** is a programming language designed to work within Microsoft Office Applications.

▶ Comments are ignored by Access when the macro or VBA code is run.

1. With the **Export_Fees_Query** open in Design view, click the first macro action to select it.

2. In the **Action Catalog** pane, under **Program Flow**, double-click **Comment**. In the comment box, type Exports Fees query to Excel Select the **Object Type** text box, and then compare your screen with **Figure 1**.

   Comments are colored green to set them apart from the macro actions. Comments begin with /* and end with */ to instruct Access to ignore all of the text between those symbols when the macro is run.

3. Point to the comment so that the **Move up**, **Move down**, and **Delete** icons display. Click **Move up** to move the comment above the first macro action.

   Comments should be displayed above each macro action.

4. Below the second action, click the **Add New Action arrow**, and then click **Comment** to insert a second comment. Type Exports Fees query to HTML

5. Repeat the technique just practiced to move the second comment between the first and second macro actions. Select the first action, and then compare your screen with **Figure 2**.

■ **Continue to the next page to complete the skill** ▶

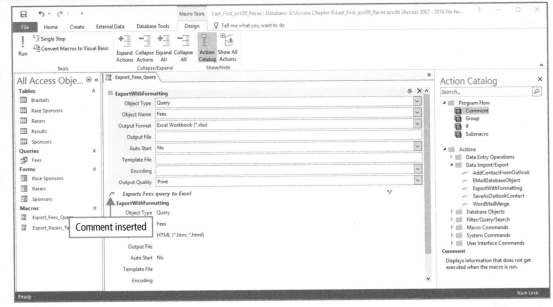

Figure 1

Access 2016, Windows 10, Microsoft Corporation

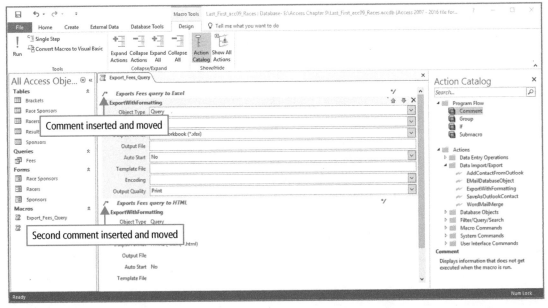

Figure 2

Access 2016, Windows 10, Microsoft Corporation

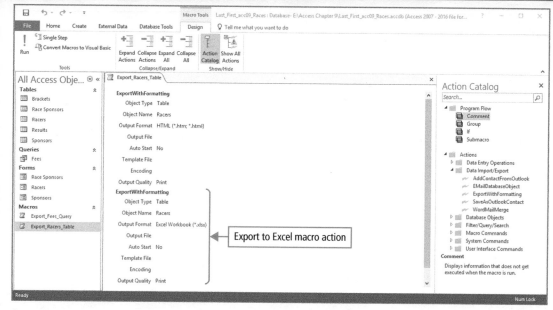

Access 2016, Windows 10, Microsoft Corporation

Figure 3

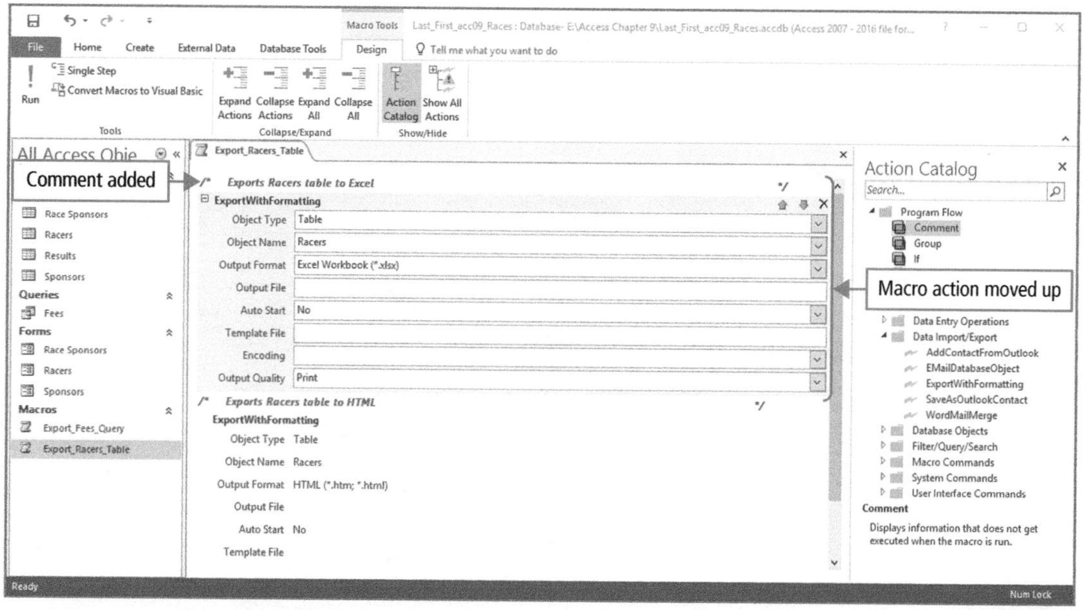

Access 2016, Windows 10, Microsoft Corporation

Figure 4

6. Click **Save** 🔲. Click **Run** to test that the comments have not affected the macro. In both **Output To** dialog boxes, click **Cancel**. **Close** ☒ the macro.

7. In the **Navigation Pane**, right-click **Export_Racers_Table**, and then click **Design View**. Compare your screen with Figure 3.

   Unless instructed otherwise, macro actions are performed in the order they are inserted in the macro. Here, the Racers table will be exported as an HTML file, and then exported as an Excel file.

8. In the macro, click to select the second macro action. Click **Move up**.

9. Use either technique practiced previously to insert a comment with the text Exports Racers table to Excel Move the comment above the first macro action.

10. Insert a second comment with the text Exports Racers table to HTML and then move the comment above the second macro. Select the first action, and then compare your screen with Figure 4.

11. Click **Save** 🔲. **Run** the macro to test that it exports the Racers table in the Excel and HTML file formats, and then in both **Output To** dialog boxes, click **Cancel**. **Close** ☒ the macro.

   If you accidentally clicked OK instead of Cancel when testing macros, you can delete any files created by the macros.

■ **You have completed Skill 2 of 10**

▶ Using message boxes and VBA expressions, you can ask for input and then have the macro perform different actions based on the results of that input.

1. On the **Create tab**, in the **Macros & Code group**, click the **Macro** button.

2. In the **Action Catalog** pane, under **Program Flow**, double-click **If**, and then compare your screen with **Figure 1**.

   An **If action** added to the macro provides a conditional expression and then performs an action or series of actions only when the result of the condition is true or false.

3. To the right of the **Conditional expression** box, click the **Builder** button 📄 to open the **Expression Builder**.

4. In the **Expression Builder** dialog box, under **Expression Elements**, expand **Functions**, and then click **Built-In Functions**. Under **Expression Categories**, scroll down, and then click **Messages**.

5. Under **Expression Values**, double-click **MsgBox**, and then compare your screen with **Figure 2**.

   The Expression Builder inserts the MsgBox action, followed by the arguments used by the MsgBox action.

6. In the expression just inserted, click the **<<prompt>>** argument, and then, including the quotation marks, type "Export Fees query?"

   The *prompt* argument is the message that displays in the message box.

7. Click the **<<buttons>>** argument, and then type 4

   The number 4 instructs the macro to display a message box with two buttons—*Yes* and *No*.

▪ **Continue to the next page to complete the skill** ▶

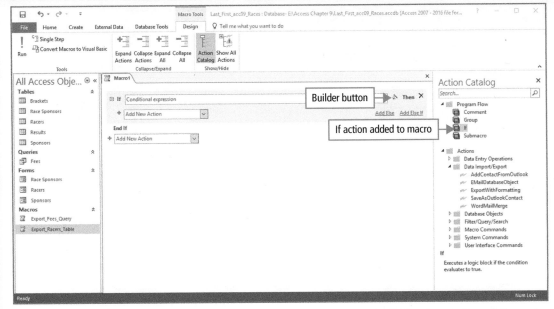

Figure 1

Access 2016, Windows 10, Microsoft Corporation

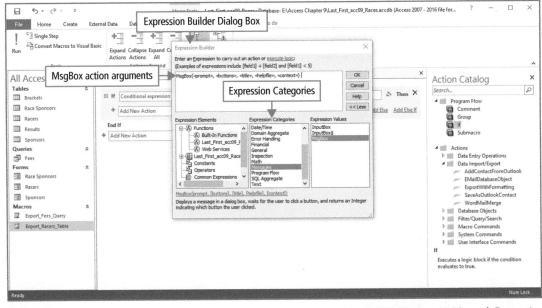

Figure 2

Access 2016, Windows 10, Microsoft Corporation

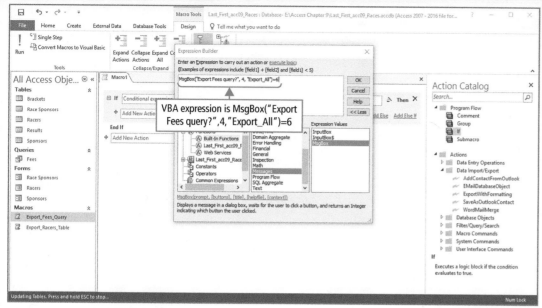

Access 2016, Windows 10, Microsoft Corporation

Figure 3

Access 2016, Windows 10, Microsoft Corporation

Figure 4

8. Click the **<<title>>** argument, and then type "Export_All" To the right of "Export_All", delete all the remaining text, commas, and spaces. Do not delete the closing parenthesis.

9. Click to the right of the closing parenthesis, and then type =6 Compare your screen with **Figure 3**.

When the Yes button is clicked, the numeric value 6 is sent to the expression, and the condition in the expression is true. When the No button is clicked, the numeric value is not 6, and the condition is false.

10. Click **OK**. If an error message displays, close it, open the **Expression Builder**, and then carefully check your typing. Be sure to include the quotation marks, commas, and parentheses as described previously.

11. Click **Save** 🔲. In the **Save As** dialog box, type Export_All and then press [Enter].

12. If necessary, click to select the **If** action. Above the **End If** statement, in the **If action** box, click the **Add New Action box arrow**, scroll down, and then click **RunMacro** to insert the action within the If action.

13. Click the **Macro Name arrow**, and then click **Export_Fees_Query**.

14. Below the **End If** statement, click the **Add New Action arrow**, and then click **If** to insert a second If action. In the lower **If** box, type MsgBox("Export Racers table?", 4,"Export_All")=6

15. Using the technique just practiced, in the second **If** action, add a new action that runs the **Export_Racers_Table** macro. Click **Save** 🔲. Click a blank area, and then compare your screen with **Figure 4**.

■ **You have completed Skill 3 of 10**

▶ When testing macros with conditions, all possible outcomes should be tested.

▶ For conditions with Yes/No message boxes, both the Yes and No buttons should be tested.

1. On the **Design tab**, in the **Tools group**, click **Run**, and then compare your screen with **Figure 1**.

    The message box title, prompt, and buttons specified in the expression display.

2. Click **Yes** so that the Export_Fees_Query runs. In the **Output To** dialog box, verify the file type is Excel Workbook, and then click **Cancel**. In the second **Output To** dialog box, verify the file type is HTML, and then click **Cancel**.

    Recall that the file does not actually need to be saved to test if the macro is running correctly.

3. Compare the second message box that displays on your screen with **Figure 2**.

4. Click **Yes** to run the **Racers** table export. In both **Output To** dialog boxes, click **Cancel**.

5. Run the macro again. In the first message box, click **Yes**.

6. In the **Output To** dialog box, navigate to your **Access Chapter 9** folder. In the **File name** box, type Last_First_acc09_Fees_Workbook and then click **OK**. In the second **Output To** dialog box, type Last_First_acc09_Fees_HTML Click **OK**.

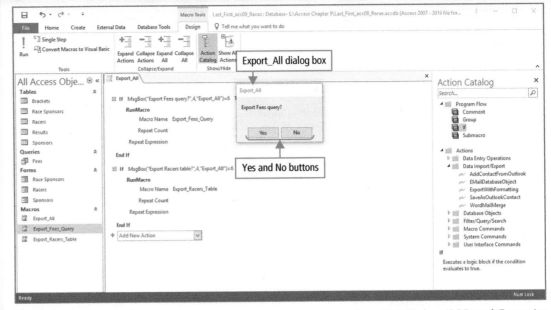

Figure 1

Access 2016, Windows 10, Microsoft Corporation

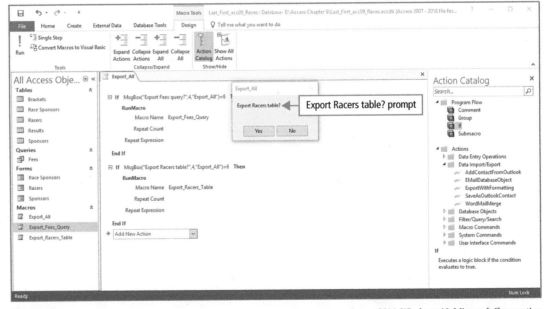

Figure 2

Access 2016, Windows 10, Microsoft Corporation

■ **Continue to the next page to complete the skill**

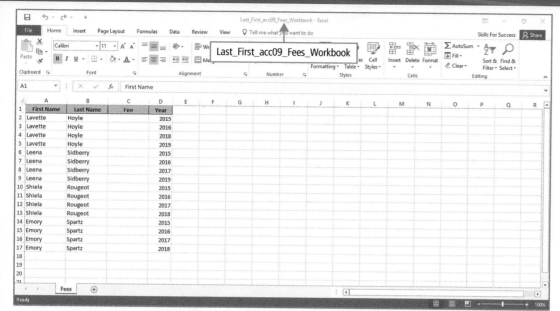

Excel 2016, Windows 10, Microsoft Corporation

Figure 3

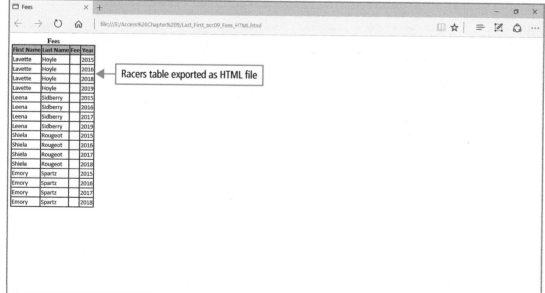

Microsoft Edge, Windows 10, Microsoft Corporation

Figure 4

7. In the **Export_All** message box asking to export the **Racers** table, click **No**.

8. **Close** ☒ the macro.

9. Click **File Explorer** ▭, and then navigate to your **Access Chapter 9** folder. Verify that the Excel file and web page were saved in the **Access Chapter 9** folder.

10. In the displayed folder window, double-click **Last_First_acc09_Fees_Workbook**. If necessary, **Maximize** the window, and then compare your screen with Figure 3.

The names and contact information for all racers are displayed in an Excel worksheet.

11. **Close** Excel.

12. From your **Access Chapter 9** folder, double-click **Last_First_acc09_Fees_ HTML**, and then if necessary **Maximize** the window. Compare your screen with Figure 4.

The names and contact information for all racers are displayed in an HTML worksheet.

13. **Close** ☒ your web browser.

14. **Close** ☒ **File Explorer**.

■ **You have completed Skill 4 of 10**

▶ Buttons can be added to forms, and actions can then be assigned to the buttons. For example, a button can be set to run a macro when it is clicked.

1. In the **Navigation Pane**, right-click the **Racers** form, and then click **Design View**.

2. On the **Design tab**, in the **Control group**, click the **Button** button. Point to the **4 inch** horizontal grid line and three grid dots below the **Detail** bar, and then click one time.

3. In the **Command Button Wizard**, under **Categories**, click **Miscellaneous**, and then under **Actions**, click **Run Macro**. Compare your screen with **Figure 1**.

   Many different actions can be assigned to a button. Buttons are used to open forms, run macros, navigate and edit records, or open reports.

4. Click **Next**, and then under **What macro would you like the command button to run?**, verify that **Export_All** is selected.

5. Click **Next**. Select the **Text** option button, and then in the **Text** box, replace the existing text with Export Data Compare your screen with **Figure 2**.

■ **Continue to the next page to complete the skill**

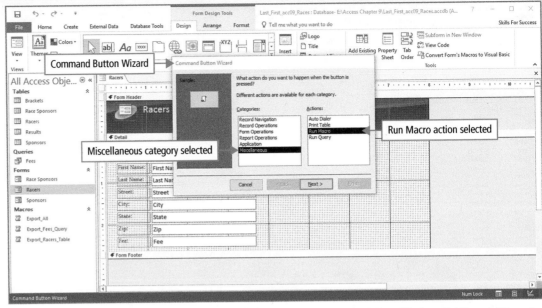

Figure 1

Access 2016, Windows 10, Microsoft Corporation

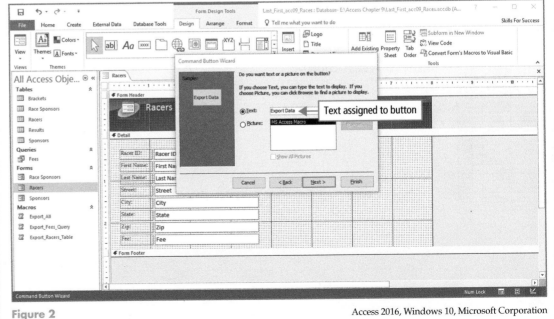

Figure 2

Access 2016, Windows 10, Microsoft Corporation

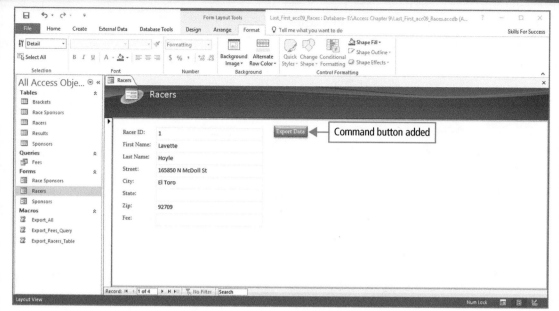

Access 2016, Windows 10, Microsoft Corporation

Figure 3

Field		Value
Racer ID		Accept Auto Number
First Name		Stephen
Last Name		Cell
Street	← Form data	15 Canadian Way
City		Aspen Falls
State		CA
Zip		93463

Access 2016, Windows 10, Microsoft Corporation

Figure 4

6. Click **Next**, and then in the **Name** box, type cmdExport_Racers

> Programmers often assign meaningful names to buttons and other objects so that they can identify them when they write VBA code. The *cmd* prefix helps programmers identify the type of object—here, a command button. Object names cannot have spaces.

7. Click **Finish** to complete the wizard and to insert the button.

8. Switch to Layout view, and then click the **Export Data** button. On the **Format tab**, in the **Control Formatting group**, click the **Quick Styles** button. In the gallery, click the sixth choice in the sixth row—**Intense Effect - Aqua, Accent 5**. Click a blank area of the form, and then compare your screen with Figure 3.

9. Switch to Form view. On the Navigation bar, click the **New (blank) record** button ▶. Use the form to enter the record shown in Figure 4.

> The *Fee* field has intentionally been left blank.

10. Click the **Export Data** button. In both message boxes displayed by the macro, click **No**.

11. **Save** 🖫 and **Close** ✕ the form.

■ **You have completed Skill 5 of 10**

▶ Buttons that perform commonly used Access commands can be placed on the Quick Access Toolbar, also known as the QAT.

▶ QAT buttons also run macros when they are clicked.

1. Click the **File tab**, and then click **Options**.

2. On the left side of the **Access Options** dialog box, click **Quick Access Toolbar**, and then compare your screen with Figure 1.

3. Click the **Choose commands from arrow**, and then from the list, click **Macros**.

4. Click the **Customize Quick Access Toolbar arrow**, and then from the list, click the choice that displays the path and name of your database file. Compare your screen with Figure 2.

> The QAT can be modified for all databases or just the currently opened database. Here, the QAT of the current database will be changed.

5. In the list of available macros, click **<Separator>**, and then click the **Add** button.

> A *separator*—a small vertical or horizontal line used to separate choices in a list, toolbar, or menu—will be added to the QAT.

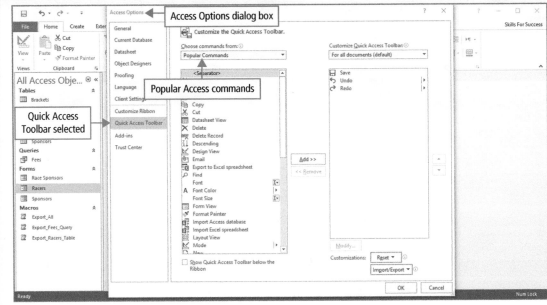

Figure 1

Access 2016, Windows 10, Microsoft Corporation

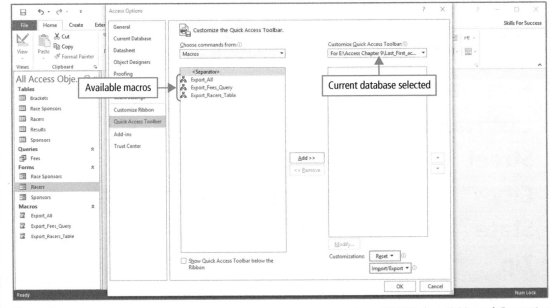

Figure 2

Access 2016, Windows 10, Microsoft Corporation

■ **Continue to the next page to complete the skill**

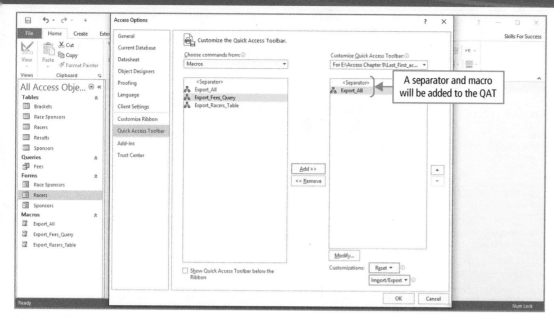

A separator and macro will be added to the QAT

Access 2016, Windows 10, Microsoft Corporation

Figure 3

6. In the list of available macros, click **Export_ All**, and then click the **Add** button. Compare your screen with **Figure 3**.

7. Click **OK** to close the dialog box. On the **Quick Access Toolbar**, to the right of the last separator, click the macro button to verify that the **Export_All** macro runs. In both of the displayed messages, click **No**.

8. Create a full-screen snip, **Save** it in your **Access Chapter 9** folder as Last_First_ acc09_Fees_Races_Snip and then close the **Snipping Tool** window.

9. Open the **Export_All** macro in Design view. Repeat the techniques practiced previously to add a comment. In the **Comment** box, using your own name, type Written by Your Name Press ⏎ Enter, and then type the current date in the format: *dd/mm/yyyy*.

10. Click the **Move Up** button as needed to move the comment above the first macro action.

11. Click **Save** 🖫. On the **Design tab**, in the **Tools group**, click **Convert Macros to Visual Basic**. In the **Convert macro: Export_All** dialog box, click **Convert**. In the message box, click **OK**.

12. In the **Project** pane, under **Modules**, double-click **Converted Macro-Export_ All**, and then compare your screen with **Figure 4**.

13. Click the **File menu**, and then click **Close** and **Return to Microsoft Access**. **Close** ☒ the **Export_All** macro.

■ **You have completed Skill 6 of 10**

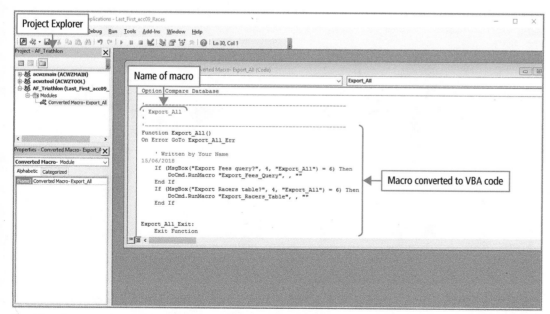

Project Explorer

Name of macro

Macro converted to VBA code

Visual Basic for Applications, Access 2016, Windows 10, Microsoft Corporation

Figure 4

▶ VBA is a subset of the Microsoft Visual Basic (VB) programming language and is used to write your own macros. *Programs* are instructions that tell a computer what to do—that run while you work with Office applications.

1. Open the **Racers** form, and then notice that the Fee field has no data.

2. Switch to Design view, and then on the **Design tab**, in the **Tools group**, click the **Property Sheet** button. On the form, click the **State** text box to display its properties. Click the property sheet **Event tab**, click in the **On Lost Focus box**, and then compare your screen with **Figure 1**.

> The property sheet Event tab displays all the *events*—actions, such as mouse clicks or typing, detected by a running program—that are associated with the control. Here, the On Lost Focus event detects when the insertion point moves out of the *State* text box.

3. On the property sheet **Event tab**, click the **On Lost Focus Build** button, and then compare your screen with **Figure 2**.

> The Choose Builder dialog box has three options for writing stored instructions: Macro Builder, Expression Builder, and Code Builder.

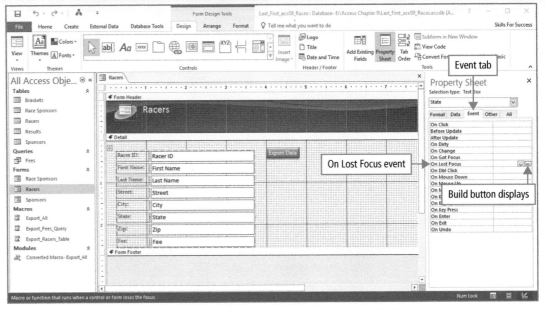

Figure 1

Access 2016, Windows 10, Microsoft Corporation

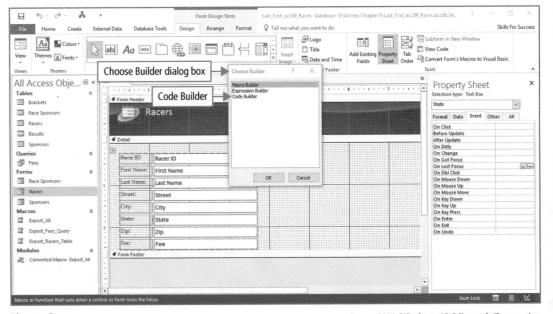

Figure 2

Access 2016, Windows 10, Microsoft Corporation

■ **Continue to the next page to complete the skill**

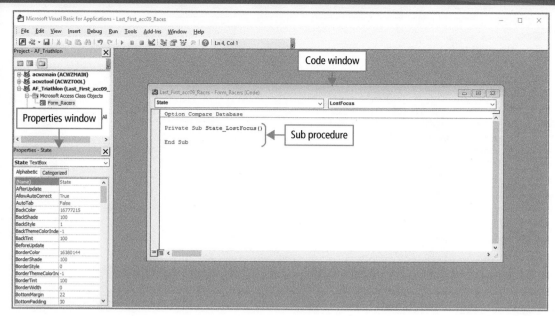

Visual Basic for Applications, Access 2016, Windows 10, Microsoft Corporation

Figure 3

4. In the **Choose Builder** dialog box, click **Code Builder**, and then click **OK**. If the **Converted Macro-Export_All** window is opened, click the window, and then click **Close** ☒. Take a moment to familiarize yourself with the Microsoft Visual Basic window, as shown in Figure 3.

The **Visual Basic Editor (VBE)** is a program for writing VBA program code.

The center of the screen is the **Code window** in which you write and edit VBA code. Here, the Code window displays the State_LostFocus **sub procedure**—a group of related statements that is a subset of a macro. Sub procedures are often referred to as subs or procedures.

In the upper left corner of the VBE window, the Project Explorer is used to manage code windows. In the lower left corner, the Properties pane lists the current properties for each database object.

5. On the Standard toolbar, click the **Save** button.

This action saves the VBA code, but does not save any changes made to the form.

6. On the Standard toolbar, click the **View Microsoft Office Access** button, and then compare with Figure 4.

The form window is the active window, and the Microsoft Visual Basic window displays as a button on the taskbar.

The On Lost Focus property displays *[Event Procedure]* to indicate that a sub procedure will run whenever the State control loses focus.

7. Save ☐ the form and keep it open for the next skill.

■ **You have completed Skill 7 of 10**

Access 2016, Windows 10, Microsoft Corporation

Figure 4

▶ In VBA, comments begin with a single quotation mark.

▶ Programmers routinely test their programs in a process called debugging. To **debug** is to find and fix errors in programming code and make sure the program functions as intended.

1. With the **Racers** form open in Design view, in the property sheet, click the **On Lost Focus Build** button to return to the VBE window. Alternatively, you can switch between windows by pressing `Alt` + `F11`.

2. In the **Code** window, with the insertion point below *Private Sub State_LostFocus( )*, type the following comments. Be sure each line begins with a single quotation mark:

   'Updates the Fee field based on the value in the State field

   'Written by Your Name

3. Press `Enter`, and then verify that the comments display in green, as shown in **Figure 1**.

4. Click **Save** 🖫, and then press `Alt` + `F11` to return to the form. Switch to Form view. Click in the **State** text box, and then press `Tab`. Compare your screen with **Figure 2**.

   The code has only comments, so screen elements were not changed, the program ran successfully, and the focus moved to the Zip field without generating an error.

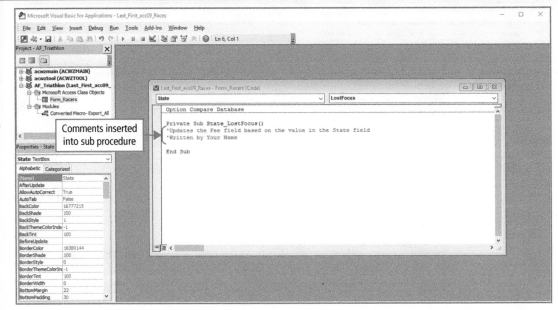

Figure 1

Comments inserted into sub procedure

Visual Basic for Applications, Access 2016, Windows 10, Microsoft Corporation

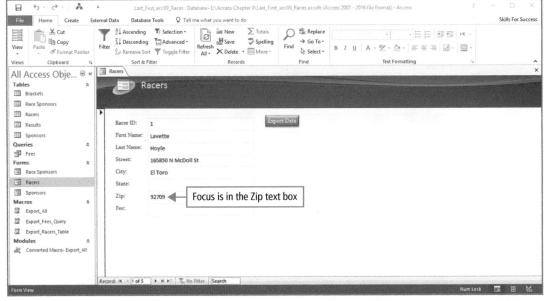

Focus is in the Zip text box

Figure 2

Access 2016, Windows 10, Microsoft Corporation

▪ **Continue to the next page to complete the skill** ▶

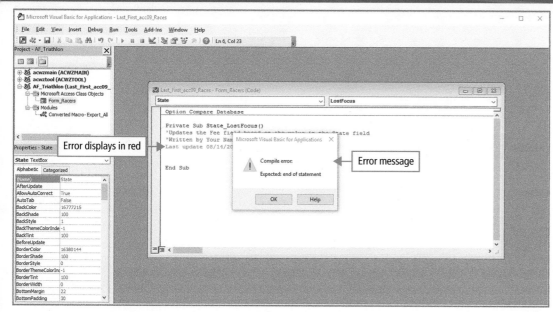

Visual Basic for Applications, Access 2016, Windows 10, Microsoft Corporation

Figure 3

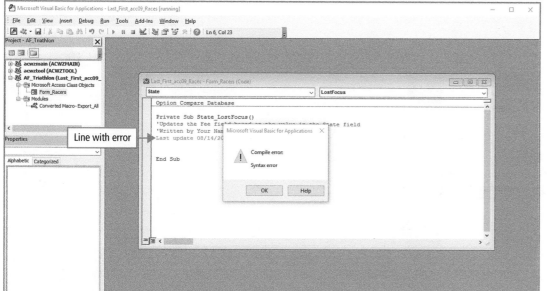

Visual Basic for Applications, Access 2016, Windows 10, Microsoft Corporation

Figure 4

5. Switch to Design view. In the property sheet, click the **On Lost Focus Build** button to return to the VBE window.

6. In the blank line below your name, type the following without a single quotation mark: Last update 08/14/2018 Press Enter, and then compare your screen with Figure 3.

7. Read the message, and then click **OK**. Press Alt + F11 to return to the form. Switch to Form view. Click in the **State** text box, press Tab, and then compare your screen with Figure 4.

    A message displays, and in the Code window, the line with the error is highlighted. The code has a *syntax error*—a code error that violates the rules of a programming language. Here, the error is that a comment does not begin with a single quotation mark.

8. Click **OK**. On the Standard toolbar, click the **Reset** button to stop the code from running. In the VBE window, to the left of *Last update 08/14/2018*, insert a single quotation mark ('), and then click **Save**.

9. Press Alt + F11 to return to the form. Switch to Form view. Click in the **State** text box, and then press Tab to verify that the focus moved to the Zip field without creating an error. Keep this form open for the next skill.

    Whenever you see error messages when working with VBA code, you can apply these techniques to reset the procedure. You can then carefully check your typing and test your code again.

■ **You have completed Skill 8 of 10**

 **WATCH** SKILL 9.9

▶ A *statement* is a line in a program that contains instructions for the computer.

▶ Programs often need to store values in the computer's random access memory (RAM). *Variables* are programming objects that refer to the values stored in RAM.

1. Switch to the **Visual Basic Editor Code** window, click at the end of the last comment, and then press Enter two times.

2. Type the comment 'Declare variable and then press Enter.

3. Type the statement Dim strState As String and then press Enter two times. Verify that Dim and As String are blue, as shown in **Figure 1**.

   Dim, As, and *String* are **keywords**—words in a programming language that have a particular meaning or purpose.

   strState is the name of the variable, and As String determines the variable's **data type**—the type of data that can be stored in a variable such as numbers, characters, or dates.

   The *str* prefix indicates to the programmer that the variable will store a **string**—a sequence of either alpha or alphanumeric characters. Many programmers practice **Hungarian notation**—a naming convention in which the prefixes indicate the type of data or type of object.

4. Type the comment 'Assigns the State field value to the variable and then press Enter.

5. Type the statement strState = Forms! Racers!State Press Enter, and then compare your screen with **Figure 2**.

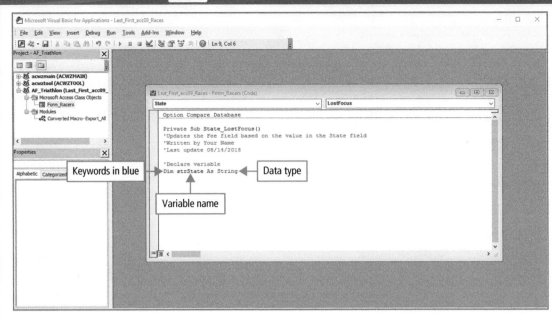

Figure 1　　　　　Visual Basic for Applications, Access 2016, Windows 10, Microsoft Corporation

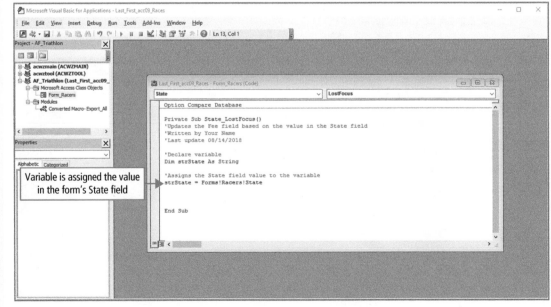

Figure 2　　　　　Visual Basic for Applications, Access 2016, Windows 10, Microsoft Corporation

■ **Continue to the next page to complete the skill**

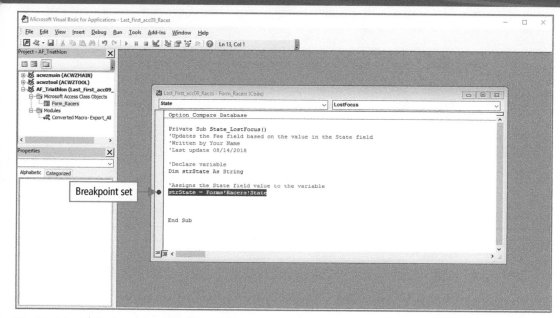

Visual Basic for Applications, Access 2016, Windows 10, Microsoft Corporation

Figure 3

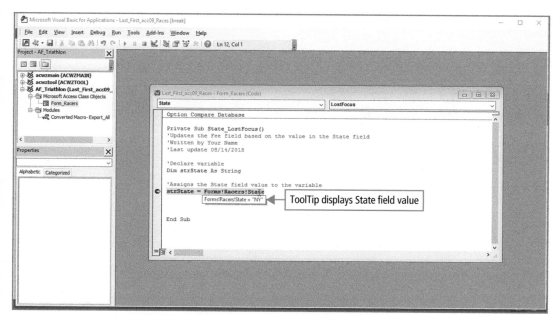

Visual Basic for Applications, Access 2016, Windows 10, Microsoft Corporation

Figure 4

6. In the **Code** window, click in the margin to the left of the statement *strState = Forms!Racers!State*. Compare your screen with **Figure 3**.

> The red dot indicates that a **breakpoint**— an intentional stop or pause inserted into a program—has been set. When the program runs, it will stop at the breakpoint so that the programmer can more precisely test the code.

7. Click **Reset**. Click **Save** ⊟, and then press [Alt] + [F11] to return to the form. If necessary, switch to Form view.

8. In the first record, type NY in the **State** field, and then press [Tab].

> The Microsoft Visual Basic window opens and the line with the breakpoint is highlighted.

9. Point to the text *Forms!Racers!State*. Read the ToolTip to verify that the **State** field equals *NY*, as shown in **Figure 4**.

10. Point to *strState* and notice the variable has not been assigned a value, as indicated by the ToolTip *strState = ""*.

11. From the **Debug** menu, click **Step Into**. Point to strState and notice the variable has been assigned the correct value, as indicated by the ToolTip *strState = "NY"*.

> In this manner, **logical errors**—errors where the program runs but does not produce the intended results—can be found. Here, the program is functioning as intended—the variable is storing the value entered into the State field in RAM.

12. On the Standard toolbar, click the **Reset** button. From the **Debug** menu, click **Clear All Breakpoints**. Click **Save** ⊟. Keep this open for the next skill.

■ **You have completed Skill 9 of 10**

▶ To make decisions, programs rely on **control structures**—methods that perform logical tests and perform actions when the conditions are true.

▶ The **If Then Else control structure** tests if a condition is true. When the condition is true, the program runs one set of statements. Otherwise, a different set of statements is run.

---

1. In the **Code** window, click in the first blank line below *strState = Forms!Racers!State*, and then press [Enter].

2. Type the comment 'Assigns a fee based on the state and then press [Enter].

3. Type the following control structure indenting the second statement, with the [Tab] key, as indicated, press [Enter], and then compare your screen with Figure 1.

   If strState = "CA" Then
       Forms!Racers!Fee = 15
   End If

   Here, the If statement tests if the variable—*strState*—is equal to CA. When it is, the Fee field will be changed to 15. The indented line adds **white space**—optional spacing that visually organizes the code to make it more readable by programmers.

4. Click **Save** 🖫, and then press [Alt] + [F11] to return to the form.

5. In the first record of the **Racers** form, change the **State** to CA and then press [Tab]. Compare your screen with Figure 2.

   The VBA code assigned the value *CA* to the variable, and then tested if the variable was equal to *CA*. This condition was true, so the statement to assign a fee of 15 was executed.

■ **Continue to the next page to complete the skill** ▶

Figure 1

Visual Basic for Applications, Access 2016, Windows 10, Microsoft Corporation

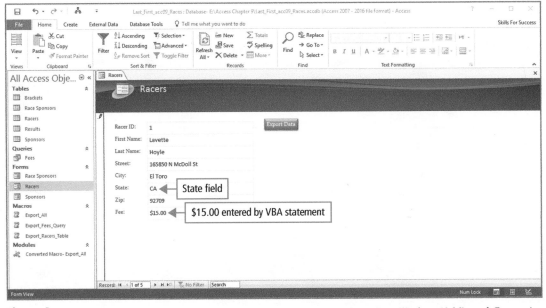

Figure 2

Access 2016, Windows 10, Microsoft Corporation

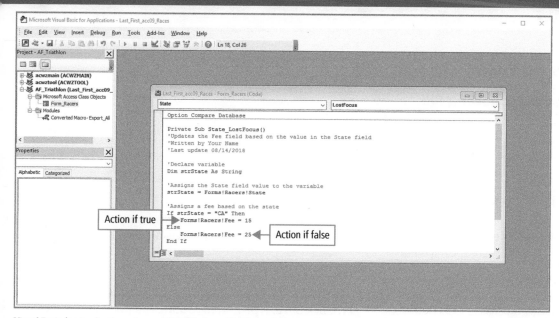

Action if true

Action if false

Visual Basic for Applications, Access 2016, Windows 10, Microsoft Corporation

Figure 3

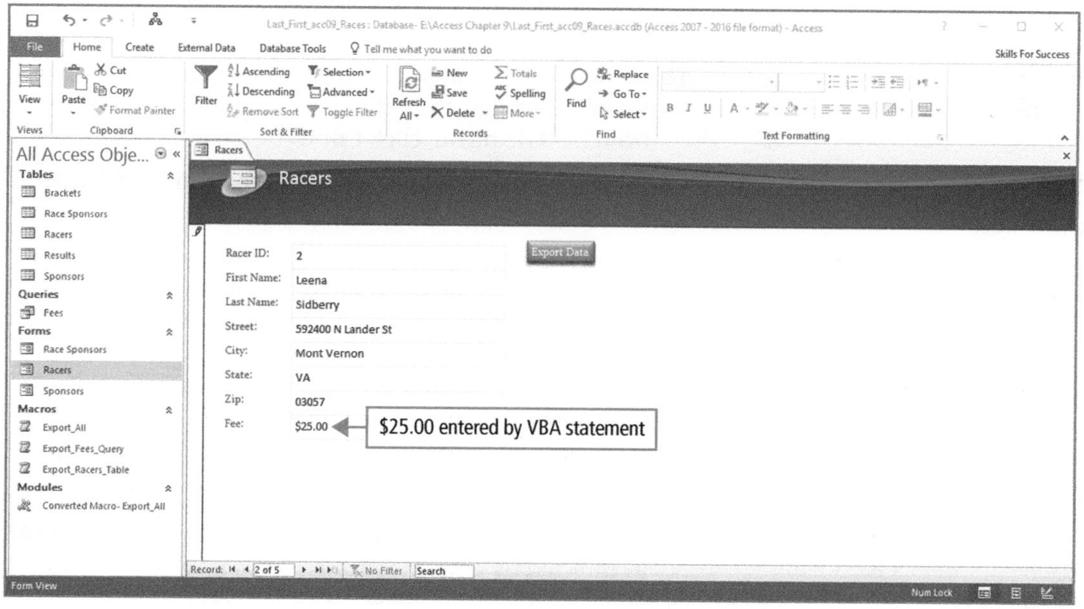

6. Press [Alt] + [F11] to return to the VBE window. In the **Code** window, click to the right of the text *Forms!Racers!Fee = 15*, press [Enter], and then press [Backspace].

7. Type the following statements, indenting as indicated:

   Else

       Forms!Racers!Fee = 25

8. Carefully compare your code with **Figure 3**.

   The Else statement specifies what statement should execute when the If condition is *not* true. Here, when the state is not *CA*, the value 25 will be entered into the Fee field.

9. Click **Save** 🖫, and then press [Alt] + [F11] to return to the form.

10. With the **Racers** form in Form view, navigate to the second record, and then in the **State** field, type VA Press [Tab], and then verify that a fee of $25.00 is entered into the Fee field, as shown in **Figure 4**.

11. Repeat the technique just practiced to change the state for record **3** to CA and the state for record **4** to MI

12. In the Navigation bar, click the **New (blank) record** button, and then enter your own name and address into the form.

13. Press [Alt] + [F11] to return to the VBE window. If instructed to print this project, from the **File** menu, click **Print**, and then click **OK. Close** ⊠ the **Microsoft Visual Basic** window.

14. **Close** ⊠ the **Racers** form and then **Close** Access. Submit your file as directed by your instructor.

   ✔ **DONE! You have completed Skill 10 of 10, and your database is complete!**

$25.00 entered by VBA statement

Access 2016, Windows 10, Microsoft Corporation

Figure 4

More Skills 11

Build Macros That Send Reports via E-Mail

To complete this project, you will need the following file:

- acc09_MS11Outings

You will save your file as:

- Last_First_acc09_MS11Outings

▶ To complete this project, Outlook needs to be installed and configured to work with your e-mail account.

▶ A macro can be created that sends reports via e-mail by exporting the report to Microsoft Outlook.

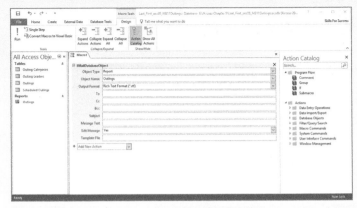

Figure 1   Access 2016, Windows 10, Microsoft Corporation

---

1. Start **Access 2016**, and then open the student data file **acc09_MS11Outings**. Click the **File** tab, and then save the file as an **Access Database** in your **Access Chapter 9** folder as Last_First_acc09_MS11Outings If necessary, enable the content.

2. Display the **Create tab**, and then in the **Macros & Code group**, click the **Macro** button.

3. In the macro, click the **Add New Action box arrow**, and then click **EMailDatabaseObject**.

4. Click the **Object Type arrow**, and then click **Report**.

5. Click the **Object Name arrow**, and then click **Outings**.

6. Click the **Output Format arrow**, and then click **Rich Text Format** (*.rtf). Compare your screen with **Figure 1**.

    With the Rich Text Format, the e-mail message will retain most of the formatting in the Access report.

7. In the **To box**, type your own e-mail address. If asked by your instructor, in the Cc box, type your instructor's e-mail address.

8. In the **Subject** box, type Outings Report from Chapter 9

9. In the **Message Text** box, type Dear Todd, Please review our latest outings. If you have any questions, then please do not hesitate to contact Julia Wagner at (809) 555-1015 or jwagner@aspenfalls.org

10. In the macro, click the **Add New Action box arrow**, and then click **Comment**. In the **Comment** box, type Created by First Last

11. Click **Save**, type E-Mail_Outings_Report, and then click **OK**.

12. On the **Design tab**, in the **Tools group**, click **Convert Macros to Visual Basic**. Click **Convert**, and then click **OK**.

13. In the **Project Explorer**, double-click **Converted Macro-E-mail_Outings_Report**. If you are printing this project, from the **File** menu, click **Print**.

14. From the **File** menu, click **Close and Return to Microsoft Access**.

15. If you have an Outlook Express account on your computer, click the **Design tab**, and then in the **Tools group**, click **Run**. Wait a few moments for the macro to prepare the message and for Outlook to display an e-mail window. If an error message displays, Outlook may not be configured to work with your e-mail address. If so, close all messages.

16. In the **Outlook Message** window, click the **Send** button.

17. **Close** the macro, and then **Close** Access. Submit your file as directed by your instructor.

■ **You have completed More Skills 11**

More Skills 12

Build Macros to Navigate Forms

To complete this project, you will need the following file:

- acc09_MS12Police

You will save your file as:

- Last_First_acc09_MS12Police

▶ A macro can automate the steps needed to open a form and navigate to a new, blank record.

1. Start **Access 2016**, and then open the student data file **acc09_MS12Police**. Save the file in your **Access Chapter 9** folder as Last_First_acc09_MS12Police If necessary, enable the content.

2. On the **Create tab**, in the **Macros & Code group**, click the **Macro** button.

3. Click the **Add New Action arrow**, scroll down the list, and then click **OpenForm**.

4. In **OpenForm**, click the **Form Name arrow**, and then click **Police Awards**.

5. Click the **Add New Action arrow**, scroll down, and then click **GoToRecord**.

6. Click the **Object Type arrow**, and then click **Form**.

7. Click the **Object Name arrow**, and then click **Police Awards**.

8. Click the **Record arrow**, and then click **New**. Compare your screen with **Figure 1**.

9. Click **Save**, and then in the **Save As** dialog box, type Award_Form_Entry Click **OK**.

10. On the **Design tab**, in the **Tools group**, click **Run**. Compare your screen with **Figure 2**.

    The Police Awards form opens with a new blank record displayed.

11. Click the **Award_Form_Entry** macro tab. Click the **Add New Action arrow**, and then click **Comment**. Type the following comment, using your own name Prepared by First Last

12. Click **Save**, and then **Close** the macro. **Close** the form, and then **Close** Access. Submit the file as directed by your instructor.

■ **You have completed More Skills 12**

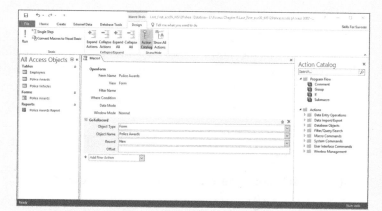

Access 2016, Windows 10, Microsoft Corporation   **Figure 1**

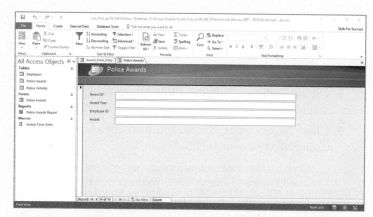

Access 2016, Windows 10, Microsoft Corporation   **Figure 2**

More Skills 13

Run Macros on Startup

To complete this project, you will need the following file:

- acc09_MS13Harvest

You will save your file as:

- Last_First_acc09_MS13Harvest

▶ *Startup macros*—macros that run automatically when an Access database is opened—can be used to automate common startup tasks such as opening forms or running queries.

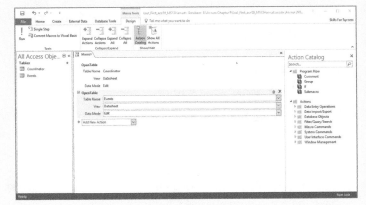

Figure 1   Access 2016, Windows 10, Microsoft Corporation

1. Start **Access 2016**, and then open the student data file **acc09_MS13Harvest**. Click the **File** tab, and then save the file as an **Access Database** in your **Access Chapter 9** folder as Last_First_acc09_MS13Harvest If necessary, enable the content.

2. Click the **Create tab**, and then in the **Macros & Code group**, click the **Macro** button.

3. Click the **Add New Action box arrow**, scroll down the list, and then click **OpenTable**.

4. Click the **Table Name arrow**, and then click **Coordinator**.

5. Click the **Add New Action arrow**, scroll down, and then click **OpenTable**.

6. Click the **Table Name arrow**, and then click **Events**. Compare your screen with **Figure 1**.

7. Click **Save**, and then in the **Save As** dialog box, type AutoExec and then click **OK**.

   For a macro to run when the database is opened, it must be saved with the name *AutoExec*.

8. On the **Design tab**, in the **Tools group**, click **Run**. **Close** the tables and the macro.

9. **Close** Access. Start **Access**, and then open **Last_First_acc09_MS13Harvest**. Compare your screen with **Figure 2**.

   When the database opens, any macro with the name AutoExec runs. Here, the Coordinator and Events tables were opened by the AutoExec macro.

10. In the **Navigation Pane**, click the **AutoExec** macro. Right-click, and then click **Design View**.

Figure 2   Access 2016, Windows 10, Microsoft Corporation

11. Click the **Add New Action box arrow**, click **Comment**, and then type the following comment using your own name Prepared by First Last

12. Click **Save**, and then **Close** the macro and tables. **Close** Access. Submit the file as directed by your instructor.

- **You have completed More Skills 13**

More Skills ⑭

Add Table Descriptions

To complete this project, you will need the following file:

- acc09_MS14Art

You will save your file as:

- Last_First_acc09_MS14Art

▶ Table descriptions identify the use and purpose of a table.

1. Start **Access 2016**, and then open the student data file **acc09_MS14Art**. Click the **File** tab, and then save the file as an **Access Database** in your **Access Chapter 9** folder as Last_First_acc09_MS14Art If necessary, enable the content.

2. Right-click the **Art Class Categories** table, and then click **Design View**. In the *Description* row, click in the **Description (Optional)** property.

3. Type Describes the purpose of the course. and then click **Save**. **Close** the table.

4. Open the **Art Class Sections** table in Design view. In the **Class Title** row, in the **Description (Optional)** property, click to the right of the word *Key*. Press Space, and then type Title of the course In the **Fee** row, in the **Description (Optional)** property, type Cost of the course Compare your screen with **Figure 1**.

5. **Save** and **Close** the table. In the Navigation Pane, right-click the **Art Instructors** table, and then click **Table Properties**. In the **Description** text box type This table contains Art Instructor information Click **Apply**.

6. Open the **Art Classes** table in Design view. In the **Category Description** property, type Class Category

7. In the **Description** row's **Description** property, type Explanation of the course

8. In the **Length Description** property, type Duration of the course

9. **Save** the table, and then compare your screen with **Figure 2**.

10. **Close** the table. Submit the file as directed by your Instructor.

- **You have completed More Skills 14**

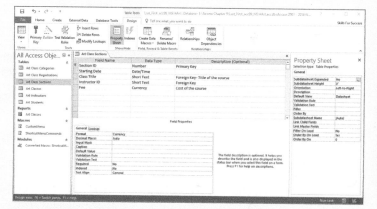

Access 2016, Windows 10, Microsoft Corporation

Figure 1

Access 2016, Windows 10, Microsoft Corporation

Figure 2

The following table summarizes the **SKILLS AND PROCEDURES** covered in this chapter.

Skill	Task	Step	Icon
1	Create a macro	Create tab → Macros & Code group → Macro → Action Catalog Pane	
2	Export with formatting	Add New Action arrow → ExportWithFormatting → Select Object type → Select Object Name → Select export format	
2	Add comment to a macro	Design view → Action Catalog pane → Program Flow → Comment	
2	Add conditions to a macro	Create tab → Macros & Code group → Macro → Action Catalog pane → Program Flow → If → Builder button	
3	Add built-in function	Expression Builder → Expression Elements → Functions → Built-in Functions → Expression categories	
4	Run a macro	Design tab → Tools group → Run	
5	Add macro Command button	Open Form in Design view → Design tab → Controls group → Button button → Command Button Wizard → Categories → Miscellaneous → Actions → Run Macro	
6	Add Quick Access Toolbar button	File → Options → Access Options → Quick Access Toolbar → Choose commands from arrow → Macros	
6	Convert macro to VBA	Open macro in Design view → Design tab → Tools group → Convert Macros to Visual Basic → Convert	
7	Add On Lost Focus	Design tab → Tools group → Property sheet → Event tab → On Lost Focus → Code Builder → OK	
7	Add comments to On Lost Focus	On Lost Focus VBE → Type comments	
8	Write VBA statement	Visual Basic Editor Code window → Include comments → Declare variable → Type statement	
9	Add Breakpoint	Visual Basic Editor Code window → Click in the left margin next to statement	
9	Debug	Visual Basic Editor → Debug menu → Step Into	
10	Add Conditions to VBA procedure	Code window → Type control structure (If) → Alt + F11 → Test in form view → Alt + F11 to return to VBE	
MS11	Macro to Send Reports via E-mail	Macros & Code group → Macro button → Add new action arrow → EmailDatabaseObject	
MS12	Open Form Macro	Macros & Code group → Macro button → Add new action arrow → Open Form	
MS13	Run Macros at Startup	Create Macro → click Save → type AutoExec	
MS14	Add Table Description	Navigation Pane → Right-click table → type table description in description text box	

Project Summary Chart

Project	Project Type	Project Location
Skills Review	Review	In Book and MIL MyITLab® Grader
Skills Assessment 1	Review	In Book and MIL MyITLab® Grader
Skills Assessment 2	Review	Book
My Skills	Problem Solving	Book
Visual Skills Check	Problem Solving	Book
Skills Challenge 1	Critical Thinking	Book
Skills Challenge 2	Critical Thinking	Book
More Skills Assessment	Review	In Book and MIL MyITLab® Grader
Collaborating with Google	Critical Thinking	Book

MOS Objectives Covered (Quiz in MyITLab®)

2.2.3 Add table descriptions

Key Terms

Online Help Skills

1. Start **Access 2016**, and then in the upper right corner of the start page, click the **Help** button ⟨?⟩.

2. In the **Access Help** window **Search online help** box, type Macros and then press ⟨Enter⟩. In the search result list, click **Create a user interface (UI) macro**. Compare your screen with **Figure 1**.

3. Scroll down to the section **Create an embedded macro**.

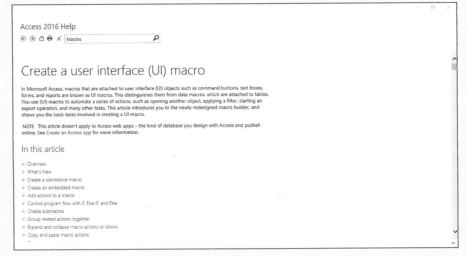

Figure 1   Access 2016, Windows 10, Microsoft Corporation

4. Read the article to answer the following questions: An embedded macro runs from which type of events? Could an embedded macro be considered a security risk? Which type of database objects typically contain an embedded macro?

Matching

Match each term in the second column with its correct definition in the first column by writing the letter of the term on the blank line in front of the correct definition.

___ **1.** An action or group of stored instructions used to automate tasks.

___ **2.** Remarks added to a macro or VBA code to provide information to those writing or reviewing the macro or VBA code.

___ **3.** A programming language designed to work within Microsoft Office Applications.

___ **4.** Added to the macro, this provides a conditional expression and then performs an action or series of actions only when the result of the condition is true or false.

___ **5.** A small vertical or horizontal line used to separate choices in a list, toolbar, or menu.

___ **6.** Instructions that tell a computer what to do.

___ **7.** Actions, such as mouse clicks or typing, detected by a running program that are associated with the control.

___ **8.** A program for writing VBA program code.

___ **9.** The area where VBA code is written and edited.

___ **10.** A group of related statements that is a subset of a macro.

A Code window

B Comment

C Event

D If action

E Macro

F Program

G Separator

H Sub procedure

I Visual Basic Editor

J Visual Basic for Applications (VBA)

Multiple Choice (MyITLab®)

Choose the correct answer.

1. What is the process of finding and fixing errors in programming code and making sure the program functions as intended?
   - A. Debug
   - B. Sub procedure
   - C. Separator

2. What is a code error that violates the rules of a programming language?
   - A. Logical error
   - B. Syntax error
   - C. Rules error

3. What line in a program contains instructions for the computer?
   - A. Variable
   - B. Statement
   - C. Data type

4. What programming objects refer to the values stored in RAM?
   - A. Data type
   - B. Keyword
   - C. Variable

5. The part of the statement that specifies whether a stored variable is a number, character, or date.
   - A. Sub procedure
   - B. Data type
   - C. Breakpoint

6. What is a sequence of either alpha or alphanumeric characters?
   - A. Data type
   - B. Macro
   - C. String

7. Which is a naming convention in which the prefixes indicate the type of data or type of object?
   - A. Hungarian notation
   - B. Syntax notation
   - C. Event

8. What is an intentional stop or pause inserted into a macro?
   - A. Breakpoint
   - B. Syntax error
   - C. Macro

9. What type of errors allow the macro to run, but do not produce the intended results?
   - A. Syntax
   - B. Logical
   - C. Both A and B

10. What type of statement tests if a condition is true?
    - A. If
    - B. If Then Else control structure
    - C. Neither A nor B

Topics for Discussion

1. In this chapter, you learned to write stored statements in the Macro Builder and in the Visual Basic Editor. Which method do you think is more efficient and why? State the reasons for your answers.

2. If VBA programs can work without adding comments, then why do programmers add them? State the reasons for your answer.

Skills Review

MyITLab®
Grader

To complete this project, you will need the following file:

- acc09_SRCars

You will save your file as:

- Last_First_acc09_SRCars

1. Open **acc09_ SRCars**, and then save the database in your **Access Chapter 9** folder as Last_First_acc09_SRCars If necessary, enable the content.

2. Open the **Cars** form in Design view. In the **Controls group**, click **Button**. In the **Form Header**, point to the **3 inch** horizontal grid line, one grid dot below the **Form Header** bar, and then click one time.

3. In the **Command Button Wizard**, click **Miscellaneous**, and then click **Run Macro**. Click **Next**, verify that **ExportCarsToHTML** is selected, and then click **Next**. Click in the **Text** box, and then replace the text with Export Cars Click **Finish**. Compare your screen with **Figure 1**.

4. Switch to Form view, and then click the **Export Cars** button. In the **Output To** dialog box, click **Cancel**. **Save**, and then **Close** the form.

5. Click **File**, and then click **Options**. In the left margin, click **Quick Access Toolbar**. Click the **Customize Quick Access Toolbar arrow**, and then click your file name and file path. Under **Choose commands from**, click **Macros**. Click **ExportCarsToHTML**, and then click **Add**. Compare your screen with **Figure 2**, and then click **OK**.

6. On the **Create tab**, in the **Macros & Code group**, click the **Macro** button. Click **Save**. In the **Save As** dialog box, type Export_Cars and then press Enter.

7. Click the **Add New Action arrow**, and then click **RunMacro**. Click the **Macro Name box arrow**, and then click **ExportCarsToHTML**. Click the **Add New Action arrow**, and then click **If**. Click in the **If** box, and then type MsgBox("Export as Excel Workbook?",4,"Data Export")=6

8. Above the **End If** statement, click the **Add New Action arrow**, and then click **ExportWithFormatting**. Click the **Object Name arrow**, and then click **Cars**. Click the **Output Format arrow**, and then click **Excel Workbook (*.xlsx)**.

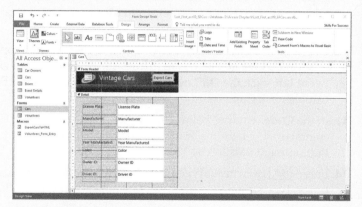

Access 2016, Windows 10, Microsoft Corporation

Figure 1

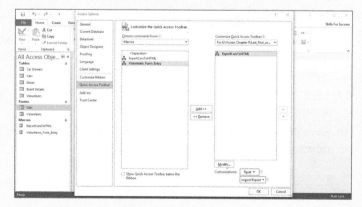

Access 2016, Windows 10, Microsoft Corporation

Figure 2

■ Continue to the next page to complete this Skills Review

9. Above the **End If** statement, click the **Add New Action arrow**, and then click **Comment**. Type Prepared by Your Name. Last updated: Current Date Move the comment to the beginning of the macro, as shown in Figure 3.

10. Click **Save**, and then click **Run**. In the **Output To** dialog box, click **Cancel**. In the message box, click **Yes**. In the **Output To** dialog box, click **Cancel**. Run the macro again, and then in the message box, click **No**.

11. In the **Navigation Pane**, click the **Export_Cars** macro once. On the **Design tab**, in the **Tools group**, click **Convert Macros to Visual Basic**. In the displayed message box, click **Convert**, and then click **OK**. In Project Explorer, double-click the module name to open its code window. From the **File** menu, click **Close and Return to Microsoft Office Access**. **Close** the macro.

12. Open the **Volunteers** form in Design view, display the Property Sheet, and then click the **State** text box to display its properties. On the Property Sheet **Event tab**, click the **On Lost Focus** box, and then click the **Build** button. Double-click **Code Builder**.

13. In the **Code** window, below *Private Sub State_LostFocus( )*, type the following comment: 'Updates the Travel_Allowance field Press Enter, and then type the comment 'Written by Your Name

14. Press Enter two times. Type Dim strState As String and then press Enter two times. Type strState = Forms!Volunteers!State Press Enter two times.

15. Type If strState = "CA" Then Press Enter, and then type Forms!Volunteers!Travel_Allowance = 25 Press Enter, and then type Else Press Enter, and then type Forms!Volunteers!Travel_Allowance = 100 Press Enter, and then type End If Compare your screen with Figure 4.

16. Click **Save**. Click **File** and then click **Close and Return to Microsoft Office Access**. Switch to Form view. Press Tab five times to update the **Travel_Allowance** field.

17. Click **New (blank) record**, and then add your information to the record. Type 5 as the Volunteer_ID

18. **Save** and **Close** all forms and macros. **Close** Access. Submit the file as directed by your instructor.

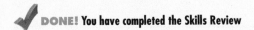

DONE! You have completed the Skills Review

Figure 3   Access 2016, Windows 10, Microsoft Corporation

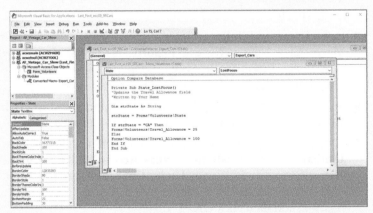

Figure 4   Visual Basic for Applications, Access 2016, Windows 10, Microsoft Corporation

Skills Assessment 1

MyITLab®
Grader

To complete this project, you will need the following file:

- acc09_SA1Events

You will save your file as:

- Last_First_acc09_SA1Events

---

1. Start **Access 2016**, and then open then **acc09_SA1Events**. **Save** the file in your **Access Chapter 9** folder with the name Last_First_acc09_SA1Events

2. Create a new macro, and then add the **ExportWithFormatting** action. Set the macro to export the **Events_For_Approval** query as an **Excel Workbook (*.xlsx)**. Add the comment Exports the Events_for_ Approval query to an Excel file and then move the comment to the top of the macro. Save the macro as Export_Events_to_Excel and then **Close** the macro.

3. Create a new macro, and then add the **ExportWithFormatting** action. Set the macro to export the **Events_For_Approval** query as an HTML document. **Save** the macro as Export_Events_to_HTML and then **Close** the macro.

4. Create a new macro, saved as Export_Events Add an **If** action that displays a message box with the text Export Events to Excel? The message box should display Yes/No buttons and the title Export Request When the **Yes** button is clicked, an action should run the **Export_Events_To_Excel** macro.

5. After the **End If** statement, add an **If** action that displays a message box with the text Export Events as a Web Page? The message box should display Yes/No buttons and the title Export Request When the **Yes** button is clicked, an action should run the **Export_Events_To_HTML**.

6. **Save**, and then compare your screen with **Figure 1**. **Run** the macro to test all possible outcomes. When the **Output To** dialog box displays, click **Cancel**.

7. Add a button to the **Quick Access Toolbar** for the current database that runs the **Export_Events** macro when it is clicked.

8. Open the **Events** form in Design view. In the **Detail** section, on the **1 inch** vertical gridline, two grid dots below the **Approval** text box, insert a command button. Use the wizard so that the button runs the **Export_Events_To_Excel** macro and displays the text Export to Excel

9. Open the **Volunteers** form in Design view, and then click the **Title** field text box. On the **Design tab**, open the **Property Sheet**. On the **Event tab**, click the **On Lost Focus Build** button, and then double-click **Code Builder**.

Access 2016, Windows 10, Microsoft Corporation

Figure 1

10. Below **Private Sub Title_LostFocus()**, type 'Updates LunchAllowance field based on the value in the Title field Press Enter, and then type the following code:

```
Dim strTitle As String
strTitle = Forms!Volunteers!Title
If strTitle = "Housekeeping" Then
    Forms!Volunteers!LunchAllowance = 20
End If
```

11. **Save**, and then **Close and Return to Microsoft Access**. **Save** and **Close** the forms and macros. **Close** Access. Submit the file as directed by your instructor.

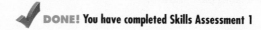

DONE! You have completed Skills Assessment 1

Skills Assessment 2

To complete this project, you will need the following file:

- acc09_SA2Rentals

You will save your file as:

- Last_First_acc09_SA2Rentals

1. Start **Access 2016**, and then open the student data file **acc09_SA2Rentals**. Save the file in your **Access Chapter 9** folder with the name Last_First_acc09_SA2Rentals

2. Open the **Renters** form in Design view, and then click the **State** text box. Display the property sheet, and then create a VBA sub procedure for the **On Lost Focus** event.

3. In the **VBA Code** window, type the comment 'Updates the Tax field based on the value in the State field Press Enter .

4. Press Enter , and then type a statement that declares a variable named strState and assigns it the string data type.

5. Press Enter two times, and then add a statement that assigns the **State** field value in the **Renters** form to the variable.

6. Press Enter two times, and then add an **If Then Else** control statement that assigns a **Tax** of 25 for renters from "CA" and a **Tax** of 85 for renters not from "CA" Compare your screen with **Figure 1**.

7. Return to the form, switch to Form view, and then test the macro by using the Tab key to go through each of the records to update the **Tax** field for each record. If asked by your instructor, print the Code window. **Close** the **Code** window. **Save** and **Close** the **Renters** form.

8. Create a macro that exports the **Reservations** table as an **Excel Workbook (.xlsx)**. Save the macro as Export_Reservations Before the first macro action, add the **Comment** Exports the Reservations table as an Excel file **Save**, and then convert the macro to Visual Basic. **Close** the Visual Basic Editor.

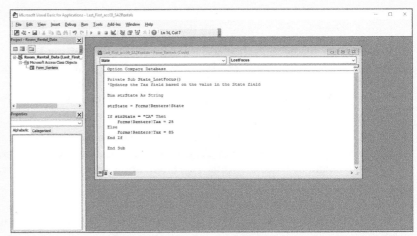

Figure 1   Visual Basic for Applications, Access 2016, Windows 10, Microsoft Corporation

9. Open the **Renters** form in Design view. In the **Detail** section, on the **1 inch** vertical gridline, and three grid dots below the **Tax** text box, insert a command button. Use the wizard so that the **Export_Reservations** macro runs when the button is clicked. The button's text should be Export Reservations to Excel and the button should be named the command button cmdExportReservations

10. **Save** and **Close** the **Renters** form and **Export_Reservations** macro. **Close** Access. Submit the file as directed by your instructor.

 **DONE!** You have completed Skills Assessment 2

My Skills

To complete this project, you will need the following file:

- acc09_MYMaintenance

You will save your file as:

- Last_First_acc09_MYMaintenance

Visual Basic for Applications, Access 2016, Windows 10, Microsoft Corporation

Figure 1

1. Start **Access 2016**, and then open **acc09_MYMaintenance**. Save the file in your **Access Chapter 9** folder with the name Last_First_acc09_MYMaintenance

2. From the **Design tab**, create a Maintenance_Table_Excel_Export **Macro**. Create an **ExportWithFormatting** action that exports the **Maintenances** table as an Excel file.

3. Open the **Vehicles** form in Design view, and then add a button at the **2 inch** horizontal gridline, two grid dots below the **Form Header** bar. Click the **Miscellaneous** category, and then click **Run Macro**. Name the button Export Maintenance Table

4. Apply the **Subtle Effect - Dark Blue, Accent 1 Quick Style** to the Export Maintenance Table button.

5. Open the **Maintenance_Table_Excel_Export** macro in Design view, and then in the **Tools group**, click **Convert Macros to Visual Basic**.

6. Open the **RepairShops** form in Design view. Click the **Zip** text box, and then on the Property Sheet, click the **Build** button on the **On Lost Focus** event. Click **Code Builder**.

7. Below *Private Sub Zip_LostFocus()*, type the following statement.

   Dim strZip As String
   strZip = Forms!RepairShops!Zip
   If strZip = "93464" Then
       Forms!RepairShops!Distance = "Within 5 miles"
   Else
       Forms!RepairShops!Distance = "More than 5 miles"
   End If

8. Above the **Private Sub Zip_LostFocus()** entry, add the following comment: 'Updates the Distance field according to the Zip value Compare your screen with **Figure 1**.

9. Switch to Form view, and then tab through the **RepairShop** entries to update the **Distance** field on each record.

10. **Save** and **Close** the form, and then **Close** Access. Submit your file as directed by your instructor.

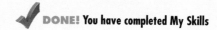
DONE! You have completed My Skills

Visual Skills Check

To complete this project, you will need the following file:

- acc09_VSGeo

You will save your file as:

- Last_First_acc09_VSGeo

Open the database **acc09_VSGeo**, and then save the file in your **Access Chapter 9** folder as Last_First_acc09_VSGeo Create two macros. Name the first macro Export_June_Events_To_Excel which exports the **June 2018 Events** query to an Excel file. Name the second macro Geocache_Table_To_HTML which exports the **Geocache** table to an HTML file. At the top of each macro, include the following comment: Prepared by Your Name On the **Events** form, create the two buttons (June events to Excel and Geocache Table to HTML) as shown in **Figure 1**. Each button has been formatted with a Quick Style of **Light 1 Outline, Colored Fill – Aqua, Accent 5**. Each button should be positioned and formatted as shown and run the corresponding macro. Submit the file as directed by your instructor.

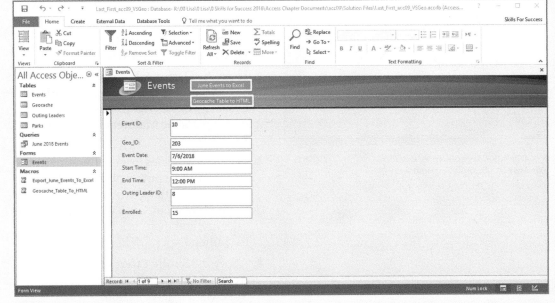

Figure 1

Access 2016, Windows 10, Microsoft Corporation

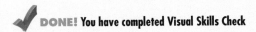 **DONE! You have completed Visual Skills Check**

Skills Challenge 1

To complete this project, you will need the following file:

- acc09_SC1Swim

You will save your file as:

- Last_First_acc09_SC1Swim

Open **acc09_SC1Swim**, and then save the database in your **Access Chapter 9** folder as Last_First_acc09_SC1Swim The **Employees** form has a VBA event procedure with four different errors in the program. Open the **Employees** form and tab through the fields until the error message appears. Debug the program so that the correct **Insurance** is entered into

the form field. Click through each record to update the entire **Employees** table.

Submit the file as directed by your instructor.

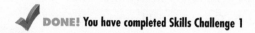 **DONE! You have completed Skills Challenge 1**

Skills Challenge 2

To complete this project, you will need the following file:

- acc09_SC2FarmersMarket

You will save your file as:

- Last_First_acc09_SC2FarmersMarket

Open **acc09_SC2FarmersMarket**, and then save the database in your **Access Chapter 9** folder as Last_First_acc09_SC2FarmersMarket On the **Farms** form, create an **On Lost Focus** event that will enter a fee of $20 for farms with a 93463 zip code, and a fee of $25 for farms with any other zip code. Add a comment to the top of the code that describes the purpose of the event. Tab through the **Farm** form entries to update the fees. Create a macro that exports an Excel file of

the **Farms** table. Add a comment to the top of the action that describes the purpose of the macro.

Submit the file as directed by your instructor.

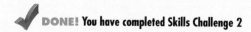 **DONE! You have completed Skills Challenge 2**

More Skills Assessment

MyITLab®
Grader

To complete this project, you will need the following file:

- acc09_MSAShows

You will save your file as:

- Last_First_acc09_MSAShows

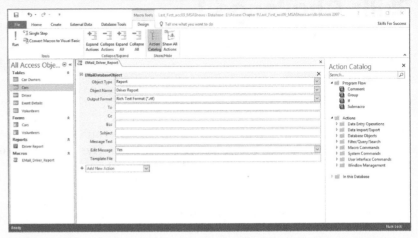

Figure 1 Access 2016, Windows 10, Microsoft Corporation

1. Start **Access 2016**. Open the file **acc09_MSAShows**, and then save the file in your chapter folder as Last_First_acc09_MSAShows

2. Add the following **Descriptions** to the **Cars** table field properties:

   Manufacturer: Car manufacturer
   Model: Model of car
   Year Manufactured: Year car was manufactured
   Color: Color of car

3. Create a macro named Email_Driver_Report that will e-mail the *Driver Report* in **Rich Text Format**. Leave all other properties blank. Compare your screen with **Figure 1**.

4. Create a macro named Volunteers_Entry that opens the *Volunteers* form to a new record. Compare your screen with **Figure 2**.

5. Create a macro named AutoExec that opens the *Car Owners* table when the database is opened.

6. **Save** and **Close** all objects, and then **Close** Access.

7. Submit the file as directed by your instructor.

Figure 2 Access 2016, Windows 10, Microsoft Corporation

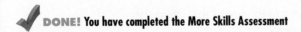
DONE! You have completed the More Skills Assessment

Collaborating with Google

To complete this project, you will need a Google account(refer to the Common Features chapter) and the following file:

- Blank Google Form

You will save your file as:

- Last_First_acc09_GPSnip

1. Open the **Google Chrome** web browser. Log into your Google account, and then click the **Apps** button.

2. Click **Drive** to open Google Drive, and then click the **NEW** button. Point to **More**, and then click **Google Forms**.

3. At the top of the form, click **Untitled form**, and then type Racers Drawing

4. In the first **Question Title** text box, type: Full Name

5. Click the **Question Type arrow**, and then click **Text**. Click **Done**.

6. Click the **Add item arrow**, and then click **Text**.

7. In the **Question Title** text box, type: Phone and then click **Done**.

8. Click the **Add item arrow**, and then click **Text**. In the **Question Title** text box, type Email and then click **Done**.

9. In the **Confirmation Page** section, click the **Show link to submit another response** checkbox to deselect it.

10. On the menu bar, click **View**, and then click **Live form**.

11. Type the following into the form:

    Full Name: Lana Shane
    Phone: 805-555-3814
    Email: lshane@aspenfalls.org

12. Click **OK**, and then click the **Racers Drawing – Google Forms tab**. On the menu bar, click **View responses**, and then compare your screen with **Figure 1**.

13. Open the **Snipping Tool**, click the **New arrow**, and then take a **Window Snip**. In the **Snipping Tool** mark-up window, click the

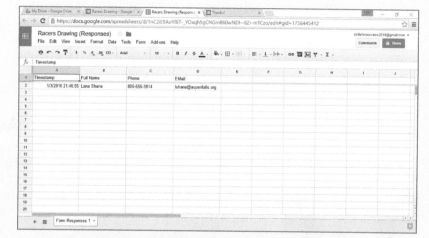

Figure 1

Save Snip button. In the **Save As** dialog box, navigate to your Access Chapter 9 folder. Be sure the **Save as type** box displays **JPEG file**. Name the file Last_First_acc09_GPSnip and then press Enter. **Close** ⌧ the Snipping Tool mark-up window

14. Close all windows, and then submit the file as directed by your instructor.

✔️ **DONE! You have completed the Collaborating with Google Project**

CHAPTER 10

Create Database Applications

- ▶ When you have groups who need to use a database in different ways, you can place the tables in one file, and create separate applications to work with the tables.

- ▶ Each database application can share a common table, but the application provides only the queries, forms, reports, or macros needed for a specific group of end-users.

- ▶ Database applications typically provide a custom interface to open objects. For example, you can customize the Navigation Pane so that it provides only the choices you want the end-user to see.

- ▶ You can place buttons on a form to provide a custom application. Each button opens the database objects you want the end-user to access.

- ▶ You can prevent end-users from changing the database design by changing Access options.

- ▶ To prevent others from gaining unauthorized access to sensitive data, you can protect the database application with a password.

michaeljung/Fotolia

Aspen Falls City Hall

In this chapter, you will create two database applications for the Aspen Falls Water Utilities department. You will work under the supervision of Diane Payne, Public Works Director. Each application will share the same database tables, but each application will contain different queries, forms, reports, and macros.

The Water Utilities department has two end-users who need to use the database differently: data entry operators and management. The data entry operators need to open forms to update data. Management will not enter data, but they do want to access several reports. For this reason, you will place the tables in one database file, the data entry data forms in a second database file, and the queries and reports in a third database file.

In this project, you will create two different applications to provide each end-user the experience they desire. You will create a custom navigation form in one application and customize the Navigation Pane in the other application. You will also change database options to prevent end-users from modifying the design of the database.

Outcome

Using the skills in this chapter, you will be able to split databases and update linked tables, create front-end databases and custom navigation forms, insert command buttons, secure and encrypt databases, and customize the Navigation Pane.

Objectives

10.1 Construct split databases and update linked tables

10.2 Create front-end databases

10.3 Modify the Navigation Pane

10.4 Apply security and encryption to databases

Student data file needed for this chapter:

acc10_Water_Master

You will save your files as:

Last_First_acc10_Water_Master_be
Last_First_acc10_WaterManagement_fe
Last_First_acc10_WaterDataEntry_fe
Last_First_Water_Master

SKILLS

Skills 1–10 Training

At the end of this chapter, you will be able to:

Skill 1 Split Databases and Update Linked Tables
Skill 2 Create Front-End Databases
Skill 3 Create Custom Navigation Forms
Skill 4 Insert, Format, and Test Command Buttons
Skill 5 Secure and Encrypt Databases
Skill 6 Customize Application Settings
Skill 7 Create Additional Front-End Databases
Skill 8 Create Macros to Verify Actions
Skill 9 Customize the Navigation Pane
Skill 10 Hide Navigation Pane Groups

MORE SKILLS

Skill 11 Analyze Performance
Skill 12 Recover Data from a Backup
Skill 13 Use Table Analyzer to Normalize Tables
Skill 14 Use the Security Wizard

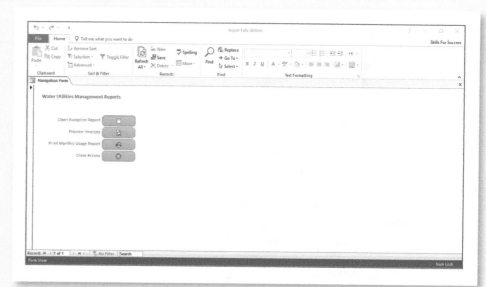

Access 2016, Windows 10, Microsoft Corporation

▶ You can move database tables to a separate database file. You can then design multiple databases that link to the tables. In this way, you can create queries, forms, and reports with different purposes using a single database file as the data source.

▶ The process of moving the tables into one database file and forms, queries, macros, and reports into a separate database file is known as splitting a database.

1. Start **Access 2016**, and then open the student data file **acc10_Water_Master**. On the File tab, click **Save As**. With **Save Database As** selected, click the **Save As** button. In the **Save As** dialog box, navigate to the location where you are saving your files for this project. Click **New folder**, type Access Chapter 10 and then press [Enter] two times. Save the file with the default file name. If necessary, enable the content.

2. Click the **Database Tools tab**, and then in the **Move Data group**, click the **Access Database** button. Compare your screen with Figure 1.

    Database Splitter is used to divide the database into two files. The ***back-end*** file contains the tables, and the ***front-end*** file contains the forms, reports, macros, and queries. ***Split database*** is the action of moving the tables into one database file and the forms, queries, and reports into a separate database file.

3. In the **Database Splitter** dialog box, read the message, and then click the **Split Database** button.

4. In the **Create Back-end Database** dialog box, navigate to your Access Chapter 10 folder. Name the file Last_First_acc10_ Water_be and then click **Split**. Compare your screen with Figure 2.

■ Continue to the next page to complete the skill ▶

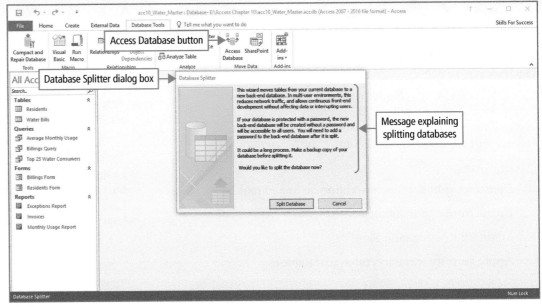

Figure 1

Access 2016, Windows 10, Microsoft Corporation

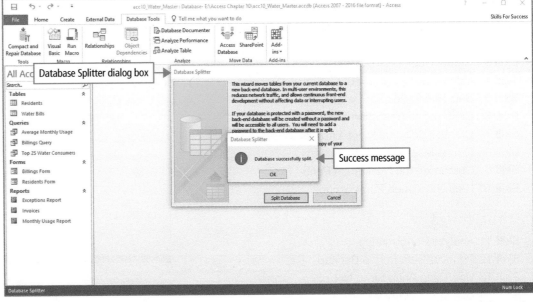

Figure 2

Access 2016, Windows 10, Microsoft Corporation

MOS
Obj 1.4.4

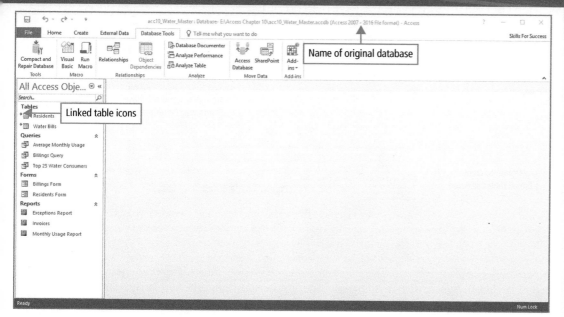

Access 2016, Windows 10, Microsoft Corporation

Figure 3

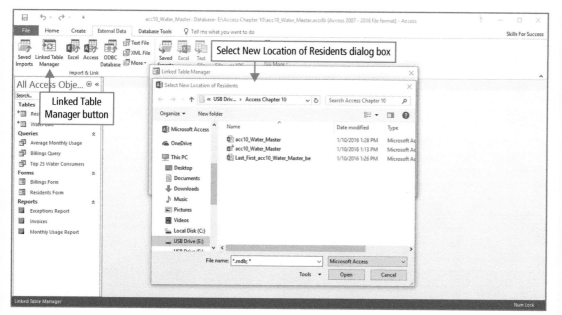

Access 2016, Windows 10, Microsoft Corporation

Figure 4

To keep split database files organized, it is a common practice to append the letters *be* in the file name of back-end databases.

5. Read the message that displays, click **OK**, and then compare your screen with **Figure 3**.

   The tables in the Navigation Pane have an arrow next to them to indicate they are linked to tables in another database file. Here, the tables have been moved to Last_First_acc10_Water_be. The name of the original database—*acc10_Water_Master*—remains the same.

6. Click the **External Data tab**, and then in the **Import & Link group**, click the **Linked Table Manager** button.

7. In the **Linked Table Manager** dialog box, select the **Residents** and **Water Bills** check boxes. Select the **Always prompt for new location** check box. Click **OK**, and then compare your screen with **Figure 4**.

   If you move or rename a back-end database file, the front-end objects will not work until the location of the back-end tables are updated using the Linked Table Manager dialog box. For example, if you save your work on a USB flash drive on one computer, you may need to update the links when you open the front-end from a different computer.

8. In the **Select New Location of Residents** dialog box, click **Cancel**. In the **Linked Table Manager** dialog box, click **Cancel**.

   The links to the tables do not need to be updated at this time.

9. **Close** ☒ Access.

   In other skills, you will import objects from the file *acc10_Water_Master* database. However, you will not need to submit this file, and you do not need to save it using a different name.

■ **You have completed Skill 1 of 10**

 **WATCH** SKILL 10.2

▶ To create a front-end database, you first link to tables in a back-end file. You then can build the front-end queries, reports, and forms.

1. Start **Access 2016**. On the **Access** Start page, click **Blank desktop database**. In the **Blank desktop database** window, replace the suggested **File Name** value with Last_First_acc10_Water Management_fe

2. Click the **Browse** button, and then in the **File New Database** dialog box, navigate to your **Access Chapter 10** folder, and then click **OK**.

3. Click the **Create** button to create the new database.

4. **Close** ⊠ Table1 without saving it.

5. Click the **External Data tab**, and then in the **Import & Link group**, click the **Access** button.

6. In the **Get External Data - Access Database** dialog box, click **Browse**. In the **File Open** dialog box, navigate to and click **Last_First_acc10_Water_be**, and then click **Open**.

7. In the **Get External Data - Access Database** dialog box, select the **Link to the data source by creating a linked table** option button. Compare your screen with **Figure 1**, and then click **OK**.

8. In the **Link Tables** dialog box, click the **Select All** button. Compare your screen with **Figure 2**, and then click **OK**.

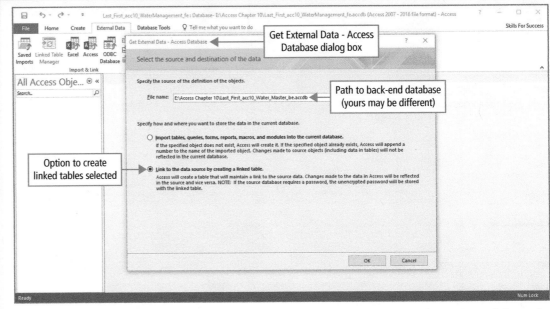

Figure 1

Access 2016, Windows 10, Microsoft Corporation

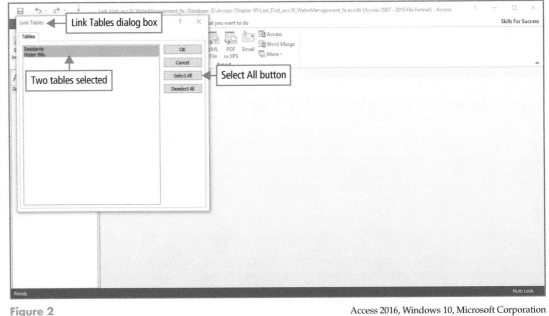

Figure 2

Access 2016, Windows 10, Microsoft Corporation

▪ **Continue to the next page to complete the skill**

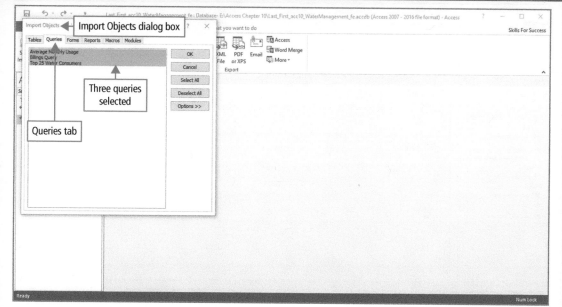

Access 2016, Windows 10, Microsoft Corporation

Figure 3

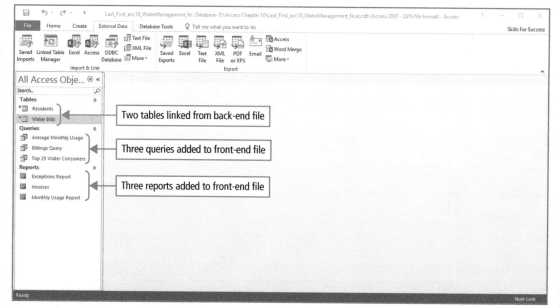

Access 2016, Windows 10, Microsoft Corporation

Figure 4

9. If necessary, click the **External Data tab**, and then in the **Import & Link group**, click the **Access** button.

10. In the **Get External Data - Access Database** dialog box, click **Browse**. In the **File Open** dialog box, navigate to and click **acc10_Water_Master**, and then click **Open**.

11. In the **Get External Data - Access Database** dialog box, verify that the **Import tables, queries, forms, reports, macros, and modules into the current database** option button is selected, and then click **OK**.

12. In the **Import Objects** dialog box, click the **Queries tab**. Click the **Select All** button, and then compare your screen with **Figure 3**.

13. In the **Import Objects** dialog box, click the **Reports tab**. Click the **Select All** button, and then click **OK** to import the three queries and three reports.

14. In the **Get External Data - Access Database** dialog box, click **Close**. Compare your screen with **Figure 4**.

15. Leave the database open for the next skill.

■ **You have completed Skill 2 of 10**

- ▶ Navigation forms have buttons that you use to quickly open forms and reports.
- ▶ To create a custom navigation form, you add buttons and assign actions to them using the Command Button wizard.

1. Click the **Create tab**, and then in the **Forms group**, click the **Blank Form** button. **Close** ☒ the Field List pane.

2. Click **Save** 🖫. In the **Save As** dialog box, name the form Navigation Form and then click **OK**.

3. On the **Design tab**, in the **Controls group**, click the **Label** button 🔲, and then click in a blank area of the form to insert a label control.

4. With the insertion point in the label control inserted previously, type Water Utilities Management Reports

5. Press Enter to accept the label text and to select the label control. Compare your screen with **Figure 1**.

6. With the label still selected, click the **Arrange tab**. In the **Rows & Columns group**, click the **Insert Below** button four times to add four blank cells to the table.

7. Click in the second row of the table—the first blank cell—and then type Open Exceptions Report to insert a label control.

8. In the third row, insert a label with the text Preview Invoices

9. In the fourth row, insert a label with the text Print Monthly Usage Report

10. In the fifth row, insert a label with the text Close Access Click a blank area of the form, and then compare your screen with **Figure 2**.

■ **Continue to the next page to complete the skill**

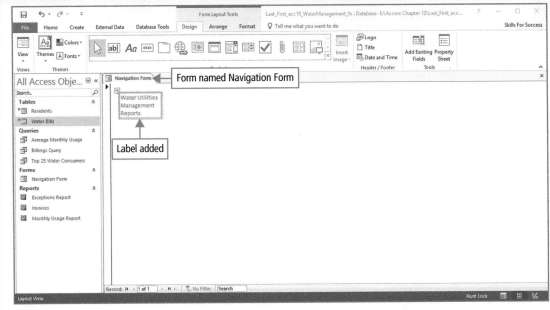

Figure 1

Access 2016, Windows 10, Microsoft Corporation

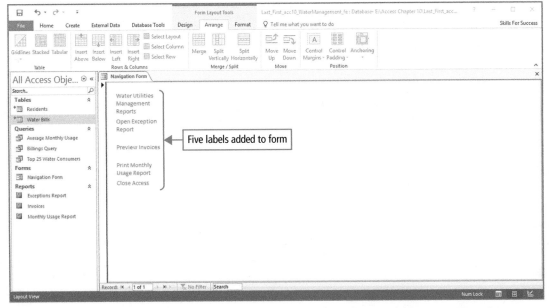

Figure 2

Access 2016, Windows 10, Microsoft Corporation

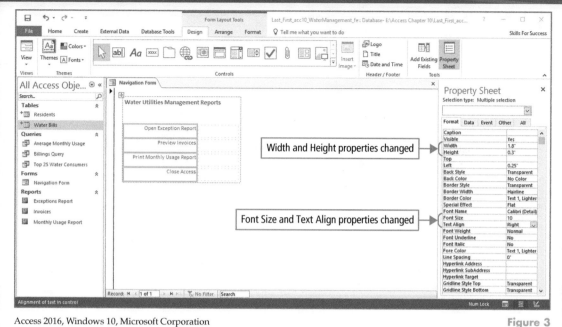

Access 2016, Windows 10, Microsoft Corporation

Figure 3

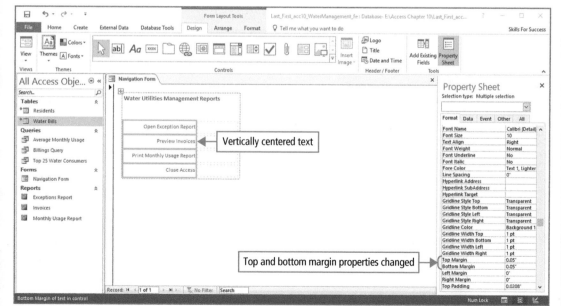

Access 2016, Windows 10, Microsoft Corporation

Figure 4

11. Click the first label to select it. Click the **Format tab**, and then in the **Font group**, click the **Bold** button ⬛.

12. With the label formatted in the previous step still selected, click the **Arrange tab**, and then in the **Rows & Columns group**, click the **Insert Right** button to add a second column.

13. With the first label still selected, press and hold ⬚Shift⬚ while clicking the first cell in the second column. With both cells selected, on the **Arrange tab**, in the **Merge/Split group**, click the **Merge** button.

14. Using the technique just practiced, select the cells with labels in rows 2 through 5. Click the **Design tab**, and then in the **Tools group**, click the **Property Sheet** button.

15. In the **Property Sheet** pane, change the **Width** property to 1.8" the **Height** to 0.3" and the **Font Size** to 10

16. In the **Property Sheet** pane, click **Text Align**, click the **Text Align arrow** that displays, and then click **Right**. Compare your screen with **Figure 3**.

17. In the **Property Sheet** pane, scroll down as needed to display the **Top Margin** and **Bottom Margin** properties.

18. In the **Property Sheet** pane, change the **Top Margin** property to .05" and the **Bottom Margin** property to .05"

    Setting the top and bottom margins in this manner vertically centers the labels within each table cell.

19. Compare your screen with **Figure 4**, and then click **Save** ⬛. Leave the form open for the next skill.

■ **You have completed Skill 3 of 10**

▶ You can insert buttons that, when clicked, complete common database tasks.

1. With the **Navigation Form** open in Layout view, click the **Design tab**. In the **Controls group**, click the **More** button ⬇. Click the **Use Control Wizards** command if needed so that its icon is selected.

2. On the **Design tab**, in the **Controls group**, click the **Button** button, and then click in the blank cell in row 2, column 2.

3. In the **Command Button Wizard**, under **Categories**, click **Report Operations**. Under **Actions**, click **Open Report**. Compare your screen with **Figure 1**.

   In the Command Button Wizard, the actions that display change depending on which category is selected.

4. Click **Next**, and then under **Which report would you like the command button to open**, verify that **Exceptions Report** is selected.

5. Click **Next**. Verify that the **Picture** option button is selected and that the *MS Access Report* option is selected.

6. Click **Next**. Accept the button name provided by the wizard by clicking **Finish**. Compare your screen with **Figure 2**.

7. In row 3, column 2, repeat the technique just practiced to insert a button control. In the **Command Button Wizard**, select the **Report Operations** category, and then the **Preview Report** action. In the second wizard screen, select the **Invoices** report. In the third wizard screen, select the **Preview** picture, and then click **Finish**.

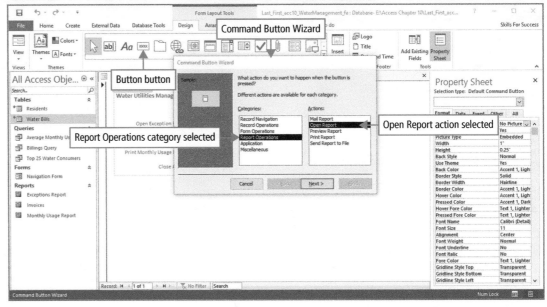

Figure 1

Access 2016, Windows 10, Microsoft Corporation

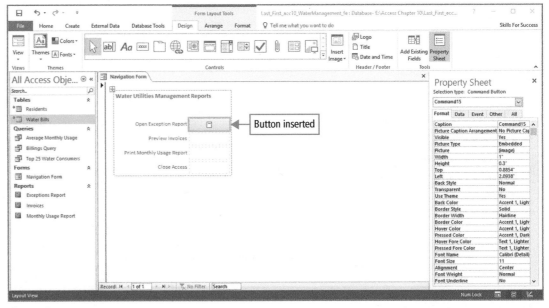

Figure 2

Access 2016, Windows 10, Microsoft Corporation

■ Continue to the next page to complete the skill

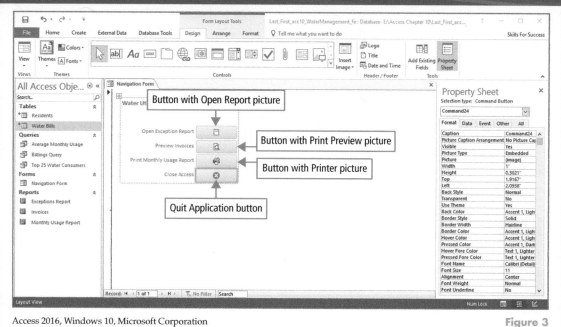

Access 2016, Windows 10, Microsoft Corporation

Figure 3

Access 2016, Windows 10, Microsoft Corporation

Figure 4

8. In row 4, column 2, insert a button control. In the **Command Button Wizard**, select the **Report Operations** category and the **Print Report** action. In the next screen, select **Monthly Usage Report**, and then accept the remaining wizard defaults.

9. In row 5, column 2, insert a button control. In the **Command Button Wizard**, select the **Application** category and the **Quit Application** action. Accept the remaining wizard defaults. Compare your screen with **Figure 3**.

10. Select the four buttons just inserted, and then click the **Format tab**. In the **Control Formatting group**, click the **Quick Styles** button, and then click the seventh style in the fourth row—**Subtle Effect - Green, Accent 6**.

11. In the **Control Formatting group**, click the **Change Shape** button, and then click the third style—**Rounded Rectangle**.

12. Switch to Form view, and then compare your screen with **Figure 4**.

13. Click the **Open Exceptions Report** button to open the report, and then **Close** ☒ the report.

14. In the **Navigation Form**, click the **Preview Invoices** button to open the report in Print Preview view, and then **Close** ☒ the report.

15. In the **Navigation Form**, click the **Print Monthly Usage Report** button, and then in the **Print** dialog box that opens, click **Cancel**.

16. **Close** ☒ the report, **Save** 🖫 the form, and then **Close** ☒ the form.

■ **You have completed Skill 4 of 10**

▶ To prevent unauthorized access to your database, you can encrypt the database.

▶ **_Encryption_** is the process of transforming information into a format that cannot be read until the correct password is entered.

1. Click the **File tab**, and then click **Close** to close the database, but leave Access open.

2. Click the **File tab**, and then click **Open**. On the **Open** page, click **Browse**.

3. In the **Open** dialog box, navigate to your **Access Chapter 10** folder, and then click **Last_First_acc10_WaterManagement_fe** one time to select it.

4. In the **Open** dialog box, click the **Open arrow**. Compare your screen with Figure 1, and then click **Open Exclusive**.

   Before a database file can be encrypted, it should be opened in **_Exclusive mode_**—a mode that prevents others from opening the database while you are working with it.

5. If necessary, enable the content.

6. Click the **File tab**, and then compare your screen with Figure 2.

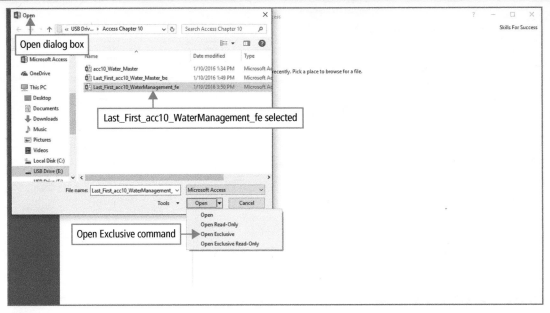

Figure 1

Access 2016, Windows 10, Microsoft Corporation

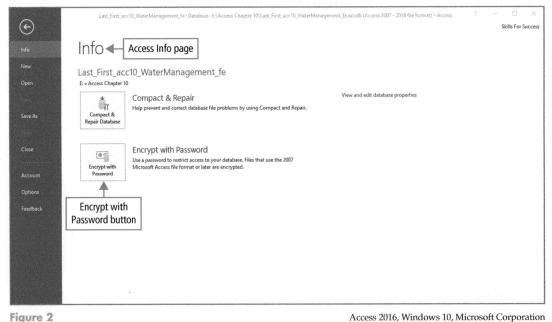

Figure 2

Access 2016, Windows 10, Microsoft Corporation

■ **Continue to the next page to complete the skill**

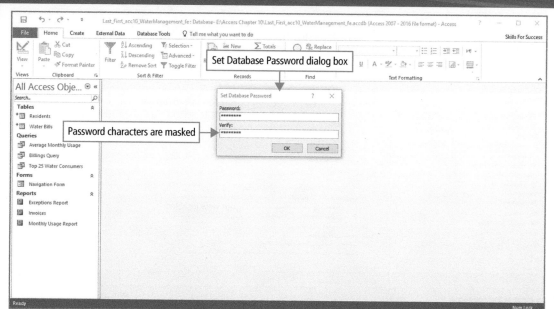

Set Database Password dialog box

Password characters are masked

Access 2016, Windows 10, Microsoft Corporation

Figure 3

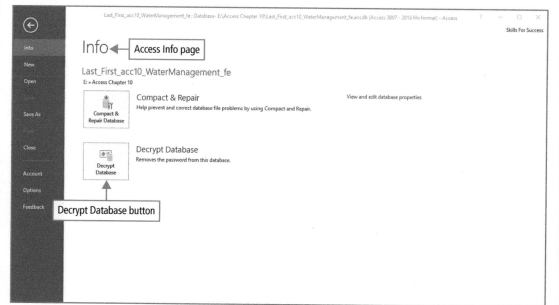

Access Info page

Decrypt Database button

Access 2016, Windows 10, Microsoft Corporation

Figure 4

7. On the **Info** page, click the **Encrypt with Password** button.

8. In the **Set Database Password** dialog box, in the **Password** box, type Success!

9. In the **Set Database Password** dialog box, in the **Verify** box, type Success! Compare your screen with **Figure 3**, and then click **OK**. If a message displays, read the message, and then click OK.

> When protecting databases, use a ***strong password***—a password that contains a combination of upper- and lowercase letters, numbers, and symbols.

10. Click the **File tab**, and then click **Close**. Click the **File tab**, and then use the **Open** page to open **Last_First_acc10_Water Management_fe**.

> Once a database file is encrypted, it does not need to be opened in Exclusive Mode unless you wish to permanently remove the encryption from the file.

11. In the **Password Required** dialog box, type the password Success! and then click **OK**.

12. Click the **File tab**, and then compare your screen with **Figure 4**.

> On the Info page, the Encrypt with Password button has changed to the Decrypt Database button. Before decryption is removed, the database must be opened in Exclusive mode.

13. Leave the database open for the next skill.

■ **You have completed Skill 5 of 10**

▶ You can change Access options to automatically open a form, hide the Navigation Pane, or prevent users from changing the design of the database.

1. On the **File tab**, click **Options**, and then in left pane of the **Access Options** dialog box, click **Current Database**.

2. Under **Application Options**, click in the **Application Title** box, and then type Aspen Falls Utilities

3. Click the **Display Form arrow**, and then click **Navigation Form**.

4. Clear the **Enable Layout View** check box, and then compare your screen with **Figure 1**.

   An *Application Title* is a value that displays in the Access window title bar instead of the file name, path, and file type. When a form is selected as the *display form*, that form automatically opens when the database is opened. When Layout view is disabled, others can use the database forms, reports, and queries, but they cannot switch to Layout view.

5. In the **Access Options** dialog box, scroll down to display the lower half of the Current Database options.

6. Under **Navigation**, clear the **Display Navigation Pane** check box.

7. Under **Ribbon and Toolbar Options**, clear the **Allow Full Menus** check box. Compare your screen with **Figure 2**.

   Disabling full menus prevents others from using Ribbon commands that can change the format or design of database objects.

8. In the **Access Options** dialog box, click **OK**. Read the message that displays, and then click **OK**.

■ Continue to the next page to complete the skill

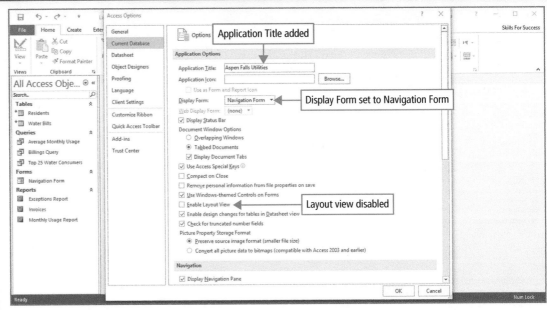

Figure 1

Access 2016, Windows 10, Microsoft Corporation

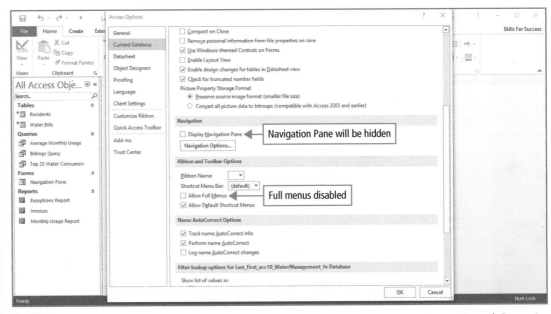

Figure 2

Access 2016, Windows 10, Microsoft Corporation

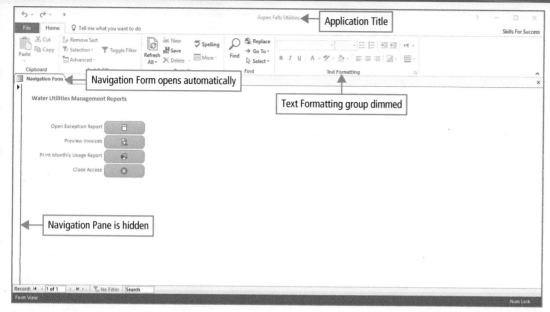

Access 2016, Windows 10, Microsoft Corporation

Figure 3

Access 2016, Windows 10, Microsoft Corporation

Figure 4

9. **Close** ⊠, and then open **Last_First_ acc10_WaterManagement_fe**. In the **Password Required** dialog box, type **Success!** Press Enter, and then compare your screen with **Figure 3**.

   This customized application provides a navigation form to open the desired options. Only the Home tab displays, and all commands that can be used to change formatting are dimmed.

10. Right-click a blank area of the form, notice that the shortcut menu can be used to switch to Design view, and then click a blank area of the form to close the menu.

11. On the **Quick Access Toolbar**, click the **Customize Quick Access Toolbar** button ⊽. Compare your screen with **Figure 4**, and then click **More Commands**.

12. In the left pane of the **Access Options** dialog box, click **Current Database**. Scroll down to display the **Ribbon and Toolbar Options**, and then clear the **Allow Default Shortcut Menus** check box.

   When full menus have been disabled, you can access the Current Database options in this manner.

13. In the **Access Options** dialog box, click **OK**. Read the message that displays, and then click **OK**.

14. Close, and then open **Last_First_acc10_ WaterManagement_fe**. Enter the password **Success!** and then right-click a blank area of the form to verify that a shortcut menu does not display.

15. In the **Navigation Form**, click the **Close Access** button that you added to the form previously to close the database and exit Access.

■ **You have completed Skill 6 of 10**

 **WATCH** SKILL 10.7

- You can create multiple front-end files that link to a single back-end database. In this way, you can create custom applications for users with different needs.

- In this skill, you will create a front-end for users that enter data into the back-end tables.

1. Start **Access 2016**. On the **Access** Start page, click **Blank desktop database**. In the **Blank desktop database** window, replace the suggested **File Name** with Last_First_acc10_WaterDataEntry_fe

2. Click the **Browse** button 📁, and then in the **File New Database** dialog box, navigate to your **Access Chapter 10** folder, and then click **OK**.

3. Click the **Create** button to create the new database. **Close** ⊠ Table1 without saving it.

4. Click the **External Data tab**, and then in the **Import & Link group**, click the **Access** button.

5. In the **Get External Data - Access Database** dialog box, click **Browse**. In the **File Open** dialog box, navigate to and click **Last_First_acc10_Water_be**, and then click **Open**.

6. In the **Get External Data - Access Database** dialog box, select the **Link to the data source by creating a linked table** option button. Compare your screen with **Figure 1**, and then click **OK**.

7. In the **Link Tables** dialog box, click the **Select All** button. Compare your screen with **Figure 2**, and then click **OK**.

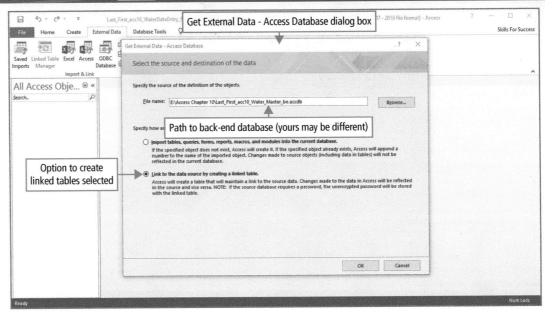

Figure 1

Access 2016, Windows 10, Microsoft Corporation

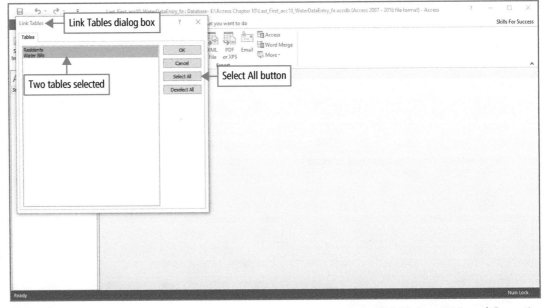

Figure 2

Access 2016, Windows 10, Microsoft Corporation

▶ Continue to the next page to complete the skill

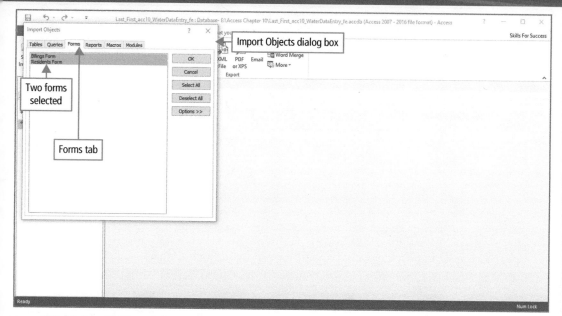

Access 2016, Windows 10, Microsoft Corporation

Figure 3

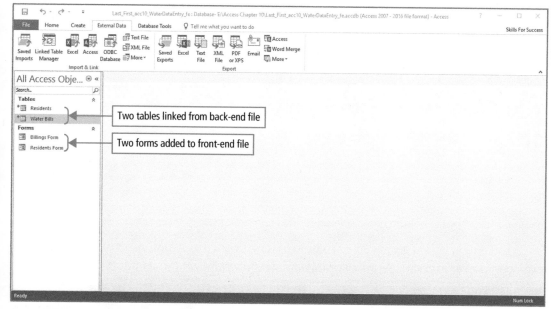

Access 2016, Windows 10, Microsoft Corporation

Figure 4

8. On the **External Data tab**, in the **Import & Link group**, click the **Access** button.

9. In the **Get External Data - Access Database** dialog box, click **Browse**. In the **File Open** dialog box, navigate to and click **acc10_Water_Master**, and then click **Open**.

10. In the **Get External Data - Access Database** dialog box, verify that the **Import tables, queries, forms, reports, macros, and modules into the current database** option button is selected, and then click **OK**.

11. In the **Import Objects** dialog box, click the **Forms tab**. Click the **Select All** button, and then compare your screen with Figure 3.

12. Click **OK** to import the two forms into the front-end.

13. In the **Get External Data - Access Database** dialog box, click **Close**. Compare your screen with Figure 4.

14. Leave the database open for the next skill.

■ **You have completed Skill 7 of 10**

▶ You can create macros that ask the user for input before continuing.

1. With **Last_First_acc10_WaterDataEntry_fe** open, click the **Create tab**. In the **Macros & Code group**, click the **Macro** button to open the new Macro Builder tab.

2. If the Action Catalog pane does not display, on the Design tab, in the Show/Hide group, click the Action Catalog button. Compare your screen with **Figure 1**.

3. In the **Action Catalog** pane, under **Program Flow**, double-click the **If** command to add the condition to the Macro1 tab. Compare your screen with **Figure 2**.

4. To the right of **If**, in the **Conditional expression** box, type the following VBA statement: MsgBox("Are you sure you want to quit Access?",4,"Please Confirm")=6

5. Below **If**, click the **Add New Action arrow**. Scroll down the list of actions, and then click **QuitAccess**.

6. Below the **QuitAccess** action inserted in the previous step, click the **Options arrow**, and then click **Exit**.

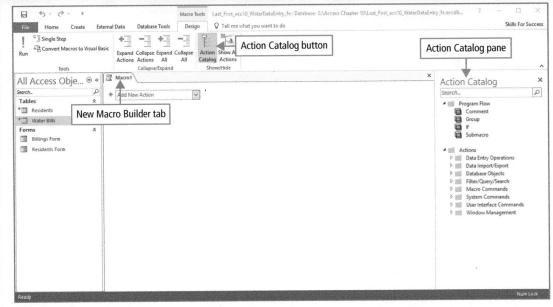

Figure 1

Access 2016, Windows 10, Microsoft Corporation

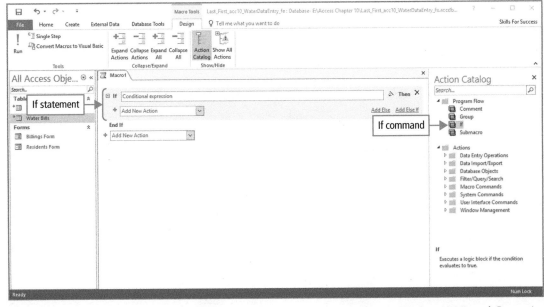

Figure 2

Access 2016, Windows 10, Microsoft Corporation

■ **Continue to the next page to complete the skill**

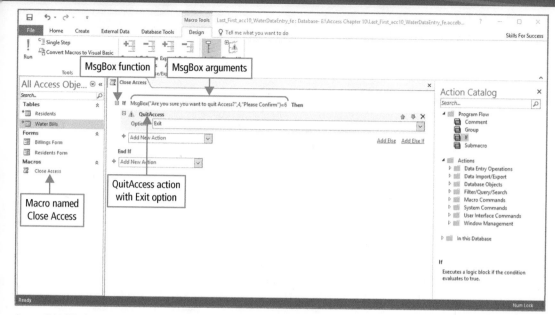

Access 2016, Windows 10, Microsoft Corporation

Figure 3

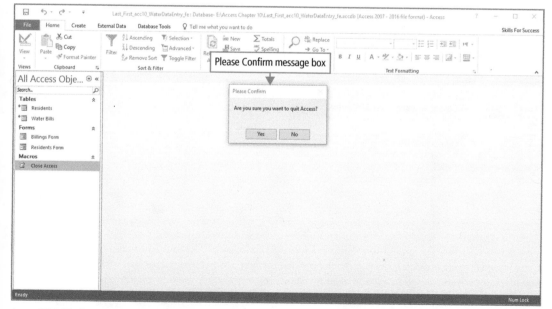

Access 2016, Windows 10, Microsoft Corporation

Figure 4

7. Click **Save** 🔲. In the **Save As** dialog box, name the macro Close Access and then press [Enter]. Compare your screen with Figure 3.

   The MsgBox function can have several arguments. Here, the first argument defines the message text, the second argument—*4*—sets the message to display Yes and No buttons, and the third argument defines the text in the title bar of the message. When the Yes button is clicked, the value 6 is returned to the macro.

8. **Close** ✕ the macro.

9. In the **Navigation Pane**, under **Macros**, double-click **Close Access**, and then compare your screen with Figure 4.

   This macro will prevent the data entry operator from accidentally exiting Access. If the user clicks the Yes button, the QuitAccess action will be executed. If the user clicks No, the macro stops and the database window will stay open.

10. In the **Please Confirm** message box, click **Yes** to close the database.

11. Start **Access 2016**, and then open **Last_First_acc10_WaterDataEntry_fe**. If necessary, enable the content.

12. In the **Navigation Pane**, under **Macros**, double-click **Close Access**. In the **Please Confirm** message, click **No** to verify the database does not close.

    When testing a macro, it is important to test all possible outcomes.

13. Leave the database open for the next skill.

- **You have completed Skill 8 of 10**

▶ You can provide a unique application interface by customizing the Navigation Pane.

1. With **Last_First_acc10_WaterDataEntry_fe** open, click the **File tab**, and then click **Options**. If necessary, in the left pane of the Access Options dialog box, click **Current Database**.

2. In the **Access Options** dialog box, scroll as needed to display the **Navigation** settings, and then click the **Navigation Options** button.

3. In the **Navigation Options** dialog box, under **Categories**, click **Custom**, and then click the **Rename Item** button. Type Aspen Falls Categories and then press Enter to accept the name.

4. Under **Groups for "Aspen Falls Categories"**, click **Custom Group 1**, and then click the **Rename Group** button. Type Data Entry and then press Enter to accept the name.

5. Compare your screen with **Figure 1**, and then click **OK** two times to close all dialog boxes.

6. Click the **Navigation Pane arrow** ⊙, and then click **Aspen Falls Categories**.

7. Point to the Navigation Pane's right border, and then with the ↔ pointer, drag to the right until the entire category name *Aspen Falls Categories* displays without being cut off. Compare your screen with **Figure 2**.

    When you create a custom category and group, the database objects first display under Unassigned Objects.

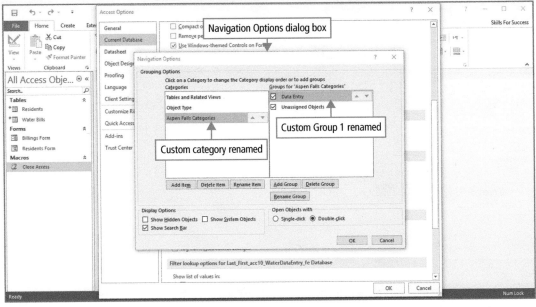

Figure 1

Access 2016, Windows 10, Microsoft Corporation

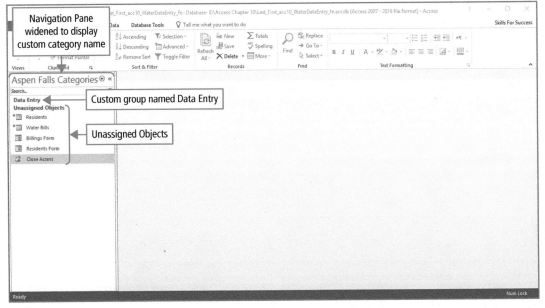

Figure 2

Access 2016, Windows 10, Microsoft Corporation

■ **Continue to the next page to complete the skill**

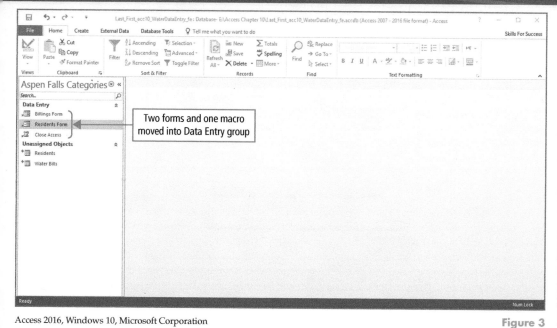

Access 2016, Windows 10, Microsoft Corporation

Figure 3

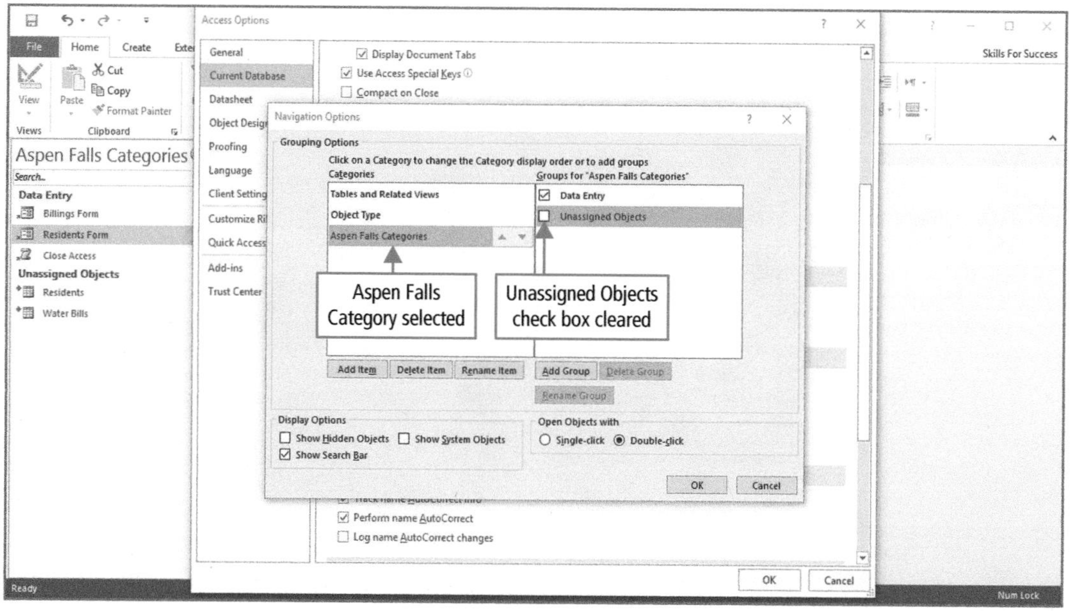

Access 2016, Windows 10, Microsoft Corporation

Figure 4

8. In the **Navigation Pane**, drag the **Billings Form** so that it displays over the **Data Entry group**, and then release the left mouse button.

9. Repeat the technique just practiced to move the **Residents Form** into the **Data Entry** group, and then move the **Close Access** macro into the **Data Entry** group. Compare your screen with **Figure 3**.

> When you move items into a custom group, they display in alphabetical order within each object type. Here, the two forms display in alphabetical order followed by the macro.

10. Click the **File tab**, and then click **Options**. If necessary, in the left pane of the *Access Options* dialog box, click **Current Database**.

11. In the **Access Options** dialog box, scroll as needed to display the **Navigation** settings, and then click the **Navigation Options** button.

12. In the **Navigation Options** dialog box, click **Aspen Falls Categories**, and then clear the **Unassigned Objects** and **Show Hidden Objects** check boxes.

13. Compare your screen with **Figure 4**, and then click **OK** two times to close all dialog boxes.

> By hiding the Unassigned Objects category, the data entry operator will only be able to access the objects in the Data Entry group.

14. Leave the database open for the next skill.

■ **You have completed Skill 9 of 10**

▶ You can hide Navigation Pane groups so that the users cannot easily find database objects you do not intend for them to use.

1. With **Last_First_acc10_WaterDataEntry_fe** open, click the **File tab**, and then click **Options**. If necessary, in the left pane of the Access Options dialog box, click Current Database.

2. In the **Access Options** dialog box, scroll as needed to display the **Navigation** settings, and then click the **Navigation Options** button.

3. In the **Navigation Options** dialog box, under **Categories**, click **Tables and Related Views**.

4. Under **Groups for "Tables and Related Views"**, clear the **Residents**, **Water Bills**, and **Unrelated Objects** check boxes. Compare your screen with **Figure 1**.

   With the groups cleared, if the data entry operator selects the Tables and Related Views category in the Navigation Pane, no database objects will be available.

5. In the **Navigation Options** dialog box, under **Categories**, click **Object Type**.

6. Under **Groups for "Object Type"**, clear all the check boxes, and then compare your screen with **Figure 2**.

   This setting prevents the data entry operator from opening objects using the Object Type category in the Navigation Pane.

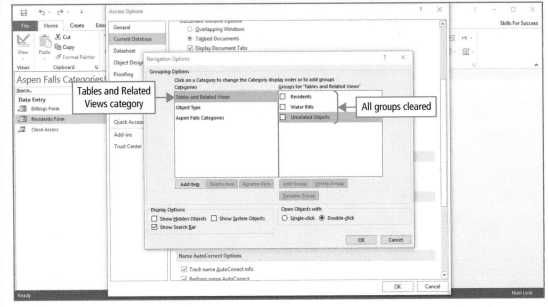

Figure 1

Access 2016, Windows 10, Microsoft Corporation

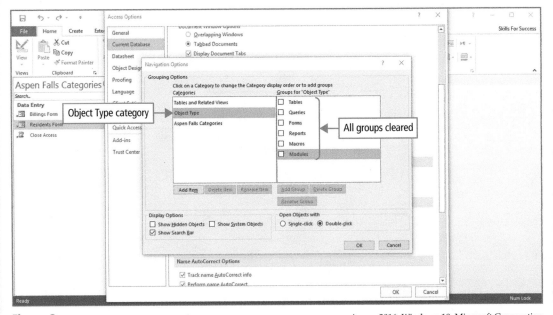

Figure 2

Access 2016, Windows 10, Microsoft Corporation

■ **Continue to the next page to complete the skill**

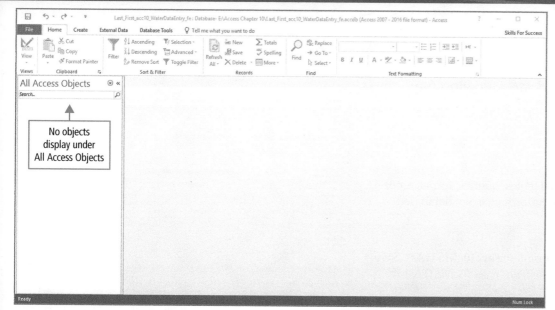

Access 2016, Windows 10, Microsoft Corporation

Figure 3

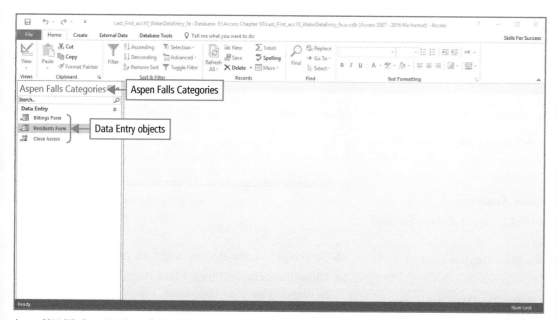

Access 2016, Windows 10, Microsoft Corporation

Figure 4

7. Click **OK** two times to close the dialog boxes.

8. Click the **Navigation Pane arrow** 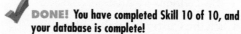, and then click **Tables and Related Views**. Under **All Tables**, verify that no database objects display.

9. Click the **Navigation Pane arrow**, and then click **Object Type**. Under **All Access Objects**, verify that no database objects display as shown in **Figure 3**.

10. Click the **Navigation Pane arrow**, and then click **Aspen Falls Categories**.

11. In the **Navigation Pane**, double-click each form to verify that it opens. Right-click the **Residents Form tab**, and then from the shortcut menu, click **Close All**. Compare your screen with **Figure 4**.

12. **Close** ⊠ Access, and then submit the files as directed by your instructor.

DONE! You have completed Skill 10 of 10, and your database is complete!

More Skills (11)

Analyze Performance

To complete this project, you will need the following file:

- acc10_MS11Art

You will save your file as:

- Last_First_acc10_MS11Art

▶ You can analyze the performance of individual tables, queries, forms, reports, and macros. You can also analyze the overall performance of a database.

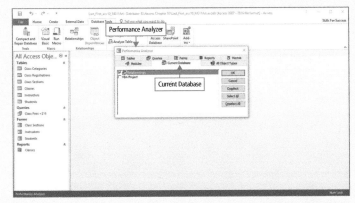

Figure 1   Access 2016, Windows 10, Microsoft Corporation

1. Start **Access 2016**, and then open the student data file **acc10_MS11Art**. Save the file in your **Access Chapter 10** folder as Last_First_acc10_MS11Art If necessary, enable the content.

2. Click the **Database Tools tab**. In the **Analyze group**, click **Analyze Performance**.

    The Performance Analyzer displays.

3. Click the **Current Database tab**.

4. Select the **Relationships** check box, compare your screen with **Figure 1**, and then click **OK.**

5. Read the message, and then click **OK.**

6. **On the Database Tools tab**, in the **Analyze group**, click **Analyze Performance**.

7. Click **All Objects Types**, and then click **Select All**. Compare your screen with **Figure 2**.

8. Click **OK.**

9. Review the suggestions made by the **Performance Analyzer**.

10. Under **Analyze Results**, Click **Table'Instructors': Change data type of field 'Zip' from 'Short Text' to 'Long Integer'.**

11. Under **Analysis Notes**, read the suggestions made by the analyzer.

12. Click **Close.**

13. Open the **Instructors** table in Design view. Click the **Zip Data Type arrow**, and then click **Number.**

14. Click **Save**, read the message, and then click **Yes.**

Figure 2   Access 2016, Windows 10, Microsoft Corporation

15. Switch to Datasheet view, and then verify the Zip values.

16. **Close** the table, and then **Close** Access. Submit your file as directed by your instructor.

■ **You have completed More Skills 11**

More Skills 12

Recover Data from a Backup

To complete this project, you will need the following file:

- acc10_MS12Classes

You will save your files as:

- Last_First_acc10_MS12Classes
- Last_First_acc10_MS12Classes_Backup

▶ Objects in a database can be restored from a backup.

▶ Databases that use switchboards usually hide the Navigation Pane so that those who use the database see only the switchboard when they open the database.

---

1. Start **Access 2016**, and then open the student data file **acc10_MS12Classes**. Save the file in your **Access Chapter 10** folder as Last_First_acc10_MS12Classes If necessary, enable the content.

2. Click the **File tab**, and then click **Save As**. In the **Save Database As** pane, double-click **Back Up Database**.

3. Save the file in your **Access Chapter 10** folder as Last_First_acc10_MS12 Classes_Backup

4. In the **Navigation Pane**, click the **Art Instructors** table, and then press Delete . Read the message, and then click **Yes**.

   The corrupt table is removed from the database.

5. Click the **External Data tab**. In the **Import & Link group**, click **Access**. Click **Browse**, and then navigate to your **Access Chapter 10** folder.

6. Double-click **Last_First_acc10_MS12Classes_Backup**. Compare your screen with Figure 1, and then click **OK**.
   MOS
   Obj 1.4.6

7. On the **Tables tab**, click **Art Instructors**, and then click **OK**.

8. Click **Close** to add the table backup to the database.

9. **Close** Access. Submit your file as directed by your instructor.

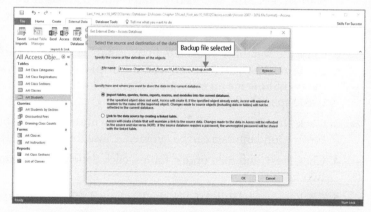

Access 2016, Windows 10, Microsoft Corporation

Figure 1

■ **You have completed More Skills 12**

More Skills 13

Use Table Analyzer to Normalize Tables

To complete this project, you will need the following file:

- acc10_MS13Outings

You will save your file as:

- Last_First_acc10_MS13Outings

▶ **Redundant data** is data duplicated in more than one location within a database.

▶ **Table Analyzer** searches a table for redundant data and, when found, suggests how to split the table into two or more related tables.

1. Start **Access 2016**, and then open the student data file **acc10_MS13Outings**. **Save** the file in your **Access Chapter 10** folder with the name Last_First_acc10_MS13Outings If necessary, enable the content.

2. Click the **Database Tools tab**. In the **Analyze group**, click **Analyze Table**. In the **Table Analyzer Wizard**, read the displayed information, and then click the two **Show me an example** buttons to learn how redundant data can waste space and lead to mistakes.

3. Click **Next**, and then click the two **Show me an example** buttons to learn how redundant data can be avoided. Close the message windows.

4. Click **Next**, and then under **Tables**, click **Scheduled Outings**. Click **Next** two times.

5. Click to select **Table 1**. Click the **Rename Table** button, type Schedule and then click **OK**.

6. Repeat the technique just practiced to rename **Table 2** as Leaders

7. Click **Next**, and then in the **Leaders** table, click **LeaderID**, and then click the **Set Unique Identifier** button.

   LeaderID will be the primary key in the Leaders table. Unique identifier is another term for primary key.

8. Repeat the technique just practiced to select the **Schedule** table and set the **ScheduleID** as the unique identifier. Click **Next**. If you receive a warning message, click **Yes**.

   The Table Analyzer has identified potential typographical errors in the new Leaders table. **Typographical errors** are errors created during data entry. Access

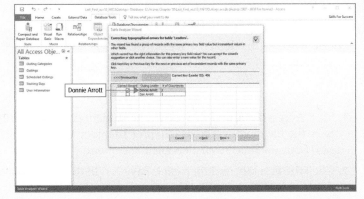

Figure 1   Access 2016, Windows 10, Microsoft Corporation

identifies potential typographical errors by comparing inconsistent values. Here, Collin Bohon's name has been spelled two different ways.

9. With *Collin Bohon* selected as the correct entry, click the **Next Key** button. Verify that *Donnie Arrott* is selected, and then compare your screen with **Figure 1**. Click **Next**.

10. In the **Table Analyzer Wizard**, select **No, don't create the query** option button. Click **Finish**.

11. Read the message, and then click **OK**. Close the **Leaders** and **Schedule** tables.

12. **Close** Access. Submit your file as directed by your instructor.

■ **You have completed More Skills 13**

More Skills 14

Use the Security Wizard

To complete this project, you will need the following file:

- acc10_MS14Cinco

You will save your files as:

- Last_First_acc10_MS14Cinco
- Last_First_acc10_MS14Cinco_WIF
- Last_First_acc10_MS14Cinco_BU

▶ The Security Wizard can be used to create user accounts, assign passwords, and assign permissions.

▶ The Security Wizard provides several prebuilt groups with permissions already defined for each group.

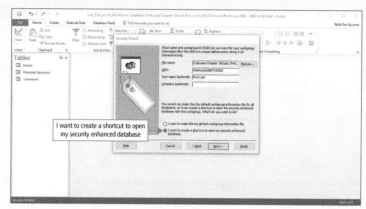

Access 2016, Windows 10, Microsoft Corporation   **Figure 1**

1. Start **Access 2016**, and then open **acc10_MS14Cinco**. Click the **File tab**, and then click **Save As**. Under **Save As**, click **Access 2002-2003 Database**, and then click **Save As**. Navigate to your **Access Chapter 10** folder, and save the file as Last_First_acc10_MS14Cinco Click **Save**. If necessary, enable the content.

2. Click the **File tab**. Click **Users and Permissions**, and then click **User-Level Security Wizard**.

3. In the displayed **Security Wizard**, carefully read the message, and then click **Next**.

4. Click the **Browse** button, and then in the displayed **Select a workgroup file** dialog box, navigate to your **Access Chapter 10** folder. In the **File name** box, type Last_First_acc10_MS14Cinco_WIF and then click **Select**.

   The database will be saved as a ***workgroup information file***—a security-enhanced database in which the user and group permissions created by the Security Wizard are applied.

5. In the **Security Wizard**, click in the **Your name (optional)** box, and then replace the existing text with First Last using your own first and last name.

6. Be sure that the **I want to create a shortcut to open my security-enhanced database** option button is selected. Compare your screen with **Figure 1**.

   The WID—workgroup ID—value is a unique value assigned by Access.

7. Click **Next**.

   The second screen of the Security Wizard is used to select the database objects where security settings will be applied.

8. Click **Next**, and then select the **Backup Operators** check box.

   A ***backup operator*** is responsible for creating backup copies of the master file. Backup operators cannot view or change any data or open any forms or reports.

9. Click **Next** two times. Click your Windows account sign on, and then in the **Password** box, type Success!1

10. Click **Add a New User**. In the **User name** box, type Staff Press Tab, and then type Success!2 Click the **Add This User to the List** button.

11. Click **Next**, and then click the **Group or user name arrow**. From the displayed menu, click **Staff**. Select the **Backup Operators** check box, and then click **Next**.

12. Click the **Browse** button, and then navigate to your **Access Chapter 10** folder. In the **File name** box, type Last_First_acc10_MS14Cinco_BU and then click **Select**.

13. In the displayed **Security Wizard**, click **Finish**. Click **Close Print Preview**. Read the displayed message, and then click **No**. Click **OK**. **Close** Access. Submit the file as directed by your instructor.

■ **You have completed More Skills 14**

The following table summarizes the **SKILLS AND PROCEDURES** covered in this chapter.

Skill	Task	Step	Icon
1	Split databases	Database Tools tab → Move Data group → Access Database	
1	Update linked tables	External Data tab → Import & Link group → Linked Table Manager	
2	Link to back-end tables	External Data tab → Import & Link group → Access → Select Link to the data source by creating a linked table option button	
4	Set Control Wizards to start automatically	Design tab → Controls More button → Select Command Button Wizard Command	
4	Add buttons to perform database tasks	Design tab → Controls group → Button. In Command Button Wizard, click the Category, and then click the Action	
4	Test buttons	Switch to Form view → Click button	
5	Password protect databases	Open the database using Open Exclusive. File → Info → Encrypt with Password	
5	Remove password protection	Open the database using Open Exclusive. File → Info → Decrypt Database	
6	Set title	File → Options → Current Database → Title	
6	Set opening form	File → Options → Current Database → Display Form	
6	Prevent changes to database	File → Options → Current Database: Clear Enable Layout View check box Clear Allow Full Menus check box Clear Allow Default Shortcut menus check box	
6	Hide the Navigation Pane	File → Options → Current Database → Clear Display Navigation Pane check box	
6	Open Access Options without using menus	Quick Access Toolbar → Customize Quick Access Toolbar	
9	Customize Navigation Pane	File → Options → Current Database → Navigation Options: Modify categories and group names Select or clear groups for each category In Navigation Pane, display custom category, and then drag and drop database objects into desired groups	

Project Summary Chart

Project	Project Type	Project Location
Skills Review	Review	In Book and MIL MyITLab° Grader
Skills Assessment 1	Review	In Book and MIL MyITLab° Grader
Skills Assessment 2	Review	Book
My Skills	Problem Solving	Book
Visual Skills Check	Problem Solving	Book
Skills Challenge 1	Critical Thinking	Book
Skills Challenge 2	Critical Thinking	Book
More Skills Assessment	Review	In Book and MIL MyITLab° Grader
Collaborating with Google	Critical Thinking	Book

MOS Objectives Covered (Quiz in MyITLab°)

1.3.4 Display objects in the navigation Pane	1.4.5 Encrypt a database with a password
1.4.4 Split a database	1.4.6 Recover data from backup

Key Terms

Online Help Skills

1. Start **Access 2016**, and then in the upper right corner of the start page, click the **Help** button ⟨?⟩.

2. In the **Access Help** window **Search Online help** box, type Split database and then press ⟨Enter⟩.

3. In the search result list, click **Split an Access database-support.office.com**. Maximize the window, and then compare your screen with Figure 1.

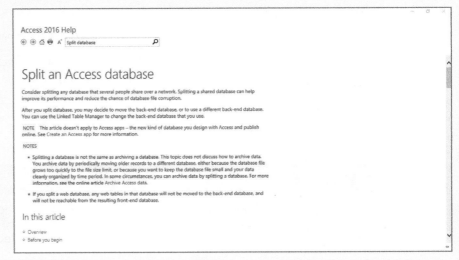

Figure 1   Access 2016, Windows 10, Microsoft Corporation

4. Read the article to answer the following questions: What is the difference between archiving a database and splitting a database? Under what circumstances would you archive a database?

Matching

Match each term in the second column with its correct definition in the first column by writing the letter of the term on the blank line in front of the correct definition.

_____ **1.** The action of moving the tables into one database file and the forms, queries, and reports into a separate database file.

_____ **2.** A database file that contains tables that are linked to from other database files.

_____ **3.** A database file that contains forms, reports, macros, and queries based on tables linked to a back-end file.

_____ **4.** The process of transforming information into a format that cannot be read until the correct password is entered.

_____ **5.** A password that contains a combination of upper- and lowercase letters, numbers, and symbols.

_____ **6.** A value that displays in the Access window title bar instead of the file name, path, and file type.

_____ **7.** A form that automatically opens when the database is opened.

_____ **8.** A function that uses the number 4 to display Yes and No buttons on a dialog box.

_____ **9.** The number returned to the MsgBox function to indicate that the Yes button was clicked.

_____ **10.** An Access feature that can be hidden so users cannot easily find database objects you do not intend for them to use.

A Application Title

B Back-end

C Display form

D Encryption

E Front-end

F MsgBox

G Navigation Pane Groups

H 6

I Split database

J Strong password

Multiple Choice   MyITLab®

Choose the correct answer.

1. What is the Database Splitter used to divide?
   A. The database into back-end and front-end files
   B. The database tables from the database queries
   C. The encryption files from the database files

2. What is the first step in creating front-end databases?
   A. Linking the tables to the front-end file
   B. Linking the tables to the back-end file
   C. Building reports and queries to link to the back-end and front-end files

3. In a custom navigation form, what tool is used to assign actions to buttons?
   A. Control Panel
   B. Command Wizard
   C. Button Wizard

4. On the Format tab, which tool can be used to change the shape of a button?
   A. Format button
   B. Quick shape
   C. Change shape

5. When encrypting a database, how many times is the password entered during the encryption process?
   A. Once
   B. Twice
   C. Encrypted databases do not use passwords.

6. When creating a customized application, which options can be disabled to restrict changes to the database?
   A. Ribbon tabs
   B. Ribbon buttons
   C. Both A & B

7. In the Last_First_acc10_WaterDataEntry_fe database name, what does fe indicate?
   A. Front-end
   B. Full encryption
   C. Final edition

8. Why is it useful to create a message box confirming that a database should be closed?
   A. It is not useful.
   B. To prevent the data entry operator from closing the database without first creating a record of the choice to close the file
   C. To prevent the data entry operator from accidentally exiting the database

9. When items are moved to a custom group, the moved items display in which order?
   A. Numerical
   B. Alphabetical
   C. They are not in any particular order.

10. What method can prevent a data entry operator from opening objects using the Object Type category in the Navigation Pane?
    A. In the Navigation Options dialog box, clear the check boxes under Navigation Pane.
    B. In the Navigation Options, under Categories, click Object Type, and then clear the check boxes.
    C. It is not possible to disable this feature.

Topics for Discussion

1. You have learned how to encrypt a database. What are the risks involved with encrypting a database? How many people should have access to the password? Who should decide which employees will have access to the password?

2. You created a navigation form. What are the advantages of using a navigation form? Should the buttons available on a navigation form also be available on other forms in the database? Under what circumstances would the same button be useful on two different forms or reports?

Skills Review

MyITLab®
Grader

To complete this project, you will need the following file:

- acc10_SRCars

You will save your files as:

- Last_First_acc10_SRCars
- Last_First_acc10_SRCars_be
- Last_First_acc10_SRCars_fe

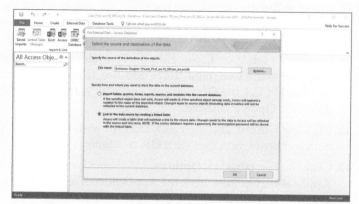

Access 2016, Windows 10, Microsoft Corporation

Figure 1

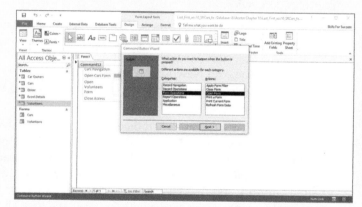

Access 2016, Windows 10, Microsoft Corporation

Figure 2

1. Start **Access 2016**, and then open the student data file **acc10_SRCars**. Save the database in your **Access Chapter 10** folder as Last_First_acc10_SRCars If necessary, enable the content.

2. On the **Database Tools tab**, in the **Move Data group**, click the **Access Database** button. In the **Database Splitter** dialog box, click **Split Database**. Save the file as Last_First_acc10_SRCars_be Click **Split**, and then click **OK**. On the **External Data tab**, in the **Import & Link group**, click **Linked Table Manager**. Click **Select All**, and then click **OK** two times. **Close** Access.

3. Open **Access 2016**, and then on the Start page, click **Blank desktop database**. Name the file Last_First_acc10_SRCars_fe Click the **Browse** button and navigate to your **Access Chapter 10** folder. Click **OK**, and then click **Create**. **Close** Table1 without saving it.

4. On the **External Data tab**, in the **Import & Link group**, click the **Access** button. Click **Browse**, navigate to the **Last_First_acc10_SRCars_be** file, and then click **Open**. In the **Get External Data – Access Database** dialog box, select the **Link to the data source by creating a linked table** option button. Compare your screen with **Figure 1**, and then click **OK**.

5. In the **Link Tables** dialog box, click **Select All**, and then click **OK**. In the **Import & Link group**, click the **Access** button. Click **Browse**, and navigate to your **Access Chapter 10** folder. Click **Last_First_acc10_SRCars**, and then click **Open**. Click **OK**. In the **Import Objects** dialog box, on the **Forms tab**, click **Select All**, and then click **OK**. Click **Close**.

6. Click the **Create tab**, and in the **Forms group**, click **Blank Form**. **Close** the Field List pane. In the **Controls group**, click the **Label** button, and click a blank area of the form. Type Cars Navigation and then press Enter. Click the **Arrange tab**, and in the **Rows & Columns group**, click the **Insert Below** button three times.

7. Press Tab, and then type Open Cars Form Press Tab, type Open Volunteers Form and then press Tab. Type Close Access Click the first label, and then

in the **Rows & Columns group**, click **Insert Right**. Hold down Shift, and then click the first cell in the second column. In the **Merge/Split group**, click **Merge**. On the **Design tab**, in the **Controls group**, click the **Button** button, and then click the blank cell in row 2.

8. In the **Command Button Wizard**, under **Categories**, click **Form Operations**. Under **Actions**, click **Open Form**. Compare your screen with **Figure 2**, and then click **Next**.

■ Continue to the next page to complete this Skills Review ➤

9. Verify **Cars** is selected, and then click **Finish**. Using the technique just practiced, add an Open Form button to open Volunteers to the empty cell in row 3.

10. Click the **Button** button, and then click the empty cell in the fourth row. Under **Categories**, click **Application**, and then under **Actions**, click **Quit Application**. Click **Finish**. **Save** the form as Navigation Form

11. On the **File tab**, click **Close**; click the **File tab** again, and then click **Open**. Navigate to **the Last_First_acc10_SRCars_fe** file, and then click it one time to select it. Click the **Open arrow**, compare your screen with **Figure 3**, and then click **Open Exclusive**.

12. Click the **File tab**, and then click **Encrypt with Password**. Type Skills5& in both text boxes, and then click **OK** two times.

13. Click the **File tab**, click **Options**, and then click **Current Database**. Under **Application Options**, click the **Application Title** text box, and then type Cars Event Scroll down to the **Ribbon and Toolbar Options** and clear the **Allow Full Menus** and **Allow Default Shortcut Menus** check boxes, and then click **OK** twice.

14. On the **Create tab**, in the **Macros & Code group**, click **Macro**. In the **Action Catalog** pane, double-click **If**. In the **Conditional expression** box, type MsgBox("Are you sure you want to quit Access?",4,"Please Confirm")=6 Below **If**, click the **Add New Action arrow**, and then click **QuitAccess**. Below the **QuitAccess** action, click the **Options arrow**, and then click **Exit**. **Save** the macro as Close Access **Close** the macro.

15. On the **File tab**, click **Options**, and then click **Current Database**. Scroll down to the **Navigation** settings, and then click the **Navigation Options** button. Under **Categories**, click **Custom**, and then click **Rename Item**. Type Cars Categories and then press [Enter]. Under **Groups for "Cars Categories"**, click **Custom Group 1**, and then click **Rename Group**. Type Data Entry and then press [Enter]. Compare your screen with **Figure 4**, and then click **OK** two times.

16. In the **Navigation Pane**, drag the **Cars**, **Navigation Form**, and **Volunteers** forms to the **Data Entry group**.

17. On the **File tab**, click **Options**, and then under **Current Database**, scroll down and click the **Navigation Options** button. Under **Categories**, click **Cars Categories**, and then under **Groups for "Cars Categories"**, clear the **Unassigned Objects** and **Show Hidden Objects** check boxes. Click **OK** two times.

18. Close Access. Submit the file as directed by your instructor.

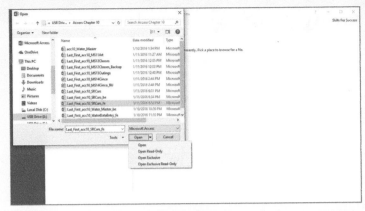

Figure 3   Access 2016, Windows 10, Microsoft Corporation

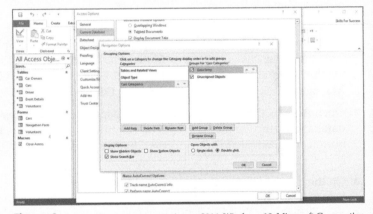

Figure 4   Access 2016, Windows 10, Microsoft Corporation

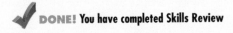
DONE! You have completed Skills Review

Skills Assessment 1

MyITLab®
Grader

To complete this project, you will need the following file:

- acc10_SA1Events

You will save your files as:

- Last_First_acc10_SA1Events
- Last_First_acc10_SA1Events_be
- Last_First_acc10_SA1Events_fe

---

1. Start **Access 2016**, and then open the student data file **acc10_SA1Events**. Save the database in your **Access Chapter 10** folder as Last_First_acc10_SA1Events If necessary, enable the content.

2. Use the **Database Splitter** to split the database and save the file as Last_First_acc10_SA1Events_be Use the **Linked Table Manager** to link all of the tables.

3. Create a **Blank desktop database**, and then save the file as Last_First_acc10_SA1Events_fe Close **Table1** without saving it. From the **Import & Link group**, use the **Access** button to navigate to the **Last_First_acc10_SAEvents_be** file. Link to the data source by creating a linked table. In the **Linked Tables**, select all tables.

4. In the **Import & Link group**, use the **Access** button to navigate to and select the **Last_First_acc10_SA1Events** file. **Open** the file, and then in the **Import Objects** dialog box, **Select All** forms, queries, and reports.

5. Create a Navigation Form that includes two columns. In the first row, **Merge** the cells and include an Events Navigation label. Include three more rows of cells. In the first column, starting with the second row, create the following labels: Open Events Report | Open Volunteers Form | Close Access Using the **Command Button Wizard**, add the corresponding buttons, accepting the default picture for each button.

6. Encrypt the **Last_First_acc10_SA1Events_fe** database using Skills3& as the password.

7. In the **Access Options**, change the database title to Sponsored Events Under the **Ribbon and Toolbar Options**, clear the **Allow Full Menus** and **Allow Default Shortcut Menus** check boxes.

8. Create a Close Access macro that uses an **If** action with the **Conditional expression** MsgBox("Are you sure you want to quit Access?",4,"Please Confirm")=6 Add an **Action** to **Quit Access** using the **Option** to **Exit**. Compare your screen with Figure 1.

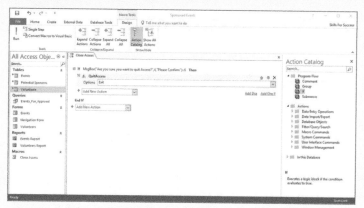

Access 2016, Windows 10, Microsoft Corporation   **Figure 1**

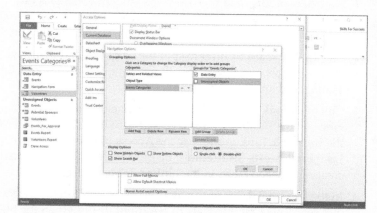

Access 2016, Windows 10, Microsoft Corporation   **Figure 2**

9. In the **Navigation Settings**, rename the **Custom Category** Events Categories Rename **Custom Group 1** Data Entry

10. In the **Navigation Pane**, drag the **Events** form, **Navigation Form**, and **Volunteers** form to the **Data Entry group**.

11. In the **Navigation Options**, under the **Groups for "Events Categories"**, clear the **Unassigned Objects** and **Show Hidden Objects** check boxes. Compare your screen with Figure 2.

12. **Close** Access. Submit the files as directed by your instructor.

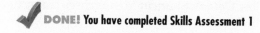

DONE! You have completed Skills Assessment 1

Skills Assessment 2

To complete this project, you will need the following file:

- acc10_SA2Rentals

You will save your files as:

- Last_First_acc10_SA2Rentals
- Last_First_acc10_SA2Rentals_be
- Last_First_acc10_SA2Rentals_fe

Figure 1   Access 2016, Windows 10, Microsoft Corporation

1. Start **Access 2016**, and then open the student data file **acc10_SA2Rentals**. Save the database in your **Access Chapter 10** folder as Last_First_acc10_SA2Rentals If necessary, enable the content.

2. Use the **Database Splitter** to split the database, and then save the file as Last_First_acc10_SA2Rentals_be Use the **Linked Table Manager** to link all of the tables.

3. Create a **Blank desktop database**, and then save the file as Last_First_acc10_SA2Rentals_fe Close **Table1** without saving it. From the **Import & Link group**, use the **Access** button to navigate to the **Last_First_acc10_SA2Rentals_be** file. Link to the data source by creating a linked table. In the **Linked Tables**, select all tables.

4. In the **Import & Link group**, use the **Access** button to navigate to and select the **Last_First_acc10_SA2Rentals** file. **Open** the file, and then in the **Import Objects** dialog box, **Select All** forms and reports.

5. Create a Navigation Form that includes two columns. In the first row, **Merge** the cells and include a Rentals Navigation label. Include three more rows of cells. In the first column, starting with the second row, create the following labels: Open Reservations Report | Open Renters Form | Close Access Using the **Command Button Wizard**, add the corresponding buttons, accepting the default picture for each button. Compare your screen with Figure 1.

6. Encrypt the **Last_First_acc10_SA2Rentals_fe** database using Success4$ as the password.

7. In the **Access Options**, change the database title to Room Rentals Under the **Ribbon and Toolbar Options**, clear the **Allow Full Menus** and **Allow Default Shortcut Menus** check boxes. Compare your screen with Figure 2.

Figure 2   Access 2016, Windows 10, Microsoft Corporation

8. Create a Close Access macro that uses an **If** action with the **Conditional expression** MsgBox("Are you sure you want to quit Access?",4,"Please Confirm")=6 Add an **Action** to **Quit Access** using the **Option** to **Exit**.

9. In the **Navigation Settings**, rename the **Custom Category** Rental Categories Rename **Custom Group 1** Data Entry

10. In the **Navigation Pane**, drag the **Renters** form, **Navigation Form**, and **Reservations** form to the **Data Entry group**.

11. In the **Navigation Options**, under the **Groups for "Rental Categories"**, clear the **Unassigned Objects** and **Show Hidden Objects** check boxes.

12. **Close** Access. Submit the files as directed by your instructor.

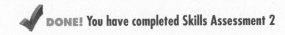 **DONE! You have completed Skills Assessment 2**

My Skills

To complete this project, you will need the following file:

- acc10_MyMaintenance

You will save your files as:

- **Last_First_acc10_MYMaintenance**
- **Last_First_acc10_MYMaintenance_be**

Access 2016, Windows 10, Microsoft Corporation   **Figure 1**

Access 2016, Windows 10, Microsoft Corporation   **Figure 2**

1. Start **Access 2016**, and then open the student data file **acc10_MYMaintenance**. Save the database in your **Access Chapter 10** folder as Last_First_acc10_MYMaintenance If necessary, enable the content.

2. Use the **Database Splitter** to split the database. Save the file as Last_First_acc10_MyMaintenance_be Use the **Linked Table Manager** to link all the tables to the database.

3. Create a Navigation Form Add the **Label** Maintenance Navigation and then use **Insert Below** to add three additional rows to the form. Include the following titles to the three labels below the title label: Open Maintenances Report | Open RepairShops Report | Close Access

4. Insert a second column in the **Navigation Form**, and then using the **Command Button Wizard**, add buttons that correspond to the labels in the first column. Use the default pictures on the buttons. **Merge** the cells in the first row. If necessary, drag the bottom of the first row up to reduce the height of the row.

5. Select all three buttons, and then on the **Format tab**, apply the **Quick Style Moderate Effect - Dark Blue, Accent 1**. Click the **Close Access** label, and then drag downward to increase the height of the label until the entire label is visible.

6. Close **Access**, and then open the database again as **Open Exclusive**. From the **File tab**, Encrypt the database using the password TireIron46$

7. From the **Application Options**, change the **Application Title** to Car Maintenance and then scroll down to the **Ribbon and Toolbar Options**. Clear the **Allow Full Menus** and **Allow Default Shortcut Menus** check boxes. Compare your screen with Figure 1.

8. Create a Close Access macro that uses an **If** action with the **Conditional expression** MsgBox("Are you sure you want to quit Access?",4,"Please Confirm")=6 Add an **Action** to **Quit Access** using the **Option** to **Exit**.

9. From the **File tab**, click **Options**, and then in the **Current Database**, under the **Navigation** settings, click the **Navigation Options** button. Under **Categories**, rename **Custom** Maintenance Categories Rename **Custom Group 1** Data Entry

10. In the **Navigation Pane**, select the **Maintenance Categories**. Drag the **Navigation Form**, **RepairShops** form, and **Vehicles** form to the **Data Entry group**. Return to the **Navigation** settings, and then click the **Navigation Options**. Under the **Maintenance Categories**, clear the **Unassigned Objects** check box and verify that **Show Hidden Objects** is unchecked. Compare your screen with Figure 2. Submit the files as directed by your instructor.

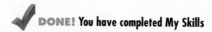 **DONE! You have completed My Skills**

Visual Skills Check

To complete this project, you will need the following file:

- acc10_VSGeo

You will save your file as:

- Last_First_acc10_VSGeo

Open the student data file **acc10_VSGeo**, and then save the database in your **Access Chapter 10** folder as Last_First_acc10_VSGeo

Create the custom Navigation Form shown in **Figure 1**. On the Navigation form, add buttons to Open Events Report | Open Geocache Report | Print Geocache Report and Close Access Using the **Command Button Wizard**, assign the appropriate action to each button. In the **Property Sheet**, change the **Width** property of the buttons to 1.8 the **Height** to 0.3 and the labels **Font Size** to 10 Use the **Picture** option button option for the button display. Apply the **Quick Style Subtle Effect – Olive Green, Accent 3**, and the **Change Shape Snip Single Corner Rectangle** to each button. Submit the file as directed by your instructor.

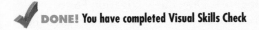 **DONE! You have completed Visual Skills Check**

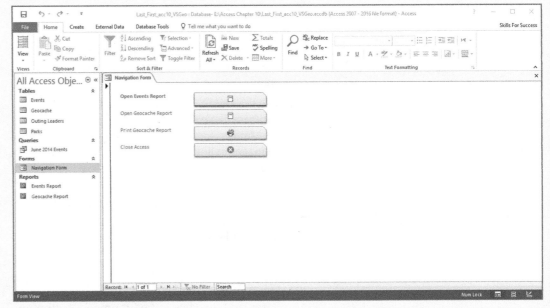

Figure 1

Access 2016, Windows 10, Microsoft Corporation

Skills Challenge 1

To complete this project, you will need the following file:

- acc10_SC1Swim

You will save your files as:

- Last_First_acc10_SC1Swim
- Last_First_acc10_SC1Swim_be
- Last_First_acc10_SC1Swim_fe

Open the student data file **acc10_SC1Swim**, and then save the database in your **Access Chapter 10** folder as Last_First_acc10_SC1Swim Use the Database Splitter to split the database, and then save the back-end file as Last_First_acc10_SC1Swim_be Create a front-end database file saved as Last_First_acc10_SC1Swim_fe Link to the **Last_First_acc10_SC1Swim** file. Using the **Import Objects** dialog box, link to all of the tables and reports. Create a custom Navigation Form that includes buttons to open the Employees Report and the Swimming

Classes Report The **Navigation Form** should also include a button to Close Access Encrypt the database using Skills1# as the password.

Submit the files as directed by your instructor.

 **DONE! You have completed Skills Challenge 1**

Skills Challenge 2

To complete this project, you will need the following file:

- acc10_SC2FarmersMarket

You will save your file as:

- Last_First_acc10_SC2FarmersMarket

Open the student data file **acc10_SC2FarmersMarket**, and then save the database in your **Access Chapter 10** folder as Last_First_acc10_SC2FarmersMarket Encrypt the database using puMpkins5& as the password. Change the **Application Title** to Farmers Market Disable the **Full Menus** on the **Ribbon** and disable the **Default Shortcut Menus**. Create a custom **Category** in the **Navigation Pane** and move the

database forms into the custom group. Remove all **Unassigned Objects** from the newly created **Navigation Pane Category**.

Submit the file as directed by your instructor.

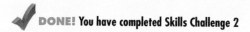 **DONE! You have completed Skills Challenge 2**

More Skills Assessment

To complete this project, you will need the following files:

- acc10_MSAActivities
- acc10_MSAActivities_Backup

You will save your file as:

- Last_First_acc10_MSASActivities

---

1. Start **Access 2016**. Open the file **acc10_MSAActivities**, and then save the file in your chapter folder as Last_First_acc10_MSAActivities

2. Restore the **Training Days** table to the database from the **acc10_MSAActivities_Backup** file.

3. Using the Performance Analyzer, analyze the **Activities** table, and then compare your screen with **Figure 1**.

4. Complete the *Performance Analyzer* suggested changes. In the *Activities* table, for the *Outing ID* field, choose the **Number Data Type**, and a **Field Size** of **Long Integer**.

5. Use the Table Analyzer to normalize the tables. In the **Table Analyzer Wizard**, rename Table1 Schedule and then rename Table2 Guides Accept *Unique identifier* value, and then select *Dan Arkson* as the **Correction** value.

6. Encrypt the database with the password Success9& Compare your screen with **Figure 2** and then click **OK**.

7. **Save** and **Close** all objects, and then **Close** Access.

8. Submit the file as directed by your instructor.

 **DONE! You have completed the More Skills Assessment**

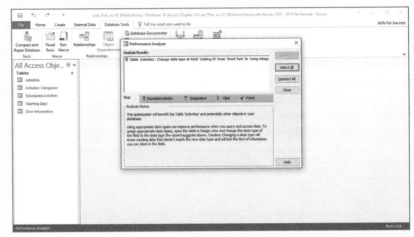

Figure 1   Access 2016, Windows 10, Microsoft Corporation

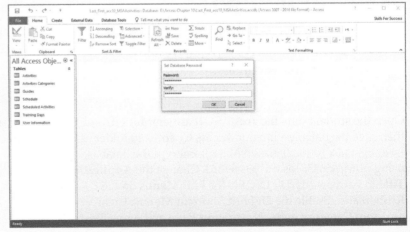

Figure 2   Access 2016, Windows 10, Microsoft Corporation

Collaborating with Google

To complete this project, you will need a Google account (refer to the Common Features chapter) and the following files:

- acc10_GPProducts_Backup (Excel)
- acc10_GPFarmersMarket (Access)

You will save your files as:

- Last_First_acc10_GPFarmersMarket
- Last_First_acc10_GPProducts_Backup

1. Open the **Google Chrome** web browser. Log into your Google account, and then click the **Apps** button.

2. Click **Drive** to open Google Drive, and then click the **NEW** button. Click **File upload**, navigate to the student data files, and then open **acc10_GPProducts_Backup**.

3. Select **acc10_GPProducts_Backup** in **Google Drive**. Click the **More actions** button, point to **Open with**, and then click **Google Sheets**.

4. In cell **A26**, type 25 and then in cell **B26**, type Plants

5. In cell **A27**, type 26 and then in cell **B27**, type Baked Goods Compare your screen with **Figure 1**.

6. Click **File**, click **Download as**, and then click **Microsoft Excel**. Save the file in your chapter folder as Last_First_acc10_GPProducts_Backup

7. Open **Access 2016**, navigate to your chapter folder, and then open the file **acc10_GPFarmersMarket**. Save the file in your chapter folder as Last_First_acc10_GPFarmersMarket

8. Click the **External Data tab**. In the **Import & Link tab**, click **Excel**. Click **Browse**, navigate to your chapter folder, and then double-click **Last_First_acc10_GPProducts_Backup**.

9. In the **Get External Data – Excel Spreadsheet** dialog box, click **OK**. In the **Import Spreadsheet Wizard** dialog box, verify the **First Row Contains Column Headings** checkbox is selected, and then click **Next**.

Figure 1

10. Change the data type to **Long Integer**, and then click **Next**. Click the **Choose my own primary key.** checkbox, and then click **Finish**.

11. **Close** the browser window. **Close** all Access objects, and then submit the file as directed by your instructor.

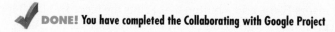

DONE! You have completed the Collaborating with Google Project

CAPSTONE PROJECT

To complete this project, you will need the following files:

acc_CAPTriathlon
acc_CAPRacers (Excel)

You will save your file as:

Last_First_acc_CAPTriathlon

---

1. Start **Access 2016**, and then open the student data file **acc_CAPTriathlon**. Save the file in your **Access Capstone** folder as Last_First_acc_CAPTriathlon If necessary, enable the content.

2. Open the **acc_CAPRacers** Excel file and delete column D. In the first row, change the column headings from **Racer** to RacerID **First** to FirstName and **Last** to LastName **Save** and **Close** the file.

3. Create a new Racers table by importing the file **acc_CAPRacers**. Save the RacerID as the primary key with a **Data Type** of **Integer**. Save the import steps with the description Import Racers Excel file Open the **Racers** table in Datasheet view, and then compare your screen with **Figure 1**.

4. Open the **2016 Race Sponsors** query in SQL view, and then change the **WHERE** clause to return values from 2017 instead of 2016. Save and run the query. Rename the query 2017 Race Sponsors

5. Create a Delete 2014 Race Marshals Query that deletes the 2014 entry from the **Race Marshals** table. Run the query.

6. Create a FullName Query that includes all the fields in the **Racers** table. Create a column that concatenates the **FirstName** and **LastName** fields in the **Racers** table. Drag the **FullName** column so it is the fourth column in the query. Run the query. Compare your screen with **Figure 2**, and then close the query.

7. Create a Race Sponsors Form that includes all of the fields from the **Race Sponsors** table. Apply conditional formatting to the **Amount** text box, which adds a **Yellow Background Color** to Amounts greater than 1000

8. On the **Race Sponsors Form**, add a button that opens the **Sponsors Form**, at the 3-inch horizontal gridline, two grid dots below the **Form Header** bar. The button should display the text Open Sponsors Form

9. On the **Sponsors Form**, add a button that Prints the record, at the 3-inch horizontal gridline, two grid dots below the **Form Header** bar. Accept the default settings for the button.

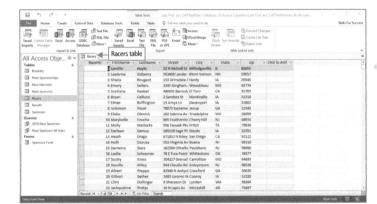

Figure 1   Access 2016, Windows 10, Microsoft Corporation

Figure 2   Access 2016, Windows 10, Microsoft Corporation

■ Continue to the next page to complete the project ➜

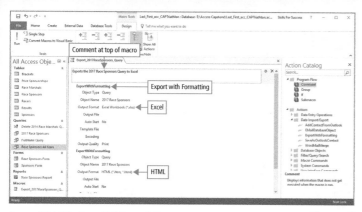

Access 2016, Windows 10, Microsoft Corporation

Figure 3

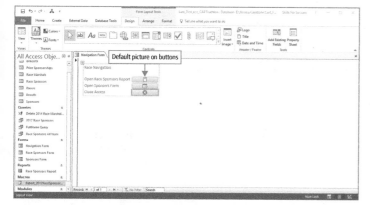

Access 2016, Windows 10, Microsoft Corporation

Figure 4

10. Create a Race Sponsors Report from the **Race Sponsors All Years** query. Change the **Width** of the **Sponsor Name** text box to 2.5 and the **Race Year** text box to 0.75 Delete the page count control at the bottom of the report.

11. On the **Race Sponsors Report**, group the records by **Race Year**, and then sort the records by **Amount**.

12. On the **Race Sponsors Report**, apply conditional formatting to the **Amount** text box, which adds a **Dark Blue 2** background color to **Amounts** between 2000 and 3000

13. Create a one-to-many relationship between the **Racers** and **Results** tables using the **RacerID** field. Enforce referential integrity.

14. Create a macro that will **ExportWithFormatting** the **2017 Race Sponsors** query in **Excel Workbook (*.xlsx)** format. Save the macro as Export_2017RaceSponsors_Query

15. Add a **New Action** that will **ExportWithFormatting** the **2017 Race Sponsors** query in **HTML format**.

16. Add the comment Exports the 2017 Race Sponsors Query to Excel Move the comment to the top of the macro, and then compare your screen with **Figure 3**.

17. In the **Quick Access Toolbar**, add a **Separator**, and then add the **Export_2017RaceSponsors_Query** macro.

18. Convert the **Export_2017RaceSponsors_Query** macro to **Visual Basic**.

19. Create a Navigation Form that includes two columns. In the first row, **Merge** the cells and include a Race Navigation label. Include three more rows of cells. In the first column, starting with the second row, create the following labels: Open Race Sponsors Report | Open Sponsors Form | Close Access Using the **Command Button Wizard**, add the corresponding buttons, accepting the default picture for each button. Compare your screen with **Figure 4**.

20. Change the **Application Title** to Triathlon Database

21. Under the **Ribbon and Toolbar Options**, clear the **Allow Full Menus** and **Allow Default Shortcut Menus** check boxes.

22. In the **Navigation Options** rename the **Custom Category** Race Categories Rename **Custom Group 1** Data Entry

23. In the **Navigation Pane**, drag the **Navigation Form**, **Race Sponsors Form**, and **Sponsors Form** to the **Data Entry group**.

24. In the **Navigation Options**, under the **Groups for "Race Categories"**, clear the **Unassigned Objects** check box.

25. **Close** Access and submit the file as directed by your instructor.

 **DONE!** You have completed the Access Capstone!

Edit an Excel Spreadsheet

- ▶ **Excel Online** is a cloud-based application used to complete basic spreadsheet editing and formatting tasks using a web browser.
- ▶ Excel Online can be used to create or edit spreadsheets using a web browser instead of the Excel program; Excel 2016 does not need to be installed on your computer.

- ▶ When you create a document using Excel Online, it is saved on your OneDrive so that you can work with it from any computer connected to the Internet.
- ▶ You can share your spreadsheet with colleagues or groups, giving them either read-only access or allowing them to edit the document.

lisovoy/Fotolia

Aspen Falls City Hall

This project assumes that you are working at two computers. One does not have the desktop version of Microsoft Excel installed, and the other has the software installed. You will edit and format a spreadsheet using Excel Online. You will also edit the spreadsheet in Excel 2016. You will edit this spreadsheet for Lorrine Deely, Community Center Supervisor. The spreadsheet includes the contact information for the Community Center art instructors.

Excel Online is used to create, edit, or open Excel workbooks from any computer or device connected to the Internet. Workbooks can be saved on your OneDrive, and you can continue working with them later when you are at a computer that has Excel 2016 installed.

In this project, you will use Excel Online to edit a spreadsheet that will be used in the Art Class database. You will delete rows and columns, fill cells, and resize columns. Finally, you will open the workbook in Excel 2016 to sort the records.

Time to complete this project — 30 to 60 minutes

Introduction

Outcome

Using the skills in this project, you will be able to create and edit an Excel Online spreadsheet.

Objectives

1 Create workbooks on OneDrive

2 Modify columns and rows in a spreadsheet

3 Modify data in a spreadsheet

> **Student data file needed for this project:**
> **acc_WAArtInstructors (Excel)**
>
> **You will save your file as:**
> **Last_First_acc_WAArtInstructors**

SKILLS

At the end of this project you will be able to use Excel Web App to:

▶ Upload Excel workbooks to OneDrive

▶ Save workbooks to OneDrive

▶ Delete columns

▶ Delete rows

▶ Fill a series

▶ Resize columns

▶ Open workbooks in Excel 2016

▶ Sort records

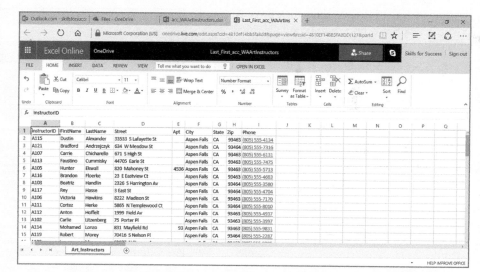

Excel 2016, Windows 10, Microsoft Corporation

Edit an Excel Spreadsheet | **Access Online Project** • **449**

1. Start **Edge**, navigate to live.com and log on to your Microsoft account. If you do not have an account, follow the links and directions on the page to create one.

2. After logging in, navigate as needed to display the OneDrive page, and then compare your screen with **Figure 1**. (Your folders may differ from the figure.)

   OneDrive and online technologies are accessed through web pages that can change often and the formatting and layout of some pages may often be different than the figures in this book. When this happens, you may need to adapt the steps to complete the actions they describe.

3. On the toolbar, click **Upload**, and then click **Files**. Navigate to your student data files, click **acc_WAArtInstructors** and then click **Open**.

4. Click the **acc_WAArtInstructors** file to open it.

5. Click the **File tab**, then click **Save As**. Click **Save**, and then type Last_First_acc_WAArtInstructors Click **Save**.

6. Click column **D** to select it, and then on the **Home tab** in the **Cells group**, click the **Delete** arrow. In the displayed menu, click **Delete Columns**.

7. Repeat the technique just practiced to **Delete** column **I** and then compare your screen with **Figure 2**.

8. Click row 16 to select it. On the **Home tab** in the **Cells group**, click the **Delete** arrow. In the displayed menu, click **Delete Rows**.

■ **Continue to the next page to complete the skill**

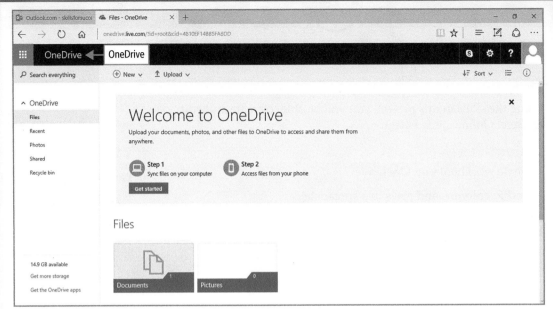

Figure 1

Windows 10, Microsoft Corporation

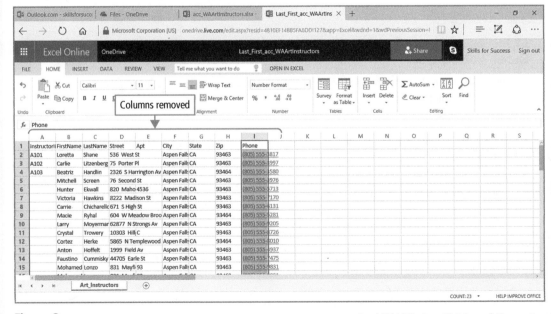

Figure 2

Excel 2016, Windows 10, Microsoft Corporation

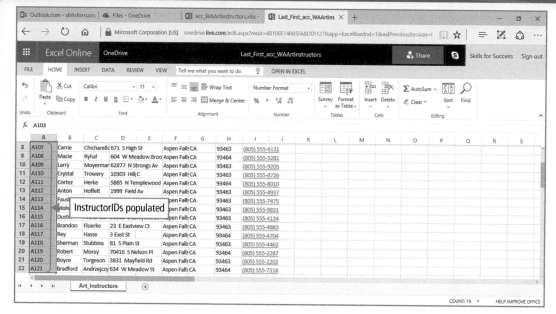

Excel 2016, Windows 10, Microsoft Corporation

Figure 3

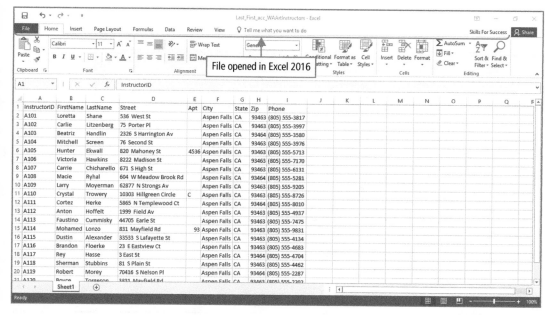

Excel 2016, Windows 10, Microsoft Corporation

Figure 4

9. Select the range **A2:A4**. In the lower right corner of cell **A4**, press and hold the fill handle and drag down through cell **A22**. Compare your screen with **Figure 3**.

10. Click the **File tab** and then click **Save As**. Click **Where's the Save Button?** Read the message and then click **OK**.

11. Select columns **A:I**. Double-click the right edge of column **I** to resize the columns to **Best Fit**.

12. **Close** the Excel workbook tab.

13. Select the **Last_First_acc_WAArtInstructors** workbook in OneDrive, and from the toolbar click the **Open** arrow.

14. Click **Open In Excel**. Read the message, and then click **Yes**.

15. Verify that the workbook opened and then if necessary, click **My workbook opened successfully**. Switch to Excel 2016 and then compare your screen with **Figure 4**.

16. Click the **Data tab**. In the **Sort & Filter group**, click the **Sort** button.

■ Continue to the next page to complete the skill

17. If necessary, select the **My data has headers** check box, and then click the **Sort by** arrow. Click **LastName**, and then compare your screen with Figure 5.

18. Click **OK** to perform the sort. Click **Save** and then **Close** the spreadsheet.

19. Switch to the browser window and double-click **Last_First_acc_WAArtInstructors**. Compare your screen with Figure 6.

> The changes made in Excel 2016 were saved to the OneDrive file. Here, notice the records are sorted by LastName.

20. **Close** the spreadsheet.

21. In the top right corner of the **Edge** window, click **Sign out**. **Close** the browser window.

DONE! You have completed the Access Online Project!

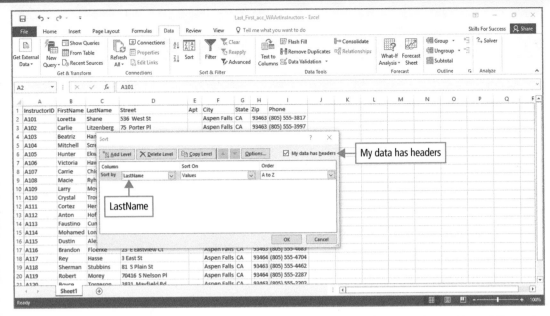

Figure 5

Excel 2016, Windows 10, Microsoft Corporation

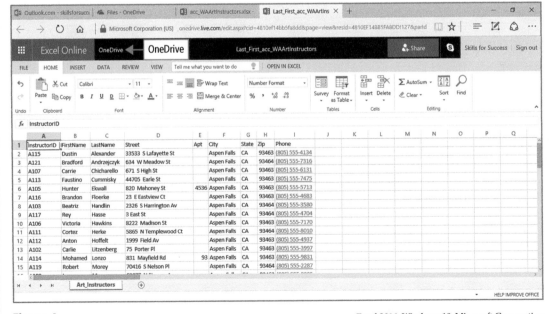

Figure 6

Excel 2016, Windows 10, Microsoft Corporation

Glossary

ActiveX control A control that enables your active applications to interact with another application across the web.

Alias A descriptive label used to identify a field in expressions, datasheets, forms and reports.

And logical operator A logical comparison of two criteria that is true only when both criteria outcomes are true.

Append query A query that adds the results of the query to an existing table.

Append row The last row of a datasheet into which a new record is entered.

Application Part Tables, forms, and other objects created from templates.

Application Title A value that displays in the Access window title bar instead of the file name, path, and file type.

Asterisk (*) In SQL, a character that selects all the fields from the table(s) listed in the FROM statement.

Asterisk (*) wildcard A wildcard character that matches any combination of characters.

Attachment data type A data type used to store files such as Word documents or digital photo files.

AutoComplete A menu of commands that match the characters you type.

AutoNumber A field that automatically enters a unique, numeric value when a record is created.

Avg An operator that calculates the average of the values in each group.

Back-end A database file that contains tables that linked from other database files.

Backstage view A collection of pages on the File tab used to open, save, print, and perform other file management tasks.

Backup operator Responsible for creating backup copies of the master file.

Between . . . And operator A comparison operator that finds all numbers or dates between and including two values.

Breakpoint An intentional stop or pause inserted into a program.

Calculated field A field added to queries, tables, or reports that derives its value from other fields. Its values from other fields in the table or query.

Caption A field property that determines what displays in datasheet, form, and report labels.

Cascading Delete A referential integrity option in which you can delete a record on the one side of the relationship and all the related records on the many side will also be deleted.

Cascading Update A referential integrity option in which you can edit the primary key values in a table and all the related records in the other table will update accordingly.

Cell A box formed by the intersection of a row and column into which text, objects, and data can be inserted.

Code window The area where VBA code is written and edited.

Columnar layout A layout that places labels in the first column and data in the second column.

Combo box A control that has a text box and a list that is hidden until you click its arrow.

Command button A control that performs an action or sequence of actions when it is clicked.

Comment Remark added to a macro or VBA code to provide information to those writing or reviewing the macro or VBA code.

Compact and Repair A process that rebuilds database files so that data and database objects are stored more efficiently.

Comparison operator An operator that compares two values, such as > (greater than) or < (less than).

Compatibility mode A mode that limits formatting and features to those supported in earlier versions of Office.

Concatenate Combine two or more values to create one single value.

Conditional formatting Changes the appearance of a control based on the display configuration related to the value that appears in a field.

Contextual tab A tab that displays on the Ribbon only when a related object such as a graphic or chart is selected.

Control Objects on forms or reports such as labels, text boxes, lines, and pictures.

Control structure Methods that perform logical tests and perform actions when the conditions are true.

Copy A command that places a copy of the selected text or object in the Office Clipboard.

Count An operator that calculates the number of records in each group.

Criteria Conditions in a query used to select the records that answer the query's question.

Crosstab query A select query that calculates a sum, an average, or a similar statistic, and then groups the results by two sets of values.

Currency data type A data type that stores numbers formatted as monetary values.

Custom Input Masks Input masks created to meet specific needs such as the number of characters entered into a field.

Data element Consists of an opening tag, the actual data, and a closing tag.

Data type The type of data that can be stored in a variable such as numbers, characters, or dates.

Database documentation Information about object properties, relationships, and permissions in a database.

Database Documenter An Access tool that creates database documentation.

Datasheet The presentation of a database table.

Datasheet view An Access view that features the data but also has contextual tabs on the Ribbon so that you can change the table's design.

Date/Time data type A data type that stores serial numbers that are converted into and formatted as dates or times.

Debug To find and fix errors in programming code and make sure the program functions as intended.

Default printer The printer that is automatically selected when you do not choose a different printer.

Delete query A query that deletes records from a table. The records selected by the query criteria are deleted when the query is run.

Delimited text file A text file in which columns are separated by a special character such as a space, comma, or tab.

Delimiter A character such as a space, comma, or tab.

DESC An SQL command that changes the sort order to descending.

Detail control The area of a report that repeats for each record in the table or query.

Display form A form that automatically opens when the database is opened.

Double-click To click the left mouse button two times quickly without moving the mouse.

Double-tap To tap the screen in the same place two times quickly.

Drag To press and hold the left mouse button while moving the mouse.

Edit To insert, delete, or replace text in an Office document, workbook, or presentation.

Edit mode A mode that selects the text inside a control, not the control itself.

Encryption The process of transforming information into a format that cannot be read until the correct password is entered.

Entity relationship diagram A visual model used to plan a database.

ERD Acronym for Entity relationship diagram.

Event Actions, such as mouse clicks or typing, detected by a running program that are associated with the control.

Exclusive mode A mode that prevents others from opening the database while you are working with it.

Expression A combination of fields, mathematical operators, and prebuilt functions that calculate values in tables, forms, queries, and reports.

Expression Builder A tool used to create expressions used in controls and fields.

Extensible Markup Language (XML) A standard that uses text characters to define the meaning, structure, and appearance of data.

Field A common characteristic of the data that the table will describe, such as city, state, or postal code.

Field size A field property that limits the number of characters that can be typed into a text or number field.

Filter A tool that displays data containing only specified values.

Find duplicates query A query that searches a field and then displays records that contain duplicate values.

Font A set of characters with the same design and shape.

Foreign key A field that is used to relate records in a second related table. The foreign key field is often the second table's primary key.

Format To change the appearance of the text—for example, changing the text color to red.

Format Painter A tool that copies formatting from selected text to apply that formatting to other text.

FROM An SQL clause that lists the table or tables the query fields are from.

Front-end A database file that contains forms, reports, macros, and queries based on tables linked to a back-end file.

Gallery A visual display of selections from which you can choose.

Group By An operator that designates which query column contains the group of values to summarize as a single record, one for each set.

Grouped records A tool that combines records with identical values from a field in a report.

HTML document A text file with instructions for displaying its content in a web browser.

Hungarian notation A naming convention where the prefixes indicate the type of data or type of object.

Hyperlink An electronic reference to another part of the same document or link to a different document or web page.

Hyperlink data type A data type that stores links to websites or files located on your computer.

Hypertext Markup Language document A text file with instructions for displaying its content in a web browser.

If action Added to the macro, If actions provide a conditional expression and then perform an action or series of actions only when the result of the condition is true or false.

If Then Else control structure A statement that tests if a condition is true.

IN An SQL operator used to select records from a list of acceptable values.

Index Stores the locations of all records for a given field in the same way that a book's index stores each location of a word in the book.

INNER JOIN An SQL clause that defines how fields from related tables should be joined.

Input mask A set of special characters that control what can and cannot be entered in a field.

Insertion point A flashing vertical line that indicates where text will be inserted when you start typing.

IntelliSense A feature that displays Quick Info, ToolTips, and AutoComplete boxes as you type.

Is Not Null An operator that tests if a field contains a value—is not empty.

Is Null An operator that tests if a field is empty.

Keyboard shortcut A combination of keys that performs a command.

Keyword A word in a programming language that has a particular meaning or purpose.

Label A control on a form or in a report that describes other objects in the form or report.

Label report A report formatted so that the data can be printed on a sheet of labels.

Landscape An orientation that is wider than it is tall.

Landscape layout The page orientation where the page is wider than it is tall.

Layout A format that determines how data and labels are arranged in a form or report.

Layout view An Access view used to format a form or report while you are viewing a sample of the data.

Linked table A table that exists in a different file from the one you are working on created by an application such as Access or Excel but that can be opened as a table in Access.

Live Preview A feature that displays what the results of a formatting change will be if you select it.

Logical error Errors where the program runs but does not produce the intended results.

Long Text data type A data type that can store up to 65,535 characters in each record.

Lookup field A field in which values are obtained from another table or from a list.

Macro An action or group of stored instructions used to automate tasks.

Make table query A query that makes a new table.

Many-to-many relationship A relationship in which one record in either table can have many associated records in the other table.

Microsoft account Personal account that you use to access your files, settings, and online services from devices connected to the Internet.

Mini toolbar A toolbar with common formatting commands that displays near selected text.

Modal When a form's Modal property is set to Yes, the Navigation Pane will collapse when the form is opened. When the form is closed, the Navigation Pane will display.

Multiple item form Displays records in rows and columns in the same manner as a datasheet.

Navigation form A form that contains a Navigation Control with tabs that you can use to quickly open forms and reports.

Number data type A data type that stores numeric values.

Office Add-in A plugin that adds extra features or custom commands to Office programs.

Office Clipboard A temporary storage area that holds text or an object that has been cut or copied.

One-to-many form A two-part form in which the main form displays in Single Form view and the related records display in a subform in Datasheet view.

One-to-many relationship A relationship in which a record in the first table can have many associated records in the second table.

One-to-one relationship Each record in one table can have only one corresponding record in the other table.

Option group A frame with a set of boxes, toggle buttons, or option buttons.

Or logical operator A logical comparison of two criteria that is true if either of the criteria outcomes is true.

ORDER BY An SQL clause that is used to sort a field.

Padding The space between controls in a report or form.

Page footer Located at the bottom of each page and can contain labels, text boxes, and other controls.

Page header Located at the top of each page and can contain labels, text boxes, and other controls.

Parameter query A query that displays an input box that asks for criteria each time the query is run.

Paste A command that inserts a copy of the text or object from the Office Clipboard.

PDF file A Portable Document Format file.

Placeholder A reserved, formatted space into which you enter your own text or object. If no text is entered, the placeholder text will not print.

Placeholder character A symbol in an input mask that is replaced as you type data into the field.

Plot area The area bound by the axes in a chart.

Pop up form A form that when opened remains on top, even when it is not the active form.

Portable Document Format file A file format that preserves document layout and formatting and can be viewed in Word, Windows Reader, or Adobe Acrobat Reader.

Portrait An orientation that is taller than it is wide.

Portrait layout The standard page orientation where the page is taller than it is wide.

Primary key A field that uniquely identifies each record in a table.

Print A command that opens the Print dialog box so that you can select a different printer or different print options.

Print Preview A command that opens a preview of the table with Ribbon commands that you can use to make adjustments to the object you are printing.

Program Instructions that tell a computer what to do.

Protected View A view applied to files downloaded from the Internet that allows you to decide if the content is safe before working with the file.

Query A database object used to ask questions about—query—the data stored in database tables.

Query Builder A tool that creates queries within database objects such as forms and reports.

Query design grid The lower half of the Query Design view window that contains the fields the query will display and the query settings that should be applied to each field.

Query design workspace The upper half of the Query Design view window that displays the tables that the query will search.

Question mark (?) wildcard A wildcard character that matches any single character.

Quick Info An IntelliSense box with a message that explains the purpose of the selected AutoComplete command.

Quick Print A command that prints the object directly. You cannot make any adjustments to the object, choose a different printer, or change the printer settings.

Quick Start field A set of fields that can be added with a single click. For example, the Name Quick Start data type inserts the LastName and FirstName fields and assigns the Text data type to each.

Quick Start table Tables created from templates.

Quick Style Prebuilt collection of formatting choices, such as background colors, font colors or shading, that can be applied with one click.

RAM The computer's temporary memory.

Record A collection of related data, such as the contact information for a person.

Redundant data Data duplicated in more than one location within a database.

Referential integrity A rule that keeps related values synchronized. For example, the foreign key value must be present in the related table.

Report A database object that presents tables or query results in a way that is optimized for onscreen viewing or printing.

Report Layout view A view that can be used to format a report while viewing the report's data.

Report view A view optimized for onscreen viewing of reports.

Ribbon Contains commands placed in groups that are organized by tabs so that you can quickly find the tools you need.

Rich Text Format file A document file format designed to work with many different types of programs.

RTF file Rich Text Format file.

SELECT An SQL clause that lists the fields the query should display.

Select query A type of query that selects and displays the records that answer a question without changing the data in the table.

Separator A small vertical or horizontal line used to separate choices in a list, toolbar, or menu.

Short Text data type A data type that stores up to 255 characters of text.

Single Form view A view that displays one record at a time with field names in the first column and field values in the second column.

Slide (PowerPoint) An individual page in a presentation that can contain text, pictures, or other objects.

Split database The action of moving the tables into one database file and the forms, queries, and reports into a separate database file

Split form Displays two synchronized views of the same form. By default, a split form displays in Form view in the top half of the form and in Datasheet view in the lower half of the form.

SQL See Structure Query Language.

Stacked layout A layout in which labels display the field names in the left column, and text boxes display the corresponding field values in the right column.

Startup macro A macro that runs automatically when an Access database is opened.

Statement A line in a program that contains instructions for the computer.

String A sequence of either alpha or alphanumeric characters.

Strong password A password that contains a combination of upper and lower case letters, numbers, and symbols.

Structured Query Language A language used to query database tables.

Subdatasheet A datasheet that displays related records from another table by matching the values in the field that relates the two tables. In a datasheet, the subdatasheet displays below each record.

Subform Form within another forms.

Sub procedure A group of related statements that is a subset of a program. Often referred to as subs or procedures.

Subqueries Queries nested within another query.

Subreport A report that is inserted into another report.

Sum An operator that calculates the total of the values in each group.

Summary statistic A calculation for each group of data, such as a total, an average, or a count.

Syntax error A code error that violates the rules of a programming language.

Table The object that stores the data by organizing it into rows and columns. Each column is a field, and each row is a record.

Table Analyzer A tool that searches a table for redundant data and when found, suggests how to split the table into two or more related tables

Table Design view An Access view that features table fields and their properties.

Tabular layout A layout in which the controls are positioned as table cells in rows and columns.

Tag Text between the < and > characters.

Text box A control on a form or in a report that displays the data from a field in a table or query.

Text file File used to store text characters, but not formatting, tables, or graphics.

The Cloud An Internet technology used to store files and to work with programs that are stored in a central location.

Theme A prebuilt set of unified formatting choices including colors and fonts.

TOP An SQL command that selects the highest values of the next field listed in the SELECT clause. The number of values to display is determined by the number that follows it.

Typographical errors Errors created during data entry.

Unicode (UTF-8) A system for representing a large variety of text characters and symbols. It is used often in HTML documents.

UNION An SQL clause that is used to combine one or more queries in a union query.

Union query A query that combines the results of two or more similar select queries.

Unmatched record Data contained in one field does not have a corresponding value in a related table.

Update query A query that adds, deletes, or modifies records. In Access, update queries are typically used to change data stored in tables.

Validation rule A field property that requires that specific values be entered into a field.

Variable Programming objects that refer to the values stored in RAM.

Visual Basic Editor (VBE) A program for writing VBA program code.

Visual Basics for Applications (VBA) A programming language designed to work within Microsoft Office Applications.

WHERE An SQL clause that identifies the query criteria.

White space Optional spacing that visually organizes the code to make it more readable by programmers.

Wildcard A special character, such as an asterisk, used in query criteria to allow matches for any combination of letters or characters.

Word wrap Words at the right margin automatically move to the beginning of the next line if they do not fit.

Workgroup information file A security-enhanced database in which the user and group permissions created by the Security Wizard are applied.

Yes/No data type A data type that stores variables that can have one of two possible values—for example, yes or no or true or false.

Appendix

Online materials can be found in the Student Resources located at www.pearsonhighered.com/skills

		Microsoft Office Specialist Access 2016		
Chapter	MOS Obj #	Objective	Skills Heading	Page
1		**Create and Manage a Database**		
	1.1	**Create and Modify Databases**		
Ch1	1.1.1	Create a Blank Desktop Database	Create Databases	40
Ch3	1.1.2	Create a Database from a Template	Create Databases from Templates	141
Ch5	1.1.3	Create a Database by Using Import Objects or Data from Other Sources	Design Databases and Modify Field Properties	208
Ch7	1.1.4	Delete Database Objects	Apply Conditional Formatting to Form Controls	299
	1.2	**Manage Relationships and Keys**		
Ch1	1.2.1	Create and Modify Relationships	Relate Tables	48
Ch1	1.2.2	Set the Primary Key	Create Tables in Design View	46
Ch1	1.2.3	Enforce Referential Integrity	Relate Tables	49
Ch1	1.2.4	Set Foreign Keys	Create Tables in Design View	47
Ch1	1.2.5	View Relationships	Relate Tables	48
	1.3	**Navigate Through a Database**		
Ch3	1.3.1	Navigate Specific Records	Use Forms to Modify Data	123
Ch3	1.3.2	Create and Modify a Navigation Form	Create Navigation Forms	139
Ch3	1.3.3	Set a Form as the Startup Option	Create Navigation Forms	139
Ch10	1.3.4	Display Objects in the Navigation Pane	Customize the Navigation Pane	424
Ch2	1.3.5	Change Views of Objects	Add Text Criteria	82
	1.4	**Protect and Maintain Databases**		
Ch1	1.4.1	Compact a Database	Compact and Repair Databases	60
Ch1	1.4.2	Repair a Database	Compact and Repair Databases	60

Chapter	MOS Obj #	Objective	Skills Heading	Page
Ch3	1.4.3	Back Up a Database	Back Up Databases	143
Ch10	1.4.4	Split a Database	Split Databases and Update Linked Tables	408
Ch10	1.4.5	Encrypt a Database with a Password	Secure and Encrypt Databases	417
Ch10	1.4.6	Recover Data from Backup	Secure and Encrypt Databases	429
	1.5	**Print and Export Data**		
Ch4	1.5.1	Print Reports	Preview and Print Reports	169
Ch8	1.5.2	Print Records	Insert Page Breaks, Change Layouts, and Modify Reports	337
Ch3	1.5.3	Save a Database as a Template	Back Up Databases	143
Ch4	1.5.4	Export Objects to Alternative Formats	Export Reports to Word	181–183
2	**Build Tables**			
	2.1	**Create Tables**		
Ch1	2.1.1	Create a Table	Create a Table in Datasheet View	42
Ch1	2.1.2	Import Data into Tables	Import Data into Tables	52
Ch2	2.1.3	Create Linked Tables from External Sources	Link to External Data Sources	102
Ch3	2.1.4	Import Tables from Other Databases	Import Objects from Other Databases	142
Ch5	2.1.5	Create a Table from a Template with Application Parts	Create Tables using Application Parts and Rich Text Fields	212
	2.2	**Manage Tables**		
Ch1	2.2.1	Hide Fields in Tables	Format Datasheets	56
Ch7	2.2.2	Add Total Rows	Create Forms from Application Parts	
Ch9	2.2.3	Add Table Descriptions	Add Table Descriptions	391
Ch7	2.2.4	Rename Tables	Add Hyperlinks to Forms	303
	2.3	**Manage Records in Tables**		
Ch5	2.3.1	Update Records	Add Lookup Fields	221

Appendix

Chapter	MOS Obj #	Objective	Skills Heading	Page
Ch2	3.1.5	Create a Multi-Table Query	Create Queries in Design View	86
Ch2	3.1.6	Save a Query	Create Queries in Design View	87
	3.2	**Modify a Query**		
Ch6	3.2.1	Rename a Query	Modify Existing Queries	255
Ch2	3.2.2	Add Fields	Create Queries in Design View	87
Ch6	3.2.3	Remove Fields	Create Delete Queries	266
Ch2	3.2.4	Hide Fields	Add Calculated Fields to Queries	94
Ch2	3.2.5	Sort Data within Queries	Work with Logical Operators	96
Ch2	3.2.6	Format Fields within Queries	Add Calculated Fields to Queries	95
	3.3	**Create Calculated Fields and Grouping within Queries**		
Ch2	3.3.1	Add Calculated Fields	Add Calculated Fields to Tables	84
Ch6	3.3.2	Set Filtering Criteria	Create Update Queries	256
Ch2	3.3.3	Group and Summarize Data	Group and Total Queries	92
Ch2	3.3.4	Group Data by Using Comparison Operators	Work with Logical Operators	97
Ch2	3.3.5	Group Data by Using Arithmetic and Logical Operators	Add Calculated Fields to Queries	94
4	**Create Forms**			
	4.1	**Create a Form**		
Ch3	4.1.1	Create a Form	Use the Form Wizard	120
Ch7	4.1.2	Create a Form from a Template with Application Parts	Create Forms from Application Parts	300
Ch3	4.1.3	Save A Form	Use Form Wizard	121
	4.2	**Configure Form Controls**		
Ch3	4.2.1	Move Form Controls	Work with Tabular Layouts	130
Ch3	4.2.2	Add Form Controls	Use the Form Wizard	120

Appendix

Index

macros, 368, 372, 388, 389, 390
many-to-many relationship, 214
queries, 249, 258, 262, 268, 270
reports, 328, 332, 336, 342, 348, 349
criteria
queries, 82–83, 90–91, 260, 261, 271
reports, 334–335, 338
crosstab queries, 103
Currency data type, 46
Customize Quick Access Toolbar, 378, 419

data elements, import XML, 222
data entry datasheets, 42, 44–45, 140
Data Entry group, 425
data entry related tables, 50–51
Data group, 227
Data Import/Export, 368
Data tab, 217, 329, 338, 451
Data Tools group, 216
data types, 218, 221, 265, 268, 384
Attachment, 62
Currency, 46
Date/Time, 50
Long Text, 61
Number, 47
Short Text, 42
Yes/No, 63, 208, 374
Database Documenter, 226–227
Database Splitter, 408
Database Tools tab, 214, 225, 226, 250, 428
split databases, 408
Table Analyzer, 430
databases
applications, 406–445
backup, 143
command buttons, 414–415
creation, 40–41
customizing, 418–419
encryption, 416–417
front-end databases, 410–411, 420–421
linked tables, 408–409
macros to verify actions, 422–423
Navigation Pane
  customization, 424–425
  hiding groups, 426–427
performance analysis, 428
recover from backup, 429
Security Wizard, 431
split databases, 408–409
Table Analyzer, 430
design, 206–245
Application Parts, 212–213
Custom Input Masks, 228
Database Documenter, 226–227

documentation, 226–227
encryption, 416–417
ERD, 208
export XML, 230
import, 142
lookup fields, 220–221
macros, 390
Make Table Query, 231
many-to-many relationships, 214–215
one-to-one relationships, 224
queries from tables, 231
split, 408–409
system, 36
templates, 141
unmatched records, 224
visual skills check, 242, 442
Google, 245, 445
key terms, 234, 434
matching, 235, 435
multiple choice, 236, 436
My Skills, 241, 441
online help, 234, 434
skills assessment, 239–240, 244, 439–440, 444
skills challenge, 243, 443
skills review, 237–238, 437–438
Datasheet View, 294, 301, 428
tables, 42–43, 54, 58, 219, 253
datasheets, 54–59, 254, 293
crosstab query, 103
data entry, 42, 44–45, 140
Excel tables as, 52
Date and Time, 299, 329
date and time criteria, 90–91
Date Filters, 256, 266
Date Picker, 50, 311
Date/Time data type, 50
Debug menu, 385
debugging, 382–383
Decrypt Database, 417
default printer, 14
Default Value, 209, 264
Delete, 9, 49, 212, 216, 217
Excel Online, 450
forms, 289, 296, 300, 309
macros, 370
Delete Columns, 450
delete queries, 266–267
Delete Record, 225
Delete Rows, 450
Delete Sheet Columns, 216
delimited text files, 210
delimiters, 210–211
DESC, 251
Description, 212, 213, 223, 228, 311, 391

Design tab
forms, 289, 294, 295, 300, 302, 303, 304, 306, 307, 309, 310
macros, 369, 374, 376, 388, 389, 390, 422
navigation forms, 412, 413
queries, 256, 268, 269
reports, 329, 331, 336, 338, 339, 340, 344, 345
tables from queries, 252
VBA debugging, 382
Design View
databases
applications customizing, 419
design and Field Properties, 208
find duplicates query, 248
forms, 288–289, 295, 296, 299, 304, 306, 311
lookup fields, 221
macros, 371, 390, 391
parameter queries, 260, 262
QAT, 379
queries, 86–87, 254, 256, 264, 265, 266, 271
reports, 160, 332–333, 336, 343, 346, 347, 348, 349, 350, 351
tables, 46–47, 253
VBA, 380, 383
XML, import, 223
destination table, 265
Detail bar, 335, 346, 376
Detail control, 165
Detail section
forms, 296
reports, 339, 344, 347, 348, 349, 350
display forms, 418
Display Navigation Pane, 418
.docx extension, 59
double-click, 9
double-tap, 9
downloads, 6
drag, 10
drag-and-drop, reports, 349

Edge, 202, 450, 452
edit
forms, 129
text, 8
keyboard shortcuts, 17
Edit list, 228
Edit Relationships, 215, 225
Editing group, 217
Else statement, 387
Enable Content, 22
Encrypt with Password, 417
encryption, 416–417
End If, 373
Enforce Referential Integrity, 225